S0-BAH-739

Educating Children and Adolescents with Behavioral Disorders

Educating Children and Adolescents with Behavioral Disorders

An Integrative Approach

Joseph V. Rizzo
Barat College

Robert H. Zabel
Kansas State University

Allyn and Bacon, Inc.
Boston   London   Sydney   Toronto

Copyright © 1988 by Allyn and Bacon, Inc.
A Division of Simon & Schuster
160 Gould Street
Needham, Massachusetts 02194

All rights reserved. No part of the material protected by this copyright notice may be reproduced or utilized in any form or by any means, electronic or mechanical, including photocopying, recording, or by any information storage and retrieval system, without the written permission of the copyright owner.

Library of Congress Cataloging-in-Publication Data

Rizzo, Joseph V., 1942–
    Educating children and adolescents with behavioral disorders: an integrative approach / Joseph V. Rizzo, Robert H. Zabel.
        p.   cm.
    Bibliography: p.
    Includes index.
    ISBN 0-205-11358-3
    1. Behavior disorders in children—United States.
2. Problem children—Education—United States.
3. Special education—United States. I. Zabel, Robert H., 1947– . II. Title.
LC4802.R59 1988
371.93—dc19   87-33491
                                              CIP

Production administrator: Annette Joseph
Production coordinator: Helyn Pultz
Editorial-production service: Nancy Benjamin
Photo researcher: Laurel Anderson
Manufacturing buyer: Bill Alberti
Cover administrator: Linda K. Dickinson
Cover designer: Design Ad Cetera

Printed in the United States of America

10 9 8 7 6 5 4 3 2 1   92 91 90 89 88

Photo credits

Page 3: Susan Lapides
Page 27: Elizabeth Crews/The Image Works
Page 59: Bob Kalman/The Image Works
Page 89: Maureen Fennelli/Photo Researchers, Inc.
Page 111: Susan Lapides
Page 145: Alan Carey/The Image Works
Page 173: Alan Carey/The Image Works
Page 192: Carolyn Hine/The Picture Cube
Page 217: David Strickler/The Picture Cube
Page 248: Mark Antman/The Image Works
Page 287: Guy Gillette/Photo Researchers, Inc.
Page 315: Rick Friedman/The Picture Cube

To Our Families

Brief Contents

Complete Contents

Preface

We believe that an integrative approach is central to intervening in and understanding the lives of children and adolescents with behavioral disorders. In this book we attempt to provide that integration.

First, the book integrates theory, research, and practice because each of these "ways of knowing" has something important to offer. We believe that theories about the nature and etiology of disordered behavior should direct interventions, that efforts to improve children's behavioral and emotional adjustment should be based on sound theoretical underpinnings, and that practice can often be guided by well-executed research.

Second, this book seeks to integrate the multiple perspectives necessary for understanding and influencing children's behavioral adjustment. No single approach holds a monopoly on defining and treating behavioral disorders, but this does not mean we have simply adopted a neutral eclecticism. Clearly, some approaches are more useful than others for understanding behavioral disorders, just as some interventions hold more promise than others. We feel we have included the best theoretical perspectives, the most useful, up-to-date research, and the proven practices of educators and clinicians. The result is a book that is both scholarly and practical.

Although this book was written with educators in mind, our concern extends beyond the classroom and school. Certainly our focus is on the youngster's educational experience, but there are additional critical influences as well. Much of our early discussion of characteristics of behavioral disorders addresses family, community, and sociocultural influences in addition to those in the classroom and school.

The content is organized under four major headings, beginning with "Basic Issues" in Part I. The first chapter sets the stage for the rest of the book by providing an introduction to classification systems, identifying current objectives and issues in educational programs for behaviorally disordered children and adolescents, and providing a rationale for our integrative approach. Chapter 2 reviews features of several major perspectives used to understand disordered behavior and to formulate interventions. We also include analyses of the family and community as behavior settings. Chapter 3 discusses the purposes and processes of assessment in behavioral disorders. We consider multiple procedures for assessing both the child and ecosystems that are relevant to intervention.

Part II focuses on the characteristics of specific populations. There are several discernible patterns or types of disordered behavior. We call these patterns personality problems (Chapter 4), conduct disorders (Chapter 5), pervasive developmental disorders (Chapter 6), and learning disorders (Chapter 7).

Part III, "Special Education Programming," stresses interventions. We recognize that the boundaries between specific methods are not discrete. However, it is helpful to distinguish between those that represent primarily a behavioral orientation (Chapter 8) and those that are psychoeducational (Chapter 9). The former focuses directly on changing disordered behavior, whereas the latter includes cognitive/emotional methods intended to change the ways children think and feel about themselves and others. We believe both approaches offer beneficial strategies for educational intervention. In Chapter 10 we place these interventions into a programming context as we look at the process of educational planning, service delivery models, and several model programs.

Part IV, "Teachers and Parents," focuses on two of the primary players in the lives of behaviorally disordered children. In Chapter 11, we discuss important traits and competencies of teachers. Because teachers of behaviorally disordered students are at risk for experiencing job-related stress and burnout, we examine these topics in depth and suggest strategies for reducing stress and preventing burnout. In our final chapter, "The School-Home Partnership," we describe possible patterns of parent involvement in educational interventions and explore ways of facilitating cooperation and collaboration between home and school.

Although each chapter focuses on specific topics, we did not attempt to limit our discussions within the confines of a particular chapter. We frequently refer to previous and, at times, upcoming themes in the book. Because of their importance in understanding and influencing children's behavioral adjustment, some topics are integrated throughout. Assessment, for example, is a concern that is included in some way in every chapter.

Our goal is to provide a critical review of relevant theory, research, and practice. We note limitations, cautions, and even flaws in some interpretations and interventions. For example, we believe it is essential for teachers and other practitioners to understand the potential shortcomings of some traditional approaches to assessment, to recognize potential adverse side effects of punitive techniques, to understand the limits of parent involvement, and to be aware of the potential wear and tear from teaching behaviorally disordered students.

Perhaps the most salient integrative feature of this book involves the professional training of the authors. Professor Rizzo has been trained in clinical psychology and worked with troubled children and their families in clinical practice and residential settings. Professor Zabel, with his special education background, has worked with special needs children in classroom settings, and with preservice and practicing teachers. Both perspectives have been integrated into this text. Although we have collaborated on the content and organization, each of us has taken primary responsibility for writing the individual chapters that reflect our areas of expertise. Thus, Professor Rizzo wrote most of the chapters dealing with basic issues and characteristics of specific populations; Professor Zabel wrote the assessment chapter and those dealing more directly with educational issues and interventions.

We believe this book provides a comprehensive, integrative treatment of the behavioral disorders of children and adolescents. We hope that it conveys information and guidance for those teachers, therapists, counselors, and others who seek to aid these troubled children and their families.

Acknowledgments

Many people have contributed directly or indirectly to the preparation of this book. The danger of naming those who have made contributions is the inadvertent omission of many others. Still, we know that certain individuals deserve special recognition.

First, we must thank the children and their families with whom we have worked and who have taught us about the complexities, challenges, and rewards of jointly striving for happier lives. Next, we thank the many teachers who have invested in our educations. Some of these teachers have been our own students, who have shared their experiences, ideas, successes, and failures as teachers of children with behavioral disorders. Some teachers are cited in the text, but most are not named. Among those whose ideas, experiences, and wisdom we can document are James Bartlett, Betty Bowling, Sheryl Grace, Elizabeth Lodge Rogers, Frank Nigro, Barb Peterson, and Katie Philp.

Several persons were involved in the preparation of this book at Allyn and Bacon. Our former editor, Jeff Johnston, encouraged us to develop and proceed with the project. John Coleman helped shepherd several chapters through review and revision, and Mylan Jaixen oversaw completion of the project and coordinated the many details of getting it into print.

Through the whole process, Beth Brooks kept careful track of everything and attended to important details.

Several reviewers provided thoughtful, critical appraisals of content, organization, and style, and many of their ideas have been incorporated. They include: Richard Fox, University of Wisconsin–Milwaukee; Mark Koorland, The Florida State University; Sharon Morgan, The University of Texas at El Paso; Rex Schmid, University of Florida; Robert Simpson, Auburn University; Craig Smith, Georgia College; Thomas Stich, Mansfield University; and Frank Wood, University of Minnesota.

We also thank our wives, Joyce Rizzo and Mary Kay Zabel, and children, David, Jeanette, Andrea and Sarah Rizzo, and Laura, Matthew, and Claire Zabel, who gave up many hours with us as we sat pounding away at our word processors, put up with our distraction, and listened to our frustration during the two-year project.

Finally, a special thanks must go to Ron and Lori Perlman, our "agents extraordinaire," who brought us together and believed in this project.

J. V. R.

R. H. Z.

Educating Children and Adolescents with Behavioral Disorders

PART I

Basic Issues in the Study of Behavioral Disorders in Children and Adolescents

The three chapters comprising Part I form a comprehensive foundation for the study of behavioral disorders in children and adolescents. An integrative perspective with emphasis on the complex ecological forces affecting children is critical to effective educational and psychological intervention. Such intervention demands the active involvement of parents and of professionals from many disciplines.

Chapters 1 and 2 investigate, through in-depth discussions, assumptions, issues, and problems in contemporary psychology and psychiatry; examine research on family interaction; and study the dramatic changes in current family life. Chapter 1 includes a detailed examination of controversies in diagnostic classification, a concept important for teachers to be familiar with in order to confer knowledgeably with their colleagues in clinical psychology and psychiatry. In planning effective intervention strategies, teachers must be aware of family dynamics, social forces acting upon the family, and the lives of children.

This initial process of foundation building leads us toward a thorough discussion of the assessment process in Chapter 3. The clinical and research foundations of psychology, psychiatry, and family studies are shown to be critically important as they are translated into practical educational applications in the lives of individual children. Such translation occurs in the process of assessment in which teachers and allied professionals first attempt to identify and to develop a comprehensive understanding of a single child living in a complex world of interacting forces.

Part I, then, is an introduction not only to the very broad clinical and research foundations of special education for behaviorally disordered children, but also to the specific assessment concepts and techniques that initiate the helping process for an individual child. Though complex and demanding, these chapters present a solid foundation for later study of specific childhood and adolescent problems and for approaches to intervention.

CHAPTER 1

Issues in the Study of Behavioral Disorders in Children and Adolescents

Overview

Introduction

For most children without behavioral disorders, learning is as natural as growing, and the work of teachers consists primarily in guiding them and channeling their energies. Without doubt, teaching demands technical skill, patience, wisdom, and tremendous stamina; yet teaching is largely a matter of fostering the development of a natural inclination in children to explore and interact with the world around them. While such potentials exist in children with special educational problems as well, their education also demands that teachers help them cope with a variety of problems in the learning process. In some children, these problems consist of limited intellectual abilities. In others, they stem from impairments of vision or hearing or neuromuscular coordination. As a society, we have come to recognize that such impairments require special modifications of the educational process in order to help disabled children fulfill their potentials.

In other children, however, problems in learning are more subtle in nature and arise not from clearly definable impairments, but from complex behavioral, emotional, and interactional characteristics that disrupt children's abilities to feel comfortable with themselves or others, to interact in satisfying or productive ways, or even to experience the world as the rest of us do. This text looks at the special educational problems of such children and explores the development and characteristics of those problems. Though a number of labels have been used to categorize these children, we will use the broad term *behavioral disorders* to include children whose ability to learn is impaired by personality problems, conduct disorders, or pervasive disturbances of development.

It is not easy for teachers to recognize or understand children and adolescents with personality problems. The features that distinguish them from their classmates are subtle and can easily go undetected. Often, children with personality problems are not understood as requiring special education services, and their needs go unmet despite their considerable suffering. Parents, teachers, and other school personnel usually perceive them as quiet, shy, often sad, unassuming, cooperative, and conscientious. If they perform well in school, children with personality problems may be stereotyped as bookish and withdrawn. If they do poorly, they are often characterized as nice, but not very bright. They endure anxiety, loneliness, self-rejection, and depression quietly and sadly. Barring some desperate cry for help in the form of a self-destructive act, a dramatic drop in grades, or an uncharacteristic act of vandalism, no one may ever notice that the child with a personality problem needs special assistance.

By contrast, parents, teachers, and others in the community are usually all too aware of children and adolescents with conduct disorders. These youngsters may display defiance, seething resentment, explosive anger, impulsive destructiveness, or various forms of drug or alcohol abuse. Often they are well known to the police and the courts. As angry loners or members of alienated groups, they may appear bent on hurting others or themselves, or both. School performance is usually poor and almost invariably their behavior disrupts the normal course of educational activities. Depending on the severity of the problems they manifest, these children may remain in regular classroom settings, or be segregated in special classrooms or schools for predelinquent or delinquent children.

Still another group of children and adolescents display such severe disruptions in their cognitive and emotional functions and behavior that they are completely unable to function in regular educational settings. Many of these children fail ever to develop language. Others have such severe language limitations or use language so peculiarly that they are unable to communicate clearly about their most basic needs and feelings. Deficits in ability are matched by idiosyncratic and nonfunctional behaviors, and such children are typically locked in a world apart from others. They may spend hours and days in self-stimulatory or self-destructive behaviors and in meaningless, repetitive rituals. Such children are marked so clearly by their behav-

ioral differences that, almost invariably, efforts to help them must take place in special settings for the most severely impaired.

At one time, the rationale for treating personality problems, conduct disorders, and pervasive developmental disorders together and apart from other problems of childhood seemed clear. These disorders appeared to stem from faulty psychosocial development rather than from genetic problems, brain trauma, intellectual deficits, or physical disabilities. Today, this rationale is no longer as clear. The lines between biophysical and psychosocial problems have blurred as we have developed deeper understandings of childhood developmental problems. While personality problems and conduct disorders do appear to stem largely from difficulties in adjusting to psychosocial expectations and patterns of interpersonal relationships, there are also, clearly, important constitutional variables now to be considered. And, though pervasive developmental disorders now clearly have their primary roots in genetic and constitutional impairments, these disorders have major ramifications for a child's ability to adapt to the psychosocial environment.

Basic Themes in the Study of Behavioral Disorders

In embarking upon the study of a broad and complex topic it is important to have a few landmarks to help maintain one's perspective and orientation. A mass of facts, names, and research conclusions is virtually useless, and therefore worthless, without some basic organizing principles. To some extent, the theories that characterize a field provide such organizing structures, and the methods of a discipline also guide our thinking. However, it is also important to be intentional and explicit about the assumptions and values that shape and organize our thinking. Perhaps the most basic assumptions that shape this text are: a commitment to an integrative framework, an emphasis upon an ecological orientation, a belief in the necessity of interdisciplinary approaches to intervention, and inclusion of parents as key resources in the special education process.

Integrative Framework

Our study of behavioral disorders in children and adolescents has demonstrated that an *integrative framework* is essential to an understanding of problems and an effective intervention strategy. This means that a wide range of concepts, theories, and techniques may offer valuable insight into childhood problems. The test of the validity and strength of concepts and ideas must always be sought in the research findings they generate and their usefulness in intervention, rather than in the intensity with which people hold them. An open, integrative perspective facilitates such ongoing testing of ideas.

Ecological Orientation

It has also become clear in recent years that a child's developmental and educational difficulties cannot be considered apart from family, school, neighborhood, and community influences. There is now general agreement that one must consider a child's total environment as a dynamic system of interrelated components in order to help that child achieve optimal developmental levels. While different disciplines have applied different terms to this kind of holistic view, psychologists and educators have come to think of it as an *ecological orientation*, in which a child's special talents or impairments must always be thought of in interaction with family, school, community, and cultural variables. Taken together, these different levels of social organization constitute the *ecosystem* in which the child grows and functions. Intervention to help a child develop and learn most effectively must take place simultaneously at these interrelated levels, each of which influences the others. Later in this chapter, we will review the development of the ecological orientation in greater depth, and this orientation will

permeate the concepts of assessment and intervention developed throughout the text.

Interdisciplinary Intervention

A necessary accompaniment to an ecological orientation is an *interdisciplinary approach* to intervention. The process of helping a child reach his or her optimal developmental potential must draw on the expertise of a variety of professionals, each of whom may provide unique concepts and perspectives to be integrated into a comprehensive plan for the child's education. Thus, teacher, psychologist, social worker, speech pathologist, pediatrician, and others may provide crucial pieces of information that foster a depth of understanding that no single discipline can provide. When these pieces are integrated into a comprehensive educational and service plan, the child stands to receive the greatest benefit.

Parental Involvement

It is important that parents be included as key members of the interdisciplinary team. While they may or may not have technical skills that are important in planning for their child's education, the parents do have knowledge and understanding of their own child. What is more, they have ultimate responsibility for the child's welfare and often must be recognized as the people who will actually implement major portions of the service plan designed for their child. While a youngster may spend five or six hours a day in school, he or she will spend the remaining hours in the home and neighborhood. It is in these settings that interactions with parents, siblings, peers, and others in the community become crucial in facilitating or hindering development, and parental responses become pivotal in structuring the child's world. School professionals must, therefore, enlist parental assistance in a partnership designed to help a child develop optimally.

In the remainder of this chapter we will develop a context for discussing the behavioral disorders of children and adolescents in terms of the major personality, conduct, and severe emotional problems that they experience. We will begin with some broad distinctions among children with personality and conduct problems and those with pervasive developmental disorders, examine the evolution of educational programs for these children, and discuss the importance of ecological and interdisciplinary approaches to the education of all behaviorally disordered children.

Issues in the Classification and Diagnosis of Behavioral Disorders

This section begins with a discussion of the commonalities and distinctions among the different behavioral disorders. The problem of appropriate classification of childhood disorders has been an ongoing one in psychology, psychiatry, and special education. While one might ask whether classification is necessary at all, the fact is that a conceptual structure is critical to organizing the vast amounts of clinical, educational, and research material that have been accumulated over the years. Furthermore, it is through appropriate classification that children are provided access to the services they may need to maximize their educational potential. Although inappropriate use of classification by branding children with an unequivocal label can be destructive, appropriate uses of classification are often the only route to educational and social services for many children (Wood, 1979).

The Medical Model of Behavioral Disorders

In one sense, the field of special education has been hampered by premature efforts at classification. Early approaches to diagnosis and classification in psychiatry and psychology were based on a *medical model* of disease. In a medical model there is an assumption that *symptom syndromes*, sets of symptoms that frequently occur together, have specific causes in the pathology of certain organs or physical systems. Thus,

for example, fever is a symptom reflecting the existence of some underlying problem. Likewise, a headache also suggests that something is wrong in systemic functioning. Neither fever nor headache alone, however, define a medical problem. They only tell us that there is some underlying physical disorder which causes both symptoms. Because clusters of such symptoms often occur together in recognizable patterns or syndromes, physicians are able to identify the underlying disorder causing the symptoms and to treat that disorder directly. Thus, for example, a syndrome consisting of fever, headache, runny nose, and sore throat may suggest an underlying infection that can be treated with antibiotics. A syndrome consisting of fever and headache with nausea and vomiting following a day in the sun suggests a different underlying cause and different treatment.

The key point in understanding the medical model of disorders is that observable signs and symptoms are only manifestations of an underlying problem, and do not themselves constitute the problem. A physician may use symptomatic treatment in some cases and try to reduce fever and headache by administering aspirin. But the physician recognizes that the underlying cause must also be remedied or the symptoms will persist. This medical model of disease is the foundation of medical diagnosis and treatment, and it has been used since antiquity.

However, while this model has been useful in understanding a variety of medical problems, its utility in understanding behavioral disorders is limited. Consequently, diagnostic classification systems based on this model have also been limited and have tended to distort approaches to understanding these problems in children. There is no evidence, for example, that conduct disorders can be traced to specific organic diseases or that personality problems can be treated by medical procedures specific to them. As we will see later, contemporary research is beginning to suggest that key constitutional and physiological factors may predispose children to respond in particular ways, but such findings bear little relationship to the traditional medical model. Nevertheless, it is important to have at least some understanding of traditional approaches to classification in order to understand the basis for the broad distinctions that we will use in our discussion as well as to understand the current terminology used by other child mental health professionals.

Clinically Based Classification

In 1980, the American Psychiatric Association published the third edition of its *Diagnostic and Statistical Manual of Mental Disorders* (DSM-III) (American Psychiatric Association, 1980). This major work was an attempt to standardize diagnostic nomenclature for mental disorders and bring systematization into the use of psychiatric terminology. Because it resulted from the collaborative efforts of psychiatrists from many different theoretical orientations and psychologists with as many different viewpoints, DSM-III is a document full of compromises (Williams, 1985). Expectably, it has met with considerable criticism and generated ongoing controversy. Nevertheless, special education professionals must be aware of DSM-III in order to communicate knowledgeably with their colleagues in psychiatry and psychology.

DSM-III presents a *multiaxial classification system*. This means that psychological disorders are classified simultaneously along several different axes or dimensions. Axis I disorders consist primarily of clinical syndromes or constellations of symptoms. A specific pattern of symptoms that occur together constitutes a clinical syndrome that is described among Axis I disorders (see Box 1.1). Thus, for example, an individual who displays a persistent, intense, and irrational fear of social situations involving potential judgment by others, a fear of doing things that might be embarrassing or humiliating, and a recognition that these fears are irrational, would be diagnosed as having a social phobia.

Axis II disorders consist of a variety of patterns in which specific personality traits become maladaptive because of their inflexibility, their impairment of social or occupational functioning, and the subjective distress they may cause. In some instances, Axis II patterns may be used to describe personality traits even when an actual disorder is not diagnosed. Thus, for example, one Axis II personality disorder is referred to as "passive-aggressive personality disorder"

Box 1.1   Some Examples of Axis I DSM-III Diagnoses Used for Children and Adolescents

The diagnostic classifications listed below are among those frequently encountered in working with behaviorally disordered children. DSM-III also includes specific developmental disorders such as developmental reading, language, and arithmetic disorders, which are coded on Axis II. In addition, any other diagnostic category normally first manifested after adolescence may be applied to children or adolescents if the specific criteria are met.

- *Mental Retardation*—mild, moderate, severe, profound, and unspecified types.
- *Attention Deficit Disorders*—those disorders with or without hyperactivity present, and a residual type manifest in older adolescents and adults.
- *Conduct Disorders*—aggressive socialized, aggressive undersocialized, nonaggressive socialized, nonaggressive undersocialized, and atypical conduct disorders not fitting any of the above categories.
- *Anxiety Disorders*—separation anxiety disorders, overanxious disorders, and others.
- *Pervasive Developmental Disorders*—infantile autism, childhood onset pervasive developmental disorders, and atypical pervasive developmental disorders.

and is characterized, among other things, by procrastination, stubbornness, inefficiency, and frequent forgetfulness. It is not uncommon to observe such a constellation of characteristics in others (and even ourselves when we are being honest), but these characteristics become psychological disorders only when their rigidity, repetition, and pervasiveness begin to interfere with social relationships and occupational effectiveness and create personal distress.

The key distinction between Axis I and II disorders is that Axis I disorders are often dramatic or florid in their behavioral manifestations. Inclusion of Axis II disorders ensures that important—but perhaps less intense—disorders are not overlooked (American Psychiatric Association, 1980, p. 23). An individual may exhibit one or more problems that can be diagnosed on Axis I or Axis II or both.

In some instances, an individual may also have a physical disorder or condition that is relevant to an understanding of personality functioning. Such physical conditions may or may not be directly related to psychological disorders on Axes I and II, but are important in the overall understanding and management of the psychological problems. For example, a child with a severe personality problem may also have a gastric ulcer or a youngster with a severe conduct disorder may have diabetes. Such coexisting physical conditions are diagnosed on Axis III.

Axes IV and V are important features of DSM-III because they constitute an explicit acknowledgement that ecological factors such as social stresses and levels of previous functioning are critical to an understanding of an individual. Axis IV includes ratings of the severity of psychosocial stressors in the child's environment such as a change of teacher, a move to a new school, the death of a peer, parental conflict or divorce, or hospitalization. Ratings on Axis IV tell something about the overall ability of the child to cope with severe pressures. A child who manifests psychological disorder in the absence of any significant psychosocial stressors is clearly more vulnerable than another child who begins to display problems in the face of a parental death or divorce.

Finally, the adequacy of an individual's social relations, occupational functioning, and use of leisure time over the course of the past year is rated on Axis V. Such ratings range from poor to superior and give some idea of the level of a person's competence prior to the emergence of psychological problems. Box 1.2 presents an example of DSM-III multiaxial diagnosis.

Limitations of DSM-III

Overall, DSM-III provides a comprehensive approach to the classification of individual problems. However, by its very nature as a classification system or taxonomy, it tends to distort the reality of problems in individual children and adolescents. A taxonomic system such as DSM-III tends to imply that the characteristics being classified exist *within* the individual being studied without any clear, concrete evidence. It is important to remember that a diagnostic label is not reality, but rather only one kind of classification.

Consider, for example, the DSM-III classification: Conduct Disorder, Socialized, Nonaggressive. The diagnostic criteria for this disorder include: (1) chronic violations of important social norms relevant to the individual's age group (e.g., persistent truancy); (2) repeated running away from home overnight; (3) chronic lying; and (4) stealing. While a child or adolescent might exhibit one or more of these behaviors and, therefore, meet some of the criteria for diagnosis, it would be crucial to understand how these behaviors fit into the child's overall pattern of adaptation to the ecological system of which he or she is a part. Although any one of these behaviors could seriously impair a youngster's ability to function adequately in mainstream society, it is also possible that they might be important ways of adapting to an unhealthy environment. Thus, a youngster with an abusive parent might be running away or lying to avoid physical and emotional damage. While such behaviors are not likely to foster

Box 1.2   An Example of DSM-III Multiaxial Classification

Don is an eleven-year-old boy currently in sixth grade. He was referred to the school psychologist for evaluation after several recent episodes of crying, frequent refusal to eat, daily refusal to go to school, and refusal to speak to anyone at school, including teachers and peers. He has attempted to run away from school on several occasions and has been forced to remain under the direct supervision of office personnel or the school nurse. School personnel report that he does not eat his lunch and instead calls his mother at lunchtime.

At home Don has been irritable and has displayed uncharacteristic anger. Don has been avoiding any contact with neighborhood children and spends most of his time watching TV or reading. In the past his grades have been quite good and, though a loner, he has always had a few friends he enjoyed.

Background information shows that Don is the younger of two brothers. His parents have a stable marriage, and they are able to express affection to each other and to their sons. Their expectations for their children and their disciplinary standards are basically reasonable, although both parents tend to be somewhat perfectionist and demanding. Both parents work and both have achieved a reasonable degree of occupational success. The family has recently moved to a new city as a result of a job transfer for Don's father, and the move was completed only two days before school opened and Don started sixth grade. Don had to give up his dog before the family's move and he was quite upset about this loss.

His parents report that Don is usually friendly, has always received good grades in school in the past, and has a good sense of humor, although

this has not been evident for several days. He is having nightmares and tends to follow his mother around the house after she returns from work, trying always to keep her in sight.

Axis I: Clinical Syndrome
Separation anxiety disorder with school refusal, avoidance of being alone in the home, apathy, sadness, nightmares.

Axis II: Personality Disorder
No diagnosis on Axis II (that is, no observed personality disorder despite some tendency toward shyness and social withdrawal).

Axis III: Physical Disorders or Conditions
No diagnosis on Axis III (a physical examination completed prior to the family's move showed Don to be in good health).

Axis IV: Severity of Psychosocial Stressors
(*1=none; 2=minimal* [e.g., family vacation]; *3=mild* [e.g., change in teachers]; *4=moderate* [e.g., parental discord or change in schools]; *5=severe* [e.g., parental divorce]; *6=extreme* [e.g., parental death or physical or sexual abuse]; *7=catastrophic* [e.g., multiple family deaths].)
Moderate to severe with move to a new home, starting a new school, and loss of a cherished pet.

Axis V: Highest Level of Adaptive Functioning Past Year
1=superior; 2=very good; 3=good; 4= fair; 5=poor.
Good to very good adaptive functioning past year.

positive development, they nevertheless do not exist simply as problems in the individual.

Further, DSM-III reflects its medical heritage in a model that views behavior and personality problems as clinical entities much like physical diseases. While there is evidence to justify such a view with regard to some kinds of childhood

problems (such as certain forms of mental retardation and pervasive developmental disorder), there is no evidence to warrant a generalized medical model of all behavioral disorders or to imply that such problems exist *within* persons (Achenbach, 1982). Despite its inclusion of Axis IV ratings of psychosocial stressors, DSM-III, nevertheless, has perpetuated the medical-disease model of disorders and is not particularly useful to special educators, although it is an essential tool for understanding and communicating with other mental health professionals.

Another major problem limiting the usefulness of DSM-III is that it fails to incorporate critical developmental considerations in the process of diagnosis. Built around a traditional understanding of adult disorders, DSM-III does not address the role of developmental processes and stages in the identification of psychological disorders. For example, during the course of normal development it is common for children and adolescents at certain ages to experience periods of unusual tension, fearfulness, or ambiguity about their identity. Such phenomena do not indicate the presence of psychological disorder, but could be misunderstood as doing so without a recognition that they are part of important developmental processes. Further, some problems may not be particularly serious at one point in development, but may be very serious at another (Bemporad & Schwab, 1986). As a comparison, mumps, a common and mild problem in children, can cause potentially serious problems during adulthood. Among behavioral disorders, a mild transportation phobia in a young child may have few consequences and disappear as the child grows, but the same problem could be disabling in an adult.

Finally, DSM-III has not eliminated problems in the reliability or consistency with which psychiatric diagnoses are applied. The concept of *reliability*, in this context, refers to the ability of those using the system to reach agreement and maintain consistency in their application of diagnostic concepts (Quay, 1986). Research studies using DSM-III have failed to demonstrate high levels of reliability among diagnosticians using the system (Mattison, Cantwell, Russell, & Will, 1979; Williams, 1985), and correlations with the earlier edition of DSM-III, DSM-II (American Psychiatric Association, 1968) are rather modest at best (Mezzich, Mezzich, & Coffman, 1985).

Empirically Based Classification

Developing alongside traditional classification systems, several research-based approaches have offered more promise of providing accurate understanding of individual children while simultaneously permitting useful classification in order to permit children to have access to appropriate education and treatment. Most of these approaches are based on descriptions of the behaviors of children rather than on theoretical or clinical preconceptions.

The basic concept underlying empirical approaches to classification is that the *description* of children's behaviors is the appropriate point of departure for understanding those behaviors. Thus, rather than beginning with preconceived notions derived from theories or historical concepts, investigators using empirical approaches typically begin their investigations with large-scale surveys in which teachers or parents are asked to describe children's behavior. Subsequently, the researchers conduct statistical analyses of these descriptions to determine what behaviors tend to occur together most frequently in children. At the same time, it is possible to see what behaviors do not occur together. Proceeding in this fashion, several investigators have been able to demonstrate commonalities and differences that permit reasonable classification of children on the basis of their behavior that does not obscure the unique abilities and needs of the individual child (Achenbach, 1966, 1978a, 1978b; Achenbach & Edelbrock, 1978; Edelbrock & Achenbach, 1980; Hewitt & Jenkins, 1946; Himmelweit, 1953; McDermott, 1980, 1981; Peterson, 1961).

Research along these lines has often used multivariate statistical methods such as factor analysis. *Factor analysis* is a technique whereby patterns among behaviors may be determined through statistical identification of clusters of characteristics that are highly correlative with each other but not with other clusters. Factor analytic research has produced consistent results indicating that it is possible to classify children's behavior reliably into a few major categories. One of these categories has variously been termed internalizing disorders, anxiety/withdrawal, overcontrolled, or personality problems (Achenbach, 1982). These problems are characterized in a child by subjective suffering, with additional specific symptoms such as anxiety, depression, phobias, worrisomeness, withdrawal, nightmares, physical concerns and pains such as nausea and headaches, frequent crying, self-consciousness, and excessive shyness.

A second major category is also known by a variety of terms: these include externalizing, undercontrolled, social maladjustment, or conduct disorders. Children with conduct disorders display such behaviors as disobedience, lying, stealing, fighting, truancy, destructiveness, sexual delinquency, and inadequate guilt feelings.

There is some question whether a further useful distinction can be made between externalizing problems that are primarily the result of cognitive and neurological deficits and those that result primarily from social deficits (Reeves, Werry, Elkind, & Zametkin, 1987; Werry, Reeves, & Elkind, 1987). This distinction is explored in detail in Chapter 5. For the moment, however, the weight of research evidence points clearly to the need for distinguishing between personality problems and conduct disorders.

A third major group of problems that occur together may involve symptoms of uncommunicativeness, ritualistic or stereotyped behaviors, distortions of sensory experiences such as seeing or hearing things that are not there, self-stimulatory behavior, self-injurious behavior, and failure to pass many expected developmental milestones. Behavior problems like these differ significantly from those in either of the other two broad categories and are most like what have traditionally been termed childhood psychoses.

One of the problems that arises in using such broad defining categories is that subtle variations among individual children are obscured and real differences may be overlooked. However, if we bear in mind that children are real people whose behaviors do not often fit our preconceived notions, it is still useful to organize our thinking about childhood problems into three broad categories, termed here as personality problems, conduct disturbances or disorders, and pervasive developmental disorders, and then to examine different patterns within them. In actual educational practice, however, it is critical always to remember that "the children haven't read those books" (Kanner, 1969), and that appropriate uses of classification should always serve the needs of individual children.

Educational Objectives and Issues

Because of the fundamental differences among personality problems, conduct disorders, and pervasive developmental disorders, there are crucial differences in educational objectives and educational interventions for these children. Not only must the classroom teacher have a clear sense of differing needs, temperamental characteristics, response patterns, and family influences, but he or she must also be aware of differences in how these children experience and so relate to their world. Further, it is important that teachers be clearly aware of the ways in which educational and social service structures and systems affect children's lives.

Children and Adolescents with Personality Problems

Most often, the needs of children with personality problems are simply ignored in contemporary education. As noted earlier, these children are not typically disturbing to others. They do not usually engage in acts of vandalism; they are not overtly defiant; they do not often steal, cheat, assault others, or display sexual delinquency.

In short, they simply do not bother classmates, teachers, or school administrators. As a result, they are an underserved group despite the fact that as many as 8 to 10 percent of school-age children may experience such problems (Joint

Commission on the Mental Health of Children, 1970), and despite the fact that children with personality problems are explicitly included among those with behavioral disorders as defined in the regulations implementing Public Law 94–142, the Education for All Handicapped Children Act (U.S. Congress, 1975). In those regulations, serious emotional disturbances (behavioral disabilities) are defined as including inabilities to learn that are not due to intellectual, sensory, or other health factors, inabilities to develop or maintain satisfactory relationships, inappropriate behaviors or feelings, pervasive unhappiness or depression, and physical symptoms of fears related to personal or school problems.

Given these facts, what educational objectives may be usefully defined for children and adolescents with personality problems? First, it is critical that these youngsters be accurately identified as in need of service. This is no simple task. The distinctions between children in need of service and those simply displaying normal developmental variations and tensions are difficult to make in practice. Extensive research has demonstrated that most children display periods of fearfulness, sadness or transient depression, shyness, and problems in interpersonal relationships (LaPouse & Monk, 1958, 1964; Werry & Quay, 1971; Bauer, 1976). Chapter 3 examines approaches to accurate identification in considerable detail, but for the moment it is important to recognize that identification is a key objective in the education of children with personality problems.

Second, identification must lead to useful interventions that will enable these children to develop the interpersonal skills, adaptive strategies, and internal confidence that permit maximal growth. There is a wide range of techniques that teachers can implement in the classroom or in cooperation with parents. In certain instances, interventions may be necessary that are beyond the scope of educational services or the competency of the classroom teacher (Wood, 1985). Some children, for example, may require skills

training, counseling, or psychotherapy outside the classroom setting with professionals trained in these techniques. In either case, assessment and identification must translate into useful intervention strategies to be meaningful.

Third, it is important that educational administrative structures be responsive to the needs of these children through the provision of appropriate preservice and in-service training, screening and identification programs, and through intervention services in the school, in cooperation with families, or by arrangement with outside professionals as necessary to meet the needs of the individual child. At the administrative level, schools must attempt to organize human, technical, financial, physical, and informational resources in such a fashion that identification and intervention are possible (Maher & Bennett, 1984).

Finally, program evaluation and revision must be integral components of educational programming for children with personality problems. As critical as program evaluation is throughout all areas of special education, it is particularly important in programs for children with personality problems since such programs remain relatively new compared with services for children with other disabilities.

Children and Adolescents with Conduct Disorders

Unlike children with personality problems, children and adolescents with conduct disorders are rarely overlooked. Their behavior is frequently disturbing to classmates, parents, teachers, and the community. The objective of accurate identification remains important, but it takes on a significantly different character. Because their behavior disturbs others, children with conduct disorders typically elicit punitive responses from those in their environment (Wood, 1979). Often there is a tendency for professionals to be overinclusive in their identification of children with conduct disorders and to attempt to exclude them from integrated educational settings by putting them into special ones to avoid dealing with their disruptiveness. On the other hand, there are also strong cultural and political pressures to view such children as essentially normal and not in need of special services (Kauffman, 1984). Their behavior may be viewed as voluntary, subject to internal controls, and therefore not requiring specialized intervention. A frequent attitude is that it is the children's fault they do not learn. Children with conduct disorders are seen as responsible for their behavior, but at the same time as requiring exclusion from normal educational settings.

But once identified, how do we work with conduct disordered children most effectively? What are the key educational objectives for such youngsters? And where do we work with them? These complex questions are at the center of ongoing debate in special education and in educational administration.

We adopt the view that educational intervention for children with conduct disorders must simultaneously address psychological, psychosocial, and academic factors. It is clear, both from educational experience and extensive research, that there is little possibility of academic growth in children whose behavior and emotions are disruptive, disordered, and filled with conflict. They confuse, frustrate, and anger both peers and teachers. Often, they hate themselves. Learning cannot take place in an atmosphere filled with such tensions. There is simply no way to avoid the fact that our teachers and schools must deal directly and immediately with the psychological and interpersonal problems that these children experience. While interventions on the part of mental health professionals may be important additional steps, the classroom teacher must take major responsibility for working to promote emotional and behavioral growth in these children and in their relationships with others.

At the same time, the teacher's primary responsibility is to teach the basic cognitive and academic skills children need to survive and to grow in society. The teacher must provide an environment that will permit both personal integration and academic achievement to take place simultaneously.

And finally, these complex tasks must take place in an environment that is as little removed from the educational mainstream as possible. Children with conduct disorders will not live apart from the rest of society as they grow through adolescence and adulthood, and they cannot be educated apart from their peers to any greater extent than is absolutely necessary for them to develop the emotional, behavioral, and cognitive skills they will need to cope in life.

Children and Adolescents with Pervasive Developmental Disorders

The educational issues that arise in working with children with pervasive developmental disorders are considerably different from those discussed thus far. In most instances, these children experience such pervasive disruption of emotional, behavioral, and cognitive functioning that the teacher's primary objective must be to establish emotional contact and communication with them. The ability to learn self-care and daily routines, survival skills, communication skills, and basic control of bodily and behavioral functions takes priority over traditional academic experiences. Special education takes the form of intensive training and care in highly structured, controlled settings. Opportunities for normalized educational experiences are sharply limited and, often, simply do not exist.

Evolution of Special Education for Children and Adolescents with Behavioral Disorders

The emergence of formal special educational programs for children with specific disabilities is historically a quite recent event. Prior to the nineteenth and twentieth centuries, social views of children tended to depersonalize them. Children were viewed in terms of their religious, military, or economic significance and treated according to their value to the family or the society in which they lived. Thus, for example, among the ancient Greeks, the people of the city-state of Sparta valued male children who could become warriors and contribute to the state's militaristic goals. Girls and those boys who displayed disabilities had little value to society because they did not further its aims. Similarly, in agrarian and preindustrial societies children were valued to the extent that they could contribute to the economic security of the family. The more children a farmer had, the more land he could work to build wealth and ensure family well-being.

Because of their impairments, children with various kinds of disabilities often had little economic value and were viewed, instead, as liabilities to their families and to society. If their disabilities could not be exploited to someone's advantage, they were left to fend for themselves or to depend on the kindness of those few men and women who could see them as individuals with intrinsic worth. Assistance for disabled children might come from a few generous benefactors or from religious societies, but there was little organized social response to their needs. What assistance there was, was provided for those children whose impairments were obvious and easily understandable. People could respond with sympathy to a sightless child or one who was physically crippled.

However, those children with emotional and behavioral problems received little in the way of understanding or assistance, either from individual benefactors or from society. Rather, they were viewed as social misfits unable to carry their own weight by virtue of their fears and inhibitions, as moral degenerates who could not conform their behavior to prevailing moral or social norms or, in the case of pervasive developmental disruption, as possessed by evil spirits. Not everyone held such views, of course (Kauffman, 1979), but they were the prevalent views that shaped social and political institutions and activities.

Early Efforts

The earliest formal educational efforts to assist children with specific impairments were directed toward those with disabilities that were more or less clearly identifiable. The intellectual spirit that spurred major social, political, and scientific changes during the first part of the nineteenth century also fostered humanistic concern for the well-being of disabled children. The remainder of the century witnessed humane and courageous efforts to educate children with vision, hearing, and intellectual impairments. Students of special education are very familiar with the names of Jean-Marc Itard, Edouard Seguin, Samuel Gridley Howe, Thomas Gallaudet, Walter E. Fernald, and Maria Montessori. These pioneers and their students produced major advances in educational concepts and intervention techniques. More important, their work was an unequivocal demonstration that educational intervention could have positive effects in helping disabled individuals function productively despite their impairments.

Unfortunately, few such strides occurred in the recognition that children with personality problems, conduct disorders, and pervasive developmental disorders could also be helped. Societal attitudes toward these children were characterized by insensitivity and blame.

What changes there have been have come slowly and sporadically, and often through the juvenile justice system, class action suits, or from psychological and psychiatric practice rather than through the educational system or systematic, forward-looking legislation.

The very first formal public school efforts to educate children with conduct problems were the streamer classes of the New Haven, Connecticut, school system in 1871. In these classes, children with conduct problems were lumped together with mentally retarded youngsters and immigrant children who did not speak English. Nevertheless, the streamer classes constituted a social recognition that disordered and disruptive behavior might reflect childhood problems amenable to professional intervention.

Another pioneering effort to recognize and treat psychological problems in children was the first child guidance clinic, established in 1896 by Lightner Witmer at the University of Pennsylvania. Three years later, in 1899, the social reform efforts of John Peter Altgeld and Julia Lathrop culminated in the establishment of the first juvenile court in the United States. Rather than adjudicating criminal responsibility in minors, the juvenile court was to act as a chancery court with responsibility for ensuring the welfare of children. Questions of innocence, guilt, or punishment were to take second place to planning for the optimal development of children.

In 1909 in Chicago, William Healy established the Juvenile Psychopathic Institute, whose mission was to work clinically with children who were under the care of the juvenile court. During the 1920s and 1930s, the child guidance movement continued to spearhead efforts directed toward understanding and helping children with psychological problems, but without major legislative support. Healy remained a major force in working toward therapeutic understanding of conduct problems and, in 1941, proposed adoption of some of the features of the British Borstal system for the correction of childhood and adolescent problems that led to conflict with the law (Healy & Alper, 1941). These efforts resulted in the development of the Youth Authority Movement during the 1940s and 1950s, which led many states and the federal government to develop forms of model legislation intended to emphasize psychological and educational intervention rather than incarceration and punishment. Vocational training, occupational therapy, individual psychotherapy, and group psychotherapy were some of the ideas incorporated into these approaches to intervention, along with the concept that a youngster's entire living situation could constitute a "therapeutic milieu" (Polsky, 1962). By midcentury an emerging ecological orientation was gaining momentum with the recognition that "antisocial behavior in children and youth may be provoked by environmental forces, by interpersonal forces,

or by a combination of both" (Richards, 1951, p. 243).

During the same period, thoughtful educators were also aware of the need for more specific educational planning and intervention for children with behavioral disorders, and many educators spoke out on behalf of troubled children (Kauffman, 1979). As early as 1938, some educators recognized the complexities involved in the classification of childhood problems and suggested the broad distinctions between conduct disorders and personality problems that were discussed earlier in this chapter. Further, they recognized the necessity for study of the individual child within a total ecological context (Baker & Stullken, 1938). Nevertheless, these insights and efforts remained sporadic and unsystematic.

Public Law 94–142

The first sweeping legislative action that explicitly encompassed the needs of children with personality problems, conduct disorders, and pervasive developmental disorders did not occur until 1975 with the passage of Public Law 94–142, the Education for All Handicapped Children Act.

The purpose of PL 94–142 is to ensure a free, appropriate, public education to all handicapped children. Most important, in the context of the present discussion, PL 94–142 explicitly acknowledges the special educational needs of children with serious emotional disturbance. The law specifies that all handicapped children shall receive adequate educational services, due process safeguards of their educational rights, placement in the least restrictive environment consistent with their needs, nondiscriminatory testing and evaluation, and individualized educational planning. Public schools must develop adequate training and staffing plans to ensure that the special educational needs of handicapped children can be met, or they must contract with private agencies to provide such services. Each of these provisions is spelled out in considerable detail, and the law is given force by tying federal funding assistance to adequate compliance on the part of the schools. While the promise of Public Law 94–142 has yet to be fulfilled, it has stirred greater efforts toward providing adequate services to special children than any other single piece of legislation.

However, PL 94–142 has not gone without criticism, and its definition of serious emotional disturbance particularly has generated confusion and heated controversy. The law defines serious emotional disturbance as:

A condition exhibiting one or more of the following characteristics over a long period of time and to a marked degree, which adversely affects educational performance: a. An inability to learn which cannot be explained by intellectual, sensory, or health factors; b. An inability to build or maintain satisfactory interpersonal relationships with peers and teachers; c. Inappropriate types of behavior or feelings under normal circumstances; d. A general pervasive mood of unhappiness or depression; or e. A tendency to develop physical symptoms or fears associated with personal or school problems. (*Federal Register*, 1977, p. 42478)

Controversy has arisen from the fact that, as currently stated, PL 94–142 is ambiguous in the definition of serious emotional disturbance (Wood, 1985). While the law mandates services for children who are seriously emotionally disturbed, it does not clearly provide for educational services to students who exhibit behavior that reflects social maladjustment, but who may not experience serious emotional disturbance (Schulz & Turnbull, 1983).

In fact, PL 94–142 reflects the ambiguities in terminology and usage that pervade the professional and scientific literature discussed earlier in this chapter. Thus, some professionals might argue that social maladjustment does not exist in the absence of some degree of emotional disturbance, while others would argue that the two terms refer to distinctly different sets of problems that could exist independently of each other. Subsequent regulations implementing the law have not successfully clarified these issues, and other questions have emerged as

well. For example, discussions of the ambiguities in PL 94–142 have led to further questions regarding the intent of Congress in the enactment of PL 94–142 and appropriate execution of its provisions (Wood, 1985).

Another controversy concerns inclusion of autism in the federal definition. Although originally included together with schizophrenia, autism is now subsumed in the category called "other health impaired." Chapter 6 will examine some of the issues involved in this controversy.

In a 1985 position paper, the Executive Committee on the Council for Children with Behavioral Disorders took a strong stand advocating that the term *behaviorally disordered* be used to replace *seriously emotionally disturbed* in PL 94–142 (Huntze, 1985). The committee reasoned that the term *behavioral disorders* (1) does not carry the confusing theoretical and conceptual connotations of serious emotional disturbance; (2) will promote more comprehensive and objective assessment of children; (3) is less stigmatizing; (4) is more representative of the kinds of children and problems that schools are currently serving; and (5) more accurately reflects professional tendencies in using observations of behavior as the basis for evaluation and intervention rather than inferred internal states.

The remainder of this text continues to use a set of terms that corresponds to research findings, follows the recommendations of the Executive Committee on the Council for Children with Behavioral Disorders, and that will help students organize and integrate their own learning in a useful way. Because of their inclusiveness, the terms *behavioral disorder* or *behaviorally disordered* are used to refer to a broad range of childhood problems. Behavioral disorders will include all of those problems explicitly addressed in PL 94–142. It is important to note how similar these components of the Public Law 94–142 definition are to what is described above as internalizing problems or personality problems. However, the term *conduct disorder* also includes what is described above as *externalizing problems*, including what is often termed *social maladjustment.* Use of the term *personality problem* continues to refer to those disorders that are primarily internalizing in nature, and *conduct disorder* continues to refer to problems that are primarily externalizing problems. Finally, the term *pervasive developmental disorder* is subsumed under the broad heading of behavioral disorders to refer to problems that involve disruptions of reality contact such as childhood schizophrenia and autism.

In brief, then, the broad category of behavioral disorders includes personality problems, conduct disorders, and pervasive developmental disorders. Each of these three subcategories is sufficiently distinct from the others in predisposing characteristics, causation, and approaches to intervention to warrant separate discussion. Part Two examines each of these groups of childhood problems in greater detail.

Educational Models for Children with Behavioral Disorders

One of the key provisions of Public Law 94–142 is the mandate that children with special educational needs be educated in the least restrictive environment consistent with their needs. This has not been the prevalent approach historically. Rather, children with special needs have often been excluded from educational services or segregated into special residential or day schools or special classrooms without clear consideration of the optimal environment for learning. In addition to the obvious stigmatization associated with such segregation, inappropriately restrictive educational models teach children little about their ability to cope with real-world problems, to control their impulses and interact effectively with others, or to make use of their potentials.

While we have recognized the need for appropriate environments in the education of children with sensory, intellectual, and physical disabilities for some time, this has not been as clear a case for children with behavioral disorders. Instead, specific educational intervention in public school systems for children with behavioral disorders has been virtually nonexistent until very recently. Most often, children with personality problems have been simply overlooked by school systems bent on dealing with more obvious kinds of problems. Since children with personality problems very often suffer in silence, they have rarely been an educational priority in the past. The impact of dramatic rises in suicide rates and psychophysiological disorders in children in recent years has served to focus attention more clearly on the needs of children who struggle with anxiety, fearfulness, and depression. However, these disorders constitute only a small fraction of the personality problems that beset children as well as adults.

Children with conduct disorders, by contrast, have received more attention from educators. Unfortunately, relatively little of this has been benign attention. Rather, children with conduct disorders have often been excluded from mainstream educational services for varying lengths of time in the hopes that suspension, expulsion, or placement in residential institutions would somehow magically give them the skills needed to function more effectively once returned to the company of their peers. Attempts at punitive control and regimentation have had little positive effect, and often these children are returned to mainstream environments unchanged except for feeling more resentment and fear, and with no greater ability to establish positive and satisfying interaction patterns.

Children with pervasive developmental disorders have characteristically been served in highly restrictive institutional settings or in private schools apart from normal peers. They have been controlled with medications or restraints, but often little has been done to try to develop the basic communicative and interactional skills that would enable them to function at optimal levels of independence. While changes in educational approaches with psychotic children have begun to emerge recently, the need to rethink intervention techniques and environments is perhaps most pressing for these children.

The key issue in developing appropriate educational placements for special children is matching the child's abilities and needs to an educational setting that is integrated as closely as possible into the educational mainstream. In a cascade model of educational services, Reynolds and Deno have proposed a multilevel organization of educational services (Deno, 1970; Reynolds, 1962, 1976).

Within this model, the least restrictive environment for special education is the regular classroom. The introduction of additional modifications ranges from the use of consultants to the regular classroom teacher through assistance by itinerant or resource specialists, part-time special classroom placement, full-time special classroom placement, full-time special day school placement, and residential placement. In any of these instances, however, the critical issue is maintenance of the child's educational program in the least restrictive setting consistent with the child's needs for the shortest time necessary to achieve the child's educational objectives.

Education in the Regular Classroom

The least restrictive educational environment for some children with behavioral disorders is the regular classroom. Children who can benefit from this setting are those whose behavior is not so markedly different from that of their peers that it disrupts either their own learning and development or that of other children. In order to be able to function in the regular classroom, the child must be able to maintain sufficient concentration and attention to listen for sustained periods, to respond to written and verbal instructions presented to a large group, and to employ the self-control necessary to follow through on assignments and to interact cooperatively with the teacher and with other children.

The teacher is the key to enabling children to learn in the regular classroom setting because it is the teacher who establishes such critical environmental parameters as clear but flexible structure, consistency, warmth, predictable consequences for behavior, and encouragement. Children with personality problems and conduct disorders can often learn within this kind of environment because they are able to see the relationships between their behavior and the consequences from the environment. Predictability provides them with a measure of control. Fearful children develop a sense that they can control the circumstances that are associated with their fears, and with encouragement they can gradually face the external stimuli and control the internal responses that produce their fear. Depressed children, similarly, come to learn that they have some measure of control over their moods and some measure of control over their environment. With a sense of control, the hopelessness that often characterizes their outlook diminishes. Children with conduct disorders, likewise, can develop a clear awareness of the relationships between their behavior and the responses of others, or the natural consequences in the physical environment. A reduction in the internal and environmental chaos that such youngsters often experience is reduced.

But behaviorally disordered children cannot develop such structure for themselves, and the intervention of a skilled, sensitive teacher is critical. Further, it is important that the regular classroom teacher have access to sufficient resources in personnel and materials to address special educational problems in the classroom. One approach that is coming into wide usage along these lines is the availability of consulting and/or resource teachers—specialists in intervention with specific kinds of childhood problems who can serve in a consultative role in the classroom, or who can work with individual children or small groups outside the classroom for brief periods throughout the day (Forness, Sinclair, & Russell, 1984). The classroom teacher must also have ready access to other support personnel including psychologists, social workers, and medical personnel.

Education in the Special Classroom: Full- or Part-Time

In some cases, a child's needs may extend beyond the services that can be provided in the regular classroom even with the support of resource or consulting teachers. One child might be unable to speak in a large group of children, while another may be unable to withstand normal classroom competition and pressure. Still another child might be unable to control aggressive impulses to the extent necessary to interact safely with other children. In instances such as these, it is in the best interests of the child to learn in an environment that is more supportive, more amenable to individualized education, or more highly structured. Some children may be able to function part of the time in a regular classroom setting and require special modifications during only a portion of the school day. Others may require full-time placement in a special classroom over a period of months or years.

There are a wide range of organizational options for special classroom placement (Morse, 1980; Sindelar & Deno, 1978), but all share a recognition that, at least for certain periods, behaviorally disordered children may require more individualized attention, more intensive structure, or the assistance of specialists that cannot be provided in the regular classroom setting.

Education in the Special Day School

An even more restrictive educational setting is the special day school, which is usually physically separate from regular school buildings. The special school setting is appropriate for those youngsters who cannot adapt to even minimal expectations for attention, communication, and cooperative interaction with others. Educational programming is intensive, highly structured, and often oriented toward establishing self-control and basic interaction and communication skills. It is unusual to find children with personality problems in such settings. Rather, environments with this level of structure and control are usually appropriate for children and adolescents with severe conduct disorders and pervasive developmental disorders.

One example of a special day school program is the Mark Twain School in Montgomery County, Maryland (LaNeve, 1980). Designed to fill the educational needs of seriously emotionally disturbed children, the Mark Twain School works with youngsters from elementary through high school in providing its students with a variety of psychoeducational alternatives. Teacher/advisers not only use traditional teaching methods, but also develop students' individual educational plans, coordinate services, counsel students, work with parents, and assist students in transitions to other programs or jobs. The broad behavior management program at Mark Twain is founded on three major principles: (1) the staff does not accept excuses; (2) natural consequences are used instead of punishment; (3) the staff does not give up on any student.

Education in Residential Schools

The most restrictive educational environment for some students is the residential school designed to meet an individual's needs for a high degree of structure, environmental control, and intensive programming. Often, educational intervention is coupled with complex behavior modification programs, individual and group psychotherapy, and chemotherapy. Educational efforts are typically directed toward establishing basic skills in self-care, communication, and the activities of daily living. Residential staff are available on a twenty-four-hour basis and programs extend into all areas of the individual's life. In effect, the residential school constitutes a totally controlled environment designed to enable the individual to return as rapidly as possible to less restrictive settings with the basic skills needed to continue learning while coping with the demands of daily life.

The TREES (Therapeutic Residential Experience for Emotional Stability) in Augusta County, Virginia, is a five-day residential school for behaviorally disordered adolescents (Heuchert, Morrisey, & Jackson, 1980). In this program, students are removed from the experiences of chronic failure that characterized their preplacement ecological environment or ecosystem, and are placed in a residential camplike environment. Simultaneously, staff members work with parents to provide training in parenting skills and to plan for the return of students to their preplacement environments. The program includes extensive individual and group counseling services, and values clarification discussions, wilderness experiences, attendance at cultural events, and vocational experiences as well as more traditional classes. Concepts underlying the TREES program include the belief that problems do not reside in students but in the interactions between students and their environments. TREES attempts to modify problems through environmental changes as well as other means, and works toward modification of the ecological system to which students will eventually return.

Subsequent chapters examine each of these educational alternatives in considerably more detail and discuss the specific educational needs of children and adolescents with different kinds of behavioral disorders.

An Ecological Orientation in the Education of Children and Adolescents with Behavioral Disorders

Our discussion of educational models and the service cascade model serves as a natural introduction to an ecological orientation in the education of children and adolescents with behavioral disorders. The term *ecology* refers to the study of the relationships between an organism and its environment. In special education, an ecological orientation reflects a commitment to the study of the reciprocal influences between a child and a particular environment. In a comprehensive discussion of conceptual models in special education, William Rhodes (1974) distin-

guished among behavioral, psychodynamic, biophysical, sociological, and ecological models. While each of the other models describes childhood problems as existing within the individual child or the environment, only the ecological approach examines the possibility that behavioral disorders may arise at the point of interaction between child and environment. This is not to suggest that the other models are invalid. On the contrary, each contributes its own valid perspective to understanding childhood problems. However, to the extent that any model neglects an intensive study of child-environment interaction, it is incomplete (Rhodes, 1967, 1970).

As an example of the distinctions among these models, consider for a moment a child who displays a consistent pattern of unacceptable, aggressive behavior toward peers in the classroom. A behavioral approach might suggest that this behavior is maintained by reinforcers that need to be identified; intervention would require altering the patterns of reinforcement that maintain the behavior. A psychodynamic view would likely posit the existence of unconscious anger (perhaps toward one or both parents) which is displaced toward peers. The appropriate intervention would involve attempts to help the child recognize and accept the unconscious anger and express it more constructively. A biophysical approach would very likely search for underlying constitutional factors or subtle neurological deficits as causative factors, and a sociological model would prompt an exploration of the child's environment as the source of the problem.

In contrast to all of these, an ecological orientation would consider several possibilities. Is there something in a particular environment that elicits aggressive responses from the child? Perhaps the child is being ostracized, teased, or bullied by peers and is simply retaliating. Or perhaps the demands of the classroom environment are creating sufficient stress to maintain a state of chronic overarousal in the child. Is it possible that the child has learned that aggressive behavior is adaptive at home or in the neighborhood, but has failed to learn that it is inappropriate in the classroom? Finally, is it possible that the child is not unusually aggressive at all, but that his teacher is unable to tolerate even minimal aggressive displays?

Obviously, an answer to any of these questions would depend on an intensive study of the child-environment interaction. But the important point is that neither child nor environment would be studied independently. Rather, it is in the interaction between them that useful intervention possibilities might emerge.

Susan Swap has outlined the key assumptions of an ecological approach to the study of behavioral disorders (Swap, Prieto, & Harth, 1982). First, the disturbance or disorder does not exist within the individual. Rather, what we describe as disturbance lies in the interaction between the child and the environment. Second, in order to be effective, interventions must affect the ecological system of which the child is a part. Interventions directed unilaterally toward changing only the child's behavior or changing only the environment will not lead to durable and pervasive change. Third, an ecological orientation is integrative, and intervention techniques may take a variety of forms ranging from behavioral interventions to altering individuals' perceptions, modifying attitudes, or changing the physical environment. Fourth, the complexity of ecological systems is such that any specific intervention may produce a range of unanticipated consequences. Finally, each interaction between child and behavior setting is unique and must be investigated with an open mind and freedom from preconceptions.

The remainder of this text repeatedly returns to these basic assumptions in considering the etiology and characteristics of behavioral disorders and appropriate interventions. However, it is worth reemphasizing here that this orientation is not intended to replace other conceptual models or intervention techniques, but rather to enrich them and enhance their effectiveness.

The Professional Team

In only a few pages of preliminary discussion, the enormous complexity of special education with behaviorally disordered children has become apparent. As in other professional fields, increasing knowledge leads to increasing awareness of the realistic limitations of any given individual or discipline. As a consequence, responsible professionals have moved toward a comprehensive team approach in the education of behaviorally disordered children and adolescents. The clear necessity for professional interdependence has even prompted lawmakers to ensure that troubled children will receive interdisciplinary services by including a provision for interdisciplinary evaluation and planning in Public Law 94–142.

The specific purpose of the professional team is to bring to bear as much expert information as possible in planning educational interventions for the individual child. Within the context of frequent team meetings, professionals from different disciplines have the opportunity to share the findings of their individual assessments and to develop integrated intervention plans that consider all aspects of the ecological systems in which the child functions. Thus, for example, the classroom teacher is able to provide data regarding day-to-day functioning, while the psychologist may be able to shed light on this data on the basis of independent cognitive and personality assessment. The team social worker, in turn, may be able to provide a context for the data provided by the teacher and psychologist with information about the child's developmental history, family background, and neighborhood characteristics. Further, the resource teacher, nurse, or physician may have additional observations that will contribute to a comprehensive picture of the child as a component in a complex ecological system.

In addition to providing each other with information, members of the professional team can also provide mutual feedback, new perspectives, ideas for intervention, and even emotional support. The team meeting becomes a forum for sharing evaluative data regarding program effectiveness and a vehicle for facilitating communication (Losen & Losen, 1985).

However, the concept of team functioning must extend beyond periodic team meetings. All too often, the team meeting becomes the only point at which team members gather to plan and evaluate. Ideally, the team meeting should be the point at which information, plans, and evaluation strategies are shared formally as the end point of ongoing intradisciplinary and interdisciplinary consultation. Intradisciplinary consultation is a process in which a professional— classroom teacher, resource teacher, psychologist, social worker, or nurse—seeks out the counsel of other professionals in his or her own discipline. Intradisciplinary consultation may occur as an individual shares a problem or experience with a supervisor, with a colleague in the same school or school system, or with a colleague working in a different setting. Such steps may help in providing fresh perspectives and new ways of thinking about a problem, access to different ideas emerging in the professional literature, innovative concepts and techniques that have not yet appeared in the professional journals, and encouragement to continue trying in the face of problems that are resistant to change. Similarly, interdisciplinary consultation can enrich the perspective of a given discipline by providing totally different ways of conceptualizing a problem or highlighting aspects of the child's ecological system that were not previously considered. The background, training, orientation, and techniques of a professional from a different discipline may help in completely reconceptualizing a problem.

But neither intradisciplinary nor interdisciplinary consultation or effective team cooperation is likely to occur unless each member of the professional team is confident of his or her own abilities and those of other team members, and of a receptive attitude on the part of other team members. It is crucial that the professional team function in a school atmosphere that is supportive and concerned about its professional staff as well as the children it serves.

In a comprehensive discussion of the special education team, Stuart and Joyce Losen (1985) outline the different roles of team members and describe ideal team functioning. For example, the chairperson of the professional team must provide clear information regarding the roles of team members and must take responsibility for informing parents of these roles. The team leader must also be aware of, and inform parents of, parental rights, be familiar with school resources, and understand what is realistically feasible within the context of school operation. The team chairperson may be from any professional discipline, but is most likely to be a member of the administrative staff. The team coordinator, by contrast, is likely to be a member of the professional staff and is responsible for communicating with team members prior to the team meeting, recommending to the chairperson who should be present, maintaining records for the team, coordinating referrals for special services and collecting reports, overseeing the development of the child's individual educational plan (IEP), and following up on team recommendations to ensure that services are delivered in a timely fashion. The team case manager is the individual (most often the classroom teacher) who has the most active contact with the child and who is responsible for day-to-day implementation of the IEP. The case manager is the primary contact person for parents and the person most immediately aware of ongoing problems, questions, and issues that arise each day. The case manager is most immediately aware of the child's overall progress and, in effect, the executor of the team's decisions.

Because the special education teacher is often cast in the role of case manager, it is clear that his or her role is much broader than classroom education. In fact, the special education teacher is not only an educator, but also serves in therapeutic, advocacy, and liaison roles as well. The complexity of these functions requires that the special education teacher be a highly skilled individual conversant with a variety of perspectives in addition to possessing patience, insight, perseverance, and a host of other qualities. Chapter 11 discusses in considerable detail the personal and professional qualities that effective special education teachers display.

The School-Home Partnership

Our discussion of the special education team has thus far treated only its professional members. However, it has become increasingly clear that parents are, and must be treated as, key members of the team. All too often, parents have been relegated to a secondary role in the process of developing and implementing special education plans. In the case of children and adolescents with behavioral disorders particularly, parents have often been viewed as primary causative agents and almost systematically excluded from educational planning for their children.

Heavily influenced by medical and psychodynamic models, educators have tended to blame parents for their children's problems. Behavioral disorders have often been seen as the result of overprotection, faulty communication engendering intense anxiety, parental conflict, neglect, and abuse. While all of these may occur at times, there is no evidence in extensive research literature to support the view that parents cause behavioral disorders in their children (Suran & Rizzo, 1983). A more useful view that does find support in research and clinical experience is a transactional model, in which the interaction between parents and child may be just one source of problems. However, within the context of an ecological orientation, a child is a member of many interacting ecological systems, and problems may arise from faulty transactions in any or all of these systems.

The emergence of behavioral and ecological perspectives has permitted the development of a more realistic assessment of parents' roles, and this assessment clearly indicates that parents play a key part in their children's education (Shea & Bauer, 1983). As the primary ecological system in which children develop, the family must be incorporated into processes of assessment and educational planning. In fact, family involvement is now recognized as so crucial to effective special education that it is acknowledged as a key component of PL 94–142.

Later chapters examine the role of parents in the child's ecosystem in detail, and discuss specific methods for promoting parental participation and cooperation. For the moment, however, it is important simply to reemphasize that effective special education for behaviorally disordered children and adolescents cannot proceed with maximal effectiveness unless parents are actively involved in the process.

Summary

The study of behavioral disorders in children and adolescents encompasses a wide range of specific problems. However, most behavioral problems in children and adolescents fall into three broad categories: personality problems, conduct disorders, and pervasive developmental disorders.

Several basic themes serve as important foundations for the study of behavioral disorders. First, an integrative framework provides a means of bringing together diverse theoretical concepts and sources of clinical and research experience. Second, an ecological orientation furthers integrative aims by showing the influences of interactions between children and their environments. An interdisciplinary approach makes explicit recognition of the concepts and techniques developed in independent but related disciplines. Finally, it is important to recognize the role of parents as key members of the interdisciplinary intervention team.

Recognizing the complexities of classification and its role in diagnosis, we examined both clinically and empirically based classification systems and discussed the advantages and disadvantages of the DSM-III model. We also presented a series of broad, empirically based distinctions among personality problems, conduct disorders, and pervasive developmental disorders and some of the key educational issues and objectives associated with these problems.

After a review of several landmark developments in the study of childhood behavioral disorders, we mentioned, briefly, a few major educational models, including education in the regular classroom, in special classrooms, education in special day schools, and education in residential schools. This discussion set the stage for detailed exploration of educational models in later chapters.

Finally, Chapter 1 concluded with a detailed examination of ecological assumptions that are basic to intervention in childhood behavioral disorders, and a review of an interdisciplinary team approach to intervention.

CHAPTER 2

A Context for the Study of Behavioral Disorders in Children and Adolescents

Overview

Introduction

The study of any complex subject is made easier with the assistance of a few basic conceptual foundations, which then provide a context for organizing clinical experience and research findings. In this study of childhood and adolescent behavioral disorders, we have chosen to work from an integrative perspective. No single theory, methodology, or research approach has yet emerged that provides all the answers to the study of childhood problems. As in other areas of human activity, the study of behavioral disorders has been subject, at various points, to faddish thinking, to naive confidence that particular methods or techniques will provide simple solutions to complex problems, and to pointless theoretical controversy. Time inevitably proves that such approaches are sadly limited.

This text develops an integrative perspective on childhood behavioral disorders. Many of the different viewpoints that have emerged over the years offer useful ways of conceptualizing problems that may have particular value in understanding an individual child. We have tried to avoid a mindless eclecticism and to develop instead a reasoned integrative context that permits the incorporation of different ideas in flexible and useful ways.

An integrative view of childhood problems means that a basic commitment to an ecological perspective, for example, does not preclude a simultaneous recognition of the value of specific theoretical orientations. Instead, such a commitment involves an interpretation of psychodynamic or social learning theories within the overall context of an ecological point of view.

Ecological Perspectives on the Development of Childhood Problems

From an ecological perspective, every child is the focus of a unique set of interacting influences and forces that shape the course of development. These forces act on a child to shape learning patterns, expressive style, attitudes, habits, and relationships—in fact, every aspect of the growing child's life. However, children are not simply inactive lumps of human material, passively molded by these forces. Children take active roles in their unique ecosystems, and in continuous vital ways they influence their parents, families, classrooms, and neighborhood communities.

As we explore the development and characteristics of different kinds of childhood problems and psychological and educational approaches to intervention with these problems, it is crucial to remember the multiple interacting forces that constitute each child's unique ecosystem. The incredible complexity of these systemic interactions partly accounts for the difficulty of developing effective interventions. However, these same complexities also create opportunities for intervention at many places in a child's life.

To illustrate these points concretely, consider the situation of a ten-year-old boy—we can call him Jerry—who is currently experiencing serious difficulties in school. In fifth grade, Jerry presents his teachers with multiple management problems. He is doing poorly in his studies. His relationships with peers are alternately characterized by withdrawal and explosive anger. Small in stature, Jerry is often teased and picked on by classmates. At times he tries to act the role of class clown and to win peer acceptance by tolerating their teasing. At other times, the jokes of his peers strike too close to home, and he becomes explosively angry, striking out physically, even going so far as to threaten classmates with a knife. Often Jerry tries daredevil stunts to prove to his classmates that he is worthy of their respect. Most often such stunts backfire.

Jerry cries easily. He thinks he is homely and is particularly sensitive about the size and shape of his nose. While he is actually a handsome youngster, there is no way to convince him of this, and the fact that classmates tease him about his nose does little to reassure him. Jerry also feels he is stupid, and his school grades reinforce this belief. Teachers think of Jerry as a vulnerable and appealing youngster who often appears sad and lonely. Yet these same teachers are easily driven to distraction by Jerry's explosiveness and the disruption he causes in the classroom when he tries to gain acceptance through clowning.

Jerry's parents have been divorced for three years. Before the divorce the family consisted of Jerry and a younger brother and sister. The parental divorce was bitter and acrimonious, and both parents continue to harbor resentment toward each other. Jerry's mother has retained custody of her children. Both parents have subsequently remarried and both have young children from their current marriages. In these recombined families Jerry often feels lost and unsure of his place. With a brother, sister, and two stepbrothers, Jerry's place is not quite clear to his parents and stepparents, let alone to Jerry himself.

Sometimes Jerry takes on the role of a big brother and tries to uphold the rules in his recombined families. However, he often finds himself being scolded for being too harsh with his stepsiblings, while at other times he is scolded for not taking on the responsibilities of a ten-year-old in keeping his younger siblings out of mischief. Often frustrated and confused, he secretly vents his hostility on his younger siblings with teasing, provocation, and, occasionally, a punch or two.

With parents and stepparents working, Jerry has often been left in the care of adolescent baby-sitters or at a neighborhood day-care center. In many ways, the "benign neglect" he has encountered from various sitters has prompted him to develop an unusual level of independence. He can prepare foods he wants; he knows how to use money and get to stores and how to get around his neighborhood independently; he knows how to wheedle, cajole, and manipulate others. However, left to his own devices so much of the time, and often unintentionally ignored in the press of family activities, Jerry is already familiar to local police, who have several times found him wandering the neighborhood late at night after frantic parental calls for police help. Both Jerry's parents and the police have also received phone calls from neighbors accusing Jerry of stealing from or bullying their children. Jerry even reports that some neighbors have quietly threatened to spank him or take his bike if he does not stay away from their families.

Jerry's behavior has attracted the attention of special education professionals at school. They consider him to have serious personality and conduct problems that may develop into even more disruptive and self-destructive patterns as Jerry moves toward adolescence and adulthood. Diagnostically, they have determined that Jerry is a bright youngster with above-average intellectual ability but inadequate grounding in basic skills, some mixed signs of possible learning disability, depressive characteristics, and disruptive behavioral patterns.

Jerry is not a real child; he represents a composite of childhood experiences and characteristics that every teacher encounters daily. Whether Jerry is placed in a special classroom, in a mainstream class with resource help, or with no assistance at all is largely a function of the community in which he happens to live or the unanticipated consequences of one or two of his escapades. Whether he develops into a productive, happy adult or moves in the direction of loneliness, depression, alienation, and destructive behavior depends on the adequacy of family, school, and community responses to him now, when he is still a child.

The scope of a ten-year-old child's ecosystem is baffling in its complexity. Parents and stepparents, siblings and stepsiblings, teachers, neighborhood peers, adult neighbors, police—all influence and are influenced by Jerry's behavior. Less directly perhaps, but no less important, Jerry's behavior is also influenced by the socioeconomic character of his community and neighborhood and by the values, mores, and prejudices of the people around him. Television programs, cartoon characters, rock stars, and film personalities shape his aspirations and define his ideas about success and failure. Media influences tell him not only what toys are desirable, but which goals and personal characteristics are important. And even as all these influences converge on this ten-year-old youngster, his own temperament, ability, and interests affect these influences and give them a unique quality that precludes any standardized, textbook descriptions.

The complexity of the ecological system in which Jerry lives is not only the wellspring of his personality but also the basis for multiple points of intervention to help him grow toward wholeness and satisfaction with his life. Effective intervention to promote healthy developmental paths depends on the creativity with which the adults around Jerry can mobilize resources in the home, school, neighborhood, and in Jerry himself.

The remainder of this chapter looks briefly at a few of the key factors influencing children's development in contemporary society. Our understanding of these influences is tentative, and in many instances the forces themselves are fluid and changing. Yet psychology and education have developed many concepts and understandings that can have important effects on the lives of children. We will look first at several influential views of child development. We will then briefly examine sources of family influence, and discuss changing aspects of contemporary family life. Finally, we will examine the broad sociocultural patterns that have a pervasive impact on the lives of children.

Theories of Child Development

Theories are models of reality, ways of ordering and understanding our observations of the world. They are not necessarily true or false, but rather more or less useful as tools for organizing knowledge and ideas. Over the past hundred years or so, several theories of child development have emerged and influenced the directions of research and thinking about the forces that control development. They have shaped educational policy and practices, and directed the course of psychological and educational approaches to intervention.

In turn, these various theories have either grown or declined in the influence of social values and in their own usefulness as tools for understanding behavior; and they have been modified by the events they sought to explain as scientists and clinicians have tested them against reality. Our purpose in the following sections is simply to review a few of the most influential views of child development as each of them highlights certain aspects of the ecological contexts in which children grow. More specifically, we will examine the psychodynamic models of development of Sigmund Freud and Erik Erikson, respectively; the cognitive model of Jean Piaget; the behavioral models of John B. Watson and B. F. Skinner; Albert Bandura's social learning model; and the ecological model proposed by numerous contemporary theorists.

Psychoanalytic and Psychodynamic Theories of Development

Psychodynamic theories are so called because they focus on the interplay of internal, unconscious motivational forces. Sometimes the term *psychodynamic* is used synonymously with psychoanalysis, though the latter refers, strictly speaking, to the views developed and elaborated by Sigmund Freud at the end of the nineteenth and into the twentieth century. Freud and other psychoanalytic theorists have discussed and influenced virtually every aspect of psychological and educational practice, and psychoanalysis has been among the most important currents of modern thought. Though declining in influence in recent years, psychoanalytic concepts still deserve mention in a discussion of child development.

Freud proposed that the newborn infant is, psychologically, a bundle of instinctual drives whose energy is derived from basic bodily needs. With birth a process begins in which the infant experiences repeated cycles of need arousal and, if the infant is to survive, need satisfaction. Because the human infant is so dependent, virtually all need satisfaction occurs in the presence of a caregiver—primarily the mother. Initially, the newborn infant is unable to distinguish internal images from external reality, and an image of need satisfaction—for example, a mental image of a nurturing breast—accompanies the internal experience of hunger because the breast has appeared in the past when the infant has been hungry. However, the infant also learns quickly that the imagined or wished-for breast

does not bring lasting hunger satisfaction. Eventually, the infant begins to differentiate internal from external experiences, to distinguish between imagination and reality, to develop an image of the mother as an external figure, and to associate her presence with need gratification. In psychoanalytic terminology, the infant begins very gradually to move from primary process thinking, in which drives and gratification occur magically through a process of internal wish fulfillment, toward secondary process, or realistic, thinking. The transition to secondary process thinking is very gradual and occurs over a period of years. In fact, even in normal adults there remain occasional traces of primitive, magical, wishful thinking, especially at times of deprivation or extreme tension or fatigue.

Because the mother is, typically (according to Freud), the most important figure in the developing infant's life, the infant invests her with tremendous power to gratify all instinctual drives. For the newborn these are associated with the lips, mouth, tongue, eating, and hunger gratification. This stage is termed the *oral stage* of development, and lasts from birth through approximately the first eighteen months of life. During the course of normal development, processes occurring at this stage form the foundation for later ability to relate appropriately to others with empathy and to give and receive without undue dependency. On the other hand, repeated frustration of oral needs or overgratification can lead to a fixation at the oral stage, with later potential for regression to this stage at times of extreme anxiety or inability to move beyond this stage in the development of adult character. Adults with an oral fixation may manifest this in extreme dependency on others or in envy, greed, brittle independence, or sarcasm.

During the second year of life, impulses and gratifications associated with eliminative processes begin to emerge. As the growing child begins to develop neuromuscular sphincter control during the *anal stage* of development, pleasurable impulses associated with retention and expulsion of feces begin to play an increasingly important role in development. During the second and third years, the child begins to experience a sense of increasing control over bodily functions and with this sense of control, a sense of autonomy and independence from the parents. During this stage, children experiment with retention and expulsion of feces, and parental reactions often form the basis for feelings of independence and autonomy or shame. Again, frustration or overgratification of infantile impulses during the anal stage may form the basis for characteristics in adulthood such as impulsivity, excessive anger, disorganization and messiness, rigidity, obstinacy, stinginess, or compulsive orderliness.

During the *phallic stage* of development, which extends from approximately three to five or six years of age, the growing child becomes increasingly aware of the pleasurable sensations associated with genital stimulation. Freud believed that during this stage of development children of both sexes become preoccupied with more explicitly sexual fantasies and masturbatory activities. Because their lives still center around their mothers, children of both sexes tend to associate pleasurable sexual sensations in vague ways with images of the mother. For boys, presumably, wishes emerge to possess the mother completely and, simultaneously, fears emerge that a punitive father may become aware of such impulses and punish the child with castration. This constellation of wishful fantasies and fears is known as the Oedipus complex. Because of castration anxiety, boys gradually push their sexual impulses out of awareness or, in psychoanalytic terminology, repress these impulses and push them into unconscious regions of the mind where they are no longer accessible to conscious awareness. At the same time, a boy at the phallic stage typically begins a process of identification with his father to further ward off danger and, simultaneously, vicariously possess his mother.

In girls, the process proceeds somewhat differently. The girl comes to believe that she has somehow been castrated and deprived of a penis. Instead of the castration anxiety experienced in boys, the girl at the phallic stage experiences penis envy, and at a wish-fulfillment level attempts to gain possession of the father's penis through identification with her mother.

Healthy development during the phallic stage forms the foundation of a normal sexual identity, adequate control and expression of impulses, an ability to relate to others with appropriate warmth and intimacy, and an ability to work productively. Frustration or overgratification may produce distortions in sexual identity, inhibited spontaneity, inability to relate with warmth and genuineness, guilt, inappropriate passivity or competitiveness, and intense anxiety.

During the *latency stage,* which extends from approximately age six through adolescence, children engage in extensive repression of the impulses and internal turbulence characteristic of the Oedipal stage; developmental energies are, instead, diverted toward mastery of basic work and interpersonal skills. The child continues to learn ways of coping with the anxieties of earlier developmental stages, and consolidates the skills and characteristics that started to develop during earlier stages.

While this constitutes only the barest outline of psychoanalytic theory, it is clear that Freud and his students viewed infancy and childhood as the most critical periods of development. During these times there is a need for the maintenance of an ongoing balance between impulse expression and inhibition. While parents can do nothing to alter the basic progression through the stages of child development, it is essential that they help the child maintain this balance by reinforcing emergent self-control without inhibiting the healthy expression of impulses. They must help their child master the anxiety arising from feared breakthrough of unacceptable impulses and provide an accepting, stable, structured atmosphere in which the child can develop controlled gratification of basic drives.

Freud made explicit and deepened our recognition of the importance of basic biological drives in early development. Although we may argue about the relative importance of sexual motivation as a cornerstone of infant and child development or about the empirical validity of Freudian concepts, there is no question that biologically rooted motivational forces and societal responses to these forces shape and color every aspect of early personality development.

During the 1940s and 1950s students of psychoanalysis began to amplify and develop various aspects of Freud's thinking. While psychoanalytic developmental theory originally focused primarily on the nature of instinctual impulses, their expression, and their role in creating anxiety, later theorists explored the social and interpersonal aspects of psychoanalytic theory. Among the most important of these students was Erik Erikson.

Without introducing major changes in the foundations of psychoanalytic thinking, Erikson concentrated more extensively on the psychosocial interplay of internal and interpersonal forces and its results on the internal psychodynamics of development. Like Freud, Erikson focused on key developmental stages, but extended these well beyond childhood into adulthood. Erikson's stages reflect many of the same issues Freud recognized as important, but he also used a social perspective. Erikson conceived of development as a series of *psychosocial crises* in which the resolution of key developmental issues shapes the emergence of subsequent stages and internal and social characteristics.

The earliest stage of development, according to Erikson, centers on the development of a basic attitude of *trust versus mistrust*. During the first year of life, interactions with caregivers in the environment form the basis for the child's sense that the world is a caring place and that the people in it will provide consistent nurturance. Such a sense of basic trust encourages development of confident self-acceptance and an optimistic orientation toward the world. If early experiences are characterized, instead, by interpersonal rejection or neglect, the child will come to doubt the self and relate to the world in a doubting, suspicious fashion.

As the growing child develops the ability to move and walk independently and to control bodily functions, the next major stage of development emerges with a focus on *autonomy versus shame and doubt*. The key issues during this stage have to do with the extent to which child and parents are able to develop mutual regulation of behavior. If parents emerge during this stage as punitive and controlling, there is every chance that the child will develop self-doubt and a sense of shame. Alternately, respect for the child's ongoing skill in regulating movement, control of body functions, and awareness of ability to make choices, produces a healthy sense of self-respect and autonomy.

During the next stage, developmental issues center on a crisis of *initiative versus guilt*. Extending roughly from age three to five or six and paralleling the Freudian Oedipal stage, this period is characterized by increased physical mobility, curiosity, and intrusiveness. Parents of children at these ages often describe them as "getting into everything," and healthy parents struggle to maintain a balance between permissiveness and control. Without a recognition of the rights of others and the need to control impulse expression, the child may become aggressive and exploitive, using others socially, emotionally, and sexually. On the other hand, self-control arising from parent-induced guilt may discourage a healthy confidence in exploring oneself and the world and lead to passivity, a fear of knowledge, and morbid self-restriction.

During the years from age five or six to adolescence, children experience tensions around issues of *industry versus inferiority* as they begin to move increasingly outside the home and into neighborhood and school environments. Ready and eager to learn during these years, children embark on an energetic exploration of their physical world and relationships with others. A safe environment encouraging interaction with the physical and social worlds enables the growing child to develop a productive sense of industry and confidence in the ability to master tasks and relationships in a satisfying way. By contrast, if the child encounters criticism and discouragement, a sense of inferiority and inability to cope are likely to be the unfortunate results.

Although Erikson discussed psychosocial crises throughout the life cycle, the final one discussed here emerges during early adolescence and continues through early adulthood. During this stage, adolescents struggle with issues of *identity versus identity diffusion.* Healthy development through the earlier stage enables the adolescent to experiment with his or her own identity, to examine role models, and to try different ways of being. An interpersonal environment that permits role experimentation with confidence permits eventual integration of various roles and styles into a stable, caring, goal-oriented adult personality. On the other hand, an adult environment that exploits adolescent self-exploration, encourages mindless experimentation for vicarious gratification of adult impulses, or ridicules the adolescent's struggles may lead to an inability to develop a stable sense of self. In instances such as these, adolescents may flounder amid unstable values and fail to develop a sense of self-worth and stable identity.

The importance of Erikson's model of human development is in its emphasis on the external, interpersonal world of the growing individual. Our interactions with important people in our lives and with their values define the paths we take as we work to build our own personalities. Where Freud focused on the importance of internal drives, Erikson emphasizes the vital roles of parents, cultural values, and social institutions as influences on development. Psychodynamic views of development have prompted us to look more clearly at the complexity of internal and external forces that interact in the lives of individuals. An awareness of these viewpoints is critical for educators and other child-care professionals because they remind us always to look beyond immediate issues, simplifications, and superficialities in dealing with children and childhood problems. Instead, psychodynamic views insist that we must always remember to consider the hidden forces inside ourselves and those embedded so deeply in our values and cultural institutions that we often fail to realize they are there.

Behavioral Theories of Development

Behavioral psychology burst on the scene in 1913 with the publication of a position paper entitled "Psychology as the Behaviorist Views It" by John B. Watson (1878–1958). Watson, at that time a professor at Johns Hopkins University, rejected what he perceived as the subjective, unscientific psychology then current, and insisted that psychology could enter the realm of genuine science with an objective study of behavior. Watson developed the position that one could learn all that was needed about human behavior through objective observation rather than subjective self-reporting. Watson's thinking both influenced and paralleled the work of a number of other U.S. psychologists of the time and prompted extensive research on the mechanisms and impact of learning. From 1913 to the present, research on learning processes has constituted the core of behaviorist psychology and is perhaps the most active field of research in U.S. psychology and education today.

Watson developed ideas about the application of behaviorist conditioning principles, particularly as related to child development. Popularizations of his ideas exerted tremendous influence on child-rearing and educational practices from 1920 through 1950 and set the stage for modern behavioral psychology.

The work of B. F. Skinner (1904–   ) focuses on the importance and complexity of the relationships between behaviors and their consequences. Any consequence of a behavior that increases the probability of the recurrence of that behavior is termed a *reinforcer.* There are two broad classes of reinforcers: positive and negative. A *positive reinforcement* is the occurrence of an event consequent upon a behavior that increases the probability of recurrence of the behavior. A *negative reinforcement* is the cessation of an event consequent upon a behavior that increases the probability of the behavior recurring. In contrast, any event whose occurrence decreases the probability of a behavior is termed a *punishment.* Finally, the complete elimination of previously occurring consequences of a behavior, leading to the cessation of that behavior, is termed *extinction.* Through the careful manipulation of behavioral consequences, it is possible to modify a wide range of behaviors; to shape new behaviors; to develop others that are personally or socially desirable; and to reduce or eliminate troublesome or disruptive behaviors.

At present, there is considerable controversy regarding both the real efficacy of behavior modification principles and techniques and the ethics of their application. However, there is no question that behavioral psychology has had tremendous impact on both approaches to treatment of psychological problems and development of educational intervention techniques. Chapter 8 discusses behavioral concepts, techniques, and applications in greater detail.

It is important to note that the key impact of behavioral psychology has been to provide a specific technology for explaining, preventing, and intervening in developmental problems in ways that are both effective and readily applicable in a wide range of ecological settings.

Although Skinner's work has been, perhaps, the single most influential force in contemporary U.S. psychology, several other researchers have developed variations on the central behaviorist themes and produced significant theoretical offshoots. Among the most important of these variations have been the similar ideas of a variety of people that are often lumped together under the title *social learning theory.*

Social Learning Theory

In general, social learning theorists have broadened the narrowly defined principles of traditional behaviorism by looking at how learning occurs in the real world, rather than in the psychological laboratory. In contrast to psychoanalytic and behavioral approaches in which new ideas revolutionized thinking about personality and behavior, social learning theory has evolved more slowly, gathering the threads of ideas from many directions gradually, to weave them into a complex and richly detailed tapestry of concepts and ideas.

It is not possible to trace the origins of social learning theory to any single researcher. Instead, in the late 1940s and early 1950s several investigators began publishing the results of research that has broadened and enriched more narrowly conceived theories. For example, in 1950 John Dollard and Neal Miller published a landmark book, *Personality and Psychotherapy: An Analysis in Terms of Learning, Thinking, and Culture,* in which they attempted to integrate psychoanalytic and behavioral learning principles, and which was an important statement of their general approach to human development. Dollard and Miller wanted to show that neither psychoanalysis nor learning theory as narrowly conceived was adequate for an understanding of personality. Rather, they attempted to show how basic human drives combined with learning mechanisms to produce chains and sequences of behavior that, in turn, interacted and recombined to produce individual behavior patterns and incredibly intricate and complex social institutions and cultural patterns. These patterns themselves then became forces shaping the directions of subsequent individual and cultural learning patterns.

At about the same time, Robert Sears was conducting investigations on patterns of child rearing that eventually led him to view individual personality as the outcome of interactions among biological forces, interactions within the family, and later interactions outside the family, all mediated through complex learning mechanisms (Sears, Maccoby, & Levin, 1957).

Along the same lines, John Whiting and Irvin Child, at Harvard and Yale respectively, were studying the ways in which cultural variations produced variations in the personality characteristics of members of a specific cultural group (Whiting & Child, 1953). Influenced strongly by Dollard and Miller, these researchers used the concepts and techniques of cultural anthropology to study differences in patterns of dependency, nursing and weaning, cleanliness training, sexual development, and aggression in different cultural groups ranging from contemporary U.S. society through native American Indian tribes and isolated cultural groups in the South Pacific. The results of their investigations showed clearly the existence of important relationships among cultural values and institutions, day-to-day child-rearing practices, and outcomes in individual personality.

These investigative lines came together in the work of Albert Bandura and Richard Walters (1963) as they explored the specific mechanisms of social imitation and identification. Recognizing the importance of learning mechanisms such as reinforcement, punishment, and extinction, Bandura and Walters extended our understanding of these concepts and showed that much, if not most, important learning does not occur directly but rather through observation of others and the consequences of their behavior. Mediated by cognitive processes and language, children learn appropriate responses, methods of problem solving, and patterns of behavior by listening to and observing others in their immediate environments, and later, through a range of cultural media. In a classic series of studies, Bandura and his associates showed not only the likelihood of occurrence, but also that specific forms of aggressive behavior can be learned through observation of unfamiliar adult and child models in film clips only (Bandura, 1969, 1974; Bandura, Ross, & Ross, 1961, 1963). Although it was no surprise to anyone that children learn by imitation, this important work began to answer questions about how and why imitation and identification occur.

The importance of the combination of thinking and research in social learning theory is that it has produced a set of concepts and principles that have become pivotal in organizing ideas from a broad range of disciplines and theoretical positions. Social learning theorists have begun a process of intellectual integration that allows psychologists, educators, sociologists, behavioral ecologists, and cultural anthropologists to communicate in common terms and develop common understandings.

Piagetian Theory of Development

Although most major theories of child development have focused largely on the development of personality and behavioral characteristics, Jean Piaget, a Swiss investigator, pioneered the study of cognitive development in children. Trained as a zoologist and ethologist, Piaget's interests turned to epistemology, that branch of philosophy that seeks to understand how we know. In attempting to understand the origins and development of human knowledge, Piaget focused his attention on the study of human thinking and learning. Many of Piaget's ideas developed from and were tested in observations of his own children as they grew from infancy into childhood.

Piaget studied the actions and responses of infants as they observed and interacted with the people and objects in their environments. Later, he examined the kinds of questions they asked and the responses they gave to his questions. Through meticulous, systematic observation he began to see regularities in the patterns of observation and understanding that growing children display, and he described the orderly unfolding of stages of cognitive development.

Initially, infant thinking is largely a reflection of bodily actions and reactions. Completely egocentric, the young infant has no real awareness of separate people or objects in the environment, or any ability to conceive of the world as though there were other points of view. Thinking consists of sensations and motor responses. Hence, Piaget termed this initial developmental stage the *sensorimotor period* of development. During this and later developmental periods, the infant's interactions consist of two primary modes: *assimilation* and *accommodation*. Assimilation is the process whereby the infant, in response to environmental stimuli, modifies internal perceptual and motor patterns in order to be able to grasp and cope with or accommodate him- or herself to the nature of reality. Beginning only with primitive human reflexes as a base, the infant gradually begins to learn the relationships among actions and their effects in the real world. Through reciprocal processes of assimilation and accommodation, the infant begins to build *schemata,* mental representations of how the world works. These schemata, in turn, are further modified and elaborated through the ongoing maturation of mental abilities and interactions with objects and people in the environment. Language begins to emerge during this period, and little by little mental and linguistic functions begin to replace the initial sensorimotor mode of thinking.

Roughly during the third and fourth years of life, the child begins to develop simple ideas about the way the world works and thinks less with the body and increasingly with the mind. During this *preconceptual period* children remain egocentric and cannot conceive of other ways of experiencing the world. Yet, the move from thinking only in bodily terms has begun, and they are able to use genuine, if primitive, ideas. Children during this period also remain *animistic* in thinking, and attribute intention and motivation to inanimate objects, as when a youngster talks about the "bad table" that has just "inflicted" a bump to the head.

During the *intuitive period,* from age four to seven, children begin to develop a simple capacity for reasoning, concept formation, and generalization, but at a level that is largely intuitive rather than logically developed. Instead of being able to reason about relationships among causes and effects, the child is able to grasp certain relationships, but is unable actually to understand or explain them.

The period of *concrete operations,* from age seven to eleven, reveals further maturation of mental abilities as the child continues learning about the world through assimilation, accommodation, and the elaboration of ever more complex mental schemata. The term *concrete operations* refers to the fact that the child begins to manipulate the world mentally through the use of ideas that are still rather concrete. Abstract ideas remain difficult to grasp, but tangible objects can be manipulated mentally so that a youngster is able to consider the concrete consequences, for example, of throwing a stone into

a pool of water. However, the child remains unable to think more abstractly about the physical relationships among solids and liquids.

This latter ability emerges during the period of formal operations, at age twelve or so, when the child's ability to think abstractly begins to unfold. At this point, most aspects of intellectual egocentrism and animism have gradually diminished as children begin to develop greater ability to think about abstract concepts, to think in hypothetical terms about how things might be rather than only about how they are, and to consider and experiment with such abstractions as justice and responsibility. At this point, the developing adolescent first becomes genuinely able to consider the consequences of actions from the points of view of others and to consider whether or not to engage in certain courses of action.

It is important to recognize that the developmental stages that Piaget outlined reflect general maturational and learning patterns. Their emergence and course differ in different individuals, and in some children become more fully differentiated than in others. It is recognized, for example, that even some adults continue to view the world in more or less animistic terms, and there are always individuals whose thinking remains more concrete and egocentric than others. Such factors are evident in the superstitious, stereotypical, and defensive patterns of thought and behavior that are all too apparent in our world.

The important point here is a recognition that emerging cognitive development is regular and systematic, and that children's day-to-day behavior and personality characteristics do not develop apart from intellectual capabilities. Thus, it is fruitless to deal with a child at a preconceptual level of intellectual development in terms of abstract concepts of right or wrong, and it is foolish to expect a child to consider any long-term consequences of a behavior as an adult might. In order to understand childhood problems, one must always consider the child's own way of grasping and understanding the world. Interventions can then be meaningful and effective.

Altogether, Piaget's careful empirical observations and his emphasis on the importance of intellectual maturation have added depth and richness to our understanding of child development and have provided a critically important perspective to educational and intervention processes. His elaboration of the processes of assimilation and accommodation shows clearly the importance of an interactional viewpoint in understanding the causes of personality problems and behavior disorders in children. His investigations force us to maintain an awareness of internal maturational processes as central components in an ecological system. (Box 2.1 shows the developmental chronologies of several major theorists.)

Ecological "Theory"

In truth, there is no ecological theory of child development. Rather, there is an ecological viewpoint or perspective on development—a specific way of looking at the emergence of problems that reflects an ecological orientation.

In contrast to most of the theoretical viewpoints discussed thus far, no single individual is responsible for developing an ecological perspective on child development or childhood problems.

Rather, this orientation has emerged gradually in the work of many dedicated researchers, who have recognized that each growing child is the focus of multiple interacting social and physical forces, and is influencing and being influenced by these forces in a process of continual change. This field of living and nonliving forces, including the individual child, is termed the *ecosystem* (Sells, 1963, 1966). Because the ecosystem is a dynamic, interacting field of forces, it is not possible to consider variations in any individual child, including severe problems, apart from the total system, both present and historical, in which the child lives (Hewett, 1981).

Put more concretely, a child is a biological organism developing in a world composed of physicochemical, psychological, social, anthropological, and historical facts whose reality for the child is partly shaped by the child's experience of them. Ecological psychology refers to the interaction between psychological and all nonpsychological forces impinging upon the individual (Lewin, 1951). Two key ideas emerge from such a conception: First, it is not possible to change any component of an ecosystem without also affecting all other components to some degree. Second, it is possible to effect change in a targeted element of an ecosystem by im-

---

Box 2.1 Chronological Age and Theoretical Developmental Stages

This chart shows the approximate chronological ages and the durations of developmental stages proposed by Freud, Erikson, and Piaget. The ages at which different abilities, issues, and concerns emerge depend on mental age and psychosocial experiences, as well as chronological age. Behavioral and social learning theorists do not usually conceive of development in stages and so are not included here. (Detailed descriptions of developmental processes are presented in the text.)

Age	Freud	Erikson	Piaget
0–1	Oral Stage	Basic Trust vs. Mistrust	Sensorimotor Period
2	Anal Stage	Autonomy vs. Shame and Doubt	
3–4	Phallic Stage	Initiative vs. Guilt	Preoperational Period
5–6	Latency Stage	Industry vs. Inferiority	
7–11			Concrete Operations
12	Genital Stage	Identity vs. Identity Diffusion	Formal Operations

plementing change in a nontargeted element.

A child's behavior cannot be changed without to some extent change being effected in the behavior of other members of the child's family. In some instances, because a level of stability may exist in the adaptations a family has made over time, family members may resist or sabotage efforts at changing a child's behavior because of an implicit recognition that other elements of the family may thereby be changed. If a rebellious youngster's behavior improves, an angry and abusive parent may no longer be able to sustain rationalizations for punishing the child and venting hostility. Alternatively, it may be possible to change the child's rebellious behavior by working indirectly with the angry parent whose own frustrations and conflicts are provoking the child's rebelliousness. Ecological psychologists have developed several basic assumptions regarding such interactions (see Box 2.2).

Behavior Settings. In developing an ecological model of childhood disturbance, Susan Swap conceptualized several levels of analysis critical to an understanding of an individual child (Swap, 1978). First, there is the *behavior setting* level, consisting of the physical environment, characteristic program of activities, human in-

habitants, and time-space location in which the child lives. The home, a classroom, a neighborhood community center, a Sunday school meeting room, or the local police station are all examples of behavior settings in which a child might be functioning at any given moment. In a way, conceptualization of the behavior setting is a function of the specificity that the observer chooses. The examples above could be narrower and more specific (family members sharing the bathroom in the morning) or broader and more inclusive (the local police station in an urban ghetto or in a rural farm community). In any behavior setting, a child's problem behavior is the product of interaction between the child and the elements of the setting.

Patterns of Behavior Across Settings. A second level of analysis consists of *patterns of behavior across settings*. At this level of analysis one searches for consistencies and variations across behavior settings. Recognition that a youngster displays problem behavior at home in the morning and throughout morning classes, is cooperative for an hour after lunch, disrupts afternoon classes, and continues to display problems throughout the day might suggest several avenues of investigation to the teacher or psychologist trying to develop effective interventions.

Box 2.2   Principles and Assumptions of an Integrative/Ecological Model

1. Knowledge is never complete. The state of our knowledge at any given moment represents only a partial understanding of how and why individuals behave as they do.
2. Different perspectives may offer useful, but limited, approaches to understanding behavioral phenomena.
3. The most useful approach to understanding behavior results from the reasoned integration of a range of theoretical concepts, research data, and clinical experience.
4. An individual child's disturbed behavior rep-

resents disturbance in the ecological system of which the child is a part rather than a disturbance in the child (Swap, Prieto, & Harth, 1982).
5. While disturbed behavior may have a variety of possible causes in any component of the ecosystem, the transactional nature of behavior immediately transforms the disturbed behavior into a disturbance of the system as a whole.
6. Interventions to modify ecological disturbance must be directed toward the ecological system, and not solely toward any component of the system.

Community and Culture. The third level of analysis consists of the *community and culture* in which the child lives, including community values and social norms, formal institutional structures such as educational, mental health, and religious systems, and informal shapers of culture such as television, magazines, and newspapers. Other variables at this level might include community socioeconomic level, population density, and patterns of nutritional adequacy in the community.

Each of these three levels consists of a variety of specific characteristics. At the level of the behavior setting, one must consider the individual child's characteristics, such as temperament or intelligence (Thomas & Chess, 1977; Thomas, Chess, & Birch, 1968). Temperamental variations in children are key factors affecting the child's responses to caretakers and their responses to the child. Characteristics of significant others (parents and teachers) in the behavior setting are also critical. And the physical milieu—ranging from family size and number of rooms in the home to adequacy of heat and light in the classroom or condition of textbooks—exerts tremendous though subtle influence on a child's behavior. Every experienced teacher knows the importance of seating arrangements and classroom neatness. Program, space, and time characteristics may include such factors as teacher skill and experience, adequacy of the curriculum, availability of play space, pace of the family schedule, and even the amount of sleep a child gets each night.

Examination of behavior patterns across settings may show that the child who is disturbing in the classroom may be a leader on the playground or the child who is withdrawn and socially isolated on the playground may be creative and imaginative in the safety and comfort of the home.

Finally, at the level of community and culture, it is important to examine the impact of such specific variables as availability and adequacy of curricular recognition (school recognition) and provision for dealing with childhood problems, community attitudes toward childhood problems, programs for recognition of problems, availability of intervention services, and responsiveness of service delivery systems. We need also to consider the broader responsiveness of our political and economic system to individuals with special needs and the informal values communicated through radio and television, advertising, magazines, and even comic books. To what extent, for example, is it reasonable to expect cooperative behavior from a youngster bombarded with messages about self-gratification, competitiveness, and the acceptability of deceit or violence in achieving one's goals?

Within the context of Susan Swap's multilevel system of analysis, it becomes apparent that an ecological perspective demands careful, systematic, and integrative consideration of a child's whole life situation to develop meaningful and effective interventions. This is by no means a simple process, but neither is it impossible. An ecological framework requires that we reject simple solutions and self-satisfying platitudes. Problems do not reside in a child and disturbance is as much a function of the perceptions of those who are being disturbed as those who are blamed for it and labeled. Although there are now available useful conceptual and methodological tools in the ideas of psychodynamic, behavioral, and social learning theorists, these tools must be applied within the context of a total ecological framework to be effective.

The remainder of this chapter briefly examines a few key ecological variables. The discussion is suggestive rather than exhaustive. Those involved in special education undertake a responsibility to become as conversant as they can not only with the technical tools of educational methodology, but also with the concepts and problems of related disciplines. Hopefully, this discussion will help provide some initial guidelines for such study.

The Family as a Behavior Setting

As the earliest behavior setting in which children develop, the family functions critically in providing love and emotional support, security, and training in acceptable social behavior as well as furnishing basic biological care and nurturance. Children need to be needed and wanted, cared for and protected, valued and cherished, accepted and given a sense of belonging, educated and guided in the directions of socially acceptable behavior, and given opportunities to feel satisfaction through useful work and creative activities (Talbot, 1976).

In a humane and insightful statement on the obligations of parents toward their children, The Group for the Advancement of Psychiatry Committee on Public Education has noted the importance of parents in the transmission of cultural values, religious beliefs, and social ideals through love, example, and discipline (Group for the Advancement of Psychiatry, 1973). Parents have a right and a duty to advocate particular values and expectations and a right to attempt to pass these on to their children. Lacking such a solid context in which to grow, children develop without behavioral norms, have little in the way of a clear sense of purpose, direction, or selfhood, and are subject to unreasoning fears of the world or equally unreasoning demands for impulse gratification.

The concepts of Freud, Erikson, and Piaget translate into several concrete ideas. First, there must be parental respect for the orderly unfolding of childhood potentials. Thus, for example, we learn from psychodynamic theory that childhood impulses must be permitted to develop at their own pace, but within an environment in which the child is protected from overstimulation. Children need parental guidance in dealing with dependent, sexual, and aggressive feelings, and they need to be certain that they will have parental help in controlling these feelings. At the same time, they also need to know that their feelings are natural and may be expressed within the context of values prevalent in their culture. An atmosphere must be provided in which children can develop the basic trust that is the foundation for all later emotional bonds; they need to experience a sense of autonomy, neither feeling ashamed of impulses nor a sense that

they can indulge impulses in unbridled fashion. Parents must provide the context for healthy curiosity, initiative, and exploration within the context of values that respect the rights of others. And parents must encourage a healthy sense of industry and an orientation toward achievement without mindless competitiveness.

Among the most important positive child-rearing practices are firmness without rigidity, direction and guidance without unreasoned dictation, rules that make sense without arbitrariness, high expectations for all family members, and mutual trust and respect between parents and between parents and their children.

Given such an environment a child can move, during adolescence and early adulthood, toward the development of a positive sense of self-esteem and a healthy, integrated identity organized around self-acceptance, tolerance, and strong personal values.

From the perspective of behavioral and social learning theories, we know that children need parental models who are secure in their own values and who can present clear, consistent messages about appropriate and acceptable behaviors by displaying such behaviors themselves. Appropriate behaviors must be reinforced through messages that such behaviors are important and highly valued. Parents must be comfortable and unstinting in praising worthy behaviors and ideals, but they must also be comfortable in appropriately discouraging behaviors that they feel are wrong, inappropriate, or unworthy.

On the whole, love-oriented rather than power-assertive methods of control and discipline appear to foster the development of individuals who are responsible for their actions, cooperative in their relations with others, and who experience guilt in appropriate ways (Becker, 1964). Love-oriented control involves praise, age-appropriate reasoning, and withdrawal of affection or separation from the parent temporarily when the child misbehaves. On the other hand, power-assertive control methods such as physical punishment and the induction of fear tend to produce aggression and noncooperation.

Effective Families

In a fascinating investigation of different patterns of family interaction that has come to be known as the Timberlawn study, volunteer families with no identified emotionally ill member were presented with a series of tasks to complete. They were then filmed in the process of working on these tasks, and the films analyzed carefully (Lewis, Beavers, Gossett, & Phillips, 1976). These families were compared with closely matched families who each had an adolescent child hospitalized with an emotional problem.

Careful study of these films by W. R. Beavers (1982) showed that families could be differentiated on the basis of how adequately they functioned together. Effective families, those whose members did not display behavior problems, showed *clear generational boundaries.* While there was openness to ideas from all family members, there was no doubt about who was the parent and who was the child. Parents did not feel they needed to disclaim their adult power, nor did the children in these families feel called upon to assume adult responsibility prematurely.

Effective families also showed relative *equality of power.* Such equality was observed between parents, who played complementary rather than competitive roles in problem solving. However, relative equality of power also existed between parents and children insofar as the children's contributions to task completion were recognized and permitted to influence the family—less so in younger and more so in older children. Power struggles were rare in these families. Beavers also noted that there was virtually no role symmetry in effective families. That is, parents did not share responsibilities, workload, and kinds of tasks equally. Beavers observed that the effective families in this study operated like a skilled sports team with each player taking roles reflecting specific talents and abilities.

Consistent *encouragement of autonomy* was another characteristic of effective or optimal families in the Timberlawn study. Family members took responsibility for their own actions; there was a "striking absence of blame or personal attack and . . . no scapegoating" (Beavers, 1982, p. 50). Mistakes were recognized as mistakes rather than as intentional malicious acts. Family members could openly admit mistakes, and there was little need for defensiveness or face-saving maneuvers.

The Timberlawn investigators saw optimal families show *joy and comfort in relating* to each other. They noted that family members could engage in *skilled negotiation,* and it was clear that despite changes in the roles each member might assume in the family system, there was a consistent presence of *significant transcendent values* shared by the family.

Lest we develop a myth that some families have magically surmounted the tensions, frustration, anger, pettiness, and jealousy that most of us have experienced in family life, it is important to note that these characteristics were also present in these optimal families. The optimal families of the Timberlawn study were by no means superfamilies. They were people with the same weaknesses and flaws that we all have. However, what is important is that they could experience sufficient love, trust, mutuality, and respect to permit them to relate in effective, growth-promoting ways.

Problem Patterns in Family Interaction and Communication

Although it is encouraging, even inspiring, to see families function in ways that promote growth and establish a sense of security and joy in their members, it is equally important to be familiar with identified patterns that contribute to the development of problems in children. An understanding of problem patterns in family interaction is essential to knowing when to intervene and how to develop effective interventions.

Centripetal and Centrifugal Family Styles. Basing their analyses on concepts of *centripetal* and *centrifugal* family styles identified in earlier studies (Stierlin, 1972; Stierlin, Levi, & Savard, 1973), the Timberlawn investigators looked at the group of families with identified emotionally disturbed members. Centripetal families look for satisfaction largely from within the family and tend to be suspicious of the world outside family boundaries. In these families negative feelings and perceptions tend to be denied or suppressed. In marked contrast, centrifugal families are less trusting of interactions and feelings within the family and more comfortable with activities and relationships outside the family. Family members are more comfortable with expressions of criticism or anger within the family and are suspicious of affection or positive feelings from other family members.

Although centripetal and centrifugal styles can be identified within many families, neither is inherently dysfunctional, and the Timberlawn investigators identified a broad range of effectiveness reflecting both styles. However, several families were specifically identified as dysfunctional and showed these patterns to a marked degree.

Severely dysfunctional centripetal families show nearly impermeable outer family boundaries. They tend to be seen as odd or unusual by neighbors and rarely leave the family either physically or emotionally. They tend to hold an expectation of complete loyalty and a belief that all family members should think and feel alike. Parents often present confusing messages to their children or speak for them; they discourage expression of feelings and any sense of individual identity.

Severely dysfunctional centrifugal families are characterized by weak and diffuse boundaries with the outer world. Parents move in and out frequently and without adequate reason. Children frequently run away from home. Occasionally nonfamily members are brought into the household to live and, at times, it is unclear who actually constitutes the family. Interactions are characterized by anger, teasing, provocation, and hostility. Parents and children attempt to control each other through manipulation and intimidation. There is little mutuality or empathic understanding. With no consistent rules or values and no sense of what behavior will be rewarded or punished, children in these families tend to experience diffuse anger, inadequate conscience development, and an orientation toward immediate impulse gratification.

Overall, dysfunctional families are inflexible and ineffective in meeting life problems. Power structures are poorly defined, and there are often intergenerational alliances in which one parent recruits support against the other from a child family member. Parents in these families have difficulty maintaining firm, consistent values and often acquiesce to the wishes of their children, allowing the children to assume parental roles. Family members feel chronic anger toward each other and live with a sense of being manipulated, blackmailed, or coerced by each other. The family atmosphere is typically one of pain, frustration, and stagnation.

Double-Bind Communication Patterns. In addition to the pervasive disturbances noted in some of the Timberlawn families, other investigators have identified equally disruptive patterns of family interaction. One of these is the *double-bind communication pattern* in which a parent communicates simultaneous contradictory messages to a child at different communicative levels (Bateson, Jackson, Haley, & Weakland, 1969). Inconsistencies between different channels of communication are subtle and difficult to comment on, and when they occur in the context of the family, escape is virtually impossible (Weakland, 1976). Thus, for example, a boy might be instructed explicitly not to fight with other children, but then experience a sense of parental disappointment when he actually refuses to fight with other children. If he comments on the double-bind message by saying he was only obeying instructions, the parent may deny disappointment, point out that the child misunderstood, or simply say that the child should not talk back. In another instance, a mother might constantly criticize her daughter for being overweight, but make high-calorie snacks continually available to sabotage her daughter's attempts to diet. If the daughter is so foolish as to comment on this apparent contradiction, the mother may deny any intent to make dieting difficult, criticize her daughter for lack of self-control, or point out her daughter's lack of gratitude for her efforts to be a good mother. Often, the victims of double-bind messages experience confusion, frustration, and tremendous irrational guilt at never being able to satisfy an insatiable parent.

In a recent experimental study of responses to double-bind communications, a group of adolescents selected from an outpatient mental health center were presented with pictures and accompanying audiotaped stories of a series of double-bind situations (Roy & Sawyers, 1986). Physiological measures of stress were taken as the adolescent subjects heard each double-bind story and looked at the picture. Responses of these clinical subjects were compared with those of a matched group of subjects without behavior disorders. In one pictured story an inconsistent message was presented in which a mother said that a card her child had made for her was very nice, but did not look up from the magazine she was reading as she said it. All subjects showed greater degrees of stress to these inconsistent message stories than to stories in which there were consistent verbal and nonverbal messages, but clinical subjects showed greater degrees of physiological stress and less ability to confront such situations with direct comments. In the example above, many clinical subjects said they would be upset but would simply walk away, go to their rooms, or try to forget the situation. Nonclinical subjects more often said they would tell the mother, indignantly, that she had not even looked at the card, or ask her to look at it before commenting.

Overprotection and Rejection. Parental *overprotection* may result in disobedience, tantrums, and excessive and unrealistic demands on the part of the overprotected child (Levy, 1966). However, although tyrants at home, many overprotected children are often timid, fearful, and withdrawn at school or at play. In these in-

stances, it seems as though overprotected children are fearful that they may be unable to cope adequately in the real world since they have rarely had to be self-reliant at home. Other overprotected children may be aggressive, cocky, selfish, and boastful. In neither case, however, is parental overprotection and overindulgence likely to promote independence, trust, and mutuality in relationships.

Curiously, parental *rejection* may have somewhat similar results. Whether in the form of physical separation, psychological distance, or inconsistency of feelings, parental rejection may contribute to anxiety, fearfulness, dependency, and timidity in some children. It is as though a feeling that one is somehow unacceptable to one's own parents creates an expectation of rejection from others. Other child victims of rejection may respond with mutual rejection of the parent, intense anger, impulsivity, aggressive behavior, or self-destructive behavior. In extreme cases, parental rejection may take the form of neglect or child abuse.

Marital Skew and Marital Schism. Other faulty patterns of family interaction include *model deficits, nuclearity failure* (Fleck, 1985), *marital schism,* and *marital skew* (Lidz, Fleck, & Cornelison, 1965). Model deficits occur when either or both parents fail to provide adequate gender and role models for their children. This might be the case, for example, when either parent displays behavior that reflects gender uncertainty, identity confusion, or extreme social ineptness or inappropriateness. Without adequate role models in the family, a child or adolescent may turn to equally inadequate peer models or to media presentations of social ideals. Unfortunately, such models usually lack character depth, and it is almost impossible to know them in the same sense as one knows a parent.

Nuclearity failure refers to those situations in which dependency or emotional illness leads a parent to turn responsibility for family leadership over to a grandparent, other relative, or to a nonfamily member. In such situations authority, responsibility for decision making, and emotional investments occur outside the nuclear family group. It is important here to distinguish situations in which traditional, extended family groups have complementary role assignments and work with parents in the nuclear family. Instead, parental abdication creates a vacuum in family leadership that is filled by someone whose presence then distorts the normal pattern of family relationships.

Marital skew and *marital schism* refer to situations in which there is intense conflict in the family system. In families where there is marital skew, conflict is not necessarily overt. Rather, in more subtle ways parents struggle to avoid responsibilities for family functions or wage a cold war for power in the family system. A dependent father might fail to protect his children from his autocratic, abusive wife because he has yielded all power and responsibility in the family to her. At the same time, the mother in such a family may denigrate and deride her husband so that their children cannot possibly develop a sense of respect for the weak and helpless father. In another instance, a mother might continually justify and excuse an alcoholic and cruel father to the children so that they are unable to reconcile what they experience with what they are told about their father's behavior. In some families this kind of behavior might go so far as to involve complete denial of the father's drinking, and the bewildered children then must guard against admitting what they know. Often skewed marital situations involve the development of family secrets or family myths that totally contradict reality, and the children of such marriages must somehow adapt to pervasive lies and fabrications.

In marital schism, conflict is manifested openly as parents are divided into warring factions engaged in ongoing overt or covert struggles. Children are recruited as allies by both parents and inevitably suffer painful consequences no matter which side they take—and they are not often given the option of remaining neutral. Parental discord may focus on finances, sex, infidelity, in-laws, disciplinary practices, and so forth, but children rarely escape the consequences of tension and anger regardless of their source or content. Numerous reports have shown that childhood problems such as excessive anxiety, withdrawal, overcontrol, aggression, and conduct problems occur with increased frequency in intact families experiencing ongoing conflict (Emery, 1982). On the whole, conflicts that are open, hostile, and long-lasting have a greater impact than those that are less overt (Porter & O'Leary, 1980).

People often speculate on whether it is better for children if their warring parents stay together or seek separation or divorce. On the whole, research evidence suggests that intense conflict has a more destructive impact on children than the fact of separation or divorce (e.g., Jacobson, 1978; Lambert, et al., 1977). However, it is also important to remember that in many families separation and divorce do not end hostility and open conflict between the separated or divorced parents. Rather, there is often ongoing conflict and resentment around the issues that led to separation, complicated by new hostilities over custody issues or child support payments.

Marital conflict affects children of both sexes and leads to an increased incidence of childhood problems, but considerable research shows that such conflict has greater impact on boys than on girls (Emery, 1982), with a greater tendency to be displayed in problems with impulse and behavior controls.

The Effects of Divorce

In many cases marital schism eventually leads to divorce, and there is extensive evidence showing that both marital discord and divorce can have a profound negative impact on children's development (Emery, 1982). Given the fact that currently nearly half of all marriages in the United States will end in divorce (Hacker, 1983), it is clear that marital schism and divorce are key ecological variables in understanding childhood problems.

Upon closer examination, U.S. Bureau of the Census data for 1980 showed that a total of 2,143,000 marriages were performed, and 1,182,000 divorces were granted in the United States (National Center for Health Statistics, 1981). This rate of divorce reflects an increase of nearly 100 percent between 1970 and 1981, and nearly 23 percent of all children in this country currently live in single-parent families (U.S. Bureau of the Census, 1982). It has been estimated that 40 percent to 50 percent of children born between 1970 and 1980 will spend some part of their lives living in single-parent families (Hetherington, 1979). These data do not include the many families that experience ongoing conflict without seeking divorce, or the 23 percent to 30 percent of couples who experience periodic separations or withdraw their divorce petitions (Kitson & Langlie, 1984).

In evaluating the effects of divorce on children, it is almost impossible to sort out the relative impact of ongoing parental conflict and the impact of divorce itself. E. Mavis Hetherington, a leading investigator in this area, suggests that it is important that separation and divorce be viewed as a stage in the ongoing deterioration of a family situation rather than as a single, isolated event (Hetherington, 1979). From this perspective, it is the fact of parental turmoil and family conflict that is more important as a factor affecting child development than the fact of divorce. Hetherington maintains, and research evidence supports, the view that living in a family with a distant, rejecting, or hostile parent is more destructive than separation from such a parent.

In a comprehensive longitudinal study of the long-term effects of divorce and remarriage on the adjustment of children, Hetherington and her associates contacted a group of divorced families in which the mother had custody, and a comparison group of nondivorced families six years after a divorce had taken place (Hetherington, Cox, & Cox, 1985). Her sample consisted of well-educated, middle-class, white families, and measures of child adjustment included parent rating scales, teacher rating scales, peer nominations, child self-ratings, and direct observations in home and school. She found that divorce has a long-term negative impact on boys' adjustment, but that girls had greater difficulty when their mothers remarried. Considering research findings showing that children tend to form closer bonds when a custodial parent is of the same sex as the child, and given that most custodial parents are mothers, Hetherington reasoned that there is greater likelihood, in most instances, that girls will maintain or strengthen ties with their mothers following a divorce. However, remarriage introduces the presence of a stepfather who is likely to interfere with the bond between mother and daughter and intensify adjustment problems.

By contrast, there is some evidence of a reduction in the behavior problems of boys when a custodial mother remarries (Santrock, Warshak, & Elliott, 1982), though not to the level of boys in nondivorced families. The possibility here, of course, is that the presence of a male role model may help boys reestablish a more solid basis for appropriate gender identification. In the case of either boys or girls, stepfathers report relationships with stepchildren as a major problem in their marriages (Hetherington, Arnett, & Hollier, 1985). However, it appears that a stepfather in a recombined family may have the most positive impact and experience the least difficulty when he provides support to the mother in her disciplinary efforts rather than trying to assume a disciplinary role himself.

While most studies have consistently found that boys respond to parental divorce with more adjustment problems and lowered academic performance (e.g., Guidubaldi & Perry, 1985) than girls, one group of investigators at the University of Michigan suggests that female children of divorced families may have equally serious adjustment difficulties, but at different stages of life. Neil Kalter and his associates studied the adjustment of elementary school girls, high school girls, and college-age women of divorced families (Kalter, Riemer, Brickman, & Chen, 1985). These investigators found no significant differences between third- and sixth-grade girls of divorced and nondivorced families. However, girls from the ages of eleven through eighteen whose parents were divorced reported significantly greater numbers of delinquent behaviors than girls from nondivorced families. They exhibited higher frequencies of drug abuse, truancy, and larceny than girls from nondivorced families. Finally, in exploring attitudes of college women from divorced families, Kalter and his associates found that these women had more negative attitudes toward men and women and were less hopeful about their futures than women from nondivorced families. These findings are consistent with those of other investigators who suggest that women whose parents had divorced were more likely themselves to marry early, be pregnant at the time of marriage, and select less adequate husbands than peers from nondivorced families.

In another longitudinal study of children of divorce, Judith Wallerstein followed up a group of forty males and females whose parents had been divorced in 1971 (Wallerstein, 1985a). At the point of initial study in 1971, about half of these children were less than eight years old, and half were between nine and eighteen years old. During the initial assessments conducted within six weeks of parental separation, these children showed acute distress with anxiety, depression, worry about one or both parents, feelings of guilt, and loyalty conflicts. About half of these children showed a significant drop in school grades, and many engaged in acting out (disruptive) behavior. At the point of follow-up ten years later, nearly 70 percent of these individuals (now adolescents and young adults) had engaged in delinquent behavior defined as participation in mild to serious illegal activity. Many continued to experience resentment about their parents' divorces and feel a sense of deprivation, yearning, and sadness. Study of a subgroup of young women from the whole sample shows that they experienced more frequent problems with heterosexual adjustment and diminished self-worth and often developed a pattern of repetitious drifting from one man to another.

A major issue often contributing to ongoing conflict between parents after divorce is child custody. Although there are a variety of custody patterns, the prevalent one in the United States is joint custody, in which parents share authority and responsibility for children after the divorce and children alternately live in both parental homes. Thirty-two states currently have enacted such legislation. Unfortunately, little research has been available in this area until recently, and it is difficult to draw clear conclusions.

One study of divorced fathers showed that those fathers who had joint custody of their children experienced less depression and more satisfaction than fathers who had visitation rights only (Grief, 1979). One might presume that, indirectly, parents' better psychological adjustment would promote healthier child development following divorce, but there is no direct evidence to show this, nor is there consistent evidence that joint custody leads to better child adjustment than other patterns (Abarbanel, 1979; Luepnitz, 1982; Steinman, 1981).

In a recent comprehensive study of joint custody, fifty-one divorcing families with seventy-five children were recruited in a combination research and service project (Steinman, Zemmelman, & Knoblauch, 1985). These divorcing parents participated in a six-week educational program and support group and were provided with up to twelve mediational/counseling sessions. Parents and children completed a variety of rating scales and checklists and participated in interviews. Schoolteachers were also interviewed and follow-up interviews were conducted at six months and one year. Preliminary results of this study show that parents who are able to negotiate the complexities of joint custody most successfully

- show respect for the emotional bonds between the child and the other spouse;
- maintain some objectivity through the divorce process;
- empathize with the point of view of the divorced spouse and the child;

- change their emotional relationship and expectations of the divorced spouse from those of a mate to those of a coparent;
- work toward establishing modified role boundaries;
- experience high self-esteem, maintain personal flexibility, and remain open to assistance.

In contrast, many parents were unable to sustain the complex relationships and interactions involved in joint custody and felt compelled to return to the courts for renegotiation of custody. Parents who have the greatest difficulty making joint custody work

- continue to feel intense hostility toward and conflict with the divorced spouse, and displace those feelings on the children;
- need to punish the divorced spouse;
- have a history of physical abuse or substance abuse;
- believe that the divorced spouse is a bad parent;
- are unable to separate their own feelings and needs from those of their children.

Unfortunately, the effects of the joint custody arrangement on the adjustment of children has yet to be reported.

Although little can yet be said definitively about the effects of different custody arrangements, it is clear that parental disputes continuing even after divorce have severe negative effects on the emotional health of children (Hetherington, 1984; O'Leary, 1984). The research on children from postseparation or postdivorce families continuing to undergo intense conflict shows that these children experience severe distress and anxiety upon witnessing parental conflicts, develop a variety of somatic symptoms such as stomachaches and headaches, sometimes become aggressive, or withdraw into themselves (Johnston, Cambell, & Mayes, 1985). Often, such symptoms in children serve to fuel further parental conflict as the separated or divorced parents blame each other for the child's behavior.

Although it is dangerous to draw premature conclusions from an area of research that is still in its infancy and characterized by tremendous methodological complexities, a few basic facts have emerged. First, it is clear that parental discord and divorce do have an important negative impact on children's adjustment and achievement; these effects are long-standing, affecting them as they grow into adolescence and adulthood. Second, although it is difficult to sort out relative influences of conflict and separation and divorce, it appears that ongoing overt hostility is the most damaging element. Third, although separation and divorce may end discord within the household, in many families conflict, arguments, and even physical fighting persist well beyond the separation or divorce to have serious negative influences on child development. Finally, although joint custody is emerging as the prevalent pattern in postdivorce families, it is by no means clear that such a pattern avoids disruptive influences on childhood development.

One wonders whether an acute and explicit awareness of the impact of marital discord and divorce on children might prompt parents to try to work in different ways toward the resolution of their conflicts. Unfortunately, such awareness appears to be the exception rather than the rule, and as a society we face a serious, pervasive legacy of divorce (Wallerstein, 1985b) whose impact is only beginning to cause the depth of concern that it merits.

A Cautionary Note

In discussing faulty patterns of child rearing and family interaction, it is easy to form an impression that parents are almost completely responsible for their children's emotional health and ability to cope with life stresses. And, indeed, it is critically important for students of childhood problems to be intimately familiar with the patterns outlined here. These patterns constitute the most important behavior settings for many students in special classroom settings, and effective intervention often requires that appropriate referrals for some family problems be made to specialists. Classroom interventions that end when a child returns to a disruptive family system are unlikely to have much permanent effect.

Before ending this discussion, however, it is important to insert a few essential disclaimers. First, most of the patterns discussed occur in varying degrees and often evolve as the family itself moves through time. Marriage relationships do not remain static, and the fact that a child is born and grows has an impact on the relationship between the parents. Second, such patterns do not affect all family members to the same extent. One child may have weathered critical developmental stages before the emergence of a faulty behavioral pattern; a boy may not encounter the same pressures in a given family as the girls in that family do. Parental ability to cope with life stresses such as economic insecurity, marital infidelity, or emotional illness in a spouse all change over time. Finally, an ecological systems approach demands that we recognize the mutual influences between parents and children as well as the influences of the larger society. From infancy on, children affect parental attitudes, feelings, and behaviors (Bell, 1968; Harper, 1975; Suran & Rizzo, 1983). The family is not a closed system. Social and economic variables and the ideas and behaviors that children bring home with them may create upheavals in the family system. Although parents are inevitably a part of their children's lives and problems, it is an oversimplification to view them as causing those problems. Rather, it is in the transactions within the family and in those between the family and the larger world that we must search for causes and solutions.

Ecological Impact of a Changing Community

It is evident that even a behavior setting as narrow as the nuclear family can involve immense complexities. Parents and children each bring to the family setting a unique heredity, a personal temperament and expressive style, a pattern of abilities and interests, and a personal history. As family members interact together, these elements of personality influence and are influenced by those of other family members to produce a human compound infinitely more complex than anything a chemist could ever develop in a laboratory. And yet the family is only the focus of a much broader set of systemic forces that influence the family unit together and individually. The sections that follow briefly summarize a few of the most important contemporary community and cultural forces that have an impact on the development and adjustment of a single child.

Changing Family Structures

In addition to the changes in patterns of marriage and divorce, the second half of the twentieth century is witnessing changes in the very way we conceive of family life. Geographic and occupational mobility, evolving attitudes toward sexuality and marriage, the wider availability of effective birth control techniques, frequent remarriage of divorced parents, increasing numbers of single-parent families, and dramatic increases in the numbers of families in which both parents work have all created tremendous changes in family life and in the way we think about the very nature of the family.

Although we cannot examine all these changes in detail, a few warrant explicit attention because of their direct impact on children's development. These include increased frequency of parental remarriage, increased numbers of single-parent families, and increasing frequency of families in which both parents work, leading to reliance on nonfamily day care.

Parental Remarriage and Recombined Families

As changes in patterns of living become widespread, new terms and concepts have been developed to describe them. With dramatic increases in the frequency of divorce since midcentury, there have also been increases in the number of divorced parents who remarry. Though remarriage has always been an option for widowed parents, this has never been so widespread a phenomenon to prompt the development of concepts, language, and research as has the upsurge in divorce rates. Currently, investigators speak of remarried parents, blended families, reconstituted families, stepfamilies, and recombined families, all referring to a situation in which at least one marital partner who is remarrying has children by a previous marriage. The term *recombined family* is used here because it does not carry the negative connotations of stepfamily, does not reflect the unrealistic ideal of blended family, nor does it hold the clinical distance of reconstituted family.

Among divorced women under thirty with one child, 75 percent remarry (Hacker, 1983). This percentage drops only slightly, to 74.9 percent, among divorced women under thirty with two children, and to 71.5 percent with three children. Among both sexes with and without children, 73 percent of divorced persons remarry. Translated into real numbers, these figures mean that approximately thirty-five million adults had assumed the role of stepparent by 1980 (Visher & Visher, 1979a) and that more than fifteen million children live in recombined families (Einstein, 1982), with the latter figure increasing at the rate of one-half million children per year.

The fact that the divorce rate among remarriages is higher than that for first marriages (Westoff, 1977) reflects, among other things, the even greater difficulties faced in working out satisfactory adjustments than in traditional, intact, nuclear families. Even though every marrying couple must develop some mode of adaptation to each other's personalities, habits, values, money management patterns, and so forth, remarrying couples and recombined families face additional challenges.

Every member of a recombined family has experienced important losses with the dissolution of the original families. For the parents there may

have been, in addition to the loss of a spouse, a loss of self-esteem in the failure of the marriage, a loss of hopes and ideals for a perfect marriage, and a loss of ability to trust another intimately. In most cases there has been some significant financial loss and accompanying insecurity. For children there has been a loss of one parent's immediate presence. There may also be a loss of relationships with grandparents and other significant adults, possibly a loss of school relationships and friendships, and the loss of stability of the nuclear family. It is quite true that these losses may well be offset by a reduction in witnessed family conflict or reduction in other parental problems; however, they are losses nonetheless.

In extensive studies of recombined families, John and Emily Visher have also observed other important characteristics (Visher & Visher, 1979b). The children in recombined families are members of at least two different family structures: the present recombined family and the family made up of the children and the noncustodial parent. The latter may also include a spouse and his or her children by a previous marriage and possibly children of this marriage. Obviously, the network of relationships can become extremely complex and difficult for parents to manage, let alone for their children.

In their psychotherapeutic work with recombined families, Frederick Capaldi and Barbara McRae (1979) have developed a useful diagrammatic tool for conceptualizing the complex issues faced by members of a recombined family, and we will digress briefly to outline their method. In essence, Capaldi and McRae ask family members to draw a stepfamily picture, with each family member drawing his or her own individual picture showing family relationships and relationships between the family and the larger world. Family members are also asked to diagram how an ideal family might look, how their original family looked, or how they would like their current family to look. Capaldi and McRae use their family diagrams therapeutically to assess perceptions and misperceptions of family relationships, alliances, and conflicts. They might, for example, ask each member of a family to diagram his or her views of family roles and relationships and use differences in diagrams among family members as a basis for facilitating mutual understanding, correcting misperceptions, or renegotiating roles. Box 2.3 illustrates the potential complexities of a child's position in a recombined family situation.

In addition to personal loss and the problems of living in recombined families, there is the excess baggage that individuals bring to a recombined family, such as past expectations, habits, ways of relating, and resentments. In contrast with the evolved patterns of shared beliefs, customs, and jokes that existed in the nuclear family, there is often a sudden clash of habits and styles without the luxury of a shared history and sometimes without even a willingness to be tolerant of each other.

In a recombined family, parent-child relationships precede the parent-parent relationships and often set the stage for conflict between the newly married couple (Visher & Visher, 1979a). In addition to the expectations of how children should behave that each parent brings from his or her own childhood, there are also expectations that they developed in their previous marriages. Disciplinary matters are often a key source of conflict as the nonbiological parent in a recombined family is viewed as intruding on the preexisting parent-child relationships. Such situations are often further complicated if the noncustodial parent intrudes into the situation by supporting the children against either or both parents in the recombined family. The situation

---

Box 2.3   Overlapping Relationships in Recombined Families

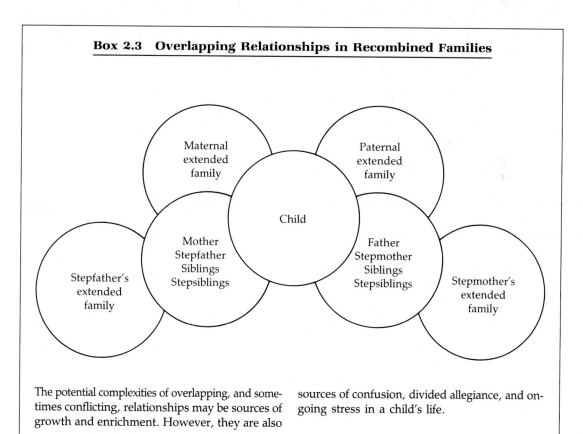

The potential complexities of overlapping, and sometimes conflicting, relationships may be sources of growth and enrichment. However, they are also sources of confusion, divided allegiance, and ongoing stress in a child's life.

may be much the same where custody is shared.

It often happens in such situations that children foster divisiveness between the newly remarried couple and exploit disagreement to ventilate their own resentment, to get their way, or to protect their relationship with the biological parent in the recombined family.

In some instances, the fact that parent-child relationships precede the parents' remarriage may also lead to other problems: concern that one's own children do not receive the attention or the material goods given to the spouse's children; envy of the nonbiological parent's children, the stepsiblings; jealousy of time and attention the biological parent gives to his or her spouse; and chronic resentment because of a belief that life would have been better if the natural parents had not divorced. Such problems are not unusual. In fact, they exist potentially in most recombined families.

Finally, no legal relationship exists between stepparents and stepchildren in a recombined family, and mutual obligations extend no further than the marriage relationship itself. Given the fact that one or both parents in the recombined family have previously divorced, that the problems of remarriage are often more difficult than those in first marriages, and that divorce rates are higher among the remarried, it is not surprising that there is often little depth to mutual commitments between stepparents and stepchildren.

Despite the hazards of remarriage, recombined families are a fact of contemporary life and it is important to consider ways of maximizing mutual satisfaction and growth in recombined families. It is critically important that children's sense of loss of a parent and the family of origin be recognized and accepted as legitimate. The fact that the parents may have had intense conflict and mutual resentment does not mean that the children must feel the same way. Sarah Einstein, in recounting her own experiences as a stepparent in a recombined family, notes that it was difficult for her to recognize that her love toward her stepchildren was conditional on their ability to think and feel the way she

wanted them to (Einstein, 1982). However, it was not until she was able to accept their feelings of love and loss toward their natural mother that their relationship moved toward mutual affection and respect. As Einstein noted, it is the parents and not the parents and children who divorce.

Recombined families also need to work toward the development of their own shared traditions and history. This involves open discussions of the "right" way to do things, ranging from how and when to cook certain dishes, celebrate holidays, or take vacations to what values and religious beliefs to hold. It is important not to try to change other family members so much as to accept and respect what they view as crucial in their lives and to work out ways of sharing and adapting and of developing family traditions in other areas.

The couple bond in remarried families must be recognized as delicate and should be cultivated carefully. A remarried parent must be sensitive to the depth and intensity of the spouse's relationship with his or her children and avoid insistence on particular relationship styles or modes of discipline. It is particularly important that each remarried parent work toward controlling the almost inevitable feelings of jealousy with regard to parent-child relationships and to avoid accusations regarding loyalty. Reciprocally, remarried biological parents must be open to their spouses' perceptions of their children and open to modifying their own perceptions (Whiteside, 1981).

Each parent in a recombined family must work actively—but not intrusively—toward establishing and cultivating a relationship with stepchildren in the family and among stepsiblings. Such relationships cannot be forced, as unfortunately is often attempted. Rather, family members must communicate a sense of acceptance, trust, and affection and permit relationships to evolve. Naturally, criticism of either biological parent, but particularly the noncustodial parent, must be avoided.

All members of the recombined family, and the children particularly, need assistance and encouragement to deal with feelings of loss, loyalty conflicts, questions about where they belong in new family systems, and feelings of anger (Visher & Visher, 1979a). In a study of 367 children living in recombined families, Helen Crohn and her associates in a remarriage consultation service found that 83 percent of the children they saw experienced significant conflict with a step-, custodial, or noncustodial parent (Crohn, et al., 1981). Impulse control problems, including substance abuse, and school problems were observed in more than a third of the children. Others experienced disturbed relationships with peers, psychosomatic problems, depression, and exclusion from the family. Only 9 percent—thirty-three children—were considered to be free of problems.

Clearly, children whose parents divorce and remarry experience intense life stress. It is critical that child-care professionals maintain sensitivity to children in recombined families and an awareness of the special problems they experience. Although it is rarely appropriate for educators to take a direct intervention role in the problems of the recombined family, it is often possible for teachers to support such indirect measures as the development of educational programs and workshops for divorced and remarried parents, to gather and disseminate information for parents on coping with divorce and remarriage, to be available if parents seek consultation or assistance, and to be familiar with professionals to whom parents may be referred for further assistance. Though the teacher's role is to teach and not to practice psychotherapy, it is nevertheless the case that the teacher may be one of the few professionals in the community with whom suffering children and their parents have ongoing contact, and it is important that teachers be available to help with information, acceptance, and appropriate referrals (Drake, 1981).

Working Mothers and Day Care

Changes in attitudes and practices regarding divorce, remarriage, and single parenting have had tremendous impact on families in recent years; however, the impact of social and economic changes leading to increased employment of both parents in first-married, recombined, or single-parent families has been of nearly equal importance. By 1981 nearly 54 percent of U.S. children under age eighteen had mothers in the labor force, and of children under age six, 45 percent had working mothers (Hacker, 1983). This means that nearly half the children in this country experience some amount of time in the care of nonmaternal, nonparental, or nonrelated professional caretakers, a 400 percent increase since World War II (Kotulak, 1986).

Although there is no lack of opinion on whether it is helpful or harmful for children to experience large amounts of time in the care of people other than their biological mothers, there is little clear evidence showing either positive or negative effects of nonmaternal care on child development. As in so many instances, however, the more ambiguous the facts, the more intense the opinions people hold and the more heatedly these opinions are expressed.

One of the reasons that there is so little clear evidence regarding the effects of nonmaternal care on children may be that research in this area is extremely difficult to conduct. One must somehow sort out, for example, the relative effects of different kinds of nonmaternal care ranging from care by the child's father and by older siblings, to care by grandparents, care by unrelated adults in a home setting, or professional day care. Further, it is only reasonable to expect that the child's age upon being first placed into care by someone other than the mother is an important variable, as is the actual amount of time the child spends in such care, both on a daily basis and from year to year. Further, it is likely that the circumstances leading the child's mother to work outside the home are also an important variable, as are the actual working conditions she experiences. Is the mother available to the child when not working? Is there continuity among caretakers? What are the physical and emotional conditions in the caretaking situation? Is the child exposed to structured and stimulating experiences or simply given basic physical care? What are the qualifications of the caretaker? Unfortunately, nearly all these variables overlap to confound and confuse the results of dozens of studies.

Another possible reason for lack of clear results showing either positive or negative effects of day care is that, by itself, it is a more or less indifferent experience and has little overall impact on children's lives. Thus it may not be the case that investigators have been unable to produce adequate research methods. Rather, adequate research has shown that it makes little difference whether a child is cared for by people other than the mother, provided the quality of care is basically adequate and appropriate and occurs within the context of healthy parental relations when the parents are present.

Perhaps the most balanced conclusion is that there is no clear evidence that nonmaternal care is harmful or beneficial (Etaugh, 1980; Siegal, 1984). Rather, the effects of nonmaternal care depend on such other factors as the age and sex of the child, the kind and quality of the child's day-care experience, socioeconomic factors, ethnic and racial characteristics, and parental attitudes. However, even these rather neutral statements are far-reaching in their implications because, in effect, they mean that there is no currently known, data-based reason for saying that mothers should not work if they choose to do so. Such a conclusion runs counter to widespread popular opinion (Etaugh, 1980; Martin, Burgess, & Crnic, 1984), but nevertheless is the only conclusion currently warranted.

Despite the fact that there is no consistent evidence of negative effects as a result of working mothers and nonmaternal care, many people voice strong objections to this pattern and many working mothers experience intense conflict and guilt because they work. If a child has physical or emotional difficulties and the mother works, others often assume that she has failed to live up to her responsibilities as a parent, and she often makes the same assumption (Nadelson, 1979). In some cases such guilt may lead to compensatory responses of overindulgence or inability to exercise appropriate discipline. However, in homes where the mother neither feels guilty nor overcompensates because she works, but instead focuses realistically on the child's needs, no such problems need develop (Hoffman, 1979). In fact, a case may even be made that maternal employment provides a context for children to learn greater independence and more appropriate sex role modeling (Hoffman, 1984).

It is important to remember that scientific research is a culture-bound activity, and the facts of one time or place may be the errors of another. Hopefully, questions regarding the effects of nonmaternal care on children will remain open and investigators will continue to examine this important issue not to prove a point, but to be sure we are doing all we can as a society to provide healthy environments for our children.

Racial and Cultural Differences

Although cultural, community, and family values are part of the ecosystem of every child from the moment of birth, some children also experience conflicts among these values that further complicate developmental processes and deeply affect their lives. Children of minority group families often face the impossible developmental task of integrating the values and institutions of the larger society with the values and institutions of their own cultural group while being denied the means to effect such integration. Many black, Hispanic, and American Indian youngsters see daily on television, in the movies, in newspapers and magazines the opportunities open to them through education and hard work. They also see the daily struggles their families face to escape a cycle of educational impoverishment and economic deprivation, discouragement, and hopelessness. If they are of school age, they may spend their days in classrooms devoid of excitement or challenges that relate to their lives outside the school. If they are older, they may recognize that realistic opportunities are out of their reach by mid-adolescence as society consigns them to menial jobs or no jobs at all.

For example, by age seven black children are aware not only of the existence of racial difference, but also of the devaluation of their own group by the larger society (Williams & Morland, 1976). Apart from the media, they have relatively little contact with the larger society, with most of the black population concentrated in forty-seven large cities in census tracts that are more than 50 percent black (Cottingham, 1975). Historically separated from the culture of the majority, often devalued in stereotyped images, many black children grow up with incomplete or negative self-images, low self-esteem, and rejection of their own racial and cultural backgrounds. Problems in the development of adequate self-concept, in turn, often set the stage for high levels of anxiety, difficulties in handling frustration and delay of gratification, low achievement orientation, a sense of limited control over one's environment and life circumstances, a tendency toward delinquency, and unrealistically high aspirations (Barnes, 1972).

Following World War II, an extensive body of research developed suggesting that racial discrimination and associated economic and educational deprivation barred black children from opportunities to develop the competencies and experiences upon which a strong, positive self-concept is based (Dreger & Miller, 1968; Kardiner & Ovesey, 1968). Substandard and segregated education led to underemployment and unemployment that, in turn, undermined the stability of black and other minority group families. Within this context, many minority group youths developed adjustment patterns which perpetuated a cycle of poverty with blocked opportunities leading to decreased motivation, dependency on social welfare institutions, and erosion of self-esteem.

Many black children and children of other minority groups continue to grow up aware that they live in the least desirable sections of their communities—ghettos, barrios, or reservations—and see hunger, poor health, and inadequate housing as their lot. They see the adults around them unable to find employment and consequently see little point in developing skills that they will never have an opportunity to use. They find little in the way of adequate transportation or recreational opportunities and, in overcrowded classrooms, encounter teachers who often view them according to their own stereotypes.

The day-to-day results of such experiences are boredom, hopelessness, and despair. These pervasive responses to racial discrimination led the Joint Commission on the Mental Health of Children to declare that racism was the most important public health problem in the United States in the 1960s and 1970s, producing discouragement, demoralization, and delinquency growing out of frustration and rage (Joint Commission on the Mental Health of Children, 1970).

These are by no means necessary developmental outcomes among black or other minority group children (Powell, 1983). Many youngsters growing up in strong families with supportive subcultures develop positive self-concepts with no significant differences from their white peers (Rosenberg, 1979). Black children, taking advantage of changes spurred by civil rights, have overcome barriers posed by economic deprivation and racial discrimination to achieve outstanding academic success and move into professional and skilled occupations (Farley, 1977; Wilson, 1978).

A key factor in this kind of proactive, healthy orientation involves positive family socialization practices that teach a youngster that blocked opportunities only provide a spur to alternative or renewed efforts. In one recent study of familial socialization practices, Phillip Bowman and Cleopatra Howard studied the family practices of a nationwide sample of three-generation black families (1985). Family messages emphasizing racial pride, ethnic heritage, black unity, individual excellence, character building, self-reliance, interracial equality, and multiethnic coexistence were important components of an individual's belief that he or she could cope effectively and achieve.

However, among other minority groups, such proactive messages may themselves be sources of conflict. For example, some American Indian families emphasize the importance of values such as sharing and generosity, cooperation with others, an orientation to time in which events happen according to their own schedule rather than according to artificially imposed deadlines, harmony with the natural order, and the importance of the extended family. In such families, it may be more important to maintain harmony and integration than to compete, to avoid meddling, and to impose one's individual will upon external events (Wise & Miller, 1983). It may be difficult or impossible for a growing child or adolescent to reconcile such values with those of a larger society that views the individual's relationship with the world in terms of struggle and conquest.

The point of this brief discussion is not to produce simplistic solutions or recommendations, but rather to emphasize the reality and difficulty of the additional stresses and conflicts that minority children must face in reconciling family and subcultural values with those of the larger society in which they live. Educators and other child-care professionals must be acutely and continually aware of the patterns of stress and internal conflict with which minority group children deal on a daily basis. They must, further, be aware of and respect the strengths that arise from distinctive subcultural backgrounds and work toward understanding the unique patterns of strength that arise from such a background of experiences.

Fortunately, the children of minority group families share a common strength in the emphasis that many of these groups place on the importance of strong family and kinship ties (Munoz, 1983; Red Horse, 1983; Vega, Hough, & Romero, 1983; Yamamoto & Kubota, 1983). The availability of the family as a resource in the face of racial and ethnic discrimination and abject poverty provides many youngsters with the support they need to cope with the stresses associated with minority group membership in this country.

Summary

Chapter 2 developed a context for studying behavioral disorders in children and adolescents. Using the composite Jerry as an example, we outlined some of the constitutional, psychological, and environmental forces that interact in each child to produce a unique pattern of characteristics and behavior. The complexity of these interacting forces requires some kind of organizing framework, and several influential theorists have provided developmental theories for just such a framework.

The psychoanalytic and psychodynamic theories of Freud and Erikson provide insight into some of the internal conflicts and anxieties that act upon children. By contrast, behavioral theories focus on the interaction of the individual with environmental stimuli in what Skinner viewed as orderly, predictable patterns. Social learning theorists have enriched both these perspectives and provided many integrating concepts that allow the useful application of psychodynamic and behaviorist theories. Piaget detailed the complexities of cognitive development, and his ideas have led to a deeper understanding of how children come to know the world around them.

Although there is no ecological theory, ecological concepts have emphasized the importance of applying theoretical concepts in the real and very complex world in which children develop. We can often isolate events in theory or even in a laboratory; however, no such isolation exists in the real world, and it is critically important to test and verify our ideas in the ecosystem in which a child grows.

Such ecosystems include the family setting, and extensive research into family functioning has helped us identify many healthy and pathological modes of family functioning. Further changes in societal values have led to changes in the very structure of the family system. In this regard, we discussed important contemporary trends in divorce, recombined families, and families in which both parents work.

Finally, we looked briefly at the devastating impact of poverty and prejudice as these affect the lives of children. Unfortunately, there are no simple solutions to the problem of economic and social deprivation. Nevertheless, they must be recognized as playing important roles in the development of childhood and adolescent behavioral disorders.

CHAPTER 3

Assessment of Children and Adolescents with Behavioral Disorders

Overview

Introduction

Assessment is a broad term for the procedures used to collect data and to make decisions. Assessment involves studying conditions in a student's environment, determining eligibility for special programming, selecting appropriate interventions and placements, monitoring student performance, and evaluating the effectiveness of programming. This chapter considers two major uses of assessment involving students with personality problems and conduct disorders:

1. procedures for determining eligibility, placement, and special education programming, and
2. procedures for ongoing monitoring of student behavior.

Because the purposes of each kind of assessment differ, some of the techniques appropriate to each purpose also differ. Referral/identification assessment, for example, focuses on how and to what extent an individual student's behavior deviates from expectations for others with similar characteristics. In contrast, monitoring student behavior may include deviation measures, but it focuses on the determination of student changes over time in response to attempted interventions.

Ecological Perspectives

Earlier chapters emphasize an ecological perspective on personality problems and conduct disorders. An individual's behavior must be considered within its ecological context. Emotional and behavioral disorders represent conflict, or a lack of fit, between the individual and his or her environment. They indicate a "disrupted pattern of individual-environment exchanges" (Rhodes & Tracy, 1974, p. 23). Rhodes and Paul (1978) proposed that the appropriateness of behavior is a function of the behavior itself as well as with whom and where the behavior occurs. From this perspective, assessment of behavioral disorders must include study of the individual and his or her environment. Consideration must be given both to the disturbing child and to the ecosystems that are disturbed (Algozzine, 1977).

This chapter presents procedures and techniques that are compatible with an ecological perspective. They include methods for measuring individual behavior as well as ecological influences, especially within classrooms and schools, on individual students. Because of the parameters of this text, the scope of the settings and perspectives that have an impact on the individual are somewhat circumscribed. The chapter emphasizes an assessment of what Deno and Mirkin

(1977) called the child's "smaller society," comprised of significant others in the child's life space.

Normality in Child Development

Judgments of emotional and behavioral deviance are always normative. They reflect expectations for what is considered normal within particular contexts. When behavior matches expectations, it is considered "normal." When it deviates from expectations, it is considered abnormal. Schools reflect societal, cultural, and community expectations for appropriate behavior. These expectations differ according to children's personal characteristics, and social and political factors (Wood, 1981). The theories of personality development of Freud and Erikson summarized in the previous chapter, as well as those of cognitive and moral development offered by Piaget and Kohlberg, reflect age-related sequential stages of development. We may, for example, expect different patterns of behavior in a preschooler, a fourth-grader, a middle school student, and a senior in high school—even under similar conditions. In addition, expectations for behavior differ according to several other characteristics, including sex (Jackson & Lahaderne, 1967), socioeconomic status (Rist, 1970), ethnicity (Coates, 1972; Prieto & Zucker, 1981), physical attractiveness (Ross & Salvia, 1975), and academic achievement (Brophy & Good, 1974). It appears that teachers respond differently to problem behavior depending on certain student characteristics.

Different ecosystems also elicit different expectations for behavior (Barker, 1968). For example, children may be expected to behave differently in a classroom than on a neighborhood playground. Quiet, attentive, studious behavior is generally expected in the former, while animated, boisterous behavior is expected in the latter. Peers, parents, and other adults may have different expectations for appropriateness even within a single setting. Parents and teachers, for example, may have divergent views about the appropriateness of discipline techniques. Of course, dramatic differences can exist in what is considered normal or acceptable behavior in one school compared

with another depending on characteristics of the students, community values, school resources, physical structures of buildings and classrooms, and faculty and administrator attitudes.

Educators in a single community can disagree about behavior, such as their students' use of profane language (see Box 3.1). The issue becomes sensitive when questions are raised such as: What is "foul" language?; where is it inappropriate?; what should be done about it? Vast differences in behavioral expectations may be apparent from one classroom to another within the same school. Even in a single classroom, teacher and student expectations for behavior may change according to the type of activity and time of day. Consequently, the assessment of personality and conduct disorders must take into account the characteristics of students' ecosystems as well as their individual characteristics.

Screening and Identification Issues

Decisions potentially leading to referral, identification, and placement of students into special education must be undertaken with great care. The mandate of the Education for All Handicapped Children Act (PL 94–142) is to identify all handicapped students, including those labeled seriously emotionally disturbed, in need of special education services. The requirement to locate and identify handicapped children has been called the zero reject principle. The purpose of identification is to design appropriate individual education programs (IEPs) for handicapped students in the least restrictive environment possible. To be eligible for special education services, a student must be formally identified as meeting diagnostic criteria for serious emotional disturbance.

Accurate, unbiased assessment is required to minimize the risks of both false negative and false positive diagnoses. False negative diagnoses are those that fail to identify students who are, in fact, handicapped. The undesirable consequence of such a diagnosis is the denial of special services to students who could benefit from them. False positive diagnoses incorrectly identify students as handicapped. The undesirable consequence is labeling a child as handicapped, with its potentially negative expectations and possible removal of that child from the educational mainstream.

Behavioral disorders face us with major challenges in trying to avoid false negatives and false positives. One is the absence of specific diagnostic criteria and quantitative measures to determine eligibility. A second challenge involves the relatively high level of stigma, or negative identity, associated with the labels emotionally disturbed, behaviorally disordered, and others used to designate this disparate category of educational exceptionality.

As noted earlier, considerations of emotional and behavioral deviance are reflections of cultural and political, as well as individual, moral and ethical values. In that sense, they are always relative. They are a matter of opinion, based upon perceptions of what is normal, typical behavior within certain settings. Thus, persons involved in behavioral assessment must be knowledgeable about normal personal, social, and cognitive development. They must be aware of the prevalent moral, ethical, and legal standards for behavior in relevant ecosystems. They must recognize that professional judgments sometimes differ from cultural, community, and family values.

Drawing on several sources, Frank Hewett and Frank Taylor (1980) have suggested a developmental model for classifying behavioral problems

---

Box 3.1   Views on "Foul Language" in Schools

According to an article in the *Milwaukee Journal*,* some teachers believe that students' use of foul language is increasing. As one teacher said, "They are less inhibited, not only in their discussions with each other, but also in class and in addressing teachers. You can put up with the damns and the hells and s– –s. Now you're getting 'f– – you' and 'get f– –,' and that's more prevalent." Another teacher commented, "Every teacher has the same complaint. There's a lack of respect and out-and-out obscenity, including the F-word. It's really a reflection of society. It even creeps into my conversation once in a while." Yet another teacher reported that after reprimanding a student for using foul language, the student told her, "I don't know why you're upset. I use this language at home all the time."

Interviewed teachers expressed different ideas on dealing with the language problems. Some proposed that schools should use detention and suspensions for foul language, while others believed it should be simply ignored unless blatant and loud and specifically directed at teachers, principals, and other students. One school board member proposed setting up a special school or classroom for children who use foul language excessively, where they could be helped to express themselves in a more acceptable manner.

This controversy over the use of foul language illustrates some of the difficulties in determining what is acceptable and deviant behavior in schools. Unresolved questions include:

What should be considered acceptable behavior in schools?

Are school standards different from those of the home and community?

Whose standards do we use—teachers', parents', students'?

Is majority or typical behavior to be considered the norm?

When behavior violates our expectations for appropriateness, do we tolerate it, tolerate some of it, punish or segregate those who engage in it, or attempt to remediate it?

*D. I. Bednarek. Schools hear a language of 4-letter words, the *Milwaukee Journal*, July 13, 1986, p. 6B.

according to both type and degree of variance from norms. (See Box 3.2.) The Hewett and Taylor sequence of optimal learning competencies includes attention, motor and verbal responses, order, exploratory, social, and mastery skills. Chapter 10 looks more closely at the Hewett and Taylor conceptualization of school behavior problems.

Paul Graubard (1973) once stated that behavioral disabilities are a variety of deviant behaviors that violate expectations of appropriateness and that the perceiver wishes to see stopped. Existing definitions of emotional and behavioral deviance reflect this relativity. Thus, diagnostic criteria are not amenable to direct and objective measurement. There is no test or measure yet developed that leads directly to a diagnosis.

The Federal Definition

Federal regulations supporting the implementation of PL 94–142 include the definition of serious emotional disturbance (SED) that was included in Chapter 1. Most states also employ this definition or an adaptation of it that conforms with the federal definition originally written by Eli Bower (1981). Although the official definition lists several traits that singly or in combination may qualify a student for the SED designation, no specific psychoeducational procedures or standards for diagnosing SED are provided. The only guidance is that the condition must be exhibited over a long period of time and to a marked degree. These qualifications mean that the listed traits cannot be temporary, transient conditions, and they must be serious in nature. However, even these qualifications are subject to debate. What constitutes a long period of time? Is it twenty days, five months, or three years? At what point does behavioral deviance become marked, as opposed to more mild or moderate, disturbance? Obviously, there are no absolute answers to any of these questions.

Meaningful identification procedures must acknowledge the absence of universal guidelines. Instead, the assessment process must build in assurances that each eligibility decision is thought-

fully and carefully undertaken. Data must be sought from a variety of sources representing a multidisciplinary evaluation of students in the context of their environments.

Labels such as seriously emotionally disturbed and behaviorally disordered are relatively stigmatizing. In the minds of many they are associated with pejorative terms such as crazy, mentally ill, delinquent, or bad. Even teachers tend to view the behaviorally disordered, and especially emotionally disturbed, labels more negatively than those for most other handicapping conditions (Wood, 1985). Pejorative labels can produce negative, self-fulfilling prophecies. Once applied, they can be difficult to remove and may continue to influence others' perceptions of a child even after they no longer are valid. Although handicap labels can provide shorthand descriptions that lead to eligibility for services, they can also be inappropriately used to explain behavior, stigmatize the person to whom they have been applied, and result in unwarranted treatment.

Incidence of Behaviorally Disordered Students

Despite the potential of false positive diagnoses, there does not appear to be an extensive over-identification of students as behaviorally disordered. The traditional estimate of the incidence of serious emotional and behavioral disorders is 2 percent of the school-age population, although considerably larger numbers of students are viewed by their teachers as presenting more mild and transient behavioral and emotional problems (Glidewell & Swallow, 1969).

Based on information collected longitudinally on a large sample of children, Rubin and Balow (1978) found that in any given year 21 percent to 31 percent are considered by their teachers to present problems of behavior and/or attitude. About 60 percent of the children in their study were considered problems by at least one of their teachers during elementary school years. However, only 7.4 percent were considered by at least three teachers to have problems, and just

Box 3.2   Common Characteristics of Disturbed Children Viewed as Negative Variants of Six Levels of Learning Competence

Too Little	◄——►	Optimal	◄——►	Too Much
Disturbances in sensory perception (sed)	Excessive daydreaming (ii) Poor memory (a) Short attention span (ii) In a world all his or her own (ii)	Attention	Selective attention (a)	Fixation on particular stimuli (a)
Immobilization (a)	Sluggishness (ii) Passivity (ii) Drowsiness (ii) Clumsiness Depression (pp)	Response (motor)	Hyperactivity (cp) Restlessness (cp)	Self-stimulation (sed)
Failure to develop speech (sed)	Failure to use language for communication (sed)	Response (verbal)	Extremely talkative (a)	Uses profanity (cp) Verbally abusive (a)
Self-injurious (sed) Lawlessness (a) Destructiveness (cp)	Disruptiveness (cp) Attention seeking (cp) Irresponsibility (cp) Disobedience (cp)	Order	Overly conforming (a)	Resistance to change (sed) Compulsive (a)
Bizarre or stereotyped behavior (sed) Bizarre interests (sed)	Anxiety (pp) Preoccupation (pp) Doesn't know how to have fun (pp) Behaves like adult (pp) Shyness (pp)	Exploratory	Plunges into activities (a)	Tries to do everything at once (a)
Preoccupation with inanimate objects (sed) Extreme self-isolation (sed) Inability to relate to people (sed)	Social withdrawal (pp) Alienates others (a) Aloofness (pp) Prefers younger playmates (ii) Acts bossy (cp) Secretiveness (pp) Fighting (cp) Temper tantrums (cp)	Social	Hypersensitivity (pp) Jealousy (cp) Overly dependent (a)	Inability to function alone (a)
Blunted, uneven, or fragmented intellectual development (sed)	Lacks self-care skills (a) Lacks basic school skills (a) Laziness in school (ii) Dislike for school (cp) Lacks vocational skills (a)	Mastery	Preoccupation with academics (a)	Overintellectualizing (a)

Key: cp   conduct problem (Quay, 1972)
   ii   inadequacy-immaturity (Quay, 1972)
   pp   personality problem (Quay, 1972)
   sed   severely emotionally disturbed (GAP, 1966; Eisenberg & Kanner, 1956)
   a   authors

Source: "Common characteristics of disturbed children viewed as negative variants of six levels of learning competence." Reprinted by permission from F. M. Hewett & F. D. Taylor, *The emotionally disturbed child in the classroom: The orchestration of success* (2nd ed.) (Boston: Allyn and Bacon, 1980), pp. 285–286.

3 percent were considered problems by all of their elementary teachers.

In this study and others (Kelly, Bullock, & Dykes, 1977; Spivack, Swift, & Prewitt, 1971) more than 20 percent of students have been viewed as being a problem by their regular classroom teachers in any year. Of the 20 percent in the Kelly, et al. study, however, teachers considered just 2 percent severely disordered and another 5 percent moderately disordered. The remainder were viewed as presenting mild behavior problems that could be addressed in the regular classroom.

A review of research on incidence concluded that only about 1.5 percent to 2 percent of school-age children present sufficiently severe and chronic disorders to require special education services (Wood & Zabel, 1978). Although this percentage corresponds with traditional estimates, nationwide the number of children and adolescents who are formally identified as SED is at present less than 1 percent (Smith-Davis, Burke, & Noel, 1984).

Some have argued that the identification of less than half of the estimated number represents a serious underidentification of behaviorally disordered children and adolescents (Grosenick & Huntze, 1980; Kauffman, 1984). There is some validity to this argument, although some students probably are identified and receive special education services under another handicap label, especially that of learning disabilities (LD). As discussed in more detail in Chapter 7, distinctions between learning and behavioral disorders are sometimes difficult to make. Many students present both kinds of problems, and determining if a child should be designated learning disabled with behavior disorders or behaviorally disordered with learning disabilities is frequently problematic.

Behavioral Disorders as Educational Handicaps

There is some question about legal requirements for providing special education services to students with serious emotional disturbances which, as stated in the federal definition, do not adversely affect educational performance. PL 94-142, its supporting regulations, and the U.S. Department of Education guidelines have not yet clarified this point. Given our limited resources and expertise, Frank Wood (1985) argues that educators' primary responsibility for students with behavior disorders should be educational interventions. Other nonschool expertise and resources should provide services for children with emotional and behavioral disorders that do not affect their educational performance.

The authors agree that schools should not, indeed cannot, assume total responsibility for treating all children's personality and behavior disorders. However, we also strongly believe that concern with educational progress cannot be strictly limited to academic performance. Certainly, special educators play a central role in the assessment and remediation of academic learning problems, but education is more than mere academics. Our public schools have always been accorded responsibility for more than teaching the three Rs. Schools not only teach academic skills to children and adolescents—their overriding goal is also the preparation of children to be good citizens. The socialization of children, including the learning and practice of personal and social skills associated with good citizenship, is central to public education. Consequently, the remediation of personal and social skills of students who present problems in these areas is a legitimate and necessary function of schools.

The Assessment Process

The Iowa Assessment Model

There are several decision-making models regarding handicapped children and youth. The Iowa Department of Public Instruction has recently published a training manual specifically designed for the assessment of students who present serious emotional and behavior problems (Wood, Smith, & Grimes, 1985). The manual outlines procedures that contribute to the efficient collection of unbiased data to assist decision making. It also includes reviews of specific procedures and instruments. The Iowa Assessment Model for Behavior Disorders emphasizes giving prior attention to the specific questions assessment is intended to answer and to procedures and instruments most likely to provide those answers. It is not bound to a particular theoretical orientation or intervention program. For these reasons, it offers an assessment model that could be adapted to a variety of settings and situations.

The Iowa model includes five sequential decision-making steps:

1. Evaluation of classroom or home adjustments
2. Prereferral activities
3. Referral for special education services—eligibility
4. Referral for special education services—placement
5. Implementation of the special education plan

Each step is distinct from the others, with a set of entry and exit criteria and questions to be answered before moving to the next step. See Appendix A for a detailed outline of the Iowa model.

Classroom or Home Adjustments. Step 1 includes informal assessment procedures readily available to classroom teachers, parents, or other significant adults who are disturbed by a student's failure to make what they consider adequate progress in school. Based upon informal observation and measures of academic performance, a teacher may view a student's behavior or academic performance as discrepant from that of other students in the class. For example, the teacher may notice that the student slowly starts and rarely finishes assignments, spends considerable time daydreaming, is readily distracted from the task at hand, bothers other students, expresses unusual thoughts, seems unusually distant and depressed, or frequently talks out and leaves his or her seat without permission.

When behaviors do not correspond with the teacher's expectations, a variety of adjustments might be attempted to deal with them. For example, the teacher might try to determine the reasons for academic difficulties, teach missing skills, and adjust curricular material and performance expectations. The teacher might verbally reprimand or deny privileges for noncompliance with behavioral expectations. Encouragement and social reinforcement might be provided for better effort and performance. The teacher might talk with the student about the perceived problems; he or she might then contact the parents to see if they are aware of or have explanations for the behavior and then perhaps enlist their support in dealing with it.

Parents, likewise, might notice a child's attitudinal, behavioral, and emotional problems and provide encouragement, incentives, punishments, and assistance to modify the problems. They might contact and consult with teachers and other school personnel. They might consult community resources such as relatives, friends, clergy, or social service and mental health agencies. If classroom and home adjustments such as these appear effective because the child responds satisfactorily to the adjustments, no further action is required.

Prereferral Activities. If adequate progress has not been made from these informal adjustments, assessment moves to Step 2—prereferral activities. A major concern at this stage is to avoid precipitously referring a student for a formal evaluation. Algozzine, Christenson, and Ysseldyke (1982) have shown that a very high percentage (92 percent) of referred students are tested, and 73 percent of these ultimately acquire a disability label and receive special services. In fact, after referral, Algozzine, et al. believe that assessment data frequently are used selectively to confirm or support a referral, rather than to test and shape it. Given the aforementioned negative and stigmatizing effects of the ED and BD labels, efforts should be undertaken to address problem situations at a prereferral stage.

In addition to a concerned teacher and parents, persons who may be involved at the prereferral step are school administrators, counselors, social workers, and school psychologists. At this stage, the regular classroom teacher retains primary responsibility for gathering information, planning and implementing interventions, and evaluating them. However, other support staff may assist the teacher in designing informal assessment procedures and interventions in addition to those routinely used in the classroom. Many schools have established prereferral teams to offer consultation and assistance to regular classroom teachers that may obviate the need for a referral. Sometimes, resource and consulting teachers of behaviorally disordered and other exceptional children participate on these teams, offering suggestions and assistance to classroom teachers.

At the prereferral step, the team studies influences in the student's environment that may encourage or allow the disturbing behavior or situation. They may offer suggestions for monitoring problem behavior, for modifying instructional and behavior management approaches, and they sometimes assist in implementing and monitoring those efforts. Prereferral adjustments include, but are not limited to, modifications of materials, instructional techniques, and aspects of the physical and social setting. The following are examples of possible prereferral activities:

- changing seating arrangements
- moving the student from one academic group to another
- adjusting the level of academic work
- providing success-oriented tasks
- arranging for peer tutoring in areas of academic difficulty
- increasing individual help from teachers
- establishing a system of reinforcement for desired performance

- ignoring the problem behavior
- providing advance organizers for assignments and regular feedback on performance
- enlisting support from the rest of the class to solve the problem behavior
- implementing class meetings for effective education and social skills training that address the problems of concern
- arranging for individual or group counseling with a school counselor, social worker, or psychologist
- meeting with parents to enlist support and follow-through for classroom interventions
- contracting with students and their families for behavioral performance
- preparing daily home-school report cards to ensure regular communication
- helping families locate and obtain counseling and other social services within the community

Prereferral interventions involve modifications that may have beneficial effects on the student's behavior within the regular classroom. They are interventions that can be provided in the context of usual services offered in regular classrooms by teachers, school support staff, and parents. In an analysis of prereferral interventions reported by teachers for students presenting behavioral problems, Sevcik and Ysseldyke (1986) found that behavioral interventions comprised a majority of their efforts. About 36 percent of these involved positive reinforcement, 32 percent were forms of punishment, and the rest were unspecified (e.g., checklists, charting of behavior) or the use of natural consequences.

Referral for Special Education Services—Eligibility. If prereferral activities are not sufficient to produce desired educational benefits to the student, the next step is to refer the student for special education services. Few school districts routinely use formal screening procedures, because behavioral disorders should be sufficiently marked and chronic to be evident in a disrupted pattern of interchange between the individual and the environment. It is usually a classroom teacher, in conjunction with a school administrator and a prereferral team, who initiates a referral. Sometimes, however, referrals come from other sources such as parents, students themselves, psychologists, psychiatrists, physicians, social workers, or other professional service providers who are involved with the student.

School districts should have established referral procedures, including appropriate forms to be completed by referrer(s). The formats differ somewhat from district to district, but they should include similar types of information. These are: (1) questions about the student's academic and social functioning in the regular program; (2) documentation of the nature and extent of the problems; and (3) descriptions of prereferral interventions that have been attempted and evaluations of their effectiveness. Appendix B shows an example of a referral form.

Multidisciplinary Assessment. A formal referral for a comprehensive evaluation requires a written notification of the student's parents or legal guardians and their consent to proceed with an individual educational evaluation. Again, school districts should have formal procedures and forms used for this purpose. Federal regulations and state guidelines attempt to protect children from unwarranted identification. Students from low socioeconomic backgrounds and those who belong to racial and cultural groups who traditionally have experienced discrimination are especially at risk for the SED and BD labels (Wood, 1981). Consequently, requirements for timely evaluation following referral (within 60 days), and, if necessary, placement following identification, are mandated. Eligibility decisions must be based on unbiased, multidisciplinary assessment. Children with limited English proficiency must be evaluated by personnel who can speak their primary language. Further protections are provided through due process rights accorded students and their families to be informed of their rights, provide consent to individual evaluations, participate in decision making, and to challenge educational decisions with which they disagree.

Unfortunately, educational practice does not always appear to correspond with the intent of

---

Box 3.3   Charges of Inadequate Assessment Practices

A *Chicago Tribune* article* reported that the Civil Rights Office of the U.S. Department of Education charged the Chicago Public School System with inadequate practices in evaluating students referred for special education. Among the specific charges were: (1) excessive delays in evaluating and placing children in special education programs, (2) severe shortages of properly trained teachers, psychologists, and other special personnel, especially for children who do not speak English, (3) missing documents such as parental consent forms, psychological evaluations, medical reports, language assessments, and classroom observations, and (4) failure to obtain parental consent before testing children and failure to include them in placement conferences.

According to a random review of district files, 77 percent were incomplete, 73 percent of referred students waited longer than the legal limit of sixty days to have their evaluations completed, and one third of the files showed no evidence of consultation with parents.

In response to the charges, school district representatives cited severe staff shortages as the primary reason for most of the problems. An explanation given for the missing documents was "creative organizing"—each member of evaluation teams kept his or her own records.

*J. L. Griffin, Group says schools neglecting disabled. *Chicago Tribune*, July 27, 1986, pp. 1, 16.

law. Recently, a U.S. Department of Education investigation of referral and identification procedures in a large urban school district raised some controversial issues (see Box 3.3).

If parents agree to have their child evaluated for special education eligibility, an individual evaluation is conducted by a multidisciplinary assessment team. The team is comprised of specialists (e.g., a regular or special education administrator, school psychologist, social worker, nurse, special education consultant, behavior disorders teacher) who are usually coordinated by a designated member of the team. Some school districts also contract for specialized assessment provided by psychiatrists, neurologists, or clinical psychologists who are not regular members of the school staff.

Assessment methods should be selected that utilize several perspectives of professional expertise and that minimize bias. When tests and measures are used that have been standardized on a population other than that of a referred student, the results should be carefully scrutinized. For example, standardized procedures that rely on fluency in standard English and include culturally biased items must be used and interpreted with an understanding of their limitations and inherent bias. In both selection and interpretation of diagnostic measures, the team should question the relevance of techniques for the particular child and situation in question. Always, procedures should be used that study the child in the context of his or her environment by comparing the student with others within the same settings.

All types of assessment are essentially formalized kinds of observation of behavior. To be useful for a diagnosis or an ongoing assessment of behavioral change, they should be valid and reliable measures of the behavior of interest. *Validity* refers to how well an assessment procedure measures what it is intended to measure (Suran & Rizzo, 1983). Thus, validity reflects the relevance and usefulness of the information provided by a specific assessment procedure. *Reliability* refers to the accuracy and consistency

of a measure. Agreement of assessment results over time and among different observers are indications of reliability.

Types of Assessment. The nature of the comprehensive evaluation depends upon the concerns expressed in the referral. The team coordinator usually makes preliminary contact with the referrers and reviews available records on the student to design an appropriate assessment plan. Every eligibility evaluation does not use the same types of data. Among the types of assessment data typically collected are psychological reports (including clinical interviews and interpretations of projective techniques), personality and self-concept data, and results of individual tests of intelligence and academic achievement. These evaluations are usually conducted by school or clinical psychologists who have specialized training in their administration and interpretation. In addition, health histories and family information may be collected by social workers, psychologists, or other personnel. Behavior ratings and interviews may be obtained from teachers, parents, and, in some cases, the referred student and peers, to help identify patterns of perceived problems and the extent they deviate from norms. Special education consultants or resource teachers may also provide data from direct observations of the student in the current placement.

All of these types of data are not always available, nor are they equally useful for identifying a student's educational needs. A 1980 study of availability and usefulness of assessment data (Zabel, Peterson, Smith, & White, 1982) found that some types of data were considered more useful than others by teachers of behaviorally disordered students. They included statements of interventions already attempted, behavior ratings, and behavior observation data. Unfortunately, these were also reported to be among the least available types of information. Apparently, they were not among the kinds of data routinely collected by school psychologists. Conversely, several more available types of

Box 3.4   Availability of Assessment Information

Type of Information	% Available
Intellectual (IQ) assessment	93.8
Standardized achievement assessment	91.3
Vision/hearing/language screening	90.2
Health history	87.3
Clinical judgment, projective tests, etc.	75.0
Behavior ratings from school personnel	72.7
Statement of intervention techniques already attempted	68.3
Formal behavior observation data	66.5
Criterion-referenced academic assessment (informal tests)	59.2
Personality and self-concept data	55.2
Description of regular classroom expectations and requirements	53.7
Behavior ratings from family	34.6
Sociometric data	32.5

information (e.g., IQ scores and reports, standardized achievement test scores, vision, hearing, and language screening) were considered to be among the least useful. A replication of this study five years later (Zabel, Peterson, & Smith, in press) indicates that some progress has been made and now some of the more useful types of data are more typically available. For example, the number of teachers who reported that formal behavior observation data are typically available increased from 45.8 percent to 66.5 percent. Box 3.4 contains a list of teacher-reported availability of thirteen types of assessment data from the recent study.

Making Eligibility Decisions. Based on the above types of data, the assessment team, together with the student's parents or guardians, must determine if the student is benefiting from his or her current placement. If the team consensus is that the student is not, the student is eligible for special education services. If they determine the student is benefiting from the present placement, yet is disrupting the learning and social environment of others, the student may be conditionally eligible for special education services.

In the latter case, Wood suggests that "any services provided to alleviate the distress being experienced by the student or others permit a continuing rate of educational progress equal to or greater than that observed in the present placement" (1985, p. 48). This condition requires that students may not be removed from regular programs solely to reduce distress to others. Certainly, all students have certain rights not to have their educational experiences diminished by the disruptions of others. James Kauffman (1984) has argued that the protections accorded disturbing students are too often given precedence over those of students whose educations are disturbed. The result, Kauffman believes, is undue reluctance to identify and place disruptive students in more restrictive educational environments. The assurance provided by Wood's aforementioned condition is that behaviorally disordered students who are benefiting from their current educational programs may be eligible for alternative placement only when they are highly disruptive to their fellow classmates.

Referral for Special Education Services—Placement. Eligibility and placement steps sometimes become blurred. Although formal identification of a student as behaviorally disordered can lead to an alternative educational placement, the Iowa Assessment Model attempts to separate these decision-making steps. After the assessment team determines the student is eligible for special education, it is faced with determining an alternative placement.

In the traditional Cascade model (Deno, 1970; Reynolds, 1962) placements have been thought of as distinct physical settings defined in terms of their restrictiveness, or distance, from the mainstream. However, placement options are better conceptualized as levels of service intensity (Peterson, Zabel, Smith, & White, 1983; Reynolds & Birch, 1982). Some students require more intense, specialized, continuous services than others. Intensity of services should be determined according to the severity of the student's handicap. Thus, some placements do require movement from one physical setting to another. Others may involve offering more specialized services such as teacher consultation on behavior management, counseling for the student, and other support services that do not require changes in the child's current assignment to a classroom or school.

In placement decisions, the kind of services that will provide educational benefits to the identified student is the primary concern. PL 94–142 and its supporting regulations specify that educational placement must be appropriate to the individual needs of the student. However, neither these requirements nor any court decisions to date have specified how appropriate placements must be. Does appropriate mean optimal or just sufficient to provide some educational benefits? Are schools bound to provide services, such as individual therapy, if they are deemed educationally beneficial? Must a rural school provide a costly self-contained program, if only a single student might benefit from it?

A U.S. Supreme Court decision (*Board of Education v. Rowley*, 1982) involving a student with a hearing impairment required that states provide access to specialized instruction and related services to identified handicapped students. The Rowley decision, however, does not speak directly to SED students and does not appear to require that services be optimal, but that they simply provide a "basic floor of opportunity" (Wood, 1985).

Although legal mandates may not require optimal placements for SED students, the authors believe that educators must design and implement programs that best serve their students. Too often, placement decisions are made on the basis of what is available rather than what is appropriate to an individual student's needs. Although it is understood that resources are always limited, we should not be content with just meeting minimal standards, with following the letter but not the intent of the law.

Involvement of Teachers. It is important in the smooth transition of students from one placement to another that the teachers who are likely to be involved participate in placement decisions. Their direct knowledge of the placement options, including a program's capacity for meeting a student's needs and the child's compatibility with others in the program, contributes to the team's deliberation. If an alternative placement is selected, the teacher will already have an understanding of the student's educational and personal history. Most important, the receiving teacher participates in designing the educational goals, objectives, time lines, and evaluation techniques in the IEP. The placement staffing also provides an opportunity to secure commitments for communication and mutual support involving staff and parents. Detailed consideration of the process and content of IEP development is included in Chapter 10.

We have presented eligibility and placement steps as if they refer to initial identification and placement decisions only. According to federal guidelines, comprehensive reevaluations must be undertaken at least every three years during the time a student receives special education services. In addition, IEPs must be prepared annually by a multidisciplinary team that includes parents. At these times, assessment data must address the student's functioning in the current placement and the documentation of progress toward IEP goals. Data collected in the referral and eligibility steps are frequently used as a baseline against which student change is measured. At periodic reevaluations, the above outlined processes for determining educational benefits of present versus alternative placements and feasibility of moving toward less restrictive placements must be considered. In addition to annual reevaluations, changes in placement may be discussed by the placement team when ongoing assessments indicate a student's readiness for a change. In such cases, the coordinator convenes the placement team to consider relevant data.

Implementation of the Plan. The final step in the Iowa Assessment Model is the actual implementation of the special education plan. During implementation, the student continues to be the joint responsibility of the multidisciplinary team, although specific responsibilities for implementing and evaluating interventions are assigned to individual team members and/or to others who have the expertise to deliver the designated services. Again, the reader is directed to Chapter 10 for more detailed discussion of IEP development.

Exceptions to the Model. Occasionally, a student's behavior threatens or actually results in injury to himself or others. Sometimes a student suddenly expresses severely disordered thoughts and emotions. The Iowa Assessment Model acknowledges the occasional necessity of moving through the decision-making steps faster than is normally desirable. In such cases, shortcuts to eligibility and placement decisions, such as bypassing Steps 1 and 2, may be justified. When this is done, the assessment team must provide written justifications for any variations in the usual procedure.

Reviews of Assessment Techniques. Implicit in each of the steps of the Iowa Assessment Model is developing a database for making decisions.

Specific procedures and instruments are not indicated, because they must be selected according to their usefulness in answering questions raised by a particular case. Several overviews of special education assessment are available that provide detailed information on both procedures and specific texts and measures applicable to all educational exceptionalities (e.g., Evans, Evans, & Mercer, 1986; Salvia & Ysseldyke, 1985; Wallace & Larsen, 1978). These sources include extensive discussions of formal and informal assessment, test construction, validity and reliability issues, and descriptions of commercially available tests and measures. Evans, et al. (1986), for example, review assessment in areas that are beyond the scope of the discussion here, such as language arts, reading, and mathematics.

In addition, the Iowa Assessment Model manual (Wood, Smith, & Grimes, 1985) contains detailed critical reviews of specific assessment procedures useful with behaviorally disordered students. The general categories are: setting analyses, pupil behavioral data (e.g., formal observation, school and home behavior checklists and rating scales), and individual trait data (e.g., projective techniques and self-report measures). The remainder of this chapter is primarily concerned with assessment strategies that teachers and other direct service providers might use to study behavior problems.

Individual Intelligence and Personality Assessment

Intelligence Tests

Some kinds of assessment contribute primarily to eligibility and placement decisions, but do not directly involve teachers. Individual intelligence tests (e.g., Kauffman Assessment Battery for Children; the Stanford-Binet; and especially the Wechsler Intelligence Scale for Children–Revised) are routinely included in comprehensive evaluations to measure global intelligence.

These tests are intended to measure cognitive skills related to academic ability. They have been normed on large populations, so that an individual's performance score can be compared with the distribution of scores for others of the same age. The resulting intelligence quotient (IQ) is a standardized measure of the child's mental age.

The role of standardized intelligence measures in special education eligibility decisions has received considerable attention. One criticism is that they rely too heavily on English language proficiency and include culturally biased items. Another criticism is that they may, in fact, not measure global intelligence, but only certain kinds of intelligence. In addition, a child's performance is compared with national norms that are not necessarily the same as local norms.

Another concern is that intelligence test scores are given undue weight in identification decisions, even though they may have little utility for designing educational interventions (Zabel, Peterson, & Smith, in press; Zabel, Peterson, Smith, & White, 1982). Thus, the value of intelligence tests is limited largely to eligibility decisions. Even there, they should always be considered in the context of multiple other measures of a student's abilities. The use of individual intelligence tests, as well as individual and group tests of academic achievement, are discussed further in Chapter 7.

Projective Techniques

Various projective techniques for studying a child's inner world are also frequently included in personality assessment. The Children's Apperception Test (CAT), the Draw-A-Person (DAP), the House-Tree-Person Test (H-T-P), and the Thematic Apperception Test (TAT) are examples of projective tests that are sometimes used to assess unconscious thoughts and feelings. In the CAT and the TAT, ambiguous pictures are shown to a child, who is then asked what he or she sees in them. The child's re-

sponses are recorded and evaluated in relation to normal and abnormal response patterns that have been found within a larger population. In the DAP the child is asked to draw a person; in the H-T-P, a house, a tree, and a person. The drawings are then analyzed according to a test protocol in which the inclusion and omission of specific features and the ways they are drawn have been related to certain personality traits.

Like individual tests of intelligence, projective techniques must be administered and interpreted by psychologists, psychiatrists, and others with appropriate training. Criticisms of projective techniques include both reliability and validity concerns. Reliability is questioned because of the difficulty of consistently scoring individuals' responses. Objective criteria against which responses can be evaluated are absent, so examiners can disagree on interpretations. The validity of these measures has also been difficult to establish, since specific personality traits are inferred from verbal or written responses that are not necessarily indicative of the individual's actual behavior.

The following sections of this chapter stress assessment procedures that teachers of behaviorally disordered students consider useful for program planning. These techniques are not necessarily limited to just one of the assessment steps outlined earlier. Some strategies useful in the school-home adjustments, prereferral, eligibility, and placement steps may also contribute to the measurement of ongoing student change and evaluation of the efficacy of educational programs. Some that are used in the diagnostic process are also useful as benchmarks, or baselines, against which to measure change.

Environmental Analyses

Ecological assessment must account for elements of the environment that affect and are affected by the individual. The analysis of complex individual-environmental interactions, even in a setting as circumscribed as a classroom or school, are difficult to delimit. Reynolds and Birch (1982) suggest assessing several dimensions of school environments. These include:

- space and facilities
- teaching and learning settings
- social environments
- responsibility for management
- classroom attention and order
- staff collaboration
- evaluation of student progress
- affective (emotional) climate
- recognizing and appreciating cultural differences
- child study processes
- parent and teacher collaboration

Wallace and Larsen (1978) believe that areas of analysis should minimally include pupil-teacher interaction, pupil-curriculum match, peer relationships, school and classroom climate, and extraneous variables outside the school setting. These areas of inquiry may be applied to both regular and special education programs.

Linda Miller, a behavioral disorders consultant in Iowa, has developed an environmental analysis procedure specifically for studying classroom influences on behavior problems (Miller, 1979; Miller, Epp, & McGinnis, 1985) (see Appendix C). Miller's procedure examines three major classroom dimensions:

1. learning setting
2. classroom social environment
3. instructional dimensions

Information is obtained from direct observation of the classroom supplemented by interviews with the teacher(s). Most information is recorded by simply checking appropriate responses or filling in blanks, although spaces are provided where elaboration may be helpful.

Learning Setting

The learning setting includes information about the type of classroom, number of students and adults, activities in progress, use of space (e.g., seating arrangements, spatial areas, locations of facilities and resources), and props (e.g., furnishings, bulletin boards, lighting, windows, ventilation, pupil's supplies, chalkboards, extraneous noise, and schedule).

Classroom Social Environment

This section of the environmental analysis includes information about the makeup of the peer group (sex, socioeconomic status, age, social maturity, ethnic mix, group climate, and other group interaction patterns). It also documents teacher characteristics and teaching styles (e.g., sex, predominant temperament, ways of working with students and expressing feelings, discipline, other interventions, and communication with parents).

Instructional Dimensions

A third section focuses on instructional methods used by teacher(s). Included are questioning techniques, planning, direction giving, discussion, evaluation, correction and marking methods, and availability outside of class. Other instructional dimensions are: lessons (e.g., nature of assignments and homework), rules and procedures of traffic regulation, and media resources (e.g., what kind and when available for use).

Of course, some types of environmental information (number of boys and girls) can be readily observed, while others (temperament of the classroom as reflected by the teacher) require considerable interpretation and inference. Certainly, not all the information that may be gathered using this form is relevant to every student in every classroom. Assessment teams and observers must judge the relative utility of the types of information they wish to obtain and design environmental analyses with a content and a format they find most helpful. Data acquired in environmental analyses should contribute to an understanding of ecological influences on individual students. These influences can be valuable data sources in making prereferral and identification decisions. They may suggest classroom adjustments that better accommodate the student or help the assessment team select and design alternative environments that provide a better individual-environment fit.

In addition to environmental analyses, several techniques can be used to provide a broad picture of the child within his or her relevant ecosystems. Among these are parent interviews, teacher and parent behavior ratings, sociometric techniques, and direct observation. These strategies are discussed in the following sections.

Parent Interviews

Parents are a valuable source of several types of information regarding their children. In assessing both the type and degree of problems, for instance, it is important to determine similarities and differences in home and school perceptions. Educators' understanding of behavior problems and the design and implementation of interventions are aided by an understanding of parents' views of their child. Parents can provide information about their child's behavior in settings other than school, about interventions that have previously been attempted at home, about family involvement in other support systems within the community, about relationships within the family and other social groupings, and about the developmental status of the child and family. These types of information may be obtained in structured parent interviews (Sodac, Nichols, & Gallagher, 1985).

Parents' perceptions of their child can be gathered in a format that is appropriate to the child and family. A parent interview may take the form of a written questionnaire, oral inter-

view, or combination of the two. Obviously, the parents' written and verbal skills and their willingness and ability to provide these types of information must be considered. Parent interviews not only contribute to the educational assessment process, but may potentially help a family understand the child and relationships between home and school behavior (Sodac, et al., 1985). In addition, the parent interview can lay a foundation for ongoing family involvement with school. Further suggestions for involving parents in the assessment process are found in Chapter 12.

Monitoring Behavior Change

There are several instruments, techniques, and strategies that may be used to monitor a student's change over time. When planning ongoing assessment, it is helpful to think in terms of three general types of measures: (1) pre-post, (2) product, and (3) process measures (Fitzgerald, 1982). Each contributes a different type of information.

Of course, some procedures for monitoring behavior fit into more than one of these general categories. For example, social skill inventories may be used as pre-post measures of global progress over time in a student's social skills, to determine specific skills the student currently performs, and/or to monitor a student's behavior in the context of a social skills training program. Special educators will probably need all three types of data to design, implement, and evaluate their interventions. The procedures they select will vary according to the kinds of data seen as most relevant to the students and settings involved, the constraints of programs (e.g., resources, personnel, available time), and the knowledge and skills of those involved in assessment. Examples of useful pre-post, product, and process measures are provided in the following sections.

Guidelines for Monitoring Behavior

It is unnecessary, as well as impossible, to measure all of a student's behavior. Instead, the goal is to sample behavior in ways that provide the most meaningful and useful information for eligibility, placement, and intervention decisions. Three guidelines for the procedures in monitoring behavioral change should be followed. These are known as the Three Rs, as they should be representative, reliable, and relevant.

First, monitoring procedures should produce representative data. The behavior studied and the conditions of measuring it should limit bias, or unverified perceptions. The times and situations for measuring behavior should be typical. Especially to be avoided is monitoring behavior when it is displayed at unusually high or low rates of intensity. Measurement should not be limited to opportunities that are convenient to the observer, if the behavior and setting variables are not typical.

Procedures should also be as reliable as possible. *Reliability* refers to the accuracy, or consistency, of measurement (Evans, Evans, & Mercer, 1986). The behavior should be measured so that others using the procedure should tend to obtain similar data. For example, formal observation techniques should utilize consistent formats and criteria so that one observer's data can be verified by that of other observers.

Perhaps most important, monitoring should focus on relevant behavior. There is no purpose served in monitoring behavior that is irrelevant to a student's functioning and is not related to interventions. Ongoing assessment should focus on those aspects of a student's functioning that are socially validated and that are relevant to his or her desired functioning.

Pre-Post Measures

Assessment procedures used to measure general traits or global characteristics at given points in time are pre-post measures. They are used to determine long-term changes from preinter-vention to postintervention. Frequently used pre-post measures of behavior problems are sociometric techniques, self-concept scales, and behavior ratings. These provide perspectives from a student's peers, from students themselves, and from teachers.

Sociometric Devices. Sociometric devices are intended to measure an individual's likability and social status in the eyes of peers or classmates. Some of these techniques are reliable measures of a student's social adjustment as well as good predictors of later social and emotional health (Cowen, Pederson, Barbigian, Izzo, & Trost, 1973).

One type of sociometric technique consists of peer nominations of classmates for particular roles. This may be a Guess Who? survey, in which students are asked to name classmates who fit descriptors such as the "most helpful," "smartest," or "meanest." Eli Bower (1981) uses nomination in his Class Play approach, designed to be used in screening for emotional and behavioral problems. It asks students to select peers for positive and negative roles (e.g., someone who could play the part of true friend) in a play situation. Each student then receives a score reflecting the total number of negative selections by classmates divided by the total number of nominations. High percentages suggest a high level of negative perceptions by peers.

The *Behavior Rating Profile: An Ecological Approach to Behavioral Assessment* (Brown & Hammill, 1978), which is discussed in the section on behavior rating scales, also uses a nomination format, with pairs of questions related to friendships, academic ability, and leadership skills. Students nominate their classmates in response to questions such as, "Which of the boys and girls in your class would you most (or least) like to help you with a problem in your school work?"

Roster peer rating scales are another sociometric device. A list of all classmates is rated on specific questions such as, "How much do you like to play with this person?" (Oden & Asher, 1977) along a negative to positive

Box 3.5   Sociometric Matrix

	Ann	Brett	Dino	Ellie	Luis	Michael	Willie
Ann			2		1		3
Brett	2		1				3
Dino	3				2	1	
Ellie	3		1		2		
Luis	1					3	2
Michael			3		1		2
Willie	2		3		1		
	11	0	10	0	7	4	10

3 = 1st choice
2 = 2nd choice
1 = 3rd choice

continuum (e.g., "not at all" to "a lot"). The Ohio Social Acceptance Scale (1979) is an example of a roster rating scale appropriate for use with junior high age students.

A sociometric matrix depicting relationships within a group may also be drawn. (See Box 3.5.) The matrix lists all group members along horizontal and vertical axes. The nominations of each student are included. Students were asked to list, in order, the three classmates with whom they would most like to work. A first choice receives a score of three, second choice, two, and third choice, one. Ann, with a total score of 11 including three first choices, and Willie and Dino, each with 10, appear to be the top peer selections. Brett and Ellie, on the other hand, were named by none of their classmates.

There are several limitations with sociometric techniques: they have unestablished reliability particularly with older students; they tell us little specifically about how a student interacts with peers; and they do not indicate the social antecedents and consequences of specific behavior. Because an entire group or class is involved in the procedures, their intrusiveness has also been a concern (O'Leary & Johnson, 1979). These techniques may also suggest or reinforce student perceptions of classmates by associating negative or positive labels or descriptions with certain peers. In addition, formats can influence results. For example, students may be asked to nominate three peers for a particular role for which fewer, or more, than three may qualify.

Sociometric techniques are useful primarily at prereferral and identification stages of assessment and can contribute information about how individuals are perceived by their classmates. There are other, less formal, ways to study peer relationships besides the techniques discussed above. Teachers may, for example, give writing assignments in which students are to use the names of classmates. The number and nature (positive or negative) of references to specific students can provide some information about social acceptance. Informal teacher observations of who plays or works with whom, who is frequently or rarely selected to participate in group activities, and who is the subject of positive and negative comments from peers can also be useful sociometric data.

Self-Concept Measures. Students' views of themselves provide yet another dimension to ecological assessment. Measures of self-concept or self-esteem have been used to reflect personal attitudes of approval or disapproval, beliefs regarding personal capabilities, significance, and worthiness (Coopersmith, 1981). Several instruments, including the Coopersmith Self-Esteem Inventory (Coopersmith, 1981), the Tennessee Self-Concept Scales (Fitts, 1965), and the Piers-Harris Children's Self-Concept Scale (Piers & Harris, 1969) have been developed for use with children.

These instruments contain descriptive statements (e.g., "I'm easy to like") or lists of adjectives (e.g., friendly, brave) that the child rates according to terms such as "like me," "somewhat like me," "not like me," or rates along a continuum such as "completely false" to "completely true." The Coopersmith Self-Esteem Inventory includes statements that reflect attitudes and feelings about home, school, and community. Roger Kroth (1975) has developed a technique called Target Behavior containing twenty-five cards describing home or school behavior ("gets work done on time," "disturbs neighbors by making noise"). The child arranges the cards in twenty-five spaces on a pyramidal chart along a nine-point continuum from "most like me" to "most unlike me."

Sentence completion formats are provided in some affective education programs (see discussion in Ch. 9), and they can also be independently prepared by teachers. They may include items such as "My favorite person is . . .'"; "Sometimes I feel . . ."; and "My teachers think I . . . ."

Measurement of self-concept is fraught with methodological difficulties. There is always the question of how perceptive a child may be about his or her own characteristics, traits, and feelings and about the child's ability to report those perceptions honestly. There can also be questions about a child's understanding of affective and behavioral descriptions, particularly when reading is involved. Still, when used in combination with other kinds of assessment and observations of a student's behavior and self-statements that reflect self-concept, they can provide another perspective.

Behavior Ratings. Behavior checklists and rating scales are a commonly used pre-post type of measure. Teachers, and sometimes parents and others who are directly involved with a student, rate an individual's behavior according to several descriptors. Behavior ratings are especially helpful in determining the perceptions of several different persons. When a rating scale has been standardized, individuals' scores can be compared with a distribution of scores to determine how they deviate from norms. Behavior checklists and rating scales are appropriately used in the screening and identification steps of the assessment process (Kerr & Nelson, 1983). They can also help determine changes in global characteristics over relatively long periods of time.

Behavior rating scales contain a large number of items describing problem behaviors. Typically, raters indicate the presence or absence of each descriptor for an individual, or rate the individual along a continuum (e.g., "always" to "never"). Usually, both total and factor scores can be tabulated based on the ratings. These factors, sometimes called scales, dimensions, or domains, are composites of items that have been found to cluster, or intercorrelate, using a statistical procedure called factor analysis.

There are perhaps 200 currently available behavior rating scales. Reviews of some more commonly used instruments are found in Sodac, Nichols, and Gallagher (1985), Spivack and Swift (1973), and Walls (1977), as well as Buros' Mental Measurements Yearbooks (1985). These reviews describe and evaluate the purpose, construction, and standardization of many instruments. Our discussion is limited to several instruments that are relatively well constructed, validated, and normed, and that are frequently used in educational assessment. Addresses of their publishers are listed in Appendix D.

The Behavior Evaluation Scale (BES), for example, is a fifty-two-item instrument for use with students in grades K through 12. Raters respond to each item (e.g., "demonstrates sudden or dramatic mood changes") in terms of its frequency of occurrence along a seven-point continuum (e.g., "never or not observed" to "continuously throughout the day"). A unique feature of the BES is that the items comprise five subscales representing the federal definition's characteristics of serious emotional disturbance.

One of the most widely used rating scales reported in the research literature is the Behavior Problem Checklist (BPC) developed by Herbert Quay and Donald Peterson. A revised scale appropriate for use with students in grades K to 8 consists of eighty-nine items, comprising five major and two minor factors. Raters indicate if each item constitutes a severe mild, or no problem for the child and tabulate total and factor scores.

The Burks Behavior Rating Scale is a 116-item instrument designed to identify immature, hostile or aggressive, and neurotic behavior patterns in children in grades 1 to 9. Responses are provided in terms of the degree to which each item describes the child in question.

Linda Brown and Donald Hammill (1978) have developed the Behavior Rating Profile. It is designed to measure behavior of children in grades 1 to 7 according to the multiple perspectives of parents, teachers, and peers. Teacher and parent rating scales consist of thirty descriptive words and phrases responded to along a continuum from "very much like" to "not at all like." A profile form shows the individual's degree of deviation on several subscales.

The Child Behavior Checklist developed by Thomas Achenbach (Achenbach, 1978; Achenbach & Edelbrock, 1979) is a 112-item scale designed for use with children between the ages of four and sixteen. Both parent and teacher rating forms are available, with responses provided according to whether items are "very true," "somewhat true," or "not true" descriptions of the child. Scores are plotted on a profile according to subscales.

In conjunction with the Devereux Foundation, Spivack and Swift (1966, 1977) have developed three rating scales to measure maladaptive behavior that may interfere with educational performance. These are the Devereux Child Behavior Rating Scale for ratings by parents of children ages eight to twelve, the Devereux Elementary School Behavior Rating Scale (DESB) for teacher ratings of children in grades 1 to 6, and the Devereux Adolescent Behavior Rating Scale for parent ratings of children ages 13 to 18. Raters indicate their agreement with descriptors along a continuum. Scores are directly plotted on profile forms to indicate degree of individual deviation from established norms on several subscales. The DESB, for example, has eleven factors, including "classroom disturbance," "inattentive-withdrawn," and "achievement anxiety."

Spivack and Swift (1973) have also developed the Hahneman Elementary School Behavior and the Hahneman High School Behavior rating scales. These fifty-four-item scales are intended to help identify and measure problem behavior in both regular and special education programs. Each of the fourteen behavior dimensions is defined by three or four items that are rated along a continuum for severity.

The Walker Problem Behavior Identification Checklist is designed for use primarily with students in grades 4 to 6. Raters circle the presence or absence of fifty classroom behavior problems comprising five factors. Factor scores are plotted on a profile analysis form.

Behavior rating scales are used to determine an individual's global behavioral traits. There are, however, some limitations in the information such pre-post measures can provide. Scores on subscales or factors are composites of ratings on several items. They are nonspecific and some detail that may be important to both identification and programming decisions is not available. Also, on standardized rating scales an individual's scores are compared with norms. These may be based on national and regional samples, according to age and sex, but they are not necessarily relevant locally. Consider, for example, how teachers' ratings might differ for a student in Manhattan, New York, and in Manhattan, Kansas, or from one school to another in each of these communities, or even from one classroom to another in a single school. When we rate a student's behavior, we are evaluating the student against some standard. It may be the ideal, the average, or the typical student. Even when we rate an individual in relation to others in the same group, we must recognize that the standards change according to the makeup of the reference group.

Standardized, norm-referenced measures like behavior rating scales provide quantified, qualitative information. They allow us to put numbers on the judgments of those doing the ratings. While they can be another important kind of measure of student characteristics, they must be used with some caution regarding their validity in the individual case. They also must be considered in the context of other types of assessment data.

Product Measures

In the course of an educational program, measures of student performance that constitute products become available. Samples of written work, time tests in math, and spelling tests collected over time are kinds of academic products. Analysis of these products can reveal what students can do as well as diagnose their difficulties. Archival records that are routinely collected are another kind of product measure. Records of school attendance, tardiness, visits to the nurse's and principal's offices, report cards, use of time out, and parent contacts are kinds of data that can document aspects of a student's functioning.

It sometimes seems easier to document academic than social and emotional products, because standard academic curricula are available. We have a fairly clear idea of what skills a first-grade, a fifth-grade, or a tenth-grade academic curriculum should include and how those skills can be measured. Criterion-referenced measures in the social and emotional domain can also be developed. However, designing comprehensive procedures to assess students' social and emotional products can be a major endeavor for an individual teacher, a special education consultant, or even a districtwide curriculum team. Such a task can involve designing a comprehensive curriculum with appropriate scope and sequence. Fortunately, some existing programs provide foundations for assessing behavioral and affective products, although they may require adaptations in other settings and situations.

Two of these curricula, Skillstreaming and Developmental Therapy, are discussed in Chapters 9 and 10, respectively. The Skillstreaming programs have been designed for adolescents (Goldstein, Sprafkin, Gershaw, & Klein, 1980) and elementary age students (McGinnis & Goldstein, 1984). Before he or she can learn social skills, the student's current ability to perform specific behaviors in several categories is assessed according to criterion-referenced measures. For example, in a group of skills for dealing with feelings, the teacher rates a student's skills such as apologizing, knowing one's own feelings, and expressing affection.

The Developmental Therapy program (Wood, 1975, 1986) includes the assessment of skills in four areas—behavior, communication, social, and (pre-) academic. In each area, specific skills are sequentially arranged in five developmental stages. Each skill is measured according to specified performance criteria. Simpler, more basic skills precede more complex, advanced skills. In the area of behavior, for example, "react by attending" is the first objective of Stage 1, while "complete individual tasks in group" is a Stage 3 objective, and "participate in group self-governance" is a Stage 5 objective. Periodic assessments of a child's performance of skills in the four areas are entered on a form that provides an overall developmental profile. This developmental assessment has also been extended for use with adolescents (Braaten, 1982a, 1982b).

Process Measures

Process measures help us understand behavioral change in relation to environmental conditions such as intervention efforts. They are used to measure short-term student progress, to determine if behavioral change is related to interventions, and to provide information about how intervention efforts should be modified. Observation of behavior is our most useful process assessment tool. Teachers of students with behavioral disorders need to have skills in a variety of direct observation techniques to supplement the kinds of behavior monitoring data collected by pre-post and product measures. They must also be able to use observation efficiently. Additional discussion of the uses and design of observation techniques is found in Chapter 8 and in sources such as Cartwright and Cartwright (1984) and Weinberg and Wood (1975).

The former baseball player Yogi Berra has been credited with saying, "You can observe a lot just by watching." When the watching is done by a trained eye and is carefully planned and conducted, there is validity to his statement. We usually distinguish between watching and observing in terms of the informality of the former, and the more structured, formal nature of the latter. There are several forms of formal observation that are useful for monitoring behavior. They include diaries, event recording, specimen records, token system data, frequency counts, and time-sampling procedures.

Diaries. One type of observation is the anecdotal record or diary. A teacher using this procedure regularly, perhaps daily, records events or experiences involving individuals or groups of students. Diaries can provide ongoing records of changes in individual and group behavior as seen by the teacher. Their limitation is that they are highly selective and qualitative in their attention to events that occur. They tend to focus on significant behavior and are general descriptions that can be difficult to distill. They can, however, be useful references to behavioral change over time, if only the specific types of behavior needed for observation are consistently documented on a day-to-day basis.

Event Records. Frequently, certain patterns of student behavior are of particular interest to teachers and other intervenors. Tantrums, fights, and crying are examples of behaviors that may not occur regularly, but may be the focus of intervention efforts. Written descriptions of such events as they occur can be a useful way of examining the environmental conditons that precede (antecedents) and follow (consequences) the incidents. Sugai (1985) has suggested that teachers maintain a critical incidents log for recording such events. They may reveal that a student's tantrums, for example, are preceded by independent seat work. Or they may indicate that the student receives considerable attention from others and does not complete assignments following his crying. Event records can lead to modifications of antecedent and consequent conditions in order to affect the behavior patterns. They also provide another type of record of ongoing change of behavior.

Specimen Records. The specimen record procedure aims to provide a comprehensive, objective record of all an individual's behavior within a unit of time. In this behavior monitoring technique, the observer does not observe only specific behaviors, but records all verbal and nonverbal behavior and social interactions involving the target student as they occur. The observer attempts to exclude interpretations, evaluations, or judgments about the behavior. Observations are conducted for predetermined blocks of time, each lasting perhaps fifteen or twenty minutes. Times and situations are selected because they are expected to be representative samples of the student's behavior. The written narrative records are then used to analyze and interpret the individual's behavior in the environmental context. By separating the objective record from the interpretation, the procedure helps intervenors avoid preconceived notions about how and why students behave as they do.

Specimen records can be very useful for revealing environmental factors that affect student behavior. They can contribute to several assessment steps and serve to document behavioral changes over time. They help to identify problem behaviors, understand how environmental variables may affect an individual's behavior, and determine how environmental factors might be modified to influence an individual's behavior.

Token System Data.   Observation of specific behaviors is built into a behavior management strategy called the token economy. (See Ch. 8 for a detailed discussion.) A token economy defines specific behaviors that are equivalent to tokens, or points, which can be earned for displaying the behaviors and later traded for rewards in the form of objects or activities. Points are awarded to students for those behaviors as they occur or within specific time periods (e.g., every ten minutes, every hour). They are typically recorded on point cards or token sheets from which individual or group behavioral data can be tabulated and recorded. The data from accumulated point cards may be graphed to show changes over time.

The token sheet shown in Box 8.5 (p. 213) is an example of a record form that could be used to monitor academic and social behavior of students integrated into departmentalized, regular classroom programs. Using this format, each teacher rates a student's academic and social behavior according to established criteria at the end of each class period. Daily and weekly point totals are compiled, and the ratings are summarized on graphs. The advantage of a process measure such as this is that it serves multiple functions. It provides a behavior management

system, it serves as a daily report card, and it is an ongoing record of student performance.

Systematic Direct Observation.   Several forms of systematic direct observation are helpful for monitoring behavioral change. Procedures can be designed that are reliable, relevant, and representative assessment devices. Some forms of direct observation that involve complex procedures, considerable training, and time are beyond what teachers with other classroom responsibilities and little assistance can reasonably handle. However, many direct observation techniques are amenable to teachers for convenient use or to specially trained special education personnel. They can be extremely useful for directly monitoring behavior in relation to interventions. Again, the reader is directed to additional discussion of observation in behavioral interventions in Chapter 8.

Frequency counts require that the teacher, or other observer, simply count the number of times a carefully defined behavior occurs in a unit of time. Frequency counts are appropriate for monitoring behavior that has a definite beginning and ending (e.g., raises hand, asks question, gets out of seat). A single behavior or several behaviors of a single student or a group may be recorded on a grid or graph paper. Box 3.6 is an example of a frequency count of the talking-out behavior of five students observed during one reading class. Because observation periods are not always of equal length, frequency records can be converted to rates. In our example, Leah talked out six times during a thirty-minute period. Thus, her talk-out rate was .2 per minute ($\frac{6}{30} = .2$).

Time sampling is a type of direct observation that incorporates features of frequency counts with additional capabilities. It involves observing a set of behaviors for a specified period of time that has been broken down into regular intervals. The intervals are relatively short, usually a few seconds in length. The shorter the interval, the more accurate the data, since some behaviors may occur more than once during

---

Box 3.6   Frequency Count

Behavior: talking out   Date: 3/18/88
Task: reading class   Time: 9:40–10:10

Matt	Joe	Leah	Robert	Nancy	Mark
|||		⊕⊕⊕⊕⊕		|||		

---

longer intervals. A six-second interval is frequently employed because it is long enough to observe and record a behavior, yet short enough to limit the number of times a behavior may occur. It also divides a minute of observation into ten intervals, making determination of behavior rates easy to compute.

Noise, as an example of a single behavior, was observed using simple time-sampling procedure (see Box 3.7). Sixty-second observations are broken into ten six-second intervals. Each time the student, Craig, made noise, the observer entered a checkmark in the appropriate space. The resulting record not only tells us the number of times (four) that Craig made noise, but the percentage of time (40%) he was noisy. A number of such samples could provide a good picture of the student's noise-making behavior.

Time-sampling procedures may be used to observe a single student, a student and one or more peers for comparison, or several individuals in a group. When more than one student is involved, observations may alternate between the target and selected peers during each interval of time. To simplify the procedure, the observer may observe the target for the entire unit of time (e.g., one minute), then observe a peer for that same amount of time, return to the target, and then repeat this alternating sequence using different peers. If several behaviors are observed, a simple code may be used (e.g., x = talks out; y = leaves seat).

In their book on data-based program modification, Deno and Mirkin (1977) include a time-sampling procedure for recording four types of behavior commonly considered problems in

---

Box 3.7   Time-Sampling Observation

Student observed: Craig   Date: February 3, 1988

Behavior: noise (humming, drumming on desk, tearing paper)

Time: independent seat work, 4th period
      1-minute observation (6-second intervals)

			✔	✔	✔	✔				4
										Total

classrooms. These are noise (e.g., talking out, pencil tapping), out-of-place behavior (e.g., unapproved absence from assigned place), physical contact (e.g., hitting, tearing, kicking, talking), and off-task behavior (e.g., staring into space, doodling). Observation periods are broken down into several-second intervals. To obtain a representative sample of an individual's behavior, Deno and Mirkin suggest initially observing a target student for ten to thirty minutes a day for five to seven days and as often as possible thereafter. Preselected peers engaged in the same setting and activity are alternately observed in the manner described above. Observational data are compiled to determine the percentage of time the behaviors are displayed both by the target student and his or her peers. From those data, a discrepancy ratio can be calculated to compare the target student with his or her peers. For example, the target may be observed on-task 20 percent of the time, while peers are on-task 80 percent of the time. Thus, the target student is on-task only one quarter the time his or her peers are.

Such information can contribute to decisions about the need for intervention. Forness (1979) has proposed that when the total percentage of a student's positive behavior falls below 70 percent, the child is at risk for serious behavior problems, and that intervention is warranted when it falls below 50 percent. Another rule of thumb for determining the necessity of intervention involves comparison of the individual's rate of relevant behaviors with those of peers in comparable situations. If a student's positive, or desired, behavior is consistently less than half that of peers, or if negative, or undesired, behavior is consistently more than twice that of peers, it may be sufficiently discrepant to warrant intervention. Although these are only guidelines that must be considered along with other assessment information, they do provide criteria that can aid decision making.

Time-sampling data may also be used to evaluate the effectiveness of interventions as measured by changes in behavior. For instance, the on-task behavior of the target student might be observed to increase from 20 percent to 50 percent during the course of some behavior change intervention. This information indicates that the intervention is having its desired effects.

Frank Wood has designed a time-sampling procedure called the Pupil Observation Schedule (POS) to measure a variety of both positive and negative student behavior. Positive behaviors are defined as:

- on-task
- at desk
- self-initiated verbalizations
- responding verbalizations
- gestures or expressions
- physical contact

Negative behaviors, on the other hand, are:

- off-task
- away from desk
- object-generated noise
- vocally generated noise
- self-initiated verbalizations
- responding verbalizations
- gestures or expressions
- physical contact

There is also a "refuses interaction" possibility. Specific operational definitions and examples of each kind of behavior are provided with the POS. Negative gesture or expression, for example, means subject waves fist, or makes a threatening or disapproving expression directed at another. Gesture or expression must be sustained for at least four seconds to be recorded.

The POS behaviors are observed during twenty 30-second intervals. Instances of the first three behaviors (on- and off-task, at and away from desk, and object- and vocally generated noise) are recorded during the first ten seconds of each interval. The other behaviors are recorded as they occur during the next twenty

Box 3.8   Pupil Observation Schedule (Form B)

Observer _____ Date _____

Description of Student Observed:

Description of Other Persons in Setting:

Description of Setting and Activity:

(During this 10-minute period.)

	1	2	3	4	5	6	7	8	9	10
On-Task	:	:	:	:	:	:	:	:	:	:
At Place	:	:	:	:	:	:	:	:	:	:
Positive Verbal Interaction	:	:	:	:	:	:	:	:	:	:
Teacher Interaction	:	:	:	:	:	:	:	:	:	:
Noise	:	:	:	:	:	:	:	:	:	:
Negative Verbal Interaction	:	:	:	:	:	:	:	:	:	:
Negative Physical Contact	:	:	:	:	:	:	:	:	:	:
_____	:	:	:	:	:	:	:	:	:	:

Reprinted with permission of F. H. Wood, Department of Educational Psychology, University of Minnesota, Minneapolis, MN.

seconds of each interval. Each occurrence is indicated by a slash entered in the appropriate box. (See Box 3.8.)

Observation procedures need not be particularly complicated and intrusive. Even with a procedure like the POS that includes several behavior categories, rarely are they all observed during a single observation session. Still, systematic observation sometimes requires assistance from someone other than a teacher who is actively working with students. Resource and consulting teachers and trained teachers' aides are potential observers.

Sometimes, however, teachers are able to conduct observations from the vantage point of their desk or while circulating a classroom. Use of systematic observation techniques does require planning, training, practice, and preparation. However, it also can result in savings of time and effort, when the observations provide data about how behavior is related to intervention efforts.

Summary

Sound assessment procedures are fundamental to understanding and intervening to change behavioral disorders. We need assessment techniques to study individual children, to examine the influences within the child's life space that affect his or her behavior, and to better understand interactions between the children and their environments. Consequently, we have emphasized an ecological assessment perspective. We have examined assessment in terms of how it can help us make decisions about the nature and degree of child deviance, about classroom adjustments to accommodate troubling students, about eligibility for special programs, about appropriate interventions, and about the effects of those interventions.

Assessment issues are so integral to our understanding of behaviorally disordered children and adolescents and to designing and evaluating interventions, that they are discussed throughout the remainder of this book. In the next four chapters, our attention turns to major patterns of disordered behavior—personality problems (Ch. 4), conduct disorders (Ch. 5), pervasive developmental disorders (Ch. 6), and interactions of behavior disorders and learning disabilities (Ch. 7). Assessment involving each of these requires strategies discussed in this chapter as well as others that are unique to those types of disorders. In our chapters on behavioral interventions (Ch. 8), psychoeducational interventions (Ch. 9), and individual educational planning and service delivery (Ch. 10), we frequently refer to the content of this chapter as we consider the design and implementation of programs for behaviorally disordered students.

PART II

Specific Behavioral Disorders in Children and Adolescents

The four chapters comprising Part II offer an introduction to the problems of behaviorally disordered children and adolescents. In these chapters, the clinical, research, and assessment foundations of Part I become focused on the different manifestations of behavioral disorders in the forms of personality problems, conduct disorders, pervasive developmental disorders, and specific learning disorders.

These chapters present detailed examinations of the characteristics and causes of childhood and adolescent problems. In providing a detailed study of specific childhood and adolescent problems, they form a bridge to other disciplines through the study of language and concepts of psychology and psychiatry. Each chapter is structured somewhat differently because of the differences in the very nature of the problems discussed, but all share in common an integration of earlier basic themes into the study of specific problems. Thus, for example, each chapter examines specific signs and symptoms to understand how these manifestations relate to causal factors in the child's ecosystem. Often this necessitates reference to earlier discussions of developmental theories or research on family interaction. In this way, the more abstract discussions of earlier chapters become meaningful as applied to the study of specific problems.

Finally, each of the chapters in Part II offers a broadly sketched preview of approaches to intervention that are discussed in detail in Parts III and IV.

PART II

Specific Behavioral Disorders in Children and Adolescents

CHAPTER 4

Children and Adolescents with Personality Problems

Overview

Introduction

Because they usually suffer in silence, children with personality problems often go unnoticed. They do not present teachers and school administrators with defiance, disruptiveness, or behavior that is dangerous or destructive. Often they are quiet and unassuming, trying to avoid attention or trouble. Occasionally, they will be mildly tyrannical in the safety and security of their own homes, becoming easily upset if things do not go their way, worrying excessively about a difficult school assignment, fearful of other children, or concerned about improbable dangers.

If their problems are noticed, it is often because their school performance does not measure up to their intellectual potential. Wrapped up in worry, self-consciousness, insecurity, physical illnesses, or depression, the child with serious personality problems may have little energy left to devote to studies or common childhood activities. Although parents may notice that something is wrong, they are prone to view any problem as a stage that the child will outgrow. At the same time, teachers may be distanced by the child's inability to be friendly and outgoing, and find it easy to ignore a youngster who does not present either easily noticed talent or problems in classroom management.

In some instances, children with personality problems may display internal conflicts, fears, and depression in ways that are more turbulent and disruptive. Periods of withdrawal may alternate with angry outbursts, tantrums, crying, or running away. Occasionally, depression is displayed in angry self-recrimination or unreasonable attempts to blame others—especially parents and teachers—for everything that is wrong in the child's life. Sometimes these children may talk about and even attempt suicide.

Anxiety as a General Characteristic

Anxiety is the single most pervasive characteristic of internalizing or personality problems in children. Ranging in intensity from uneasy apprehension about the future through a sense of unnamed dread of what may happen to episodes of acute, paralyzing panic, anxiety seems to permeate all aspects of life. Children with personality problems spend large parts of their waking hours worrying about whether they can cope with schoolwork, whether other children will like them, whether teachers will think they are stupid, or whether their parents may die unexpectedly. And for many, there is no respite; even sleep is often characterized by nightmares, restlessness, fear of the dark, and a host of nameless terrors.

All of this is not to say that children with personality problems have lives of unmitigated misery. All children play, laugh, lose themselves in toys and games, and feel love for important people in their lives. However, children with personality problems experience more frequent and more intense periods of fearful concern about the future and about their own ability to handle life tasks.

Additional Characteristics

In addition to experiencing chronic, pervasive anxiety, children and adolescents with personality problems share a variety of attitudinal and behavioral characteristics. Although it is important to remember that every child is uniquely individual, it is also true that characteristic attitudes, styles, and behaviors constitute recognizable patterns within the context of individual differences.

Timidity. For example, youngsters with personality problems tend consistently to be timid in their approach to other people and to life tasks. Apparently apprehensive about possible negative reactions from others, they are shy, diffident, unassuming, and unassertive. Rather than asking for what they need or want, they may sit in frozen silence hoping that someone will be intuitively sensitive to their needs. At the same time, they are usually pessimistic about the likelihood that this will occur. In the event that someone does notice their needs, however, they may also be disappointed because what they get is not quite what they had hoped for. Alternatively, some youngsters experience such pervasive, and usually unfounded, guilt that having wants or needs met simply adds to a sense of worthlessness.

Even those children perceived by others as spoiled, selfish, or overprotected often manifest a sense of conflict as they alternate among being demanding, disappointed, and guilty. Again, getting what they want only adds to a sense of helplessness or inability to cope as they perceive others as responsible for taking care of them.

Hypersensitivity. Children with personality problems are often unusually sensitive to the subtle nuances of normal interactions with people. They may feel easily slighted or offended, and they often withdraw from tentative attempts to approach others at the slightest hint of distance or possible rejection. Rather than experience emotional hurt, they pull back prematurely from even the possibility of being hurt, and thus fail to learn the extent of their own abilities to cope or to find acceptance in relationships.

Self-Consciousness. Sensitivity to others' reactions also creates a disproportionate sense of self-consciousness and easy embarrassment. Rather than risk the possibility of looking foolish or being teased or ridiculed, such children avoid trying new tasks, going new places without the protection of parents, or meeting new people. Better to sit in class unnoticed than have a teacher say that an answer is wrong or have a classmate giggle at a statement. Children with personality problems are sometimes perceived as extremely shy. Often they will be unable to respond even to a simple greeting, and an invitation to actual spontaneous interaction may be unthinkable.

Pessimism. As noted above, children with personality problems are generally not hopeful that their needs will be met or that others will respond positively to them. On the contrary, they tend to expect the worst from others and from life in general. These youngsters operate with the expectation that whatever can go wrong will go wrong, and they are unable to enjoy many positive events because they continue to expect something to spoil their enjoyment. In many cases, their own behavior leads to a series of self-fulfilling prophecies in which pessimism causes them to avoid an active pursuit and therefore achievement of their goals. This, in turn, reinforces a sense that nothing in life ever works out well. For the child with personality problems disappointment, self-blame, and hopelessness are constant life companions.

Characteristics versus Symptoms

Thus far, we have been discussing several general traits that are characteristic of children with personality problems. It is important, however, to emphasize that characteristics are *not* symptoms. Though timidity, hypersensitivity, self-consciousness, and pessimism are typical in children with personality problems, they are also characteristics of people without definable problems. However, when these characteristics begin to interfere with normal habits, the ability to feel comfortable, to develop mutually satisfying relationships, to perform in school at a level commensurate with ability, and to feel able to cope with the future, then they have evolved into problems that require intervention by responsible adults in the child's life.

Causes of Personality Problems

The causes of personality problems in children and adolescents include a multitude of complex factors ranging from hereditary and constitutional characteristics to the child's experiences within the family to influences from the school, neighborhood, and community. From an ecological perspective, many factors exert mutual influences in an ongoing fluid system in which the individual child is the focus of these convergent forces. As we examine some of the causes of personality problems, it is important to remember that they are looked at in isolation here only to highlight some of their aspects. In reality, they are not separable, and distinctions among biological, psychological, sociological, economic, and cultural-political influences are no more than artificial analytical distinctions (Feagans, 1974).

Genetics and Temperament as Causal Factors

While debate will always rage regarding the relative importance of heredity and environment in human development and in the causation of psychological problems, in this text it is sufficient to note that both factors are inextricably related in child and adolescent development. Environment can have no effects except upon an individual human being with a particular set of genetic and constitutional characteristics; and likewise a person, as a biological organism, cannot exist apart from an environmental system with its multiple impacts. Given these initial assumptions, the following examines recent research findings regarding the roles of genetics and temperament in childhood and adolescent personality problems.

In 1971 David Rosenthal, then Chief of the Laboratory of Psychology at the National Institute of Mental Health, published a review of the research examining the effects of heredity on a range of psychological disorders (Rosenthal, 1971). What Rosenthal found was that very little research had been conducted about the genetic elements in psychoneurotic disorders—a term roughly equivalent to the label personality problems. However, in reanalyzing the results of a few earlier studies, Rosenthal did find that first-degree relatives (parents, siblings, and children) of individuals with diagnosable personality problems experienced about twice the frequency of similar problems as second-degree relatives (grandparents, aunts, uncles, nephews, and nieces). This is the sort of result that would be predicted if, in fact, heredity is a factor in the causation of personality problems since it means that closer biological relationship is correlated with greater likelihood of having the problem. Of course, there is an important confounding factor in such a finding since closer biological relationship also correlates with more intense and pervasive environmental influence. In other words, first-degree relatives, in addition to being genetically more similar to the proband (person who is identified as the subject under study) than second-degree relatives, also tend to interact with the proband more often and with greater influence.

Rosenthal also examined the results of several twin studies in which investigators compared the incidence of personality problems in identical and fraternal twins. Identical, or monozygotic, twins share identical hereditary endowments. In comparison, fraternal, or dizygotic, twins are no more similar in heredity than nonidentical brothers and sisters. If heredity is a key component in the causation of personality or psychoneurotic problems, one would expect monozygotic twins to show a higher rate of similarity, or concordance, in the occurrence of such problems than dizygotic twins. In fact, several studies had demonstrated a higher concordance rate in monozygotic twin pairs (Eysenck & Prell, 1951; Shields, 1954), but the results of these studies were not sufficiently clear to yield strong conclusions. Furthermore, environment continued to be a major confounding variable in these studies as well.

More recently investigators at the Yale University School of Medicine have found that first-degree adult relatives of individuals with depression and panic disorders showed increased risk of developing similar problems (Leckman, Weissman, Merikangas, Pauls, & Prusoff, 1983), and the six- to seventeen-year-old children of such individuals also showed significant increased risk of developing depressive, panic, and anxiety disorders similar to their parents (Weissman, Leckman, Merikangas, Gammon, & Prusoff, 1984). These studies also demonstrated a consistent relationship between depressive and anxiety disorders, so that the presence of one is associated with the increased probability of the other.

Among the most comprehensive investigations of the role of hereditary factors is a recent study of Australian twins (Kendler, Heath, Martin, & Eaves, 1986). In this comprehensive study investigators mailed questionnaires evaluating anxiety and depressive symptoms to 5,967 pairs of twins, eighteen years old and older, listed in the Australian National Health and Medical Research Council Twin Register. They received responses from 3,810 pairs of twins, and verified whether the twins were monozygotic or di-

zygotic by photograph. Questionnaire items included, among others, assessment of feelings of agitation, panic, sleeplessness, hopelessness, loss of interest in activities, and thoughts of suicide. This study is of interest for several reasons. It shows that personality traits and psychiatric symptoms tend to be continuous characteristics with no clear demarcation between them. Thus, there is no easy distinction between a strong individual characteristic and a mild symptom. Rather, characteristics and symptoms must be evaluated within the context of the individual's total personality and functioning. Further, these investigators examined the complex question of whether monozygotic twins show higher concordance rates in the occurrence of personality problems than dizygotic twins because of environmental forces rather than hereditary factors. Examination of their own results and those of other studies led them to conclude that there are, in fact, greater similarities in the environmental forces having an impact on identical twins than on fraternal twins. However, they were also led to conclude that these *greater environmental similarities are the result rather than the cause of similarities in the twins' behavior.*

The most important result of the Australian twin study in relation to the present discussion is the investigators' conclusion that genetic factors play an important and substantial role in the causation of anxiety and depression.

Overall, then, it seems relatively clear at this point in time that genetic factors play a key role in the causation of personality problems in children and adolescents. Although it is not yet possible to sort out either the extent of genetic influences or the mechanisms by which they operate, we must acknowledge that some individuals experience constitutional predispositions to develop anxiety and depression as characteristic responses to the complex ecosystem in which they develop. We will return to discussions of genetics and temperament as causal factors in other psychological problems in children and adolescents, but for the moment, it is important simply to recognize that children and adolescents bring important response characteristics and tendencies to the person-environment system and are not simply passive recipients of environmental forces.

Psychological Factors in the Causation of Personality Problems

Although we do not yet have useful concepts of the interaction between mind and body, we do know that genetic and biological factors are somehow represented psychologically in the ways that we think, feel, and act. However, lacking an understanding of how body and mind interact, we tend to focus on them separately. This section examines some of the psychological mechanisms that may be operative in the development of personality problems. We cannot specify exactly how these are related to a child's biological characteristics; however, it is nevertheless important to recognize that genetically influenced response patterns underlie an individual's psychological functioning. It is also important to remember that many concepts regarding psychological factors in the causation of personality problems remain theoretical in nature and are guides to understanding rather than established facts.

Psychodynamic Views of Causation. As noted in Chapter 2, psychodynamic theories have evolved in several directions from the seminal work of Sigmund Freud. Although Freud did not himself work with children, his theoretical views exerted strong and pervasive influences on our understanding of childhood and the development of psychological problems. To recap briefly, psychoanalytic theory suggests that anxiety is the pivotal concept in understanding personality problems. As the developing infant and young child encounter demands from parents and others to conform to social conventions, they try to inhibit primitive drives toward immediate impulse gratification. Responding to parental training pressures, the child tries to repress and avoid any awareness of unacceptable

impulses, most particularly of aggressive and sexual wishes. However, because the intensity of these drives does not permit complete repression and because the pressures associated with them continue to mount, it often happens that these impulses threaten to force themselves into awareness.

It is this threatened breakthrough of impulses into consciousness and potential action that creates anxiety in the child, leading to further efforts to avoid not only consciousness of these base impulses but also the associated anxiety. The failure of repression to avoid impulse awareness leads to acute anxiety or panic in some individuals. In others, attempts to strengthen repressive defenses lead to the development of symptoms such as physical complaints or specific fears of environmental objects that may symbolize the repressed impulses. In some individuals, the threatened breakthrough of aggressive impulses leads the child to redirect aggression inward, and such internalized aggression may be manifested as depression. Thus, directly experienced anxiety and panic attacks result as a youngster unconsciously senses the possible breakthrough of unacceptable impulses into awareness. Other symptoms such as physical complaints without organic cause, fears of the dark, or separation from parents or school may result as the child tries to strengthen repressive defenses. Depression may result as the child tries to control unconscious anger and rage by redirecting it inward against the self.

Other psychodynamic theorists have modified these original conceptions in different ways. Otto Rank, for example, suggested that the trauma of birth is the wellspring of all later anxiety and is reexperienced in situations that threaten individual well-being (Rank, 1929). Melanie Klein, a pioneer in the psychoanalytic treatment of children, hypothesized that as early as the first year of life, the infant experiences powerful unconscious fantasies involving sexual and agressive impulses and fears of losing the mother because of these impulses (Klein, 1932).

However, Erik Erikson has undoubtedly exerted the most pervasive influence on current psychodynamic theory regarding childhood and adolescence. As noted earlier, Erikson's conception of infantile experiences of basic trust versus mistrust sets the stage for later relationships with others and with the world. If the infant's earliest experiences do not provide a sense of basic security and connection with others, then the developing child will see the world as a fearsome place offering little safety, security, or acceptance. Anxiety thus becomes a central fact of the child's existence and shapes responses related to independence, confidence, and identity development. During the stages of autonomy versus shame and doubt, initiative versus guilt, industry versus inferiority, and identity versus identity diffusion, destructive outcomes leave the child feeling anxious, ashamed, and worthless. Unable to cope with the world in confident terms, the child feels chronically anxious, defensive, and withdrawn. The result is the development of pervasive personality problems manifested in timid behavior, social isolation, and depression.

Social Learning Views of Causation. Learning theorists have consistently maintained that faulty learning experiences form the basis for a variety of psychological disorders, including personality problems in children and adolescents. Almost all of these theories take one of three basic departure points. First, there are approaches that emphasize classical or respondent conditioning processes as the bases of personality problems or psychoneurotic disorders. Such views suggest that fear is a crucial unconditioned response that can easily become associated with a wide range of both subtle and obvious environmental stimuli. For example, a boy experiencing intense anxiety upon separation from his parents on the first day of school might come to associate such fears with school attendance and then, later, with a variety of school activities and expectations. By a process of stimulus generalization, the youngster may

eventually experience anxiety in a wide range of situations and activities extending even beyond the initial experiences of separation from parents or school attendance.

A second major perspective focuses on operant conditioning processes. From this perspective, a youngster learns to avoid any situations in which anxiety occurs because avoidance reduces aversive stimuli and is, therefore, reinforcing. A girl, upon finding that a stomachache allows her to avoid going to school, may quickly learn that physical illness is a means of avoiding many situations that cause anxiety. Alternatively, she may learn that anytime she is away from her mother or father she feels nervous, but that her anxiety subsides as soon as she is back with her parents. Under such circumstances, she will rapidly learn to avoid social situations in which she does not have parental support.

Finally, social learning perspectives emphasize the importance of modeling processes in the development of personality problems. Thus, a youngster may learn to be fearful in particular situations or to use physical illness as a way of avoiding stress simply by observing parents and other family members as they cope with anxiety. A child easily learns to fear social encounters by watching a parent or other significant person who is nervous or shy in social situations; a parent who approaches life tasks fearfully can easily transmit the message that the world is a fearsome place; and a parent who talks and behaves in helpless, hopeless, and depressed ways will often transmit such ideas and feelings to an observant child.

The reality, of course, is that respondent and operant conditioning and modeling are much more complex in their influences than depicted in the examples above. In fact, these various learning processes may all interact in the development of any single behavior or complicated sequence of behaviors, which in turn may combine to form characteristic reaction patterns.

The situation is further complicated by the fact that learning processes interact with individual constitutional characteristics and environmental forces. One theorist who has attempted to incorporate these complexities into a theoretical model of neurotic problems is Hans Eysenck. In a varied program of provocative studies dating from the 1950s, Eysenck has challenged traditional views of personality and conduct problems, and recently developed a comprehensive model of personality problems integrating constitutional factors and learning processes. Eysenck (1976) has suggested that some individuals may have innate sensitivities to environmental stimuli that facilitate the development of conditioned fear responses. In other words, these persons are emotionally volatile and predisposed to the development of anxiety, which may easily become associated with various environmental cues through classical conditioning and modeling. At the same time, individuals also vary in the ease with which they form conditioned responses. That is, in some individuals conditioned responses are formed unusually easily and extinguish slowly. In other persons, conditioned responses are formed slowly and extinguish easily. In individuals who are emotionally volatile and predisposed to anxiety and who, at the same time, form conditioned responses easily, the stage is set for the development of strong anxiety responses to many environmental stimuli. Thus, the interaction of easy conditionability and intense emotionality interact with past conditioning and modeling processes to produce constellations of symptoms that we describe as anxiety disorders and depression.

Although Eysenck's model of personality problems, like any theory, must withstand extensive empirical testing, it is a useful device for integrating information and guiding our thinking about personality problems. Useful as it is, however, this model does not yet account for all the relevant variables because it does not explicitly address the impact of family influences and ecological variables.

Family Influences and Causation of Personality Problems. Although it is a truism to say that

children tend to be much like their parents, the fact is that empirical research supports this statement, and research studies show consistently that children with personality problems come from homes in which one or both parents also have such problems (Hetherington & Martin, 1972).

One of the key characteristics that has emerged in studies of families of children and adolescents with personality problems is a tendency for the parents to be excessively constraining and controlling (Rosenthal, Finkelstein, Ni, & Robertson, 1959; Rosenthal, Ni, Finkelstein, & Berkwits, 1962). Although specific characteristics obviously vary among these parents, they tend to be overprotective, hypercritical, domineering, rigid, and to use excessive discipline (Lewis, 1954). Parents of children with personality problems seem, intentionally or unintentionally, to teach their children that the world at large is to be feared, that spontaneity may bring criticism, and that mistakes are disastrous and will lead to rejection by others. Such messages force the growing child to develop an excessive and painful self-awareness. For many youngsters an important life goal is simply to avoid doing anything that draws others' attention, because such attention can only bring criticism and rejection. It is not surprising that children who hear such messages repeatedly become timid and socially withdrawn (see Box 4.1).

In some families, parents repeatedly and explicitly warn their children that others will not think much of them if they are poorly behaved or loud or if they ask for things they need. With the kind of insensitivity that they would abhor in themselves if they recognized it, such parents may be critical of their children's physical appearance, their clothes, their habits, their personal characteristics, their abilities and schoolwork, and their friends. Philip Zimbardo is a psychologist who has worked extensively with shy individuals. In reporting the comments of his students and research subjects, Zimbardo (1977) notes frequent comments by adults

Box 4.1   Peggy V.: Family Influences in the Development of a Personality Problem

Peggy V. was referred for psychological evaluation shortly after graduation from the eighth grade. The referral was made by Peggy's physician after a series of referrals to other medical specialists had failed to show any physiological basis for severe stomach problems that Peggy had been suffering for more than a year. She had frequent, sharp pains in her abdomen and chronic diarrhea with as many as twenty bowel movements per day. Her appetite, which had never been good, had dwindled during her last year of grammar school to virtually nothing. She was extremely thin and medical efforts to help her gain weight had failed. While several medical specialists had diagnosed her problem as mucous colitis, or irritable colon, none had been able to develop an effective treatment regimen. Irritable colon is a disorder of the colon characterized by frequent bowel movements, stomach pain, loss of appetite, and sometimes nausea and headache. The disorder is often viewed as functional rather than organically based and a result of chronic anxiety.

The interviewer found Peggy a very pretty girl whose appearance was spoiled by severe emaciation. She did not speak spontaneously at all during the interview and, initially, did not even raise her head or make eye contact with the psychologist working with her. She responded to questions with one- or two-word answers at first, and the psychologist tried to help her feel comfortable by providing reassurance and moving very slowly.

Eventually a picture emerged showing that Peggy was afraid of nearly everyone and everything. She had never been able to make friends at school because she was so withdrawn and timid. She described how she often longed to talk to other children but was afraid to approach them. On the rare occasion when another youngster spoke to her, she would panic, freeze, and simply stare at the ground until they walked away.

School had been nothing more than eight solid years of terror. Peggy felt that she was stupid, and said that she simply did not understand things. She dreaded tests and examinations, expected to fail, and often did. When called upon in class she would stand up to acknowledge her name, but in eight years she had rarely answered a teacher's question. She described how some teachers became impatient with her, felt she was stubborn, and would berate her in front of the whole class. She learned to stare at a spot on the floor or wall in order to avoid crying until the harangue was over.

Peggy described a day near graduation when class prophecies were read. When it was predicted that, in ten years, Peggy would be Miss America, the entire class—including her teacher—burst into prolonged laughter accompanied by many stinging jokes. She remembered this as the most devastating moment in her thirteen years.

Peggy's earliest memory was of standing near her parents—seeing only their legs—as they engaged in bitter argument. Her father left home before she was five, and thereafter she remembers seeing him only twice. On both these occasions, when he came to pick her up she remembers her mother creating terrible scenes, accusing him of being with other women and neglecting his family. He never returned after the second time. Her mother seemed to take pleasure in noting that Peggy's father cared nothing for his children and clearly did not like them since he never came to see them.

Peggy's mother took a job to support her family, and Peggy was left in the care of an elderly neighbor woman who did not speak any English. Although cared for physically, Peggy could not communicate with her caretaker and learned, eventually, not to talk. Her mother showed little interest in her and did not converse with Peggy. The only communication Peggy received from her mother was nightly harangues on her father's abandonment of them.

Occasionally, when friends or relatives visited

continued

Box 4.1   continued

and Peggy had difficulty speaking to them, her mother would make a point of how backward Peggy was and engage in a battle to make her speak. Although her mother rarely won these battles, Peggy always lost because it became more and more difficult for her to communicate. Given such an environment, it is not surprising that Peggy developed intense fear of others.

It is not surprising that only with ongoing support in a psychotherapeutic setting from a caring adult she was eventually able to develop some greater ability to relate to others. The therapist's genuine involvement with her, constant encour-

agement, and Peggy's own resources eventually helped her begin to learn how to cope with her fears without withdrawing completely into herself. When she had made a few friends, Peggy seemed to blossom, and she became more outgoing. Her irritable colon symptoms subsided somewhat, and she gained some weight. Although she developed into a very attractive young woman, she was unable ever to believe her mirror and remained timid and withdrawn. However, she was able to interact with others more effectively and to develop a sense that she could cope with most life problems.

---

whose parents told them, as they were growing up, that they were boring, homely, or stupid.

Still other parents, determined to protect their children from the dangers that they themselves see everywhere in the world, warn them against any and all strangers, caution them to avoid dogs and other animals, and paint dreadful pictures of what happens to children who do not stay close to their parents. Under such circumstances, children not only model parental attitudes and behavior, but often see the parents themselves avoiding "dangerous" people and situations.

In some instances, the child may face even more complex issues as parents simultaneously encourage assertiveness and independence and punish any steps toward that independence by labeling the child as inadequate. Most of us can recall situations in which a parent encourages a youngster to use her own judgment, and then punishes the child for making a mistake; and nearly everyone can recall seeing a parent encourage a child to speak up, while telling others how shy the child is and pointing out a whole catalog of inadequacies to others. Such double-blind communications can produce confusion, anxiety, anger, and immobility (Bateson, Jackson, Haley, & Weakland, 1969).

In brief, then, the key family characteristics that appear to influence the development of personality problems in children include family tendencies to be fearful, worrisome, overprotective, critical, and to communicate conflicting messages to the growing child. Those children prone to experiencing high levels of emotionality and anxiety respond to such parental characteristics in expectable ways by developing a variety of different manifestations of personality problems.

Varieties of Personality Problems in Children and Adolescents

Personality problems in children take many forms. Ranging from general anxiety that imposes mild limitations on a youngster's ability to make friends through paralyzing depression that may prompt attempts at suicide, these disorders share in common that the child experiences internal, subjective distress as well as displays overt signs of disturbance. In most cases, however, the child does not engage in disruptive or antisocial behavior that is disturbing to others.

The distinctions drawn in the following sections relate primarily to the ways in which a child experiences and manifests anxiety. Although some problems are characterized by vague, encompassing fearfulness, others may be manifested in intense specific fears, and still others may result in severe physical health problems. Although specific approaches to psychological and educational intervention vary among these problems, interventions almost always include attempts to reduce fear, build self-confidence and hopefulness, and develop coping skills.

Anxiety Disorders

Personality characteristics such as timidity, hypersensitivity, self-consciousness, and pessimism become personality problems when they begin to cause chronic severe anxiety and to impose limitations on a child's ability to cope with normal developmental tasks. The child with a generalized anxiety disorder is not simply timid; he or she is paralyzed by fear in the face of simple interpersonal tasks. Greeting a family friend, asking a question in class, or talking to another child are impossible demands. Self-consciousness pervades the child's awareness to the extent that a small mistake or a social error are experienced as humiliating blunders. In the face of such intense self-focus, a youngster may simply withdraw from any interaction at all and make every attempt to become invisible in the classroom or on the playground.

For some children and adolescents, generalized anxiety may be manifest as constant worrisomeness or apprehensive expectation, as it is called in DSM-III. These youngsters worry about whether they will be able to find the right classroom at school, whether there will be enough time to eat lunch, whether their mother will have an accident and be hurt or killed during the day, whether they will drop a book during class, whether life will simply swallow them up.

Reassurance does not typically help such a child, because present reassurance only postpones disaster and never forestalls it com-

pletely. Thus, the child lives in constant expectation that something terrible waits just around the corner. In fact, this kind of apprehensive expectation appears to be the hallmark of generalized anxiety disorders (Barlow, Blanchard, Vermilyea, Vermilyea, & DiNardo, 1986).

For those who perceive the world more realistically, such fears and worries are often exasperating. Frustrated parents often try to force the child into confronting difficult situations, and irritated teachers may simply decide to ignore the anxious child. Neither course typically helps very much, and the anxious child may continue to struggle with vague fears and worries for many years.

Panic Disorders. For some children and adolescents, chronic generalized anxiety and worrisomeness may periodically erupt into severe, acute panic attacks. Such symptoms as rapid heartbeat; shallow, rapid breathing; queasiness or nausea; sweating; lightheadedness and dizziness; frequency or urgency of urination; faintness; or fear of losing control may appear with sudden intensity and no warning at all. Beset by such unexplainable symptoms, some youngsters begin to fear that they are "going crazy" or becoming "mental," and the anxiety that underlies the panic attack is even further intensified. Even when the acute panic subsides, intervening periods are often characterized by apprehension about whether such an experience may recur and when. For many children, the terror of an acute panic attack is further complicated by an inability to talk about it because the experience feels so completely strange and alien. One youngster, in finally discussing such an attack, said to his psychotherapist that he did not talk about it with his parents because he simply did not know how to describe it or what to say about it. In another case, an eleven-year-old boy would simply bolt and start running aimlessly when struck by feelings of panic until, exhausted, his symptoms subsided.

To outside observers, panic attacks sometimes appear weird and strange and so they respond to them in ways that reinforce the youngster's already serious concerns about losing control or behaving in ways that will be humiliating and embarrassing. Thus, cyclical patterns are often established that contribute to ongoing anxiety and further recurrences of panic episodes.

Phobic Disorders. Panic attacks often occur unexpectedly, without apparent provocation, and with no particular environmental association; the experience of acute anxiety in phobic disorders is more narrowly directed. The intense fear involved in phobic disorders usually has a specific focus, is out of proportion to the realities of the phobic object, persists over time, causes avoidance of the phobic object, and is maladaptive in the limitations it imposes on the child's behavior (Miller, Barrett, & Hampe, 1974).

Phobic responses may be directed toward virtually any object or event imaginable. There are even reported cases of fear of chocolate and fear of vegetables. However, in school-age children most fears can be grouped into three broad categories: (1) fears of physical injury or loss, such as having an accident or injury or losing a parent through death or divorce; (2) fears of natural or supernatural dangers such as fear of thunder and lightning, fear of the dark, or fear of ghosts or monsters; and (3) fears relating to psychic stress, such as fear of school, exams, making mistakes in public, social events, doctors, or dentists (Miller, Barrett, Hampe, & Noble, 1972). As children grow older, the content of their fears changes too, so that fears of monsters and nightmares, common in kindergarteners, are replaced by fears of injury or social events in older children (Bauer, 1976).

Perhaps the most common phobias in school-age children center around fear of separation from family and fear of school or particular school-related demands and expectations. In an exhaustive study of severe fears in children, Anthony Graziano and Ina De Giovanni (1979) reviewed more than fifty years of research and found that the overwhelming majority of reported phobias in children (86%) were school phobias.

In many respects, the emergence of these specific fears is readily understandable because they relate to key areas of a child's experience. Dependent and unable to cope without parental support, children in our culture are both physically and emotionally in need of immediate parental presence. From infancy through adulthood, individuals progress developmentally toward increased independence, but during school years, children clearly recognize their dependency and display it in varying degrees of discomfort when separated from their parents. In fact, for younger children particularly, it is often difficult to determine whether school phobia is a function of fear of school or fear of separation from parents while at school (Veltkamp, 1975; Yates, 1970). Later, however, school phobic reactions appear to stem more clearly from the child's fear of the school situation itself and all the demands it represents. In either case, however, the basic fear underlying phobic responses appears to be fear of inability to cope with threatening situations (Beck & Emery, 1985). The unifying thread that ties anxiety problems, panic disorders, and phobic responses together is connected to the child's appraisal that the world is potentially dangerous, and that he or she is inadequate to cope with this danger.

Somatoform Disorders. Some children and adolescents experience anxiety directly through anxiety reactions and panic disorders; others respond with intense, situation-specific fears as in phobic reactions. Still other children react to perceived threats with primarily physical responses. Individuals with somatoform disorders exhibit physical symptoms without demonstrable organic findings or known physiological mechanisms linking the basis of these symptoms to psychological factors (American Psychiatric Association, 1980, p. 241). This broad definition encompasses a variety of different problems. When strictly defined, these problems are relatively unusual in children and do not occur with any frequency until adolescence. However, they are quite common among adults. It is important to discuss them briefly here because precursors of adult somatoform disorders are evident in some children for whom anxiety takes on a physical character: complaints of headache, stomachache, nausea, muscle pain, dizziness, chest pains, and so forth.

Physical complaints are often a legitimate way, in the eyes of these children, of avoiding situations that provoke anxiety and fear because, in our culture, illness is often permitted as a reasonable excuse for not participating in difficult tasks. Further, since many reactions caused by anxiety do, in fact, have physical manifestations, it is not uncommon for a youngster to have a headache or feel nauseous in the face of perceived threat. If feelings of illness are effective in avoiding the threat, it is not surprising if they occur again in similar situations.

Psychological Factors Affecting Physical Condition. Historically, psychiatrists and psychologists have long recognized disorders that have been variously termed psychosomatic or psychophysiological disorders. These terms came into use because it appeared that there was a direct relationship between psychological factors and physical illnesses that had a demonstrable organic basis. The view often held was that psychological conflicts or stress somehow caused deterioration of a physical organ or system. However, it was never possible to demonstrate a clear, direct, causal relationship between psychological characteristics or experiences and such physical problems as asthma, ulcers, colitis, skin inflammations, cancer, and others. This is not to say that there are no relationships between psychological and physical functioning and malfunctioning. Rather, it has not thus far been possible to show that psychological factors are causes that precede and lead to specific physiological problems.

Thus, it has become more acceptable to speak of psychological factors as affecting physical conditions, as when stress aggravates a condition, such as an ulcer, that may have causes independent of current stressful situations. While there is acknowledgment of a relationship between psychological and physical functioning, mental health professionals currently understand that these relationships are much more complex and less clearly understood than once thought (see Box 4.1, the case of Peggy V.).

One example of the complexity of these relationships is recurrent abdominal pain in children (McGrath & Feldman, 1986). Specifically defined as the occurrence of at least three attacks of pain severe enough to affect activities over a three-month period with no known organic cause, recurrent abdominal pain may occur in as many as 10 to 19 percent of older children and adolescents (Apley, 1975). Research on this disorder suggests that a complexity of factors is involved in the causation and maintenance of recurrent abdominal pain. These factors could include any combination of: (1) unidentified organic causes, such as autonomic nervous system instability; (2) operant learning in which complaints of pain are reinforced by parents or others; (3) environmental stress creating or intensifying anxiety; or (4) modeling of parental behavior. Thus, although psychological factors may not directly cause recurrent abdominal pain or other physical disorders, they may be crucial in considering the persistence of the problem or the child's ability to cope with it (Levine & Rappaport, 1984).

Another example of a physiological disorder with strong psychological components producing severe physical symptoms is asthma. For years investigators searched for parental and family characteristics that were common to asthmatic individuals. Others hypothesized that certain personality features—such as intense dependency—were typical of asthmatics. Still others speculated about the gains to the individual associated with asthmatic symptoms and experiences. However, little clear research support has been found for these hypotheses, and investigators currently take a much more cautious view. At this time no more can be said than that a variety of causal factors appear operative in most illnesses including family and environmental factors, personality characteristics, and stress; that physical illness is not a necessary outcome of psychological malfunction or stress; and that stress may aggravate the severity of preexisting physical problems (Purcell, 1975; Werry, 1972).

In brief, then, in this group of childhood problems there is real illness, accompanied by demonstrable physiological changes, which may be aggravated by psychological and environmental factors in the child's life. Perhaps more clearly with this group of disorders than any other, approaches to intervention must address the entire ecological system in which the child lives and functions, since we see in these problems the explicit interaction of all aspects of the child's life from temperament and physiological functioning to learning and environmental stressors.

Depressive Disorders

There is no simple or clear way to separate emotional responses such as anxiety and depression. Some investigators try to distinguish among states of feeling, emotions, and moods, but these distinctions typically have little value to the classroom teacher or the practicing clinician, and they are utterly meaningless to the child experiencing internal distress. While we can speak of them distinctly and know that they reflect different states of feeling, in real life anxiety and depression are inextricably related (Weissman, et al., 1984). Feelings of anxiety typically produce at least some depression in mood, and depression rarely occurs without some component of anxious expectation about the future. Thus, it is important to remember that the distinctions we make here have more to do with focus than with absolute differences. An anxious child may also be depressed about real or imagined personality flaws, and a depressed child is almost always anxious about

his or her ability to cope with life. With these cautions in mind, we can turn to a discussion of depressive disorders, the second major group of internalizing or personality problems in children and adolescents.

Symptoms of Depressive Disorders in Children and Adolescents. Strangely enough, there is considerable controversy regarding the symptoms that characterize depressive disorders in children and even argument about whether depression occurs in children at all. There are several reasons for such controversy (Cantwell, 1982). One reason is that, historically, psychology and psychiatry have been strongly influenced by psychoanalytic theory, which suggests that depression results from internalization of aggressive impulses as a result of intense superego prohibitions against aggression. However, it was theorized that superego development in children is too primitive and weakly structured to cause the intense conflict and internalization of aggression that underlie depressive disorders in adolescents and adults (French, 1979; Poznanski, 1979; Rie, 1966). Thus, theoretically, children were viewed as developmentally incapable of experiencing depressive disorders as these occur in adults, and symptoms that might look like depression were really manifestations of other problems or of transient developmental phases.

Others believe that depression does occur in children, but that depressive symptoms in children differ from those in adults. Thus, for example, some researchers suggest that enuresis and encopresis may be symptoms of depression in children (Frommer, 1967), while these rarely occur in adult depressive disorders. Still others described a phenomenon in children called masked depression, in which aggression, disruptive behavior, and a variety of antisocial behaviors were thought to be possible childhood equivalents of depression in adults (Cytryn & McKnew, 1972; Leese, 1974).

However, in a comprehensive review of research on childhood depression, Dennis Cantwell (1982) concluded that depression in children is manifested very much as it is in adults through such symptoms as melancholy, hopelessness, feelings of worthlessness, a desire to run away or escape from the current environment, thoughts of suicide or suicide attempts, irritability and aggression, sleep disturbances, deterioration in school performance, social withdrawal, physical complaints, change in appetite, and loss of energy and interests. (Box 4.2 presents a comprehensive checklist of signs and symptoms that may indicate the presence of depression in children and adolescents.) Further, it is possible to classify childhood depressive disorders into several more or less distinct subtypes, as is the case with adult forms of the problem. An exhaustive discussion of these different types of depressive disorders is beyond the scope of the discussion here, but several important distinctions must be made.

First, it is important to understand the difference between exogenous and endogenous depression. Exogenous depression, sometimes termed reactive depression, refers to disturbances in mood that appear due primarily to major disruptions in the individual's development or current ecosystem. The death of a loved one, parental separation or divorce, repeated physical, sexual, or emotional abuse, rejection by friends, and school failure are commonly occurring precipitants of exogenous depression in children and adolescents. Endogenous or chronic depression appears to have a substantial foundation in genetic makeup and temperament. In instances of endogenous depression, there is often no identifiable ecological stressor. Rather, the individual's mood is largely dependent on internal processes that seem to be biochemical in nature. While the individual's mood may

---

Box 4.2   A Checklist of Behaviors and Background Factors Often Seen in Depressed Children and Adolescents

- Frequent sadness, moodiness
- Easy discouragement
- Feelings of worthlessness
- Guilt feelings
- Excessive worrying
- Perfectionism
- Loss of interest in previously enjoyed activities
- Drop in school grades; absence of usual school effort
- Easy and/or frequent crying
- Personality inhibition (shyness, timidity, fearfulness)
- Social withdrawal; social isolation
- Unusual or unusually intense anger; irritability
- Feelings of being unloved or picked on
- Poor appetite and weight loss

- Inability to sleep; disturbed sleep
- Excessive fatigue; excessive sleeping
- Impaired attention and concentration
- Self-injurious behavior
- Suicidal ideation or attempts
- Loss of or separation from parents or other significant persons
- History of physical abuse or sexual abuse
- History of parental rejection
- Excessively demanding and perfectionist parents
- Family disorganization
- History of depression in one or both parents
- Suicide of a sibling or friend
- Suicide, suicidal ideation, or suicide attempts by a parent

Cantwell, 1983; Costello, 1981; Kovacs, 1986; Robinson, 1984; Schafii, Carrigan, Whittinghill, & Derick, 1985.

vary over time, variations are less clearly related to life events than in exogenous depression.

Another important distinction in understanding depression is that between unipolar and bipolar depressive disorders. Unipolar depressive disorders are characterized by continuous or intermittent periods of depressed mood. Bipolar disorders, by contrast, are characterized by alternating episodes of depression and inappropriate euphoria, excessive energy, grandiosity, impulsivity, and poor judgment. There is no necessary pattern to these alternative episodes, and they may even be interspersed with periods of normal mood and behavior.

The final distinction is between major affective or mood disorders, cyclothymic disorders, and dysthymic disorders. This distinction is based primarily on the severity of depression. Major affective disorders typically involve very intense disturbances of mood and may even be of such psychotic proportions that a child or adolescent loses touch with reality and displays hallucinations, delusions, loosening of associations, and bizarre behavior. Major affective disorders may be unipolar, bipolar, endogenous, or exogenous.

Cyclothymic disorders involve alternating depressive and dysphoric moods of at least two years' duration, but of lesser severity than major affective disorders. Low self-esteem may alternate with inflated self-esteem; social withdrawal may alternate with an indiscriminate need for contact with people; and excessive sleeping and loss of energy may alternate with reduced need for sleep and increased energy (APA, 1980). A dysthymic disorder (or depressive neurosis) is characterized by the depressed mood lasting at least one year in children and adolescents, but with no loss of contact with reality or exhibition of bizarre behavior. Specific symptoms may include feelings of sadness and loss of interest and pleasure in usual activities, disturbed sleep patterns, low energy or chronic fatigue, feelings of inadequacy and loss of self-esteem, impaired concentration, withdrawal from social contacts, increased irritability or anger, pessimism, frequent episodes of crying, and frequent thoughts of death or suicide.

While these various distinctions are occasionally useful descriptively, it is not clear that they have strong current research support except for the distinction between unipolar and bipolar disorders. However, because they continue in wide usage, it is important to be familiar with them.

As distressing as these symptoms and signs are in any person, it is particularly disturbing to see them dominate the life of a child or adolescent and drain the energy and enjoyment of life necessary for healthy, growing youngsters. In some cases, a youngster's suffering may be so intense that it eventually leads to consideration of and attempts at suicide.

Suicidal Behavior in Children and Adolescents. Concern about childhood and adolescent suicide has risen steadily in recent years. Suicide is the second leading cause of death among adolescents (Gadpaille, 1980), and the suicide rate among this age group doubled between 1961 and 1975 (Robbins & Alessi, 1985). About twelve thousand children between five and fourteen years of age are admitted to psychiatric hospitals each year because of suicidal behavior (Rosenthal & Rosenthal, 1984), reflecting increases in both suicidal attempts and completions among prepubertal children (Myers, Burke, & McCauley, 1985). Recent studies have even depicted the occurrence of suicidal behavior in preschool children (Rosenthal & Rosenthal, 1984).

Although there has been a steady rise in suicide rates among adolescents and young adults (ages fifteen to twenty-four) since 1970, it is not clear whether this rise reflects an overall population trend or a phenomenon specific to younger age groups (Hodgman, 1985; National Center for Health Statistics, 1984; Schaffer &

Fisher, 1981). Other research, however, has shown increases of as much as 80 percent in suicide rates among children ages ten to fourteen, and as much as 100 percent in adolescents from fifteen to nineteen (Shafii, Carrigan, Whittinghill, & Derrick, 1985). In either case, it is clear that suicidal behavior among children and adolescents is a matter for intense concern, and research in this area has surged in recent years. To work toward prevention, the key questions at this point concern identifying potentially suicidal children and adolescents and understanding the reasons for such behavior.

One important approach to identifying and understanding suicidal behavior among children and adolescents is the psychological autopsy in which investigators systematically examine the recent behavior, psychiatric history, and family history of suicide victims. In one such study, a team of researchers set out to explore and identify factors contributing to suicide in order to prevent future suicides and to serve as a point of contact for intervention with potential suicide victims (Shafii, et al., 1985). These investigators scanned local newspapers and maintained contact with the community coroner's office to learn of suspected child or adolescent suicides. While attempting to maintain sensitivity to the loss of the grieving families, these researchers conducted unstructured interviews with bereaved family members and explored suicide victims' medical, psychiatric, school, and developmental histories. They examined significant life events and reconstructed the victim's behavior during the days immediately preceding the suicide. In addition, they interviewed other relatives, friends, and people of significance in each victim's life.

Between 1980 and 1983 this team of researchers studied the lives of twenty suicide victims between the ages of twelve and nineteen. They compared the suicide victims with a group of matched controls and found many statistically significant differences between the control subjects and suicide victims. Among

other findings, suicide victims had (1) been exposed to suicide through a parent, friend, or adult relative; (2) had parents who had serious emotional problems; (3) had been exposed to parental absence or physical or emotional abusiveness or both; (4) had expressed suicidal ideation; (5) had made suicide threats; (6) had made suicide attempts; (7) had displayed antisocial behavior in the form of involvements with legal authorities, shoplifting, fighting, school suspension, and frequent use of drugs or alcohol; and (8) had displayed inhibited personality characteristics such as social withdrawal or extreme sensitivity.

Using different methods, Douglas Robbins and Norman Alessi used a structured scale to interview sixty-four adolescents who were hospitalized on a psychiatric unit in an attempt to determine the psychological, ecological, and behavioral correlates of suicidal tendencies and behavior (Robbins & Alessi, 1985). Not surprisingly, they found a high level of correlation between depressive mood and suicidal tendencies. In addition, they found that youngsters with suicidal tendencies had poor self-concepts, could no longer find pleasure in previously enjoyed activities, showed impaired concentration, were indecisive, slept poorly, and were involved in drug or alcohol abuse. The level of seriousness expressed in the intent to commit suicide was a good indicator of the actuality to commit suicide.

In still another approach to exploring the sources of suicidal behavior in children, a team of New York investigators studied a randomly selected group of 101 normal schoolchildren in Yonkers, New York, and compared them with a group of sixty-five children in an inpatient psychiatric unit (Pfeffer, Zuckerman, Plutchik, & Mizruchi, 1984). In addition to studying demographic characteristics, Pfeffer, et al. had each child and a parent interviewed individually by a psychologist or psychiatrist and several rating scales were completed. In an initial analysis of data, the schoolchildren were divided into a nonsuicidal group who had no evidence of suicidal tendencies and a group who had mentioned either suicidal ideas, threats, or actual attempts. In contrast to non-suicidal schoolchildren, the suicidal group showed a preoccupation with death, current depressed mood, a history of depression in the past, more signs of emotional problems, and a greater likelihood of suicidal impulses in the mother. Hospitalized suicidal children showed more instances of recent aggression, more intense death preoccupation, higher frequency of parental separation, parental depression, parental psychiatric hospitalization, and suicidal impulses of the mother.

Other factors that have been related to suicidal behavior in children and adolescents include family disruption with suicidal impulses in one or both parents, a family history of suicidal behaviors, acute stressful life events, abuse toward the mother, social isolation, and social contagion in which there has been exposure to suicide in the school, neighborhood, or local community (Hodgman, 1985; Myers, 1985). Box 4.3 presents a discussion of recent research on suicidal contagion.

In summary, then, recent research provides strong evidence that suicidal behavior in children and adolescents is often associated with family disruption, psychiatric problems in one or both parents, a history of separation from parents, suicidal impulses in parents, acute stressful events in the child's or adolescent's life, depressed mood along with usual signs and symptoms of depression, low self-esteem, social withdrawal or isolation, aggression, excessive use of drugs or alcohol, and suicidal ideation, threats, and attempts.

Unfortunately, though we are now in a position to identify individuals at risk for suicide, there are few explanations about why some individuals are more likely to attempt suicide than others. Explanatory theories take a variety of forms. For example, demographic analyses have led some investigators to suggest that issues of competition and failure may account for increases in suicide rates among children and adolescents (Holinger & Offer, 1982). With recent increases in the child and adolescent population, there are likely to be increases in competition for jobs, class rank, positions on sports teams, places in desired schools, and access to social services. Increased competition obviously results in increased frequencies of experiences of failure along with increased stress, increased frequency of impaired self-esteem, and reduced access to various forms of assistance. Further, an increase in child and adolescent population is also likely to result in an intensified sense of isolation, loneliness, and hopelessness. The traditional psychoanalytic view that suicide results from the internalization of intense rage that cannot be directed toward environmental objects remains a viable hypothesis. Alternatively, suicide may represent the end point of a long period of hopelessness and helplessness with no sense of ability to make one's life any better either because environmental circumstances are experienced as absolutely devastating or because the individual has such poor self-esteem (Sudak, Ford, & Rushforth, 1984). Clearly, there are familial, modeling, and social facilitation effects at work as well, in view of family and community correlates of suicidal behavior.

The fact is that any of these hypotheses singly or in combination remain plausible in attempting to understand suicidal behavior in children and adolescents.

Educational Issues and Strategies

It is clear that children and adolescents with personality problems share a variety of common characteristics. Despite each youngster's uniquely patterned temperament, self-perception, expectations, response style, ecological context, and experiences, there are consistencies among these children that require special understanding and sensitivity on the part of the teacher. Children with personality problems consistently perceive the world around them as dangerous and potentially hurtful, and they doubt their own capacity to deal with life experiences in an effective and satisfying way. Their pessimistic expectations extend to schoolwork and interpersonal interactions as well as most other tasks and relationships, and school thus becomes an important setting in which the child's potential can be maximized through positive experiences, left untouched by a school setting oriented only toward policies and procedures, or further damaged by an insensitive and uncaring environment.

Box 4.3   Contagion and Adolescent Suicide

In the spring of 1987, a dozen teenage suicides within a period of less than two weeks attracted more than usual amounts of attention nationwide. Beginning with a suicide pact among four adolescents, a rash of suicides across the country followed within days. In at least one of these instances the victim's family found newspaper clippings under the child's bed describing the earlier suicides.

Police, mental health experts, and school authorities rushed suicide prevention programs into place and encouraged teachers and parents to be alert for suicidal talk, marked personality changes, abrupt gain or loss of weight, lack of attention to personal appearance, sleep disturbances, giving away of prized possessions, and unusual risk taking in adolescents in their care. The broadcast media reported new suicides almost daily, and newspapers published interviews with leading experts.

Eventually, mental health experts began to call on the media to suppress detailed reports describing the methods and circumstances of teen suicides. And, as abruptly as it began, the epidemic stopped.

Two recent research studies have shown a clear relationship between media reports and depictions of suicide and subsequent elevations in suicide rates. In one of these studies, researchers examined data on more than 12,000 adolescent suicides occurring between 1973 and 1979 (Phillips & Carstensen, 1986). On the basis of their data these investigators were able to develop expectancy rates for adolescent suicides and then to compare these with periods following media reports of suicides. Their results showed an average increase above expected levels for three suicides following media coverage of a suicide. They found, further, that the number of suicides correlated with the number of news stories covering the initial suicide. That is, the more news stories describing a suicide, the more suicides followed the report.

An even more alarming study shows that there is an increase in suicide rates following fictional television films involving suicide (Gould & Shaffer, 1986). Suicide rates among individuals nineteen years old and younger were studied in New York City and four adjacent counties. The study extended over a twenty-five-week period that included four television movies involving a suicide. Suicide rates among adolescents increased above expected levels during the two-week period following three of these four movies. However, there was no increase following the fourth movie, which focused on the impact of suicide upon survivors.

Even though the data clearly show contagion effects in adolescent suicide after strong media influences, unfortunately we have little understanding of the mechanisms influencing these imitative phenomena. Are suicidal ideas implanted that might not otherwise have occurred to these youngsters? Do media influences serve to release inhibitions on already suicidal individuals? Do the reports dramatize suicide in such a way that it is seen as a legitimate means of coping with problems? We have no answers to these questions. There is no doubt, however, that we have a responsibility to monitor carefully the means by which we report these tragic events.

The key issues in the education of children with personality problems include: (1) the establishment of an environment in which the characteristics and needs of the individual child are of foremost importance and never mindlessly subjugated to routines, schedules, and the requirements of orderly institutional functioning; (2) a clear recognition that these children are inhibited in functioning by intense anxiety, fearfulness, or depressed mood, and not by desires to be stubborn, willful, or manipulative; (3) a commitment to education through the active and intentional rewarding of successful ventures rather than inattention to nonproblem children or through punishment of curiosity, exploration, experimentation, and hesitant ventures; and (4) explicit, consistent, but gentle pressure toward assertiveness, self-exploration, and self-acceptance.

An explicit recognition of these priorities in the education of children and adolescents with personality problems creates an environment in which youngsters can begin, perhaps tentatively and fearfully at first, to look at the world around them realistically. They can risk the possibility of making mistakes. They can try new ways of interacting with others. They can experiment with assertiveness, learn that they can fail without being destroyed, that they can cope independently and even see what it is like to feel good about themselves. Such an educational environment can provide a springboard for teaching children that their worth is not dependent on how much they have, how they look, what their parents do, or what they are able to achieve, but rather on their own personal qualities and the values they bring to their activities and relationships.

In brief, the key educational strategies in the treatment of childhood and adolescent personality problems and depression must emphasize support, reassurance, protection, and avoidance of criticism and confrontations (Weinberg & Rehmet, 1983). Repeated experiences of effective coping, independent achievement, and management of inevitable life failures are critical.

Role of the Teacher

Chapter 11 examines specific teacher characteristics and behaviors as they apply to the special educational needs of children with personality problems, conduct disturbances, and pervasive developmental disorders. At this point, we will concentrate on the broader attitudes, values, and strategies that constitute the teacher's role in educating children with personality problems.

In a general way, the teacher plays the role of facilitator in helping children with personality problems. Because children with personality problems are so often inhibited in their reactions to activities and to other people and so often constricted in emotional responsiveness, they require encouragement and assistance in "testing the water" at the outset of virtually any activity. It is often the case that they do not need assistance so much in learning how to work or how to interact, but rather in developing the courage simply to try. In the case of depressed children, this may be more accurately restated as needing assistance *to persist* at tasks and relationships long enough to experience success or satisfaction.

As a facilitator, the classroom teacher has several more specific tasks. For one thing, the classroom teacher must be prepared to recognize a child with personality problems through familiarity with the various symptoms and syndromes that have been identified. This is not to say that either the regular classroom teacher or the special education teacher should be a diagnostician or psychotherapist. Rather, it is the classroom teacher who is typically the front-line professional who will first have the opportunity to observe the behavior patterns and symptoms that indicate a need for more specialized intervention. The teacher must be intimately familiar with the patterns outlined in earlier sections and be prepared to initiate a referral for more formal assessment and, if necessary, advocate on the child's behalf for appropriate services. It is at this initial level that the kind of informal screening and assessment discussed in Chapter 3 is critically important.

Further, the classroom teacher—in the regular classroom, the self-contained special class, or as an itinerant resource person—must also initiate preliminary attempts to determine what kinds of interventions may be applicable. Again, this is not to imply that the teacher is either a psychologist or psychiatrist implementing psychotherapeutic procedures or deciding on appropriate medications. Rather, the classroom teacher is in the best position, on a day-to-day basis and in consultation with other professional members of the interdisciplinary team, to develop and implement preliminary behavior management plans.

In the case of children with personality problems, such plans and objectives must often be specially designed educational experiences that will ensure success, foster assertiveness, and build confidence. It is important to remember that these children approach the world fearful and discouraged and need repeated experiences of effective coping as well as praise and encouragement from others. It is also important for the classroom teacher to remember that no amount of external praise can ever substitute for the child's own direct experience of effectiveness and accomplishment. Thus, it is always critical to plan the educational environment in such a fashion that objectives are largely attainable and that failures are never beyond the child's capacity to manage. While such a managed educational setting is far more difficult than simply offering words of praise and encouragement, it is likely to be far more effective as a corrective emotional experience.

In the role of facilitator, the teacher must also take an active part in encouraging the development of a total ecological context that will assist the child in developing a sense of competence, self-worth, and self-confidence. In some cases this may involve consultation with parents and family, and may require little more than interested discussion and encouragement to permit a youngster more independence or

to lower perfectionist expectations. In other cases, teacher facilitation may take the role of encouraging more comprehensive treatment of the family ecosystem by appropriate professionals.

Teacher impact on the child's school ecosystem may require subtle encouragement of activities and relationships that will give a child a sense of acceptance and belonging by peers. A youngster who does well in art may find an increased sense of personal worth and peer acceptance in a classroom in which the teacher genuinely values artistic talent. Or the youngster who is fearfully diffident may develop increased confidence in being asked to help others. A sensitive and caring teacher can find multiple opportunities to arrange the classroom setting and classroom experiences in ways that build confidence and optimism.

Examples such as these could be multiplied endlessly, but the key point to be made is that the teacher as facilitator can make an important impact not only directly in interaction with a child, but as importantly through the total ecosystem within which the child functions.

Role of the Family

The role of the family in helping a youngster with personality problems is both more and less easily defined than that of the teacher. In some cases, the family will have recognized the child's problems before they are identified by school or other professionals. In these fortunate instances, it is often the parents who will first express concern or initiate steps toward assessment and intervention. The teacher, other school personnel, and mental health professionals may then become consultants and partners with the family as all work together toward useful intervention steps. Parents may need education, guidance, and behavior management suggestions that can be implemented at home and in the neighborhood. Ongoing communication not only permits useful planning, but also permits fine-tuning of plans and actions on the child's behalf.

For parents who are open to change in the interests of their child, many opportunities are present to enhance the youngster's developmental experiences. Parents can, by example and by more explicit teaching, show a youngster that the world need not be a fearful place. Commonplace examples of such parental teaching are evident in every family as parents teach their children to handle normal fears, to face challenges and difficulties, and to cope with failures. In the case of a child or adolescent with personality problems it is a matter of undertaking such child-rearing activities more explicitly, with greater awareness of objectives, and with professional consultation. All this is not to say that parental actions can substitute for professional planning and intervention. If this were the case, the child would not likely be displaying problems of an intensity that disrupts normal development. Nevertheless, parents who are aware, caring, and open can, with appropriate assistance, play a key therapeutic role for the anxious or depressed child or adolescent.

In other instances, parents may not really recognize the existence of a problem. Sometimes the fearfulness, lack of confidence, self-deprecation, and pessimism that the child experiences are only extensions of parental attitudes and characteristics. In such instances, the teacher's role is much more delicate and efforts must be expended to modify the entire family system in subtle ways through encouragement of some behaviors, through appropriate and sensitive referrals, and through generous praise of appropriate parental activities. At times, it may even be impossible to modify family convictions sufficiently to be of value to the child. Nevertheless, an awareness that the family system displays important problems is a key step in planning for the child's development.

In still other cases, a deprecating, discouraging, and hostile family attitude may be a primary causal factor in the child's problems. While attempts at initiating changes in the family system through appropriate referrals and suggestions are still important, it may be that the teacher as facilitator can do little more than attempt to compensate for an unhealthy family system.

Summary

Intense and pervasive anxiety is the key distinguishing characteristic of children and adolescents with personality problems. Often manifested as timidity, shyness, fearfulness, hypersensitivity, self-consciousness, or pessimism, anxiety affects their outlook on life itself. When these characteristics reach a severity that affects the day-to-day ability to function, we see the emergence of clinical symptoms.

Although the possible causes of personality problems range from constitutional endowment to environmental stresses, most researchers agree that a combination of faulty patterns of learning in youngsters constitutionally prone to anxiety leads to the emergence of personality problems. Such problems may take the form of generalized anxiety disorders, panic disorders, phobias, somatoform disorders, or stress-related physical problems. In many children, severe depression is the primary indication that development has gone awry.

At this point educational and behavioral interventions are the prevalent modes for helping children with personality problems. Perhaps with these children more than any others, the teacher can play the key role of facilitator in helping them develop confidence in their ability to cope, self-esteem, and good interpersonal skills. Because their anxiety is so painful, many youngsters with personality problems are eager to find more effective ways of coping with life stresses, and even small modifications in the environment along with patient encouragement may lead to dramatic changes.

CHAPTER 5

Children and Adolescents with Conduct Disorders

Overview

Introduction

Children and adolescents with conduct disorders present parents, teachers, and the community at large with a wide range of quite serious problems. Surveys show that one-third to one-half of all referrals for professional services emanating from parents and teachers are for youngsters displaying conduct difficulties, and these numbers are probably conservative (Atkeson & Forehand, 1981). Unlike youngsters with personality problems who are most often quiet, fearful, and withdrawn, children and adolescents with conduct disorders tend to be disruptive, impulsive, angry, destructive, and aggressive. This does not mean that they do not also experience anxiety, fearfulness, and concerns about social rejection. On the contrary, many children and adolescents with conduct disorders also experience these feelings, and often the behavior problems they present are no more than confused and angry responses to their own internal conflicts.

For many years child mental health professionals tended to categorize youngsters with conduct disorders as morally deficient and incapable of learning from experience. They were viewed as acting out their internal conflicts against society. Thus, it was assumed that they did not suffer the internal anxiety, self-condemnation, and guilt that seemed to characterize children with personality problems.

However, it is clear at this point in time that such an assumption was an unfortunate oversimplification. In fact, although children and adolescents with conduct disorders do show ongoing problems in interaction with the world, many also experience significant internal suffering as well. Although their problems are often manifest in angry defiance of social conventions or destructive and aggressive behavior, they also experience much of the same internal suffering that characterizes children with personality problems. It is not as though there are two distinct sets of childhood difficulties known separately as personality problems and conduct disorders; rather, disturbances in conduct further complicate already complex internal conflicts and resentments and fears. Although the internalizing and externalizing distinctions we drew in Chapter 1 remain valid, it is clear that human problems do not always fit into neat categories, and one must always allow for the complexity of real persons.

General Characteristics of Conduct Disorders

A repetitive and persistent violation of the rights of others or of age-appropriate social norms is the essential defining characteristic of childhood and adolescent conduct disorders (APA, 1980). Several aspects of this diagnostic definition bear specific examination. First, the behavior patterns that characterize children and adolescents with conduct disorders are repetitive and persistent. Although most children engage in behavior of one kind or another that might be described as noncompliant, impulsive, or even aggressive at some time during the course of development, children with conduct disorders display patterns of aggression, destructiveness, and impulsivity that persist despite most efforts at correction including even punitive consequences. As noted earlier, the behavior patterns included under the current classification of conduct disorders were once viewed as a kind of "moral imbecility" because individuals with these behaviors seemed unable to learn from experience, persisting in behaviors that had repeatedly brought negative consequences in the past. Youngsters with such problems were often viewed as incorrigible by their parents, school authorities, and police because no efforts at correction seemed to have any effect on their repetition of inappropriate behavior.

Further, youngsters with conduct disorders did not seem to experience any consistent sense of guilt. They might be contrite momentarily as they observed the results of aggressive or destructive behavior, but parents, teachers, and others often viewed such remorse as a sham, because the behaviors would be repeated again and again with no apparent guilt. Today, it is clear that children and adolescents with conduct disorders often do experience genuine remorse over some behaviors, but, though it may be genuine, this guilt is not sufficient to prevent recurrences of the very same kinds of behavior. As a result, an important line of investigation, which we will discuss later, involves attempts to understand the development or morality and conscience in children with conduct disorders.

A second aspect of the diagnostic definition of conduct disorders that warrants emphasis is the fact that these behavior patterns consistently involve violations of the rights of others. Youngsters with conduct disorders often fail to recognize that their behavior has an effect, usually negative, on the rights and feelings of other people. This has led investigators to question whether these individuals are able to empathize with others or to form normal interpersonal bonds and attachments. In fact, one of the dimensions along which children and adolescents with conduct disorders are distinguished has to do with adequacy of socialization. Thus, despite considerable controversy, conduct disorders are divided into two categories: socialized and undersocialized.

Youngsters with socialized conduct disorders appear able to form close attachments with others and display a capacity for intimacy and loyalty, but only toward selected persons with whom they have a social bond. Toward outsiders their behavior may be completely callous and ruthless, with little sense of others' feelings or suffering. The classic example of socialized conduct disorder is the delinquent or criminal gang in which there is strong adherence to the norms and social code of a deviant subculture, but virtually no acknowledgment of the legitimacy of others' rights beyond the subcultural group (Empey, 1967).

By contrast, the individual with an undersocialized conduct disorder has, at best, superficial relationships with others. There is little capacity to empathize with another person and an inability to develop genuine affectional bonds. Such youngsters have little hesitancy in manipulating or exploiting others to their own advantage and are insensitive to the feelings of others. They rarely feel guilt or remorse regarding their behavior because they do not experience concern for the rights or well-being of other people. Their behavior is characterized by impulsive egocentricity, and they care little for the consequences of their behavior except to the extent that those consequences affect their own lives (see Box 5.1).

Another dimension along which individuals with conduct disorders differ is whether the behavior they display is aggressive or nonaggressive. Nonaggressive youngsters do not typically engage in behavior involving direct physical con-

Box 5.1 Marla M.: A Case of Undersocialized Aggressive Conduct Disorder

By the time she reached her fifteenth birthday, Marla M. had been in a correctional institution for juvenile girls for two months. In fact, she might have been there since she was eleven, because that was the first time she had assaulted an elderly woman. She had tried to snatch the woman's purse, became infuriated when the woman held onto it, and hit her repeatedly until she let go. But Marla had not been caught that time nor the many subsequent times she had engaged in similar activities. No one had ever reported her to the police for shoplifting, though she had been caught twice and reprimanded by store personnel. This was a surprisingly low incidence because she had stolen regularly since she was in the sixth grade—anything from candy bars to liquor, makeup, clothes, and jewelry. If Marla wanted something, she watched for an opportunity to take it, and then did so.

School records showed that Marla was a management problem from third grade onward. At first, she was simply uncooperative and occasionally defiant. Teachers were surprised to hear her vulgarity with classmates and shocked at her aggressiveness on the playground, because these behaviors were more typical of the boys in her school. But Marla could easily compete in aggressiveness with most boys as she had an explosive, uncontrollable temper that made her heedless of consequences. Although most youngsters sized up potential opponents before getting caught in a fight, Marla never cared how big the other person was, and the fury of her attacks even caused adults to hesitate to thwart her. Thus, for the most part, teachers and classmates alike left Marla alone.

When left largely to herself with no demands made upon her, Marla did not seek out conflict. She was not a bully; she simply could not accept not having what she wanted when she wanted it. When asked about her inability to handle frustration, Marla was really unable to present any analytical response. She blamed others when things did not go her way and tended to adopt a somewhat paranoid view of the world. Things did not just happen; someone was always to blame. Similarly, her world view was quite egocentric so that all that mattered to Marla was how events affected her.

Marla's overall intellectual ability was average. She could have done better at school than she did, but instead spent her time daydreaming. She fantasized about being a model or a movie star, but her fantasies were limited to visual imagery. Marla had no real conception of what she would do differently if she were wealthy and famous.

Marla had some interest in boys, but her attachments were superficial and transient and generally directed toward how tough she thought a boy was and how impressed he was by her looks. Though she had been sexually active since she was twelve, she had little real enjoyment of sex and tended to use her sexuality as a way of manipulating people and getting her way. Similarly, though she used alcohol and drugs liberally, her usage was occasional and she made no great effort to obtain mind-altering substances.

It was difficult for Marla to determine what actually was important to her beyond a moment's fancy. She had no particular affection for her divorced mother, and she had never known her father. She had no loyalty to a boyfriend and would respond to whomever made her feel attractive at the moment. She had no goals beyond whatever vague fantasies she indulged in about being a star, and she never really tried to do anything that might turn such a fantasy into reality apart from spending hours in front of a mirror experimenting with makeup. Her appearance was the only thing she seemed consistently to care about. She spent any money she had on cosmetics and clothes and shoplifted these items when she had no money. Others were important to her only in the sense that they were living mirrors who might tell her she was pretty.

In trying to understand and motivate Marla, teachers and psychologists over the years had explored her development and background. Although her home life was hardly ideal, she had

Box 5.1   continued

neither been neglected nor abused. Her mother had had little control of her since Marla was in the fourth grade and she never really knew when Marla would comply with a request, ignore it, or fly into a rage. As a result Marla's mother concluded to leave her alone sooner than most parents would. While Marla might, on rare occasions, be mildly affectionate toward her mother, there was little depth to her feeling, and a hug might be followed shortly by a spate of name-calling and abuse.

Surprisingly, the only emotion that Marla exhibited with some intensity and regularity was guilt. Yet even here, proclamations of seemingly genuine remorse could be followed within minutes by an angry outburst or even a repetition of the same behavior. And even in the midst of teary apologies Marla would blame others for her behavior.

At fifteen, Marla's future was bleak. She hated the regimentation of institutional life, and yet continued to display the same impulsive aggressiveness that brought her there. One promising note emerged during the first two months of her institutional stay. Observing Marla's preoccupation with her appearance, an attractive female teacher—clearly strongly interested in her own personal appearance—had been able to negotiate a behavioral contract with Marla. In exchange for cooperative behavior, temper control, avoidance of aggression, and compliance with institutional rules, Marla was able to earn points on a daily basis to be used toward the purchase of cosmetics and beauty magazines. In addition, long-term adherence to the daily behavior contract would earn a bonus reinforcer consisting of a trip to a department store cosmetic counter in the community.

At this point in Marla's behavior program it would be too early to tell whether any durable changes will occur in her behavior. However, it is important to note that her relationship with the teacher who shared her interest in cosmetics and fashion was the only relationship that had maintained genuine significance for Marla for more than a few weeks.

---

frontation with others. Rather, their behavior is characterized by the persistent violation of social norms. Nonaggressive conduct disorders may involve behaviors ranging from persistent noncompliance and failure to perform in the home or in school to substance abuse, repeated truancy, running away, vandalism, promiscuity, prostitution, or theft not involving physical confrontation.

Aggressive conduct disorders, by contrast, involve repeated episodes of violent confrontation with others, including acts of physical assault, robbery or theft involving physical confrontation, or sexually assaultive behavior. Such behaviors may fall anywhere in a range from repeated excessive bullying of peers and fighting at home or in school to assault, mugging, rape, and homicide. Box 5.2 summarizes current conceptualizations of conduct disorders.

Some investigators question the validity of distinctions among these subvarieties of conduct disorders. Indeed, some question the validity of the entire concept of conduct disorders as a useful diagnostic category. In one recent study, for example, investigators compared a group of sixty-six psychiatrically hospitalized adolescent boys with a randomly selected group of adolescent boys hospitalized for physical illness (Lewis, Lewis, Unger, & Goldman, 1984). Background information and school records were collected for all the boys in the study as well as data on the presence of such signs and symptoms as auditory and visual hallucinations, thought disorders, delusions, withdrawal, sadness or crying, suicidal behavior, sleep problems, learning disabilities, fire setting, cruelty to animals, and neurological soft signs, such as unusual patterns in walking, running, or jumping; peculiar

Box 5.2 Characteristics of Conduct Disorders

	Aggressive	*Nonaggressive*
Socialized	Nondefensive acts of aggression or destructiveness Thefts involving confrontation with a victim Has one or more friendships lasting more than 6 months Extends self for others even in absence of personal advantage Sometimes feels appropriate guilt or remorse Avoids informing on or blaming friends Is concerned for welfare of friends Persistence of theft or violence for more than 6 months	Repeated violations of reasonable, age-appropriate rules (e.g., truancy, substance abuse) Repeated running away from home and staying away overnight Repeated serious lying to parents and others Stealing without victim confrontation Friendship(s) lasting more than 6 months Extends self for others even in absence of personal advantage Sometimes feels appropriate guilt Avoids blaming or informing on friends Is concerned for welfare of friends Persistence of pattern for more than 6 months
Undersocialized	Nondefensive acts of aggression or destructiveness Thefts involving confrontation with a victim Absence of friendship(s) lasting more than 6 months Does not extend self for others unless there is a personal advantage Rarely, if ever, feels guilt or remorse Informs on friends if to own advantage Unconcerned about the welfare of others Pattern persists for more than 6 months	Repeated violations of reasonable, age-appropriate rules (e.g., truancy, substance abuse) Repeated running away from home and staying away overnight Repeated serious lying to parents and others Stealing without victim confrontation Absence of friendship(s) lasting more than 6 months Does not extend self for others unless there is a personal advantage Rarely, if ever, feels guilt or remorse Informs on friends if to own advantage Unconcerned for welfare of others Pattern persists for more than 6 months

postures; irregularities in rhythmic actions; extreme restlessness; and other unusual motor activities. These investigators found that youngsters who had at some time been given a diagnosis of conduct disorder also showed a multiplicity of other symptoms, all of which were also shared by boys who had not been so diagnosed—with one exception. The single characteristic consistently leading to a diagnosis of conduct disorder was aggressive behavior. However, aggressive behavior can also occur in psychotic disorders, in some neurological disorders, and occasionally in individuals who show no specific psychiatric disorder. Thus, one might legitimately question whether conduct disorders, whose only consistently present feature is aggression, should be distinguished from other psychiatric disorders, which may also include aggressiveness as a characteristic.

The question is intriguing and must remain implicit in any discussion of conduct disorders. Nevertheless, the concept of conduct disorders as a diagnostic classification is widespread and useful at present, and we will continue to employ it in the remainder of our study. The point, however, is that contemporary diagnostic usage is neither precise nor foolproof. Diagnoses are no more than mental tools to help us organize our thinking and research. In the real world, things can always be different from our conceptualizations, and we must remain sufficiently flexible to adapt our thinking to reality.

As we consider the problems of children and adolescents with conduct disorders it is important to remember that we are discussing a broad range of difficulties that vary considerably in their nature and severity. A six-year-old and an eighteen-year-old, both with severe conduct disorders, will inevitably show different kinds of problems simply by virtue of their respective ages. Negativism and defiance, frequent fighting on the school playground, bullying of peers, petty extortion, swearing at home, and threatening teachers may reflect a pattern of behavior as severe as that of a repeatedly assaultive and dangerous adolescent. Unfortunately, it is often the case that the six-year-old's behavior is left untreated because it simply does not present the kind of social danger and disruptiveness that the same behaviors do in an adolescent.

It is important that we consider not only specific behaviors and patterns of behavior, but also the overall personality context in which these behaviors occur. Truancy and armed robbery are of clearly different severity, yet both are manifestations of an underlying problem in relating adequately to others and to social expectations and both, depending on circumstances, may be considered conduct disorders.

It is important to remember that delinquency and criminality are legal concepts rather than psychological or educational ones. An individual is adjudged to be delinquent or a criminal depending on whether he or she has become involved with police and judicial authorities, and depending on the outcomes of those contacts. However, apart from legal considerations, it is the occurrence of specific behaviors and behavior patterns within the context of overall personality functioning and psychological makeup that are the key factors in determining the presence of a conduct disorder.

Causes of Conduct Disorders in Children and Adolescents

A problem as complex and varied as the range of conduct disorders in children and adolescents cannot be reduced to a few simple factors. In fact, the causes of conduct disorders are almost as diverse as the problems themselves. Psychodynamic theorists, elaborating on the thinking of Freud and Erikson, have proposed a number of causative factors in early childhood development and ongoing intrapsychic functioning. Behavioral and social learning theorists have investigated aspects of learning and social influence that have a clear impact on the emergence of these problems, and sociologists have made major contributions to an understanding of conduct disorders. Hereditary and constitutional factors have also been linked as causes to the development of conduct disturbances. In recent years, research on possible neurological deficits has led to new ideas about the etiology of these problems and new ideas about intervention.

However, it is important to remember that our understanding of these problems is far from complete. One may be a diligent student of the causes and treatment of conduct disorders and still experience considerable uncertainty and confusion when faced with the problems of an individual child and family.

Genetics and Temperament as Causal Factors

Although genetic theories of the etiology of conduct disorders have a long history, there is little clear supporting evidence that these disorders have a strong, narrowly defined genetic component. However, there is strong and increasing evidence that broadly conceived temperament characteristics may play an important causative role in conduct disorders. Though related, these two perspectives are, nevertheless, distinct, and we will examine them separately.

Genetic Factors. Theories espousing the view that heredity is a prime causative factor in conduct disorders have been debated throughout history, from Hippocrates to the present. Generally, there is the idea that there exists a "bad seed" that causes antisocial behavior. One example of such a view was the study of the Kallikak family, published by H. H. Goddard in 1912. Goddard reported that he had traced two lines of descent of a young man named Martin Kallikak, a fifteen-year-old orphan who had enlisted in a military company at the beginning of the American Revolution. Kallikak fathered a child by (in Goddard's terminology) a feebleminded young girl who worked in a tavern he visited, initiating one line of hereditary descent. After the war, Kallikak married a "respectable girl of good character" and had a child by this woman, forming another line of descent. In tracing these two lines, Goddard found that the liaison with the tavern girl produced descendants who included thirty-three prostitutes, twenty-four confirmed alcoholics, three criminals, and eight proprietors of brothels. In addition, mental disorders of various kinds were frequent among this line of descendants. Offspring of the "legitimate" family line included only "three men who were somewhat degenerate," two alcoholics, and one individual who was "sexually loose."

Unfortunately, Goddard's study failed to consider adequately the tremendous impact of family environment, socioeconomic deprivation, and other ecological variables. Goddard's study appeared to stack the deck in favor of hereditary explanations for complex and multifaceted problems and, eventually, contributed to considerable suspicion of hereditary explanations of complex problems.

In subsequent years, other investigators continued to explore the possibility of genetic causation of conduct disorders. In 1929, a German researcher reported the frequency of antisocial behavior among pairs of monozygotic, dizygotic, and opposite-sexed twins (Rosenthal, 1971). He found that concordance rates for antisocial behavior were six times higher in monozygotic twins than in either dizygotic or opposite-sexed twins. Although other investigators reported similar results in the 1930s, none of these studies really considered what it was that was supposedly inherited in the transmission of conduct disorders and delinquent behavior. In a review of genetic studies and antisocial behavior, David Rosenthal (1971) concluded that there were several possibilities, including brain abnormalities of one kind or another, low intelligence, constitutional characteristics such as body build, or actual genetic anomalies such as an extra male sex chromosome (XYY syndrome).

However, none of these factors is, by itself, really credible as a hereditary cause of conduct disorders. For example, although brain abnormalities may be involved in the causation of conduct disorders, there is no necessary implication that brain disorders are hereditary. Rather, the likelihood is that such abnormalities, if they are important, are of intrauterine, perinatal, or postnatal origin. Later we will examine the relationships between possible neurological deficit and conduct disorders in detail.

Although low intelligence may also be one causal factor in some cases of conduct disorder, the majority of individuals with low intelligence do not develop conduct disorders. Other causal influences must operate in interaction with intelligence in order for this to be considered an important etiological agent. In all likelihood, such additional influences are more important than intelligence itself in producing conduct disturbances. For example, although delinquent youngsters as a group have been shown to have lower intelligence than nondelinquent comparison groups (Hirschi & Hindenlang, 1977; Moffitt, Gabrielli, Mednick, & Schulsinger, 1981), they may also experience more frequent and more intense frustrations in school, have shorter school careers, experience more frequent social rejection from authority figures and peers, be more easily influenced by others, and have greater difficulties finding satisfying work.

Constitutional factors such as body build may play a role in the origin of conduct disorders, but like low intelligence must interact with other variables before eventuating in a specific behavior disorder. In fact, the very concept of physical constitution itself refers to an interaction among hereditary, intrauterine, and perinatal factors.

Finally, the notion of an extra male sex chromosome producing hyperaggressive behavior as an important factor in antisocial behavior and conduct disorders is no longer widely held. Extensive research has failed to show that XYY males are any more aggressive than others, though they may have lower intelligence (Segal & Yahraes, 1979).

Overall, there is currently no strong evidence to suggest that there is any direct hereditary causation of conduct disorders. Further, there is general agreement that conduct disorders, delinquency, and criminal behavior are genetically heterogeneous patterns of behavior resulting from the interaction of multiple, complex variables (Rosenthal, 1971).

Constitutional Factors. Constitutional factors are those characteristics that are present at birth or shortly thereafter as a result of interaction among hereditary, intrauterine, perinatal, or neonatal variables. Thus, constitution is a broader concept than heredity and subsumes hereditary characteristics. Physical makeup or physique and temperament are two important aspects of constitution and both have received

considerable theoretical discussion and research attention in recent years.

In 1950 Sheldon and Eleanor Glueck reported a study of 500 delinquent and 500 nondelinquent boys. Beginning in 1948 the Gluecks had conducted comprehensive studies of the background, personality, and physical characteristics of boys from socioeconomically deprived areas of Boston. Although the Gluecks recognized that poverty, poor schools, and economically deprived homes were important factors in the causation of conduct disorders among their delinquent subjects, it was clear that they had to look for causal explanations beyond such environmental factors, since their nondelinquent subjects were selected from the very same environment.

Upon further investigation, one clear difference that emerged between the family background of delinquent and nondeliquent boys was family stability. Delinquent youngsters came from families that were unstable and erratic. The parents in these families themselves displayed delinquent behavior. Many had diagnosable psychological disorders and alcoholism. Family life was disorganized and confused; mothers were often lax in discipline and fathers often harsh and overly strict with conflicting standards of behavior. There was overt conflict, frequent parental divorce, and poor household maintenance. The Gluecks characterized these parents as displaying slipshod patterns of family living (Glueck & Glueck, 1962).

Even more important in relation to our present discussion, the Gluecks also found distinct constitutional differences in the physical makeup of their delinquent and nondelinquent groups. The delinquent boys generally had stronger physical builds, more harmonious body structures, and more masculine physiognomy than their nondelinquent peers. Despite matching with nondelinquent subjects for age, race, socioeconomic background, and specific neighborhood, the delinquent boys continued to show distinctly more muscular, rugged physiques. As a result of their research, the Gluecks concluded that physical constitution played a role in the genesis of delinquent behavior.

It is important to note that the Gluecks made no claim that physical makeup or constitution was the only or even the most important variable involved in the development of conduct disorders. In fact, they felt it important to emphasize that physical constitution could not be construed as a direct causal factor at all. Rather, it was their interpretation of their research evidence that physical constitution played, at most, an indirect role in causing conduct problems. A strong, rugged physique, they reasoned, is likely to make aggressive behavior functionally more effective than it would be for a less sturdy youngster. Thus, a youngster experiencing the frustrations and deprivations characteristic of the backgrounds of these boys might find that occasional aggressive displays against peers or even parents and other authority figures were effective in achieving the ends he desired. If such behavior proved successful on many occasions, it is not at all surprising that it might emerge into a consistent pattern for relating to the world (Glueck & Glueck, 1968).

Although the Gluecks' research on constitutional causes in delinquency was provocative, there has been little programmatic follow-up research either to validate or to contradict their findings. The reasons for this are not really clear, and so the idea remains intriguing and awaits further development.

By contrast, another line of research on constitutional factors in the etiology of conduct disorders has stimulated extensive research leading to a fairly clear picture of the role of temperament in these problems. In 1968, Drs. Alexander Thomas, Stella Chess, and Herbert Birch published a landmark book, *Temperament and Behavior Disorders in Children,* summarizing the results of their study of temperament and development in young children. It is interesting to note that these investigators encountered considerable reproach and discouragement from colleagues who felt that research on constitution and hereditary factors was outdated and discredited.

Perhaps such resistance in the professional community was also a factor leading to the lack of response with which the Gluecks' research was met.

Thomas, Chess, and Birch reported on their twelve-year follow-up study of 136 children from eighty-five middle- and upper-middle-class families living in and around New York City. Although the families of these children were predominantly white and predominantly Jewish, there were some Protestant and Catholic families represented. The parents were generally well-educated and permissive. By three or four years of age 89 percent of the children were in various private nursery schools. Data collection techniques included periodic interviews with parents, various report schedules of parenting practices and household procedures, standardized testing, observations at home and at school, and interviews with teachers. Different staff members were used for different phases of these assessment procedures to minimize effects caused by their expectations and biases, or halo effects.

One set of findings to emerge from the New York longitudinal study, as it has come to be called, related to a range of relatively stable response dimensions along which children could be distinguished. The first of these was termed *activity level* and refers simply to the amount of movement or activity that characterizes an individual child. Children with high activity levels were often described by their parents as wriggling, squirming, crawling, fidgeting, grabbing, and so forth. Children with low activity levels were generally described as quieter and more placid.

Rhythmicity refers to a tendency toward regularity in basic, repetitive biological functions. Regularity of sleep, eating, and elimination patterns are characteristic of youngsters with a high degree of rhythmicity. A youngster who naps at different times of day, has variable eating patterns, and unpredictable bowel and bladder habits is characterized as being low in rhythmicity.

The New York investigators noted that some children in their sample tended to approach new people, objects, and situations in an interested, enthusiastic fashion. They smiled at strangers, reached for toys, and enjoyed new foods. Others tended to be aloof and distant in response to people and situations, slow to warm up and quick to withdraw. Such children might cry when meeting strangers or prefer to play with old familiar toys rather than new ones or to cling to their mother in new situations. This dimension of temperament was called *approach or withdrawal*.

Children in the New York longitudinal study sample varied in *adaptability*. This dimension refers to the ongoing responses an individual makes to situations. In contrast to approach or withdrawal, adaptability refers to the sequence of responses a child makes in different situations rather than initial responses. Although some youngsters were observed to be flexible and to adapt their behavior to changed circumstances, others tended to have difficulty changing and to insist on having things continue in familiar patterns.

Children were also observed to vary in the *intensity of reaction* they displayed to people and situations. In describing this dimension of temperament, the New York investigators noted that some children displayed intense reactions to varied situations. Such intense responses might be positive or negative, but the key consistent component was the intensity of the response itself. Although one child might have been observed to wince in response to loud noises, for example, another might emit a hearty scream. One child might love to take a bath so much that she would run into the bathroom and try to climb into the tub whenever she heard the water running, even while she was fully dressed; contrast this with another child who might simply smile or walk eagerly to the tub at bathtime.

Threshold of responsiveness refers to the intensity of a stimulus necessary to evoke a response. For some youngsters even mild stimuli might elicit a response, whereas for others a stimulus might have to be fairly intense to do so. Such thresholds were observed to vary among different children and to vary within the same child for different classes of stimuli. Thus, one child might have a high threshold for auditory stimuli, and a low threshold for visual stimuli.

Quality of mood differed from child to child. Where one youngster might be characteristically joyful, friendly, and pleasant, another might be consistently irritable and unfriendly. Again, this dimension varied independently of others. For example, a child might have either high activity level and negative mood quality or high activity level and positive mood quality.

Distractibility was noted to differ among children. Some displayed a capacity to maintain focused attention on directional behavior and to remain relatively oblivious to external distracting stimuli. Others, however, were more readily distracted by outside stimulation.

A related dimension was termed *attention span and persistence* and referred to the length of time a youngster might attend to a particular activity. Obviously a less distractible youngster would be more likely to show a long attention span and persistence. However, the two dimensions remain distinct in that attention span refers to the length of time a child might persist in directional activity even without external distraction.

Altogether, then, Thomas, Chess, and Birch identified nine rather stable temperament dimensions along which children could be observed to vary. Although the children in the research sample were not unchanging, they did exhibit fairly consistent and predictable response patterns to internal and external stimuli over time. Characteristics observed in a child at one point in the study tended to persist at subsequent points of observation.

As the New York study progressed and while the children in the sample were still under two years of age, three distinct subgroups began to emerge, characterized by different constellations of temperament characteristics. One of these groups of youngsters came to be called *difficult children* (or, according to some of the research staff, "mother killers"). These youngsters exhibited a constellation of characteristics that included low rhythmicity, predominating withdrawal responses, slowness in adapting to new situations, prevailing negative mood, and high intensity of reactions. Their parents found such children stressful and demanding and were often bewildered about explanations for what appeared to be unhappiness in their children.

Although one might speculate that difficult children were spoiled by indulgent parents, the fact is that the study team was unable to find any significant differences in the sample between parents of difficult children and parents of other children. However, it is also important to note that the attitudes and reaction patterns of parents of difficult children did begin to change later in the study as it became increasingly difficult for them to deal with the special demands of these children. More and more often, these parents found themselves experiencing guilt, helplessness, and eventually resentment in one or several areas of interaction with a difficult child. In some cases, the ongoing demands of managing a difficult child led to power struggles between parents and child or to inconsistent disciplinary patterns, or even to abdication at attempts to maintain parental control.

All these problems were even more intense when the parents' own temperament characteristics tended to exaggerate those of their children. Thus, for example, a child whose prevailing mood quality is negative and who has a high intensity of reaction along with easy distractibility is likely to be particularly difficult for a parent who has similar temperament characteristics. Such a youngster might be able to develop with less stress on both parent and child if the parents tend to be flexible with low reaction intensity, positive mood quality, and an ability to persist in goal-directed attempts at control.

Another group of youngsters in the study sample were characterized as *easy children*. These boys and girls were generally positive in mood, had low reaction intensity, were readily adaptable, and showed tendencies for positive approach toward new situations.

A third group of children tended to adapt slowly to new situations after initial withdrawal tendencies. They had mild reaction intensity and generally low activity level. Mood, too, tended to be mild rather than strongly negative or positive. These youngsters were observed to make good adaptations to a variety of situations if permitted to adapt at their own pace without undue parental pressure. Such children were described as *slow to warm up*.

During the course of the first twelve-year period of the New York longitudinal study, forty-two children developed some problems of sufficient severity to warrant a psychiatric judgment that a significant behavioral disturbance was present. In almost all cases such judgments occurred after parents had noted a concern about their child's development, which led to special evaluation by the research staff. The kinds of behaviors that led to a conclusion that a significant problem was present included:

- delayed development in one or several areas
- self-destructive or self-endangering behaviors in one or several areas beyond an age that the child could clearly comprehend danger
- inadequate contact with the environment or lack of responsiveness
- flouting social conventions in a flagrant manner at a point at which they could be clearly understood
- disturbed language or speech development
- signs of perceptual motor problems
- social isolation from or aggressive behavior toward peers
- school failure despite adequate intellectual ability to perform

It should come as no surprise that the preponderance of children who developed behavioral disturbances had been previously identified as difficult children. Further, the similarity between many of the temperament characteristics of difficult children and characteristics of youngsters with conduct disorders is also readily apparent.

It is important here to note that identification of a difficult temperamental style in a child does not mean, inevitably, that the child will later develop significant behavioral disturbances. Nor does recognition of an easy or slow-to-warm-up pattern mean that a child will not later have problems of one kind or another. Rather, such early identification of temperament styles only means that interactions with parents, other persons, and the physical environment are more likely to be difficult or easy as a function of the child's temperament. However, parental adaptability and other environmental circumstances can be regulated to the child's temperament style and, in many cases, minimize later developmental problems.

Overall, the New York longitudinal study had several important implications. First, the results of the study showed clearly that infant and child temperament styles vary from child to child, can be identified, and remain stable over time. Second, these temperament styles appear basically constitutional in nature and are present prior to significant modifications as a function of interactions with parents and the physical world. Third, certain temperament styles are associated with a greater probability of later behavioral disturbance, though such disturbance is by no means inevitable. Fourth, there is no evidence that parents of difficult infants differ initially in any essential respects from parents of other children. However, the care of such infants and children makes unusual demands upon parents for consistent, patient, tolerant, and firm child management, and in some cases parents unable to cope with such demands may eventually display changes in attitudes and behavior (Chess, Thomas, & Birch, 1967). Finally, and most importantly, the New York longitudinal study offered concrete practical means whereby difficult interactions between temperament and environment could be modified by helping parents identify their own children's response styles and work toward reducing stressful interactions.

Hopefully, intervention could then take the form of advice and guidance to parents before problems emerge, instead of as treatment after disturbed patterns of behavior and interaction had developed.

Temperament and Conduct Disorders

We noted briefly earlier that there are important similarities between the temperament characteristics of difficult children and those of children and adolescents with conduct disorders. This similarity, quite naturally, has also been noted by many clinicians and investigators, and dozens of research studies have explored possible relationships between the dimensions of temperament identified by the New York longitudinal study and behavioral disturbance.

In 1976 Thomas and Chess reported on the continuing follow-up of ninety youngsters from their original study sample who had, by that time, reached adolescence. At the time of the follow-up, forty-eight of these boys and girls had displayed significant behavior problems. Of these, twenty-four had shown recovery or improvement from earlier adjustment problems, and the remainder had either begun to display such problems during adolescence, continued along a prior developmental course with problems unchanged, or developed problems for the first time. In most cases, the nature of the problems observed conformed to the DSM-III diagnosis of conduct disorder, although several of the individuals showed symptoms, instead, of personality problems.

A study of the older fifty-eight children in the New York longitudinal study sample who attended fifty different nursery schools showed that teacher descriptions of behavior, instead of parent descriptions or clinical evaluations, could provide a basis for accurate prediction of which children would later develop behavioral disorders (Terestman, 1980). Interviews with teachers and direct observations of children's behaviors showed that those children among the sample who were rated highest by teachers on negative mood quality and reaction intensity were most likely to display significant behavioral disorder by nine years of age.

Although the original New York longitudinal study sample consisted of predominantly Jewish middle- and upper-middle-class families living in and around New York City, other investigators have extended these findings to different groups including Swedish, Australian, and French Canadian children (Brown, et al., 1986; Maziade, Cote, Boudreault, Thivierge, & Caperaa, 1984; Oberklaid, Prior, & Sanson, 1986; Persson-Blennow & McNeill, 1979). In each case, the basic dimensions outlined in the original study and the distinctions between difficult and easy temperament patterns have been replicated. One of the more comprehensive of these studies was conducted by a team of Canadian researchers who randomly selected a group of 984 children from a larger population of 6,253 second-graders in Quebec City (Maziade, et al., 1984). These researchers confirmed the findings of the New York study and also found that boys tend to be higher in activity level, have a higher response threshold, and are more often classified as difficult than girls (Maziade, et. al., 1985). In addition, they confirmed previous findings that difficult children are at increased risk for psychiatric disorder later during development, and that temperament can be used to predict later behavioral disorder as long as five years before actual diagnosis. Explorations of family characteristics showed that there is even greater risk of later disturbance for difficult children if parents show little agreement in child-rearing practices or lack firmness and consistency. By contrast, risk was reduced in families that functioned with adequate integration, agreement, and behavioral control of their children.

Despite the fact that many investigations have confirmed and extended the findings of the original New York longitudinal study, other studies have brought new factors to light. For example, a team of researchers at Indiana University, although finding evidence to support the construct of infant temperament, also found that

mothers who were more experienced as parents and who were more extroverted tended to rate their children as easier than mothers who were less experienced or more introverted (Bates, Freeland, & Lounsbury, 1979). In another study of temperament and cultural variation, researchers discovered that, although relationships between temperament and behavioral disturbance among a group of middle-class five-year-olds living in New York were similar to those found in the original New York longitudinal study, no such relationships emerged among a group of Puerto Rican children living in low-income housing (Korn & Gannon, 1983).

There are two important cautions raised by these studies. First, research findings always remain tentative and cannot be generalized without looking at various levels of influence. Second, it is critical to remember that research findings on temperament must be interpreted within the context of the *goodness of fit* between a child's temperament and environment. Goodness of fit refers to that interaction between a child's temperament and environmental circumstances that results when environmental characteristics and expectations match the child's abilities, motivation, and style of behaving (Thomas & Chess, 1984). Temperament and environment always interact in an ongoing complex fashion, each affecting the other continually as new developmental levels emerge and, though there is stability over time, there is also change.

At this point, then, it seems clear that it is possible to identify consistent temperamental characteristics in children and to distinguish among difficult, slow-to-warm-up, and easy temperament constellations. Further, there is strong evidence suggesting that temperament constellations are somewhat stable and useful predictors of later behavior disorders. This does not mean, however, that temperament causes conduct problems in any simple or straightforward fashion. Rather, like a geological fault line, temperament probably creates a vulnerability to later environmental strains that can eventuate in serious conduct disorder or other problems

(Cameron, 1978). When there is poor goodness of fit between parental and child characteristics, family life is disorganized and stressful, or when environmental settings outside the family impose additional strains, the likelihood of conduct disorder increases.

Neurological Dysfunction as a Causal Factor

Heredity, constitution, and temperament all refer to presumed biological substrates of personality and behavior. Another such biological factor that must be considered as a possible cause of conduct disorders is neurological dysfunction. Neurological dysfunctions may take many forms. For example, some dysfunctions may be anatomical in origin with demonstrable changes in brain tissue. Such dysfunctions are usually attributable to trauma of some sort occurring perinatally or later during development, and resulting in brain damage. Such structural damage may, in turn, affect a wide variety of cognitive and emotional responses and result in learning problems, perceptual problems, memory problems, or disinhibition of control functions. In a smaller number of cases, structural damage may result from hereditary anomalies or prenatal causes. Other neurological dysfunctions may be a function of physiological aberrations in the electrochemical processes of brain metabolism.

In addition to anatomical or physiological variations, neurological dysfunctions also vary in severity. Severe neurological dysfunctions are usually manifest in easily observed motor, perceptual, or cognitive disabilities. For example, severe brain damage may lead to seizures, inability to make controlled voluntary movements, or memory loss. Subtle neurological dysfunctions, however, may be barely noticeable and difficult to diagnose. Often, such mild neurological problems produce only soft neurological signs such as mild motor incoordination, subtle perceptual problems, or difficulty with right–left discriminations.

In the context of our discussion of conduct disorders, we are concerned with a wide range of mild neurological dysfunctions that do not lead to easily and directly observable behavioral signs, but instead may interfere with normal intellectual and emotional functions. Such problems have often been referred to as minimal brain damage, hyperactivity syndrome, hyperkinetic syndrome of childhood, and, most recently, attention deficit disorder. We will use this last term because it has been formally included in DSM-III and is currently most widely used.

Attention deficit disorders are characterized, behaviorally, by a constellation of signs including short attention span and easy distractibility, impulsiveness and low frustration tolerance. Onset typically occurs about age three, but always before seven, with the peak age for referrals between eight and ten years of age. Hyperactivity may or may not be present (APA, 1980; Varley, 1984a).

Attention deficit disorders, both with and without hyperactivity, are the subject of considerable research controversy. Investigators disagree on diagnostic characteristics, on essential defining characteristics, on causation, and on relationships to other disorders. For example, U.S. clinicians diagnose the presence of attention deficit disorder fifty times more often than British clinicians (Rutter, 1982), reflecting considerable disparity in the way the problem is conceptualized. When identical questionnaires are used to assess children, U.S. and British investigators can reach agreement on the presence or absence of specific behaviors, but differ in what they regard as the defining characteristics of the disorder.

There is disagreement about whether attention deficit disorders are, in fact, the result of mild neurological damage. A neurological disorder is clearly present in only about 5 percent of children and adolescents diagnosed as having attention deficit disorder. In most studies, the presence of neurological dysfunction is presumed because of the presence of inattention, impulsivity, and hyperactivity, and because such youngsters often respond to treatment with medication (e.g., Hechtman, Weiss, & Perlman, 1984a), but actual evidence is not often available (Kauffman & Hallahan, 1979). Thus, we are faced with a situation in which research studies report frequent strong correlations between attention deficit disorders and conduct disorders. Some researchers then use such correlations as a basis for assuming the presence of neurological dysfunction in children with conduct disorders because such dysfunctions cause attention deficit disorders. However, there is no clear evidence that attention deficit disorders result from brain dysfunction.

Further, research has shown that among children with known head injuries, hyperactive behavior prior to the injury could be used as a predictor of the probability of injury (Rutter, 1981). In other words, one might suggest that hyperactive behavior associated with attention deficit disorder signs was a factor leading to brain injury rather than the result of such injury.

Finally, although many studies have shown correlations between attention deficit disorders and conduct disorders, the nature of this relationship is not at all clear. Do attention deficit disorders contribute to the development of conduct disorders? Do both result from some common causal factor such as brain damage? Are the two simply different manifestations of the same problem at different developmental stages? Is there basically a single problem whose manifestations vary because of environmental factors?

Unfortunately, there are no clear answers to any of these questions. However, there is considerable clinical and research information available, and it is important for the student of conduct disorders to be familiar with current conceptual and research problems despite the lack of satisfying conclusions. The following paragraphs review a few representative studies to illustrate some of the recent attempts to answer these complex questions.

The descriptions of attention deficit disorders in DSM-III indicate that all of the characteristics of attention deficit disorders with hyperactivity are the same as those without hyperactivity except for the hyperactivity itself. However, there is some research evidence suggesting that this may not be the case (Edelbrock, Costello, & Kessler, 1984; King & Young, 1982). In one study of 241 Georgia schoolchildren in second through fifth grades, teacher ratings were used to select two groups of children displaying attention deficit disorder, one with hyperactivity and one without hyperactivity (Lahey, Schaughency, Strauss, & Frame, 1984). Additional measures of popularity among peers, self-reported depression, and self-concept were also administered. A comparison of these two groups of children showed important differences in addition to hyperactivity. The youngsters with hyperactivity were aggressive, had disordered conduct, showed an absence of guilt feelings, and displayed bizarre behavior. Children with hyperactivity described themselves as having poor behavior in school, poor performance, and as being disliked by peers. Perhaps most importantly, children with hyperactivity had remarkably high frequencies of conduct disordered behavior. By contrast, children without hyperactivity were more likely to be anxious, shy, and socially withdrawn. Both groups of children showed poor school performance. They were rated as unattractive by teachers and peers, and they were generally unpopular. Both groups of children described themselves as depressed and both had poor self-concepts.

Findings such as these suggest that attention deficit disorders with and without hyperactivity are not subvarieties of a single problem but different disorders, with the former much more similar in characteristics and course to conduct disorders. In fact, many investigators have found results suggesting that attention deficit disorder with hyperactivity should be placed in the same diagnostic class as conduct disorders (Gittelman, Mannuzza, Shenker, & Bonagura, 1985; Satterfield, Hoppe, & Schell, 1982; Shapiro & Garfinkel, 1986).

Given these ambiguities in the research on the relationships between attention deficit and conduct disorders, some investigators have attempted more direct studies of neurological dysfunctions and conduct disorders. A commonly used diagnostic technique for the detection of neurological abnormalities is the electroencephalogram (EEG), a recording of electrical activity in specific brain areas. It has often been hypothesized that at least some forms of aggressive behavior result from disinhibitions of control due to abnormal brain activity and that such abnormal activity can be detected through use of EEG studies. In one such study a group of investigators examined the EEG records of groups of adjudicated juvenile delinquents, conduct disordered adolescents, and nonconduct disordered adolescent psychiatric patients (Hsu, Wisner, Richey, & Goldstein, 1985). It is important here to remember that the key difference between juvenile delinquents and conduct disordered adolescents is only that the former have been so classified because of legal adjudication processes. These investigators were unable to find any systematic EEG abnormalities distinguishing adolescents with conduct disorders from those with other psychiatric problems.

A similar study using neurological soft signs rather than EEG recordings, by contrast, showed that, though such signs occur even in unselected normal populations, they occur with higher frequency in violent conduct disordered adolescents, suggesting the presence of mild neurological dysfunction (McManus, Brickman, Alessi, & Grapentine, 1985).

A study of seventy-one male and female adolescents convicted of violent felonies, who had a history of multiple placements in the Michigan state training school system, likewise produced similar results (Brickman, McManus, Grapentine, & Alessi, 1984). These youngsters exhibited problems with motor activities, language usage, memory, rhythmic functioning, and other indicators of neurological dysfunction. Furthermore, among these adolescents there was tendency for higher levels of neuro-

logical abnormality to correlate with more violent behavior.

Overall, the evidence linking conduct disorders with mild neurological dysfunction remains ambiguous. Direct evidence of the presence of soft neurological signs suggests that children and adolescents with conduct disorders do have a higher frequency of some sort of minimal brain dysfunction. At the same time, attempts to confirm the presence of neurological disorder using EEG recording have failed to show a clear or durable relationship. Likewise, studies of the relationship between attention deficit disorders—often presumed to have a basis in neurological dysfunction—and conduct disorders have not yet produced unequivocal findings. There is strong evidence that the two groups of disorders overlap considerably, and some studies suggest that attention deficit disorders with hyperactivity may even be indistinguishable from conduct disorders. Yet, there is not sufficient evidence to reach conclusions in this regard.

About all that can be said with certainty is that conduct disorders constitute a complex and heterogeneous group of problems, at least some of which may be partly caused by mild neurological dysfunctions. At an applied level this means that diagnostic and treatment interventions with conduct disordered children and adolescents must always consider the possibility that neurological dysfunction is a component of these problems. Medical as well as psychological and educational perspectives must be integral components of a comprehensive program of assessment and intervention for children and adolescents with conduct disorders. Additional discussion of the relationships between attention deficit disorders and learning disorders is found in Chapter 7.

Psychological Factors in the Causation of Conduct Disorders

Attempts to understand conduct disorders from psychological perspectives run the gamut from pyschoanalysis and psychodynamic theories to the complexities of social psychology research. Clinical and research efforts have focused, variously, on internal and motivational conflicts, faulty learning experiences in the family, aberrations in processes of cognitive and moral development, and the effects of social pressures in the community.

As we examine these different perspectives, however, it is important to remember that these views of causation do not exclude heredity, constitution, and neurological explanations of conduct disorders. Rather, they build upon possible explanatory factors in individual constitution and biological functioning. Thus, for example, a child's characteristics of temperament inevitably produce unique patterns of motivation and responsiveness that interact with learning experiences in the family and provide a foundation for strengths and weaknesses as the child encounters the larger communities of neighborhood and school. Genuine understanding of an individual child or adolescent displaying a serious conduct disorder requires a balanced consideration of all these levels of influence.

Psychodynamic Views of Causation. From a psychodynamic perspective, conduct disorders represent the external behavior that results from intense internal conflicts over the expression or inhibition of basic impulses.

Within the first moments after birth, the infant embarks on an endless cycle of need arousal and need gratification that continues throughout life. During the process of normal socialization the child learns socially acceptable means of gratifying basic biological needs and learns to defer immediate need gratification until appropriate times, places, and situations are available. The impulsive scream of a hungry infant gradually gives way first to the anxious anticipation for food in the toddler and then to patient (or maybe not so patient) contemplation of mealtime in the child, adolescent, and adult. The process is one whereby external controls imposed by parents or other caretakers are

replaced, over time, by internalized controls representing the disapproval, displeasure, and sanctions—in short, the values—of these caretakers. The growing child learns to inhibit bowel and bladder elimination and to control other basic impulses because of internalized messages representing parental approval and disapproval. And as the child learns appropriate and realistic means of impulse gratification, psychodynamic theorists speak of the emergence of *ego functions,* the time-place-mode-object formulas for meeting personal needs.

Because much of this critical learning occurs prior to the acquisition of language and as so much of it takes place at nonverbal, emotional levels anyway, it remains unconscious, or inaccessible to rational thought. Though perhaps unconscious, such learning is, nevertheless, emotionally intense, based upon infantile desires for approval and fear of punishment. The gradual development of these internalized representations of social prohibitions constitute the individual's *superego.*

By the time a child is four or five years old, most of these basic, critical processes of ego and superego development have been completed, and a foundation for later personality functioning has been laid (Fenichel, 1945; Freud, 1930, 1936; Waelder, 1960).

Disturbances of this developmental process can occur in several ways. In some infants and young children, constitutionally predisposed in unspecified ways, the intensity of needs and impulses may be so strong that the individual has difficulty learning to inhibit them appropriately (Bergman & Escalona, 1949). Alternatively, it may be that caretakers have failed to protect the child against the buildup of such intense biological needs so that, again, the individual cannot learn to inhibit them. In either case, the infant or growing child fails to learn how to defer gratification and wait until needs can be appropriately met. The result of failure to learn appropriate means of need gratification may then result, during childhood, adolescence, and sometimes into adulthood, in impulsive behavior, constant restlessness when any need is aroused, and low frustration tolerance. All other considerations become secondary to immediate need gratification. There is little in the way of normal moral development because such development requires consideration of the consequences of one's behavior or of the rights and feelings of others. For the conduct disordered individual, bent on immediate impulse gratification, such considerations simply do not come to mind.

An alternative psychoanalytic conception, not necessarily mutually exclusive of the first, suggests that the developing child or adolescent has made some internalization of parental and societal values, but again has failed to develop adequate ego strength to control impulse expression. In such individuals there may be considerable emotional turmoil because of internal conflict between intense superego prohibitions and weak ego control functions (Feldman, 1964). There may be tremendous anxiety over possible punishment for prohibited impulse expression, and yet an inability to defer gratification. Eventually, the internal struggle is aborted by the individual's acting out the forbidden impulse. In a sort of "damn the torpedoes, full speed ahead" approach, such individuals simply abandon themselves to impulse gratification in an episodic, unfulfilling manner. Self-abandonment is followed by a kind of pointless guilt, only for the cycle to be repeated over and over again.

The use of acting out behavior to resolve internal conflicts is often engendered in family situations in which parents alternate between unpredictable, harsh, erratic punishment and simply ignoring the problem behavior. Parental responses to a given behavior are more a function of parental mood and energy than of the importance of the behavior itself. Under these circumstances, the child cannot learn to distinguish between acceptable and unacceptable behavior because rewards and punishment are unrelated to specific behaviors, or may not occur at all.

In still other cases, parents may employ their children in a process of vicarious impulse gratification. In these situations, a youngster may be subtly encouraged to engage in aggressive or socially inappropriate behavior by a parent who is unable to deal adequately with need satisfaction. Although there is no overt or explicit encouragement to engage in inappropriate or illicit behavior—and perhaps even strong threats against such behavior—a father may nevertheless chuckle at his son's "manly" sexual aggressiveness or willingness to take what he wants from others. A mother may tacitly approve of her daughter's shoplifting or feel a vicarious thrill of sexual excitement at her son's or daughter's promiscuous sexuality. In the end, the child fails to learn consistent, appropriate social roles and experiences a sense of confusion at alternate parental encouragement and criticism at being caught.

For some youngsters, caught between parental and societal values emphasizing achievement and material wealth and the means to gain access to such rewards by limited ability or by opportunity limits imposed by the same society, another solution may present itself. In such cases the individual may maintain a marginal and superficial morality, adhering to social norms only to the extent that this is socially necessary. However, when an opportunity for impulse gratification presents itself, the individual takes it, regardless of any social considerations, as long as he or she can avoid getting caught. Psychodynamic theorists note that such "superego lacunae" are readily observed in many individuals whose moral fabric is riddled with holes.

Erik Erikson's psychodynamic studies of adolescent development have offered important insights into the processes of identity development (Erikson, 1959, 1963, 1964, 1968). Many youngsters who have had difficulty working through earlier psychosocial crises approach adolescence with a sense of mistrust, shame, and guilt. With little self-esteem or confidence in their ability to master life situations, such youngsters may develop a hostile and mistrustful cynicism that pervades their self-concept and approach to others. Feeling that they have been ill-treated by life, they may attempt to compensate for feelings of inadequacy by building an identity around such negative social models as criminals, gangsters, or superficial exploiters of others. Power over others may replace equality with others as a basic value, and all that matters is getting one's own way.

Other adolescents, in a desperate attempt to forge a personal sense of identity against social pressures for conformity and mechanization, may also experiment with and perhaps eventually develop an identity founded on rebelliousness, resistance, and rejection of social values. Unfortunately, it all too often happens for such youngsters that an important developmental struggle to resist mindless conformity ends in a surrender to conformity with one or another subcultural group whose only meaning rests in its own rejection of society.

In reviewing these few psychodynamic formulations of the development of conduct disorders, it is important to remember that they do not necessarily preclude other causal explanations. In fact, in many cases there is an important convergence of observations among different theoretical approaches, despite the fact that terms and language may differ. Careful review of these psychodynamic concepts will show that many of them dovetail neatly and often amplify research findings relating to constitution, temperament, and neurological dysfunction. Still others are easily integrated with research on moral development and social learning. Despite many weaknesses, psychodynamic theory and the clinical observations derived from it continue to provide a valuable body of astute thinking and analysis for the understanding of conduct disorders.

Social Learning Views of Causation. From a social learning perspective, conduct disorders in children and adolescents result either from a failure to learn appropriate social skills, or from learning inappropriate social behaviors, or both; and as we noted in Chapter 4, such learning takes place according to principles of respondent conditioning, operant conditioning, and modeling.

Social skills are learned responses first developed in the context of interactions with parents and other caretakers and later in interactions with other adults and peers. However, the most crucial early learning occurs within the first two to three years of life in the process of attachment formation between child and mother (Ainsworth, 1973). This early learning appears to involve both respondent and operant processes as the child associates primary drive reduction with the presence of the mother or other key caretakers. If there is a failure of attachment formation for some reason, the presence, attention, and love of parents may not embody the intense reinforcing properties that they do in normal development. Some research has shown that if the child's mother is rejecting because of inadequacies in her own personality or stresses in her life, or if she is insensitive to the child's responses, her ability to control the developing child's responses may be impaired (Stayton, Hogan, & Ainsworth, 1971). In turn, the ongoing acquisition of social skills in the child may be disrupted, eventuating in later severe adjustment difficulties (Michelson, Foster, & Ritchey, 1981; Wachs & Gruen, 1982). Such disruptions of early social attachment formation or bonding appear to be an important factor in the development of some conduct disorders, particularly those involving undersocialization (Wilson & Herrnstein, 1985).

As the child moves beyond toddlerhood into the preschool years, operant learning and modeling become increasingly important processes in the acquisition of appropriate social skills. During this period of development, it is important for the child to experience consistency and predictability in parents' responses to the child's behavior. Consistent, expectable patterns of reinforcement for specific behaviors permit the child to develop a sense of competence in controlling responses from others. Without such consistent reinforcement, responses from others are unpredictable and unrelated to the child's behavior. Parents and others are perceived as erratic and the child's own experience is one of helplessness in bringing about desired responses from others.

Additional problems in the development of socially appropriate responses may occur if parents or others model hostility, aggressiveness, inconsistency, impulsiveness, or disregard for the rights and feelings of others. In these cases the child may learn, imitatively, that one can coerce others into desired responses by force or aggression. However, as the child develops, parents are not the only models for such behavior, and children may readily learn aggressive or coercive behavior from peers or other adults.

Ample sociological research has shown that association with peer models displaying antisocial behavior is a key factor influencing an individual in the direction of aggression, stealing, or other coercive social responses (Sutherland & Cressey, 1966). The interaction of differential patterns of association with undesirable adult and peer models and reinforcement for socially deviant behavior by the peer group often results in antisocial behavior in the individual (Akers, 1985). Conformity to the norms and behavior patterns of deviant subcultural groups may bring about deviant social reinforcement in the form of conferred status within the group, associated self-esteem, and often the immediate gratification of material desires as well. This is the kind of pattern that often occurs in socialized conduct disorders where the individual has formed social attachments and experiences a sense of loyalty, but these are directed at individuals or groups whose behavior is at odds with normative social standards.

For an integrative overview of the role of social learning processes in the development of conduct disorders, we again return to the model developed by Hans Eysenck (1976, 1977). You will recall, from our discussion of personality

problems in Chapter 4, that Eysenck developed a comprehensive model of personality development based on the interaction of constitutional variations among individuals and complex conditioning processes.

In the context of discussing conduct disorders, Eysenck's model suggests that some individuals have greater difficulty than others in forming conditioned emotional responses, and in these persons such responses are easily extinguished. Eysenck termed these individuals extroverts. People also vary along an independent dimension called emotional arousability; some individuals are rather stable and placid while others tend to be emotionally labile and intense with a low tolerance level for frustration.

During the process of development, children learn that certain behaviors bring about disapproval or punishment from parents or other caretakers. These punishing responses from others are associated with anxiety, and eventually, children learn to experience anxiety in response even to mental images of prohibited behaviors. The association of conditioned anxiety responses with forbidden or previously punished behaviors is the core of what is called conscience.

For those individuals in whom conditioned anxiety responses develop slowly and extinguish quickly, there is likely to be inadequate or inconsistent conscience development. At the same time, the intense and labile emotions of such individuals prompt immediate responses to stimuli. With little inhibition of conditioned anxiety responses, or conscience, behavior may be impulsive and erratic, and the individual may pay little heed to the feelings or needs of others. Box 5.3 presents a schematic outline of Eysenck's model.

If we add to this basic model the complications presented by inadequate social attachments, inconsistent reinforcement by parents, associations with deviant subcultural groups, and imitation of deviant models, we can readily see how the interaction of constitutional factors

Box 5.3   Eysenck's Model of Personality Problems and Conduct Disorders

Emotional Instability

Emotionally unstable extroverts form conditioned emotional responses slowly and extinguish rapidly. They are more easily emotionally aroused and respond with higher intensity.	Emotionally unstable introverts form conditioned emotional responses rapidly and extinguish slowly. They are more easily emotionally aroused and respond with greater intensity.
Emotionally stable extroverts form conditioned emotional responses slowly and extinguish quickly. They are less easily emotionally aroused and respond with less intensity.	Emotionally stable introverts form conditioned emotional responses rapidly and extinguish slowly. They are less easily emotionally aroused and respond with less intensity.

Extroversion   *Introversion*

Emotional Stability

and faulty learning can result in the development of serious disturbances of conduct.

Family Influences and Causation of Conduct Disorders. Although family influences operate through the processes of conditioning and modeling, there is enough research exhibiting the negative effects of specific family interaction patterns to warrant separate discussion.

One such pattern that has been repeatedly noted in research studies on adolescents with conduct disorders, from the Gluecks' early studies to the present, is inadequate parental supervision. When adolescents are allowed to make decisions on day-to-day activities without parental involvement, there is a greater likelihood of disordered conduct as reflected in teacher ratings of behavior, frequency of police contacts, and arrest rates (Goldstein, 1984). This holds true even when social, economic, and racial characteristics are held constant, and regardless of whether the parent marriage is intact.

In a comprehensive review of seventy studies of early childhood predictors of later delinquency, the adequacy of overall family functioning proved to be a key variable (Loeber & Dishion, 1983). Children from families that demonstrated poor parenting skills, few rules, inadequate supervision, and failure to exercise discipline were more likely to be involved in delinquent activities than those from more cohesive families. In fact, family functioning proved to be the single best predictor of later conduct disturbances.

In an ongoing series of studies of families with conduct disordered children, Gerald Patterson (1982, 1986) has shown that parents in these families tend to use coercive patterns of mutual control. Patterson's research suggests that such mutual coercion often begins with parental demands presented in intrusive and aversive ways. These responses, as one might expect on the basis of modeling principles, are likely to elicit similarly negative responses from the child. If the child's aversive responses are sufficiently intense to cause the parent, at least occasionally, to back away from the interaction, it is clear that the child's response has been negatively reinforced (that is, the aversive stimulus stopped as a consequence of the child's behavior).

Stated briefly, if parents frequently use aversive, pain-eliciting means of inducing child compliance, the child is very likely to use the same kinds of behavior to force compliance in others including siblings, peers in school, and the parents themselves. These mutually aversive behaviors further contribute to general patterns of dissatisfaction within the family including marital dissatisfaction, mutual blame, and negative self-perceptions.

In addition to coercive patterns of interaction, Patterson observed that parents of conduct disordered children tend also to have difficulty stating clear rules for their children and difficulty following up on whether their children have complied. They tend not to enforce rules consistently and spend much time nagging, scolding, and belittling their children rather than matching child behavior with stated consequences.

In summary, available research findings consistently and repeatedly show that particular patterns of parental behavior increase the probability of conduct disorders in children and adolescents. These include parental conflict, inconsistent, harsh, and erratic disciplinary practices, absence of adequate supervision, aversive parental behaviors such as nagging, verbal abuse, and physical abuse, parental delinquencies including criminal behavior, alcoholism, or drug addiction, and parental mental disorders (Baumrind, 1978; Conger, 1981; Wahler, 1976, 1980).

Moral Development and Conduct Disorders. In 1932 Jean Piaget published a study entitled *The Moral Judgment of the Child,* in which he outlined a developmental and structural conception of childhood morality. Piaget's observations convinced him that children at preoperational levels of development tend to comply with rules because of a combination of fear and affection. The binding power of rules initially depends, for the young child, on the presence of the person who makes the rules. Gradually, the child is able to maintain compliance with rules because of the internalized presence of the rule-maker rather than actual physical presence. Piaget termed this phase of moral development *heteronomy.*

During the period of concrete operations (age seven to eleven), heteronomy is eventually replaced by a phase called *moral realism* in which the child believes that rules contain their own inherent moral force that exists apart from intent or situational circumstances or even the rule-maker. Piaget notes the example of a child who lived with the maternal order that one must always finish a certain part of a meal. When the youngster was ill, and her mother said it was unnecessary to finish all the meal, the child nevertheless felt duty-bound to finish it (Piaget & Inhelder, 1969).

Only as the child moves into the stage of *moral autonomy* is moral realism completely replaced by an awareness that rules govern relationships and therefore involve principles of mutuality and justice.

More recently, Lawrence Kohlberg has conducted a series of studies that have delineated more specific phases of moral development (1976). According to Kohlberg, the earliest forms of morality are based, much as Piaget suggested, on obedience and fear. Morality does not extend beyond the immediate consequences for a behavior. During the stage of *instrumental relativism,* morality becomes a matter of advantage in a process of mutual exchange with the purpose of gratifying one's own needs. It is as though the child makes moral decisions by considering "What's in it for me?" These two stages comprise what Kohlberg called the *preconventional* or *premoral level* of development in which morality is basically self-serving.

At the *conventional level* of moral development, moral judgments are initially a function of conventional expectations of what is "nice" or appropriate. Moral behavior is behavior that is approved by others. This is the stage of *interpersonal concordance.* During the stage of *law and order,* moral judgment is based on

---

Box 5.4 Examples of Kohlberg's Stages of Moral Development

Preconventional Stage

Punishment/obedience	I should do what is right so I won't be punished.
Instrumental relativism	I should do what is right so I can get what I want from others.

Conventional Stage

Interpersonal concordance (Good boy/good girl)	I should do what is right so others will see that I am good.
Law and order	I should do what is right so I will feel good when obeying rules and laws.

Postconventional Stage

Social contract	I should do what is right so others will do what is right for me in return.
Universal ethical principles	I should do what is right so that justice and order are preserved in human relationships on the basis of universal principles of mutuality, trust, respect, and equality.

---

a conception of duty and respect for authority.

The *postconventional level* of moral development is based on a recognition of abstract moral principles derived from a shared *social contract*. The final stage that Kohlberg described is that of *universal ethical principles*, which recognizes mutuality, trust, respect, justice, and equality. (See Box 5.4.)

Research based on Kohlberg's delineation of moral development consistently shows that delinquent youngsters display moral reasoning at more primitive and immature levels than nondelinquent youths (Jurkovic, 1980). Although there is considerable variability and overlap between delinquent and nondelinquent populations, adolescents with conduct disorders tend to make moral judgments at preconventional or premoral levels. One significant variation from this general pattern, however, is that adolescents whose delinquency is a result of identifiable external or internal stressors tend to show more sophisticated moral reasoning and, expectably, experience more internal moral conflict and guilt.

The key question arising from studies on morality is, of course, whether assessments of moral reasoning in controlled situations correspond to moral judgments in the real world. Research results do not provide a clear answer to this question, and various studies report different findings (Jurkovic, 1980). In one recent study, for example, a group of forty-eight thirteen- to seventeen-year-old male and female adolescents were chosen by their teachers for displaying unruly, aggressive, impulsive, and disruptive behaviors (Arbuthnot & Gordon, 1986). Among other things, these adolescents had engaged in theft, vandalism, and fire setting. In addition to teacher ratings, data were gathered on the frequency of referrals to the principal's office for disciplinary action, frequency of police and court contacts, and absenteeism. These adolescents were then randomly assigned either to a control group or to a treatment group involving discussion meetings over a period of sixteen to twenty weeks. During these meetings the students were presented with situations of moral dilemma that they discussed under the direction of a group leader. Following the training, students in the treatment group showed a significant decrease in referrals to the principal's office, while control students showed a slight increase. Contacts with police or juvenile court authorities among the treatment group students dropped to a rate of only ten percent of that for control group students. However, teacher ratings of behavior did not change.

By contrast, a similar program of moral development discussion groups was conducted with groups of conduct disordered students living either in a residential institutional setting or attending a day school for adolescents "in need of supervision" (Niles, 1986). Although these students showed an ability to engage in moral reasoning at more sophisticated levels as a result of training, these changes were not reflected in improvements in actual classroom behavior.

Although one might hope that training in moral reasoning might offer promise of facilitating changed behavior among conduct disordered children and adolescents, there is as yet no convincing evidence that such training leads to consistent improvements in conduct.

Substance Abuse Disorders

Although conduct disorders and substance abuse disorders are distinct sets of problems, the two occur together with enough frequency to warrant discussion here. There is a wide range of views in our society about what constitutes substance abuse. Some groups in our society frown on the use of any substances that alter mood or behavior and reject even such widely used stimulants as coffee, tea, or cola drinks. Others find such stimulants acceptable but do not approve of tobacco or alcohol use. Still others find the recreational use of the above and other illicit substances such as marijuana or cocaine acceptable. Still others reject tobacco

and alcohol as debilitating but accept the use of marijuana and cocaine.

Given such a range of views, any definition of substance abuse is bound to be unacceptable to some group. Nevertheless, the professionals involved in developing DSM-III definitions of substance abuse decided that three major characteristics distinguish substance abuse from substance dependence and from nonpathological use (APA, 1980). First, substance abuse disorders are characterized by *pathological use of a substance.* Pathological use might be characterized by remaining drunk or high throughout the day, repeated unsuccessful efforts to cut down on the substance or to restrict use to certain times or places, or usage to the point of complications such as alcoholic blackouts, drug overdoses, or smoking despite chronic bronchitis or emphysema. The specific substance in question may range from tobacco to hallucinogens (Box 5.5 describes some commonly abused substances).

The second defining characteristic of substance abuse is the presence of *impaired social or occupational functioning* resulting from pathological use of the substance in question. Impaired functioning may be reflected in the failure to keep social commitments, patterns of social withdrawal or aggression, criminal activity to obtain the substance or the money to buy it, missing school or work obligations, deterioration in the ability to make reasonable judgments, and more or less complete domination of the individual's life by need for the substance.

Third, the abuse must exist for at least one month and must occur enough to display *a pattern of activity.* Use of the substance need not occur daily or even weekly, but only sufficiently often that a pattern is discernible.

Substance dependence is an even more severe pattern of abuse and includes the above characteristics plus either substance tolerance or withdrawal symptoms during abstinence. *Tolerance* refers to a marked increase in the amount of the needed substance to reach comfortable

Box 5.5 Commonly Abused Substances

Substance	Mode of Use	Street Name	Desired Effects
Opiates			
Opium, morphine	Smoking, inhalation, injection	Hop, tar, Miss Emma, M, monkey	Sense of calm, peace; euphoria
Heroin	Smoking, inhalation, injection	H, Harry, horse, schmeck, slag	Sense of calm, peace; euphoria
Barbiturates			
Amobarbitol	Orally, injection	blues, blue devils, bluebirds	Sedation; sleep induction; tranquility
Pentobarbitol	Orally	nemmies, yellow jackets, yellows	Sedation; sleep induction; tranquility
Stimulants			
Amphetamine sulphate	Orally, injection, inhalation	Bennies, beans, peachies, roses, uppers	Antidepressant; energizer; appetite suppressant
Cocaine	Inhalation, orally, injection	Coke, snow, crack, flake	Antidepressant; psychic energizer
Hallucinogens			
Cannabis (Marijuana)	Smoking	Grass, hash, pot, reefer, Mary Jane	Relaxation, euphoria
Phencyclidine	Orally, smoking, inhalation, injection	PCP, angel dust, rocket fuel	Excitement; relaxation
Alcohol			
Alcohol	Orally		Disinhibition; relaxation

levels of mood or behavior change. Thus, for example, the cigarette smoker who moves from one to two packs of cigarettes per day is displaying tolerance. In the same manner, the consumer of alcohol who needs more and more liquor before showing signs of intoxication is displaying tolerance.

Withdrawal is characterized by an identifiable syndrome upon cessation of substance use. Some theorists suggest that excessive use of an artificial substance eventually replaces normal biochemical functions and cessation of the substance causes uncomfortable imbalances that are reduced by the resumption of substance use. In essence, substance abuse becomes self-reinforcing because it reduces the discomfort associated with abstinence from the substance (Bakalar & Grinspoon, 1984). The alcoholic who takes a drink to reduce his tremors and the heroin addict who injects himself to reduce nausea, tremors, chills, and cramps are both displaying withdrawal symptoms.

Characteristic Patterns of Substance Abuse

For years mental health professionals hypothesized that there were identifiable sets of characteristics that typified addictive personalities. Researchers conducted dozens of studies in the quest for a recognizable alcoholic personality, for example. Unfortunately, no such patterns have been consistently demonstrated in the research literature for any substance addiction pattern.

The fact is that in contemporary western industrialized society, drug usage is quite common and not restricted to any particular group. In one study, fully one-third of a nationwide sample of adolescents between twelve and seventeen years old reported some use of illicit drugs (Fishburne & Cisin, 1980). Two-thirds of those between eighteen and twenty-five reported such illicit usage. It is important to note that these figures do not include alcohol and tobacco. Other investigators have found almost identical rates (Johnston, Bachman, & O'Malley, 1977). It is important to remember, of course, that these figures refer only to use of an illicit substance rather than to substance abuse as defined earlier.

Although no specific addictive personality has yet been clearly defined, it does appear likely that among children and adolescents, the presence of significant maladjustment in the form of conduct disorders, rebelliousness, depression, and social alienation precede the emergence of substance abuse disorders (Kandel, Kessler, & Margulies, 1978). And, although substance abuse personalities have yet to be identified, there are characteristic patterns of drug usage (Brill, 1981).

Some individuals use illicit substances on one or more occasions on an *experimental* basis. Subject to peer and media pressures, and perhaps having observed parents or other role models use illicit substances, many adolescents simply want to see what effect such substances have. Depending on their reactions to experimental use of alcohol or drugs they may or may not move to different patterns of usage.

Other individuals develop *social or recreational patterns* of usage. For these persons, alcohol or drug use is confined to social occasions with other individuals, and substance use is incidental to the social situation. That is, a youngster attending a party may use alcohol or drugs because they are available and their use is implicitly or explicitly encouraged. However, it is the social situation rather than the substance that the individual seeks out.

Youngsters who engage in experimental and social or recreational substance usage often experiment with what have been termed *gateway drugs:* alcohol, marijuana, and cocaine (DuPont, 1984). These three substances are the drugs through which the overwhelming majority of U.S. substance abusers are introduced to patterns of abuse. Because they are readily available, thought to be harmless and nonaddictive, and often socially accepted, alcohol, marijuana, and cocaine are drugs of choice for occasional and social or recreational drug users. However, despite much scientific and media controversy about progression from occasional use of gateway drugs to substance addiction, it is likely that experimental and recreational drug usage do serve as steps toward more serious substance abuse problems.

A more pervasive pattern has been attributed to *seekers* who search out occasions and opportunities to indulge in substance use. These individuals are more likely to be identified as substance abusers since many of their activities are centered on obtaining and using drugs or alcohol. In DSM-III terminology, such individuals display pathological use, although they may not yet show a full-blown substance abuse disorder.

Finally, a pattern of regular use of alcohol or drugs may develop in which the substance becomes the focus of existence, and all relationships and activities exist primarily to aid in ob-

---

Box 5.6   Signs of a Developing Substance Abuse Disorder

Although there are no absolute means of identifying a substance abuse disorder apart from biochemical testing, the presence of the following patterns and characteristics in children and adolescents often signals the presence of a problem. Of course, some of these characteristics also typify normal adolescent experiences in our culture, and teacher and parental judgment and knowledge of the individual become key factors.

- More or less abrupt loss of interest in family and long-standing friendships
- Association with unconventional friends and acquaintances
- Deterioration in grades

- Mood swings; depression
- Diminished alertness
- Irritability; excessive anger; unusual conflict with other family members
- Slowed or slurred speech
- Weight loss or gain
- Coming home drunk or stoned
- Presence or flaunting of drug paraphernalia
- Frequent lying
- Stealing
- Unexplained possession of more money than usual
- Warnings from teachers, neighbors, parents of friends
- Arrest for driving under the influence or possession of illicit substances

---

taining the needed substance. This pattern of *dysfunctional drug usage* is identical to a substance abuse or substance dependence disorder with social or occupational impairment, tolerance, or withdrawal. Box 5.6 is a checklist of the possible signs of a developing substance abuse disorder.

Causes of Substance Abuse

Any discussion of the causes of substance abuse is bound to produce some frustration because there is such a wide diversity of potential causal factors and because substance abuse disorders often coexist with other disorders as well. Further, it is often impossible to determine whether a substance abuse disorder is the result of other psychological problems, whether it causes other problems, whether both sets of problems stem from some common underlying cause, or all three. The fact is that there is no simple causal explanation of substance abuse disorders. However, there is evidence showing the partial roles of many factors.

One of the key ecological factors related to

the occurrence of substance abuse disorders is family background. Among drug users there is a high frequency of poor relationships between parent and child often involving parental coerciveness and rejection and child rebelliousness and antisocial behavior. In addition, drug users report high frequencies of families disrupted by discord and divorce, and often one or both parents also use psychoactive drugs (Oppenheimer, 1985). It is clear that there are important common ecological characteristics in the family backgrounds of both substance abusers and individuals with conduct disorders.

Peer group affiliations are also important contributing factors. Research has shown that the most important single predictor of marijuana use among high school students is reported marijuana usage by a best friend (Kandel, 1973, 1974). One important question here, however, is whether an adolescent with a propensity to become a substance abuser seeks out peers already engaged in substance abuse or whether peers cause the emergence of drug taking behavior. The answer to this question is unclear.

Although social class and ethnic or racial

characteristics may at one time have been important causal factors in the development of substance abuse disorders, it is no longer clear that this is the case. Some research has suggested that frequency of drug usage remains higher among adolescents of black or Hispanic origin than among whites. However, these findings are ambiguous and have not been replicated. At this point neither frequency of occurrence, pattern of usage, nor drugs of choice are clearly related to socioeconomic or ethnic and racial background (Oppenheimer, 1985).

We have barely scratched the surface of the voluminous research on causes of substance addiction; however, these few paragraphs do indicate the extent of the research. There are few findings that point clearly to specific causal factors. Those that do exist suggest only that expectable family discord and personal maladjustment are associated with substance abuse disorders.

Discussion of the treatment of substance abuse disorders is beyond the scope of this book. Although individual and group psychotherapy and behavior modification attempts at intervention have been extensively reported in clinical and research studies, none of these approaches has been consistently effective. Comprehensive treatment approaches involving psychotherapy, behavior modification, changes in the individual's social milieu, and family intervention offer the best hope for effective intervention.

Educational Issues and Strategies

Undoubtedly because they are the most frequent reasons for referrals for special intervention from parents and in school settings, conduct disorders have been subject to more experimental intervention approaches than any other area of childhood psychopathology. Such interventions have run the gamut from medical treatment with psychopharmacological agents (drugs) to psychoanalytic treatment,

behavioral treatment in residential settings, parent training in child management techniques, and literally dozens of classroom intervention programs.

However, the diversity of causes, overlapping with other problems such as attention deficit disorders, and the heterogeneity among youngsters displaying conduct disorders have defied any simple solution to these problems. This section briefly examines the effectiveness of medical interventions and the respective roles of families and teachers. Chapters 7, 8, 9, and 10 present detailed discussions of a variety of intervention techniques in home, classroom, and community.

Medical Intervention with Conduct Disorders

As noted earlier, there is as yet no clear evidence that neurological dysfunctions are a major causal factor in conduct disorders. Although there is considerable diagnostic evidence of overlap of attention deficit disorders with hyperactivity and conduct disorders, research evidence has not yet proved that attention deficit disorders are caused by neurological or neurochemical problems. Nevertheless, medical intervention with stimulant drugs has been used extensively in the treatment of both attention deficit disorders and conduct disorders.

There is intense debate over the appropriateness of drug treatment for both attention deficit disorders and conduct disorders. The fact is that there is no clear rationale for the use of medication in the treatment of problems that do not have a consistently demonstrable medical basis. Although it might be reasonable to use medications in the treatment of an individual child for whom there is reason to suspect neurological malfunctioning, there is little justification for applying such methods to treatment of these classes of problems. Further, many argue, medications do not change the problems but only mask them by making these youngsters more tractable and easily managed.

Despite such controversy, however, the fact is that treatment of attention deficit disorders with hyperactivity and conduct disorders through stimulant medications has been shown to reduce the frequency and intensity of disruptive and aggressive behavior repeatedly in dozens of studies (Kavale & Nye, 1984). Further, improvement occurs in 70 percent to 80 percent of children treated with stimulant medications, independent of whether neurological dysfunction can be demonstrated (Campbell, Cohen, & Small, 1982; Halperin, Gittelman, Katz, & Struve, 1986). Stimulant medications have been shown to reduce levels of motor activity, increase attention, decrease restlessness, and improve cooperativeness (Werry, 1982). Despite demonstrable symptomatic improvement in many children and adolescents, however, there is no evidence that medication effects any permanent change in the nature or intensity of conduct problems or hyperactivity (Varley, 1984a). For further discussion of drug treatments and side effects see Chapter 7.

Recently the belief that dietary additives may play an important causal role in hyperactive and aggressive behavior has attracted considerable popular attention (Feingold, 1975). Many parents have responded to this causal hypothesis by imposing a dietary regimen on their children in the hopes of seeing improvements in attention and behavior.

Unfortunately, systematic reviews of controlled studies in this area have not shown that dietary restrictions produce any measurable improvement in child behavior beyond the possible placebo effects related to parental expectations (Gross, Tofanelli, Butziris, & Snodgrass, 1987; Varley, 1984b; Wender, 1986). Although it is unlikely that eliminating food additives from a child's diet can have any direct negative effects, there are potential problems with indiscriminate recommendations of a regimen that has no foundation in empirical research. For one thing, imposition of severe dietary restrictions on a child who is unaccustomed to firm parental control may simply create an ad-ditional battleground on which parent and child can struggle daily. Further, if faith in a dietary regimen causes parents to abandon other intervention efforts, time is wasted and problem behaviors become even more entrenched.

Educational Objectives

In one sense the development of educational objectives for children and adolescents with conduct disorders is a simple and straightforward process. Those who are constantly arguing and scrapping with peers need to learn more adequate interactional skills. Those who behave impulsively need to learn self-control techniques to prompt them to stop and think before acting. Those who are aggressive need to increase their level of tolerance for frustration and alternative ways of getting what they want from others. And those who find social acceptance among subculturally deviant peers through acts of theft or vandalism need to learn that they can find self-esteem and social acceptance through behaviors that are socially acceptable and useful.

Simple enough, it might seem, and yet literally hundreds of intensive experimental programs, billions of dollars spent on correctional institutions and personnel, and countless hours of parent, teacher, and clinician effort have not yet produced practical and consistently effective techniques for preventing and correcting conduct disorders.

The qualifications in the preceding sentence are important. Psychological and educational researchers have developed powerful technologies for intervention with conduct disordered children and adolescents. However, practical techniques that parents and teachers are able to implement in careful, consistent fashion and that result in significant changes in behavior are not easy to find. The key problem seems to be that parents and teachers themselves need to change their approach to these children and to develop the kind of self-control, consistency of attitudes and behavior, and commitment expected of the children they are trying to help.

In our view, effective intervention with conduct disordered children requires several major elements in their ecosystems. First, caretakers must recognize explicitly that, despite hereditary, constitutional, and possible neurological causal factors, the socially unacceptable behaviors that constitute conduct disorders are largely learned in interaction with others. Conduct disordered children and adolescents have not made a simple choice to behave the way they do, and we cannot evaluate or change such behaviors effectively if we respond as if they have, requiring only strong enough punishments to coerce them to change. This is not to say that punishment is never appropriate or effective, for it sometimes may have an important place in systematic programs of change. However, punitive attitudes growing out of anger are almost always inappropriate.

Disordered behaviors are learned and maintained by internal reinforcers such as self-rewarding feelings and attitudes, by material reinforcers, or by social reinforcement from others. If destructive and aggressive behaviors were inherently more strongly reinforcing than social acceptance and recognition, these would be the normative behaviors in a society. They are not. And this means that a child displaying high frequencies of such behaviors has failed to find reinforcement in the social attachments that characterize most individuals or has learned to find it in alternative, less appropriate areas.

Second, all the available intervention technologies that have been developed require at least as much energy, effort, commitment, and investment as displayed in the disordered behaviors themselves. Effective intervention with conduct disordered youths requires hard work over extended periods with little immediate reward. Because these disordered behaviors are reinforcing, they are strongly resistant to replacement or extinction. Programmatic intervention efforts may need to persist for months and years, and do so in the face of discourage-ment and repeated setbacks before hoped-for results begin to materialize.

Third, interventions must be comprehensive and include thoughtful consideration of the child's total ecosystem. Interventions developed at school that consider only schooltime behaviors will simply not work in producing durable changes in the attitudes or behavior of conduct disordered youths. Similarly, conduct disordered children and adolescents do not develop changed attitudes or improved behavior in a clinician's consulting room during weekly sessions or at home between dinnertime and bedtime. Comprehensive, coordinated efforts that give simultaneous consideration to all major components of a youngster's daily life are most likely to produce enduring improvement.

Finally, effective interventions involve thoughtful, planned changes in the behavior of those responsible for conduct disordered children and adolescents. Coercion must give way to persuasion, and random punishment to planned discipline. The single most important component of effective intervention with conduct disorders is the consistent application of planned behavior consequences. It is critical that caretaker and child are both aware of a systematic relationship between the child's behavior and that of the caretaker. Variations because parent or teacher is having a bad day or because the child needs a break will undermine programmatic efforts and, in some cases, even make matters worse.

The Role of the Teacher

The teacher of conduct disordered children, whether in mainstream or special classroom or even in special day or residential school programs, faces the complex task of providing a structured, predictable learning environment in which these children can learn that their behavior and the choices they make determine the consequences they experience. As noted earlier, for many of these youngsters the relationships between behavior and consequences often appear (and often are) arbitrary and whimsical. Often the result, for the individual, is increased frustration, a feeling of being picked on or singled out, and increased resentment at being treated unfairly. Such feelings only serve to make matters worse by increasing resentment and reducing any sense of attachment to adult authority figures.

Provision of a structured, predictable environment means that rules must be explicit and clearly stated and consequences specified clearly and in advance. It means, further, that consequences must, within reason, be realistic and invariant. An expectation that quiet seat work will be followed by a specified amount of free playtime must be fulfilled consistently. Likewise, an expectation that hitting a classmate—no matter what the reason—will be followed by a parent/teacher conference must also follow without exception.

Because conduct disordered youngsters are trying and exhausting, teacher attitudes and behavior *must* remain within strict professional boundaries by controlling punitive impulses and avoiding sarcastic, belittling, or humiliating comments, no matter how provocative a child may be. It is critical to remember that the teacher is also a behavioral role model. Meeting provocation with anger is only a repetition of a cycle that has already been repeated countless times in the child's development.

In addition to providing structure, predictability, and a model of appropriate social behavior, the teacher also serves as liaison between home and classroom and between the classroom and the rest of the school. In effect, the teacher is also a case manager coordinating intervention efforts on a day-to-day basis and facilitating communication between parents and other professionals involved with the child. This does not mean that the teacher must function as principal, psychologist, truant officer, and so forth. It does mean, however, that the teacher is the only school professional who will be involved with the child on a daily basis, and therefore must work toward ensuring that other professionals are aware of what is happening in the child's educational and behavioral programs and maintaining ongoing communication.

Finally, the teacher is an educator. Within the context of helping to develop and implement behavioral programs, the teacher must also perform basic educational tasks in ways that are stimulating, involving, and challenging. Often overlooked in interventions with conduct disordered children is the fact that educational materials and the process of learning can themselves be sources of reinforcement, self-esteem, and confidence if appropriately presented.

The Role of the Family

Parents of conduct disordered children must play a role much like that of the teacher if interventions are to be effective. Like the teacher, they must provide an environment that is predictable and fosters the development of a sense of self-control and environmental control. Like the teacher, they must forsake punitive, coercive measures in favor of systematic, planned responses to their children's behaviors. And like the teacher, they must work toward helping the child recognize alternative sources of reinforcement in more acceptable behaviors.

Such statements may seem pointless initially because in the preponderance of cases, families of conduct disordered children are least equipped to provide such an environment. As we noted earlier, parents of conduct disordered children often have difficulty with family organization, consistency, impulse control, and aggressiveness. However, the existence of these problems and deficiencies does not change the fact that the child with severe behavior problems still needs a predictable, orderly home environment characterized by cooperation rather than coercion, and by mutual reinforcement rather than mutual pain (Patterson, 1986).

However difficult the task of helping parents develop more adequate child management skills, it is nevertheless a key component in the prevention and treatment of conduct disorders. Perhaps because it appears to be an impossible social task, we have as a society avoided facing the fact that inadequate parenting is likely to produce children and adolescents who have significant problems. Instead, we address the incredible waste of human potential resulting from disordered behavior only after the fact.

There is no lack of research evidence showing that parents can be trained in effective child management skills. Parents can learn to recognize mistakes in their interactions with their children; they can learn to respond more effectively to disturbances in conduct; and they can themselves be effective intervention agents. But efforts along these lines must extend beyond experimental studies. We now have effective methods for training parents, but we have no systematic social programs bringing such training to those who need it most. Government agencies at local and state levels do not hesitate to intervene in family lives after problems have come to the attention of police or other child welfare authorities. We have no governmental agencies providing systematic training or assistance in child management and family organization *before* a problem erupts.

In effect, as a society we deal with parents as coercively as many parents deal with their children. We do not provide them with assistance, training, encouragement, or role models. Instead, when they do not behave as we believe they should, we punish them, often with the harshness, inconsistency, and erratic impulsiveness that we see them direct toward their children.

Summary

Conduct disorders are characterized by a wide range of behaviors. Generally, the two specific ones are externalizing behaviors and persistent violation of social norms. Recent research shows that there are distinctions between socialized and undersocialized conduct disorders and between aggressive and nonaggressive conduct disorders.

Heredity and constitution may play important roles in the causation of conduct disorders, but research evidence does not yet provide clear evidence of how these factors influence behavior. By contrast, there is extensive evidence showing the important role of temperament as a causal factor in conduct disorders. Beginning with the New York longitudinal study, investigators have replicated and broadened findings linking characteristics of the difficult child with disordered behavior.

The role of neurological dysfunctions in conduct disorders remains highly controversial, and the relationship between conduct and attention deficit disorders is unclear. Some studies suggest that there is considerable overlap between attention deficit disorders with hyperactivity and conduct disorders, and different investigators do not always maintain clear distinctions in their research. It is possible that neurological dysfunctions in the form of mild brain damage may play an etiological role in both sets of problems, but clear, widespread evidence of neurological disorder is not available.

Psychological views of causation include psychodynamic concepts of distortions in impulse control mechanisms and inadequate ego functions permitting the occurrence of acting out behavior. Social learning views of causation suggest that failure to learn adequate social skills, reinforcement of inappropriate behaviors, and poor role models may all play important roles in causing conduct disorders. Investigators studying moral development in children also point to primitive patterns of moral reasoning in delinquent youngsters.

Substance abuse disorders, though distinct from conduct disorders, often occur in association with them. Substance abuse disorders are characterized by patterns of pathological use of a substance, social and occupational impairment, and duration for longer than one month. Substance dependence, in addition, may involve tolerance and withdrawal symptoms.

Patterns of substance use include experimental use, social or recreational usage, seeking the substance, and pathological usage. Although there are no clear and consistent causal factors specific to substance abuse disorders, research has shown relationships with conduct disorders and other patterns of maladjustment, strong peer influences, family discord, and substance abuse in other family members as frequent background characteristics.

Approaches to intervention with conduct disorders include administration of stimulant medications, educational strategies, and parent training. Medications have been shown to have consistent impact in reducing hyperactivity and aggressiveness, in helping children to focus their attention, and in reducing restlessness. However, the use of medications is controversial and some suggest that medications are prescribed too readily.

The teacher plays a critical role in intervention with conduct disordered children through the establishment of an orderly, predictable classroom environment in which cooperative rather than coercive interactions are emphasized. The teacher works toward showing children how to find sources of social reinforcement and self-esteem, as well as presenting educational material in a way that shows the practical importance of learning.

Parents can also be important intervention agents and, like teachers, must establish consistent, predictable relationships between a child's behavior and its consequences.

CHAPTER 6

Children and Adolescents with Pervasive Developmental Disorders

Overview

Introduction

The most disturbing and puzzling of childhood psychological problems are *pervasive developmental disorders*. These problems involve distortions in the whole range of psychological functions during childhood development including attention, perception, learning abilities, language, social skills, reality contact, and motor skills. There is no aspect of the growing child's abilities or development left unaffected by these impairments, and because they are so pervasive and so severe, there is rarely hope of complete improvement. Rather, some children with these disorders can usually hope for little more than to be able to sustain the most basic levels of need satisfaction, ability to relate, and freedom from anxiety.

The classroom teacher of children with pervasive developmental disorders (PDD) faces a challenging, exhausting, and physically grueling task in trying to help these boys and girls achieve basic self-care, communication, and social skills sufficient to allow them to live with minimal loneliness, frustration, and pain. Gains with these youngsters are measured in months and years rather than days, and progress is marked by periods of massive regression into withdrawal, aggression, and self-abuse.

Yet measurable progress does occur regularly in the training and education of children with pervasive developmental disorders, and often a teacher will be able to experience clearly a sense of genuine agency and effectiveness in the child's progress. Such change may be seen through the healing of scars on a boy who had previously spent years continually clawing at his own flesh, or watching a previously withdrawn and emotionally vacant girl smile at her teacher's gentle teasing. Teachers who find satisfaction in their own awareness of the value of human struggle against tremendous odds for the sake of helping another person can find such satisfaction in educating these children.

The Study of Pervasive Developmental Disorders

Nowhere else in the study of childhood psychological problems is a historical perspective so important as in the study of childhood pervasive developmental disorders. This area has been—and continues to be—marked by diagnostic imprecision and confusion, changing terminology, and theoretical argument. Perhaps because these disorders are so devastating, there has always been an urgency and intensity in trying to unlock the puzzles of causation and intervention, which in turn has led to premature conclusions and numerous blind alleys. In order to avoid getting hopelessly mired in such confusion, it is important to spend some time tracing the historical development of current thinking and defining current terminology as concretely as possible.

Historical Perspectives on Pervasive Developmental Disorders

Toward the end of the nineteenth century efforts at classifying mental disorders led to the work of a German physician named Emil Kraepelin. Kraepelin devised a classification scheme in which he described and categorized varieties of *dementia praecox,* an early term for schizophrenia, and related disorders. Kraepelin was not wedded to his classification scheme, and accepted modifications made by others in the course of further research and discussion.

One of the most important of these for our purposes, because it included key discussions of childhood variants of dementia praecox, was a paper by Sante De Sanctis, a professor at the University of Rome (De Sanctis, 1906/1971). In his 1906 paper, De Sanctis outlined a series of questions that still trouble investigators. Are severe psychological disturbances in childhood qualitatively different from severe adult disturbances or are they variants of the same disorder? Is there continuity between childhood manifestations of these problems and adult manifestations? Is there a single major form of early childhood severe psychological disturbance, or are there several forms? Are severe disturbances of childhood distinct from mental deficiency or are they subvarieties of intellectual impairment? What is the earliest age at which such disorders appear? Is there a period of normal development followed by deterioration, or are such problems present from birth?

De Sanctis found no definitive answers to these questions, but he described instances of what he called *dementia praecocissima,* a severe psychological disturbance occurring prior to puberty, distinct from mental retardation, but qualitatively similar to schizophrenia as it had been described in late adolescents and adults. He felt the problem was characterized by emotional withdrawal, anxiety, agitation, and bizarre behavior, and intellectual deterioration following a period of more normal development.

At about the same time, a German investigator, Theodor Heller, observed several children who began displaying signs and symptoms of a serious disorder by the age of three or four years (Heller, 1930/1969). Without any evident preceding illness that might have caused intellectual deterioration, these children began to display moodiness, disobedience, destructiveness, anxiety, and deterioration of intellectual abilities—often with a loss of language. There were also evidences of deterioration in motor functions, loss of continence, and peculiar tics and grimaces. The condition came to be known as *dementia infantilis,* and some termed it Heller's Syndrome. Heller and others maintained that this disorder was distinct from dementia praecox or schizophrenia as it occurs in adults and from childhood schizophrenia.

Other investigators in Europe and the United States focused more directly on childhood schizophrenia and tended to minimize the distinctions that Heller made. Lauretta Bender was among the most influential of these researchers, and by the late 1930s she had developed a view that childhood schizophrenia is a pervasive psychobiological disorder affecting every area of functioning. By 1948, Bender had further refined this concept, and she suggested that childhood schizophrenia involves a genetically determined maturational lag occurring at the embryonic level of development. In other words, lack of appropriate differentiation of embryonic structures and functions sets the stage for pervasive disruption of all developmental functions should some sort of crisis occur that precipitates the actual disorder prior to birth, in infancy, or during early childhood. Neither in her work nor her review of other research was Bender able to find consistent evidence pointing to social or environmental causation (Bender, 1971).

During this time period, however, psychoanalytic theory began to have extensive impact on European and U.S. child psychiatry with the work of investigators such as Rene Spitz (1945), J. Louise Despert (1938, 1965, 1968), Margaret Mahler (1952), Melanie Klein (1932), and Bruno Bettelheim (1955a, 1955b). Central among the results of their efforts was the evolution of a view that negative environmental influences and traumatic psychological events are the major causative factors in the development of severe emotional disturbances in childhood, most notably childhood schizophrenia. Whether born into poor and disorganized family environments blighted by poverty and ignorance or into middle-class families where destructive emotional influences were more subtle, the view was that these children, unable to cope with physical and emotional deprivation and parental rejection, withdrew into lonely, terror-plagued worlds of their own. In numerous clinical reports and research papers, a wide range of parental characteristics were enumerated as potentially devastating to the developing child, and treatment efforts focused on modifying parental behavior as well as treating the disturbed child.

Historically, some children with serious emotional disturbances were treated in expensive, private, residential settings with intensive psychiatric, psychological, and social work interventions with them and their families. During the same period others were lumped together with mentally retarded children or those with severe neurological impairments and placed in large public institutions with little more in the way of intervention than custodial care by marginally trained attendants.

However, scientific controversies made little difference in the lives of these children and their families, and there was seldom real change in their lives.

In 1943 Leo Kanner, a U.S. psychiatrist, published a landmark paper entitled "Autistic Disturbances of Affective Contact" (Kanner, 1943). Kanner described his work with eight boys and three girls, none of whom was older than eleven. These children shared several characteristics, the most prominent of which was the inability to relate normally to people or situations from the very beginning of life. This *autistic aloneness* was manifested in a complete absence of any physical or emotional response to others in the world except for distress when others attempted to intrude into the child's world.

Kanner also observed that these children never assumed anticipatory postures prior to being picked up nor did they adjust their bodies to the posture of a person holding them. Although eight of the original eleven knew how to speak, they did not use language to communicate. Some of these youngsters had excellent rote memories, but their memory feats carried no communicative meaning to others. Some of the children displayed *echolalia*—echoed repetitions of speech—and were unable to use speech spontaneously. They could not use the word Yes as an affirmation, but would affirm by repetition. In other words, "Do you want a cookie?" was answered with "Do you want a cookie?" complete with the same intonations and inflections. Some of the children would reverse pronouns (pronominal reversal) using You for I. These children manifested a compulsive desire to maintain sameness in their environments. Any change in the location of objects, or removal of or introduction of things into the immediate environment might precipitate panic. An extension of this characteristic concern with sameness was the endless repetition of the same actions over and over, even to the smallest detail. Many of these youngsters would spend hours twirling or spinning objects, watching records revolve on a turntable with no sound, or spinning the wheels of a toy car.

Kanner (1943) believed all the children he observed were "unquestionably endowed with good cognitive potentialities." They looked intelligent and serious-minded, and those who spoke had "astounding" vocabularies. Because the children did not permit others to have real access to them in the sense of genuine interaction, formal intelligence testing was not possible. All the children came from highly intelligent families. Because their profound disturbance was present from birth with no intervening period of normal development, these children with *early infantile autism* were seen as having a disorder different from childhood schizophrenia or any other previously described severe emotional disturbance.

A massive body of research has subsequently grown from this initial description of the eleven young children, and definitional and diagnostic considerations have changed so radically that current descriptions often bear little resemblance to those originally presented by Kanner. Investigators have debated whether early infantile autism and childhood schizophrenia are the same disorder or whether they are different. They have argued about what the essential defining differences might be. And they continue to argue about the etiology of both autism and childhood schizophrenia.

The past few years have also seen the emergence of attempts—not always successful—at greater definitional and diagnostic precision. Research-based findings have increasingly replaced theoretical arguments, and present terminology is far different from that which was current ten years ago. Yet, these problems are so complex that contemporary research reports are still characterized by argument and debate. Nevertheless, there is slow, steady progress in understanding these most devastating problems of childhood and the hope of eventual effective intervention.

DSM-III and Pervasive Developmental Disorders

The DSM-III category of pervasive developmental disorders replaces a whole range of terms that had previously been common in the literature on severe emotional disturbances in childhood. Childhood psychosis, childhood schizo-phrenia, Heller's Syndrome, dementia infantilis, symbiotic psychosis, and other terms have been discarded. Instead, the term pervasive developmental disorders encompasses problems characterized by distortions in basic psychological processes, such as attention, perception, learning, reality testing, and motor development, that underlie the development of social skills and language. The term is used to emphasize the fact that many key areas of functioning are affected simultaneously and to a severe degree. These problems reflect a severe qualitative disturbance in development that is neither a regression to an earlier stage nor a delay, but a distortion that is not normal at any stage.

One might well ask, "What happened to all the other problems that researchers have been studying for the past hundred years?" The answer is that nothing has happened to them. Rather, in many cases they had never been defined clearly; the distinctions among them were imprecise; and they meant different things to different investigators. Thus, they were more or less useless scientifically, and they offered no real hope of being clinically helpful in the development of intervention techniques. The current situation is that child psychiatrists and psychologists have finally recognized that they were artificially drawing distinctions and building arguments with no consistent framework and no solid data for mutual communication and understanding. Scientific progress can occur only where there is mutual understanding built upon clear, operational definitions of terms and consistency in the application of concepts.

At this point there are fewer terms and definitions, and intensive research is offering the promise of more useful conceptual tools that can help us move toward greater depth of understanding and the development of effective techniques for prevention and intervention.

The broad category of pervasive developmental disorders includes five subcategories: infantile autism, full syndrome present; infantile autism, residual state; childhood onset pervasive developmental disorder, full syndrome present;

childhood onset pervasive developmental disorder, residual state; and atypical developmental disorder. The following sections of this chapter examine the evolution of the concept of infantile autism and explore ideas regarding its causation. Subsequently, we will look in detail at what are now termed childhood onset pervasive developmental disorders.

Infantile Autism

The term *infantile autism* currently reflects some of Kanner's early conceptions, but there are also significant differences (DeMyer, Hingtgen, & Jackson, 1981). For example, as noted above, Kanner stated clearly that the children in his sample had "good cognitive potentialities," "strikingly intelligent physiognomies," and "good intelligence." Subsequent researchers have sometimes operated as though mental retardation and infantile autism are therefore mutually exclusive diagnoses. However, others have not adhered to this distinction, and most contemporary researchers do not insist on it.

Although Kanner described autism as involving an innate inability to relate to others, he also noted that it did not resemble any known neurological impairment and implied that the children in his sample were neurologically intact. However, there is no way of knowing whether any or all of his original eleven children indeed experienced some degree of neurological damage or dysfunction. In fact, other investigators have found evidence suggesting that neurological dysfunction may coexist with or even be a component of infantile autism. For example, one follow-up study of a different sample of autistic children nearly twenty-five years after Kanner's original report showed that 18 percent of this sample had developed seizure disorders by adolescence (Rutter & Lockyer, 1967). Other studies of possible neurological correlates of infantile autism have shown that as many as 80 percent of children with infantile autism eventually develop seizure disorders (Deykin &

McMahon, 1979). The authors of DSM-III (APA, 1980) take the position that autism may be associated with organic conditions, although they are silent on the related question of whether autism is in fact a manifestation of neurological dysfunction.

In the nearly fifty years since Kanner originally described infantile autism, multiple diagnostic systems have emerged to the point that "there are nearly as many different systems as there are investigators" (DeMyer, Hingtgen, & Jackson, 1981). However, in order to maintain the terminological and diagnostic consistency essential to progress in this area, we will adhere closely to the system proposed in DSM-III.

Signs and Symptoms of Infantile Autism

By definition, infantile autism is characterized primarily by autistic aloneness, a serious and pervasive lack of responsiveness to other people. Autistic children function without seeming to be aware of the presence or absence of other people. When people are present, they may be perceived and used as objects rather than as persons. It is not uncommon for an autistic child to use part of another person's body as though it were a tool—for example, using someone's hand to turn on a light switch without interacting at all with the person the hand is attached to. There is often little apparent interest in or attachment to them.

Infants with autism do not develop expectable responses to caretakers: they do not cuddle, do not smile in response to their mother's presence, do not seek or make eye contact, and do not appear to like being held or touched. Often they do not show the stranger anxiety so typical during the latter part of the first year. As they grow older, autistic children may duplicate the play activities of other children, but without any interaction or relatedness.

Language may be absent or present, but when it is present it is often, as Kanner noted, used peculiarly. Approximately half of all autistic children never develop any useful speech (Campbell & Green, 1985). Those autistic children who do have language are echolalic. Another of the peculiarities of autistic speech is pronominal reversal. Most autistic children who have language tend to use it literally, concretely, and idiosyncratically so that meanings are unclear. Apart from the mimicry in echolalic speech, autistic children may use speech tones and inflections in unusual ways. One common tonal distortion among autistic children is the use of questionlike rising inflections at the end of statements. Sometimes there are stereotyped repetitions of meaningless phrases in a singsong tone.

Some autistic youngsters develop habits of using unusual nonspeech sounds. These may include tongue clicking, repetition of nonsense syllables, screeches, and screams. There is no apparent attempt to communicate through such sounds, and often they seem to be no more than self-stimulatory behavior.

One of the key characteristics of infantile autism noted by Kanner and subsequently confirmed by many other investigators is an obsessive concern with maintenance of sameness in the environment (Rimland, 1964). Many autistic children develop an acute awareness of the placement of objects and, sometimes, even of people in their environment, and insist that there be no changes in these objects. The arrangement of furniture, placement of toys, the way books are shelved, even table settings may become issues of major importance to an autistic child who will resist changed arrangements or even be thrown into a rage or panic when changes occur.

Some autistic children develop strong attachments to or preoccupations with odd or peculiar objects—a wheel detached from a toy, a dead flashlight battery, a piece of yarn or string. Other youngsters become trapped in repetitive cycles such as flipping a light switch, twirling an empty record player turntable, clutching a piece of wood, or staring at a fan.

Still other autistic children may become obsessed with a particular topic such as weather and listen to weather reports, watch for changes in weather, and talk only about weather. Those with higher intelligence may show fascination with rote topics such as train schedules or lists of dates. In his classic study of autistic children, Bernard Rimland (1964) described one youngster who developed a preoccupation with water heaters. This child would stare at water heaters, search them out in a new building, and leaf through magazines and catalogues looking for pictures of water heaters.

A few autistic youngsters have been described as showing *idiot savant* performance. Literally translated as "wise idiot," the term refers to youngsters who show islets of normal or even brilliant ability while most other areas of functioning are severely impaired. Kanner described autistic youngsters with the ability to do rapid and accurate rote calculations, and others have mentioned children with unusual musical ability, rote memory, or mathematical talent. However, these abilities are most typically useless, because they do not involve goal-oriented performances or genuine involvement with other people or with the remainder of the child's environment.

Other commonly occurring behaviors in children with infantile autism include self-abusive behavior, unprovoked episodes of laughing, crying, or rage, unusually high or low pain thresholds, failure to recognize dangers, hand and finger twirling, and constant rhythmic body movements and rocking.

Finally, and contrary to early speculations about infantile autism, most autistic children also show severe cognitive deficits, reflected in scores on standardized intelligence tests. Because the children Kanner studied looked intelligent, sometimes had striking vocabularies, often showed unusual rote memory abilities, and became easily preoccupied with aspects of their environments, Kanner believed autistic children were at least of normal intelligence, and perhaps typically brighter than average. Unfortunately, subsequent research has not borne out Kanner's expectations about the intelligence of autistic children. In one of the most comprehensive studies of the intelligence of autistic children, Marian DeMyer and her associates examined 135 autistic boys and girls at an average age of 5.2 years (DeMyer, et al., 1974). Nearly three-fourths of these children had test IQs below 52, and fewer than 3 percent had IQs above 85. Retesting of seventy of these children six years later showed remarkable stability in test IQs, and even those who did show some improvement remained in the retarded range of intellectual functioning. Others present slightly more optimistic figures and estimate that approximately half of all children with infantile autism are moderately, severely, or profoundly retarded; one-fourth are mildly retarded; and one-fourth have IQs above seventy (Campbell & Green, 1985). In any case, it is clear that infantile autism is associated with severe and pervasive deficits in intellectual functioning.

Causes of Infantile Autism

Speculation about the causes of infantile autism has covered the entire spectrum of possibilities from those that are frankly environmental to others that look entirely at genetic and constitutional factors, with virtually every combination in between. Nearly three dozen distinguishable theories regarding the causation of infantile autism have been presented since the original delineation of this syndrome in 1943.

Most theories of the causation of infantile autism can be viewed as organic, organic and experiential, or experiential (Hingtgen & Bryson, 1972). Organic theories generally focus on possible causes in the child's hereditary endowment, interaction between genetic factors and intrauterine environment, or some form of organic trauma occurring prior to birth, during delivery, or shortly after birth. These *nature theories* (DeMyer, Hingtgen, & Jackson, 1981) assume that the autistic child is biologically abnormal, and that parental or other environmental influences have little impact on the child's condition. By contrast, *nurture theories* develop

from a premise that the autistic child is biologically normal, but very early in life encounters malignant influences that lead to the development of severe psychological deficit. Such theories generally place major responsibility for the development of the disorder specifically upon the child's parents. *Nature-nurture theories* of causation suggest that autism develops when a biologically vulnerable child encounters early negative environmental influences such as emotional deprivation or extreme parental rejection.

It would be impossible as well as pointless to enumerate all of these views here. However, it is important that students of this disorder have some familiarity with the evolution of theory and research, and so we will examine a few of the more influential etiological views. At the same time, we will summarize relevant historical and current research.

Experiential/Nurture Theories. The earliest concepts of causation in infantile autism were heavily influenced by psychoanalytic or psychodynamic theories of personality as well as by Kanner's observations. Because the defining characteristics of infantile autism included failure to relate to people and profound aloneness, it is not surprising that Kanner also examined the social characteristics of the parents of autistic children. In concluding his report he noted that the parents of autistic children tended to be highly intelligent people—four fathers were psychiatrists, one a prominent lawyer, one a chemist, and others were successful businessmen and academics. Nine of the eleven mothers were college graduates at a time when relatively few women completed college. Among grandparents and other relatives, many were prominent scientists and business people. These parents were also described as rather obsessive and as rather coldhearted, and even the successful marriages among then tended to be "cold and formal affairs" (p. 648).

Considering these early descriptions of the parents of autistic children as cold, aloof, distant, and formal, a theoretical view developed suggesting that emotional deprivation was the key factor leading to the development of autism. Autistic children seemed to have developed in families characterized by "emotional refrigeration" in which there was little genuine warmth or easy spontaneity (Eisenberg, 1957; Eisenberg & Kanner, 1956). In the absence of warmth, affection, and loving support, it was presumed that autistic children failed to develop adequate emotional bonds to their parents and remained locked inside themselves, relating more adequately to things than to people.

Despite a lack of empirical evidence, the view that deficient parenting is the key causal factor in the development of infantile autism has undergone many variations. Various theorists have suggested that infantile autism stems from inadequate stimulation from the mother, failure to satisfy infant needs and maternal repression of infant impulses, deprivation of sensory stimulation during critical periods of development, and deficient physical contact and touching of the infant by the mother (DeMyer, Hingtgen, & Jackson, 1981).

It is important to note that many nurture theorists have clearly stated that the autistic child, as an infant, probably had innate deficiencies in the ability to form normal emotional bonds with his or her parents or hypersensitivity to environmental stresses (e.g., Betelheim, 1967; Kanner, 1943). Nevertheless, the impact of these theories has been strong enough that the ideas filtering down to individual clinicians, teachers, and parents erroneously emphasize—almost to the complete exclusion of other factors—the role of defective parenting in the causation of infantile autism.

Organic/Nature Theories. In marked contrast to theories emphasizing the role of parents in the causation of infantile autism are those that view the disorder as the result of biological abnormalities. Most of these theories postulate an anatomical or structural defect in the infant that, in turn, interferes with normal perceptual, cognitive, affective or emotional, or linguistic development.

An early proponent of an organic theory of infantile autism was Bernard Rimland (1964). In Rimland's view, children with infantile autism are "grossly impaired in a function basic to all cognition: the ability to relate new stimuli to remembered experience" (p. 79). Thus, an autistic child is unable to develop meaningful concepts or to integrate experiences into comprehensible wholes. Experiences are individual, discrete, meaningless. What is more, because of this deficit the autistic child cannot relate emotional experiences with cognitive ones. For most infants and children, bonding with the mother and other significant figures seems to occur because positive emotions are experienced in the presence of those figures. But for the autistic child who cannot relate and integrate experiences no such expectations develop. As Rimland put it: "No association between 'pleasure' and 'mother'; no affection for mother" (p. 82).

This view of cognitive deficits in infantile autism goes a long way toward explaining many characteristic features of the disorder. Echolalic speech, pronominal reversal, and extreme concreteness could be reflections of the autistic youngster's inability to develop a concept of "I" or "you," and thus to inappropriate language usage. For example, a child may store the sentence, "Do you want some milk?" literally and without analysis of all its components. Subsequently, the child simply repeats, "Do you want some milk?" to express a desire for milk, with no awareness of the multiple, distinct components of meaning involved in this simple sentence. Similarly, the child's insistence on preservation of sameness and preoccupation with repetitive mechanical manipulation could well stem from a need to maintain order in what, otherwise, is a highly unpredictable and chaotic experiential world.

Building on this hypothesized deficit in the ability to relate new and remembered stimuli in a meaningful way, Rimland then speculated about the neurological structures that mediate such functions normally and considered what defective neurological structures could cause the problems observed in autistic children. A likely structural candidate, in his view, was the reticular activating system of the brain, a neural system that serves as a kind of central relay system or switchboard that controls awareness of incoming stimuli.

Although other investigators have also suspected that defects in the reticular activating system are responsible for autistic phenomena (e.g., Hutt & Hutt, 1970), this is by no means the only neural structure that has been implicated. Some feel that the key problems may be motivational, emotional, or attentional defects rather than cognitive ones (Fein, Skoff, & Mirsky, 1981). And apart from structural defects, many investigators have suggested physiological malfunctions including faulty metabolism as potential organic causes of infantile autism. Unfortunately, there is still no evidence, after more than forty years of intensive investigation, showing clear and specific organic causes of the disorder.

Organic–Experiential/Nature–Nurture Theories. Organic/experiential or nature/nurture theories of the causation of infantile autism have grown out of attempts to reconcile conflicting sets of research findings and to integrate these with clinical observations. Most often investigators pursuing this line of investigation have hypothesized that biologically vulnerable infants encountering less than optimal parenting are most likely to develop infantile autism. Infants with an innate vulnerability but exceptionally effective parenting would not actually develop the disorder, while those with milder organic defects but less effective, or even pathological parenting, would exhibit the signs and symptoms of autism. The specific defects postulated by organic/experiential theorists run the gamut of those hypothesized by organic theorists, but with the key addition that biological factors are seen as only predisposing and not as actually causing the disorder in the absence of traumatic early experiences or defective parenting.

Research Findings on the Causation of Infantile Autism

Ideally, theory and research should develop apace with each other. Unfortunately, the realities of clinical research do not often conform to ideals, and theorizing often outpaces solid research foundations. This has been the case with the study of infantile autism.

Following Kanner's 1943 report on the eleven autistic children, studies on the causes of this mystifying disorder began gradually to appear in the literature. Many theorists, struck by the consistencies that Kanner (1949) observed in the parents of autistic children, focused their attention on parental pathology or mishandling as the causes of the problem. Despite his own description of autistic children as innately incapable of forming emotional attachments, Kanner's subsequent reports noted that parents of autistic children were cold, humorless, perfectionist individuals. Surprisingly, in view of characteristics suggesting patterns of emotional distance from others, parents of autistic children were noted to have unusually low rates of mental illness, and were consistently described as highly intelligent. Further, there were also strikingly low rates of divorce and separation among these couples. Nevertheless, the view emerged that absence of parental warmth and closeness caused the autistic infant to turn away from parental distance or rejection and "to seek comfort in solitude" (Kanner, 1949, p. 424).

Despite extensive theorizing about parental causation of autism, however, actual research evidence supporting such a view failed to materialize. Instead, when adequately controlled research studies began to appear in great number, they showed that parents of autistic children were neither colder nor less responsive than parents of nonautistic children (Cox, Rutter, Newman, & Bartak, 1975), nor did they have a significantly higher degree of psychopathology than other parents (McAdoo & DeMyer, 1978).

In one study, Marian DeMyer (1972) and her associates interviewed parents of autistic children and parents of a carefully matched group of normal children. They found that parents of autistic youngsters did not differ from other parents in acceptance of their children as infants, in warmth, nurturance, feeding practices, or physical contact with their children. Nor is there evidence that parents of autistic children differ in cognitive characteristics from normal parents. Investigators comparing the cognitive characteristics of parents of a group of fifteen autistic boys with parents of a matched group of normal boys found no meaningful differences between them (Lennox, Callias, & Rutter, 1977). A wide range of other studies have failed to reveal any differences between parents of autistic children and parents of nonautistic children in socioeconomic status (Schopler, Andrews, & Strupp, 1979), linguistic interactions with their children (Frank, Allen, Stein, & Meyers, 1976), or maternal age (Steinhausen, Gobel, Breinlinger, & Wohlleben, 1984).

Views regarding the parental role in the etiology of infantile autism have changed so significantly since the syndrome was first described in 1943 that clinicians are currently advised that "parents should be assured and convinced that they are not responsible for the child's apparent refusal to interact with the world" (Morgan, 1984).

Although the influence of views suggesting parental behavior as a major causal factor in infantile autism has declined, research on other aspects of the disorder has burgeoned since 1970. The number, range, and diversity of these studies defies classification or simple summary. Instead, we will try to sample a few of the more significant studies in order to understand current thinking about this disorder.

Research on the prevalence of infantile autism has consistently shown that it is, fortunately, an infrequent problem. Kanner said that he had diagnosed only 150 cases of infantile autism among the approximately 20,000 children he had seen during his thirty years of professional practice.

In 1970, Darold A. Treffert (Treffert, 1970), then superintendent of a Wisconsin state hospital, conducted a comprehensive survey of Wisconsin treatment facilities to determine the frequency of autism during the five-year period from 1962 to 1967. Treffert was able to find only 280 unduplicated cases of autism and childhood schizophrenia from among an estimated population of 899,750 children in Wisconsin between the ages of three and twelve. Selecting from this total of 280 children only those who fit the classical symptoms of infantile autism, Treffert found only seventy cases, a rate of occurrence of 0.7 cases per 10,000 children. Treffert found that males suffering from autism outnumbered females by more than three to one. The average age of fathers at the time of the autistic child's birth was 33.5 years and the average of mothers was 28.6 years, higher than the average ages for parents of nonautistic psychotic children. Parents' educational achievement was also higher than for nonautistic psychotic children, providing mild support for early notions about parents of autistic children. By contrast, rates of psychiatric disorder were also higher for these parents, a finding directly contrary to early speculations.

A recent investigation of the prevalence of infantile autism (Steinhausen, Gobel, Breinlinger, & Wohlleben, 1986) involved a survey of children of Berlin, West Germany. This study identified fifty-two autistic children who met rigorous research criteria for the diagnosis of infantile autism suggested in 1978 by Michael Rutter, a British investigator. These criteria include (1) onset before thirty months of age; (2) impaired social development; (3) delayed and deviant language development; and (4) insistence on the maintenance of sameness in the environment (Rutter, 1978).

Based on a total population of 279,616 children under the age of fifteen, Rutter's identification of fifty-two autistic children yielded a prevalence rate of 1.86 cases of infantile autism per 10,000 children. This rate is more than double that found by Treffert, but is quite close to the results of other studies in England and Sweden (Gillberg & Schaumann, 1982; Wing, Yeates, Brierly, & Gould, 1976). As in other studies, the disorder is more frequent in males than in females, but there were no significant differences in family socioeconomic background between autistic and nonautistic children.

At this point in time it is clear that infantile autism is a rare disorder, but there is no consistent evidence to show that parents of autistic children differ significantly from other parents in any respects, except, possibly age—parents of autistic children on the average are perhaps five or more years older than parents of nonautistic children (Links, 1980). Even this difference, however, is questionable (Stinehausen, et al., 1984).

In the absence of clear family or environmental differences, investigators have explored a range of other etiological possibilities. Several studies of possible genetic causation in infantile autism have failed to show strong evidence, although concordance rates for autism may be slightly higher in monozygotic twins than in dizygotic twins (Folstein & Rutter, 1977; Ritvo, Freeman, Mason-Brothers, Mo., & Ritvo, 1985). However, even this evidence may not show genetic influence so much as problems in prenatal environment, since even identical twins do not share identical uterine environments.

Extensive research has focused on neurobiological defects as possible causal factors in infantile autism. These studies have ranged from examinations of the reticular activating system, as suggested by Rimland, to other brain structures such as the limbic system, ventricles, and temporal lobes.

In one such study, reported cases of children who had been diagnosed as psychotic or autistic, had died, and had subsequently been autopsied were investigated (Darby, 1976). Of thirty-three such cases, twenty-seven showed identifiable neuropathology, though the specific nature of pathological findings varied. Some of the individuals had clear structural changes, but many showed generalized, nonspecific atrophies or degeneration.

Another approach to the study of possible neurological deficit is through electrical activity in the brain. The general format of such studies is to take electroencephalograms (EEGs) of children diagnosed as autistic and to compare these with EEG recordings from other groups of children. In one such study, EEG recordings of children classified as autistic were compared with EEG recordings of nonpsychotic mentally retarded youngsters, hospitalized mentally ill children, and a group of normal controls (Small, 1975). In this study, 64 percent of the autistic children showed EEG abnormalities as compared with 54 percent of hospitalized mentally ill children, 40 percent of retarded children, and less than 6 percent for normal control subjects. Unfortunately, the results of other, similar studies do not provide consistently similar results, and in many cases the results of different studies directly contradict each other. In reviewing EEG studies of autistic and other psychotic children, Angela James and Robert Barry, a pair of Australian investigators, found that reported EEG abnormalities in various studies ranged from 13 percent to 83 percent (James & Barry, 1980). They noted that such discrepancies can stem from factors as varied as misdiagnosis, differences in classification systems, EEG artifacts, and the difficulties inherent in examining young, disturbed children who are uncooperative, inattentive, and constantly moving.

A third approach to exploring differences in neurological integrity and functioning in children with infantile autism is to examine brain metabolism (Rumsey, et al., 1985). Using modern positron emission tomography (PET), a group of investigators studied brain metabolic functions in autistic men. PET scanning is a technique for examining actual brain functioning in different brain areas by measuring amounts of radioactive material as it is metabolized. Adults were used in this study rather than children because of hazards associated with exposure to radiation for children. A group of ten men with histories compatible with DSM-III criteria for infantile autism were subjects in this study. Results of PET scanning in autistic men were then compared with those of age-matched normal, healthy men. These investigators found no deficiencies in resting cerebral metabolism in autistic men. There were diffuse elevations in resting metabolic rates in the autistic group as a whole, but there was also sufficient overlap with the normal group to obscure the meaning of any differences. Finally, autistic men showed greater extremes in relative metabolic rates in specific regions as compared with whole brain rates and greater asymmetry in one or more brain regions. Thus, as with EEG studies, there are findings suggestive of differences in brain functioning, but with no strong conclusions yet possible.

Finally, one might also attempt to determine the presence of neurological damage by looking for evidence of pre- , peri- , and postnatal injuries as documented in medical records. Investigators at the UCLA Neuropsychiatric Institute examined records of 181 individuals in the Registry for Genetic Studies of Autism at UCLA (Mason-Brothers, et al., 1987). These researchers looked for the presence of thirty-four different possible complicating factors in the pregnancies and deliveries of mothers of autistic children. These factors included, for example, presence of bleeding during pregnancy, threatened abortion, toxemia, rubella, complications during delivery, prematurity, infant jaundice, and need for oxygen administration after birth. No pre-, peri-, or postnatal event was uniquely associated with later diagnosis of autism, although mothers who had only one autistic child showed a higher frequency of events such as bleeding, flulike symptoms during pregnancy, and taking of medications when compared with mothers of more than one autistic child.

The few studies we have outlined here are representative of extensive recent and current research on organic causation in infantile autism. In most instances, differences can be demonstrated between autistic individuals and controls on such variables as EEG functioning, cerebral metabolism, brain stem functioning (Ornitz, Atwell, Kaplan, & Westlake, 1985), and brain biochemistry (Young, Cohen, Brown, & Caparulo, 1978).

The fact remains, however, that we still have no clear understanding of the organic mechanisms contributing to the development of infantile autism, though there no longer seems any doubt that greater technical sophistication will eventually reveal such mechanisms.

However, we do know, with reasonable certainty, that autistic children differ from others on a wide range of linguistic, intellectual, perceptual, and learning variables. Children with infantile autism show loss of speech or failure to develop speech (Kurita, 1985); they display severe cognitive deficits (DeMyer, Hingtgen, & Jackson, 1981); and they are terribly isolated, locked inside themselves by impaired abilities to relate to others (Fein, Pennington, Markowitz, Braverman, & Waterhouse, 1986).

Sadly, the outcomes of this devastating disorder have been very poor (DeMyer, et al., 1983; Rutter & Lockyer, 1967). At best, only 1 percent to 2 percent of autistic children ever develop normal functioning, and 5 percent to 19 percent achieve borderline normal functioning (DeMyer, Hingtgen, & Jackson, 1981). Despite some symptomatic improvement in adults with residual autism, the overwhelming majority continue to exhibit severe social impairments, and many continue to display the behavioral peculiarities and stereotyped movements characteristic of children with autism (Rumsey, Andreasen, & Rapoport, 1986). In one of the most thorough follow-up studies to date, investigators at the National Institute of Mental Health examined fourteen adult men between the ages of eighteen and thirty-nine whose developmental histories showed clearly the presence of infantile autism (Rumsey, Rapoport, & Sceery, 1985). These individuals and their families were interviewed, the autistic adults observed over time, structured rating scales were completed, and psychological tests were administered. The results of this comprehensive study showed that, as adults, these individuals retained many social and behavioral peculiarities that continued to mark them as different. They had many stereotyped and inappropriate behaviors including peculiar hand movements, perseveration, the smelling of objects, and episodes of nudity or partial undress. They had occasional temper outbursts and were occasionally aggressive and destructive. They did not show typical schizophrenic symptoms, but instead continued to manifest behaviors and thought processes characteristic of autistic children and adolescents. Although a few had developed normal language, most showed ongoing language deficits, in some cases as severe as complete mutism. In every case adaptive functioning was below normal or at the lowest end of the normal range. Only a few had competitive jobs, and only one had friendships outside his family. None was married, nor was there any likelihood that they ever would be. The parents of these adults suffering from autism showed a high level of commitment to their children, and the researchers found them warm,

dedicated, and unrelenting in their efforts to help their sons.

Childhood Onset Pervasive Developmental Disorders

No less devastating in their overall impact on the lives of afflicted individuals and their families are *childhood onset pervasive developmental disorders*. Like infantile autism, this disorder affects virtually every aspect of a child's existence and a family's life. And like infantile autism, childhood onset pervasive developmental disorders also have an impact on a child's intellectual, emotional, social, and behavioral development and leave no area of functioning undamaged. Prognosis for improvement is poor, and for normal functioning virtually nonexistent. Box 6.1 summarizes distinctions between infantile autism and childhood onset pervasive developmental disorders.

Even in the face of enlightened approaches

Box 6.1 DSM-III Distinctions Between Infantile Autism and Childhood Onset Pervasive Developmental Disorders

Infantile Autism	*Childhood Onset Pervasive Developmental Disorders*
1. Onset before thirty months	Onset between thirty months and twelve years of age
2. Bizarre responses to different environmental stimuli; insistence on sameness; unusual interest in or attachments to objects or people who are treated as objects	At least three of the following responses: sudden, catastrophic anxiety in response to everyday events; inappropriate or constricted emotions; sudden rages; resistance to change; oddities of motor movements; abnormal speech and/or voice tone; over- or underreactivity to sensory stimulation; self-injurious behavior
3. Gross deficits in language development and peculiar speech patterns including pronominal reversal, echolalia, metaphorical language	Idiosyncratic use of language as noted above
4. Absence of delusions, hallucinations, loosening of associations	Absence of delusions, hallucinations, loosening of associations

to the care of disturbed and retarded children and adolescents, these unfortunate youngsters show such terrible disruptions of development and functioning that most often they continue to be cared for in institutional settings in which adequate controls can be provided to ensure their safety, though there is little yet that can be done to provide much hope of eventual normal functioning.

DSM-III and Childhood Onset Pervasive Developmental Disorders

According to DSM-III, the key characteristics of childhood onset pervasive developmental disorder (hereafter referred to as COPDD) are profound and pervasive disruptions in social relations and multiple behavioral peculiarities with onset after thirty months and before twelve years of age.

Prior to the publication of DSM-III in 1980, COPDD did not exist as a diagnostic category. Instead, there were a multiplicity of diagnostic terms encompassing a broad range of severe childhood disturbances. The most commonly used of these terms was *childhood schizophrenia*, reflecting a belief that early and severe disruptions of functioning were similar in etiology, characteristics, and course to adult forms of schizophrenia. In fact, it is still legitimate to use the term *schizophrenia occurring in childhood* to refer to severe childhood disorders if the characteristics match diagnostic criteria for adult forms of schizophrenia, with the additional provision that schizophrenia occurring in childhood typically includes hallucinations, delusions, loosening of associations or incoherence in thought and language that are not present in infantile autism or COPDD (APA, 1980, p. 89). Hallucinations and delusions do not, by definition, occur in infantile autism or childhood onset pervasive developmental disorders.

Changes in DSM-III leading to the definition of COPDD have generated considerable controversy and confusion among clinicians and researchers. The distinctions among infantile autism, COPDD, atypical pervasive developmental disorder, and childhood schizophrenia are quite clear as outlined on paper in DSM-III, but they are by no means so clear when we are confronted with real problems in real children.

A key problem has been the use of age as a criterion for differential diagnosis. By definition, infantile autism begins prior to thirty months of age, while COPDD begins after thirty months but before twelve years of age. Onset of schizophrenia occurs typically during adolescence or early adulthood, but a specific age of onset is not defined. However, many investigators have noted that it makes little sense to distinguish, diagnostically, between two individuals who manifest problems that are virtually identical in all respects except that one occurs at twenty-nine months and another occurs at thirty-one months, particularly when there are no empirical data to support such an age-based distinction (Cantor, Evans, Pearce, & Pezzot-Pearce, 1982; Volkmar, Cohen & Paul, 1986; Volkmar, Stier, & Cohen, 1985).

Further, it is not clear that COPDD children differ in any consistent way from children with infantile autism. In a comprehensive study designed to explore differences among the subgroups of the broad category of pervasive developmental disorders, researchers at the Yale University Child Study Center evaluated 390 children under seventy-two months old (Dahl, Cohen, & Provence, 1986). These investigators interviewed parents, evaluated the children in individual sessions, and completed comprehensive rating scales for each subject. They examined factors such as age, demographic characteristics, behavior, physiology, environment, intellectual ability, and parental characteristics. They recorded the age of actual diagnosis, and the age at which a diagnosis could reliably have been made. Their results showed that the age of onset did not distinguish among subgroups of pervasive developmental disorder. Infantile autism and COPDD could be distinguished from other problems on the basis of impairments in social interaction, need for the preservation of sameness, bizarre thought content, and stereotyped or odd behaviors. However, autism and COPDD could not be so readily distinguished from each other, with the exception that children with autistic disorders manifested more severely disrupted development.

At this point, some investigators have come to view COPDD as a wastebasket term as it is defined in DSM-III, with little clinical usefulness (Fein, et al., 1986; Waterhouse, Fine, Nath, & Snyder, 1986). Nevertheless, the similarities between current definitions of COPDD and traditional discussions of childhood schizophrenia suggest that both labels may refer to the same disorder. In fact, if we take the step (for purposes of the present discussion) of eliminating exclusionary criteria regarding absence of hallucinations, delusions, and incoherence or marked loosening of associations, then COPDD and childhood schizophrenia become descriptively identical. There is some empirical justification for ignoring the exclusionary criterion regarding hallucinations and delusions because it is virtually impossible to determine the presence or absence of these features in mute or communicatively limited children, and because verbalizations of autistic individuals who can function at a higher level suggest the possibility of hallucinations and delusions (Volkmar & Cohen, 1985).

DSM-III also includes another diagnostic term, *atypical childhood onset pervasive developmental disorder* (ACOPDD), to refer to severe disturbances not included under the rubrics either of infantile autism or COPDD. While ACOPDD might be an appropriate category for discussions of what has been termed childhood schizophrenia, it is unlikely that two wastebasket categories are more helpful than one, and we will not explicitly use this term in the remainder of our discussion, recognizing, however, that it too could encompass research findings on childhood schizophrenia.

An early and still viable description of childhood schizophrenia was developed by a group called the British Working Party under the direction of Mildred Creak (Creak, 1961; Piggott & Gottlieb, 1973). For these investigators, childhood schizophrenia was characterized by: (1) gross and sustained defects in emotional relationships; (2) unawareness of personal identity; (3) preoccupations or fascinations with particular objects apart from the normal uses of these objects; (4) resistance to change; (5) abnormal perceptual experiences such as excessive, diminished, or unpredictable responses to sensory stimuli; (6) acute, excessive, and unreasonable anxiety responses; (7) failure to develop speech or loss of speech; (8) unusual movement patterns; and (9) serious retardation of intellectual functioning with islets of normal, near normal, or exceptionally high intellectual functioning.

There have also been reports indicating that as individuals grow older, those who showed early, severe symptomatology of infantile autism or COPDD may later come to resemble adult schizophrenics. For example, a group of Canadian investigators studied the developmental course of nineteen children and eleven adolescents who had received early diagnoses of childhood psychosis (Cantor, Evans, Pearce, & Pezzot-Pearce, 1982). These investigators found significant differences between the signs and symptoms characteristic of pre- and postpubertal individuals. Few adolescents, for example, showed the severity of language disturbances seen in the children, although more than half of them had exhibited such symptoms during childhood. Alternately, adolescent subjects showed delusional and hallucinatory behavior more like that characteristic of adult schizophrenics.

Thus, in the remainder of our discussion of COPDD, we will deal with this diagnostic category as functionally equivalent to traditional views of childhood schizophrenia, recognizing that such usage must remain tentative and subject to revision based on the results of future research.

It is important to be absolutely clear that while we have decided to treat COPDD and childhood schizophrenia as functionally equivalent terms, we do not mean to imply that COPDD is simply an early form of the same disorder recognized as adult schizophrenia. There are several reasons why this currently seems unlikely: (1) there are differences in the symptomatology of COPDD and adult schizophrenia; (2) adult schizophrenia represents a decline from a considerable period of more adequate development; (3) there is strong evidence of heredity in adult schizophrenia so far not seen in schizophrenia occurring in childhood (Achenbach, 1982).

Rather, we intend only to say that at this point in time descriptions of COPDD are enough like descriptions of childhood schizophrenia in available clinical and research literature to understand them as the same disorder, distinct from infantile autism and other childhood problems.

Signs and Symptoms of Childhood Onset Pervasive Developmental Disorders

Childhood onset pervasive developmental disorders are characterized most importantly by extensive, severe, and ongoing defects in interpersonal relationships. Following a period of more or less normal development, children with COPDD, sometimes in response to a traumatic event, begin to manifest early signs of problems in relating to others (Eggers, 1978). These may range from the self-imposed utter isolation characteristic of children with infantile autism to less severe but more bizarre derangements in relationships. The child with COPDD may recognize and respond to others, but in peculiar ways such as clinging to a parent or caretaker with inappropriate intensity and responding with terror at separation or, alternatively, remaining aloof and distant. The COPDD child may show lack of empathy for others, not recognizing their feelings or pain; he or she may be labile in responsiveness, at one moment clinging and the next withdrawing from contact or displaying

severely aggressive behavior. Emotional responses to others are often inconsistent and unpredictable and tears or laughter may be completely inappropriate to the events occurring in an interaction.

In addition to impaired interactions, the child with COPDD may display intense, free-floating anxiety with little apparent cause or experience sudden, unprovoked panic attacks. In some cases, children with COPDD may be phobic toward specific objects or situations. Normal everyday occurrences may act to trigger catastrophic reactions with uncontrollable terror and crying.

At other times, inappropriate emotional responses may be displayed in mood swings or intense sadness. Some COPDD children will display episodic rage reactions accompanied by destructive behavior or physical aggression including hitting, kicking, biting, and scratching.

Insistence on maintenance of sameness in the environment, also a characteristic of infantile autism, often leads to compulsive rituals in which objects need to be kept in the same place all the time or events have to be repeated in a rigidly ordered sequence. Variation from such routines is often the trigger for panic or rage.

Children with COPDD also show peculiarities of voice and movement. Again, as with autistic children, there may be echolalic speech, peculiar intonations, or strange and repeated noises and sounds. In the occasional instance in which the child has some language, he or she may eerily carry on both parts of a bizarre dialogue in different voices. Peculiar mannerisms may include handflapping in fear or excitement, self-stimulatory finger twiddling, peculiar birdlike walking, hopping, or twirling. In some cases, the child may display strange posturing.

Some children have been noted to be either hypo- or hypersensitive to sensory stimulation.

Finally, there may be either episodic or continual displays of self-injurious behavior. These children may engage in head slapping, head banging against floors, walls, objects, or people, self-scratching, or self-biting. In many cases such behavior is of sufficient severity to constitute a serious threat to the child's physical safety. In others, it may lead to chronic ulcerations, scarring, or calloused body parts.

As we noted earlier, the DSM-III definition of COPDD indicates that hallucinations or delusions should not be present in COPDD. However, it is not clear that this is a useful criterion. Some children who meet all other diagnostic criteria for COPDD and who do not fit criteria for adult schizophrenia may have hallucinations or delusions (Eggers, 1978).

Causation of Childhood Onset Pervasive Developmental Disorders

As noted earlier, we are treating COPDD as equivalent to what has been traditionally termed childhood schizophrenia. The reason we are doing this is because there is a large body of literature suggesting that infantile autism and childhood schizophrenia are different disorders while, at the same time, there is also convincing evidence that infantile autism and COPDD as currently defined are distinguished essentially only by age of onset. Thus, currently, there are two diagnostic terms for what may be the same disorder while another disorder described often and in detail in the research has essentially been defined out of existence. It is important to note that, while such usage is conceptually and empirically defensible, it is not—strictly speaking— the way DSM-III uses this terminology. However, only further refinement of concepts will determine eventual correct understandings. In the meantime, there is an extensive body of research on childhood schizophrenic disorders that cannot be ignored simply because of changes in terminology (Cantor, et al., 1982).

As with infantile autism, various theories of causation have emerged in the study of childhood schizophrenia. These include, again, experiential theories, organic theories, and experiential/organic theories. And as with infantile autism, experiential and experiential/organic

theories have failed to withstand the tests of close scrutiny and empirical study. Without going into extensive detail, experiential theories of causation in childhood schizophrenia have generally taken one of several courses. Some theorists have suggested that extreme parental rejection may cause a child to withdraw from painful reality into a world of fantasy and desperate loneliness. Some have suggested that extreme marital tensions between parents can cause a youngster to become terrified at the prospect of allying with one or the other parent or losing either or both of them. Others have suggested that intense maternal smothering accompanied by paternal passivity and withdrawal may be so overwhelming that they cause a child to withdraw from the natural course of maturation. And still others have pointed to the presence of distorted double-bind communication patterns in which parents simultaneously communicate contradictory messages at different levels, generating such intense confusion, rage, fear, and guilt, that the developing youngster alternates between withdrawal and intense dependency in a psychological reality that is muddled and hopeless.

However, research efforts have failed to show consistent differences in the family backgrounds of schizophrenic and control children (Jacob, 1975), and every characteristic that has been found in empirical studies of the family backgrounds of childhood schizophrenics has also been observed in the families of normal control subjects (Frank, 1965). Further, it has not yet been possible to show that observed variations in parental behavior are causes rather than effects of disturbed child behavior. Thus, there is at present no solid research basis to support experiential theories of the causation of childhood schizophrenia (Hingtgen & Bryson, 1972).

Although it appears that experiential/organic theories, representing an intermediate position, may hold more promise for an explanation of childhood schizophrenia, the fact is that they are no more tenable than experiential views until solid research evidence shows that the life experiences of schizophrenic children differ in some consistent way from those of nonpsychotic children.

The theoretical position currently most tenable appears to be that youngsters suffering from childhood schizophrenia have a biological predisposition for the disorder, although the nature of such predisposition is by no means clear. One rather general theory suggests that childhood schizophrenics suffer from a maturational defect that is caused either by inherited predisposition or early organic trauma of an unspecified nature (Bender, 1947, 1956, 1971). These children experience an embryonic plasticity in every aspect of development including motor, perceptual, cognitive, and emotional functions. These disturbances, in turn, produce the impairments in relational ability, self-identity, body image, and orientation in time and space so characteristic of childhood schizophrenia. However, although this broad theoretical view provides a kind of explanation of the symptomatic characteristics of childhood schizophrenia, it is too vague to be of practical use.

Nevertheless, there is support for a view that biological abnormalities may play a key role in the etiology of childhood schizophrenia. There have been frequent reports of complications in the prenatal periods and births of individuals later diagnosed as schizophrenic during childhood (Hingtgen & Bryson, 1972; White, 1974). Complications during the mothers' pregnancy such as toxemia, severe maternal illness, and maternal vaginal bleeding have been noted with significantly greater frequency in the histories of childhood schizophrenics than in those of normal children (Gittelman & Birch, 1967; Pollack & Woerner, 1966). Further, psychotic children have been noted to show a higher frequency of neurological signs than other children, suggesting the presence of central nervous system deficit (Pollack, et al., 1970).

Further support for the view that organic dysfunction is a primary causative factor in childhood schizophrenia comes from multiple studies showing a higher frequency of electroencephalogram abnormalities in psychotic children than in other children (James & Barry, 1980). Again, however, the specific nature of underlying neurological problems remains unclear.

An alternative organic hypothesis raises the possibility that childhood schizophrenia may be a genetically based disorder. This hypothesis arises because there is now extensive evidence showing strong genetic influences in adult forms of schizophrenia. Numerous studies showing higher rates of schizophrenia in the adult offspring of schizophrenics, higher concordance rates for adult forms of schizophrenia in monozygotic than in dizygotic twins, and studies of twins reared together as compared with twins reared apart all point in the direction of a strong inherited component in adult schizophrenia (Kessler, 1980).

What does the research evidence say about genetic influences in childhood psychotic disorders? In fact, as noted earlier, this is one of the key distinctions between adult schizophrenia and childhood schizophrenia. Although rare forms of dominant gene mutations or polygenic inheritance may contribute to the causation of childhood schizophrenia, the weight of research evidence does not support a strong genetic influence in childhood schizophrenia (Hanson & Gottesman, 1976).

At this point in time, the most plausible view of causation in childhood schizophrenia is that subtle central nervous system deficits, most likely resulting from pre- or perinatal damage, produce an unusual vulnerability to environmental stressors that may trigger the actual onset of psychotic symptoms sometime during early childhood. The specific mechanisms by which this happens remain obscure, but the overall weight of research evidence points in the direction of impaired integrity of central nervous system processes, whether these be structural or neurochemical (Friedlander, Pothier, Morrison, & Herman, 1982).

One very intriguing direction emerging in recent research is the study of the possible role of endorphins in the causation of childhood psychosis. Endorphins are brain chemicals apparently involved in the brain's response to physical pain and emotional stress. Functioning very much like natural opiates, endorphins appear involved in mood control as well as stress control. In one recent study of autistic and nonautistic psychotic children investigators examined endorphin components of cerebrospinal fluid and compared these with extracts from the cerebrospinal fluid of normal children (Gillberg, Terenius, & Lonnerholm, 1985). The results of this study showed higher concentrations of an endorphin component in psychotic children as compared with normal children. Unfortunately, the results of this study are highly tentative and only suggestive of potential future directions. Nevertheless, they do indicate the continuing creativity and energy as well as the increased technical sophistication with which investigators are pursuing answers to the riddles of severe emotional disturbances in children.

For the present, however, the prognosis for children with COPDD or childhood schizophrenia remains as dismal as it is for infantile autism, with little hope of eventual recovery of normal functioning. Yet despite the apparent hopelessness for children afflicted with infantile autism and COPDD, many special educators, psychologists, and physicians continue to work toward improving the day-to-day lives of these children. Although the results of their efforts are often small and painfully won, even tiny changes make important differences in the lives of these children and their families.

Intervention in Pervasive Developmental Disorders

The key approaches to intervention in infantile autism and childhood onset pervasive developmental disorders have been and continue to be educational in nature. However, there have also been important efforts to treat these problems through use of medication and psychotherapy as well. Before looking in detail at approaches

to educational intervention, we will briefly examine the effects of psychopharmacology and psychotherapy in the treatment of pervasive developmental disorders.

Medication in the Treatment of Pervasive Developmental Disorders

Although the weight of research evidence suggests that pervasive developmental disorders are basically aberrations of biological functioning, medical science has not yet produced either an understanding of their causes or consistently effective medical interventions. Nevertheless, a few promising experimental approaches have been reported. Clinicians and researchers have experimented with a wide range of psychoactive medications in the hopes of reducing the intensity of symptoms and making psychotic children more responsive to alterations in their ecological milieu and to educational intervention.

Although initially it might seem that studying the effects of drugs on childhood behaviors should be simple and straightforward, the study of psychopharmacological treatment of psychotic children is, in fact, complicated and confusing. Magda Campbell, a respected child psychiatrist, has enumerated a range of problems in the study of drug treatment for childhood psychosis (Campbell, 1975). For example, it is usually quite difficult to sort out the relative effects of drugs and intentional behavioral treatment or the incidental environmental changes that are always occurring. Further, it is necessary to set up controls for such variables as age, diagnosis, relative severity, intelligence, social class, and prior treatment in order to determine the specific effects of a specific medication. One must determine therapeutic dosage ranges with medications that are, by definition, being used experimentally in these studies, and there must be adequate controls for observer biases such as double-blind administration. One must have available adequate numbers of trained observers and careful baseline data against which to compare the effects of different dosage strengths on behavior. Finally, all of these variables must be accounted for within the context of day-to-day treatment in home or institutional settings.

Even when all these variables are considered, there is also a need for the consideration of ethical issues, and one must have reasonable certainty that the proposed experimental drug treatment will produce no harmful effects. In fact, ethical issues are of central importance in experimentation with drug treatment because one must consider not only potential immediate harm, but also unanticipated long-term side effects. Thus, it should not be surprising that, despite more than twenty years of research on the use of antipsychotic medications, results remain tentative and unclear.

Several antipsychotic medications, such as trifluoperazine and haloperidol, that have proven effective in the treatment of schizophrenic adults have been used to treat children with pervasive developmental disorders with generally promising results in reducing hyperactivity, stereotypic behavior, withdrawal, and anxiety (Claghorn, 1972; Faretra, Dooher, & Dowling, 1979; Rock, 1974). Haloperidol (Haldol), particularly, has shown promise in reducing maladaptive behavior and facilitating learning (Campbell, et al., 1982). Although haloperidol was not shown to be superior to contingent reinforcement in facilitating imitative speech, the combination of haloperidol and reinforcement has been shown to be superior to either alone (Campbell, et al., 1978). Trifluoperazine has also been shown to be helpful in the control of social, language, and affective symptoms (Campbell, Fish, Shapiro, & Floyd, 1972).

A few investigators have experimented with the administration of lysergic acid diethylamide (LSD) to psychotic children. In one study Lauretta Bender, a prominent child psychiatrist, administered LSD to fifty children with pervasive developmental disorders (Bender, 1966). The children in her sample ranged from four through fifteen years old, and generally responded to this treatment with improved

mood, more positive facial appearance, increased responsiveness, and more appropriate perceptual responses. Other investigators using LSD in the treatment of childhood psychosis reported that children receiving LSD were able to become more involved with their psychotherapists, and they showed more emotional responsiveness, increased speechlike behavior, and fewer stereotyped behaviors (Mogar & Aldrich, 1969).

Some investigators have hypothesized that there are wide individual differences in optimal levels of nutrient substances in the body, and that idiosyncratic, individual needs for specific vitamin substances may contribute to the causation of childhood psychoses. Thus, for example, an individual child might experience a specific vitamin deficiency despite the fact that he or she is receiving typically needed amounts of that substance in a normal diet. As a result of such speculation, several investigators have experimented with megavitamin therapy, the administration of massive doses of specific vitamins, in the treatment of childhood psychoses (Osmond, 1973; Pauling, 1973).

In one such investigation, Bernard Rimland (1973) reported the results of a twenty-four-week study of 300 psychotic children. Parents of these children were given schedules according to which they administered vitamin combinations including B_1, B_2, B_6, folic acid, niacinamide, and vitamin C. Parents also completed extensive behavior reports on their children in conjunction with megavitamin administration. Rimland reported that tentative analyses of data from this study showed either definite or possible improvement in as many as 86 percent of the children participating in the study. However, numerous methodological problems in such research have caused other investigators to remain skeptical of the beneficial effects of megavitamin therapy.

Numerous studies with a variety of antipsychotic medications have been reported in the experimental literature on treatment of infantile autism and childhood onset pervasive developmental disorders and, in fact, many medications have beneficial effects in reducing specific symptomatic features of childhood psychoses. Hyperactivity, stereotypic behavior, self-injurious behavior, impulsivity, and aggressiveness have all been shown to respond to chemical treatment, although often with cognitive blunting (Mikkelsen, 1982). This is particularly problematic in children because of the central importance of learning processes in ongoing development. Nevertheless, at times even learning must take second place to safety for children whose self-injurious behavior may be of life-threatening proportions.

Despite their efficacy in symptom reduction, it has become clear in recent years that drugs also pose major problems in terms of the serious side effects that they produce. As mentioned above, cognitive blunting is one frequent concomitant of treatment with psychoactive medications. Research has shown that treatment with neuroleptic drugs may produce deterioration of performance on even simple tasks, slowed psychomotor speed, increased response time, and impaired memory (Sprague & Werry, 1974).

Other side effects of psychotropic medications may include blurred vision, dry mouth, urinary retention, constipation, irritability, depression, and weight gain (Winsberg & Yepes, 1978). Instances of liver damage have been reported and cardiovascular effects may occur, although the evidence in this area is less clear.

Perhaps the most serious of the many potential side effects of psychopharmacological treatment of childhood psychoses, however, is tardive dyskinesia (TD). Tardive dyskinesia is a syndrome characterized by involuntary movements, and was initially observed in adults who had been treated on a long-term basis with psychoactive drugs. With cessation of drug treatment, the effects are reversible in some cases; in other cases tardive dyskinesia has been irreversible, with an implication that structural brain changes occur after long-term neuroleptic chemotherapy (Berger & Rexroth, 1980). It

is not clear whether tardive dyskinesia in psychotic children is associated with long-term drug treatment. However, clinical and research reports have shown the emergence of TD symptoms in children following the withdrawal of psychoactive medications (Mikkelsen, 1982).

Several studies have shown that, after treatment periods ranging from six months to fourteen months, cessation of antipsychotic medications in children was followed by the emergence of involuntary tongue and jaw movements, choreiform (rapid, jerky, involuntary) and athetoid (slow, sinuous, purposeless) movements of the arms, trunk, and head, posturing, body rocking, and disturbances in balance manifested as a kind of drunken gait (e.g., Engelhardt, Polizos, & Waizer, 1975; Polizos, Engelhardt, Hoffman, & Waizer, 1973). In addition, cessation of drug treatment in these children virtually always resulted in total clinical relapse, and TD symptoms persisted in some cases for as long as twelve months. It is not clear whether the symptoms of TD may be irreversible in some children, and there have been reports of symptoms persisting for the duration of a four-year follow-up study (Paulson, Rizui, & Crane, 1973).

Yet despite the potentially dangerous side effects for some children of long-term treatment with psychoactive medications, for others they represent a means of reducing the devastating symptoms that inhibit any semblance of adequate development.

Behavioral and Educational Interventions in Pervasive Developmental Disorders

Although descriptions of children with pervasive developmental disorders have appeared intermittently since the nineteenth century, little progress in systematic treatment occurred until the twentieth century. As noted in the previous section, the emergence of psychopharmacological approaches to the treatment of adult psychoses led quickly to experimentation with drugs in the treatment of childhood disorders. Equally important, however, was the emergence of intensive efforts at psychotherapeutic treatment of children.

As with chemotherapy, early work in the psychotherapy of pervasive development disorders evolved alongside an intensive investigation of severe emotional disturbances in adults. By the 1930s psychoanalysis had developed considerable influence in the United States as a method of treating adult psychological disorders, and many offshoots of traditional psychoanalytic treatment concepts and methods began to appear. Most of these psychoanalytic offshoots saw severe psychological disturbance as the result of aberrant and destructive emotional experiences and ongoing family pathology. Clinicians believed that, if severe disturbance resulted from unhealthy environmental experiences, then positive environmental experiences might reverse the terrible effects they observed. As we noted earlier, there is little contemporary support for such views, and some key investigators have stated categorically that no known factors in a child's psychological environment can cause autism (Ornitz & Ritvo, 1976). Nevertheless, such views were critically important in stimulating efforts to provide children with corrective emotional experiences in the context of individual psychotherapy and residential treatment providing "healthier" environments for growth.

One early proponent of environmental intervention along psychodynamic theoretical lines was Bruno Bettelheim. At the Orthogenic School at the University of Chicago, Bettelheim established a therapeutic milieu, a setting in which severely disturbed children were exposed to an interpersonal environment that was accepting and permitted regression and redevelopment in a safe and controlled setting (Bettelheim, 1955a, 1955b, 1967). Another program, called the League School program, was also founded on psychodynamic principles, but emphasized the importance of structure in the child's school environment with predictable rules, directive guidance, and structured academic programs (Fenichel, 1974).

An alternative point of view that became influential during the 1960s recognized that pervasive developmental disorders, and especially infantile autism, have a neurophysiological basis, but also recognized that corrective emotional experiences could, perhaps, compensate for constitutional deficits (DesLauriers, 1978; Des-Lauriers & Carlson, 1969). This approach to treatment, called *theraplay*, focused on the importance of high impact, intrusive approaches to treatment with emphasis on emotional interaction with the psychotic child (Zabel, 1982).

The optimism of this period regarding the effects of psychotherapy on pervasive developmental disorders provided the impetus for exploration and intervention that eventually produced more systematic and empirically based concepts of treatment and educational intervention. Investigators began to think in terms of providing consistent structure, guidance, and nurturance to severely disturbed children in long-term residential treatment centers and in individual, psychodynamically oriented psychotherapy. They offered warm, caring, controlled settings in which children could begin to learn the rudiments of personal identity and interpersonal interaction. Some believed that severely withdrawn children needed intrusion into their worlds; others, recognizing that psychotic children might need assistance in controlling sensory stimulation, tried to provide such stimulation in graded doses. All in all, mid-twentieth century psychology, education, and psychiatry saw the development of intensive treatment efforts, and many reports of improvement appeared in the literature of the time. Subsequent research has not proven such efforts to be as effective as originally thought, but such initial optimism was crucial in forming the basis for current efforts for systematic education of psychotic children.

By 1960, behavior modification began to emerge as a powerful influence in the U.S. mental health and education communities, and systematic, empirically based approaches to behavioral and educational intervention gained widespread influence. Later chapters review these approaches in detail. However, it is important to note some of the specific behavioral and educational approaches to intervention with pervasive developmental disorders at this point.

Perhaps the earliest systematic attempts at intervention in the pervasive developmental disorders of childhood were the efforts of investigators who noted that many severely disturbed children could be brought to a point of consistent and purposeful interaction with their environments through operant conditioning (Ferster, 1961; Ferster & DeMyer, 1961). Using reinforcer vending machines in isolated training rooms, these researchers noted that the behavior of autistic children could be brought under the control of environmental stimuli. Later, operant conditioning approaches were used in more normalized settings with reinforcers often consisting of attention, smiles, physical contact such as touching or holding, and verbal praise (DeMyer & Ferster, 1962).

It became clear that, apart from theoretical rationales, severely disturbed children could be helped to more appropriate behaviors through the systematic reinforcement of those behaviors. In some instances efforts at teaching imitative and even meaningful use of language were shown to be effective (Lovaas, Berberich, Perloff, & Schaeffer, 1971; Lovaas, Freitas, Nelson, & Whalen, 1967; Lovaas, Schaeffer, & Simmons, 1965). Severely disturbed children could even learn to engage in appropriate social exchanges with parents and others within the context of mutually reinforcing behaviors (Kozloff, 1973).

Since these early studies of behavior modification as a treatment modality for pervasive developmental disorders, literally hundreds of treatment reports have appeared in the literature reflecting the ingenuity and persistence of clinicians in trying to help these profoundly disturbed children. Generally, behavior modification approaches to the treatment of childhood psychoses make no assumptions regarding causation. Rather, the approaches taken are almost completely empirical in nature and based on demonstrated behavioral principles rather than on theoretical assumptions.

From this perspective, behavioral approaches are quite consistent with ecological principles because emphasis is placed on the observed responses of children to changes in their environments. Rather than looking for deficits within children, behavioral investigators have looked instead toward the environmental manipulations that might prompt and encourage more normalized development. Although investigation into the causes of these disorders continues with energy, clinicians also have powerful behavioral tools that can help children function more productively until a better understanding of the nature of these problems is reached.

It is impossible to summarize the vast literature on behavioral interventions with pervasive developmental disorders. However, certain trends are clear. One such trend is the increased use of behavioral techniques in special classroom settings by teachers working in consultation with behavioral specialists rather than the one-on-one treatment approaches by specialists so often prevalent in experimental reports (e.g., Frankel, 1976). With contemporary educational thrusts in the direction of least restrictive environments, normalization, and mainstreaming, it has become apparent that the treatment and education of children with pervasive developmental disorders cannot be left to isolated university laboratories and clinics. Rather, such intervention efforts must occur as often and as intensively as possible in the educational settings in which we expect these children to function (see Box 6.2).

A second important trend is the systematic training of parents and other family members in behavioral technology so that implementation of therapeutic techniques can be used in the home as well as the classroom (Graziano, 1978; Harris, 1982; Rutter, 1985). Of particular interest in this area are efforts to train siblings

Box 6.2   Donny F.: A Case of Childhood Onset Pervasive Developmental Disorder

Donny F. is eighteen years old. Currently he spends his days in a day-care prevocational program where he learns to perform simple sorting tasks, to stuff envelopes, and to count out small pieces for simple assembly. Donny is able to attend to these tasks for periods of forty-five minutes or longer, provided his teacher or supervisor is in the immediate vicinity to give him occasional verbal reinforcement for on-task behavior. Most of the time a periodic, "Good work, Donny," is sufficient to keep him going for another five- or ten-minute span of time.

In Donny's prevocational program, work periods alternate with activities such as listening to music, going for walks to local stores under teacher supervision, and playing simple games. Donny is on a token reinforcement program, and he is able to earn colored plastic disks for on-task behavior, appropriate use of language, and compliance with teacher requests. (See Chapter 8 for a complete discussion of token economies.) At the end of each program day, Donny is allowed to exchange these tokens for his choice of a soda, a candy bar, a walk with his teacher, small toys, or magazines.

After his day-care program, Donny is transported by private bus to a residential facility where he lives with fourteen other young men and women. Most of these people are functioning at a level of moderate to mild mental retardation, although there is a wide range of causal factors limiting their abilities. A few others, such as Donny, have had diagnoses of early infantile autism or childhood schizophrenia. All the members of Donny's program are involved in some simple maintenance and group living chores and training programs.

Donny is currently working on independent showering, shaving, and shampooing, and group home staff work to help him through a guided series of prompts on these self-care activities. He is also working on bed-making tasks and learning to sort clothes to be laundered. In the evening when he returns home he is involved in learning to use a vacuum cleaner and learning to prepare a bag lunch for the next day. Evenings are spent in a variety of educational programs and Donny is learning to count, to recognize numbers, and to dial a telephone. He responds well to structured training and to adult attention. Generally he is cooperative and seems to enjoy living in a group setting.

Donny has made important developmental strides in his residential program. Prior to enrollment in this program he displayed volatile and explosive behavior. Since early childhood he had shown episodes of aggressive, destructive, and self-injurious behavior. Sometimes these episodes were precipitated when Donny did not get his way or when he was scolded. At other times, there were no apparent provocations and Donny would simply begin hitting those nearest him, biting his hand, and smashing furniture until physically subdued.

Although his parents had been involved in a variety of treatment and behavior management programs, they had never been able to maintain consistency in their responses to Donny. They were well intentioned and repeatedly tried to follow recommended management programs, but there were always things that interfered with their follow-through. At times they became frustrated with Donny and angry with him, and their responses were more a function of their own feelings than his behavior. At other times they were simply too discouraged and exhausted to be consistent. And at still other times, their own sense of guilt and failure (though actually unfounded) caused them to undermine their own efforts. "I knew it was the wrong thing to do while I was doing it," was a frequent complaint from Donny's father.

Eventually Donny's parents recognized that they could no longer cope with his rages and explosive behavior, and they sought residential placement for him. This was a difficult decision for them and they felt as though they were aban-

continued

Box 6.2   continued

doning their son. Yet, they both recognized that Donny was physically stronger than they, and his uncontrolled outbursts constituted a real danger—to Donny as well as themselves.

At this point they recognize clear progress in Donny and know that residential services have provided a structure and consistency that they could not. They see Donny for brief visits two or three times a month, and these are generally enjoyable times for the family. Mr. and Mrs. F. recognize that Donny will never be normal, but feel some reassurance that he will be cared for in a setting that they feel good about and that he will continue to develop at his own pace.

---

as behavior therapists for their autistic brothers and sisters. Laura Schreibman and several associates wondered whether normal siblings of autistic children could be taught to carry out behavior modification procedures correctly and implement them in naturalistic settings during unstructured play activities (Schreibman, O'Neill, & Koegel, 1983). Using three sibling pairs as subjects, these investigators had the normal siblings observe videotaped training films of behavior therapy procedures with autistic children. The siblings learned concepts of reinforcement, shaping, chaining, and extinction. Trainers and siblings discussed potential applications of behavior therapy techniques in everyday situations, and the siblings had actual practice sessions under supervision with corrective feedback. The results of this study showed that normal siblings can become proficient in behavioral teaching skills and can generalize their teaching skills to situations that were never actually practiced. Further, there were genuine improvements in the behavior of the autistic siblings, and the normal siblings were observed to make fewer negative and more frequent positive statements about their autistic brothers and sisters.

Similar studies using normal and mildly handicapped students as peer trainers for other students with pervasive developmental disorders have likewise shown that students can implement behavioral approaches with resultant improvement in behavior and in interaction between mildly handicapped and severely handicapped youngsters (Lancioni, 1982; Shafer, Egel, & Neff, 1984).

A third important trend involves the clear recognition that generalization of training effects has to be planned for systematically so that changes that have been implemented in specific settings continue to occur in new and different settings (Franks, Wilson, Kendall, & Brownell, 1984). Research and therapeutic efforts more and more consistently include explicit plans to facilitate generalization even prior to the research study or implementation of the behavioral program plan (e.g., Gaylord-Ross, Haring, Breen, & Pitts-Conway, 1984).

Investigators are increasingly aware of the importance of incidental teaching as a means of facilitating skills acquisition in children with pervasive developmental disorders as well as other problems. *Incidental teaching* means that particular skills are taught within the context of other simultaneously occurring activities. Teaching a child about the value of a balanced diet within the context of normal mealtime conversation is an example of incidental teaching. Thus far, most examples of incidental teaching have occurred during the course of training in functional language usage. However, in one recent study, efforts were made to teach two autistic children sight-word reading skills within the context of play activities (McGee, Krantz, Mason, & McClannahan, 1986). During the course of a twenty-five-minute play period, a trainer offered an autistic child a toy. When the child asked for or reached for the toy, the trainer requested that the child first indicate recognition of the written name of the toy. Results of this study showed that incidental teaching promoted the acquisition and retention of a sight-word vocabulary. For children having difficulty dealing with typical structured curricular activities, incidental teaching offers an additional avenue of approach.

Finally, programs for autistic children are beginning to move from private or community-sponsored institutional settings into public school classrooms (Frank, et al., 1984). For example, at Rafael High School in Marin County, California, autistic children are exposed to operant training procedures in the classroom, in the gymnasium, in the cafeteria, at school functions, and in nearby neighborhood shops (Gaylord-Ross & Pitts-Conway, 1983).

Although trends in the education and treatment of children with pervasive developmental disorders are promising and offer hope of increased normalization and integration into the educational and social mainstream, it is important to remember that we are nowhere near solutions to these problems. We have developed medical and behavioral technologies that offer assistance in the amelioration of specific symptoms and the acquisition of specific skills. Yet the tools that will permit genuine normalization have yet to be developed.

Summary

The study of pervasive developmental disorders shows clearly the fluid and evolving nature of our understanding of human behavioral problems. Systematic clinical descriptions of severe disruptions of development in infants and young children led eventually to early attempts to understand these unusual phenomena.

The work of such pioneer investigators as De Sanctis and Heller showed that there was a consistent constellation of signs and symptoms that reflected severe disturbance of reality contact and sharply limited developmental potential in some children. The terrible developmental consequences of these disorders prompted other investigators to look for potential causes in the child's heredity, in possible developmental trauma, and in the child's environment.

By the middle of the twentieth century investigators had described a variety of different psychotic disorders of childhood, and papers describing childhood schizophrenia and infantile autism stimulated research efforts leading to greater diagnostic precision and more effective interventions. In recent years we have begun to think of three broad syndromes: infantile autism, childhood onset pervasive developmental disorders, and atypical developmental disorders.

Questions raised in explorations of the etiology of childhood psychoses have led to the development of organic/nature, experiential/nurture, and nature/nurture theories of causation. Although intensive research efforts into the causation of pervasive developmental disorders continue to this day, the weight of current evidence suggests that children with pervasive developmental disorders are born with constitutional vulnerabilities to severe disturbance. Parents are no longer viewed as somehow involved in the causation of these disturbances, though the family disruption caused by such devastating problems may, in turn, cause or contribute to the development of adjustment problems in other family members.

Currently, we know that the use of medication is an important, if controversial, component in the treatment of many children with pervasive developmental disorders. Active research programs around the United States are dedicated to developing more effective forms of chemotherapy. Equally important, however, are behavioral and educational interventions in special school settings that help severely disturbed youngsters reach their maximum developmental potential. Although the prognosis for children with pervasive developmental disorders remains grim, combined medical, behavioral, and educational interventions continue to provide important tools for their treatment.

CHAPTER 7

Personality and Behavior Problems and Learning Disorders

Overview

Introduction

In an initial advising conference with a special education faculty member, a prospective student was asked about her interests in teaching handicapped students. The student expressed a strong interest in teaching learning disabled or mentally retarded children, but not behaviorally disordered students. She explained, "I don't want to deal with lots of discipline problems." Considerable counseling followed in which the faculty member pointed out that teachers of children with either specific or general learning problems frequently must also address the behavioral problems of their students, just as teachers of behaviorally disordered students must engage in academic remediation.

The link between learning and behavior problems is firmly established. In fact, the differential diagnosis between behavior disorders, learning disabilities, and mild mental retardation is a relatively recent phenomenon. Today, we often use these labels to refer to distinct categories of educational exceptionality, when in reality we frequently have difficulty distinguishing among these groups. Debate continues over how these groups differ from one another and whether there are really educationally relevant distinctions that merit the assignment of different diagnostic labels. In practice, however, students with these different diagnoses are often educated in the same special education programs.

As we have noted in earlier chapters, behaviorally disordered children often experience learning difficulties. They may, for example, have more difficulty in specific academic skills such as reading, mathematics, and spelling than other students. They may have normal or above normal abilities, but their academic performance is not commensurate with their ability. Some of these children are also described as inattentive, impulsive, and distractible. They may be considered to have *attention deficit disorders* and are frequently called *hyperactive*.

Other children and adolescents experience more general learning problems. Their performance lags behind same-age peers across all academic areas. In addition, their measured intellectual abilities are also below normal. They may be considered *slow learners*, or, if their measured intelligence is significantly below normal and there are associated *adaptive behavior* problems, they may be considered *educable mentally retarded*.

Although not all learning disabled, slow learner, and educable mentally retarded students have behavioral disorders, many do. The commonly accepted definition of mental retardation prepared by the American Association of Mental Deficiency (AAMD), for example, addresses problem behavior. *Deficits in adaptive behavior* and *subaverage general intellectual ability* form the central diagnostic criteria. At different developmental ages, adaptive behavior reflects the ability to interact with others, to participate in group activities, and to perform vocational social responsibilities (Grossman, 1973).

Some of the more prevalent behavioral and emotional characteristics associated with learning problems are dependency, distractibility, perseveration (inappropriate repetition of behavior), disruption, withdrawal, hyperactivity, inconsistent behavior, irritability, antisocial behavior, and poor social perception (Wallace & McLoughlin, 1979).

Parents, teachers, and peers often perceive particular patterns of social-emotional problems in learning disabled children and adolescents (Algozzine, 1979). Parents, for instance, frequently describe their learning disabled children as anxious, unable to receive affection, having poor impulse control, and less tactful and cooperative than their siblings. Teachers often see LD students as less able to accept responsibility; less able to cope with new situations; as being hyperactive, angry, and hostile; and as having more problems with peers. Peers describe LD children as more worried, frustrated, and rejected, and as less clean, neat, good-looking, and popular than their other classmates. Clearly, many of these views of children with learning problems are similar to characteristics of children with personality and, especially, conduct problems discussed in earlier chapters.

This chapter examines some of the relationships between behavioral and learning prob-

lems. First, we will look at definitions and characteristics of children with learning disorders, particularly those considered to have learning disabilities. Special emphasis will be given to the characteristics and treatment of children who have attention deficit disorders with hyperactivity—a pattern of behavior we also considered in our discussion of conduct disorders (Chapter 5). We will also review some of the literature that has examined similarities and differences between learning disabilities and other educational exceptionalities, including behaviorally disordered, educable mentally retarded, underachievers, and slow learners. We will consider procedures and issues in assessment of learning problems. Finally, we will review some promising strategies for remediating learning disorders.

Definitions of Learning Disabilities

Early Views

As both a distinct category of exceptionality and an area of special education, learning disabilities has a relatively brief history. Still, there has been considerable evolution in the prevalent views regarding learning disability. About forty years ago, Alfred Strauss and Laura Lehtinen published *Psychopathology and Education of the Brain-Injured Child* (1947). In it they reported their studies of children who were distinguished by their perceptual problems and hyperactivity. The perceptual problems were presumed, though not proven, to be organic and to result from dysfunctions within a child's central nervous system, possibly minimal brain damage (MBD). The brain damage might be hereditary, or result from injury or disease. However, the presumed brain damage was so minimal that it could not be directly located and detected.

There has been considerable emphasis placed upon possible neuromedical causes of learning disabilities. Most of this has been speculative and probably largely irrelevant to intervention. More than twenty years ago, Sam Kirk stated that "the term 'brain injured' has little meaning to me from a management of training point of view. It does not tell me whether a child is smart or dull, hyperactive or underactive. It does not give me any clue to management or training. . . . It is not a basic cause, since the description of a child as brain injured does not really tell us why the child is brain injured or how he got that way" (1963, pp. 2–3). Others, too, have criticized the use of terms such as *minimal brain damage* as a disease rather than a disorder model. Gallagher (1976), for example, called MBD a useless term for educators, who need educational diagnoses to help them deal with children's educational needs.

As an alternative to the medical and neurological interpretations, Kirk suggested the use of the term *learning disabilities* to designate those children who have disorders in language, speech, reading, and associated communication skills. This learning disabilities (LD) label, which does not imply any particular causation, became the fastest growing category of exceptional children during the 1960s and 1970s. LD rapidly came to serve as an umbrella term for students whose previous designations included minimal brain damage, dyslexia, neurological disorders, perceptual disorders, and hyperactivity.

Ever since the introduction of the LD label, however, a lack of consensus has persisted regarding the specific types of behaviors and conditions that comprise the category. Nevertheless, the absence of precise eligibility criteria coupled with the relatively low stigma attached to the label, have enabled it to become a rallying point for various advocacy efforts. Today, it constitutes the largest single category of educational exceptionality, encompassing approximately 40 percent of all identified handicapped children (Keogh, 1986).

The Federal Definition of Learning Disabilities

In 1968, the National Advisory Committee on Handicapped Children, headed by Kirk, presented several recommendations concerning learning disabilities and proposed a definition.

Box 7.1 Federal Criteria for Specific Learning Disability

(a) A team may determine that a child has a specific learning disability if:

(1) The child does not achieve commensurately with his or her age and ability levels in one or more of the areas listed in paragraph (a) (2) of this section, when provided with learning experiences appropriate for the child's age and ability levels: and

(2) The team finds that a child has a severe discrepancy between achievement and intellectual ability on one or more of the following areas:

   (i)   Oral expression;
   (ii) Listening comprehension;
   (iii) Written expression;

   (iv) Basic reading skill;
   (v)   Reading comprehension;
   (vi) Mathematics calculation; or
   (vii) Mathematics reasoning.

(b) The team may not identify a child as having a specific learning disability if the severe discrepancy between ability and achievement is primarily the result of:

   (1) A visual, hearing, or motor handicap;
   (2) Mental retardation;
   (3) Emotional disturbance;
   (4) Environmental, cultural, or economic disadvantage.

Source: *Federal Register* (December 29, 1977), Washington, DC: U.S. Government Printing Office, 65083.

Their definition was very similar to the one that was later included in PL 94–142, The Education for All Handicapped Children Act of 1975. That definition read as follows:

"Specific learning disability" means a disorder in one or more of the basic psychological processes involved in understanding or in using language, spoken or written, which may manifest itself in an imperfect ability to listen, think, speak, read, write, spell, or to do mathematical calculations. The term includes such conditions as perceptual handicaps, brain injury, minimal brain dysfunction, dyslexia, and developmental aphasia. The term does not include children who have learning problems which are primarily the result of visual, hearing, or motor handicaps, of mental retardation, of emotional disturbance, or of environmental, cultural, or economic disadvantage (Federal Register, 1977).

In addition, several criteria were added for determining a child's eligibility for the specific learning disability designation (see Box 7.1). One criterion is a discrepancy between a child's ability and achievement in one or more areas: oral expression, listening comprehension, written expression, basic reading skills, reading comprehension, mathematics computation, and reasoning. Another criterion is the so-called exclusionary clause: the discrepancy may not be the result of sensory handicaps, mental retardation, emotional disturbance, or environmental, cultural, or economic disadvantage. Most states have adopted the federal definition, or an adaptation of it, although there are a variety of formulas used to determine the existence of discrepancies between ability and achievement.

An Alternative Definition

Other more recent definitions have also been proposed. For example, the National Joint Committee for Learning Disabilities, representing several advocacy groups, suggested an alternative definition to reduce confusion and to provide additional clarity (Hammill, Leigh, McNutt, & Larsen, 1981). This group acknowledged that the heterogeneous makeup of learning disabilities is manifested by "significant difficulties in the acquisition and use of listening, speaking, reading, writing, reasoning, and mathematical abilities" (p. 336). This definition further reaffirms an etiological interpretation by stating that the disabilities are "intrinsic to the individual and presumably due to central nervous system dysfunctions." It also points out that learning disabilities may occur together with sensory impairments, mental retardation, social and emotional disturbance, and be affected by, but not the result of, environmental influences.

Criticisms of Learning Disability Definitions

Some criticism of these definitions has been directed at their exclusionary phrases. Hallahan and Kauffman (1977), for example, note that "whenever it is necessary to say what something is *not* in order to say what *is* suspicion must be aroused regarding whether the 'definers' are sure what the problem is" (p. 140). As we have pointed out earlier, when a child presents both learning and behavior problems, it is often impossible to determine which causes the other. We believe that instead of phrases that exclude students with emotional disturbances, mental retardation, and environmental disadvantages, it is more helpful to think in terms of primary disability. A critical question concerns aspects of the child's functioning (academic learning, social behavior, emotional adjustment, intellectual ability, etc.) that most affect school performance. Only when these are identified can interventions be designed and implemented.

Characteristics of Learning Disabilities

According to researchers at the Minnesota Institute of Learning Disabilities, "After five years of trying, we cannot describe, except with considerable lack of precision, students called LD. We think that LD can best be defined as 'whatever society wants it to be, needs it to be, or will let it be' at any point of time" (Ysseldyke, Thurlow, Graden, Wesson, Algozzine, & Deno, 1983, p. 89). Their research led them to conclude that LD students are those who experience academic difficulties, who create major disturbances for regular classroom teachers, and who are removed from the educational mainstream after being classified by socially sanctioned labelers. Some of the learning and academic problems, disturbing social behavior, and processes leading to the designation of students as learning disabled are discussed in the following sections.

Types of Learning Problems

It should be apparent from the discussion above that specific learning disabilities encompass diverse types of academic learning problems, including problems in reading, spelling, use and understanding of spoken and written language, as well as attention deficit disorders. By definition, the learning problems are specific to certain areas rather than general in nature. This is how LD students are differentiated from slow learners and mildly retarded students.

Reading. Most learning disabled students have reading problems. The term *dyslexia* has traditionally been used to indicate pronounced and persistent difficulties in learning components of words and sentences and being able to integrate them with other representational systems such as telling time and following directions (Bryan & Bryan, 1978). Problems with spelling, punctuation, and grammar pose language-related difficulties for many learning disabled students that affect both reading and writing.

Language. Problems in receptive language (understanding) and expressive language (verbal production) constitute another general cluster of learning problems. Kirk, McCarthy, and Kirk (1968) designed the Illinois Test of Psycholinguistic Abilities (ITPA) to diagnose children's language problems. The ITPA contains several subtests that purportedly identify specific language

problems and prescribe remedial strategies. Although psycholinguistic approaches were popular for a number of years, the relationship of specific psycholinguistic abilities and academic performance has been questioned (e.g., Arter & Jenkins, 1979; Sternberg & Taylor, 1981).

Mathematics. Disabilities in mathematics have not received as much attention as other areas; however, problems in mathematics computation and comprehension are sometimes evident. These include difficulty with spatial and size relationships, left-right confusion, distractibility, perseveration (excessive repetition or difficulty shifting from one process to another), understanding symbols, and abstract thinking.

Perceptual and Motor Skills Gross motor, fine motor, and perceptual-motor disorders constitute other types of learning disability. Gross motor skills include coordination of movements such as walking, running, and throwing balls. Fine motor skills include such activities as handwriting and cutting with scissors. Visual perceptual motor skills include activities that require eye-hand coordination such as copying or tracing patterns, and auditory perceptual skills include such abilities as distinguishing among consonant blends such as *th*, *sh*, and *ph*.

Auditory or visual memory disorders have also been related to academic difficulties. Children who have difficulty remembering what they have previously learned, such as a sequence of orally read numbers or a written passage in a text, may have memory disorders. Some students cannot recall information they have recently heard or seen; others have difficulty remembering auditory and visual information from the more distant past.

Although perceptual difficulties may seem to indicate sensory impairments with learning disabled children, their senses actually appear to be intact. Their vision, hearing, and other senses are normal, yet they seem to have difficulties processing what they see and hear. This leaves us with the presumption of some kind of underlying perceptual problems to explain learning disabilities. Because of failures in the direct remediation of the processes that underlie academic learning, direct instruction in academic areas such as reading, mathematics, and spoken and written language have been found more effective interventions. More will be said about direct instruction in specific skills later in this chapter.

Attention Deficit Disorders and Hyperactivity

As noted in Chapter 5, the Diagnostic and Statistical Manual (DSM-III) of the American Psychiatric Association uses the term *attention deficit disorders* (ADD) as a category of problem behavior that is similar to the educators' use of learning disability. Attention deficits and poor task orientation are characteristics of many children considered learning disabled, but DSM-III distinguishes among three types—with hyperactivity, without hyperactivity, and residual. Thus, some children who have ADD are also considered hyperactive, while others are not. In addition, some children seem to outgrow the hyperactivity, yet still experience its residual effects.

Characteristics of Hyperactivity

Hyperactivity refers to a constellation of conduct problems that tend to go hand in hand. These are *hyperactivity* (excessive motor movement), *impulsivity* (acting without considering consequences), and *distractibility* (or inattention to relevant stimuli). As James Kauffman (1986) has pointed out, these types of behavior reflect judgments about appropriate amounts of activity, attention, and control of behavior. Consequently, determination of hyperactivity is related to expectations of what is developmentally, or age-, appropriate behavior in certain situations.

The construct of hyperactivity is closely tied to that of self-control. Children described as hyperactive appear to have inadequate control over their physical movements, attention, and impulses. Although symptoms of hyperactivity vary according to a child's age and the situation, common behavioral features include the following: stubbornness, bossiness, mood lability, temper outbursts, low self-esteem, and low tolerance for frustration.

In school hyperactive children appear to have difficulty staying on-task, organizing, and completing their school work. They may seem not to listen to instructions, and their work may be sloppy and careless. They may be excessively fidgety, impulsively talking out and leaving their seats without permission. Obviously, this constellation of behavior can have implications for academic performance as well as social behavior (Keogh, 1971). In many classrooms, children are expected to sit relatively still for long periods of time, to pay attention to learning tasks, to follow instructions, and to complete tasks. These children may also experience problems outside of school. They may not follow parents' instructions or stick with activities considered appropriate for their age.

Prevalence

The prevalence of ADD may be as high as 10 percent of the school-age population (Gadow, 1979), although the DSM-III estimate is just 3 percent. Hyperactive children are well represented in certain other diagnostic categories. Ross (1974), for example, reported that approximately one-third of diagnosed psychiatric disorders of school-age children involve hyperactivity. A large proportion of students in LD and BD programs are considered hyperactive by their special education teachers (Sindelar, et al., 1985). In LD programs, teachers consider 30 percent to 40 percent hyperactive; in BD programs, 50 percent to 60 percent are considered hyperactive.

Etiology

A number of etiological factors for hyperactivity have been proposed (Johnson, 1981). Although specific genetic determinants are unknown, there are higher rates of hyperactivity, as well as other types of problem behavior, among close relatives of hyperactive children (McMahon, 1980). In one study, 20 percent of hyperactive children were found to have a parent who also had been hyperactive, compared with only 5 percent of nonhyperactive children (Morrison & Stewart, 1971). Families with hyperactive children also have higher rates of alcoholism, depression, and schizophrenia (Johnson, 1981).

Of course, family environments in which there is an occurrence of conduct disorders affect children's behavior and adjustment. However, some evidence derived from studies of hyperactivity in twins and in biological and adoptive parents has helped clarify the role of heredity. For example, a higher concordance rate for hyperactivity has been found for monozygotic than for dizygotic twins (Lopez, 1965). When one identical twin is hyperactive, the other is more likely also to be hyperactive than is the case with fraternal twins. Recently, Alberts-Corush, Firestone, and Goodman (1986) compared biological and adoptive parents of groups of children who were diagnosed hyperactive according to DSM-III criteria, and parents of nonhyperactive children. They found a strong familial association. Biological parents of hyperactive children exhibited more attentional deficits than either the adoptive parents of hyperactive children or parents of normal children.

Other research has examined the influence of organic factors, such as pregnancy and birth complications, minor physical anomalies, abnormal electroencephalograms (EEGs), and soft neurological signs (e.g., coordination problems, speech disorders). Although all of these have been linked by some researchers to hyperactivity, none has been unequivocally associated with the syndrome (Johnson, 1981). Pregnancy and birth complications are part of the history of some hyperactive children, but certainly not all. By the same token, some nonhyperactive children have also experienced prenatal and birth complications.

The role of psychogenic factors has also been explored. Some believe that many hyperactive children have difficult temperaments from an early age that place them in conflict with others (Graham, Rutter, & George, 1973; Stewart & Olds, 1973). Some have received social reinforcement in the form of attention for high activity levels. Because a relatively high proportion of the parents of hyperactive children are also hyperactive themselves, observational learning by children of behavioral patterns may also play a role. However, as the Alberts-Corush, et al. adoption study indicates, modeling and reinforcement are not sufficient explanations for all children's hyperactivity.

Several environmental factors, such as lead poisoning and chemical food additives, have also been implicated in attention deficit disorders with hyperactivity. David, Clark, and Voeller (1972), for example, found that some hyperactive children have significantly higher levels of lead in their blood compared with nonhyperactive controls. Feingold (1976) and others have said that hyperactivity is related to the consumption of artificial flavorings, coloring, and preservatives, and natural salicylates found in many foods. In some early studies in which these substances were systematically removed from children's diets, parents reported behavioral improvements. As noted in Chapter 5, more controlled experiments, however, have not provided convincing evidence to support the Feingold hypothesis (Kavale & Forness, 1983).

It is reasonable to conclude that a variety of factors can contribute to hyperactivity. In most cases, there is no clear etiology and in any event, knowing the etiology might contribute little to an intervention plan.

Long-Term Adjustment

Considerable attention has been given to the long-term status of hyperactive children, since a common assumption is that at least some outgrow their hyperactivity. In a review of this literature, Hechtman and Weiss (1983) concluded that the majority of hyperactive children continue to exhibit various symptoms into adolescence and young adulthood. Several studies have shown that adolescents continue to have significant academic difficulties as well as problems with impulsivity, distractibility, and poor self-esteem. Followed into young adulthood, some of those with hyperactivity are found to function normally, although the majority continues to display poorer social skills, lower educational achievement, more impulsiveness, irritability, emotional lability, and lower self-esteem than nonhyperactive comparison groups. A relatively small group experiences more severe antisocial problems, including psychoses, depression, suicidal behavior, and drug and alcohol abuse (Hechtman & Weiss, 1983).

Drug Treatment

A common treatment of hyperactivity has been the prescription of central nervous system stimulants, such as Ritalin (methylphenidate), Dexedrine (dextroamphetamine), and Cylert (pemoline). Pharmacological treatment has been controversial, with some advocating its benefits and others criticizing its indiscriminate use. Critics argue that medications are too readily prescribed, dosages are often too high, and effects and side effects are not carefully monitored.

Considerable research has examined the effectiveness of drugs, especially Ritalin, on a variety of measures. Some research has compared treated and untreated hyperactive children (e.g., Reid & Borkowski, 1984; Rie, Rie, Stewart, & Ambuel, 1976). Some has compared drugs with other treatments, particularly behavior modification (e.g., Backman & Firestone, 1979; O'Leary, 1980; Sprague, 1983). The research has generally shown that the drugs can be effective with many hyperactive children by reducing activity level, disruptiveness, distractibility, and increasing attention.

However, drug treatment has not been found directly to improve learning or academic achievement of hyperactive children (Barkley & Cunningham, 1978; Lambert, Windmiller, Sandoval, & Moore, 1976; Rie, et al., 1976). Although drug treatment may seem "easier" and have more immediate effects, drugs appear to have few long-term benefits (Firestone, Crowe, Goodman, & McGrath, 1986). Behavior modification techniques, such as are discussed in Chapter 8, appear more effective for improving academic performance (Ayllon, Layman, & Kandel, 1975).

Some researchers have questioned whether children treated with Ritalin experience concomitant undesirable behavioral changes that result in new problems. Rie, et al. (1976), for example, questioned whether the drugs may reduce children's curiosity of and involvement with their environment, thereby cancelling out the benefits of reduced activity level and increased attention. Others, however, have found that curiosity levels of hyperactive children are not significantly reduced for students on relatively low dosages of Ritalin (Fiedler & Ullman, 1983).

Several reviews have differentiated among types of hyperactivity and their implications for intervention. Barbara Keogh (1971), for example, offered three hypotheses to explain the academic difficulties of hyperactive children. One group has neurological impairments, the second has information processing problems due to accelerated motor activity, and the third is impulsive, which affects decision making and reaction time. Only the first group, Keogh believes, is likely to benefit from drug treatment.

Even when medication helps hyperactive children pay better attention, learning problems often persist. "A youngster in the fourth grade with first-grade skills will not suddenly read at grade level if he is better able to attend to the fourth-grade text. A child who has failed in school and who has had painful and unrewarding relationships with others will not automatically reverse his negative attitudes toward himself as a result of being able to attend for a longer period of time" (Sandoval, Lambert, & Sassone, 1981, p. 118).

Side Effects

Gadow (1979) has reviewed the side effects of stimulant drugs. Two of the most common are loss of appetite and insomnia, although the latter can often be averted if the drugs are not given late in the day. Others are headaches, stomachaches, drowsiness, increased heart rate, elevated blood pressure, nausea, moodiness, irritability, and talkativeness. For some, decreases in activity level are extreme, and children acquire a zombie-like appearance. Long-term use of Ritalin and Dexedrine have also been associated with reduced weight gain and growth in height, although there are usually growth spurts when medications are discontinued. Some medicated children experience a rebound effect and seem even more irritable and hyperactive when the drugs wear off.

There is concern that one of the long-term side effects is a predisposition of hyperactive children to later drug abuse. However, in a follow-up study of hyperactive children as young adults, they were not found to be heavier users of nonprescription drugs than nonhyperactive comparison groups (Hechtman, Weiss, & Perlman, 1984a). Alcohol and marijuana were the only such substances regularly used by large numbers of either group. Use of stimulants, hallucinogens, cocaine, and heroin was only slightly higher among hyperactive young adults.

A potential danger of drug treatment is that it may be viewed by parents, teachers, and physicians as a panacea for hyperactivity and associated learning problems. When behavioral improvements are observed, additional behavioral and academic interventions may not be implemented. In a manual for teachers on the use of medication, Gadow (1979, p. 22). has stated, "drugs do not teach the child anything . . . It is quite possible that without remedial instruction medication may not facilitate school achievement." Treatment of hyperactivity requires more than a single approach. Medication, behavior modification stressing self-control techniques, direct academic intervention, and individual and family counseling may all play a role in remediating hyperactivity (Backman & Firestone, 1979).

There appears to be widespread use of psychotropic drugs, particularly central nervous system stimulants for children and adolescents considered hyperactive. Other behavior-altering drugs, including antidepressants, antipsychotics, and lithium are less common, yet sometimes prescribed for other disorders such as the pervasive developmental disorders discussed in the previous chapter. Epstein and Olinger (1987) have suggested several guidelines for school personnel who work with students medicated with psychotropics. These include the following:

- become informed about the drugs
- follow school policy for administration of medications at school
- develop a communication system for physicians and parents
- collect behavioral data before, during, and after drug therapies
- monitor side effects
- discuss medication directly with students
- use parent groups to teach behavior management skills

Learning Disorders and Other Diagnoses

Behavior Patterns

Comparisons among learning disabled, behaviorally disordered, educable mentally retarded, and other diagnostic groups have appeared frequently in the research literature. In an early study, McCarthy and Paraskevopoulos (1969) compared behavior patterns evidenced by LD, ED, and a normal comparison group. They examined teacher ratings on three dimensions of the Quay-Peterson Behavior Problem Checklist—unsocialized aggression, immaturity/inadequacy, and personality problems. The teachers saw unsocialized aggression, characterized by behaviors such as restlessness, disruptiveness, attention seeking, fighting, and hyperactivity, as the most pronounced problem area for both ED and LD students. The ED students were rated significantly more deviant than LD students on all three dimensions. Further, the LD students were rated more deviant on each scale than the average students. The ratings were completed by teachers who were aware of their students' diagnoses; however, it is unclear how the teachers may have been influenced by knowledge of those labels. Other researchers have also found that teachers judge behaviorally disordered students to be more maladjusted than either LD or EMR students (Cullinan, Epstein, & Dembinski, 1979).

Differences have also been found in the observed frequency of specific classroom behaviors of ED and LD students. Barr and McDowell (1972) observed out-of-seat, negative physical contact, and vocalizations of matched groups of ED and LD students in special classes. The ED students exhibited significantly more negative physical contact and vocalizations, although they were not significantly more often out of their seats. Again, setting variables, such as classroom behavioral expectations in the two different settings, was not controlled.

Differences in deviant behavior of LD and BD students have been found to be a function of age level and placement. Sindelar, King, Cartland, Wilson, and Meisel (1985) compared teachers' judgments of the proportion of their students who exhibited five deviant behavior patterns—withdrawal, anxiety, hyperactivity, aggression, and lying, cheating, and stealing. The BD students were viewed more deviant on all five, although students' age and placement mediated those differences. Generally, more secondary students and those in self-contained programs were considered deviant compared with elementary and resource program students. As in the research cited earlier, behavioral distinctions between LD and BD students were found to be more quantitative than qualitative. That is, the same types of problem behavior were apparent in both groups, but they were more pronounced for BD than LD students.

Intelligence and Achievement

It has been difficult to pin down differences in intellectual functioning and achievement among identified LD, BD, and other populations. Several researchers have found median IQs of LD students to be in the mid- to upper-90s—similar to those of students identified as BD (Kavale & Forness, 1984). Gajar (1979) compared ED, LD, and EMR students on measures of intelligence and achievement. She found that all three groups had IQ score distributions below population norms and they were underachievers in reading, spelling, and arithmetic. However, there were also differences among the groups. For example, both ED and LD students had median IQ scores that were significantly higher than those of EMR students. Although the average ED and LD IQ scores were similar, LD students' IQ scores showed significantly more scatter, or variance, in subtest scores on the WISC–R than those of the ED students.

Demographic Comparisons

Gajar (1979) also noted some demographic differences among the ED, LD, and EMR groups, most notably that there was a higher percentage of black students in the EMR sample (53%) than in either the LD (27%) or the ED sample (18%). Others, too, have found that minority children are more likely to be considered EMR than LD (Tucker, 1980). By following ethnic representation in EMR and LD categories during the late 1970s, Tucker found that minority students, particularly blacks, increasingly made up a larger proportion of the EMR population. White students, by contrast, constituted a majority of students considered LD.

In a recent analysis of the emergence and growth of learning disabilities since the late 1950s, Sleeter (1986) calls learning disabilities a "socially constructed" category. She contends that it has been developed to accommodate white, middle-class students whose learning problems could not be ascribed to intellectual, environmental, emotional, or sociocultural factors. She asserts that the clauses in the LD definition excluding children whose learning problems may be due to environmental influences has resulted in de facto exclusion of many minority children from the category.

In considering the categories of ED, LD, and EMR, Hallahan and Kauffmann (1977) believe that the three groups have a great deal in common. They cite the three broad areas of educational concern for these groups as personality and social adjustment, underachievement, and intelligence. Hallahan and Kauffman conclude that the three categories show more overlap than uniqueness. Children in all three groups present personal and social adjustment problems, display below-average IQ scores, and are underachievers. As an alternative to standardized measures for determining educational needs, they suggest direct measurement of student performance of specified social and academic skills

Underachievement

Ysseldyke, Algozzine, Shinn, and McGue (1982) view learning disabilities as primarily problems of academic underachievement. In an interesting study comparing identified LD students and non-LD underachievers on a variety of measures commonly used to diagnose learning disabilities, they found few distinctions. In fact, an average of 96 percent of the scores of the two groups overlapped. That is, some of the underachievers scored more deviantly than some learning disabled students. Ysseldyke and his colleagues conclude that schools are either identifying too many students as LD who are not, or they are failing to identify many underachievers who should be considered LD. They believe that as many as 40 percent of these students may be misclassified.

On the Quay-Peterson Behavior Problem Checklist, the measure of personal and social adjustment used in the Ysseldyke, et al. (1982) study, there was also considerable overlap in the scores of some members of each group. However, the average score of the LD group was approximately twice as high as that of the underachievers. Thus, it appears that a key factor in distinguishing between underachievers and learning disabled students is teacher perceptions of behavioral problems in the latter group.

Assessment of Learning Disabilities

Formal assessment of students suspected of having learning disorders should follow the assessment steps outlined in Chapter 3. At each step, questions should be raised about the student's functioning in relation to the educational environment. For example, the early steps of assessment should examine features of the current educational placement (e.g., appropriateness of expectations, curricular materials, environmental influences, instructional strategies) that might affect academic performance. Pre-referral adaptations, such as those suggested in Chapter 3, should be implemented in regular classrooms. If these do not ameliorate the learning problems, assessment may advance to a formal evaluation. Here, the types of data that should be collected by the multidisciplinary assessment team would also be those discussed in Chapter 3 for students referred due to behavioral problems.

As we noted in an earlier section of this chapter, learning disabilities are defined in terms of discrepancies between ability and achievement in specific areas. LD students are underachievers whose performance lags significantly behind their measured abilities. Some states have adopted specific formulas for determining discrepancies between ability and achievement. Ability is usually based on scores from standardized individual intelligence tests; achievement is based on scores from standardized, individual, and group tests of academic performance.

Because of the exclusionary clauses in the LD definition, additional types of information are also required. Lerner (1981) has discussed five types of diagnostic data that should be included in a comprehensive evaluation: case histories and interviews, observation, informal testing, formal standardized testing, and criterion-referenced testing. If the concern is primarily with the child's academic performance, intelligence and achievement assessment are often stressed.

Ability Measures

Measures of ability or intelligence include individually administered tests such as the Stanford-Binet (Form L–M, ages 2 to adult), the Wechsler Intelligence Scale for Children—Revised (WISC –R, ages 6.0 to 16.11), and the more recently developed Kauffman Assessment Battery for Children (K–ABC, ages 2½ to 12½). These tests are based upon a concept of global intelligence. The Stanford-Binet, for example, yields an intelligence quotient (IQ), which is calculated by comparing the child's chronological age (CA) with mental age (MA).

IQs are actually deviation scores that indicate how an individual's scores compare with a normal distribution of scores for other children of the same age. The tests are constructed so that the average score is 100. For example, if a ten-year-old child's scores equal those of the average nine-year-old who has been tested, the child's IQ would be 90 (MA = 9, divided by CA = 10).

Performance on individual intelligence tests is frequently used as a critical diagnostic criterion to differentiate types of learning problems. The designation of learning disabled is generally limited to children whose measured IQs are average or above, although the average IQs for this population fall slightly below population averages. Children whose overall IQs are below 90 but above about 70 are more likely to be ineligible for the LD designation and may be considered slow learners. Children whose measured IQs are significantly below average (below about 70, but above about 55), may be considered educable mentally retarded (EMR).

The WISC–R is frequently used in the assessment of learning disabilities because, in addition to its global score, it has separate verbal and performance scales comprised of twelve subtests. WISC–R subtest results can be examined to determine possible uneven patterns of performance. Discrepancies are sometimes found in an individual's performance on subtests, with relatively high performance on some and low performance on others. A child's overall IQ score may be below average, yet there may be areas of relatively high and low abilities.

Achievement Measures

Measures of academic achievement are also necessary for the determination of discrepancies. Commonly used standardized achievement measures include the Peabody Individual Achievement Test (PIAT), Stanford Achievement Test, the Brigance Diagnostic Inventories, the Woodcock-Johnson Psycho-Educational Battery: Achievement Section, and the Woodcock Reading Tests. The psychometric properties of these and other measures of academic achievement are discussed in several sources (e.g., Evans, Evans, & Mercer, 1986; Salvia & Ysseldyke, 1981).

Determining Ability–Achievement Discrepancies

Although learning disabilities are defined as discrepancies between ability and achievement, there is a lack of consensus about how they should be determined or how large they must be. Janet Lerner (1981, pp. 113–114) suggests trying to answer the following questions: "(1) What has the child actually learned and what is the child's present achievement level? (2) What is the child potentially capable of learning and how can this potential be measured? (3) What amount of discrepancy between achievement and potential should be considered significant?" To date, no universally acceptable answers to these questions are available. Schools and, ultimately, the multidisciplinary teams charged with determining eligibility for special education must determine their own standards if they are not determined in state guidelines.

Problems with Standardized Discrepancy Measures

Some of the difficulties encountered in diagnosing learning disabilities include problems with measurement errors on standardized tests that limit the certainty that a child's test scores actually represent his or her ability and achievement. For many students considered learning disabled, test performance is unstable. For at least one subgroup, scores on both aptitude and achievement decline following formal identification (White & Wigle, 1986). In addition, questions have been raised about the validity and reliability of standardized, norm-referenced measures of intelligence and academic achievement. These questions include the relationship between the factors measured by intelligence tests and actual capacity for learning, the stability of intelligence measures over time, and the comparability of different measures of intelligence.

There are also the concerns we noted in Chapter 3 about the validity of measures of intelligence with minority children. Most tests tend to rely on the use of standard English, reflect narrow cultural experiences and values, and sometimes have not included minority representation in their norming procedures. Thus, the performance of minority children on these tests may represent biased underestimates of a child's ability. Low performance may be due to factors such as poor test-taking skills, lack of motivation, and lack of exposure to the skills tested (Harrington, 1984).

Suffice it to say that there are both advantages and disadvantages of standardized tests. Advantages include the following:

- standard procedures for administration and scoring
- ability to compare an individual score with group norms

- measurement of ongoing changes in performance
- measurement of individual variability in specific areas

Potential disadvantages include:

- low reliability and validity for some tests
- overgeneralization of findings
- emphasis on total or global scores rather than on the performance of specific skills
- lack of relevance to educational program design and implementation
- discrimination against minority groups

Certainly, standardized tests have a place in the educational assessment process. They are particularly useful in making decisions about a student's eligibility for special education programs. However, even when used for this purpose, they must be administered and interpreted by qualified examiners, their results should be viewed in the context of multiple measures, and they should be related to educational programs.

In addition, there is no generally accepted procedure or standard for determining discrepancies between ability and achievement. Indeed, this is a thorny issue. If, for example, a discrepancy of one year is the accepted standard, consider how much greater that discrepancy would be for a six-year-old than a sixteen-year-old. The six-year-old's underachievement probably represents a more serious problem than the sixteen-year-old's.

Discrepancy formulas (e.g., Bond, Tinker, & Wasson, 1979; Hanna, Dyck, & Holen, 1979) have been developed using scores on norm-referenced tests. In addition to comparisons of scores on intelligence and achievement tests, discrepancies are sometimes tabulated by computing differences between a child's achievement level in a subject area and the child's grade level, or between a child's chronological and mental age.

Such standard formulas should always be used with some healthy skepticism about the validity and reliability of the scores that are used. Scores derived from formulas are no more meaningful than the test scores that go into them. In addition, these scores alone cannot account for many variables such as students' educational background, motivation, and environment. Still, some criteria are necessary to help multidisciplinary teams determine a child's eligibility for services. Quantitative data from standardized measures and scores derived from discrepancy formulas must always be evaluated in the context of multiple measures of a child's functioning. These should include criterion-referenced and informal testing of specific problem areas, direct observation of student performance in the educational settings, and information obtained from case histories and interviews.

Interventions with Learning Disabilities

Process Approaches

Early efforts to remediate learning disabilities emphasized approaches such as perceptual-motor and psycholinguistic training. Instruments such as the Illinois Test of Psycholinguistic Abilities (ITPA) were developed to measure visual, auditory, and motor processes underlying communication skills required for successful academic learning. From these assessments, interventions were designed to directly remediate the psycholinguistic disabilities. Despite their popularity, these process approaches have not generally been found to result in corresponding improvement in academic skills (Arter & Jenkins, 1979; Kavale & Mattson, 1983). Kavale (1981), however, did find that psycholinguistic approaches appear to improve verbal expression. Some advocates of psycholinguistics have argued that in many of the studies reviewed to discredit such training, psycholinguistic training was inappropriately used in isolation from other academic instruction (Kirk & Chalfant, 1984).

Clinical Teaching

Janet Lerner (1981) has proposed that a special kind of instruction, which she calls *clinical teaching*, is necessary for children who are handicapped by learning problems. Clinical teaching emphasizes a continuous diagnosis and treatment of learning problems using a cycle of diagnosis, planning, implementation, evaluation, and modification of the diagnosis. Clinical teaching has its roots in applied behavior analysis. Many of the behavioral interventions discussed in Chapter 8 are also derived from applied behavior analysis. Clinical teaching involves a process similar to designing individual educational programs (IEPs) that will be discussed in Chapter 11. Lerner has outlined the following eleven steps:

1. identify behavior
2. establish goals
3. arrange learning situations
4. gather baseline data
5. study baseline data
6. analyze performance
7. decide on necessary changes
8. select intervention techniques
9. use the techniques
10. remove the techniques
11. help generalize the behavior

Direct Instruction

Direct instruction in specific academic skills incorporates some features of the clinical teaching model and appears to be an effective approach to remediation of learning disabilities (Gersten, Woodward, & Darch, 1986; Lloyd, 1987). It, too, follows the procedures of individualized educational programming. Mercer and Mercer (1985) identify the following instructional sequence in direct instruction:

1. identify target skills
2. determine factors likely to facilitate learning
3. plan instruction
4. use data-managed instruction for presentation, controlled practice, and independent practice

Direct instruction is based partly on research by Rosenshine (1976) involving students performing at low levels in regular classrooms. It utilizes a process of teacher demonstration, guided practice by the student, and feedback from the teacher (Gersten, et al., 1986). *Demonstration* refers to teacher modeling of skill. *Guided practice* refers to teacher questioning, prompting, and checking the student's understanding during practice of the skill. *Feedback* refers to the teacher's evaluation and reinforcement of performance.

Recently, Lloyd (1987) synthesized research literature involving direct instruction. He identified three distinct approaches—behavioral, instructional, and cognitive—although they sometimes overlap and are used in combination. An example of the behavioral approach is modeling of desired academic behavior (e.g., fluent reading) by the teacher and reinforcement of its performance. An example of the instructional approach is using task analysis to break down the steps necessary to perform a given task and making them explicit to the student. Cognitive approaches make covert operations more overt. For example, a student may be taught to verbalize the steps for checking the accuracy of academic work.

Identification of target skills to be taught through direct instruction may be determined by student performance on standardized, norm-referenced tests, as well as criterion-referenced measures. In the course of intervention, the teacher must determine if task difficulty levels are appropriate, since learning tasks must be sufficiently demanding to engage student interest while allowing a relatively high success rate. The continuous collection of data on student performance in learning tasks is also necessary to monitor progress and provide information on how teaching strategies might be modified.

The importance of generalization of learned skills is widely recognized (Blankenship & Lilly, 1981; Deshler, Schumaker, & Lenz, 1984; Stearns & Rosenshine, 1981). Generalization refers to the maintenance of a skill across time and set-tings so that a student can perform the learned skill outside of the remedial environment. Deshler, et al. (1984) suggest a sequence of presentation, controlled practice, and independent practice of academic skills. The teacher first presents the need for learning a target behavior to the student and breaks it down into its component parts. The teacher then models each skill and explains each step. Next, the student practices the task in controlled materials with prompts, cues, and reinforcement from the teacher. The student then practices the skill independently, but with reinforcement and feedback from the teacher. Finally, the student practices the skill in other settings and with other materials, as in the regular classroom and curriculum, while the teacher continues to provide reinforcement and feedback.

Effective Teaching

Stearns and Rosenshine (1981) have identified several factors that appear related to student academic success in regular classrooms. Some of these are included in the broader literature about effective teaching, but may have particular relevance for students with learning problems (Behling, 1986).

One of the conclusions from the effective teaching literature is the importance of focusing on academic instruction. Engaged time, or the amount of time students actually spend on academic tasks like reading and computing, is positively correlated with achievement. Ysseldyke, et al. (1983) suggest that increasing the amount of time LD students are actively engaged in academic work is a relatively easy, yet perhaps critical, factor for improving their academic performance.

In addition, providing ongoing feedback helps students distinguish between correct and incorrect performance and informs them of their progress. Ensuring success is also important. High success rates appear to contribute to higher student self-esteem, better retention of learning, higher scores on achievement tests, and more positive attitudes toward school.

Stearns and Rosenshine (1981) believe it is critical that teachers express positive expectations for student performance and provide reinforcement for desirable academic and social behavior. It is apparent that a disproportionate amount of the interactions between teachers and LD students pertain to behavior management (Dorval, McKinney, & Feagans, 1982; Feagans & McKinney, 1981). They are largely teacher initiations in response to student inattention and rule infractions that do not involve positive interchanges and reinforcement.

Teachers' expectations also inadvertently affect student performance in both positive and negative directions. Based on an extensive review of research, Good (1981) found that expectations translate into teacher behavior toward students. For example, teachers tend to pay less attention to poorly achieving or slow students, and smile at and call on them less frequently than better students. They seat slower students further away from themselves, and provide more criticism and less feedback of their performance. They interrupt them more frequently, require less effort from them, and praise them less. The unfortunate result is that, over time, poorly achieving students conform by "living down" to their teachers' expectations. Consequently, strategies for effective teaching may be particularly important for students with learning disorders.

Learning Strategies for Adolescents

An approach related to direct instruction that is especially appropriate to teaching adolescents is the *learning strategies* approach (Alley & Deshler, 1979; Deshler & Schumaker, 1986). Rather than teaching a specific academic curriculum, learning strategies teach students how to learn and perform tasks. For example, a student may be taught strategies for summarizing and mem-

orizing material in social studies, rather than specific social studies content. Sometimes called *metacognitive* skills, learning strategies are seen as particularly relevant for adolescents. Adolescents with learning problems typically have a long history of academic failure, and they often display minimal academic motivation. In addition, the amount of time they need to acquire deficient skills becomes more limited as they get older.

Schumaker, Deshler, Alley, and Warner (1983) have prepared several strands of a learning strategies curriculum. One includes strategies for acquiring information from written materials, such as word identification, self-questioning, and paraphrasing. Another strand includes strategies to help students identify and remember important information. Strategies for listening, note taking, and preparation for tests are included. A third strand includes strategies to facilitate written expression and demonstration of competence, such as formulas for sentences, paragraphs, and theme writing, error monitoring, and assignment completion.

A sequence of steps is used to teach learning strategies. It includes elements of the steps in direct instruction outlined earlier. Modeling of skills by teachers and rehearsal supported by metacognitive exercises involving verbalizing and thinking about tasks are included. The specific steps are:

1. testing to determine current habits on a particular task
2. breaking down the task into its component parts and providing a rationale for the task
3. teacher modeling of the task from start to finish, while verbally explaining each step
4. student verbal rehearsal of each step in the task
5. student practice with controlled material in a controlled setting
6. practice in materials and situations similar to regular classrooms, with corrective feedback and reinforcement from teacher
7. post-tests of student performance

A central goal of teaching learning strategies this way is to better ensure generalization and maintenance of learned skills. This approach attempts to systematically provide skills that students can apply to a variety of learning situations. Although the learning strategies approach is used to teach academic skills, the process is the same as the cognitive behavior modification approaches involved in social skills training programs that are discussed in Chapter 9.

Summary

In this chapter, we have added another dimension to our ecological perspective by examining some relationships between behavioral and learning disorders. Behavioral disorders cannot be considered in isolation from learning problems. Although not all behaviorally disordered children also experience academic failure, many do. Likewise, not all children with learning difficulties present behavioral and emotional problems, although many do. In fact, some educators view learning disabilities as primarily indicative of a child's difficulty in social perception. In some cases, personality and conduct problems contribute to difficulties with academic learning. The child may be too depressed or distracted to attend to academic work. In other cases, a child's problems with learning result in frustration, anger, and loss of self-esteem, which in turn are expressed in disruption or withdrawal in school.

For some behaviorally disordered students, learning problems affect performance in limited academic skill areas. For others, the difficulties are more pervasive and many exist across all academic areas. For some children, the learning problems are relatively mild; for others, academic ability and performance are more discrepant from age and grade expectations.

It is difficult to generalize about the contribution of learning disorders to behavioral problems and, conversely, of behavioral problems to learning disorders. Even when studying an individual case, we can usually only speculate about how one type of problem might have led to the other. However, it is clear that problems in one area place a child at higher risk for the other.

In this chapter, we have examined characteristics of learning disorders, particularly those called learning disabilities. We have studied definitions, characteristics, diagnostic procedures, and some of the difficulties in distinguishing between learning disabilities and other educationally relevant categories. We have given particular attention to definition and treatment of attention deficit disorders—a pattern of disordered behavior that has both academic and behavioral implications. Finally, we examined some strategies for remediating learning disabilities.

In the following chapters, we will discuss other interventions, most focusing on changing behavior and improving emotional adjustment. Just as some of the techniques of clinical teaching and direct instruction are relevant to intervening with behaviorally disordered children, many of the behavioral and psychoeducational approaches covered in forthcoming chapters are also relevant for children and adolescents with learning disabilities.

PART III

Special Education Programming

In one sense, Chapters 8, 9, and 10 constitute the core of this book because they present a broad range of specific intervention methods and techniques. The chapters in Part III translate into action the broad foundational concepts of Part I and the in-depth understanding of specific childhood disorders of Part II.

For example, our earlier understanding of community and family influences contributing to an undersocialized, aggressive conduct disorder will now be directed toward establishing specific interventions with an individual child or adolescent. We will examine methods for identifying points of intervention and methods for collecting data. In turn, these techniques will be used to develop plans for behavioral

and psychoeducational intervention at the classroom level.

In Chapter 10 we will also examine the characteristics of service delivery systems in order to understand the complex relationships among child, teacher, and school system. Although teacher understanding may lead to identification of specific problems and a plan for intervention, all these must in turn fit within the constraints of the educational system. No matter how complete one's understanding or how comprehensive an intervention plan one develops, it must be workable within prevailing models and practices.

In essence, then, Part III constitutes a set of action plans for turning knowledge and understanding into day-to-day teacher behavior.

CHAPTER 8

Behavioral Interventions

Overview

Introduction

In earlier chapters we have presented information concerning *who, what,* and *why* questions about children and adolescents with behavioral disorders. We discussed definitions and major theoretical perspectives on emotional and behavioral deviance. Next, we considered the assessment process and strategies that contribute to making decisions about who requires special interventions and the nature and extent of their social and academic difficulties. Then, we examined several patterns of behavioral disorders. We now turn our attention to the *how* questions: the intervention processes and strategies most helpful for improving the social, emotional, and academic functioning of behaviorally disordered children and adolescents.

This chapter discusses behaviorally oriented educational interventions. Chapter 9 addresses psychoeducational interventions. The distinction between interventions as behavioral or psychoeducational is largely determined by the target of the intervention process. Richard Whelan (1977) has noted that the two orientations can be distinguished by their assumptions about the sources of behavioral deviance and the focus of intervention. Implicit in behavioral approaches

is the assumption that disordered behaviors are themselves the problem. Thus, behavioral interventions are directed at changing (or modifying) a child's disordered behavior. By contrast, psychoeducational approaches assume that disturbed emotions and thinking produce disordered behavior. Consequently, these interventions focus on changing the ways children feel and think about their behavior.

Despite our separate consideration of behavioral and psychoeducational interventions, we recognize that the distinction is sometimes arbitrary. We have chosen, for example, to discuss social skills training programs in Chapter 9, despite their common foundation in learning theories. Although there are some identifiable differences between the two approaches, there are also areas of overlap. In most special education programs for students with personality and conduct disorders, methods that could be characterized as both behavioral and psychoeducational are employed.

The Behavioral Approach

Over the past twenty-five years, behavioral interventions have been increasingly employed in educational programs for behaviorally disordered students. The growth in the use of such techniques has corresponded with the development of applied behavior analysis (the study of how antecedent and consequent events affect behavior). Today, a variety of such interventions are used to teach and modify a variety of behaviors under a variety of conditions. The discussion of conceptual models of emotional and behavioral deviance in Chapter 2 included the behavioral model as a major approach for explaining deviant behavior. These behavioral, or learning, theories provide explanations of how disordered behavior can be learned. Each learning theory also provides the theoretical underpinnings for specific behavior modification strategies. However, those based upon operant learning theory and social learning theory have had the widest application in school-based programs. Techniques derived from operant learning theory (behavior modification through the systematic, contingent reinforcement or punishment of behavior) constitute a major constellation of behavior modification strategies presented in this chapter. Because of their emphasis on understanding and deliberate decision making, methods derived from social learning theory (modeling or imitative learning) are discussed in the next chapter.

An extensive amount of literature on the application of behavioral interventions has appeared in the past twenty-five years. For additional information beyond what is provided in this chapter, several comprehensive overviews of behavioral interventions with behaviorally disordered students are available (e.g., Kerr & Nelson, 1983; Neel, McDowell, Whelan, & Wagonseller, 1982; Nelson & Rutherford, 1987; Polsgrove & Nelson, 1981; Simpson & Sasso, 1982; Zabel, 1981).

Assumptions

Neel, et al. (1982, p. 102) have summarized five basic assumptions of behavioral approaches:

1. nearly all behavior is learned

2. principles of behavior can be used to change disordered behavior
3. the focus is on current rather than past situations
4. the focus is on observable phenomena rather than internal states
5. the techniques used in a behavioral approach are subjected to testing each time they are used

According to a behavioral perspective, both desirable and undesirable behaviors are learned. Behaviorally disordered children have been characterized as exhibiting "deficits of those behaviors considered desirable and/or excesses of those behaviors considered undesirable by teachers, parents, peers, and society in general. In other words, they engage in too many inappropriate, disruptive, disagreeable behaviors, and too few appropriate, cooperative, agreeable behaviors" (Zabel, 1981, p. 192). The behavioral model provides methods by which such undesirable behaviors can be "unlearned" and desirable behaviors can be learned.

Behavioral approaches do not dwell upon past causes of behavior, but instead examine how current conditions influence and maintain behavior. This does not mean that behavioral approaches totally discount the importance of the effect of past learning on behavior. It does mean, however, that behavior managers believe that solutions to problem behaviors can be developed within the child's current environment. Thus, behavioral approaches are amenable to educational programs because of their practical emphasis on changing aspects of the immediate environment to modify behavior.

In addition, although behavioral approaches do not discount the existence of internal functions, such as thoughts and feelings, they generally assume that these internal states can only be determined by observable behavior. Thus behavior managers generally concern themselves only with changing observable, measurable behavior.

The emphasis on the measurement of behavioral change is a central feature of this approach. A variety of procedures exist for assessing the effectiveness of behavioral interventions, but the ultimate measure of success is documented change in pupil behavior. "Accordingly, irrespective of other changes that may occur concomitantly in behaviorally disordered students (e.g., improvement of self-concept, better understanding of self), educators must be able to demonstrate that their interventions significantly modified these excesses and deficits initially associated with special program placement . . . " (Simpson & Sasso, 1982, p. 47). In the latter part of this chapter, we will discuss some commonly used means of measuring behavior change.

Increasing and Decreasing Behavior

Behavioral interventions can be used to increase and/or decrease behaviors. Zabel (1981) noted three ways that behavioral interventions are employed by teachers of behaviorally disordered students. First, they are used to improve academic performance by breaking down academic tasks into their component parts and sequentially teaching these by providing prompts and reinforcement for correct responses. The direct instruction strategies we discussed in Chapter 7, for example, include these behavioral elements. Second, behavioral interventions are used to improve the student behavior that contributes to academic performance. These conditions for learning include, for example, increasing the amount of time a student spends working on-task or reducing the number of days a student is absent from school. Third, behavioral interventions are also used to directly increase behaviors considered socially desirable, such as sharing or cooperating, and to reduce behaviors considered undesirable, such as fighting or arguing.

In each of these uses, behavioral change usually occurs gradually. Changes in behavior often must be *shaped*. Shaping refers to reinforcement of successive approximations of a terminal behavior. For example, a desirable behavior for a socially withdrawn child might be interactive play with classmates. However, it may not be immediately possible to reinforce that terminal behavior, since the child avoids any interaction with peers. To shape the behavior, a hierarchy of behaviors that lead to interactive play must be determined. Then, each successive approximation of the behavior must be reinforced until it occurs spontaneously. In this example, it may first be necessary to reinforce the child simply for staying in the same room with classmates, then for watching classmates play, then for sitting at the same table, and so on, until the terminal behavior of interactive play can be reinforced.

As we have discussed earlier, learning and behavior problems frequently go hand in hand, with problems in one area contributing to problems in the other. A student experiencing academic difficulties is more likely to have social problems; one experiencing social problems is more likely to encounter academic difficulties. Thus, improving a child's functioning in either the social or academic arena may improve performance in the other. Behavioral interventions offer several strategies for increasing and decreasing behavior.

Determining Goals and Objectives

Prior to the implementation of any intervention, behavioral or otherwise, it is necessary to determine appropriate goals and objectives. Specific guidelines for preparing individual educational programs (IEPs), including written goals and objectives, are included in Chapter 10. The framework for behavioral interventions corresponds with steps in the IEP process and includes the following phases:

- selection of target behaviors
- observation and recording of baseline data
- development of a rationale for intervening
- selection of method(s) for modifying target behavior

- implementation of the intervention
- monitoring effectiveness of intervention
- communication of intervention outcomes to relevant participants

This multiphase process means that behavioral interventions must be systematically planned, implemented, and evaluated.

The A–B–C Analysis

As we saw in Chapter 3, evidence of relationships between a child's behavior and environment frequently can be determined. Information based on direct observation and setting analyses can help us recognize functional relationships between antecedent conditions, resulting behavior, and consequences of that behavior. The relationships are considered functional because behavior is seen as dependent upon controlling antecedent and consequent events. Antecedents are conditions preceding behavior that set the stage for the behavior or prompt its occurrence (Walker, 1979). They include the physical and social settings in which behavior occurs (e.g., behavior of others, the curriculum, and even a child's own self-reported feelings and thoughts preceding the behavior of interest). Consequences are events (e.g., environmental conditions, reactions of others) following behavior that maintain, strengthen, or weaken it.

This so-called A–B–C (antecedent–behavior–consequence) analysis always recognizes the context in which behavior occurs. In a classroom where certain student behaviors may be of particular concern, a behavioral analysis would seek answers to the following questions: "What are the antecedent conditions that prompt, or set the occasion for the behavior?" and "What consequences—reinforcements, punishments—maintain, strengthen, or weaken the behavior?"

For example, a student's frequent interruption of class proceedings by talking without permission may be a concern to the teacher. Observation of antecedents and consequences of the problem behavior may reveal that when the

teacher leads a class discussion she seldom responds to the student's raised hand (antecedent), the student talks without permission (behavior of concern), and the teacher and other students respond by paying attention to the talking out (consequence). In this scenario, the student's talking-out behavior has probably been strengthened. This analysis of antecedents and consequences for a troubling behavior points to conditions in the immediate environment that may require modification if the problem behavior is to be changed.

Lest this functional analysis appear too simplistic, remember that antecedents and consequences of deviant behavior also occur beyond the immediate environment of the classroom. For instance, some behaviorally disordered students have received little approval for their appropriate behavior and have, in effect, learned undesirable behavior because it results in attention from others. Such behavior may be well established in the child's repertoire as a result of previous or current reinforcement in other environments (e.g., family, neighborhood), making it more resistant to modification in the school.

Selection of Target Behaviors

The kinds of questions that can be asked about potential target behaviors are the *what, who, where, when,* and *how* questions. Box 8.1 includes questions that can contribute to an understanding of problem behavior. To answer these questions, the behavior modifier may have to engage in additional study of the behavior to understand its functional relationship with antecedents and consequences. Such an analysis can also contribute to a rationale for intervening.

In the Box 8.1 example, Tom's disruptiveness includes frequent talking out, poking other students, and verbal insults toward others. These behaviors have been observed throughout the school day, but especially during math class, before lunch, and just before the end of the day. They are most pronounced during independent seat work, disturb students near Tom and

---

Box 8.1   Studying Problem Behavior

Student: Tom
Program: Middle School Self-Contained BD Class

---

1. What is the problem behavior?

   Tom's provocative verbalizations. He insults and teases other students; he also tries to poke, trip, and bump other students.

2. What does the problem affect?

   It disrupts other students' working, makes students angry, demands teacher attention.

3. Where does the behavior occur?

   Tom's verbal behaviors are directed anywhere in the classroom; poking and other physical behaviors are primarily within Tom's arm- and leg-reach from his desk.

4. When does the behavior occur?

   It occurs throughout the day, especially during math (3rd period), before lunch, and in late afternoon.

5. How often (long) does it occur?

   Tom makes approximately 3 to 4 provocative comments per 45-minute period, and more during times mentioned above; 2 to 3 physical contacts each day.

6. How do others react to it?

   Other students, especially Dennis and Jaimee who are frequent targets, respond with counter-insults and threats. The teacher tells Tom to stop it and takes away points. None of this seems to have any beneficial effect on Tom's behavior.

---

draw the teacher's attention away from working with others. In addition, the teacher reports her own anger and frustration in dealing with Tom. Once potential target behaviors have been studied in terms of their functional relationship with antecedent and consequent conditions, the process of selecting methods for modifying those behaviors can begin.

Methods for Increasing Behavior

Reinforcement

Reinforcement refers to consequences of behavior that increase the future rate of that behavior. There are two general categories of reinforcement—positive and negative—that can be used to increase behavior. Positive reinforcement is more commonly employed in programs for behaviorally disordered children (Maheady, Duncan, & Sainato, 1982). It involves presenting a stimulus following a particular response that has the effect of maintaining or increasing that response (Sulzer-Azeroff & Mayer, 1977).

There are several forms of positive reinforcement, including tangible rewards (e.g., objects, edibles), tokens (e.g., checkmarks, stars), activities (e.g., special privileges, free time), and social reinforcement (e.g., attention, compliments). A particular object or event is not considered reinforcing unless it contributes to an increase in the behavior of interest. Of course, some consequences are reinforcing for some students, while different consequences are reinforcing for other students. Thus, a teacher's attention or praise for the desired behavior of one student may effectively increase that behavior. Other students may require the kinds of tangible or token reinforcement described below to modify their behavior.

Any number and kind of items and experiences may potentially serve as positive reinforcers. For some students, snacks, stickers, pencils, and toys are effective. For others, privileges like taking attendance, delivering messages, sitting in special places, using a tape player, or enjoying free time may be more effective. Other students may respond to accumulating points in a token economy, a system of awarding symbolic rewards, such as checkmarks, that are later exchanged for actual reinforcers, and seeing graphic representations of their progress. Teacher attention and praise for performance are low-cost, easily used, yet powerful forms of reinforcement for many students. Even for a single student, however, different types and strengths of reinforcers may be necessary to modify different behavior at different times.

The best ways to select reinforcers are to observe what students like to do and to ask what they find rewarding. If a student has been observed visiting with other students, chewing gum, reading magazines, drawing pictures, or listening to rock music, then any of these may be used as potential reinforcers. If a student expresses interest in reading in a designated quiet area, playing board games with other students, working with the janitor, or working on a special project, these may be potential reinforcers.

Reinforcers can be systematically employed to change behavior using the Premack Principle (Premack, 1965). This principle states that a higher frequency behavior (i.e., one that the student engages in independently) can be made contingent upon a low frequency behavior (i.e., one that the student does not engage in independently) to increase the latter. For example, several students may frequently talk with one another (high frequency behavior), but seldom complete assigned work (low frequency behavior). The Premack Principle may be employed by providing a designated time for talking that is contingent upon the completion of assignments. Specified amounts of completed work could earn specified amounts of talking time.

Token Economies

One commonly employed application of the Premack Principle is the *token economy.* It can be an effective method for modifying behavior both of individuals and groups (Kazdin, 1982; Kazdin & Bootzin, 1972). Tokens are symbolic rewards used as temporary substitutes for the more substantial reinforcers for which they may later be traded. Tokens may take the form of checkmarks, points, poker chips, colored strips of paper, or play money, and are assigned a predetermined value and are earned for performing specified behavior.

An advantage of a token system is that symbolic rewards can be awarded immediately following the performance of a desired behavior with minimal interference in the ongoing program. Later, tokens can be cashed in for the actual reinforcers at convenient times. Token economies require a prior determination of the behaviors that will earn tokens, the token value of specific behaviors, the procedures for awarding tokens, the exchange rate for the actual reinforcers, and the opportunities for exchange.

Token economies have been used with both individuals and groups of students with personality and conduct disorders. Even group systems can be individualized. Some behaviors earn rewards for all members of the group, while additional behaviors are specified for individuals within the group. Token value, exchange rate, and types of actual reinforcers may differ from student to student. Box 8.2 contains a sample token card listing token-earning behavior common to the group ("raises hand before talking" and "stays in seat") as well as individually as-

Box 8.2   Sample Token Card Resource Room

Name: *Marcia*   Date: *April 6*

| | Behaviors | | | |
Time	raises hand	in-seat	hands to self	minds own business
10:15– 10:30		✓	✓	
10:30– 10:45		✓	✓	
10:45– 11:00	✓		✓	✓
11:00– 11:15	✓	✓	✓	✓
11:15– 11:30	✓	✓	✓	✓
Totals:	3	4	5	3

Points Earned: *15*   Points Spent: *10*   Points Saved: *5*

signed behavior ("keeps hands to self" and "minds own business").

It is common practice to provide choices for the actual reinforcers. Sometimes teachers organize this in the form of a store with a variety of snack foods, toys, games, and activities that may be purchased for different prices, with the relative cost determined by real-world values. Thus, some items and activities may be relatively inexpensive, but provide more immediate gratification for those who need it. Others may be more costly, requiring an accumulation of tokens over a longer period of time.

A menu of reinforcers can provide choices and help students avoid becoming satiated by the same reinforcers. Just as one's appetite for turkey may be strong on Thanksgiving Day, but

severely dissipated after several meals of leftovers, the continuous use of the same reinforcers sometimes lessens their desirability. Managers of token economies should also provide sufficient opportunities for students to purchase reinforcers to ensure that associations are made between behavior and reinforcement. Especially with younger children and when token economies are initiated, purchasing opportunities may need to be more frequent than with older children or when the token economy is a long-established intervention. It is also critical to the success of a token economy that access to actual reinforcers outside of the system is limited, since access to unearned reinforcers will deflate the value of the tokens.

Teachers can be creative in their selection of

actual reinforcers. They may be as simple as a sticker or a piece of candy or as elaborate as a ride in an airplane. The key is to identify what has reinforcing potential for the participants, what is within the teacher's ability to provide, and then to determine token values and exchange rates. Reinforcers need not be things. Frequently, activities are powerful reinforcers. One teacher in a self-contained class for behaviorally disordered students negotiated a group reward of having his beard shaved when the class collectively earned a certain number of points for classroom behavior. Several weeks later, the class achieved the targeted number of points and accompanied the teacher to the barbershop, where they reaped their reward.

In an early study of a token economy, Graubard (1969) showed how the group can be used to help disturbed delinquents to learn. Given the influence of peer approval among teenage students, Graubard determined it was necessary that they buy into the token system. The class was told it could earn points to exchange for rewards such as sports equipment, money, and time to listen to records only when the entire group followed specified classroom rules and completed assignments. Rules governing attendance, destruction of property, and the use of physical force were mandated to the group. Other rules concerning talking and discussion procedures were negotiated. The students themselves were taught to manage the token system, while the teacher assigned work, awarded points, and ignored inappropriate behavior. In just twenty morning sessions, Graubard found that the group's inappropriate behavior fell to less than one-half of its previous level and there was a corresponding increase in the group's academic production.

Although no particular problems were noted in the Graubard study, group token systems should be used with some caution. When rewards are contingent upon total group participation, teachers should be aware of the possibility that the group will coerce, rather than encourage, participation from its individual members.

An advantage of token economies is that they can also be used across settings. In a departmentalized program, for example, students can carry their point cards from class to class. At the end of each period, the teacher awards a specified number of points for several categories of behavior. These might be quality of academic work, punctuality and attendance, amount of work completed, and social behavior. Points can be tabulated daily and weekly, with actual reinforcers made available at predetermined times. Similar procedures can be used for students who are integrated in regular classes, with a resource teacher overseeing a token system to help maintain a student's appropriate behavior in the mainstream program.

When tokens are provided for qualitatively judged behaviors (e.g., "cooperation with others"), care must be taken to ensure that both teachers and students are clear about what the behavior means and how it will be evaluated. When a token economy is used in a single setting, such as a special classroom, the system manager must establish objective standards and clarify them with students. When the token economy operates in several environments, a good deal of communication may be required to ensure consistency.

Token economies can be extended beyond classroom walls to provide more consistent behavior management in other environments (e.g., on the school bus, in the lunchroom, at home). For example, in a secondary program the teacher arranged for parents to deposit students' allowances in a special bank checking account. Students could then earn that money through predetermined academic and social behavior in the classroom and receive weekly checks written by the teacher in accordance with their performance.

A token system serves the dual purpose of a motivational support system and behavior monitoring system that can provide ongoing information about social or academic performance useful for developing and modifying students' programs. This data collection capability is built into token economies. Later in this chapter, we will discuss how tokens that are systematically assigned and awarded can translate into behavioral data for evaluating intervention effectiveness.

Generalization

A concern with any intervention is the degree to which it generalizes over time and across settings. That is, the degree to which the behavior of concern continues to be performed beyond the setting in which it has been learned. Unfortunately, relatively little attention has been given to maintenance and generalization of behavioral gains in the research literature. The same criticism can be leveled at nonbehavioral interventions, but the weakness may be more apparent with behavioral interventions because of their emphasis on measurement. Patterson (1974), Stokes and Baer (1977), and Walker and Buckley (1972) have analyzed factors involved in generalization and maintenance of treatment gains. One strategy is called *fading.*

Fading Type of Reinforcement. Fading can involve a gradual change in the stimulus presented to prompt a behavior. For example, a teacher's verbal prompt, "Look at me," prior to beginning a learning task may be gradually dropped when the student looks at the teacher spontaneously.

Fading can also refer to the gradual reduction of dependence upon external reinforcement for behavior. It may involve moving away from more external forms of reinforcement toward social reinforcement and intrinsic, or self-reinforced, behavior. Even when immediate, tangible, or token reinforcement is necessary, it should usually be paired with social reinforcement, so that associations can be made between the tangible and social reinforcement. The award of a token, for example, can be accompanied by a positive statement regarding performance, such as "good work" or "nice job." Eventually the social reinforcement alone may replace the token.

Thinning Reinforcement Schedules. Another procedure for encouraging generalization is called *thinning* the frequency of reinforcement. Several reinforcement schedules, or ratios of reinforcers to target behaviors, are possible. There are no hard and fast rules for the type of reinforcement schedule that should be used. Like the type of reinforcers themselves, the schedule is determined by the needs of the target student. When a new behavior is being taught, continuous reinforcement may be necessary. That is, every time the behavior is performed, it should be reinforced. However, once a behavior has been learned, an intermittent, less frequent schedule of reinforcement is appropriate. Bandura (1977) and Skinner (1974) have illustrated that behavior is most persistent when it is reinforced at a low, variable level.

Intermittent schedules take several forms. For example, a fixed interval schedule makes reinforcement available following a predetermined interval of time, such as every fifth or tenth minute. Variable interval schedules provide reinforcement at irregular intervals of time, such as following the third, seventh, and twelfth minutes during a fifteen-minute period. Fixed ratio reinforcement follows a predetermined number of target responses, such as the completion of each row of math problems. A variable ratio schedule provides reinforcement for irregular numbers of target behaviors, such as following completion of the third, fifth, and ninth problems. Alexander and Apfel (1976) have shown how schedules of reinforcement can be systematically altered in token systems to improve classroom behavior.

To determine an appropriate schedule, teachers must consider the degree to which the target behavior requires reinforcement, as well as the logistics of providing reinforcement. Some experimentation may be necessary to determine an initial, effective schedule. As interventions are implemented, the schedule can be thinned or faded as feasible. When target behavior appears to require less external reinforcement, less needs to be provided.

Relatively little attention has been given to preparing the student's natural environment to support generalization of behavioral gains made in special programs. Training regular classroom teachers and parents to provide consistent reinforcement for a prescribed behavior represents one such effort. Gerald Patterson (1974) has been a pioneer in training parents to implement behavioral interventions. More recently, Rhode, Morgan, and Young (1983) have taught behaviorally disordered students to use self-evaluation procedures to promote generalization and maintenance of treatment gains. In chapter 10 on educational programming and chapter 12 on working with parents, we will examine some additional strategies for maintenance and generalization of improved behavior in other settings.

Negative Reinforcement. A less commonly used behavioral method for increasing behavior in programs for behaviorally disordered students is negative reinforcement. Negative reinforcement is the cessation of an aversive stimulus contingent upon a specified response. A frequently used example of negative reinforcement is twisting someone's arm to increase the probability that they will say "uncle." Obviously, such physically aversive techniques have no place in special education programs, although other types of negative consequences are sometimes employed. One example might be to allow a student to skip some already assigned work if the student receives a perfect grade on a current assignment. Called *contingent skipping,* reinforcement is avoiding work that the student considers aversive.

Negative reinforcement is generally perceived as more coercive than positive reinforcement. Consequently, it provides greater risk for provoking oppositional behavior from students. Many behaviorally disordered students have encountered considerable negative reinforcement in their lives; some have developed considerable resistance to it, adopting a belligerent "make me" stance that sometimes leads to an escalation of negative consequences for noncompli-

ance. Thus, negative reinforcement can set a negative tone for interaction between student and teacher.

Methods for Decreasing Behavior

There are several behavior modification methods for decreasing undesirable behavior. These include reinforcement of behaviors that are incompatible with or are alternatives to the undesirable behavior, and several forms of punishment.

Reinforcement of Incompatible or Alternative Behavior

Differential reinforcement of incompatible (DRI) and differential reinforcement of alternative (DRA) behavior are nonaversive methods for reducing undesirable behavior. They are positive approaches for decreasing behavior. For example, a student may disrupt a class by frequently leaving his seat without permission. Rather than intervening directly to reduce the out-of-seat behavior, the teacher may be able to reduce it indirectly either by reinforcing behavior that is incompatible with out-of-seat behavior (i.e., in-seat) or by reinforcing alternative behavior (e.g., completion of academic work that can only be done at the student's desk). As Dietz and Repp (1983) point out, DRI and DRA can both reduce inappropriate behavior and build appropriate behavior.

McAllister, Stachowiak, Baer, and Conderman (1969) showed how a combination of teacher praise for being quiet and disapproval for talking out and turning around could be used with a low-track, high school English class. Although nondisruptive, appropriate classroom behavior does not ensure academic learning, there is considerable evidence that increasing completion of academic work can be associated with decreased disruptiveness (Kaufman & O'Leary, 1972).

In some situations, teachers unintentionally reinforce behavior that is incompatible with the behavior they desire. For example, a teacher may respond to student misbehavior with a disapproving comment in order to interfere with it. Buckley and Walker (1971) have found that "free operant teacher attention" to deviant behavior can maintain deviant student behavior as well as occupy a disproportionate amount of the teacher's time. They have also shown, however, that a teacher can turn this situation around by deliberately ignoring students' deviant behavior, while paying attention and responding to more desirable behavior.

Extinction

The above-mentioned technique of deliberately ignoring behavior in order to reduce it is called *extinction*. It is particularly applicable to reducing attention-seeking behavior, especially when alternative, incompatible behavior is reinforced. Extinction can consist of nonreaction to unwanted behavior; for example, when a teacher consistently does not call on students who do not raise their hands before talking. Sometimes, extinction may involve an obvious form of nonresponse, such as turning away, in order to make the student aware of disapproval of the behavior of interest.

In one junior high program for behaviorally disordered students, for example, the teacher uses a type of extinction. She responds to student griping, tattling, and unfounded complaints with a bland, noncommittal "thank you for telling me," to remind them that their complaints will receive no gratification from her. When one frustrated student complained, "You know what I hate? When I tell you something you just say, 'Thank you for telling me' but you don't do anything about it." Predictably, the teacher replied, "Thank you for telling me." The message to the student was that his behavior was unacceptable and would receive no response.

Ignoring undesirable behavior is not the only form of extinction. Removing existing reinforcement is another. Autistic children's repetitive, self-stimulating behavior has been extinguished by reducing or removing its reinforcing properties. For example, the auditory stimulation of spinning a plate on a hard surface such as a floor has been reduced by placing the plate on a rug where it can make no sound. The result has been extinction of the behavior.

Extinction is not effective for reducing all types of undesirable behavior. Some behavior simply cannot be ignored because it poses threats to other students, property, or the students themselves. Severe forms of attention-seeking behavior, such as threatened self-abuse or suicide, cannot be ignored because of the potential horrific consequences. In addition, some undesirable behavior is self-reinforcing. For example, nose picking, daydreaming, and masturbation are unlikely candidates for reduction through extinction. Reinforcement from other sources, such as attention and approval from classmates, even intermittently, can also undermine the effectiveness of extinction efforts by a teacher.

Successful use of extinction frequently requires perseverance by the teacher, since attention-seeking behavior often initially escalates when there is no response from the intended audience. The teacher may have to endure an upgraded, persistent display of the undesired behavior before it begins to diminish. Although deliberately not attending to unwanted behavior is one measure, other procedures, such as increasing reinforcement for others who are behaving appropriately can prompt an alternative, more desirable behavior. In most cases, as soon as the attention-seeking behavior ceases and appropriate behavior is displayed, that behavior should be reinforced.

Punishment

Several forms of punishment have been used to reduce some kinds of problem behavior. However, for each of these techniques there are limitations and ethical concerns. Consequently, extreme caution must be exercised when any form of punishment is considered. Aversive procedures have deservedly received considerable attention, and the debate continues regarding ethical and practical considerations in their use (McGinnis, Scott-Miller, Neel, & Smith, 1985).

According to a behavioral definition, punishment is a consequence of behavior that reduces its future probability. Such consequences reduce behavior because they are experienced as physically or psychologically aversive or unpleasant. Corporal punishments such as paddling, slapping, pinching, arm twisting, and even tickling have sometimes been used by teachers and other school authorities to reduce undesired student behavior. In some school districts, corporal punishment is endorsed by the community and school authorities as an acceptable method of discipline (Rose, 1983). In fact, the U.S. Supreme Court (*Ingraham* v. *Wright*, 1977) acknowledged historical and contemporary approval of "reasonable" corporal punishment. A variety of studies and polls "indicate that strong majorities of parents, teachers and school administrators, and in some cases, even students favor the use of corporal punishment in schools" (Wood, 1978, p. 30). Nevertheless, a punisher often finds scant support for challenged actions after the fact.

Aversive consequences such as assigning extra work, staying in from recess or after school, and standing in the hall are some noncorporal forms of punishment. More commonly employed, although often not recognized as punishment, are consequences such as scolding and shaming students and removing privileges.

Frank Wood and several colleagues have given considerable attention to the legal and ethical issues in the use of punishment and aversive techniques in schools (Wood & Braaten, 1983; Wood & Hill, 1983; Wood & Lakin, 1978). Wood and Hill asked regular and special education teachers to rate the aversiveness of thirty commonly used interventions for problem behavior. Among those considered most aversive were:

- physically restrain, push, or hold a student firmly

- require a student to do time-out in special isolation room
- paddle or switch a student on buttocks or legs
- request police to come to school to remove a student
- require student to go to school office or place of detention
- vigorously shake student or tightly squeeze flesh (arm, ear, neck, etc.)
- refer student for placement in in-school suspension.

It is significant that the teachers reported that they themselves rarely used these techniques. Other researchers have reported similar findings (Elliott, Witt, Galvin, & Peterson, 1984; Salend, Esquivel, & Pine, 1984).

Ethical and Practical Concerns. We strongly discourage the use of punitive approaches to reduce undesired student behavior in most instances and, instead, encourage the use of more positive approaches to behavior change discussed above. Our stance is based on both ethical and practical considerations.

Rubenstein and Rezmierski (1983) and Wood (1978) have convincingly argued that behaviorally disordered children are at risk of being punished. Such children elicit impulses from adults both to punish and to heal. The former impulse frequently prevails when disordered behavior is perceived as threatening. Because of its apparent effect of quickly reducing undesired behavior, it seems easy to punish behaviorally disordered children. We believe such tactics require great scrutiny.

There are limits to the effectiveness of punishment. Although punishment has been shown to be effective in producing immediate reductions in undesired behavior, improvements are often short-lived and the behavior for which the child was punished reappears. Because punishment interrupts problem behavior, it seems to work, reinforcing the punisher. Wood and Braaten (1983) note that punishment has a seductive appeal, despite the absence of any evidence of long-term effectiveness. Also, punishment alone does not teach alternative, desired behavior. When a teacher yells, "Be quiet," a student's talking may be temporarily suppressed, but the student has not learned an alternative behavior. Subsequently, the punished student may try to avoid the punishing situation or the punisher rather than engage in an alternative behavior.

Sometimes punishment is actually antagonistic to its intended purpose. Loud verbal reprimands (e.g., "Stop that! You're interrupting the class!") may call classmates' attention to the misbehavior, thus inadvertently reinforcing it. O'Leary, Kaufman, Kass, and Drabman (1970) have found soft reprimands, audible only to the target child, to be more effective than loud reprimands in reducing disruptive classroom behavior.

In-school suspension is a punishment for breaking school rules through such acts as truancy, fighting, swearing, and displaying disrespect for teachers. Conditions of in-school suspension are meant to be aversive: students are closely monitored, social interaction is not allowed, movement is limited, and all time must be spent working. School may be made doubly aversive to students who already find it disagreeable. In the case of a truant student, it is hard to see how such a consequence might encourage school attendance. Contingencies such as assigning extra school work or staying after school should generally not be used, since they can reinforce the notion that studies and school are aversive.

An additional concern about punishment is its potential immediate and long-term side effects. Punishment may deflect a student's attention from his or her behavior to the encounter with the punisher. Anger, distrust, and antagonism are frequently directed toward the punisher and may generalize to school, to teachers, and to adults. Sometimes, this anger develops into retaliation. Furthermore, teachers and others who use punishment provide models for settling differences that can be destructive for the punished child as well as others who observe the punishment. Students learn that "might makes right" as more powerful people prevail over less powerful.

A seldom discussed, yet real concern about punishment is its effect on the punisher. Particularly when it is not used in an open, unemotional way, the punisher may experience a sense of failure for not solving the problem more positively and may feel guilt for inflicting pain on another.

Many behaviorally disordered students have experienced large amounts of punishment in their lives. Some have been physically abused. Consequently, some have developed particular sensitivity or resistance to being punished. It is important for teachers and other school authorities to recognize that their own perceptions of aversiveness may be quite different from those of their students. What we may consider aversive may be reinforcing for some students. Being paddled or sent to time-out, for example, can confer a certain status that may strengthen, rather than weaken, the target misbehavior. As with reinforcement, consequences that are experienced as punishing vary among individuals.

Obviously, the above discussion raises serious ethical and practical concerns that must be considered before employing aversive techniques with behaviorally disordered students. It is also important to remember that there can be legal hazards for educators who use aversive techniques. "In the most narrow sense, special educators making use of punishing procedures have a selfish interest in planning protections against the more severe civil, criminal, and social penalties that might result. Beyond that, most will recognize the positive value in social pressures that push us toward better ways of educating children with special needs" (Wood, 1978).

Does this mean that aversive techniques should never be used with behaviorally disordered students? All teachers probably employ strategies that are perceived by some students as aversive. Interfering with the self-stimulating behavior of an autistic student, or including a socially inept, withdrawn student in a group activity may be experienced as aversive by those students. Nevertheless, the interventions may provide potential benefits that are judged to outweigh their aversiveness. When punishing and aversive techniques are used, it is essential that they be carefully selected, tailored to the individual needs of the target student, openly and systematically implemented, and continuously monitored and evaluated. Below, we discuss some forms of punishment that have been found to have efficacy for reducing forms of disordered behavior.

Response Cost. Response cost is a type of punishment used in some token economies. In addition to giving tokens, for engaging in specified behaviors, they can be removed for a specified misbehavior. In effect, participants are fined for breaking rules. Kaufman and O'Leary (1972) compared the effectiveness of reinforcement and response cost procedures in a token economy used in special classes in a psychiatric hospital and found both to be effective in reducing disruptive behavior without producing undesirable side effects. Phillips, Phillips, Fixsen, and Wolf (1971) found a combination of positive reinforcement and response cost more effective than response cost alone.

If response cost is used as part of a token economy, procedures for its use should be consistent with the reinforcement procedures. Hill Walker (1983) has offered several guidelines for implementing response cost. They include the following:

- it should be implemented immediately after and applied each time the target behavior occurs
- a child should not accumulate negative points
- the ratio of earned points to lost points should be controlled
- subtraction of points should not be punitive or personalized
- positive, appropriate behavior should be praised as it occurs

Among the most important of these guidelines is the avoidance of any accumulation of negative points, because the student may perceive his situation as debtor hopeless and give up on the token system.

Time-out. Time-out is a commonly used procedure for decreasing undesired behavior in programs for behaviorally disordered students (Maheady, Duncan, & Sainato, 1982; Zabel, 1986), but it is also one of the most controversial. Time-out is a procedure where "access to the sources of reinforcement is removed for a particular time period contingent upon the emission of a (maladaptive) response" (Sulzer-Azeroff & Mayer, 1977, p. 281). Brantner and Doherty (1983) define time-out as a change to a less reinforcing environment. The implication is that "time-in" must be a reinforcing environment for time-out to be an effective punisher.

A variety of forms of time-out are used by teachers (Gresham, 1979; Harris, 1985; Zabel, 1986), but not all correspond to a behavioral definition. Time-out may take the form of the physical segregation or isolation of a student in a specially designed facility for a short period of time so that behavior can be closely monitored. Time-out may also mean the exclusion of a student from ongoing class activities without his or her removal from the classroom. For example, a student might be required to sit facing the wall or behind a partition. Nonexclusionary time-out is yet another application in which the student is not physically segregated from reinforcing activity, but participation is limited. For example, a student is not allowed to earn tokens for a specified period of time or participate in class activities.

C. Michael Nelson and colleagues (Gast & Nelson, 1977a, 1977b; Nelson & Rutherford, 1987; Nelson & Stevens, 1983; Rutherford & Nelson, 1982) have provided detailed analyses of time-out. Based upon their review of forty studies of time-out with behaviorally disordered students in educational settings, Rutherford and Nelson (1983) classified time-out into six categories: planned ignoring, planned ignoring plus restraint, contingent observation, reduction of response maintenance stimuli, exclusion, and seclusion. However, there is no consensus on the inclusion of planned ignoring (or extinction) as a form of time-out. Gresham (1979) and Harris (1985), for example, assert that time-out is different from extinction because time-out involves at least mildly aversive consequences, while extinction involves removal of reinforcement.

Gast and Nelson (1977a, 1977b) have offered guidelines for the use of time-out. These include systematic planning of its use, careful supervision of implementation, assurance of safety features in time-out facilities, and continuous evaluation of effectiveness in producing desired results. In addition, behaviors resulting in time-out should be explicitly stated and communicated beforehand to students, and records of time-out's use and effectiveness maintained. They and others (e.g., Barton, Brulle, & Repp, 1983; Harris, 1985; Neel, 1978; Nelson & Stevens, 1983) have discussed legal and ethical implications of time-out in light of the "least restrictive alternative" doctrine of PL 94–142. Court cases have explicitly ruled against the isolation of handicapped persons for lengthy periods of time. Nelson and Rutherford (1983) consider time-out one of the most easily abused forms of intervention. Among potential shortcomings are the following: time-in environment is insufficiently reinforcing; time-out is inappropriately applied; the teacher cannot enforce the time-out contingency; and effectiveness is not established.

According to the Zabel study (1986), only about one-fifth of teachers of behaviorally disordered students report that their districts have written guidelines for time-out, and only about one-half maintain written logs of its use in their programs. Gast and Nelson (1977a, 1977b) urge the development of concise, written procedures delineating behaviors that result in time-out, the use of warnings, duration, conditions for release, and procedures for reentry into the program.

As far as the length of time-out is concerned, Gast and Nelson suggest using no more time than is necessary to accomplish a reduction in behavior, since longer periods have not been found to produce better results. Our guideline is no more time-out than the number of minutes equivalent to the child's age in years. Thus, for a six-year-old, six minutes would be the maximum, and for a twelve-year-old, twelve minutes would be the upper limit. In addition to time limits especially for isolation time-out, it is essential that facilities be free of dangers, well ventilated and lighted, appropriately heated and cooled, and continuously supervised.

Other Aversive Techniques. Additional behavioral methods of reducing disordered behavior, including corporal punishment and overcorrection, have been presented in the research literature, but have been studied primarily with severely impaired subjects in institutional settings. When less aversive forms of intervention have failed to modify behavior that seriously endangers (e.g., self-abuse) or significantly interferes (e.g., self-stimulation) with the subject's functioning, such techniques have been tried. Corporal punishment may take such forms as slapping, mild electric shock, or spraying lemon juice in the subject's mouth. Wood and Braaten (1983) advocate against the use of corporal punishment in school-based programs due to the absence of empirical support for its therapeutic value.

According to Sulzer-Azeroff and Mayer (1977), overcorrection involves two components — restitution, where the individual must restore the environment to a condition vastly improved from that which existed prior to the punished behavior, and positive practice, where the individual must repeatedly practice a substitute, positive behavior. These techniques are not commonly used in school programs for behaviorally disordered students and have been insufficiently studied at this point. Thus, they should be used only after careful study of the research literature to determine their appropriateness and limitations for the behavior of interest and to establish guidelines for their use. Even then, such strategies should be implemented under the strictest scrutiny from fellow members of the educational team, parents, and advocacy groups.

Guidelines for Punishment. To protect both punished and punisher, Wood and Braaten (1983) encourage the following guidelines for the use of any form of punishment: a policy statement, including the place of aversive procedures within a therapeutic education program, definitions of permitted and prohibited aversive procedures, and citations of relevant local, state, and federal laws, regulations, and court opinions; procedural guidelines, including promotion of awareness of aversive procedures and their use and misuse; staff training requirements; descriptions of appropriate use of aversive procedures; maintenance and retention of records; procedures for handling complaints and appeals, coupled with specific cautions; a list of useful resources; and procedures for periodic review. Wood and Braaten (1983, p. 73) also stress the role of individual teacher sensitivity to the use of aversive procedures: "Teachers should never attempt to continue in a role requiring use of aversive procedures for which they are untrained or with which they are extremely uncomfortable."

Methods for Increasing or Decreasing Behavior

There are some behavior modification methods that can be used either to increase or to decrease behavior. Self-monitoring, for example, by self-recording, tabulating, and graphing behavior is reinforcing for some students. Gottman and McFall (1972) found that disruptive adolescents who recorded their contributions to class discussions increased them, while a comparison group that recorded the times they did not make contributions when they felt like speaking up, decreased their contributions. Self-recording can

also reduce behavior such as disruptive talking out, although without backup reinforcement, self-recording appears to lose its appeal over time (Broden, Hall, & Mitts, 1971).

Contracting

A strategy that incorporates many behavior modification features previously discussed and that has numerous applications with behaviorally disordered children is *contingency contracting*. Contracts are formalized reciprocal arrangements between two or more parties that establish the conditions for the exchange of behavior, goods, and services. They are negotiated agreements about how individuals will treat one another. When used with behaviorally disordered students, they are usually formal, written documents. Although they are not legally binding, contracts can help individuals modify their behavior to enhance interpersonal relationships and ultimately develop better self-control.

Homme, Csanyi, Gonzales, and Rechs (1969) outlined the following elements of a behavioral contract:

1. specification of behavior to be changed
2. performance criteria for the behavior
3. reinforcing events and the ratio between the behavior to be performed and the consequences to be received
4. time for delivery of payoffs
5. bonus clause for near-perfect performance
6. penalty clause specifying aversive consequences for breaking the contract
7. method used to determine whether the behavior meets selected criteria

Box 8.3 contains a sample contract between a student, teacher, and the student's mother in which the Homme, et al. criteria are identified by the numbers listed above.

A major advantage of contracts is that they can be adapted to a variety of behaviors and situations. The procedure is flexible and can be renegotiated and revised as conditions change.

Box 8.3   Sample Contract

① ③   Phillip agrees to refrain from using profanity when talking to others and to himself in school. If Phillip does this for one week with no more than three profanities he will receive 50 extra points to be used during Friday "Activity Time." ② ④

⑤   If Phillip uses no profanities during the week, he may select one item of his choice from the "Prize Box" and a "Certificate of Merit" will be sent to his mother.

     If Phillip swears more than three times, he will not participate in "Activity Time." ⑥

⑦   Mr. Johnson will keep a posted record of Phillip's behavior.

     I understand and accept the conditions of this contract.

Signed: **Phillip**   Date: **November 14**

Signed: *Mr. Johnson*   Date: *11/14*

Signed: *Mrs. De Avila*   Date: *November 14*
        (witness)

Perhaps contracting's most appealing feature is removal of the onus of responsibility from the teacher's shoulders. All parties to a contract share responsibility for behavioral change. Everyone agrees to the type of desired behavioral change, who will be responsible, what benefits each party will receive, and how it all will be accomplished. If individual participants do not live up to the conditions of the contract, they must accept responsibility.

Measuring Behavior

Procedures for precise, objective measurement of behavioral change are implicit in behavior modification methods. Most of the behavioral methods discussed above contain built-in procedures to enable the teacher or other behavior modifier to determine the current status of target behavior and to evaluate the success of the interventions.

Several benefits of behavioral assessment have been discussed in the literature (Axelrod, 1977; Hall, Hawkins, & Axelrod, 1975). They include the following:

- precise definition of target behavior
- precise information of performance that is relevant to diagnosis
- teacher efforts that focus on specific behavior, rather than global traits
- frequent measurement and charting of behavioral data that encourages persistence in implementing an intervention

Efficiency and Quality Issues

Accurate measurement of behavioral change is necessary in any educational programming. Certainly, data collection demands teacher time, effort, and ingenuity, but without accurate assessment of intervention effectiveness, there is no way of knowing the efficacy of one's efforts. Teachers should adopt assessment techniques that are efficient in the context of their programs and minimize disruptions of their programs and demands upon their time. All student behavior cannot, and need not, be monitored. Only that which is truly useful to program design and evaluation should be collected. We already have plenty of information about behaviorally disordered students that teachers do not view as useful in program planning (Zabel, Peterson, Smith, & White, 1982). As we stressed in our discussion of behavior monitoring techniques in Chapter 3, data should be representative, reliable, and relevant.

Among the general types of data that can be used to monitor student change are pre-post testing (e.g., standardized measures of interpersonal skills, self-concept), product measures (e.g., checklists, file records, teacher ratings, team consensus), and process records (e.g., point cards, graphs, and observational data) (Fitzgerald, 1982).

Types of Data

Process records, including direct observational data, are the most amenable to documenting change due to behavioral interventions. They include frequency, interval, and duration recording, token system data, and self-ratings. Such process measures can be used to measure shorter-term progress than either pre-post or product measures. Thus, they can contribute information for making continuous adjustments of interventions.

Teachers should have a repertoire of process measurement skills that can be adapted to different behaviors and situations. Fitzgerald (1982) has suggested guidelines to improve the qual-

ity of information that is collected. She says that teachers must be realistic about how much behavior they can monitor. Teachers should sample student's behavior, focusing on one or two students during certain times of the day or use the same system for several students. Establishing routines for collecting representative data and preplanning observations during critical phases of interventions contribute to efficient behavior monitoring. In addition, Fitzgerald suggests building observation procedures into lesson plan books to assure commitment to the plan.

Frequency Recording. Frequency recording is used when the observer is interested in the number of times a particular behavior occurs during a certain period of time. For example, a teacher may record each time a student raises her hand, swears, leaves her seat, or smiles. Each behavior can simply be recorded with a checkmark or slash on a piece of paper as it occurs.

Duration Recording. For some types of behavior, it is more meaningful to know the duration, or length of time, the behavior occurs. On-task and off-task behavior are more relevantly measured in terms of their duration rather than in terms of their frequency. Latency in performing behavior, such as length of time between receiving assignments and beginning work or between a teacher's request and student's response, is another type of duration recording that is frequently important for behaviorally disordered students. For example, knowing that a student is late for class twelve days out of twenty provides one kind of data. Records indicating that the duration of the student's tardiness diminished from a weekly average of eight minutes to less than one minute over a four-week period provides yet another type of behavioral data.

Interval Recording. In most instances, other demands on a teacher's time preclude continuous observation and recording. Consequently, it is necessary to sample behavior at predetermined points. Using a procedure called *interval record-*

ing, an observer can simply indicate when a target behavior occurs within a unit of time. Teachers frequently find it most convenient to use interval recording when short observation sessions provide sufficient data, when the behavior occurs relatively infrequently, and when the behavior is easily detectable (Hall, et al., (1975).

Time Sampling. Time sampling provides even greater flexibility and convenience for the observer. When using this procedure, the observer looks for the target behavior only at the end of regular, usually predetermined, units of time. The teacher, for example, may scan her class for off-task behavior for twenty seconds at five randomly selected points during a thirty-minute study period. The rest of the time, she can attend to other responsibilities such as providing instruction or grading papers. Of course, she must take care to select representative times to sample the behavior so that student behavior is not adjusted to bias her observations. To avoid such situations, the teacher may preselect irregularly scheduled observation points.

There are many permutations of the behavior monitoring techniques just summarized. Different behaviors, settings, and observational resources require different procedures. For more detailed discussions of practical approaches for monitoring behavior, the reader should study sources such as Cartwright and Cartwright (1984) or Fitzgerald (1982).

Graphing Data. In most cases, observational data are summarized and graphically depicted to better illustrate the process of behavioral change. Box 8.4 contains a graph on which the rate of talking out of four students during one week is displayed.

Rate is often a more meaningful way to summarize observational data than frequency, especially when the length of individual observations varies. It is not always possible to observe for the same amount of time from session to session. Rate is computed as follows:

$$\text{rate} = \text{counted behaviors/time}$$

Thus, if fifteen talk-outs were recorded during a twenty-minute period, the talk-out rate would be .75 per minute (fifteen talk-outs/20 minutes).

Data from token economies are readily amenable to graphic representation when they are carefully designed and objectively and consistently implemented. The tokens themselves are a kind of observational record, although they usually represent qualitative (ratings) as well as quantitative (counts) information about student behavior. In the example in Box 8.5, teachers' ratings of social behavior and academic performance of a student in several mainstream classes are recorded on a daily report card. These daily and weekly point totals can be charted to reveal patterns of behavior over time.

A key to the effective measurement of behavior is careful planning. Target behaviors must be defined, observers trained, procedures established, and observation forms prepared. The procedures must then consistently be carried out. Although this demands teacher time and energy, once the systems are in place, essential behavioral data can be collected smoothly and efficiently. The resulting information can be reinforcing for students and teachers alike as changes are documented over time.

Research Designs

In addition to selecting appropriate and efficient data collection procedures, behavioral interventions require decision-making procedures. Among the research designs that are helpful in this process are the reversal and multiple baseline formats. Although these are often single-subject research designs, they are increasingly used to determine changes in the behavior of multiple subjects or groups.

Reversal Designs

The reversal, or ABAB, design has perhaps been the most widely used behavioral research de-

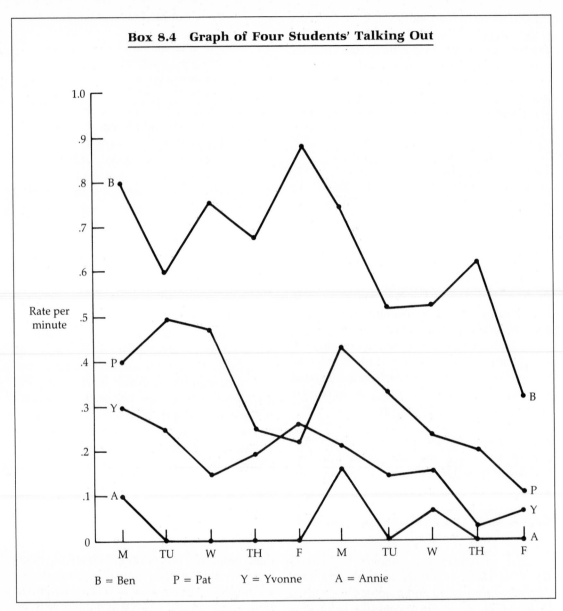

Box 8.4   Graph of Four Students' Talking Out

B = Ben   P = Pat   Y = Yvonne   A = Annie

sign. It consists of several sequential phases (as illustrated in Box 8.6). First, a baseline (A1), or base rate, for the target behavior is determined. This is the rate of the behavior prior to implementation of an intervention against which subsequent rates of behavior can be compared. The experimental phase (B1) follows, which begins with the introduction of the intervention. For example, a specific target behavior may be reinforced, or a token economy or a contract implemented. Once a pattern is observed during this phase of the reversal design, there is a return to baseline conditions (A2). The intervention is temporarily reversed to assess its influence on observed behavior change. Following this brief return to baseline conditions, the intervention is reinstated (B2). When the target behavior appears relatively stable, the intervention may

Box 8.5   Daily Report Card

	Social	Academic
1: Social Studies Comments: good behavior today, but homework not finished Signed: N. McGrew	④ 3 2 1 0	4 3 ② 1 0
2: Resource - Reading Comments: Worked hard all period! Signed: Mrs. Wallace	④ 3 2 1 0	④ 3 2 1 0
3: Resource - Language Arts Comments: argued about assignments, made noises for first 15 min. – settled down but didn't finish work Signed: Mrs. Wallace	4 3 ② 1 0	4 3 2 ① 0
4: Science Comments: participated in lab - got along great with the group Signed: M. Berg	④ 3 2 1 0	4 ③ 2 1 0
5: PE Comments: "Forgot" gym suit again Signed: W. Henderson	4 3 2 1 ⓪	4 3 2 1 ⓪
6: Math Comments: came in argumentative and angry - turned in only ½ of work Signed: Barbara Winfield	4 3 2 ① 0	4 3 2 ① 0
Daily Totals:	15	11

4 = excellent; 3 = good; 2 = average; 1 = poor; 0 = unacceptable

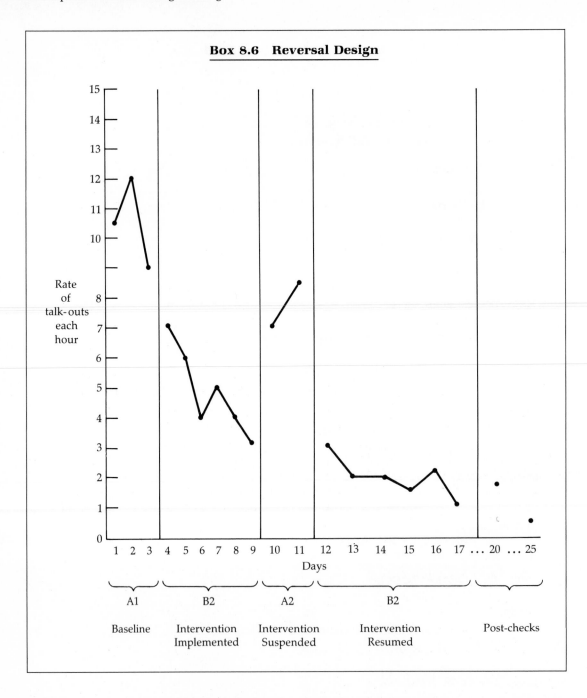

Box 8.6   Reversal Design

again be discontinued to determine the stability of the target behavior, with postchecks made periodically over time.

During each phase of the reversal design, averages (means or medians) can be figured to determine behavior trends. In Box 8.6, the mean number of talk-outs during three days of baseline (A1) is about 10.3. It falls to about 5.0 when the intervention is first implemented (B1) during days 4 to 9. It increases to about 7.8 when the intervention is suspended during days 10 and 11 (A2), but falls below 2.0 when the intervention is reinstated (B2) for several days. Postchecks on days 20 and 25 indicate continuing low rates of talk-outs. In this example, the graphed data appear to indicate effectiveness of the intervention.

There are no hard-and-fast rules for determining the length of each phase. If a particular intervention is working, a pattern (e.g., an increase or decrease in the behavioral rate in the desired direction) should be apparent on the chart. If no pattern can be determined, the intervention is probably ineffective and needs adjustments. Teachers must use their judgment in determining the length of each phase on the basis of desirability of observed changes in behavior, the apparent stability of the changes, and correspondence with predetermined behavioral objectives.

It is not always appropriate or feasible to use a complete reversal design. For example, when modifying self-abusive or disruptive behavior, the teacher may not wish to return to baseline conditions to test the effect of the intervention. Any reduction in these behaviors is too desirable to reverse. In addition, some types of behavior are not readily reversible. For example, a student's accuracy in spelling a list of words may not diminish when an intervention (the reinforcement of correct spellings) is discontinued.

Multiple Baseline Designs

The multiple baseline design is an alternative that can allow for the measurement of several behaviors, the same behavior with several students, or behavior in several settings. For example, a contingency contract may be implemented with one student to increase his school attendance. If successful, another contract may be prepared to increase his participation in class, as well as other behaviors of interest. Or, extinction might be used to decrease one student's talking-out, then extended to other students for whom this behavior is also a concern. The multiple baseline design could be used to evaluate the effectiveness of an intervention to increase positive student interactions with peers in a resource room and then subsequently in several mainstream classes.

Summary

In this chapter, we have presented an overview of behavioral interventions with behaviorally disordered students. We cited general features of behavioral approaches and stressed the importance of selecting interventions that are consistent with identified therapeutic and educational goals for individual students and that ultimately contribute to improved self-management of behavior.

Behavioral methods consist largely of procedures for increasing or decreasing the frequency, rate, or duration of specific behaviors. Most means of increasing behavior involve some form of reinforcement. Consequently, we discussed selection and implementation of different types of individual and group reinforcement systems, such as token economies, as well as schedules of reinforcement and generalization and maintenance of behavioral improvements.

Behavioral methods for decreasing behavior include differential reinforcement of incompatible (DRI) or alternative (DRA) behavior and various forms of punishment. Response cost and time-out are two punitive techniques used in some school programs to reduce disordered behavior. When techniques such as these are used, they must be employed carefully, openly, and humanely. Consequently, we stressed some of the limitations and potential side effects of punishment, together with the importance of following strict guidelines for its use.

Some behavioral interventions can be used either to increase or decrease behavior. Procedures such as self-monitoring and self-recording by students and contingency contracting are examples.

An important feature of any behavioral intervention is accurate measurement of behavioral change. Thus, several techniques for monitoring and graphing behavior and common research designs for evaluating treatment effectiveness were presented.

In this discussion of behavioral methods, we have emphasized caution regarding their use. Behavioral interventions can appear deceptively easy to use. Consequently, they are also easy to abuse. Appropriate, effective use of behavior modification techniques is anything but simple. Frank Wood (1968) has said that they are like a two-edged sword that can be used for good or ill. Always, they require extreme care in planning and implementation to ensure they are used in the best interest of the child. They offer no panacea, but simply technology that can be intelligently and humanely used to improve the status of behaviorally disordered children and adolescents.

In the next chapter, we will examine another category of interventions for students with behavioral and personality disorders—psychoeducational interventions. Together with behavioral interventions, they constitute the most widely used school-based intervention approach.

CHAPTER 9

Psychoeducational Interventions

Overview

Introduction

The foundations for psychoeducational interventions were provided primarily by psychodynamically oriented educators and clinicians, including Bruno Bettelheim, Fritz Redl, David Wineman, and Carl Fenichel. They combined psychotherapeutic and educational approaches in the treatment of children with personality and behavior disorders. Through the 1950s, most intervention efforts were offered in residential treatment centers and psychiatric facilities in which education was considered of secondary importance in the central mission of psychotherapeutic treatment.

Over the past thirty years, interventions for children and adolescents with personality and behavioral disorders have been increasingly focused on education in school settings. Individuals such as William Morse, Nicholas Long, Stanley Fagen, Peter Knoblock, and Peggy Wood have guided the evolution of psychoeducational approaches from the traditional approach, in which psychoeducational interventions have contrasted with behavioral approaches. That distinction is no longer so clear. For example, in *Conflict in the Classroom* (Long, Morse, & Newman, 1980) and in journals such as *The Pointer*, behavioral perspectives as well as psychodynamic interventions have increasingly been incorporated. In addition, behaviorists have advanced theory and practice that are more compatible with the traditional cognitive-affective concerns of psychoeducators.

According to Knoblock (1983, p. 107), the goal of psychoeducation is "to understand the many complex ways children interact with environmental forces, including the significant persons inhabiting their world—particularly parents and teachers. Today, psychoeducation focuses both on the needs and feelings of children (either as observed or inferred) and on a range of environmental factors, including facilitative relationships between children and teachers." This, Knoblock says, requires an ecological frame of reference for solving children's problems that does not place responsibility for change totally upon the individual child, but recognizes the influences of multiple environmental factors as well. Hence, psychoeducational interventions include efforts to change the individual both directly and indirectly by adjusting aspects of the environment.

In this chapter, we include a variety of interventions under the general rubric of *psychoeducation*, including some that do not have their basis in psychodynamic understandings of human behavior. Psychoeducational interventions are no longer mutually exclusive from the behavioral interventions discussed in the previous chapter. Many of the goals and some of the strategies employed in behavioral and psychoeducational approaches overlap. However, the interventions presented in this chapter tend to place greater emphasis on the impact of children's cognitive and affective functioning on their behavior. *Cognition* refers to activity of the mind—what a person has learned and the process of learning; *affect,* to the feeling or emotional aspects of experience and learning. Dembinski, Schultz, and Walton (1982) suggest the following as a major tenet of psychoeducational approaches: "Intellectual learning always involves some sort of feeling, and feelings always have an intellectual concomitant" (p. 209).

The interventions presented in this chapter are drawn from a variety of theoretical perspectives. Some are derived from psychodynamic perspectives (i.e., feelings produce behavior). Some are based on cognitive developmental theories, such as those of Piaget and Kohlberg, emphasizing stages of development. Others originate in behavioral theories, particularly social learning theory as proposed by Bandura. In fact, interventions such as cognitive behavior modification and social skills training rely on social learning theory explanations of how behavior is learned through the observation of models.

A unifying theme among the interventions in this chapter is the recognition of relationships between how individuals think and feel and how they behave. They stress methods for improving students' self-awareness of feelings, thoughts, and behavior. Common goals of psychoeducational approaches are helping students increase self-control and enhancing self-concept.

Aspects of Psychoeducational Interventions

Fagen, Long, and Stevens (1975) have outlined the following fundamental principles of psychoeducational approaches:

- relationships between teachers and students are central to success
- educational environments must consider factors that influence student interactions with peers, staff, and curriculum
- learning must be invested with feeling
- emotional conflict can be used to teach new ways of understanding and coping with stress
- cognitive, affective, and psychomotor processes continuously interact
- students vary in learning styles
- behavior may have many causes, and one cause may produce many behaviors
- collaboration among the significant adults in students' lives is necessary

In the early 1950s, Fritz Redl and David Wineman (1951) described characteristics of predelinquent boys at Pioneer House, a residential treatment center in Detroit, Michigan. They characterized them as "children who hate," whose egos were "pauperized" as a result of missing links in their lives—disorganized families, lack of community ties, and inadequate financial security. Given deficits of normal internal control over behavior, Redl and Wineman (1952) proposed special approaches for helping emotionally disturbed children develop controls from within. Their work, together with that of other early psychoeducators, has led to the development of four major psychoeducational interventions. These are:

1. design of a therapeutic milieu
2. programming for ego support
3. antiseptic manipulation of surface behavior
4. clinical exploitation of life events

The Therapeutic Milieu

Several psychoeducators have emphasized the impact of the environment, including both the physical setting and psychological atmosphere, on the mental health and behavior of children. Bruno Bettelheim (who escaped from a Nazi concentration camp and immigrated to the

United States) utilized a psychodynamic perspective in designing the Orthogenic School at the University of Chicago as a therapeutic milieu for severely emotionally disturbed children and adolescents. In books, such as *Love Is Not Enough: The Treatment of Emotionally Disturbed Children* (1950) and *A Home for the Heart* (1974), he describes the care given to ensure that the physical environment and staff understanding of emotional disturbance and attitudes toward treatment are in accordance with a psychodynamic view of emotional development.

Structure. A pervasive feature of a therapeutic environment is structure. Carl Fenichel (1971), founder of the League School in New York, considered structure to include predictable, consistent rules and routines that provide external support and stability for students whose lives have been disorganized and chaotic. Most psycho-educators agree with Fenichel that "disorganized children need someone to organize their world for them" (1971, p. 339).

Behaviorally oriented researchers, too, have emphasized the importance of structure provided by routines and rules. Madsen, Becker, and Thomas (1968), for example, found that rules are most effective when they are (1) few in number, (2) relatively short, (3) stated positively (e.g., "Work quietly" rather than "Do not make noise"), and (4) regularly reviewed with students. They also found rules work best when students are rewarded for following them and when inappropriate behavior is ignored.

Environmental Stimulation. The influence of various aspects of the physical environment on student academic performance and social behavior has received considerable attention. Over the years, there have been some dramatic shifts in views about the effects of some environmental factors, particularly the influence of various types of sensory stimulation.

Strauss and Lehtinin (1947) and Cruickshank, Bentzen, Ratzeburg, and Tannhauser (1961) proposed an *overflow theory* of the effects of sensory stimuli on hyperactive and other neurologically impaired students. They believed that high levels of auditory, visual, and other sensory stimuli have the generalized effect of increasing activity and distractions. Proposed solutions included isolating hyperactive students from peers, using study cubicles, eliminating extraneous furniture, and reducing decorations and windows. Classrooms were to be bland and nonstimulating, on the assumption that less sensory input would produce less behavioral output.

More recent research has not supported this assumption. Based upon her review of studies involving normal, hyperactive, behaviorally disordered, and autistic subjects, Zentall (1983) has proposed an *optimal stimulation theory*. According to this view, the level of arousal is determined by three factors: individual child differences in need of arousal, task and environmental stimuli, and fatigue and time exposed to a setting or task (degree of novelty). It is not simply more sensory stimulation that results in more behavior, but that a combination of individual, environment, and task characteristics determine arousal. Further, it appears that both extremely low and extremely high levels of sensory stimulation produce adverse behavioral responses in normal children, with exceptional children even more sensitive to the extremes.

Contrary to overflow theory, Zentall has found that brighter colors, color contrasts, and novel tasks and experiences, unless too difficult or inadequately planned, have a calming effect on both normal children and, especially, hyperactive children. In addition, social and psychological advantages may be produced by color novelty and access to windows. Less convincing findings have been reported for the effects of noise, but it appears that moderate levels of noise in familiar settings generally produce greater performance gains than do quiet conditions.

Social stimulation can also be beneficial. Generally, increased student proximity to the teacher results in improved task-related and social behavior, and increased peer density (more students in same space) increases both performance and social problems. Hood-Smith and Leffingwell (1984) have experimentally demonstrated the effects of different classroom seating arrangements on maladaptive behavior, finding traditional row and column seating less desirable than some other arrangements. Research on the use of cubicles (study carrels) with emotionally disturbed students indicates they may help students pay attention, but do not necessarily improve their academic performance (Shores & Haubrich, 1969).

The length of time students are exposed to a setting or a task has also been found to have differential effects. Longer and more familiar tasks and settings are more beneficial for withdrawn and nonactive students, and greater variation seems to benefit hyperactive students.

Zentall (1983) recommends several accommodations to individual needs for environmental stimulation. These include

- organizing classrooms into various work settings
- use of earphones with access to sound (e.g., music) or no sound
- requiring active versus passive task responses
- use of varying time periods for tasks
- reduction of seating density
- teacher proximity

She says, "Low stimulation tasks should be performed in highly stimulating, pleasant settings that have windows and music and are cheerfully painted and frequently redecorated by students (e.g., with subject-related themes). Furniture and classroom structure should encourage clear patterns of movement. Children should work with different partners, in different seats, with alternate vantage points to provide additional stimulation. When students and teachers are performing complex, unusual tasks, they should be assigned to familiar, pleasant, low stimulation settings with low peer density" (1983, p. 109).

Attention should be given to the physical design of classrooms. Features of the physical setting contribute to the psychological environment and may influence student behavior and feelings as much as behavior management strategies and curricular adjustments. Classrooms should be pleasant, inviting environments for students and teachers alike. They should be designed and decorated to communicate acceptance, caring, and expectations for behavior. Student involvement in the decorating of classrooms and the display of student work increases their sharing in the environment. Rarely can teachers start from scratch in designing the physical structures where their programs are housed. However, they usually have considerable control over the arrangement and decoration of the physical environment, and so can help make it a therapeutic milieu.

Programming for Ego Support

Some psychoeducators have stressed the need for building student self-esteem by programming opportunities for success, or what Redl and Wineman (1952) call *ego support*. As our earlier discussions of characteristics of students with personality and conduct disorders have emphasized, many of these children and adolescents have extensive histories of failure in social relationships and academic achievement. Consequently, it is necessary to arrange experiences in which they can be successful. Of course, this effort requires a careful assessment of the student's current status and capabilities for social and academic skills. Based on that assessment, educational programs can be prepared to ensure that failure and frustration are minimized and new challenges are gradually and sequentially presented.

Fagen, Long, and Stevens (1975) have proposed the following steps for organizing academic instruction to ensure success:

1. Start at or below the students' functional level.

2. Increase difficulty by small steps.
3. Place teaching tasks in a developmental sequence.
4. Provide positive feedback.
5. Strengthen by repetition.
6. Show appreciation for real effort.
7. Enhance the value of the skill area.
8. Maintain flexibility and enjoyment.
9. Prepare for real-life transfer of training.
10. Plan short, frequent, regular training sessions.

Antiseptic Manipulation of Surface Behavior

Teachers face challenges in how to respond to students whose behavior is destructive to themselves, disturbs others, or disrupts classroom routines. Teachers must continuously ask, "How directive, how intrusive, and how supportive should I be when attempting to control students' behavior?" Long and Newman (1976) offer four intervention choices along a continuum from less overt to more intrusive: permitting, tolerating, preventing, and interfering.

Permitting. There are times when behavior should be *permitted*. Teachers, parents, and other adults readily inform children of what they may not do—particularly after proscribed behaviors have been performed. Although rules for behavior should be explicitly presented to students, it is also important to be explicit when informing them about what behavior is permissible. For example, students might be told, "It is OK to run and yell on the playground," or "Smoking is allowed in the designated area between 12:20 and 12:30." Such explicit determination of what behavior is permitted, as well as what is not, lessens the need for students to experiment to see what happens. Establishing clear expectations for academic standards, behaviors, and classroom procedures during the first few class meetings of the school year can have long-lasting effects on student behavior. Behaviorally disordered students who lack suffi-

cient self-control and self-direction are supported by clear expectations and classroom routines.

Tolerating. Long and Newman (1976) also propose that some deviant behavior should be tolerated when it is indicative of a student's developmental level or symptomatic of a personality or conduct disorder. Some examples might be thumb sucking in an anxious, immature ten-year-old or cigarette smoking in a conduct disordered fourteen-year-old. Although such behaviors are not endorsed by responsible adults, they may be extremely difficult to extinguish, and there may be more pressing problem behavior to address. The teacher's decision may be to treat undesirable, yet understandable, behavior with benign neglect.

Preventing. Another major intervention choice is *preventing* problem behavior. Too often, we focus on modifying existing behavior problems, when our efforts might be better spent on preventing their occurrence. As discussed earlier, considerations in designing a therapeutic environment (structure, arrangement of the physical setting, consistency, support from rules and routine) help establish conditions that are not conducive to deviant behavior.

In addition, group management methods that increase student involvement in class activities allow minimal opportunities for students to interfere with others, and the efficient use of instructional time helps prevent behavioral problems. The research of Jacob Kounin of Wayne State University in Detroit and his colleagues (Kounin, 1967, 1970; Kounin, Friesen, & Norton, 1966; Kounin & Gump, 1974) has provided important insights about the role of teacher behavior. Based upon analyses of videotaped records of regular classrooms, they have documented relationships between specific teacher behaviors and student work involvement.

An important teacher behavior is one that Kounin calls *with-itness*. With-itness is the degree to which a teacher is aware of individual student behavior within the group and verbally and nonverbally communicates that awareness. Another teacher behavior, called *overlapping*, refers to paying attention to more than one activity or issue at a time. The teacher who overlaps might simultaneously have several students doing seat work, while offering individual instruction to another student, and nonverbally signalling another student to get back on-task.

Maintaining smoothness through a lesson by not interrupting with information that is not absolutely relevant, and maintaining the group's momentum by not overinvestigating a topic, are additional teacher skills related to student behavior. Kounin found that effective teachers alert the group to pay attention. They use such techniques as randomly calling upon students to recite, creating suspense for activities ("Can you imagine what might happen next?"), and signaling students that they will be called upon ("Chad, Terry is going to read this paragraph and then I'm going to ask you to tell me . . . ").

More effective teachers demand accountability from their students, who are required to show their work or recite in the group as the teacher circulates among them, checking performance. Kounin also found that valence and challenge arousal increases student involvement, particularly at transition times. For example, the teacher might introduce an activity by saying, "The next exercise is different from anything we've done before." Finally, Kounin found that seat work and recitation variety and challenge are generally conducive to better student behavior when activities are well planned and transitions handled smoothly.

Kounin stressed the importance of a ripple effect on students who observe teachers reacting to others' misbehavior. He classified teacher admonitions in three categories: clarity, firmness, and roughness. *Clarity* involves naming the student, specifying the behavior, and the reasons it is unacceptable. *Firmness* involves communication that the behavior will not be tolerated. *Roughness* involves the use of threats or punishment. Each of these teacher responses affects students who are observing the teacher. Clarity tends to increase conformity within the entire group, while firmness affects only those directly involved in the misbehavior. Roughness, however, has little effect on other students' overt behavior, but it does upset them.

Borg (1976) has produced a set of specific activities and resources to train teachers in the use of techniques based on Kounin's research and behavior modification principles. Borg's own research suggests that teachers can learn the strategies, and that those who systematically apply them encounter fewer incidents of disturbing behavior in their classrooms.

Interfering. Some student behavior cannot be tolerated, permitted, or prevented. In these cases, the teacher may need to *interfere* with it. Redl and Wineman (1952) described several interfering techniques for "antiseptically manipulating surface behavior." By that, they mean stopping disruptive or potentially disruptive behavior in relatively simple, straightforward ways with no therapeutic intent. The techniques are considered antiseptic because they prevent contagion of the behavior to others and further infection within the individual.

Planned ignoring is one of these techniques. It is similar to extinction as discussed in the last chapter. Based upon prior experiences with students, the teacher may decide not to call attention to a behavior that is attention seeking and is likely to diminish when ignored. Many times, it is not necessary to confront directly every annoying, transient problem behavior. Simply calling attention to the behavior may inadvertently reinforce it. In addition, challenging relatively minor behavior problems can frequently lead to power struggles between teacher and student that neither can win.

Signal interference is a relatively nonstigmatizing method to communicate nonverbally with students about their behavior. Eye contact, gestures, and facial expressions are common forms. *Proximity control* involves moving close to students who may benefit from supportive closeness or whose behavior needs to be interfered with. As discussed earlier, there is empirical support (Etsheidt, Stainback, & Stainback, 1984; Kounin, 1970; Zentall, 1983) for teacher proximity, as well as verbal and tactile contact. *Touch control*, gently touching a shoulder, for example, frequently can redirect or calm a student. However, teachers must be alert to students and situations where proximity and touch control may not be effective. Some students are especially sensitive to being touched or may interpret an adult's touching differently than intended. Some students feel pressured by physical closeness. Hence, teachers should exercise caution with these techniques, be tuned to students' verbal and nonverbal cues about receptiveness, and be alert to situations when it may be best to back off.

Redl and Wineman (1952) also discuss "tension decontamination through humor." Faced with a tense situation, a teacher may find and communicate the humor in it. Humor can sometimes diffuse the situation, helping to clear the air. Generally, the humor should not be forced or at a student's expense. When directed at themselves, teachers communicate their security. It is not realistic, of course, that humor can be found in every tense situation, or that it can be sincerely communicated.

Several of Redl and Wineman's techniques revolve around the relationship between teacher and students. There are times when a student may need a "hypodermic of affection" in the form of extra attention or expressions of concern to help him or her realize that the teacher cares. Sometimes, students will benefit from "hurdle help"—encouragement and assistance getting started on a lesson or entering into an activity. For example, the teacher may review a daily assignment sheet and help a reluctant student complete the first few activities.

Teachers' "interpretation as interference" can help avoid a potential crisis. For example, the teacher may explain to an angry student that a classmate's knocking books off his desk was accidental. At other times, the teacher may appeal directly to a student's sense of values. For example, to a student who monopolizes the use of some class equipment, the teacher might say, "You know it isn't fair to the rest of the group for you to use the tape player during the whole period." Although the student may not yet possess a value like fairness, affirming it may provide an educational function.

"Involvement in an interest relationship" is an interfering technique with many permutations. It may simply mean sharing students' interests in sports, music, and hobbies, or it may consist of more grandiose efforts to capitalize on student interests to increase involvement and motivation. For example, in one junior high BD program, the teacher was able to capitalize on and develop a student's interest in caring for the many plants in the room. Each day, the student donned a lab coat supplied by the teacher, and watered, fertilized, trimmed, and otherwise cared for the plants. Math, science, and language arts activities were infused in the activity, as the student measured and charted plant growth, studied botany, and prepared reports on his work.

A useful interfering, as well as preventive, technique is the "limitation of space and tools." Because of their seductive properties for many behaviorally disordered students, it is important that teachers be cognizant of objects and situations that draw students into deviant behavior and attempt to minimize them. Certainly, potentially dangerous objects that could be used as weapons or for self-injury, drugs, and pornography have a high valency for behavioral problems and should be forbidden in schools. In addition, objects that can contribute to distraction or be misused, yet have legitimate uses in the program (e.g., scissors) may be controlled, with student access limited to appropriate times and situations. Valuable personal and school property that might be at risk for disappearance or damage (e.g., teacher's purse, tape players) should be kept in locked compartments. The appeal of such objects may be too strong for some students. Likewise, it is helpful to have clear designations for the appropriate use of space within a classroom. Certain areas (the reading corner, the game area) may be used only for specified activities. Rules governing mobility through the classroom, entering others' desks, lockers, and so on should be made explicit to prevent problems.

Several programmatic adaptations can also interfere with problem behavior. *Regrouping* involves changes in seating arrangements to control group contagion. It may mean removing an individual from a group by assigning him or her to another program or rescheduling the student when group dynamics are less volatile. *Antiseptic bouncing* refers to nonpunitive removal of an individual from the group. This strategy may be appropriate when the student is threatened, teased, intimidated, or made a scapegoat by other group members, needs a break from a stressful activity, precipitating or drawn into group contagion, or others in the group are bothered by the individual. A student may be sent to a designated quiet area within the classroom, to a time-out area, or even out of the room. In the last instance, the student might be asked to carry a message to the office. It might say something like, "Alicia needs to calm down. Send her back in a few minutes when she is more settled."

Antiseptic bouncing is not intended to be punishing, but rather an opportunity for students to gain control of their emotions and behavior or to escape threatening situations. In fact, many teachers of behaviorally disordered students consider their use of time-out to be nonaversive to the student (Zabel, 1986b). Smith (1982) contends that time-out can serve as a "confirming" strategy. In effect, the student may think, "I broke that rule so now I'm going to the quiet area." How antiseptic bouncing is perceived by students probably depends largely on how its purpose is communicated by the teacher. Regardless of the teacher's intent, however, time-out procedures outlined in the previous chapter should be prepared and followed.

Physical restraint may be necessary when a student is out of control and dangerous to self, others, or property. In most cases, preventive and other interfering techniques as discussed above obviate the need for physical control. Physical restraint should be used only as a last resort in a crisis situation. When used, the central concern should be minimizing potential injury to everyone involved.

Dealing with Crises

Every behavioral crisis is unique in terms of its precipitating circumstances, characteristics of involved student(s), the teacher, and available assistance. Consequently, it is hazardous to prescribe a rigid set of procedures that should always be followed. Our discussion represents considerations for handling potentially dangerous crises that have been adapted from guidelines provided by Bents, Lakin, and Reynolds (1980).

In crisis situations it is important that teachers attempt to maintain self-control without overreacting with physical controls. Despite student behavior such as verbal threats, obscenities, throwing or breaking objects, and actual physical assaults on others, they can frequently be helped to regain control without resorting to physical restraint.

A sequence of strategies can be attempted in response to crisis behavior. The teacher should first firmly state the consequences of not following instructions, saying something like, "I can't let you do that. If you are not in time-out by the time I count to five, I will call the principal to have you removed from the room."

If the student does not respond and the teacher is unable to contain the behavior, the teacher should send for help. If another adult is unavailable to send, a student may be sent. Where the potential for crisis exists, prior arrangements should be made with administrators, counselors, and other teachers. When no one in a school building can provide physical control, the student should be told that police or other appropriate personnel (e.g., ward staff in an institution, parents) will be called. If dangerous incidents are probable in a program, these contingencies should be clearly communicated to students at noncrisis times.

When other students are in danger of being hurt, they should be sent from the setting to the principal's office or another designated location. Even when physical danger to other students is not imminent, some students are extremely frightened by an out-of-control classmate. In some cases, potential contagion of the behavior for others exists. If another adult is available, that person may accompany the rest of the group to a safe location. Sometimes, it is best for the teacher to also accompany the class from the setting where the student is out-of-control, returning with support as soon as possible.

Teachers should use physical restraint only when absolutely necessary, and only if they have sufficient strength and skill. Bullock, Donohue, Young, and Warner (1985) have illustrated some defensive techniques for handling physical aggression that minimize injury to the student and teacher. Restraint should not be punishing or inflict pain on the offending student. It is usually most effective to firmly grasp the student's hands or arms. If necessary the teacher can maintain control by holding the student's wrists from behind, crossing his or her arms over the student's abdomen. Even in this position, however, care must be taken to avoid being struck by the student's head. While restraining the student, the teacher should calmly encourage him or her to regain control. The student should be asked if he or she is in control and then observed for physiological signs of control (e.g., coherent speech, relaxation of muscles, cessation of struggling). Once released, the student should be accompanied to an appropriate setting, such as a time-out area or hallway. In no instance should other students be asked to help physically restrain an out-of-control student.

Following the crisis, it is usually important to calm and soothe the rest of the group. Teachers' remarks should be relatively brief at this time,

although the incident may be addressed at more length later, in appropriate forums such as group meetings. A teacher's comments about the incident can include an explanation of where and how the offending student is now, what precipitated the incident, and how it could have been avoided. Classmates who behaved appropriately during the crisis should be praised for their control. The teacher should attempt to return the class to its normal routines and activities as soon as possible.

Obviously, physical restraint is a high-risk intervention with the potential for injury to its participants. There are many situations in which its use is more dangerous than the alternatives. For example, attempting to physically prevent an adolescent who is intent upon leaving a classroom or school from doing so is not recommended. It is likely that the student who cannot get around an obstacle (the teacher), may go over it.

Life Space Interviewing

Despite efforts to prevent behavioral problems or to interfere with them, crisis situations sometimes develop in programs for behaviorally disordered students. These include fights, tantrums, arguments, destruction of property, stealing, teasing, and cheating. When such behavior reaches crisis proportions, some psychoeducators have suggested that they can be used to help students learn from the experience. William Morse (1959, 1963) and others have proposed strategies for the clinical exploitation of life events, or the Life Space Interview (LSI). These procedures are essentially methods to establish communication between adults and children around behavior, feelings, and perceptions aroused in crises. The purpose of the LSI is to help a child develop a better understanding of how his or her behavior and feelings contributed to the incident and to develop better strategies for the future.

There are two major forms of the LSI: emotional first aid and the more therapeutic clinical exploitation of life events. The form selected depends largely upon the teacher's or interviewer's decision of what to make of the precipitating crisis. It is not always clear, even at the outset of the interview, which form will be pursued. It depends upon the interviewer's goal at that time, constraints of the setting and other responsibilities, and the readiness of the student to benefit from the interview.

Emotional First Aid. *Emotional first aid* can be used to meet several goals. These include providing an opportunity for sympathetic communication with students about their feelings, offering emotional support and reassurance to help get students back on track, reminding students of policies and routines, keeping lines of communication open, and serving as an umpire.

Clinical Exploitation of Life Events. Sometimes the crisis can be used in more therapeutic ways that contribute to students' understanding of the effects of feelings on behavior, developing values about behavior, learning new behaviors, and gaining greater self-control, even in the face of group pressures. This *clinical exploitation of life events* consists of several sequential steps. Step 1 is getting the geography of the situation by asking who, what, when, where types of questions to help the child gain an accurate picture of what events led to the crisis and what happened in the crisis. This initial step is critical to helping students understand their role in the incident and reaching a consensus between the students and interviewer about what happened.

Step 2 focuses on students' feelings during and following the incident. To do this, the interviewer may note physiological signs and nonverbal behavior such as trembling, crying, tense muscles, and facial expressions and relate them to particular emotions. Some behaviorally disordered students are deficient in their abilities to recognize emotions (Zabel, 1978) and need help developing a vocabulary of feelings and relating feelings to behavior.

Next, the interviewer "tests for depth and

spread" of feelings and behavior (Step 3) by questioning students about other times and places where similar incidents have occurred. Together, they can determine if the current crisis is an isolated event or part of a persistent pattern.

Step 4 requires "developing solutions and alternatives to behavior." The goal here is to design solutions that students can realistically accomplish together with specific plans for achieving them.

Finally, the interviewer "offers assistance, support, and feedback" during implementation of the plan for avoiding, or more favorably handling, potential future crises. Box 9.1 contains examples of the kinds of questions asked in each phase of the interview.

Obviously, teachers must be selective in using this strategy. It can be time consuming and draw the interviewer away from involvement with the rest of the group. Still, arrangements can sometimes be made to use the LSI when timely and appropriate. Some empirical support exists for the academic and social benefits of the LSI with behaviorally disordered children (DeMagistris & Imber, 1980). Even if the entire procedure is not used in the format presented here, it can provide direction for analyzing crises. Too often, we are eager to arrive at solutions to problem behavior before the participants fully understand and accept their roles in the development of crisis situations.

Affective Education

Affective education is a curricular area that has been emphasized in some psychoeducational programming. It is based on the notion that overt behavior is a reflection of internal cognitive-affective views of oneself and others. The purposes of affective education are to help students to improve awareness of their own and others' feelings, to learn to appropriately express feelings, to respond to others' feelings, and to develop personal values (Mosher & Sprinthall, 1971).

Box 9.1 Possible Questions in a Life Space Interview

Step 1. Getting the geography of the situation:
"John, would you tell me what just happened in the classroom?"
"Were you at your desk when Paul bumped you?"
"What kind of fight were you having? What were you doing to each other?"

Step 2. Identifying feelings:
"Now that you're here and we're talking about the fight, how do you feel?"
"You were shaking and breathing hard. What does that mean?"
"You felt hurt. What else did you feel?"

Step 3. Testing for depth and spread of behavior and feelings:
"You mentioned you've been in other fights this year. When?"

"Does this happen in other classes, too?"
"What's so bad about crying?"

Step 4. Developing solutions and alternatives:
"If this is a problem, and we agree that it is, what can we do about it?"
"Is there someone in the class who could help?"
"What else could you do? What could you say to Ms. Meyer?"

Step 5. Offering assistance, support, and feedback:
"We'll talk with Ms. Meyer about what you plan so she knows."
"I'll check with you last period every day for the next week to talk about how your plan is working."

In a comparison of affective education and social skills training, Frank Wood (1982) has noted considerable overlap and believes the two approaches should be considered complementary. They have the similar general goals of increasing independence, self-direction, responsible behavior, and a flexible, creative value system. However, affective education curricula place greater emphasis on the experience and exploration of thoughts, feelings, and interpersonal relationships. Social skills curricula, alternatively, emphasize the acquisition of skills that will enhance the individual's acceptance by others.

Developers of affective education curricula provide experiences intended to relate cognitive and emotional development to enhance student self-concept and social skills. From this perspective, positive, constructive behavior is the result of healthy, age-appropriate cognitive-affective development; destructive behavior results from unhealthy, inadequate development. The goal of affective education is the deliberate promotion of personal growth. Both Wood (1982) and

William Morse (1982) have commented on the unsystematic teaching of values—the "hidden curriculum"—that exists in schools. Morse (1982, p. 210) says, "Affective education requires consciously directing our affective interventions and not leaving the matter to happenstance or haphazard efforts."

The Pupil Stress Cycle

Affective-oriented educators tend to stress the importance of empathic relationships between teachers and students. An example is Nicholas Long and Stanley Fagen's (1981) psychoeducational approach to therapeutic behavior management based upon the Pupil Stress Cycle (Long, 1979). According to this model, a key consideration in pupil stress is the student's self-concept—collected perceptions of self, including values, beliefs, and images. That self-image is affected by various sources of stress (economic, developmental, psychological, and reality) both external and internal to school. Stress is a personal, subjective reaction to specific life events, whether real, anticipated, or imagined, that cause physiological discomfort.

Long believes that stressful incidents arouse strong feelings in students, but because they have been taught that certain feelings are bad and unacceptable, they may deny them or act them out in disguised forms. Thus, troublesome behavior generated by those feelings often creates problems in school even when the source of stress is outside school. For example, a student's hostility generated by a conflict with a parent may be directed at a teacher. Regardless of the source, however, there is a likely reaction from the teacher and others in the school environment. The insensitive teacher may react personally to the student's hostility, inadvertently reinforcing it. In this way, a pupil stress cycle often begins to develop into a power struggle between student and teacher in which there are no winners.

To prevent such a no-win situation, Long and Fagen (1981) have suggested several strategies that emphasize an understanding of the Pupil Stress Cycle and the improvement of teachers' empathic relationships with students. Strategies include verbal and nonverbal communication with students about feelings, labeling and accepting feelings, lowering school pressure, and redirecting students' feelings into more acceptable behavior. They also suggest helping students complete one task at a time, encouraging them to help less fortunate classmates, temporary separation from stressful settings, and encouragement to seek professional help when necessary.

Another approach to promote student understanding and management of feelings is the Rational-Emotive Education (Ree) approach developed by Albert Ellis (Zionts, 1983). The underlying assumption of Ree is that many individuals are disturbed because of their inaccurate and distorted perceptions of events. Intense emotions often accompany irrational beliefs that are expressed in an individual's negative self-talk. Some common forms are generalizing from particulars (e.g., "I failed the test, so I'm stupid"), exaggerating events (e.g., "I failed the test because the teacher is unfair"), and placing unrealistic demands on oneself and others (e.g., "I should get As on all my tests").

To correct irrational and destructive self-perceptions, a process called *disputation* is used. Disputation is a joint problem-solving venture in which the teacher challenges student beliefs through questioning. Throughout the process, the teacher displays empathy and warmth toward the student, is actively directive, and keeps the discussion on-task. When the student accepts the irrationality of a particular belief, he or she is taught to practice more rational self-talk with the expectation it will improve both feelings and behavior.

Group Programs

Affective education may take a variety of forms, but in programs for students with behavior and personality problems, it frequently takes place in a group format. In his Reality Therapy approach, for example, Glasser (1965, 1969) has stressed the importance of developing responsible decision-making skills through structured group discussions. He has described three types of group functions: social problem solving, diagnostic meetings, and open-ended meetings.

In social problem solving, the group discusses a particular problem behavior or situation of concern to the group or to one or more of its members. For example, in a group where one member is regularly used as a scapegoat, the meeting may be used to encourage discussion of individual perceptions of the problem and jointly to develop solutions. Discussions are directed at solving problems rather than fault finding or punishment. Diagnostic meetings can be used to help determine the extent of the participants' understanding of curriculum. For example, in a group studying the U.S. Constitution, the teacher may lead a discussion of current events related to Constitutional issues involved in civil rights. Open-ended meetings permit the group members and leader to select any thought-provoking topic for discussion.

Glasser and others have offered guidelines for effective formation and implementation of group meetings. Of key importance is that groups be part of the regular routine. They should meet regularly, preferably several times each week at a specified time. This regularity makes the meeting an important part of the curriculum. Students can anticipate the opportunity for group participation. Generally, participants sit in a tight circle with no structural barriers to interfere with communication. Sometimes it is beneficial for students to move away from desks or work areas to a designated group area. A few rules should be established early in group formation (e.g., always raise your hand and wait to be called on, listen carefully when others are talking), and those who break meeting rules should be moved outside of the circles.

There are no absolute guidelines for the length of meetings, although they are generally short (10 to 20 minutes) for elementary students, but may last longer (20 to 30 minutes) for secondary students. The group leader (teacher, counselor, social worker) must maintain the pace and interest of the group, noting individual involvement, keeping the discussion on target, and recognizing signs of flagging interest and fatigue in the group members.

An additional benefit of class meetings is the opportunity they provide for students to develop communication skills. "The more we teach children to speak clearly and thoughtfully, the better we prepare them for life. When a child can speak satisfactorily for himself, he gains confidence that is hard to shake" (Glasser, 1969, p. 144).

Supportive peer groups, such as the Positive Peer Culture for delinquent adolescents (Vorrath & Brendtro, 1974), have emphasized the problem-solving capability of the group. A similar program has been designed for elementary school students (Virden, 1984). Among the types of problems addressed in these support groups are "hurting problems," "lying problems," "misleading others," "being easily misled," "small feel-

ings," "aggravation," and "showing disrespect to self and others." During support group meetings, participants recount relevant problem experiences and explain what happened. Other members of the group, guided by the group leader, offer suggestions and support for coping with the problems.

Although problem solving is a legitimate concern of groups, meetings should not dwell on problems to the exclusion of other group interests and concerns. A varied discussion menu should help maintain participant interest and avoid their becoming satiated with the discussion of problems.

Affective Curricula

Several affective education curricula are available that may be used in whole or in part in regular or special education programs. *Curriculum* implies a more comprehensive approach to affective education—one consisting of a specific content, with determined scope and sequence, as well as processes for teaching the content. One of the pioneers in developing affective education curricula is Ralph Ojemann (1967). His program, Dealing with the Causes of Behavior, is intended to be included in regular social studies, reading, English, math, and other subjects. The curriculum is presented in four books organized by topic and grade level. Small group discussion, brainstorming, role-playing, buzz groups, and other processes are used to help students explore causes and motivations, as opposed to surface aspects, of human behavior.

Other affective education curricula for elementary-age students include Developing Understanding of Self and Others — Revised (DUSO–R) (Dinkmeyer, 1982) and Toward Affective Development (TAD) (Dupont, Gardner, & Brody, 1974). These programs are intended to teach an understanding of feelings, interpersonal relations, and communication skills using illustrative stories, puppetry, role-playing, and discussion. DUSO–R is designed for use with children in kindergarten through fourth grade. TAD is intended for somewhat older children (grades 3 to 6). Both the DUSO–R and TAD programs include developmentally sequenced activities. Instructor manuals provide detailed instructions and suggestions for elaboration. They may be used as the core of an affective education program or as supplemental activities.

For secondary level students, the Coping With series, Revised (Wrenn, 1984) is a collection of paperback books about adolescent problems and concerns such as personal identity, making decisions, and communication. Also primarily for adolescents, the Transition program (Dupont & Dupont, 1979) provides sequenced packages of group activities intended to improve communication skills, understanding of feelings, and exploration of values.

The Self-Control Curriculum (Fagen, Long, & Stevens, 1975) is a process-oriented, affective skills-development program. Its goals are to provide elementary students with skills for coping realistically and flexibly with life situations and to gain a better understanding and appreciation of their own and others' feelings. The curriculum consists of four cognitive and four affective skill clusters. Cognitive skills include activities to improve students' skills in selection, storage, sequencing and ordering information, and anticipating consequences. Affective skill areas are appreciating feelings, managing frustrations, inhibition and delay, and relaxation. Each curriculum area consists of two to four units. For example, activities for anticipating consequences include units on developing alternatives and evaluating consequences. For the area of appreciating feelings, the units are identifying feelings, developing positive feelings, managing feelings, and reinterpreting feeling events. Goals and learning tasks in each curriculum area are discussed by the group, with games, role-playing, discussions, and lessons used to present the skills.

Values clarification (Raths, Harmin, & Simon, 1966; Simon, Howe, & Kirschenbaum, 1972) is a procedure that can be used in group discussions to help students learn to recognize their values. Its use with students who have learning and behavior problems in special education programs has also been discussed (Simon & O'Rourke, 1977). Values clarification exercises are not intended to instill a particular set of values, but to help students clarify and act upon their values. The result, according to its adherents, is an enhancement of students' sense of identity. The approach uses a sequential process of prizing, choosing, and acting upon values. Students first practice identifying what is important to them, setting priorities, and expressing their values. Next, they practice choosing from among alternative values after considering the possible consequences of their choices. Finally, students practice acting consistently in ways that reflect their values.

Teaching techniques used in values clarification include clarifying (asking students to consider what they value), use of value sheets (provocative written statements and questions requiring responses from students), and value-clarifying discussions (nonjudgmental, accepting, teacher-led examinations of alternative values, behavior, and consequences). Simon, Howe, and Kirschenbaum (1972) provide a variety of values clarification exercises that can be adapted to different ages and settings. Although many of the exercises can be done independently by students, they are also frequently included in group discussion formats.

In the St. Paul, Minnesota, school district, Hlidek and colleagues (Hlidek, 1979; McCauley, Hlidek, & Feinberg, 1977) developed a collection of affective-oriented strategies to enhance classroom environments by combining relationship-building activities with group behavior modification. The basis of the program is to catch the child being good, rather than to react to misbehavior and to correct mistakes. A group token system provides reinforcement for following group directions, completing assigned work, and helping, encouraging, sharing, praising, and complimenting one another. Examples of those behaviors are first provided by the teacher, who also models them and reinforces performance by students. Points are awarded for individual positive behaviors and added to a group pot. Points are added, never taken away, and bonus points awarded when everyone in the group displays positive behavior, such as helping a classmate. Tokens are tabulated daily and visually displayed on a posted number line, as the number of beans in a jar, or slash marks on the chalkboard. The group and the teacher negotiate weekly group rewards together.

Relationship-building activities are an integral part of the program. They provide structured opportunities for students to practice positive interpersonal interactions. Groups meet three times each week for thirty to forty-five minutes to practice a sequence of activities focusing on the concept of *fuzzies*—positive behavior that produces good feelings. Activities include choosing positive descriptive names for each other, drawing group portraits using each other's features, interviewing and collecting biographical information about classmates, brainstorming positive attributes of each other, and discussing activities and behavior that make students feel good.

Evaluating Affective Curricula

Dembinski, Schultz, and Walton (1982) have discussed the evaluation of psychoeducational curricula; that is, the measurement of changes in student knowledge, performance, and behavior as a result of a series of activities. They point out that the success of any program is a function of the appropriateness and relevance of the activities, the teacher's skill in organizing the activities, and the application by the student of the skills to real problem-solving situations.

Not the least of the problems in evaluating affective curricula is determining an operational definition of *affect*. Some programs, such as the Self-Control Curriculum (Fagen, Long, & Stevens, 1975), have attempted to define and categorize self-control skills so they can be rated

by teachers. For example, Expresses Feelings Through Acceptable Words and Behavior (Appreciating Feelings) is assessed by criteria such as "Can use words to describe feelings (e.g., looks sad, happy, angry, etc.)" (Fagen, Long, & Stevens, 1975, pp. 254-255).

Affective skills do not lend themselves to precise definition and quantification. Students may only occasionally display affective skills, and even then, they may not be readily observable. Thus, determination of the efficacy of affective education remains elusive. This does not mean that these programs do not have any value, but that questions of their efficacy have not been, and perhaps cannot be, completely answered. The social skills training programs discussed in the following section have tended to include the measurement of effectiveness as a basic feature.

Social Skills Training

In the past few years, increasing emphasis has been placed on the importance of social skills training (Cartledge & Milburn, 1980, 1986; Gresham 1984; Stevens, 1978). The basis for this effort is the recognition that social skills may be as important as academic skills to success in school and other, broader environments. Appropriate skills for positive acceptance by others are missing in the repertoires of some children and must be deliberately and systematically taught.

Social skills training combines some of the traditional psychoeducational concerns about cognitive-affective influences on behavior with more recently developed behavioral technology. Relationships exist between social skills training and programs such as progressive education (Dewey, 1938), character education (Chapman, 1977), and moral education (Kohlberg, 1976), as well as the affective education approaches discussed above. However, social skills curricula tend to emphasize teaching behavior that will be accepted and reinforced by others (Wood, 1982).

Specific behavioral strategies drawn from social learning theory are used to teach social skills. Social learning theory (Bandura, 1977), as described in Chapter 2, emphasizes the role of vicarious learning by observing behavior models. According to this perspective, both socially acceptable and unacceptable behavior can be acquired through observing others' behavior. Behavior learned this way is cognitively stored and may be performed in appropriate situations when it is likely to be reinforced. Although social learning occurs naturally as individuals observe others, social learning principles can also be used as a deliberate and systematic method to teach behavior.

In Chapter 7, we presented some applications of social learning theory to the teaching of academic skills. The direct instructional approach (e.g., Deshler & Schumaker, 1986) to academic and cognitive interventions has much in common with the strategies presented here.

Cognitive-Behavioral Strategies

Carpenter and Apter (1987) and Glen, Rueda, and Rutherford (1984) have reviewed interventions that they characterize as cognitive-behavioral or social-cognitive. The former, cognitive-behavioral strategies, have the principal goal of increased self-control of behavior through self-monitoring, self-evaluation, and self-reinforcement (Kanfer & Karoly, 1972).

Self-Monitoring. Self-monitoring involves teaching students to consciously examine their own behavior. Used alone, self-monitoring has been successfully used to increase behaviors such as studying (Broden, Hall, & Mitts, 1971) and contributions to class discussion (Gottman & McFall, 1972). Self-monitoring appears to have the most effect on behavior when "(1) it occurs early in a behavioral chain; (2) children record both target and competing behaviors; (3) it is used continuously in initial phases; and (4) it is supported by additional procedures such as self-evaluation, self-reinforcement, and intermittent

external reinforcement" (Polsgrove & Nelson, 1982). In most classroom applications, self-monitoring is just one aspect of more multi-faceted efforts to teach social skills. For example, the Think Aloud (Camp & Bash, 1981) and the MARC (Francescani, 1982) programs teach self-monitoring as an initial self-control strategy.

Self-evaluation. In the same manner, self-evaluation, or teaching students to compare their behavior against predetermined standards, is usually part of a larger program. Students are taught how to compare their performance of a behavior of interest to their own rate prior to instruction (base rate). For example, the student may learn to say, "I talked out just three times today, compared with twenty times when I started last week."

Self-Reinforcement. Self-reinforcement (and self-punishment) teaches students to provide positive and negative feedback to themselves (e.g., "I did it right" or circling a happy, neutral, or unhappy face on a recording form). Rutherford, Howell, and Rueda (1982) have shown that it is possible to teach self-reinforcement techniques to behaviorally disordered students. Compared with a group receiving only external reinforcement for nondisruptive behavior, Bolstad and Johnson (1972) found that students employing both self-evaluation and self-reinforcement exhibited less disruptive behavior. Although self-reinforcement can encourage adaptive classroom behaviors, it does not appear as effective for managing aggressive behavior.

Social-Cognitive Approaches

Social-cognitive interventions are intended to teach students to deal more effectively with social and interpersonal events through self-instruction and problem-solving strategies (Harris, 1982). Self-instruction typically involves verbal prompting, or self-talk, by an individual concerning his or her performance of a particular behavior. This verbal prompting, whether overt (aloud) or covert (silent), has been effective in helping children and adolescents exercise better control over behavior, such as paying better attention and improving performance on tests.

Meichenbaum and Goodman (1979) have outlined four basic steps for teaching self-instruction to children. These are:

1. cognitive modeling of the behavior by an adult while talking aloud
2. child's imitation of the behavior while talking aloud and guided by the adult
3. faded guidance by the adult with the child whispering the instructions while going through the behavior
4. child performing the behavior guided only by covert speech

Turtle Technique. The Turtle Technique (Robin, Schneider, & Dolnick, 1976; Schneider & Robin, 1974) is a program that has used self-instruction to reduce aggressive interchanges among elementary level, behaviorally disordered children. When frustrated or angry, about to throw a tantrum, or close to verbal or physical aggression, students practice the turtle response: "pulling their arms and legs in close to their body, putting their heads down on the desks, and imagining that they were turtles withdrawing into their shells" (Robin, et al., 1976, p. 450). The turtle technique is first modeled to the group by the teacher, who guides student practice in typical problem situations. The teacher provides praise and sometimes other reinforcement for correct imitation. Students also practice muscle relaxation techniques to help them defuse strong emotions and problem-solving strategies to help them cope with emotionally arousing situations. They are instructed in generating alternative solutions to problems, anticipating the possible consequences, and developing step-by-step plans of action. In addition to group practice, the teacher or other students intermittently may say "turtle" to a student in an appropriate situation. Students are encouraged to support use of the technique by their classmates.

Think Aloud. The Think Aloud program (Bash & Camp, 1980; Camp & Bash, 1981; Camp, Blom, Hebert, & VanDoornick, 1977) is intended to train impulsive young children to go through a practiced series of steps to deal with difficult situations. The core of the program is the practice of self-guided speech in problem solving. Students practice asking and answering the following four questions (Bash & Camp, 1980, p. 145):

1. What is my problem? or What am I supposed to do?
2. How do I do it? or What is my plan?
3. Am I using my plan?
4. How did I do?

To help judge if their solutions are good ideas, students are taught to ask, "Is it fair? Is it safe? How does it make you and others feel? Does it solve the problem?" Specific scripts, supported by illustrations and suggested activities, are provided to demonstrate how teachers can provide models for students to *think aloud* their problem solving. The Think Aloud program has been reported to improve students' performance on cognitive tests, promote social behavior, and reduce aggressive behavior.

Coaching. Oden (1980) has proposed guidelines for teaching withdrawn and socially rejected children using a similar sequence of modeling, rehearsal, and feedback. This program includes *coaching* by the teacher in social skills such as participation (e.g., getting started, paying attention); cooperation (e.g., taking turns, sharing materials); communication (e.g., talking with the other person, listening); and validation support (e.g., looking at the other person, giving a smile, offering help and encouragement).

Social problem-solving interventions are

based upon the assumption that some children and youth are deficient in metacognitive processes, or in thinking about their thinking. Thus, they have difficulty reacting flexibly to social problems in three key ways: they are unable to generate alternative solutions; they do not anticipate the possible consequences of their behavior; and they do not develop plans for successful action. Several programs have been designed to address these needs. Elias (1983), for example, used Inside/Out a commercially available videotape program depicting children coping with problems such as teasing, peer pressure, and expressing feelings. Videotape viewing is followed by group discussions guided by the teacher.

Making Better Choices. Another example of a social-cognitive program is Making Better Choices (Harris, 1984). It provides a sequence of group lessons and activities intended to improve cognitive planning and social skills of behaviorally disordered students between the ages of nine and sixteen. The first six lessons focus on giving forethought to behavior and examining consequences. The following cognitive sequence is taught:

- Stop (inhibit impulsive response)
- Plan (a sequence of behavior to accomplish goals)
- Do (follow the plan and monitor behavior)
- Check (reflect on success of the plan)

These steps are then practiced and reinforced in nineteen subsequent lessons dealing with various social skills such as temper control, apologizing, and conversation skills.

The Visalia Program. One of the early attempts to teach social skills in a systematic fashion was implemented and studied in the Visalia, California, school system (Rosenberg, 1973; Rosenberg & Graubard, 1975). Its purpose was to facilitate the reintegration of early teenage mildly retarded and behaviorally disordered students

from special programs into the mainstream. Counseling sessions were used to model socially reinforcing behavior that was coached and practiced by group members. Simulation and role-playing, sometimes with videotape recording, were used. For example, one student who grimaced in a threatening way when he thought he was smiling in a friendly way was coached, and then he practiced smiling in front of a mirror. Students were taught strategies to modify both their own and others' (teachers, peers, and parents) behavior. Behaviorist skills such as extinction (not responding to provocation by others) and reinforcement (paying attention, giving compliments, sharing), behavioral monitoring, and recording were taught and practiced. According to data collected by the students themselves, they were able to improve the reactions of teachers, peers, and parents toward them by modifying their own social behavior. The result was greater social acceptance in the mainstream.

Skillstreaming

A comprehensive social skills program that incorporates many of the features of the programs discussed above and that is particularly applicable to students with personality and behavior disorders is Skillstreaming (Goldstein, Sprafkin, Gershaw, & Klein, 1980, 1983; McGinnis & Goldstein, 1984). In this program, social skills are clustered in several groups, each with several specific skills. Different programs for adolescent (Goldstein, et al., 1980) and elementary (McGinnis & Goldstein, 1984) populations have been developed with similar content and procedures, although specific training activities are geared to the different age levels. In Skillstreaming for adolescents, for example, the skill categories are as follows:

- Beginning Social Skills (e.g., listening, giving a compliment)
- Advanced Social Skills (e.g., asking for help, convincing others)

- Skills for Dealing with Feelings (e.g., knowing your feelings, rewarding yourself)
- Skill Alternatives to Aggression (e.g., asking for permission, keeping out of fights)
- Skills for Dealing with Stress (e.g., making a complaint, dealing with group pressure)
- Planning Skills (e.g., deciding on something to do, concentrating on a task) (Goldstein, et al., 1980)

Explicit directions are provided for forming the Skillstreaming group. A group of five to eight students with two trainers (teachers, aides, social workers, psychologists, etc.) is the recommended optimal size. Groups meet regularly (20 to 30 minutes, three times each week) with approximately ten additional minutes provided for group members to record practiced skills. On nonmeeting days, related skills are pursued. In the first meetings of the group, the trainer explains the purpose of the group and jointly develops several rules for the group (raise your hand before talking, listen to whomever is talking).

Specific skill deficits of the individual members of a group are determined using a social skill checklist completed by the teacher. Box 9.2 contains a sample of the checklist. Individual student ratings are entered on a group chart that may also be used for forming groups with similar skill deficiencies. In some cases, children also rate their own proficiency on the same skills.

There are several phases of Skillstreaming: modeling, role-playing, feedback, and transfer of training. Modeling involves a demonstration of the particular social skill to the members of the group. This typically requires live depictions by the trainer(s), but may sometimes include audio, video, or film models. The component steps of each skill are demonstrated and verbally recited by the trainers' self-talk. The setting for the modeling should be as similar to real-life situations as possible, using relevant props. In some cases, social skills are depicted in the actual settings where they would occur (playground, lunchroom, bus, etc.).

Modeling is followed by role-playing by group members. First, the trainer leads a discussion of what they have observed, and when and where the skill might be used. Then, members of the group are coached as they role-play, or practice imitating, the modeled behavior. These rehearsals receive feedback in the form of praise, encouragement, and constructive criticism from other group members. The feedback is intended to reinforce the correct performance of the skill and follows guidelines for effective reinforcement as discussed in Chapter 8. In addition to social reinforcement, token reinforcement may be provided for participation in the group.

A final and crucial step in Skillstreaming is transfer of training to other settings. Several strategies are employed to ensure the generalization of newly learned skills. These include overlearning through repeated practice. Relatively simple skills (e.g., listening, how to ask a question) may be introduced every week or so; more complicated skills, such as dealing with anger, may require three weeks or longer for rehearsal and practice. Rehearsals also incorporate the practice of each skill in a variety of scenarios with identical elements (similar props and settings) to those found in real-life environments.

In addition, homework assignments are provided for students to practice and monitor their own performance of the skills. Homework may be completed in nongroup settings in school, at home, or in other relevant environments. There are several phases of homework, depending upon the degree of students' mastery of a skill (McGinnis, et al., 1985). Students may first be asked to think of school or home situations where, with whom, and when they can practice the skill. In school, Red Flag situations are provided in which a child will be set up by the trainer to practice a skill. For example, the teacher may assign work that is too demanding so a student can practice dealing with frustration. Students also write down the steps of each skill on a self-recording sheet, record when the

Box 9.2   Elementary Social Skills Checklist

Student _____

Date _____

Circle 1 if the student is *never* good at using the skill.

Circle 2 if the student is *seldom* good at using the skill.

Circle 3 if the student is *sometimes* good at using the skill.

Circle 4 if the student is *almost always* good at using the skill.

Group I: Introductory Social Skills

1. Listening: Does the student appear to listen when someone is speaking and make an effort to understand what is said?
   a) In a one-to-one setting? 1 2 3 4
   b) In a small group setting? 1 2 3 4
   c) In a large group setting? 1 2 3 4

   Problem Situation: _____

2. Asking for Help: Does the student decide when he/she needs assistance and ask for this help in a pleasant manner? 1 2 3 4

   Problem Situation: _____

3. Saying Thank You: Does the student tell others he/she appreciates help given, favors; etc? 1 2 3 4

   Problem Situation: _____

4. Beginning a Conversation: Does the student know how and when to begin a conversation with another person? 1 2 3 4

   Problem Situation: _____

5. Asking a Question: Does the student know how and when to ask a question of another person (i.e., how to ask and convey what he/she means)? 1 2 3 4

Problem Situation: _____

6. Asking a Favor: Does the student know how to ask a favor of another person in a pleasant manner? 1 2 3 4

   Problem Situation: _____

7. Following Instructions: Does the student understand instructions and follow them?
   a) Related to academic task? 1 2 3 4
   b) In the general classroom environment? 1 2 3 4
   c) In social situations? 1 2 3 4

   Problem Situation: _____

8. Joining In: Does the student know and practice acceptable ways of joining an ongoing activity or group?
   a) In the classroom? 1 2 3 4
   b) In social settings (i.e., the playground?) 1 2 3 4

   Problem Situation: _____

9. Giving a Compliment: Does the student tell others that he/she likes something about them or what they have done? 1 2 3 4

   Problem Situation: _____

10. Accepting a Compliment: Does the student accept these comments given by adults or his/her peers in a friendly way? 1 2 3 4

    Problem Situation: _____

Group II: Skills for Dealing with Feelings

11. Apologizing: Does the student tell others he/she is sorry for

continued

Box 9.2 continued

doing something in a sincere manner? 1 2 3 4

Problem Situation: _____

12. Knowing Own Feelings: Does the student identify feelings he/she is experiencing? 1 2 3 4

Problem Situation: _____

13. Express Own Feelings: Does the student express his/her feelings in acceptable ways? 1 2 3 4

Problem Situation: _____

14. Recognizing/Understanding Other's Feelings: Does the student try to figure out how others are feeling in acceptable ways? 1 2 3 4

Problem Situation: _____

15. Dealing with Own Anger: Does the student know ways to express his/her anger in acceptable ways? 1 2 3 4

Problem Situation: _____

16. Dealing with Other's Anger: Does the student try to understand another's anger without getting angry himself/herself? 1 2 3 4

Problem Situation: _____

17. Expressing Affection: Does the student let others know he/she cares about them in an acceptable manner? 1 2 3 4

Problem Situation: _____

18. Dealing with Fear: Does the student know why he/she is afraid and know strategies to reduce this fear? 1 2 3 4

Problem Situation: _____

19. Asking Permission: Does the student know when and how to ask if he/she may do something? 1 2 3 4

Problem Situation: _____

20. Sharing: Is the student agreeable to sharing things with others or offer reasons why he/she cannot in an acceptable manner? 1 2 3 4

Problem Situation: _____

21. Helping Others: Can the student recognize when someone needs or wants assistance and offer this help? 1 2 3 4

Problem Situation: _____

22. Using Self-Control: Does the student know and practice strategies to control his/her temper or excitement? 1 2 3 4

Problem Situation: _____

23. Responding to Teasing: Does the student deal with being teased in ways which allow him/her to remain in control? 1 2 3 4

Problem Situation: _____

24. Avoiding Trouble: Does the student stay away from situations that may get him/her into trouble? 1 2 3 4

Problem Situation: _____

25. Staying Out of Fights: Does the student know of and practice other ways of handling difficult situations? 1 2 3 4

Problem Situation: _____

continued

Box 9.2   continued

26. Making a Complaint: Does the student know how to say that he/she disagrees in acceptable ways?   1 2 3 4

    Problem Situation: _____

27. Answering a Complaint: Is the student willing to arrive at a fair solution to someone's justified complaint?   1 2 3 4

    Problem Situation: _____

28. Dealing with Losing: Does the student accept losing at a game or prize without becoming upset or angry?   1 2 3 4

    Problem Situation: _____

29. Showing Sportsmanship: Does the student express a sincere compliment to others about how they played the game?   1 2 3 4

    Problem Situation: _____

30. Dealing with Being Left Out: Does the student deal with being left out of an activity without losing control?   1 2 3 4

    Problem Situation: _____

31. Dealing with Embarrassment: Does the student know of things to do that help him/her feel less embarrassed or self-conscious? 1 2 3 4

    Problem Situation: _____

32. Responding to Persuasion: Does the student consider the conse-quence of what may happen if he/she goes along with what another is asking him/her to do? 1 2 3 4

    Problem Situation: _____

33. Reacting to Failure: Does the student figure out the reason(s) for his/her failure, and how he/she can be more successful the next time?   1 2 3 4

    Problem Situation: _____

34. Dealing with an Accusation: Does the student know ways to deal with being accused of something?
    a) When he/she is falsely accused?   1 2 3 4
    b) When he/she is justifiably accused?   1 2 3 4

    Problem Situation: _____

35. Dealing with Group Pressure: Does the student decide what he/she wants to do when others pressure him/her to do something else?   1 2 3 4

    Problem Situation: _____

36. Deciding on Something to Do: Does the student find something to do when he/she has free time? 1 2 3 4

    Problem Situation: _____

Note: This checklist is a modification of the "Structured Learning Skills Checklist" presented in *Skillstreaming the Adolescent*.

Source: E. McGinnis, "Teaching social skills to behaviorally disordered youth," in J. K. Grosenick, S. L. Huntze, E. McGinnis, & C. R. Smith (Eds.), *Social/affective interventions in behavioral disorders* (Columbia, MO: Department of Special Education, University of Missouri, 1984).

skill is practiced, and rate their own success. Box 9.3 includes a sample, self-recording homework form. The data can also be tallied on 3 x 5 inch file cards for a long-term record. In the elementary level program, tokens are provided on an intermittent schedule along with verbal reinforcement for active, appropriate participation in the group and for practicing social skills. Tokens go into a group "pot" and are used for activities that involve practice of social skills (playing group games, working on joint projects).

Considerable empirical evidence has been collected to demonstrate the efficacy of Skillstreaming. According to a summary of this research reported by Goldstein, et al. (1983), the program has been successful in teaching important social skills. Across diverse populations and targeted skills, over 90 percent of Skillstreaming trainees have learned new social skills. In addition, they claim that transfer of those skills to relevant real-world environments has been documented in approximately 50 percent of the cases. This, Goldstein and his colleagues say (1983), is considerably higher than the average successful transfer of improvements reported for several other forms of psychotherapy involving different types of psychopathology.

However, a comprehensive review of research on social skills training with behaviorally disordered students has found that existing research has not yet demonstrated that social skill improvements generalize to other settings or that they persist over time (Schloss, Schloss, Wood, & Kiehl, 1986). Schloss, et al. (1986) also note a lack of agreement by researchers on a comprehensive view of what constitutes social competence. In addition, researchers often have not related specific social skills interventions to specific subject characteristics. Rather, social skills training is frequently directed at presumed general needs of behaviorally disordered persons. Despite the promise of these training programs for improving social skill acquisition, the reviewers conclude that many questions about their efficacy remain unanswered.

Cooperative Learning

Many students with personality and conduct problems have difficulty functioning as members of a group, particularly within the competitive structure of traditional classrooms. Some are disruptive, easily influenced by others, or distractible. Others withdraw, fail to participate, or do not interact with others in groups. In special education programs for behaviorally disordered students, the emphasis is often on individualized instruction. The required individual education program (IEP) specifies individual goals, objectives, and instructional procedures to be used with each student. Although an individualized approach is often appropriate for determining a student's unique educational requirements, most behaviorally disordered students also need opportunities to practice participating in groups. Unfortunately, overemphasizing individualization serves to isolate students from interaction with peers even within a special program, thus effectively limiting their opportunities to learn and practice skills necessary for effective participation in the educational mainstream.

The social skills and affective education strategies discussed above are deliberate attempts to remediate social skill deficiencies. Cooperative learning strategies also offer methods of adding cooperation skills to the curriculum. Sapon-Shevin (1980), for example, has shown how cooperative games and literature can be used with young children to deliberately teach skills such as talking nicely with classmates, sharing and taking turns, and including others who have been left out. She also suggests ways cooperation can be infused in other curricular areas.

Cooperative, as opposed to either competitive or individual, learning strategies have been developed to improve both academic and intragroup relations of students, including the mildly handicapped (Schniedewind & Salend, 1987). Considerable research has explored the efficacy of cooperative approaches with different ages,

Box 9.3   Skillstreaming—Self-Recording Report

Student: *Michelle*   Date: *Sept. 30*

Skill: *Staying Out of Fights*

Steps: 1. *Stop and count to 10.*
2. *Decide what the problem is.*
3. *Think of other ways to deal with the problem:*
   a. walk away for now
   b. talk to the person in a friendly way
   c. ask someone for help.
4. *Act out your best choice.*

When I Practiced   How did I do?

on the bus

morning recess

music

after school

Source: E. McGinnis & A. P. Goldstein, *Skillstreaming the elementary school child* (Champaign, IL: Research Press, 1984) p. 93.

Box 9.4   A. Sample Lesson Worksheet

Goal: To develop appropriate interaction skills in participating students based on conforming to game rules.

Objectives:
1. All students will follow game rules.
2. The game will be completed so that everyone agrees that all have participated and the rules have been followed.

Group Size: 4–5 students per group.

Room Arrangement: Students will be seated at round tables in the play area.

Materials: One deck of UNO cards for each group.

Task-Goal/Structure Skill: Play UNO. Read and establish the rules of the game before you start. Students must watch the game and pay attention so they will know when their turn comes. The teacher will be looking for positive partici-

pation and attention paid to the rules of the game. If someone has a question, group members should take time to answer it.

Teacher Observation: All rules were reviewed. Group decided who was to deal cards by picking a number. As game was played, one student began to dominate the action. This was allowed to occur for 5 minutes to see if the others would solve it. After they did not, the teacher intervened and reminded the students that *all* must participate on an equal basis. Game progressed well.

Teacher Interventions: Ten minutes into the game, the teacher reviewed the rule about equal participation.

Teacher Evaluation: Name-calling behavior needs more work. Equal participation will continue to be stressed. Students did feel that the one dominant student was better after the teacher intervention.

---

groupings, and exceptionalities. Reviews by Johnson and Johnson (1983) and Slavin (1980, 1983) have confirmed generally positive academic and behavioral outcomes for classrooms using cooperative learning rather than traditional programs.

Although much of the research and development has involved cooperative learning in regular education and with other types of exceptional children, cooperative learning strategies have also been adapted to programs for behaviorally disordered students. Knight, Peterson, and McGuire (1982), for example, used the cooperative learning program of Johnson and Johnson (1981) to develop positive interdependence among behaviorally disordered students. Knight et al. (1982) say, "Within the cooperative social structure the goals of individuals are linked together so there is a positive correlation

among their goal attainments." Activities may be structured to promote cooperation by having groups work together "against the clock," for example, instead of competing with one another. Lessons are systematically taught with specific participating behaviors monitored and recorded as shown in Box 9.4.

Huber (1976) has suggested several ways that common group games can be modified to reduce competition. Recently, more board games have been designed that are either minimally competitive or noncompetitive. A company called Animal Town Games in Santa Barbara, California, for instance, publishes a catalog of commercially available noncompetitive games appropriate for a wide range of ages.

Since many behaviorally disordered students have difficulty coping with the competitive challenges of both losing and winning, it is

Box 9.4   (cont.)   B. Cooperative Group Monitoring Sheet

Group: Red #1   **Teacher's Name:** Knight
Activity: UNO Game—Rules   **Observer's Name:** Burkey—Aide
Duration of Observation: 45 min.   **Date:** 1/6/82

Observation Sheet

	Steve	Susan	Glenn	Martha	Randy
Participating	‖‖ ‖‖		‖‖ ‖‖	‖‖ ‖‖ ‖‖ ‖‖ |||	‖‖ ‖‖
Helping: "Let me show you."				‖	‖‖
Put-downs: "That's not right."	‖‖	‖‖ ‖	‖‖ ‖‖	‖‖ ‖	‖‖
Off-task	‖‖ ‖	‖‖			‖
Questions: "I need help."					
Encouragement: "I really liked what you did."				‖	‖

Other Comments: Martha too dominant. Doing for others too much. Too many put-downs.

Source: C. J. Knight, R. L. Peterson, & B. McGuire, "Cooperative Learning: A New Approach to an Old Idea." *Teaching Exceptional Children, 14,* (1982). 233–238. Copyright 1982 by the Council for Exceptional Children. Reprinted with permission.

usually beneficial to reduce competition within their school programs. However, competition permeates our culture, and students must also learn skills to handle themselves in competition. As students gain self-confidence from successful experiences, competitive experiences can gradually be reintroduced.

Adjunct Therapies

A variety of adjunct, or supportive, therapies are sometimes employed in educational programs for students with personality and con-

duct disorders. They include art, music, writing, and bibliotherapy, relaxation, and exercise, as well as photography, drama, and dance therapy. According to Phillips (1981, p. 382), supportive therapies are often used "without regard to how the therapies arose, what their essential functions might be, how they could be improved upon, how they could be explicitly woven into other therapeutic contents, how they might be researched, or how they might be applicable to selective types of fairly well-defined patient or client populations." Despite the lack of empirical proof of their efficacy, some teachers and therapists use art, music, writing, and other experiences in ways they believe contribute to the emotional and cognitive growth of their students.

These adjunct therapies tend to be practiced in hospitals, rehabilitation centers, and in conjunction with other individual and group therapies, although they are also sometimes used in educational programs. Some school districts, for example, employ trained art and music therapists. In others, regular and special education teachers select and adapt these therapies to their programs.

The emphasis of artistic adjunct therapies is on encouraging participants to express feelings, attitudes, and experiences nonverbally. Features of emotional release are emphasized. Through both appreciation and performance, the arts allow nonverbal expression in situations in which verbal expression may be limited or inhibited.

Art Therapy

Art therapy, unlike some other forms, yields tangible products that can be used to help evaluate individual change over time when related to other measures. Self-portraits and students' drawings of their families, for example, sometimes provide insights about how they perceive themselves and others. Case study accounts, such as those found in Bettelheim's *The Empty Fortress* (1967), include examples of how art has been used to provide an outlet for deeply suppressed feelings and thoughts. Bettelheim also used patients' drawings as the basis for elaborate and fascinating psychoanalytic interpretations of their clinical progress.

Music Therapy

Music therapy (Alvin, 1975; Purvis & Samet, 1976) is another prominent supportive therapy through both appreciation and performance. Few would deny that music can catch and reflect moods, but we do not yet know how effectively it can be used to alter psychological states or change behavior. We do know that it is a source of reinforcement for many children and adolescents. For example, used with adolescents in group therapy, it has been found to promote interest in the group, encourage expression of opinions and feelings, and promote more social contacts (Frances & Schiff, 1976). In addition, as a medium of self-expression music has been used in educational settings to help students relate music to moods and feelings.

Both music and art have been employed to promote students' self-expression and group discussion of emotions. For example, teachers sometimes ask students to name feelings and moods elicited by musical and artistic compositions or to draw pictures of how music makes them feel. Even if no therapeutic purpose is served, such activities may at least help students develop a vocabulary of feelings and provide opportunities to practice verbal communication of feelings.

Writing Therapy

Forms of writing therapy are also used in some clinical and educational programs. Phillips and Weiner (1966) offered the following criteria for writing therapy: participants should write freely about any topic of interest; writing should be regularly scheduled and limited to specified time periods; written products should be confidential and kept in a secure place; the therapist should reply, in writing, to the writer, when asking for additional information, relating previous to present writing, pulling together ideas, and marking and numbering significant phrases or passages for easier reference. In some school programs, interested students write daily logs about whatever is on their minds. The teacher then reads and responds in writing. Used this way, personal writing can provide an opportunity for interchange between student and teacher or other adult that may otherwise be unavailable because of students' verbal inhibition or reluctance to share feelings, thoughts, and experiences in front of other members of the group. Likewise, some teachers feel more comfortable providing thoughtful reactions to students in writing.

Bibliotherapy

Bibliotherapy, or therapeutic use of reading, involves referring students to printed material dealing with their problems or concerns. The rationale for bibliotherapy is that others have experienced and written about these issues and that vicarious sharing of the authors' experiences provides emotional relief, aids in problem solving, and helps develop better attitudes. Providing poetry experiences for students with emotional problems has been suggested as a way of encouraging more flexible and creative views of life experiences (Harms, Etscheidt, & Lettow, 1986). They have described a variety of poetry experiences and provided a list of contemporary poetry to explore and extend emotional responses.

In a monograph prepared for Phi Delta Kappa, a national educational honorary society, Cornett and Cornett (1980), advocate the use of bibliotherapy in a preventive way to help children deal with a variety of common problems. These include starting school, being left out, and not liking something about one's appearance. They outline the following steps in preparing and implementing a bibliotherapy program:

- identify student needs
- match students with appropriate materials
- decide on a setting, time, introductory, and follow-up activities
- prepare materials
- motivate students with introductory activities
- provide reading experiences
- allow incubation time
- provide follow-up
- conduct evaluations and direct students toward closure

A key, of course, is matching individual student interest with reading proficiency. Several topi-cally indexed, annotated bibliotherapy sources are available, including *The Bookfinder* (Dreyer, 1985).

Relaxation Training

Relaxation training in the treatment of behavioral disorders has recently received attention and might be considered an adjunct therapy. Relaxation scripts and tapes, usually involving guided imagery of peaceful and calming experiences or practice in tensing and relaxing muscles are available. Richter (1984) reviewed the efficacy of relaxation training used by teachers, counselors, and others in school settings. In addition, Cobb and Evans (1981) have reviewed relaxation training used in conjunction with biofeedback techniques such as electromyograph (EMG) measurement of muscle tension.

Some cognitive-behavior modification programs, such as the previously discussed Turtle Technique (Robin, Schneider, & Dolnick, 1976) and the Self-Control Curriculum (Fagen, Long, & Stevens, 1975), include relaxation training as a component. According to the Richter review (1984), well-controlled studies of relaxation training are still uncommon, but the research literature does include reports of successful reduction of hyperactivity, specific academic and test anxieties, and general anxiety as a result of relaxation training. Used in schools, Richter concludes that relaxation training is most successful when it is continued over longer periods of time, receives environmental support from parents, and has extended involvement of teachers. Relaxation training, however, does not appear to have a significant impact on behavioral disorders when used to the exclusion of other treatments.

Exercise

Another physiological therapy that may benefit some students is exercise. Anderson (1985) has shared her experience in developing a running group, the A.M. Club, for her junior high behaviorally disordered students. She details planning the location, schedule, and accoutrements (club T-shirts, logo, ribbons) that were initially used to encourage student involvement. Although Anderson acknowledges the equivocal research on the psychological benefits of exercise, she provides anecdotal evidence for its beneficial effects on individual student's self-esteem and group cohesiveness.

The relationship between physical exercise and mental functioning is widely accepted, yet little empirical evidence exists to support the relationship. However, Evans, Evans, Schmid, and Pennypacker (1985) experimentally tested the effects of jogging and other vigorous exercise on middle school behaviorally disordered boys. A single subject research design was used to determine changes in student performance following exercise. They used three measures: teachers' rating of student behavior, number of talk-outs, and number of math problems completed. Measurements were taken following exercise and compared to student performance prior to the exercise intervention and following an alternative activity (outdoor reading). Although exercise affected individual students to varying degrees, it appeared beneficial for all as teacher behavior ratings improved, number of talk-outs decreased, and the number of math problems completed increased following exercise. In addition, the authors noticed an unanticipated decrease in student absences during the course of the sixty-nine-day study.

Efficacy of Adjunct Therapies

Despite innovative research, the question of the therapeutic value of adjunct therapies is a long way from being answered. Phillips (1981, p. 357) commented, "At this time, the supportive therapies are more challenging than they are convincing, more novel than proven, and more varied than formalized or structured; whether all these postures are useful and fruitful remains to be seen." When the therapeutic goal of a particular adjunct therapy is something like the

enhancement of self-image, determination of efficacy is elusive. It is difficult to measure self-image, let alone relate it to a particular supportive therapy that is only part of a more comprehensive intervention program.

However, one must also remember that the absence of any proof of efficacy does not necessarily mean that a procedure cannot be beneficial. Empirical support for some other interventions is also limited. Still, a degree of skepticism is warranted by those who use these approaches, and the expectations of what they will independently accomplish should not be too grand.

Teachers and others involved in educational programs for students with personality and conduct disorders should not reject adjunct therapies out of hand. Opportunities for students to appreciate and participate in musical, artistic, and recreational activities should be provided in special education programs. William Morse (1971, p. 336) has discussed the importance of music, art, organized sports, play, and other activities in programs for behaviorally disordered students. "Because these children always strain the educational programs, they are frequently cheated out of the extracurricular fun of a regular school. This is in reverse to the order of their need for such experiences." Whether with therapeutic intent or not, the inclusion of such activities in the curriculum can be justified.

We agree with Morse that school programs, regular or special, should provide more than strictly academic experiences for students. Unfortunately, in some special programs the interesting, potentially fun aspects of school are deleted, because students are not viewed as having handled them well in the past or because academic remediation is a more pressing concern. However, experiences included in the various adjunct therapies can enliven the school experience. They can be the "hook" that keeps students coming back, maintains their interest, and encourages active participation. Art, music, drama, reading, and exercise, for example, can each provide some students with opportunities for self-expression, self-satisfaction, and a sense of competence that may not be realized through more strictly academic pursuits. In his work at the League School, Carl Fenichel (1971, p. 341) found that improvement in one area is likely to result in improvement in other areas. "Achievement can do for the disturbed child what it does for any other human being: make him feel more self-confident and motivate him toward further achievement." The adjunct therapies can also provide the media through which educators and others working with students can enthusiastically communicate and share special interests and talents.

Summary

The psychoeducational approaches included in this chapter—designing therapeutic educational environments, programming for success, managing surface behavior, interviewing techniques, affective education, social skills training, cooperative learning, and the adjunct therapies—provide procedures for structuring safe, satisfying educational experiences. They are strategies intended to promote more empathic relationships between teachers and students, more acceptable social behavior, and greater self-control. Some psychoeducational approaches emphasize systematic teaching of behavior that directly and indirectly benefits students with

personality and conduct disorders. To do this, they focus both on changing the ways students think and feel about themselves and others and on remediating academic skills.

This frequently requires that the teacher assume a therapist as well as a teacher role (Nichols, 1986). Indeed, as Fenichel (1971, p. 345) commented, the distinction between teacher and therapist is blurred and may be largely a semantic one. "Any educational process that helps to correct or reduce a child's distorted perceptions, disturbed behavior and disordered thinking, and that results in greater mastery of self and one's surroundings is certainly a therapeutic process."

Probably, none of the strategies presented in this chapter will always be effective with all students. Likewise, none of the approaches are compatible with every teacher's personal teaching style or with every school and community educational philosophy. However, together with the behavioral approaches discussed in the previous chapter, they provide numerous possibilities for designing educationally relevant interventions for behaviorally disordered students. In the next chapter, these interventions are placed into the context of designing and implementing individual educational programs and selecting appropriate models for delivering those services.

CHAPTER 10

Educational Planning, Service Delivery, and Model Programs

Overview

Introduction

In this chapter our attention is on planning and implementing educational programs for students with personality and conduct disorders. Two of the guiding principles for special education programming—designing programs appropriate to individual student needs and delivery of those programs in the least restrictive environment—are the focus of our discussion. We will begin by addressing the need for adopting an ecological approach to intervention that appreciates the dynamic relationships among the various arenas of a student's life within and beyond the ecosystem of the school.

Rhodes (1967, 1970), Hobbs (1974), and more recently Apter (1977), Apter and Conoley (1984), and Swap, Prieto, and Harth (1982) among others, have contributed to our appreciation of an ecological perspective for understanding and treating behavioral deviance. These ecologically oriented educators have explained how both individual and environment are involved in a condition of emotional disturbance. Hence, effective treatment requires interventions directed both at the disturbed individual and the disturbed environment. Swap, Prieto, and Harth (1982) have identified the following key assumptions of an ecological approach for behaviorally disordered children:

- disturbance results from disturbed interactions between a child and his or her environment
- interventions must alter the ecological systems in which disturbance occurs
- ecological interventions are eclectic
- interventions may have unanticipated consequences
- each intervention between a child and setting is unique

The design of Individual Education Programs (IEPs) is presented from an ecological perspective as both a process and a product. It is a process of collaborative planning by those involved with the child. It is also a product—a written document that outlines the plan for educational interventions. A central feature of the IEP is the determination of the appropriate placement of students within an educational service delivery model. The principle of Least Restrictive Environment (LRE) requires the determination of the educational ecosystem, or service delivery model, that most therapeutically meets a student's needs and facilitates movement toward more normalized educational placements. The final section of this chapter presents overviews of three comprehensive model programs that have incorporated features of the ecological approach: the Engineered/

Orchestrated Classroom (Hewett, 1968; Hewett & Taylor, 1980), Developmental Therapy (Wood, 1975, 1986), and Project Re-Ed (Hobbs, 1978; Lewis, 1975).

The Ecology of Educational Intervention

An overriding concern of special educational interventions for students with personality problems and conduct disorders is the improvement of their social and academic functioning. Not only is the goal improved performance within a special program but also better adaptation within the other environments where students interact, including regular school programs, the family, the community, and society. From an ecological perspective adjustments that are made in one interaction system may have an impact on others. Box 10.1 depicts the interactions that can exist across a child's ecosystems.

School-based interventions for behaviorally disordered students do not take place under laboratory conditions, in which all extraneous variables that may affect the students can be controlled while treatments are applied. Conditions that are largely beyond the direct influence of educators may affect their efforts both positively and negatively. Conversely, special educators' interventions may affect a student's life well beyond the special program. In this chapter, our attention is focused primarily on educational interventions within schools and classrooms. The approaches discussed in previous chapters will be considered in the context of the educational delivery models where they may be used.

Relationships among three major elements—the students, the intervenors, and the environment—must be considered. For each of these elements, a variety of factors may affect interventions. They include, for example, a student's personal and social adjustment, physical and

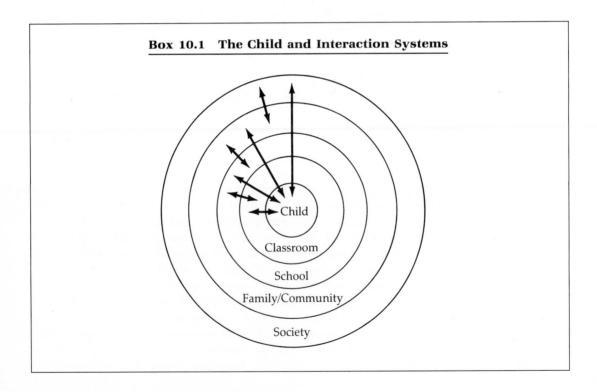

Box 10.1 The Child and Interaction Systems

Child

Classroom

School

Family/Community

Society

mental abilities, and previous educational experience. They also include teachers' and other intervenors' personal and social adjustments, physical and mental abilities, experiences, and training. All interchanges between students and teachers occur within school contexts consisting of a variety of constellations of other students, physical settings, support systems, resources, and psychological climates.

Drawing from several sources, Coleman (1986) has listed some of the factors that can affect students in classrooms. They include characteristics of teachers, peers, the physical environment of the classroom, the curriculum, and the school, as well as factors beyond the school in the realm of the family, community, and larger society in general. Consequently, the selection, use, and effectiveness of a single intervention is potentially influenced by several variables outside and inside the classroom proper.

To illustrate how some of these factors influence an intervention, the therapeutic value of the procedure of isolation time-out (as discussed in Chapter 8) is used as an example. Both practical and ethical factors are then of concern. Some general considerations for using time-out include the determination of an individual student's need for such external control, physical ability to resist placement in time-out, and previous experience with the procedure. The teacher's understanding of and experience with the technique, acceptance of time-out as a behavior management strategy, effectiveness with alternative and additional behavior control methods, and actual physical ability to place the student in time-out are additional considerations. Setting considerations include the availability of an acceptable time-out facility, support staff to assist in supervising and monitoring time-out, school district guidelines for time-out use, acceptance of the technique within the school, and reactions of classmates.

Under certain conditions and for certain kinds of aggressive or disruptive behavior, time-out might be a treatment of choice. Under other conditions, it may be inappropriate. Questions that might be asked relevant to this intervention are:

- Can the student control behavior without such external control?
- What other interventions have been attempted to control the behavior?
- Does an appropriately constructed and arranged time-out facility exist?
- Are appropriate procedures for the use of time-out established and followed?
- Has time-out been previously used with this student? How has it worked?
- Does the teacher have the training and skills to use the procedure properly?
- Are other personnel available to assist in implementing and monitoring the intervention?
- Is the procedure accepted and supported by other personnel within the school?
- Is the procedure understood and considered acceptable by the student's family and the community?

A negative response to any of these questions may preclude the use of time-out. Such practical and ethical considerations will affect the selection and use of any intervention in special education programs, although the ethical questions are perhaps most critical in the case of interventions that are aversive or punishing.

Designing Individual Education Programs

The Individual Education Program (IEP) is a central feature of school-based interventions for students with personality problems and conduct disorders. There are several procedures required by PL 94–142 for inclusion in an IEP, including multidisciplinary assessment, involvement of relevant school personnel (regular and special education teachers, administrators, school psychologists, and other support personnel) and parents or guardians, and approval of the plan by all of these interested parties. The IEP is a means of coordinating planning, support, implementation, and involvement of representatives of the various ecosystems in which the student participates. Several resources provide instruction for preparing IEPs (e.g., Fiscus & Mandell, 1983; Lovitt, 1980; Turnbull, Strickland, & Brantley, 1982).

An IEP must be prepared for every student who is identified as handicapped and has been determined to need special education services. IEPs must be written at least annually, but must also be prepared whenever a student's special program requires any substantial modification, such as a change in placement. The IEP is the document that specifies what special needs a student has, how that has been determined, what will be special about a student's program, and how the special program will be enacted.

Unfortunately, the IEP has sometimes been perceived as a mandate requiring extensive record keeping and other paperwork, but serving no useful function. However, the purpose of the IEP is to ensure that special education programs are designed on the basis of sound assessment, that all relevant parties to the special intervention are involved in planning an appropriate program, that direction is provided for program design and implementation, and that responsibilities are assigned. In short, the IEP should provide the overall design of the special program.

An IEP represents a commitment among those persons who prepare it to provide educational interventions appropriate to an individual student's needs. To ensure this, the process must conform with the due process requirements spelled out in PL 94–142. Thus, formal IEP development is a possible outcome of the assessment process outlined in Chapter 3:

1. classroom and home adjustments
2. prereferral activities
3. referral for special education services—eligibility
4. referral for special education services—placement

Due process requirements for the notification and approval by parents at several stages sometimes appear to place school personnel and parents of exceptional children in adversarial roles. It is important for educators to recognize that these procedural safeguards are intended to lessen the risk of improper or inappropriate identification and educational placement. Due process requirements present an opportunity to encourage meaningful cooperation among all of those involved in designing and implementing special educational programs. In fact, the process of IEP development may be as important as the product itself, since it is the vehicle for school personnel and families to determine and work toward common goals for the student.

Parents, of course, can play a critical role in the process. Their long-term experience and knowledge of their children make them key resources in IEP development. Parents' support elicited during IEP development can be critical to its successful implementation. The IEP process can be a way of improving parents' perceptions of their children's school experiences. Frank Wood (1973) has urged that the process of developing educational programs for behaviorally disordered students should be one of "negotiation and justification." It should involve negotiation among all relevant parties and justification of programs to be provided.

Requirements for the makeup of the IEP committee vary somewhat from state to state and from district to district. At minimum, they typically include the following:

- The student's parent(s) or guardian(s).
- A representative of the local education agency other than the student's teacher(s) who is designated to supervise the provision of special education. At an initial IEP conference, this person should report and interpret the results of the comprehensive evaluation of the

student. Sometimes this person is a school psychologist or a special education administrator or coordinator, who also serves as the chair of the IEP conference and maintains records of the proceedings.

- The student's teacher(s). If the student is being considered for an initial special education placement, this person would probably be one of the student's regular education teachers. If the student is already receiving special education services, this person would probably be the student's current special education teacher(s). Whenever possible, the potential receiving teachers participate in IEP development, since they have primary responsibility for implementing the plan.
- Additional persons who have had some relevant involvement with the student in the past, who have specialized expertise that may contribute to designing the educational program, or who may be involved in the implementation of the program. School psychologists and clinical psychologists, social workers, building administrators, nurses, and others often participate in the conference. Frequently, however, all of these persons may not be in attendance, but their written reports and recommendations are shared at the meeting. Sometimes, when the IEP team considers it appropriate, the student participates directly in the IEP meeting. In addition, in some instances, the parents may bring nonschool personnel, such as other family members, independent psychologists, or lawyers, or their written evaluations of the situation.

Elements of the IEP

The IEP document has several required parts. These are statements of:

1. present level of performance
2. long-term goals
3. short-term objectives for each of those goals
4. special education and support services, materials, and techniques

Present Level of Performance. Based upon multidisciplinary assessment as described in Chapter 3, a student's current level of functioning must be determined. In our discussion of assessment, we outlined ecological strategies for screening, identification, and monitoring behavioral change. Information should be gathered using a combination of sources, including formal and informal testing, interviews and case history information, setting analyses, and formal observation.

For students with personality problems and conduct disorders, personal and social, as well as academic, strengths and weaknesses should be addressed in the statement of present level of performance. For example, if inappropriate talking out is one major cause of concern for a student named Robert, it may be identified as a weakness in his IEP. However, evidence must have been provided in the formal evaluation process to determine the size and scope of that problem. In this case, both the frequency and quality of Robert's talk-outs may be of concern. Direct observation samples of his behavior during times of concern may have shown that he talks out an average of 30 times during each 50-minute period. Thus, the rate of talking out is 0.6 per minute (30 talk-outs/50 minutes). Additional observational data may indicate that approximately 50 percent (a rate of about 15 per hour) of Robert's talking out is considered inappropriate in school, since it consists of whining, complaining, and threatening, hostile, or profane comments directed at other students and teachers. It provokes angry verbal responses and arguments by others, distracts other students and teachers, and sometime leads to shoving matches and fights. Observation of classmates reveals that Robert's talking out is substantially discrepant from his peers. Their mean talk-out rate is only about 0.1 per minute, and few of those incidents are considered inappropriate.

In addition, based upon reports from Robert's teachers and the school principal, inappropriate talking out has been a chronic problem, and one that is getting worse. Robert's mother reports that she is encountering similar behavior at home and that he gets into frequent disputes and fights in the neighborhood. Based on these kinds of information, the IEP team may conclude that Robert's talking out interferes with his educational performance, causes considerable distress and threatens others, and is indeed a major behavioral weakness to be addressed in his IEP.

Identifying a student's weaknesses sometimes seems easier for the IEP team than identifying strengths. The student, after all, has been referred and formally identified as behaviorally disordered on the basis of perceived problems of one kind or another. Focusing on those problems may distract the multidisciplinary team from recognizing some areas of strength or achievement. When a student's social and academic strengths are not readily apparent, the IEP team may think in terms of relative strengths. Thus, a student's performance in some academic areas may be strong relative to his performance in other areas.

It is also sometimes helpful to look for strengths *within* weaknesses. For example, in the case of another student, Henry, whose frequent talking out is considered a problem, the nature of the talking out may actually be a strength. Although Henry's talk-outs are disrupting his class, most of the verbalizations are not provocative, are relevant to what is going on in class, and are even indicative of his involvement in the educational program. In Henry's case, the frequency of his talking out may be a weakness, but the nature of his talking may be viewed as a strength.

As we have stated in earlier chapters, every behavior problem must be studied within its context. In our earlier example of Robert, talking out 0.6 times per minute is not necessarily a weakness, any more than being on-task 99 percent of the time is necessarily a strength. The expectations for behavior within a classroom environment and comparisons with the behavior of others in that setting must be considered. In one classroom, informal verbal in-

teraction may be strictly prohibited; in another, considerable verbal interaction among students is allowed. If classmates are observed to talk out inappropriately 0.8 times per minute, a rate of 0.6 might even be considered a strength. A talk-out rate of 0 times per minute might be considered a weakness, because it constitutes insufficient verbal interaction with others. We are not simply suggesting that "It's all relative," but that contextual conditions cannot be ignored in determining strengths and weaknesses.

A good statement of a student's present level of performance should also include previously attempted interventions and their success rates. Teachers of behaviorally disordered students see this type of information as most valuable for educational programming, yet it is frequently unavailable when students are placed in their programs (Zabel, Peterson, Smith, & White, 1981). Parents are sometimes valuable resources in identifying their child's strengths and weaknesses and providing information on the effectiveness of interventions that have been used in the past. Their insights into what has worked outside of school can also contribute to the development of future interventions.

Long-Term Goals. The determination of annual goals should be derived directly from the statement of the present level of performance. All stated weaknesses must be addressed in these goals. They must be listed in order of priority, with weakest area addressed first. It should be noted that each identified weakness does not necessarily lead to a single goal; two or more goals may address a weakness.

There is no single way of determining appropriate educational goals, but it can be helpful for the IEP team to think in terms of the personal, social, and academic competencies that will benefit the student over the long run and in multiple settings. Annual goals should include the IEP committee's estimate of what the student should be able to accomplish within a one-year period. They should be fairly broad in scope, yet specific enough to focus on one instructional area.

An ultimate goal of schooling is to prepare students to function more independently as adults and to enhance their self-sufficiency. Brown, Nietupski, and Hamre-Nietupski (1976) have suggested using the "criterion of ultimate functioning" for severely handicapped students. Such a guideline may help IEP teams focus on important educational goals for the entire range of students with personality problems and conduct disorders. Planning instructional settings, curricula, and methods for meeting goals in the context of "ultimate functioning" may better ensure relevancy of special education programs. As Donnellan points out (1984, p. 142), "the goals of educational programs for handicapped students include maximal participation, productivity, and independence in a wide variety of community environments."

Goals, then, are the general statements of what the IEP team agrees should be attempted. They usually are stated positively, in terms of what the student should be able to do. For example, instead of "Robert will reduce his threatening, arguing, and provocative interactions with others," a long-term goal might be "Robert will increase the number of his acceptable verbal interactions with others."

A much debated issue in determining annual goals concerns their level of specificity. Some concerns are more amenable to specification than others. Two guidelines might be helpful: (1) annual goals should lead directly to specific short-term objectives, and (2) annual goals should be mutually understood and agreed upon by all members of the IEP team, including parents.

Short-Term Objectives. Short-term objectives are statements of the specific, measurable means of meeting the long-term goals. Each goal requires at least one objective, but may have more than one objective listed in the sequence in which it will be attempted. The conditions under which the desired behavior is to be demonstrated and the criterion level it is to occur

should be included in each objective. Exact dates for the expected accomplishment of each short-term objective are not always specified in the IEP. Since each objective may be built upon earlier accomplished objectives, difficulty in accomplishing one objective would alter a predetermined schedule. Objectives can be written to be accomplished during periods of time, such as weeks, months, or quarters of the school year. For our earlier talking-out example, for instance, the following might be objectives to be attempted in sequence over a ten-week period:

1. During independent seat work, Robert will raise his hand at least 75 percent of the time to get Ms. Anders's (self-contained BD teacher) permission before speaking.
2. During independent seat work, Robert will raise his hand at least 90 percent of the time to get Ms. Anders's permission before speaking.
3. During group discussion in social studies and English, Robert will raise his hand and receive permission before talking 75 percent of the time on five consecutive days.
4. Robert will write a list of ten positive statements (fuzzies) that could be directed at peers.
5. Robert will verbally list ten positive statements that could be directed at peers and teachers.
6. Robert will verbally list at least twenty positive statements that could be directed at peers and teachers.
7. Given written lists of statements and requests directed at him, Robert will write positive verbal responses for each.
8. When Ms. Anders reads requests and commands to him, Robert will provide positive verbal responses for each.
9. Robert will engage in at least ten positive verbal interactions per day with Ms. Anders and his classmates.
10. Robert will engage in at least twenty positive verbal interactions per day with Ms. Anders and his classmates.

The IEP team should write objectives that are relevant to the student's identified needs and that they believe can be achieved at the levels of performance and in the time periods specified. Goals and objectives should not be selected primarily because they can be easily accomplished, but because they are important competencies for the student to acquire.

Special Procedures, Support Services, and Techniques. The special procedures for accomplishing short-term objectives must also be indicated on the IEP form. In our talk-out example, several strategies would be possible, and the IEP team should select those they believe will work best. For example, Robert may be included in group meetings in the special classroom in which the teacher or school social worker lead discussions of relationships between how people treat others and how they are treated in return. Social skills training programs, including modeling, rehearsal, and applied practice of acceptable verbal communication may be implemented for Robert. Positive teacher feedback and, if necessary, tokens for positive practice might contribute to his skill development.

In addition, teacher and student self-monitoring systems might be designed to record the number and nature (i.e., positive and negative) of talk-outs during designated times in the special class. Results could be graphed to display to Robert his progress toward more acceptable verbal interactions. A three-party contract is another strategy that could involve the student, teacher, and parent. The teacher awards points to the student, based on teacher- or self-recorded data, and the parents provide privileges at home when the specified criteria levels are met.

Support, or related, services are those additional resources deemed necessary by the IEP team to implement a successful program for the student. The regulations for implementing PL 94–142 give school districts responsibility for providing related services, when they are necessary, to assist a handicapped child benefit from special education. In the case of students

with personality and conduct disorders, related services may include medical services for diagnostic or evaluation purposes as well as "psychological and counseling services" (Federal Register, August 23, 1977).

However, there is some dispute over the extent of the school's responsibility (Wood, 1985). Because schools have not traditionally provided psychotherapy, some educators have resisted the suggestion that schools should be required to provide this service (Smith, 1981). Although the U.S. Supreme Court has not dealt directly with this issue and the U.S. Office of Special Education Programs has not made a clear policy statement, lower court decisions have generally been supportive of a full range of related services for behaviorally disordered students (Grosenick, Huntze, Kochan, Peterson, Robertshaw, & Wood, 1982b). Some school districts provide or pay for psychotherapy as a related service (Wood, 1985).

School counselors, social workers, and psychologists may also provide assistance to the student in mobilizing community resources for recreation activities, academic tutoring, medical treatment, and other services. The nature of these services depends largely on the needs of the individual student and the availability, abilities, and willingness of school personnel to provide them. If the IEP team agrees that a support service, such as individual counseling, is essential to a student's special education program and includes it in the IEP, the school system is obligated to provide that service or to pay the costs of providing it.

Other IEP Information. In addition to the above information, the persons who are identified as primarily responsible for implementing each aspect of the IEP and the sequence in which each will be accomplished, should be specified. Names and signatures of participating team members, signifying their approval of the program, must also be included. In addition, the administrative service delivery model (special education placement) must be determined with a statement of the amount of the student's involvement in the regular and special programs.

Both the process and the product of the IEP should facilitate the implementation of an appropriate special education program. As a process, the IEP provides an opportunity to share information and ideas, and to arrive at some consensus about an appropriate educational plan for the student. It also formalizes the commitment of team members to work toward common goals. As a product, the document should lead directly to implementation of interventions. For teachers, specification of objectives and descriptions of the ways they will be accomplished are not the same as daily lesson plans but they should direct development of lesson plans.

Student Involvement in the IEP. In most cases, the student is not directly involved in IEP development, although occasionally students are invited to participate in some aspects. Even when students are not directly involved, we believe that it is usually important that they be informed about the meeting, have its purposes explained, and are provided opportunities to ask questions and perhaps provide input. This is particularly true for older students, whose ideas and concerns should be solicited and considered by the IEP team. The student, after all, is the lead player in the IEP and frequently has insights into his or her educational needs. It is important to communicate the concern and consideration that go into developing the program. The student should be informed that it is a task the adults take seriously, and one about which they concur. This communication can help dispel any sense of mystery or the appearance of collusion among the adults. The message to the student should be, "We are all working together to design an educational program that will benefit you," rather than "We adults are meeting secretly to decide what we will do to you."

Following the preparation of an initial IEP and following its annual update, it is also good practice to review it with the student. The rationales for strengths and weaknesses, goals, objectives, and special procedures should be explained in ways that the student will understand. Efforts to incorporate the student's special concerns should be highlighted. It is usually helpful for students to be informed about the IEP by a teacher or another appropriate member of the team, as well as parents. It may be beneficial, when possible, for a teacher, parent, and student to review the IEP together. Such a meeting can demonstrate to the student that this is indeed a collaboration between students and adults, and can reinforce the team's acknowledgment of the student's key role.

The Continuum of Services: Administrative Arrangements

The Cascade Model

Based upon the determination of a student's special educational needs, the IEP team must specify an appropriate educational placement. As stated earlier, the document must include a statement of the percentage of time the student will be placed in regular education. Of course, the percentage can range from zero, when the student is totally segregated from the regular program, to 100 percent, when the student is totally integrated into a regular educational program. The Cascade Model, or continuum of services (Deno, 1970; Reynolds, 1962), shown in Box 10.2 has traditionally been used to illustrate the potential placement options.

When originally proposed, the Cascade Model replaced an existing two-box system, in which regular and special education placements were seen as separate systems. In the Cascade Model, educational placements include regular or mainstream programs and are distinguished in terms of the degree of student integration implicit at each level along a continuum from less restrictive (or more integrated) to more restrictive (or more segregated) settings. "It is a system which facilitates tailoring of treatment to individual needs rather than a system for sorting

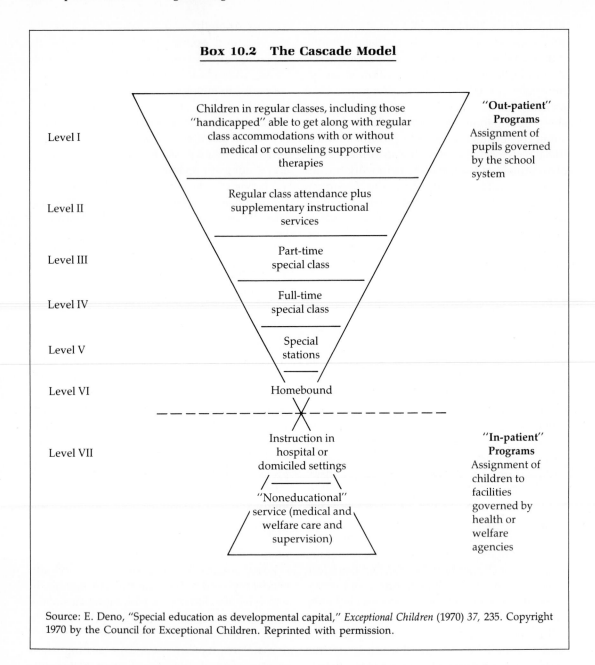

Box 10.2   The Cascade Model

Level I — Children in regular classes, including those "handicapped" able to get along with regular class accommodations with or without medical or counseling supportive therapies

Level II — Regular class attendance plus supplementary instructional services

Level III — Part-time special class

Level IV — Full-time special class

Level V — Special stations

Level VI — Homebound

Level VII — Instruction in hospital or domiciled settings

"Noneducational" service (medical and welfare care and supervision)

"Out-patient" Programs Assignment of pupils governed by the school system

"In-patient" Programs Assignment of children to facilities governed by health or welfare agencies

Source: E. Deno, "Special education as developmental capital," *Exceptional Children* (1970) *37*, 235. Copyright 1970 by the Council for Exceptional Children. Reprinted with permission.

out children so they will fit conditions designed according to group standards not necessarily suitable to a particular case" (Deno, 1970, p. 23). Each level of the Cascade Model is a possible placement for students with behavioral disorders.

There are several assumptions of the model that have implications for students with personality problems and conduct disorders. One is that some educational placements are more restrictive than others. The term *Restrictiveness* is typically used to refer to the degree of segregation, or separation, from regular or mainstream programs. According to this view, the more segregated, the more restrictive.

A second assumption is that more severely handicapped students should be served in more restrictive environments; more mildly and moderately handicapped students in less restrictive environments. Also implicit in this assumption is the view that it is generally desirable for students to move toward less restrictive placements. This Least Restrictive Environment (LRE) principle is based upon the goal of normalization (Wolfensberger, 1972), and was incorporated in PL 94–142, and its predecessor, PL 89–390. Thus, special classes within schools are considered preferable to institutional settings; regular classes are preferable to special classes.

A third assumption is that a student's movement through the continuum of educational services should be orderly and sequential. A student who has been placed in a residential facility should be sequentially reintegrated into less restrictive levels of the continuum—from residential program to special school, from special school to self-contained class, from self-contained class to part-time reintegration in regular school programs with resource program support, and ultimately from resource program to full integration in the regular, or mainstream, program with consultant support.

Limitations of the Cascade Model

A true continuum of services does not always exist for many students with personality problems and conduct disorders. Frequently, no more than one or two service delivery options are provided. Where distinguishable levels of the continuum do exist, the assumptions are not always met. Peterson, Zabel, Smith, and White (1983) have found that the severity of students' emotional and behavioral handicaps is not necessarily related to their educational placement. Some more severely behavior disordered students are placed in less restrictive programs, while some less disordered students are in the most restrictive placements. One of the most re-

strictive or segregated placements is in the youth correctional facility. However, there is currently wide variance across states even in the consideration of incarcerated children and youth as handicapped (Rutherford, Nelson, & Wolford, 1985). Some states consider this population behaviorally disordered or emotionally disturbed by virtue of their placement in the institution, while other states do not.

Peterson, et al. (1983) also found that students in allegedly more restrictive placements (i.e., self-contained classrooms) are not necessarily less integrated into regular programs than those in less restrictive placements (i.e., resource programs). Apparently, many resource programs are more self-contained than many self-contained programs. In addition, teachers at various levels of the continuum do not report using their time differently. For example, despite different role designations, Peterson, et al. (1983) found that resource and self-contained teachers spend about equal amounts of time each week on assessment, instruction, preparation, and planning. The only area of significant difference for these two delivery models is time spent consulting with other teachers and support personnel. Surprisingly, self-contained teachers spend more time in consultation than resource teachers (Zabel, Peterson, Smith, & White, 1983). Taken together, these findings indicate that the Cascade Model has not yet been completely or consistently realized for behaviorally disordered students.

Placement decisions are not always made on the basis of what is most appropriate for individual students, but, rather, on what is available. Many factors can determine the availability of service delivery models. In a rural area, for example, low incidence of identified students, wide geographical distribution and inherent transportation problems, difficulty recruiting and retaining trained teachers, lack of support services, and lack of social acceptance of certain labels can discourage identifying and providing services for behaviorally disordered students (Wood & Lininger, 1982). The result can be students who are unserved, underserved, or receiving other types of services. There may be reluctance to identify students as behaviorally disordered when there are insufficient programs. A single, efficient delivery model (i.e., one that serves a large caseload and a wide variety of students), such as consulting or itinerant services, may be provided. Although these service delivery alternatives are appropriate for some behaviorally disordered students, they cannot meet every student's educational needs. Some students may require the more continuous structure and support of special classrooms or special school placements.

Unfortunately, in situations where a continuum of services is unavailable or where only a single less restrictive model is provided, the only alternative for a student who cannot function in a regular program even with some consultant support may be placement in a more restrictive model than necessary, such as a state hospital or residential treatment facility. It is not only rural areas that may not provide a true continuum of services. In some urban areas with higher incidence populations, the ease and convenience of segregated groupings of students in special self-contained classrooms and schools can discourage the use of the less restrictive delivery models that are more appropriate for some students.

An assumption of the Cascade Model is that delivery of services is guided by established educational need (typically based on severity of handicap). In reality, placements are sometimes determined by economic and political realities as well. Some litigation since PL 94–142 (e.g., *Board* v. *Rowley*, 1982) has served to strengthen the position that placements and programs need not be the MOST appropriate possible, but that they simply provide an appropriate educational program (Wood, 1985).

Determination of appropriate placements is not usually an easy decision even when a range of options exists. Factors, such as the skills and experiences of the special and regular teacher(s), the suitability and location of facilities, acceptance by other students (Sabornie & Kauffman,

1985), and available support services need to be considered. Judgments must be made about the relative costs and benefits of situations such as a student traveling long periods of time by bus to a special school or classroom versus receiving resource support in his home school. Even where viable options are available, the IEP team must carefully consider the advantages and disadvantages of each placement.

Frank Wood (1985) has urged that IEP teams take a conservative approach in the placement of behaviorally disordered students in more segregated settings. He cites the limited proven benefits from special programming together with the potentially damaging effects of the label(s) and expectations that are elicited in the process. Wood advocates a bias against removing students from regular programs until all reasonable alternatives have been tried.

There is some reason to support this bias. Based upon a review of research on the efficacy of special programs for behaviorally disordered students, Skiba and Casey (1985) found the programs produce gains in academic and social functioning while students are in them, but it is unclear how well those gains generalize to other school and community settings and how well they persist over the long run.

Alternatively, there are those who assert that we have been too conservative in identifying and placing behaviorally disordered students in special settings and too eager to return such students to the educational mainstream (Kauffman, McCullough, & Sabornie, 1984). As a result, they believe that we often do a disservice to nonbehavior disordered students whose educational programs are diminished. Resolving this dilemma involving the right to education in the least restrictive environment of BD and non-BD students is troublesome.

To guide placement decisions concerning severely handicapped students, Ann Donnellan (1984) has suggested using a "criterion of least dangerous assumptions." We think this criterion may be equally valid for the whole range of students with personality and conduct disorders. It states that when programming options are available, decisions should be made in favor of those that appear to pose the least harm to students. Such a principle accepts the following assumptions:

- it is generally preferable to place students in less, rather than more, segregated settings
- interaction in a heterogenous group is preferable to a homogeneous group
- education should occur in nonschool or natural settings as well as school or artificial settings
- instruction using naturally occurring antecedents and consequences is preferable to use of artificial strategies

Despite our general reluctance to place students in more restrictive educational settings, we agree that some observations of James Kauffman (1984) and William Morse (1984) should be heeded. Conventional interpretations of restrictiveness according to the Cascade Model are not always valid for behaviorally disordered students. The distance from the regular program or mainstream per se does not define restrictiveness. Some regular classrooms are more restrictive, in the sense that they may restrict a child's social and emotional development, than some self-contained or institutional programs. The major concern for IEP teams should be finding or designing the educational program that seems most appropriately to meet a student's individual needs. Where the program is delivered may not be as important as what the program will be and how it will be implemented.

Disciplinary Exclusion

Policies for the exclusion of students for disciplinary reasons exist in most school systems. Disciplinary exclusion typically takes the form of suspension or expulsion. *Suspension* refers to a temporary exclusion of a student as the result of an emergency situation. It is usually relatively brief (three to ten days), although serial suspen-

sions, involving two or more consecutive suspensions, are sometimes used. *Explusion* refers to more permanent exclusion from school as a result of severely disruptive, threatening, or dangerous behavior toward other students or faculty. Expulsion may be for a specified period of time (e.g., the remainder of the school year), permanent, or for an indefinite period.

Grosenick, Huntze, Kochan, Peterson, Robertshaw, and Wood (1982) have discussed legal implications of these procedures for handicapped students, including those labeled seriously emotionally disturbed. They reviewed federal legislation and court cases that have addressed disciplinary exclusion. PL 94–142, for example, specifically requires free appropriate public education for all children in the least restrictive environment. It also requires that any change in a student's placement toward more restrictive environments requires procedural safeguards. Other federal laws, such as Section 504 of Public Law 93–112 (the Rehabilitation Act of 1973), have also specifically addressed the illegality of excluding handicapped individuals from receiving benefits of any federally supported programs due to conditions related to their handicaps. Although some states have statutes concerning disciplinary exclusion, the federal laws take precedence over these.

According to an analysis by the National Center for Law and Education in 1980, suspension and exclusion of identified handicapped students, as well as those who have been referred for evaluation, may be illegal for the following reasons (Grosenick, et al., 1982, pp. 10–11):

"1) the right to a free appropriate public education which includes specially designed instruction to meet the student's individual needs.
2) the right to have any change in placement occur only through the prescribed procedures.
3) the right to an education in the least restrictive environment with maximum possible interaction with non-handicapped peers.

4) the right to continuation of current educational placement during the pendency of any hearing or appeal, or during any proceeding relating to the identification, evaluation, or educational placement of the child or the provisions of a free appropriate public education.

5) the right not to be excluded from, denied benefits, aids, or services, or be discriminated against on the basis of one's actual or perceived handicapped status."

Most existing court cases concerning the disciplinary exclusion of handicapped students have found the offending behavior resulting in exclusion to be related to the child's handicap. In the case of seriously emotionally disturbed students, Grosenick, et al. believe that it is virtually impossible to separate misbehavior from the handicapping condition.

Does this mean that behaviorally disordered students cannot be excluded from school regardless of their behavior? Several court cases cited by Grosenick, et al. appear to indicate that exclusion is a possible option in situations of emergency under stringent conditions. Exclusion may not be for a period of more than three days and educational services must be continued during that period. This implies that either homebound or in-school suspension is a possible option. If disciplinary exclusion is used for more than three days, a change in the student's placement has been made that requires the following procedural safeguards:

1. prior written notification to parents
2. reevaluation of the student's IEP by an appropriately constituted IEP committee
3. opportunity for a due process hearing if parents object to the change of placement

In other words, decisions to use any long-term exclusion, including in-school suspension, or placement in a homebound program, require due process safeguards.

Groesnick, et al. (1982) conclude that disciplinary exclusion is an appropriate disciplinary tool with handicapped children *only* when it is included in the student's IEP, when procedural requirements are followed, and when suspension does not result in complete or permanent cessation of educational services.

Reintegration: Planning and Facilitating Movement Along the Continuum

Since a key educational goal for behaviorally disordered students is the increased ability to participate in less restrictive environments, it is essential that reintegration be carefully planned and implemented. A student's movement toward more restrictive, more segregated placements is often more carefully charted than movement in the other direction.

Determining a student's readiness for a change in placement is not always easy. A student's relatively good performance in a more restrictive environment, such as a special school or self-contained classroom, does not necessarily indicate how well that student will be able to perform in less restrictive settings. One challenge of special programs at any level of the Cascade Model is providing necessary support and structure to allow a student to succeed, and subsequently weaning the student of dependence on that support.

Special educational placements must provide a therapeutic milieu in which students can thrive, and then help those students move beyond reliance on that structure and support. Of course, this is no easy task. It requires behavioral and academic preparation for the student—remediation of problems that will impede the student's successful reintegration. It also requires careful planning of the transition process, involving preparation both of the student and environment in which the student will be received.

Preparation of the Student

Reintegration should be a process of gradual transition. However, limitations in available service delivery models sometimes preclude this. In a recent statewide examination of the reintegration of students with severe emotional and behavioral disorders in Georgia, fully one-third were found to move directly from highly segregated programs into regular classrooms (Swan, Brown, & Jacob, 1987). Ideally, each phase of reintegration should provide challenges that the student can handle without being overwhelmed. Most behaviorally disordered students have failed to adapt in one way or another in regular educational programs. Consequently, they often do not eagerly leave a special program in which they have experienced greater academic success, in which their deviant behavior may be tolerated, in which they may have received more individual attention, in which a program's external structure provides more support for their school behavior, and where the environment provides less opportunity to get into trouble.

Preparation of the student for reintegration, or for movement in any direction along the continuum, should be provided within the special program. The message communicated to students should be that a major goal of special programming is to prepare them for reintegration. This expectation should be formally incorporated into IEPs with statements of criteria for reintegration. It should be built into academic and social interventions that are used and regularly communicated to students by their special teachers and other personnel.

Expectations can also be communicated by the structure of the special program. Student privileges and responsibilities can correspond to a system of levels within a program (Braaten, 1979, 1982b). As students meet increasingly higher levels of personal and social expectations and academic performance, privileges are increased and external controls are reduced. For example,

at Capital City High School, a special secondary school for behaviorally disordered students located at Topeka (Kansas) State Hospital, students are promoted from self-contained classrooms to the more normalized departmentalized program when they have consistently earned specified numbers of points in the school's token behavior management system. The less restrictive departmentalized program simulates the operation of a regular high school in many respects. It allows for greater student mobility, less supervision, and more privileges than the self-contained program. In addition, considerable status is associated with movement from the self-contained program. When students demonstrate consistently high levels of academic and behavioral performance in the departmentalized program, they become eligible for reintegration into regular secondary school programs.

Several model reintegration programs have addressed the necessity of preparing both the student and the receiving environment for reintegration. Programs that will be described later in this chapter, the Engineered/Orchestrated Classroom (Hewett & Taylor, 1980), Developmental Therapy (Wood, 1975, 1986), and Project Re-ED (Hobbs, 1978; Lewis, 1975) have emphasized reintegration procedures.

Recently, Muscott and Bond (1985) discussed several concerns that are important to the reintegration of behaviorally disordered students. These are:

- defining treatment goals
- planning to ensure transfer of training from one program to another
- improving the attitudes and training of receiving teachers
- interfacing and coordination of service delivery systems
- providing social skills training

The first step in planning for reintegration is defining the affective, behavioral, social, and academic criteria to be used to determine each student's readiness for reintegration. Given the problems already cited with the generalization of improved performance from special to regular programs, it is particularly important to implement strategies that will promote generalization and maintenance of improved behavior. Strategies suggested in Chapters 8 and 9, such as thinning reinforcement schedules, fading external reinforcement, moving students toward self-monitoring and self-management of behavior, and training, practice, and evaluation of social skills in a variety of settings are some of the promising approaches to preparing students for reintegration.

To promote the generalization of behavioral improvement, Judith Grosenick (1971) has recommended providing experiences within special programs that come close to or mirror those found in regular classrooms. Some of her suggestions are:

- locating special classrooms among regular classrooms, rather than isolating them
- using typical arrangements of furniture, rather than arrangements such as isolating students in study carrels
- using similar and same instructional materials when possible
- using a curriculum similar to that in regular classrooms
- using similar grading systems
- including students in school programs, extra-curricular activities, and assemblies
- sharing recess and lunch times
- including activities in the special curricula that encourage self-control and independent study habits
- using group instruction when possible
- familiarizing students with routines and expectations in regular programs

Preparation of the Receiving Program

Preparation of the receiving school, including teachers, administrators, other staff, and students, is another factor in successful reintegra-tion. Too often, regular educators, including teachers, administrators, and other support staff are only minimally involved in the process. In about 90 percent of the districts in a nationwide study, most regular educators were only somewhat involved in reintegration (Grosenick, 1986). It is no wonder that in a majority of those districts regular educators were found to be no more than barely accepting of the philosophies of their behavior disorders programs.

As a group, behaviorally disordered students are among the least welcome handicapped students by regular classroom teachers (Schloss, Miller, Sedlak, & White, 1983; Vacc & Kirst, 1977; Williams & Algozzine, 1980; Wood, 1985; Zabel, 1978a) and by regular classmates (Sabornie & Kauffman, 1985). Indicative of the nonacceptance of behaviorally disordered students is the evidence that behavior disorders classrooms tend to be physically located farther from regular classrooms than LD, EMR, or cross-categorical programs (McDaniel, Sullivan, & Goldbaum, 1982).

Thus, it is not surprising that only about 20 percent of behaviorally disordered students are returned from special programs to regular class-rooms each year (Grosenick, 1986). This non-acceptance, coupled with the evidence that regular educators are typically not included in programming and reintegration planning and do not support BD program philosophies, suggests that special educators must attempt actively to involve regular educators in reintegra-tion.

Several strategies directed at receiving programs have been suggested to facilitate reintegration (Hersh & Walker, 1982; Kauffman, McCullough, & Sabornie, 1984). Hersh and Walker outline these steps:

1. determine the social and behavioral standards and expectation of regular educators prior to mainstreaming
2. develop procedures to provide correspondence between the social and behavioral concerns of receiving educators and the social

and behavioral repertoires of reintegrated students

3. teach students a social and behavioral repertoire consistent with the demands of the receiving environment

4. provide frequent follow-up consultation to the receiving program, and

5. implement procedures to train receiving teachers and administrators to manage student behavior and instruction with minimal support after an initial adjustment period

Muscott and Bond (1985, 1986) have incorporated these strategies in a cooperative transitional program between two residential treatment centers (RTCs) and a public school system in Oregon. As a model, they used the system of program levels developed in a special secondary school in Minneapolis for seriously behaviorally disordered adolescents (Braaten, 1979, 1982). The transition between RTCs or other institutional settings is particularly hazardous, because students must adjust not only to a new school environment, but to new home and community settings as well. Consequently, the involvement of parents, community, and other service providers, together with the sending and receiving school programs, is critical to successful transitions.

It is important to begin preparation of both the student and the receiving program well in advance of any placement change. Students need an opportunity to adjust psychologically to leaving the current placement and entering a new environment. It is not unusual for students to regress to old patterns of behavior when faced with an impending change. Prior to the actual change, the student can be taken to visit the new class and school, to meet new teachers, administrators, and other support personnel. The student can be informed about schedules, routines, and other expectations, and become familiar with a new physical setting. When possible, the sending teacher or a person responsible for coordinating the transition should accompany the student and parent(s) on the visit.

Teachers and administrators in the receiving program, and even future classmates, must also prepare for the addition. The teachers, especially, must consider the adaptations that will be necessary to programs, must clarify plans for implementation of the IEP with other support personnel, must consult with sending program representatives about past intervention efforts, and must plan academic and social curricula for the new student. When adequate preparations are made, the student is more likely to make a successful transition.

Selection of Programs

Selecting classroom situations in which and teachers with whom reintegrated students are most likely to succeed would not be so difficult if there were unlimited possibilities from which to select. There are always constraints on potential placements. However, most teachers of behaviorally disordered students report that there is typically more than one choice of potential reintegration sites. The IEP team must decide what is the best combination of conditions for the student given the available alternatives.

Special education teachers of behaviorally disordered students believe that several factors can be important in selecting a reintegration site. In descending order of importance are the following (Peterson, Zabel, & Smith, 1986):

- teacher's willingness and skill to modify curriculum
- degree of classroom structure
- teacher's rapport with this particular student
- teacher's personality
- level of curriculum and materials
- teacher's proficiency in the use of behavior management techniques
- number of students in the class
- number of other integrated students in the class
- teacher's training to integrate students
- location and convenience of the classroom

As this list indicates, factors relating to the receiving teacher's personal traits and skills tend to be considered more important than such demographic characteristics of the class as number of students and location.

Unfortunately, according to the Grosenick study (1986), only about one-half of all school districts have any written procedures concerning reintegration. Without generally understood (and followed) procedures, reintegration can be seriously impeded. Appropriate procedures should include placement options available, criteria for determining readiness, specification of those who should be involved in planning the transition, and the kinds of follow-up support and evaluation that will be provided. Those persons who are sending, receiving, overseeing the transition, and providing follow-up support should collaboratively plan it with the expectations of all parties specified. In sum, responsibilities and roles must be clear before the move.

- encouraging and counseling students
- encouraging and counseling teachers
- collecting and explaining assessment information on student performance
- providing direct academic remediation
- helping design and implement behavior management programs
- providing curricular ideas and materials
- providing assistance in instruction of the integrated student and classmates
- coordinating involvement of parents and other support services within and beyond the school

When reintegration decisions are made, follow-up responsibilities should be specified. White (1980) has suggested a system that designates *who* is responsible for each aspect of the program, *when* the tasks will be accomplished, and *how* they will be assessed. See Box 10.3 for a breakdown of some typical reintegration responsibilities.

Follow-Up Support

Follow-up support is often crucial to successful reintegration. It can involve direct support to the student, consultation to the receiving teacher(s), as well as an evaluation of the success of the reintegration plan. The nature of the follow-up support to be provided depends on the individual situation: the needs of the student, skills of the teacher(s), and resources and support services available to the receiving program. Generally, follow-up support for regular classroom teachers is provided by specialists operating in a resource or consulting role (Heron & Harris, 1982). Some school districts have consultants who operate in a variety of support roles assisting both regular and special education teachers. One of their major responsibilities is overseeing student transitions across educational placements (McGlothlin, 1981; Nelson & Stevens, 1981).

Support may take many forms:

Transitions for Secondary Students

As critical as successful transitions are for younger students to succeed in less restrictive educational programs, major challenges exist for secondary students moving from school to community life, particularly to employment.

In a recent follow-up study of special education students who graduated or dropped out of school, Eugene Edgar (1987) has presented a rather dismal picture of post-school adjustment. Among BD and LD students who graduated from high school, only 60 percent were employed, and most of those in low-paying jobs. Among the sizeable group (42%) who had dropped out of school, just 30 percent were employed, with another 10 percent enrolled in some kind of postpublic school education program. This means that fully 60 percent of the BD and LD dropouts who could be located for the study were involved in no formal activity at all! One can only speculate about the level

Box 10.3   Responsibilities in Facilitating Reintegration Plans

The following listing is intended to serve as a guide in assigning responsibilities to those involved in reintegrating students from an ED classroom. Agreement should be reached among all involved in the process as to who is responsible for seeing to it that each of these tasks is completed. Setting of timelines is also desirable. In order to ensure that all are aware of the responsibilities each has been assigned, a completed copy of a form such as this could be distributed to all.

Task	Assigned to	By When	Monitored by
Placement Information			
Provide preplacement information to ED teacher.	_____	_____	_____
Request information from regular teacher.	_____	_____	_____
Provide preplacement observation class.	_____	_____	_____
Monitoring Progress in ED Class			
Write and update IEP.	_____	_____	_____
Conduct observation in ED class.	_____	_____	_____
Maintain records of academic progress.	_____	_____	_____
Maintain records of social-emotional progress.	_____	_____	_____
Provide information to parents.	_____	_____	_____
Maintain contact with mental health agencies (if appropriate)	_____	_____	_____
Send progress reports to home school.	_____	_____	_____
Determining Readiness for Reintegration			
Provide objective evaluative data, progress reports, placement information.	_____	_____	_____
Invite parents to meeting to discuss reintegration possibility.	_____	_____	_____
Invite principal and/or regular class teacher.	_____	_____	_____
Determine rationale for reintegration—social, behavioral, or instructional.	_____	_____	_____
Determine areas in which to reintegrate in relation to reasons for reintegration.	_____	_____	_____
Write goals and recommendations for reintegration.	_____	_____	_____
Select the teacher and classroom.	_____	_____	_____
Select date to begin reintegration.	_____	_____	_____
Notify any persons affected who were not in attendance.	_____	_____	_____
Select person(s) responsible for follow-up.	_____	_____	_____
Select methods for follow-up.	_____	_____	_____
Full-time Reintegration in Home School			
Contact the principal.	_____	_____	_____
Set a meeting date with home school personnel.	_____	_____	_____
Invite the parents to attend the meeting.	_____	_____	_____

continued

Box 10.3   continued

	Assigned to	By When	Monitored by
Provide information at the meeting:			
1. Successful methods and materials used in part-time reintegration and in ED classroom.	_____	_____	_____
2. Type and length of involvement in the regular classroom.	_____	_____	_____
3. Child's academic and behavioral strengths and weaknesses.	_____	_____	_____
4. Evaluative reports.	_____	_____	_____
5. Written recommendations.	_____	_____	_____
Decide to initiate reintegration in home school.	_____	_____	_____
Write objectives for reintegration.	_____	_____	_____
Select the teacher and the classroom.	_____	_____	_____
Set the date to begin reintegration.	_____	_____	_____
Arrange for transportation changes.	_____	_____	_____
Send records to the home school.	_____	_____	_____
Set tentative date to staff out after successful trial reintegration.	_____	_____	_____
Discuss follow-up methods and schedule with home school personnel.	_____	_____	_____
Responsibility for follow-up.	_____	_____	_____

Follow-up

Provide follow-up report for regular class teacher as scheduled.	_____	_____	_____
Schedule informal contacts between written follow-up report times.	_____	_____	_____
Inform the regular class teacher who should be contacted if problems arise.	_____	_____	_____
Set date for staffing student out of the ED program after successful reintegration.	_____	_____	_____
Share follow-up information with parents and principal.	_____	_____	_____

Source: M. A. White, Iowa Monograph: *Strategies for planning and facilitating the reintegration of students with behavioral disorders.* (Des Moines, IA: Iowa Department of Public Instruction, 1980). Reprinted with permission.

of productive activity of the dropouts who could not be located in the follow-up.

From these data, Edgar (1987) concludes that many BD and LD students are not benefiting from their secondary programs. Most secondary special education programs emphasize remedial academic instruction in support of mainstream coursework. For many students, Edgar believes, this curriculum is unmotivating, nonfunctional, and contributes to high dropout and unemployment rates. As an alternative, he suggests reevaluating the principle of least restrictive environment for many secondary BD and LD students. Alternative, vocationally oriented programs may actually hold more promise in preparing many of these students for transitions from school to work. An unresolved dilemma, however, is between the placement of students who are often poor, minority males, in more segregated, vocational programs and their placement in more integrated remedial academic programs in the mainstream that are unsuccessful.

Obviously, a successful transition from school to work cannot be accomplished solely by schools, let alone by individual teachers. It requires the involvement of other agencies, employers, and families. Johnson, Bruininks, and Thurlow (1987) have discussed some of the obstacles to, as well as the ingredients of, transition programs for handicapped students. They are similar to some of those we discussed above that affect reintegration within schools. They include joint planning and management of transitions, evaluation of individual student needs and readiness, and evaluation of outcomes.

Programs for secondary students with behavioral disorders who are not succeeding academically in mainstream programs even with the support from special education should probably emphasize vocational training. At the high school level, particularly, on-the-job experiences should be included. A critical feature of the vocational program should be social skills training that promotes generalization and maintenance in other settings (see our discussion of these programs in Chapter 9). Employability is determined not only by knowing how to do a job, but also by social skills such as following instructions, decision making, performing independently, self-evaluation, and cooperating with others.

Another important feature of secondary programs is the involvement of families, when possible, in planning and supporting post-public school employment and or additional education and training. Unfortunately, many parents of secondary behaviorally disordered students are not very involved in their child's educational program. Chapter 12 includes some strategies for facilitating greater family involvement.

A third key ingredient of secondary BD programs is the coordination with the other systems, including other community and state agencies, where vocational experiences and training can occur. Collaborative planning and implementation of programs is necessary to ensure smooth transitions. In most secondary programs, this collaboration will require persons with specific job assignments in this area.

Comprehensive Model Programs

Many programs for behaviorally disordered students have served as models for special educational programming. A program is a comprehensive plan for delivering services to students. It includes attention to multiple aspects of the intervention process, including philosophy, program goals, population definition, procedures for program entry, methods, curriculum, materials, exit procedures, and evaluation (McCauley, 1977). When Grosenick and Huntze (1983) attempted to use these criteria to review the literature on existing descriptions of programs for behaviorally disordered students, they encountered frustration. Most programs mentioned in the professional literature do not include even the most minimal elements of program description. Others who have attempted to review programs have met with similar difficulties. Zabel and Wood (1977), for example, found the professional literature replete with studies of various methods and techniques, but few comprehensive attempts to evaluate the efficacy of entire programs.

A model program is often the brain child of an innovative individual or group who has designed, implemented, and then, perhaps, disseminated information about the model. Some of these programs have been presented in the professional literature, at conferences and workshops, and through other dissemination efforts. Some programs are known through their association with teacher education programs or participation in research projects. There are also, of course, some excellent programs that have not been well publicized and consequently are not well known to those who have not been directly involved with them.

The diversity of some well-known programs for children and adolescents with personality problems and conduct disorders is suggested in the following list (which by no means includes all model programs):

- Achievement Place (Phillips 1968; Phillips, Fixsen, Phillips, & Wolf, 1979) — a behaviorally oriented educational and residential treatment program, associated with the University of Kansas, for delinquent and behaviorally disordered students.
- Father Flanagan's Boys' Home (Michael, 1987) — a campus center near Omaha, Nebraska, for troubled youth who live in small residential groups with family teachers who serve as liaisons with the center's educational program. The Father Flanagan High School is a therapeutically designed, alternative school for inner-city, high-risk students that employs a humanistic approach.
- Jowonio, The Learning Place (Knoblock, 1983) — an integrated open school for emotionally disturbed, other exceptional, and nonexceptional children in Syracuse, New York.
- The League School (Fenichel, 1974) — a private psychoeducationally oriented day school for emotionally disturbed students in New York City.
- The Madison (Harrison) School (Braaten, 1979, 1982) — a special public school for behaviorally disordered adolescents in Minneapolis, with a developmental perspective and a structured level system using both behavior modification and counseling interventions.
- The Mark Twain School (LaNeve, 1979) — a public, secondary day school with a psychoeducationally oriented program in a specially designed facility in Montgomery County, Maryland.

- The Sonia Shankman Orthogenic School (Bettelheim, 1974) — a psychodynamically oriented residential treatment center at the University of Chicago that attempts to provide a total therapeutic milieu for severely disturbed children.

Of course, these programs serve only as samples of the variety of programs that have been described in the literature. For more information, the reader is encouraged to probe the above references or to contact the programs directly. Most model programs designed specifically for behaviorally disordered students tend to employ more restrictive delivery models (e.g., self-contained, special school, or residential and institutional programs). Consulting (Heron & Harris, 1982; Nelson & Stevens, 1981) and resource (Wiederholt, Hammill, & Brown, 1983) program models have been described, but they tend to serve multicategorical populations and thus are not necessarily identified as programs for students with personality and conduct disorders.

Each of the three model programs we will profile in this section is a comprehensive program that utilizes an ecological perspective and has had far-reaching influences on educational programming for students with behavioral disorders. In addition, they have each addressed most of the criteria to be considered a program discussed above (McCauley, 1977). The model programs are the Engineered/Orchestrated Classroom, Developmental Therapy, and Project Re-ED.

The Engineered/Orchestrated Classroom

Philosophy. Perhaps one of the most copied educational programs for emotionally disturbed children has been the Engineered Classroom (Hewett, 1968), or what its developers later came to call Orchestrating Success (Hewett & Taylor, 1980). First developed in the 1960s by Frank Hewett, Frank Taylor, and their colleagues at

---

Box 10.4   The Learning Triangle

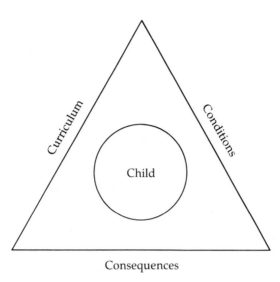

Source: F. H. Hewett & F. D. Taylor, *The emotionally disturbed child in the classroom: The orchestration of success,* 2nd ed. (Boston: Allyn & Bacon, 1980), p. 109. Reprinted with permission.

UCLA and in the Santa Monica, California, school system, this model program has seen many elements become commonplace in special education programs for behaviorally disordered students. The Engineered Classroom used behavior modification techniques, including a token economy, as its central motivational system. However, it also employed a developmental framework for assessing students and designing individual programs. From the beginning, it incorporated an ecological perspective with attention to the multiple influences upon a child's behavior.

The idea of Orchestrating Success advances the ecological theme even further with a program consisting of diverse elements that must perform in concert if behaviorally disordered children are to be successfully educated.

The Learning Triangle in Box 10.4 is illustrative of the ecological perspective. For Hewett and his colleagues, successful intervention is a matter of finding the right match between a child and a curriculum, the conditions under which the child learns, and the consequences of learning. *Curriculum* is defined as any activity, lesson, or assignment given to a child to assist him or her in achieving competence in one of six levels of learning competence. Arranged hierarchically, from most basic to most advanced, the levels are attention, response, order, exploratory, social, and mastery. The term *conditions* refers to the time (when) and setting (where) in which the curriculum will be taught. *Consequences* are the kinds of rewards or punishments that are contingent on student learning and behavior. Failure to teach any child is viewed as a failure to determine the right curriculum, conditions, and consequences. Referring to the orchestration of success, Hewett & Taylor say, (1980, p. 12) "Harmony. You can tell when it is there in a classroom. Things are in tune. Tasks, working conditions, and consequences are synchronized with the children. The teacher conducts. Everyone is playing their part. You can also recognize disharmony in the classroom. Things are out of tune. Tasks, working conditions, and consequences are not synchronized with the children. The teacher may be trying to conduct, but the results are off-key."

Two guiding principles in orchestrating success are *shaping* and *desensitization*. Each is based upon a different explanation of how learning may occur. The first, shaping, represents an operant learning approach of gradual, sequential teaching of new behavior by providing rewards contingent upon performance. Hewett and Taylor (1980) advocate using a "thimbleful" rather than a "bucketful" approach with behaviorally disordered students. That is, improvement is usually evident in small increments rather than dramatic changes. Educational expectations should be geared to the level of performance the child can currently achieve, with more advanced, complicated tasks gradually added.

The second principle, desensitization, is based upon respondent (or association) learning principles. Emotionally disturbed students must "unlearn'" some fears and negative attitudes that have impeded their success. This unlearning occurs through their association with consistent, safe, environments that produce success.

To create harmonious learning environments, Hewett and Taylor have incorporated attempts to promote the nine assumptions in Box 10.5.

Curriculum. The six levels of learning competence (attention, response, order, exploratory, social, and mastery) provide a developmental hierarchy for assessing the academic and social status of the student, determining appropriate goals and objectives, and implementing specific strategies to teach those skills. In Box 10.6 for example, two subcategories for social level skills—Relationships with Others and Self-Concept—are displayed. Determination of a stu-

dent's current performance of each subskill can be used to identify strengths and weaknesses, to determine long-term goals, and short-term objectives.

Examples of specific activities for teaching each subskill are supplied. For example, to teach the social skills in Box 10.6, any of the following may be classified as group listening activities—a regular teacher reading to the group, using story records or tapes, or group games that minimize competition and promote waiting and turn-taking skills.

Conditions. Considerable attention is given to the actual physical design of classrooms to promote the acquisition of the skills and to communicate behavioral expectations in the learning task hierarchy. In sample floor plans for the Engineered/Orchestrated Classroom, a variety of individual and group instructional arrangements are used to meet individual student needs. Although elementary and secondary level models differ somewhat, each is designed to accommodate up to twelve students, a teacher, and an aide.

In addition to an individual desk for each student, there are several areas or centers in the classroom to promote different types of individual and group learning experiences. (See Box 10.7). A Communication Center includes activities, games, and a record player with headphones. An Exploratory Center offers science and art activities, together with appropriate equipment and materials. An Order Center provides individual tasks requiring students to practice organizing skills. A Master Center consists of student desks, a group teaching station, and study carrels for students who may be distractible at certain times or with certain assignments. In a real sense, "the medium is the message" so the physical arrangement of the classroom is designed to accommodate and promote individual student learning needs.

Consequences. The third side of the Learning Triangle, consequences, is another key feature of this program. At lower stages of the learning

Box 10.5   The Establishment of a Harmonious Learning Climate

1. *Every Child Is a Learner.* Despite the seeming unreadiness of some children to learn, there is never a child who is not ready to learn something. Children who learn nothing in school are clearly teaching failures, not child-failures.

2. *Give the Child the Dignity of Being Expected to Learn.* If all children are learners, we must expect them to learn. Allowing them to continuously wallow in the confusion of self-directed learning is a questionable approach. How many disturbed children are going to "discover their way" out of their learning and behavior problems without our careful and thoughtful guidance?

3. *Don't Ask if the Child Is Ready to Learn, Ask if the Classroom Is Ready to Teach.* The classroom environment should be ready to spring to life at a moment's notice in order to engage the child in a successful learning experience. Don't rummage through cupboards and drawers to find alternative tasks when problems arise, have an instant intervention-oriented classroom set up well in advance.

4. *Recognize that Time Is Often Our Enemy.* While some disturbed children "grow out" of their problems during the elementary years, a substantial number do not. Autistic children who have not acquired communicative speech by age five usually never learn to talk. The second grade hellion who never settles down to learn to read is in serious trouble in the upper elementary grades and a disaster in junior high school if we aren't effective in teaching him or her.

5. *Think Thimblefuls.* We may fail with children if we conceive of learning in bucketful amounts. No task is too small to be considered legitimate if it moves the child even slightly ahead on the learning track. Try to have a specific set of A-B-C goals with each child. If we don't plan our strategy in advance and prioritize, we may miss our chance to truly help the child.

6. *Think Sequentially.* There is a building-block logic in the use of shaping techniques. Identify the bottom block and build your learning tower step by step. Be willing to use smaller or even larger blocks if it seems appropriate. Be prepared to back up and dismantle your tower block by block if necessary. But start building again as soon as possible.

7. *Consider Conditions.* Don't let children fail because they are asked to work too long or to do too much in the wrong place or at the wrong time. And don't let concern for correctness or accuracy eliminate the child as a candidate for some level of success. Be flexible. Move quickly to alter when, where, how, how long, how much, or how well.

8. *Consider Consequences.* Don't be squeamish about rewards. They are a fact of life. Be sure there is something that makes it worth the child's while to try in the program. Don't use candy if the child is rewarded by praise or multisensory stimulation and activities. But don't not use candy if it offers a quick and efficient means of rewarding the child. Punishment is a risky business. While it may be effective at times, exhaust all positive possibilities before considering it. Withholding rewards is probably the most appropriate negative consequence for use in the classroom.

9. *Keep the White Rabbit of Schoolness Moving.* Try to establish each child's tolerance level for handling demands, schedules, competition, rules, tests, assignments, and directions. Expect the child to function toward his or her highest tolerance level by moving the rabbit closer. But when bad news develops, gracefully and imaginatively move the rabbit back until a reassignment or alteration reduces the child's discomfort.

Source: F. M. Hewett & F. D. Taylor. *The emotionally disturbed child in the classroom: The orchestration of success,* 2nd ed. (Boston: Allyn & Bacon, 1980), pp. 214–215. Reprinted with permission.

Box 10.6   Hewett and Taylor's Social Level Skills

A. Relationships with Others
  B. Relationships with Others Outside School
    C1. Relates positively with members of family
    C2. Is accepted by others in community (e.g., postman, grocery clerk, etc.)
    C3. Relates positively with others in community
    C4. Has playmates when playing at home
    C5. Has one close friend
    C6. Has many close friends
    C7. Assumes responsibilities at home and follows through with them independently
    C8. Understands how people live together in family units
    C9. Other _____
  B. Relationships with Peers
    C1. Readily seeks out peers in school
    C2. Readily seeks to participate in group activities
    C3. Is accepted by peers in school
    C4. Relates positively with peers in school
    C5. Respects the rights of others
    C6. Does not bully others or physically abuse them
    C7. Participates cooperatively in group activities
    C8. Willingly waits turn
    C9. Does not lie to others
    C10. Readily shares with others
    C11. Has one close friend in school
    C12. Has a number of close friends in school
    C13. Is popular with most other children
    C14. Exhibits leadership abilities
    C15. Is turned to by other children for leadership
    C16. Readily accepts praise from peers
    C17. Other _____
  B. Relationships with Teachers and Others in School

    C1. Is accepted by the teacher and other school staff
    C2. Relates positively with teacher and other school staff
    C3. Seeks contact with teacher
    C4. Does not demand excessive attention or time from teacher
    C5. Respects teacher's authority
    C6. Readily follows teacher's requests
    C7. Does not lie to teacher
    C8. Appears to want to please teacher
    C9. Readily accepts praise from teacher
    C10. Other _____

A. Self-concept
  B. Degree of Self-confidence
    C1. Enters into activities even when unsure of what is expected
    C2. Enters into activities that are competitive
    C3. Will respond without constant reassurance
    C4. Recognizes school problems but demonstrates confidence that he or she can learn
    C5. Realistic with respect to expectations for own achievement
    C6. Other _____
  B. Reaction to Frustration
    C1. Adjusts easily to changes in routines or activities
    C2. Takes responsibility for own problems
    C3. Communicates positive attitude toward school
    C4. Communicates positive attitudes toward work that is assigned
    C5. Other _____
  B. Emotional Mood
    C1. Facial expression communicates lack of fear or sadness
    C2. Body position communicates lack of tension (e.g., not slouching in chair or hiding face)
    C3. Other _____

Source: F. M. Hewett & F. D. Taylor. *The emotionally disturbed child in the classroom: The orchestration of success,* 2nd ed. (Boston: Allyn & Bacon, 1980), pp. 146–147. Reprinted with permission.

Box 10.7   The Floorplan of an Elementary Level Special Day Classroom

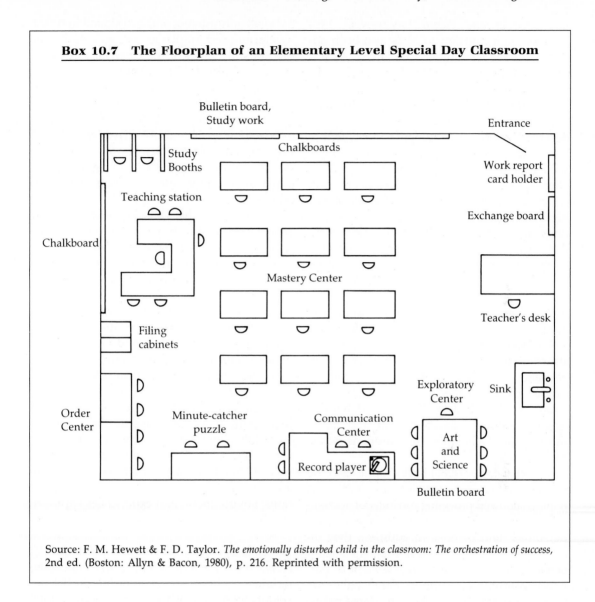

Bulletin board,
Study work

Entrance

Chalkboards

Study
Booths

Work report
card holder

Teaching station

Exchange board

Chalkboard

Mastery Center

Teacher's desk

Filing
cabinets

Order
Center

Exploratory
Center

Sink

Minute-catcher
puzzle

Communication
Center

Art
and
Science

Record player

Bulletin board

Source: F. M. Hewett & F. D. Taylor. *The emotionally disturbed child in the classroom: The orchestration of success,* 2nd ed. (Boston: Allyn & Bacon, 1980), p. 216. Reprinted with permission.

hierarchy, the motivational system takes the form of a token economy. Each morning as students enter the classroom, they pick up their work record card from a bulletin board holder. Throughout the day, the student can receive up to ten check marks during each fifteen-minute period. Check marks are awarded for task accomplishments and learner behaviors during the five-minute period following each fifteen-minute session. Two check marks are awarded for starting an assigned task, three for following through, and five for being a student (i.e., respecting the rights of others, following classroom rules). Regular opportunities are scheduled for students to use check marks to buy a variety of goods, services, and activities that have been determined to be individually appropriate.

Reintegration and Parent Involvement. Programming for reintegration has also been addressed in the learning task hierarchy. As students progress to higher developmental levels, they receive less external control and participate in more normalized school programs. The Madison School Plan (Hewett & Forness, 1977) was designed to facilitate a student's movement to less restrictive environments. Within a single school, different levels of programming are offered. These include a Preacademic I program, which emphasizes the student behaviors of paying attention, responding, and following directions and classroom rules. Instruction is individualized and student motivation supported by the token system. Preacademic II continues to provide considerable external structure for students, with an additional emphasis on individual and small group academic learning and appropriate behavior for school. Academic I is a simulated regular classroom, with group instruction and part-time integration in regular education programs within the school. Finally, Academic II is total integration in the regular program. As described by Hewett and his colleagues, students can move up and down through the levels of the continuum as necessary.

Hewett & Taylor (1980) have emphasized the role of the resource specialist in coordinating reintegration and providing consultation to regular classroom teachers, other special education personnel, and parents. In addition, they include direct instruction and assessment responsibilities in that role. The involvement of parents in planning and support of their children's educational programs is also considered necessary in the orchestration of student success, so Hewett and Taylor suggest strategies to improve parental involvement.

Developmental Therapy

Philosophy. Developmental Therapy (Wood, 1981, 1986; Wood & Swan, 1978) is a comprehensive program for emotionally disturbed, behaviorally disordered, and autistic children that was formulated, implemented, and studied at the Rutland Center of the University of Georgia under the leadership of Mary M. Wood. Like the Engineering/Orchestrated Classroom, it uses a developmental framework to assess individual student instructional needs, and to determine intervention goals and objectives, educational strategies, and placements. However, Developmental Therapy employs a more psychoeducational, or cognitive-affective, than behavioral orientation.

According to the Developmental Therapy model, successful functioning involves the arenas of doing, saying, caring, and thinking. Thus, the program includes four curricular areas: behavior, communication, socialization, and (pre)academics. Box 10.8 presents the five sequential developmental therapy goals in each of the four curriculum areas. The developmental scheme is based upon theories of personality, cognition, language, and morality including those of Erikson, Anna Freud, Piaget, and Kohlberg. According to this view, children's skills and compentencies develop in a hierarchical fashion; the acquisition of high-level skills is dependent on the mastery of low-level skills. In Box 10.9 is a summary of Developmental Therapy stages, with the corresponding adult roles, prominent techniques, interventions, environment, and experiences appropriate for each stage.

The Developmental Therapy Objective Rating Form. Following formal referral, assessment determines a child's status according to the developmental framework. The Developmental Therapy Objective Rating Form (DTORF) is used both for initial assessment and evaluation of change over time. A total of sixty-two specific competencies, or objectives, across the four curricular areas are included in the DTORF. The assessment determines which of these objectives the child currently performs and which remain to be learned. A child's performance may be uneven, with relatively advanced or retarded development in each of the curricular areas. For

Box 10.8   **Developmental Therapy Goals for Each Curriculum Area at Each Stage of Therapy**

	Behavior	*Communication*	*Socialization*	*Academic Skills*
Stage I	To trust own body and skills	To use words to gain needs	To trust an adult sufficiently to respond to him	To respond to the environment with processes of classification, discrimination, basic receptive language concepts, and body coordination
Stage II	To successfully participate in routines	To use words to affect others in constructive ways	To participate in activities with others	To participate in classroom routines with language concepts of similarities and differences, labels, use, color, numerical processes of ordering and classifying; and body coordination
Stage III	To apply individual skills in group processes	To use words to express oneself in the group	To find satisfaction in group activities	To participate in the group with basic expressive language concepts; symbolic representation of experiences and concepts; functional semi-concrete concepts of conservation; and body coordination
Stage IV	To contribute individual effort to group success	To use words to express awareness of relationship between feelings and behavior in self and others	To participate spontaneously and successfully as a group member	To successfully use signs and symbols in formalized school work and in group experiences
Stage V	To respond to critical life experiences with adaptive-constructive behavior	To use words to establish and enrich relationships	To initiate and maintain effective peer group relationships independently	To successfully use signs and symbols for formalized experiences and personal enrichment

Source: M. M. Wood, *Developmental therapy in the classroom: Methods for teaching students with social, emotional, or behavioral handicaps* (Austin, TX: PRO-ED, 1986), p. 56. Reprinted with permission.

example, a child may be functioning at Stage 4 or 5 in (pre)academics, but at only Stage 2 or 3 in social skills.

Box 10.10 contains a sample DTORF for a boy named John. John's developmental levels have been jointly determined by a parent, a regular education teacher, and a special education teacher. A check mark next to each objective indicates that the skill is consistently displayed by the child. An "X" indicates the child is currently

Box 10.9 Summary of Developmental Therapy Stages

STAGE I: Responding to the Environment with Pleasure

General Description:	Responding and Trusting
Adult's Role:	Arouser and satisfier of basic needs
Techniques:	Body contact and touch; physical intervention; classroom structure and consistent routine; control of materials by teacher; controlled vocabulary
Intervention:	Constant physical contact; caring, arousing
Environment:	Routine constant, luring rather than demanding; stimulating, arousing sensory activities

STAGE II: Responding to the Environment with Success

General Description:	Learning Individual Skills
Adult's Role:	Motivator; redirector of old coping behavior to successful outcomes; reflector of success; predictable point of reference
Techniques:	Classroom structure; consistent routine; verbal interaction between lead and support teachers; physical and verbal redirection; holding limits; reflection of action, feelings, and success
Intervention:	Frequent, both physical and verbal; supportive
Environment:	Structured, successful exploration; activities leading to self-confidence and organization; communication activities; beginning cooperative activities, simple group experiences

STAGE III: Learning Skills for Successful Group Participation

General Description:	Applying Individual Skills to Group Procedures
Adult's Role:	Model for group participation; stimulator and encourager of appropriate group interaction; upholder of limits and group expectations; reflector and interpreter of behavior, feelings, and progress
Techniques:	Redirection; reflection; verbal interaction between lead and support teachers; individual Life Space Interview; predictable structure and expectations; reflection of feelings; predictability; frequent verbal intervention, consistency
Intervention:	Frequent, primarily verbal, group focus
Environment:	Group activities that stimulate cooperation, sharing, and beginning friendships; focus on group procedures and expectations; approximate real-life situations and conditions as much as group can tolerate

STAGE IV: Investing in Group Processes

General Description:	Valuing One's Group
Adult's Role:	Group leader; counselor; reflector of reality
Techniques:	Interpretation of feelings and behavior; individual and group Life Space Interview; reality reflection
Intervention:	Intermittent, approximating real life
Environment:	Reality-oriented environment; activities, procedures, and expectations determined by the group; emphasis on group academic learning experiences, role play, field trips, elements of normal competition

continued

Box 10.9   continued

STAGE V: Applying Individual and Group Skills in New Situations

General Description:	Generalizing and Valuing
Adult's Role:	Counselor, teacher, friend
Techniques:	Normal expectations; relationships between feelings, behaviors, and consequences; nonclinical
Intervention:	Infrequent
Environment:	Normal childhood settings; conversations about real-life experiences; support in solving problem situations; independent skill building

---

Source: M. M. Wood (Ed.), *Developmental therapy in the classroom: Methods for teaching students with social, emotional, or behavioral handicaps* (Austin, TX: Pro-ED, 1986), p. 14. Reprinted with permission.

---

developing that skill, and "NR" means he is not yet ready to attempt that objective. As John's baseline DTORF indicates, he successfully displays all Stage I objectives. He performs some, though not all, Stage II objectives in the Behavior, Communication, and Socialization areas. In the (pre)academics, he performs some Stage III skills.

Baseline DTORF information is used to design appropriate, individual educational programs for students and provides a built-in procedure for ongoing assessment. Every five weeks, a similar rating is completed to determine changes that have occurred during that period. Each skill or objective translates directly into specific intervention strategies. Developmental Therapy sourcebooks (Wood, 1981) include suggestions for teaching and testing performance on each objective.

Program Structure. As in the Engineered/Orchestrated Classroom, considerable attention has been given to the structure of the Developmental Therapy program, including staffing, physical arrangement of the environment, materials, and schedule. Teacher-pupil ratios are kept low with about two teachers for every six children, who are carefully grouped to achieve compatible developmental levels. Although the focus of the program is on the educational interventions, a variety of adults may participate in a child's program. Parents, mental health professionals, paraprofessionals, and volunteers contribute the interventions.

In addition to the overview of Developmental Therapy (Wood, 1975, 1986), several other Developmental Therapy resource books have outlined the uses of fantasy, storytelling, arts, recreation, music, sociodrama, adaptive physical education, and play for reaching Developmental Therapy objectives (Wood, 1981).

Project Re-ED

Philosophy. Project Re-ED (for Re-Education of Emotionally Disturbed) was conceived in the early 1960s as an ecologically oriented alternative to traditional psychotherapeutic treatment in institutions and residential treatment facilities (Hobbs, 1974, 1978; Lewis, 1975). Project Re-ED does not so much attempt to treat emotionally disturbed children as to reeducate them and their ecosystems (home, school, and community), so there is a better fit between the child and his or her environment. Since the 1960s,

Box 10.10 Developmental Therapy Objectives Rating Form (DTORF)

Name __John_____ Class Stage __2_____ Raters _____

Date __Nov. 5_____ Type Rating (Check One)   Baseline ☒ _____ Week ☐ _____ Week ☐ Final ☐

Behavior	*Communication*	*Socialization*
Stage I	**Stage I**	**Stage I**
☑ 0. Indicate Awareness	☑ 0. Produce Sounds	☑ 1. Aware/Others
☐ Tactile ☐ Aud. ☐ Motor	☑ 1. Attend Speaker	☑ 2. Attend/Other's Behavior
☐ Taste ☐ Visual ☐ Smell	☑ 2. Respond Verbal Stimulation	☑ 3. Respond to Name
☑ 1. React by Attending	Motor Behavior	☑ 4. Interact/Adult Non-Verbal
☑ 2. Respond by Sustained	☑ 3. Answer/Verbal Approx.	☑ 5. Solit. Play
Attending	☑ 4. Spontaneous/Verbal Approx.	☑ 6. Respond Request Come
☑ 3. Simple Stim./Motor Behavior	☑ 5. Recognize Wd/To Adult	☑ 7. Dem. Underst./Sing. Request
☑ 4. Complex Stim./Imit.	☑ 6. Recognize Wd/To Child	☑ 8. Same as C5
☑ 5. Assist in Self-Help	☑ 7. Word Sequence	☑ 9. Same as C6
☑ 6. Respond Independent Play		☑ 10. Same as C7
Material		☑ 11. Begin Emergence Self
☑ 7. Indicate Recall of Routine		☑ 12. Contact Adult Spontaneous
Stage II	**Stage II**	**Stage II**
☑ 8. Use Play Material Appropri-	☑ 8. Answer/Recognize Word	☑ 13. Parallel Play
ately	☑ 9. Receptive Vocabulary	☑ 14. Same as B9
☑ 9. To Wait/No Intervention	☒ 10. Command, Question/Word	☑ 15. Initiate Minimal Movement/
☒ 10. Participate/Sitting: No Inter-	Sequence	Child
vention	☒ 11. Share Minimum Information/	☒ 16. Sharing Activity
☒ 11. Participate/Movement: No In-	Adult	☒ 17. Interactive Play
tervention	☒ 12. Describe Characteristics Self,	☒ 18. Coop. Activity/Child in
☒ 12. Spontaneous Participation	Others	Organ. Activ.
	☒ 13. Share Minimal Information	
	Child	
Stage III	**Stage III**	**Stage III**
NR 13. Complete Individual Tasks in	NR 14. Spontaneous Description	☒ 19. Model Appropriate
Group	Personal Experiences	Behavior/Child
☐ 14. Accept Success Without Loss	☐ 15. Show Feeling Response	NR 20. Share/Turns Without
Control	Appropriately	Reminders
☐ 15. Awareness/Expected Conduct	☐ 16. Participate Group Discussions	☐ 21. Lead/Demonstrate For Group
Vb.	Appropriately	☐ 22. Label Situation/Simple Values
☐ 16. Reasons for Expectations	☐ 17. Describe Attributes In Self	☐ 23. Particip. Activ./Sugges./
☐ 17. Tell Other/Appropriate	☐ 18. Make Positive Statement/Self	Child
Behavior	☐ 19. Describe Attributes Others	☐ 24. Sequence Own Experiences
☐ 18. Refrain Inappropriate	☐ 20. Recognize Others' Feelings	☐ 25. Develop Friendship
Behavior When Others	☑ 21. Verbalize Pride Group	☐ 26. Seek Assistance, Praise Child
Inappropriate	Achievement	☑ 27. Assist Others/Conforming
☑ 19. Control in Group		
Stage IV	**Stage IV**	**Stage IV**
NR 20. Respond Appropriately/	NR 22. Channel Feelings Non-Verbal	NR 28. Show Identification/Adult
Leader Choice	Creativity	Role
☑ 21. Aware of Own Progress	☑ 23. Same as B21	☑ 29. Sequence Group Experience

continued

Box 10.10   continued

Behavior	*Communication*	*Socialization*
Stage IV continued	**Stage IV** continued	**Stage IV** continued
NR 22. Implement Alternative Behaviors	NR 24. Explain How Behavior Influences Others	NR 30. Spon. Suggestions to Group
23. Flexible/Modify Procedure	25. Verbal Praise/Support Others	31. Aware of Others' Different Actions
24. New Experience With Control	26. Verbal Feelings Spon., Approp./gp.	32. Respect Others' Opinions
25. Provocation With Control	27. Verbal Initiate Positive Relation	33. Interest/Peer Opinions/Self
26. Interpersonal/Group Problem Solving	28. Spon. Express Cause-Effect/ Self, Others	34. Suggest Solution to Problems
		35. Descrim. Opposite Values
		36. Inferences/Social Situations

Behavior	*Communication*	*Socialization*
Stage V	**Stage V**	**Stage V**
NR 27. Seeks Work Skills	NR 29. Complex Verbal Structures/ Content	NR 37. Underst./Respect Others' Feelings
28. Seeks Desired Role	30. Verbal Conciliatory Skills	38. Reciprocal Skill/Multiple Roles
29. Accept Responsibility/Self	31. Rec. Others' Contributions	39. Personal Choices/Values
30. Law/Order Concepts	32. Describe Multiple Motives/ Values	40. Self Understanding/Goals
31. Participate/Group Self-Governance	33. Spontaneous Expression/ Ideals, Values	41. Sustain Mutual Relations
32. Apply Rational Process/ Problem Solving	34. Sustain Interper/Gp. Relations	

(Pre)Academic

Stage I	**Stage II**	**Stage III**
1. Same as B1	18. Recognize Use of Objects	32. Eye-Hand Coordination/Left-Right/6 year
2. Same as B2	19. Recognize Detail in Pictures	33. Body-Coordination/6 year
3. Same as B3	20. Recognize Different Object	34. Read 50 Primary Words
4. Same as B4	21. Count to 5 (1 to 1)	35. Recognize, Write Numerals For Groups 1–10 (Sets/Subsets)
5. Fine/Gross Motor/24 months	22. Recognize Same/Different Pictures	36. Write 50 Basic Words/Mem., Dictation
6. Imitate Acts of Adults	23. Count to 10 (1 to 1)	37. Recog. and Write Numerals For Groups/100
7. Discrim. of Objects	24. Eye-Hand Coordination/5 Year Level	38. Add, Subtract/1–10 (Union/Sets; Commut. Prop.)
8. Same as C3	25. Recognize Shapes, Symbols, Numerals, Words/Same, Different	X 39. Listen/Story/Comprehension
9. Same as C4	26. Categorize Different Pictures/ Similar Assoc.	40. Read Sentences/Comprehension
10. Short-Term Memory/Sound, Object, and People	27. Tell Story Sequence/Pictures	41. Physical Skills/Games
11. Match Object with Different/ Same Attri.	28. Discriminate Opposites	42. Identify Illogical Elements
12. Wrd./Label Pictures	29. Body Coordination/5 Year Level	43. Add, Subtract/10–20/Regroup/ Place Value
13. Body Coordination/3–4 Year Level	30. Recognize Groups to 10	X 44. Write Sentences/Memory, Dictation
14. Match Identical Pictures	31. Give Reasons Why	45. Multiplication, Division to 25
15. Recognize Body Parts		46. Read, Write Quantitative Words
16. Fine-Motor Coordination/3–4 Year		X 47. Read, Write/Third Grade Comprehension
17. Recognize Colors		X 48. Size Seriation/Relationship

continued

Box 10.10 continued

(Pre) Academic

Stage IV	Stage V	Notes
NR 49. Write to Communicate	NR 57. Seek Others' Opinions/Current Issues	
☐ 50. Multiply, Divide to 81 (Prime Numbers)	☐ 58. Discriminate Fact Opinion	
☐ 51. Read for Pleasure/Information	☐ 59. Recognize/Explain Illogical Ideas	
☐ 52. Compute Money to $10.00	☐ 60. Rational Numbers/Problems	
☐ 53. Explain Story Characters	☐ 61. Same as B32	
☐ 54. Use Grammatical Rules/Writing	☑ 62. Use Academic Tools/ Citizen, Worker	
☐ 55. Same as S35		
☑ 56. Measurement Problems		

_____   _____
         Parent's Signature   Parent Worker's Signature

_____   _____
  Teacher's Signature – Regular Education   Teacher's Signature – Special Education

Source: M. M. Wood (Ed.), *Developmental therapy in the classroom: Methods for teaching students with social, emotional, or behavioral handicaps* (Austin, TX: Pro-ED, 1986), pp. 47–48. Reprinted with permission.

Re-ED programs have been established in several states.

Program Structure. Children are referred to Re-ED by school systems, social service agencies, or child guidance clinics. In preliminary conferences between the referring agency and a Re-ED liaison teacher, the nature of the child's problems and past treatment within the family, school, and community are reviewed. If the child's needs match the Re-ED program, the child and his or her family visit a Re-ED school to meet with teacher-counselors, examine the program, and begin to plan an individualized program of remedial education and social learning experiences.

Re-ED facilities serve about forty children, divided into groups of about eight who live to-gether. Since improved adaptation to the home, school, and community is the central treatment goal, students spend weekdays at the school but return home on weekends. Unlike some long-term residential programs, Re-ED intends to be an intensive, relatively brief, placement in which intervention lasts a few months.

The daily schedule in a Re-ED school corresponds with a typical school day, with emphasis placed on teaching basic academic skills and the development of language skills. Programs are individualized according to the determination of the child's greatest social and academic needs. After school, a recreation program stresses the improvement of students' recreational skills. In the evenings, group skills are practiced in rap sessions and group discussions. Other parts of the daily routine, including mealtimes, dressing, and bedtimes, are also used as opportunities for reeducation. Re-ED staff attempt to deal therapeutically with children's behavior and to teach more adaptive behavior. In addition to the cognitive-affective methods of individual and group discussion and the structured school and living environment, token economies and other forms of reinforcement are sometimes used to help teach new social and academic behavior.

Teacher-Counselors. Re-ED has emphasized two professional roles. One is the teacher-counselor. Two teacher-counselors are assigned to each class and group who live together and work as a team setting goals, implementing programs, and evaluating student progress. Typically, one serves as teacher in the classroom, and the other runs the recreation and living experiences. The teacher-counselors attempt to provide consistency across these environments.

Liaison-Teachers. Liaison-teachers are the other unique Re-ED professional role. They provide the critical link between Re-ED and the child's home, school, and community. Responsibilities of the liaison-teacher depend upon the needs within the child's ecosystems. Specific duties may include assisting parents to develop alternative, and more accommodating, views of their children and to implement consistent, effective strategies for managing their children's behavior and maintain the gains made in the Re-ED program. Liaison-teachers may also help families to obtain economic, social, and mental health resources that will support their efforts to meet their family's and children's needs.

One of the most important tasks of the liaison-teacher is working with teachers and administrators of the home school. They determine the curricular and behavior management efforts that have been effected in the home and school and what skills will be necessary for the child to make it there. They communicate about the interventions implemented in the Re-ED school and provide consultation to home and school

personnel about ways of better accommodating the child. The liaison-teacher oversees the planning of the transition back to the home and school environment, and provides ongoing consultation and support following reintegration.

The Re-ED approach appears to be successful in helping behaviorally disordered children function more successfully in their various ecosystems (Lewis, 1975). Its unique feature lies in its multifaceted interventions to change the child and those arenas—the home, school, and community—where the student has been maladapted. Project Re-ED has acknowledged that changing both child and environment are necessary to correct a condition of emotional disturbance.

Summary

In this chapter, we considered issues of educational programming for students with personality problems and conduct disorders. Educational programming must be approached from an ecological perspective, because of the multiple factors, both within and beyond the school, that affect the success of interventions.

We discussed operationalizing the principles of appropriate education and least restrictive environment from an ecological perspective. The Individual Educational Program (IEP) was presented as both a process for involving all relevant persons in planning the program, and as a product, a document specifying the rationale, design, and service delivery system. Despite its limitations, the continuum of services, or Cascade Model, was presented as a useful model for conceptualizing appropriate placements for delivering services.

In order to achieve a central goal of special education programming—reintegration—it is necessary to facilitate successful movement of students to less restrictive environments. Reintegration efforts should include strategies both for sending and receiving programs. The former must prepare students for reintegration; the latter should increase involvement of the receiving program in the reintegration process and to support maintenance of student progress.

Although comprehensive descriptions of programs are few and far between, we provided overviews of three special programs for behaviorally disordered students—the Engineered/ Orchestrated Classroom, Developmental Therapy, and Project Re-ED. Each of these programs meets most of the criteria for an adequate program description, each has developed and field tested its program, and each has been a model, in whole or in part, for other programs for behaviorally disordered children and adolescents.

PART IV

Teachers and Parents of Children and Adolescents with Behavioral Disorders

This section of the book is directed toward encouraging teacher self-awareness and self-understanding as well as development of an understanding of the partnership between school and home.

Special education for behaviorally disordered children is among the most demanding careers an individual can choose. It requires understanding, patience, caring, creativity, and tremendous energy. An individual choosing such a profession must be well equipped not only with a knowledge of concepts and techniques, but with self-knowledge as well. Chapter 11 helps students develop such self-awareness and make wise career choices. Further, effective special education and mental health professionals must be shrewd conservationists

and know how to use personal and system resources while avoiding self-depletion and conflicts with the system. The ideas presented in Chapter 11 will help students begin the career-spanning process of developing such awareness.

Finally, it is critical to recognize that effective, enduring changes in behaviorally disordered children and adolescents are most likely to occur with active parental and family involvement. The concepts and ideas in Chapter 12 are designed to help the teacher and other child care professionals facilitate processes of parental involvement and change through an understanding of the problems parents face.

CHAPTER 11

Teachers of Students
with Behavioral Disorders

Overview

Introduction

"One of my students recently asked me, 'What is red and green and goes two hundred miles an hour?' The only answer that immediately came through my mind was that it must be a first year teacher of exceptional children trying to keep ahead of them. Of course, as the student quickly told me, 'It's a frog in a blender.' . . . According to the rough tally I keep in my head, he's about the 40th student I've worked with who has told me I'm crazy. On the last day I worked with the first student to tell me that, he said, 'I hope you come back to see us again. I like you, You're as crazy as we are.' It is a high compliment in this profession to be accepted" (Bell, 1979, p. 168).

As the above observation by a teacher of behaviorally disordered adolescents attests, the professional experiences and sources of satisfaction for such teachers may be quite different from those of other teachers. To successfully teach students with personality and behavior problems demands some special personal and professional attributes. Some of these characteristics are largely determined by individual personality factors that have developed even prior to formal professional training. Others are acquired in the course work of professional programs that contribute to the student's understanding of behavioral disorders and of effective interventions. Additional important competencies may be learned in practicum experiences in which students observe experienced teachers and have opportunities to apply what has been learned in course work. Of course, teaching competence continues to evolve as teachers apply their personal and professional skills to the ongoing demands and challenges of their jobs.

As noted throughout this book, the development of educational interventions requires an ecological perspective. Children with behavioral disorders exist within the context of ecosystems both internal and external to the school. Within the school ecosystem, the interrelationships of three major factors must be considered. These are the student(s), the teacher, and the environment. In the early chapters of this book, we discussed the special characteristics and needs of students in terms of behavior patterns. We presented procedures for assessing the educational needs of these students. This was followed by overviews of behavioral and psychoeducational approaches to intervention. In the last chapter, we focused on individual educational programs, educational service delivery arrangements, and model programs.

In this chapter, we will address several topics concerning teachers of behaviorally disordered students. First, we will discuss special competencies that have been considered important for teachers and look at the ways they may be acquired. Attention will be given both to what might be considered technical skills and to personality factors. Next, we will look at some demographic characteristics of these teachers, issues relating to supply and demand, professional preparation, and certification. Finally, we will examine factors related to the very real problems of stress and burnout among teachers, and strategies for coping with stress and preventing burnout.

Teacher Competencies

Over the past thirty years considerable attention has been given to delineating important or necessary competencies for teachers of students with behavioral disorders. However, a recent review of literature on teacher preparation points out that relatively little research has addressed the issue of competencies (Zabel, 1987). That review points out that relatively little research has addressed the issue of competencies for teaching children with personality and behavioral disorders. As Blackhurst, McLoughlin, and Price (1977, p. 168) acknowledge, trainee competencies are largely "based upon professional judgment, logic, opinion, speculation, hunches, and/or faith."

Relationship with Regular Education

Competencies needed by teachers of students with emotional and behavioral disorders cannot be considered separately from those that are important for regular classroom teachers. Rather, they consist of those skills plus additional kinds of understandings, skills, and personal traits. In most cases, special education teacher preparation occurs either concurrently with or subsequent to professional preparation to teach in regular classrooms. Certification requirements typically require preparation to teach in regular as well as special classrooms.

There are several reasons it is important that special education teachers receive professional training for regular classroom teaching. As we have seen, most students receiving special education due to their behavioral disorders continue to participate, at least part of the time, in the regular education program. Most of these students come out of regular programs in which they have experienced difficulties. In addition, a goal for most students is eventual return to regular classrooms. For these reasons, it is incumbent upon special education teachers to have professional training for regular classroom teaching. Special education teachers need to understand regular education environments. They must be knowledgeable about normal patterns of cognitive, physical, and social child development, about academic curricula, and grade and age level expectations. In addition, they must be able to communicate with regular educators.

Over the past few years there has been considerable concern about the quality of U.S. education. Some of the criticism has been directed at the quality of teachers and their professional preparation to teach (e.g., National Commission on Excellence in Education, 1983, 1985). Concern has been expressed about falling scores on measures of aptitude, evidence that many talented teachers are leaving the profession, charges of insufficient background in general liberal arts, low standards for admission to teacher education, and minimal standards for teacher certification in preservice teacher education programs.

Although many teacher educators have agreed with some of these charges and of the necessity for reform, some have pointed out that these apparent problems cannot be solved solely by teacher educators (Imig, 1982; Kerr, 1983). Rather, they require some basic changes in the ways that institutions of higher education view teacher preparation and the resources our society is willing to devote to education. There also are conditions beyond the immediate control of teacher educators that have an impact on the quality of teachers and teacher preparation. For example, the pool of undergraduate students from which teachers have traditionally been drawn is shrinking. There are simply fewer persons in the college-age population, and alternative professional opportunities, especially for women, have increased in recent years, attracting many who might previously have been drawn to teaching as a career. At the same time, there has been a relative decline in teacher salaries together with a decline in the status of teachers.

Essential Teaching Skills

There is considerable uniformity in the content and organization of regular, preservice teacher preparation programs. Typically, they consist of four components—general education or liberal arts, advanced study in one or more academic areas (the major), professional studies in foundations (child development, learning) and methods of teaching, and student teaching experiences (Rice, 1984). Professional preservice teacher preparation typically constitutes only about one-fourth to one-third of a classroom teacher's undergraduate program.

In spite of the uniformity of preservice preparation, there have been few attempts to address qualitative issues in regular teacher preparation. That is, what should be the content and the means of teaching pedagogy, or teaching skills? In a review of several aspects of the professional preparation of teachers, Evertson, Hawley, and Zlotnick (1984) conclude that despite criticism of existing methods of teacher preparation, the available research suggests the value of professional preparation. Teachers who have completed professional preparation programs are more likely to be effective teachers, as measured by the academic achievement of their students, than those who have not had such professional preparation. They also identify five core teaching skills that are important to good teaching. They are skills that can be adapted to variations in the content of what is taught, to the learning objectives, and to student needs. These basic pedagogical skills are (Evertson, Hawley, & Zlotnick, 1984, pp. 27–28):

1. Maximizing academic learning time by providing opportunities to learn and cover academic content.
2. Managing and organizing the classroom, by arranging physical space, planning rules and procedures, providing consequences and rewards, monitoring students' work, planning lessons, and grouping students.
3. Utilizing interactive teaching strategies with emphasis on frequent lessons presenting information, developing concepts through lecture and demonstration, and elaborating with feedback to students.
4. Communicating high expectations for student performance for both high and low achievers.
5. Reinforcing appropriate student behavior that is related to academic achievement and providing students with feedback and knowledge of the results of their efforts.

Although we know little about how well these basic teaching skills are taught in regular teacher preparation programs, or the extent they are actually employed in classrooms, all of the above skills could also be considered important for special education teachers of students with behavioral disorders. The relationship between regular and special education teacher preparation requires additional attention. Certainly, the nature and quality of the preparation of regular classroom teachers is critical to behaviorally disordered children and adolescents.

Special Competencies to Teach Behaviorally Disordered Students

If all regular classroom teachers were proficient in the above teaching competencies identified by Evertson, Hawley, and Zlotnick (1984), and they were interested in and willing to work with behaviorally disordered students, the need for special programs would undoubtedly diminish. However, there is some question about the skills and willingness of many regular classroom teachers to work with such children. "Clinical observation indicates that one educational problem relating to the diversity of human behavior is that adults, including teachers, vary in their abilities to cope with, manage, and teach groups of differing ranges and intensity of diversity. Some adults can cope well with larger numbers of youths behaving in more divergent ways than others can" (Mesinger, 1985, p. 511).

Thus, the topic of special competencies for teaching students with behavioral disorders is a critical one. Most literature on the topic has consisted of what teacher educators or special education teachers themselves view as important professional characteristics and skills. Consequently, the determination of important or necessary competencies is ultimately a matter of the expert opinions of those who would be expected to be most knowledgeable on the topic.

In an early study of the qualifications and preparation of teachers of "socially and emotionally maladjusted" children, Mackie, Kvaraceus, and Williams (1957) asked seventy-five "superior" teachers from across the country who were working in a variety of educational environments to rate the importance of eighty-eight individual competencies that had been compiled by a special study group. Twenty competencies received overall ratings of "very important" and were categorized in the following six areas:

1. Knowledge and ability to establish and operate stimulating, flexible, tension-free classrooms capable of meeting a child's individual needs.
2. Ability to use differential diagnosis and to interpret psychological tests, reports, and case histories.
3. Ability to counsel students with regard to their attitudes and problems.

4. Ability to manage a child's individual social behavior and develop self-control.
5. Knowledge of the causes of behavior problems and of students' psychological needs.
6. Ability to work with other professional groups.

Mackie, et al. (1957, p. 26) concluded that "above all, the teachers should provide a flexible school program to permit individual student adjustment and development and provide experiences in which they can be successful." They also commented on the necessity of certain personal teacher characteristics. "The teacher, all agree, should be a well-adjusted, warm, and accepting person . . . objective and supporting. He must have achieved a high degree of maturity himself. In addition, he must be able to 'take it' " (p. 33). This study was later updated with similar results (Bullock & Whelan, 1971).

Pearle Berkowitz and Esther Rothman (1960) emphasized personal qualities needed by teachers of emotionally disturbed children. They observed, "The teacher of the disturbed child should be a strange, hybrid creature who is emotionally mature, well grounded in education and psychology, talented in the arts, has a wide range of interests, and with all these attributes is aware of personal limitations. Teachers who are most successful with disturbed children are genuine human beings who have insights into their own needs and have the capacity to become an integral part of a treatment team" (p. 129).

Several years later, Frank Hewett (1967) suggested a hierarchy of seven important teacher competencies, based upon his experiences directing teacher training at the Neuropsychiatric Institute School at UCLA. Although he considered all of them important, Hewett placed them in the following descending order of importance:

- objectivity
- flexibility
- structure

- resourcefulness
- social reinforcement
- curriculum expertise
- intellectual model

A more behaviorally oriented approach to teacher competencies focusing on the acquisition of specific skills was provided by Haring and Fargo (1969), who identified eight specific skills for implementing behavioral interventions:

1. observation and behavioral analysis
2. use of academic, verbal, social, physical, and behavioral assessment information for program planning
3. selection of appropriate instructional materials
4. identifying motivational requirements of the child
5. use of contingency management procedures
6. procedures for establishing and maintaining learning activities
7. continuous monitoring of student progress
8. application of teaching skills to individuals and groups

Kerr, Shores, and Stowitschek (1978) asked graduates of their behaviorally oriented program at Peabody College to identify the most useful competencies for teaching behaviorally disordered students. According to their former students, the most frequently used competencies included task analysis, criterion-referenced testing, instructional programming, concept analysis, observation skills, behavior modification skills of prompting, modeling, and shaping, and skill in direction giving and questioning.

About the same time, Frank Feinberg and Frank Wood (1978) analyzed field procedures used in a teacher training program at the University of Minnesota. They proposed the thirteen goals for teachers shown in Box 11.1. These goals emphasize skills in assessing, designing, and implementing educational programs that include both behavioral and psychoeducational interventions. They also recognize the importance of being able to work with students, parents, and colleagues.

One of the most comprehensive attempts to identify important competencies was provided by Lewis Polsgrove and Herbert Reith (1979).

Box 11.1 Goals for Teachers

1. Employ assessment techniques in the classroom
2. Assist students in describing their goals and preferred behavior objectives
3. Work constructively with parents
4. Write an IEP for a student described as emotionally disturbed/behavior disordered
5. Demonstrate effective and positive interpersonal skills with students
6. Work cooperatively with team members
7. Develop and implement plans for systematic teaching of social behavior
8. Conduct interpersonal communication/problem solving interviews and group discussions
9. Develop and implement contracts with individual students
10. Develop and implement group reinforcement plans
11. Use a variety of preventive procedures
12. Use a variety of crisis management procedures to control/contain problem behavior and redirect pupils in desired direction
13. Use time-out and isolation procedures appropriately

Source: F. C. Feinberg & F. H. Wood, "Goals for teachers of seriously emotionally disturbed children." In F. H. Wood (Ed.), *Preparing teachers to develop and* *maintain therapeutic educational environments* (Minneapolis, MN: Dept. of Psychoeducational Studies, University of Minnesota, 1978), p. 21.

Based upon a review of previous studies of teacher competencies and their experience as teacher educators, Polsgrove and Reith prepared a list of 138 competencies in seven categories— assessment, behavioral management, communication/consultation, personal, instructional, administrative, and cognitive. The competency statements were written so that student performance could be measured in field-based settings. The list was then submitted to twenty-three special education teacher educators who rated the importance of each competency based upon frequency of use by teachers of emotionally disturbed students. Although many of the competencies received average ratings of "important," only thirty-four were rated as "greatly needed." That is, at least one-half of the teacher educators gave them their highest rating. Box 11.2 lists those competencies most highly regarded by the teacher educators.

According to Polsgrove and Reith, teacher educators value skills in direct intervention with children more than understanding disordered behavior. They conclude that there are four major skill areas necessary for teachers of emotionally disturbed and behaviorally disordered students. These are:

1. Skill in establishing a structured classroom environment, providing clear-cut expectations and limits, yet with flexibility in meeting the needs of students.
2. Ability to work with other professionals in the treatment process.
3. Ability to effectively manage children's behavior.
4. Objectivity, warmth, tolerance, and emotional stability.

Recently, Cullinan, Epstein, and Schultz (1987) reported consistent results in a study of competencies for teachers of behaviorally disordered adolescents. They asked university teacher educators, directors of residential treatment centers, and local special education administrators to rate fifty-five competencies developed from some of the above studies. The competencies

were arranged in five categories: assessment, behavior management, instructional programming, interaction with parents, interactions with other professionals, administration, knowledge, and personal/professional characteristics. Most of the competencies were considered at least "fairly important," but in two areas—behavior management and personal/professional characteristics—a majority of the competencies were rated "highly important."

Several trends are apparent in the way the issue of teacher competencies has been dealt with over the years. The emphasis has shifted from understanding or explaining disordered behavior to learning specific skills for effective intervention. This movement has corresponded with the development of applied behavior analysis and various behavior modification techniques presented in Chapter 8.

Still, it should be mentioned that the distinction between *understanding* and *intervention skills* is somewhat artificial. It is necessary to have some understanding, some explanations, some theories about the nature of students' behavior problems. Strategies for teaching such students cannot be indiscriminately applied, but should be directed by an understanding of the student's condition and needs. Although the causes of problem behavior need not, and in many cases cannot, be determined, an understanding of each student is basic to designing interventions.

It is important to remember that documented mastery of specific competencies by a student does not ensure that a student will be an effective teacher. However, the absence of a demonstration of prescribed competencies and reliance on subjective judgments of competence certainly do not ensure teaching competence. As Robert Bloom (1979, pp. 68–69) observed, "The very best that can be said of the competencies we enumerate is that they are the set of propositions by which we reduce the complexity of teaching to manageable proportions."

It is beyond the scope of any single course, practicum experience, or even entire teacher education program to fully prepare prospective

---

Box 11.2   Teacher Trainers' Views of Greatly Needed Competencies

Assessment Competencies

1. Correctly selects, administers, and interprets various informal and standardized instruments for assessing students' social performance (e.g., behavioral checklists, sociograms, anecdotal records).
2. Correctly administers and interprets various informal measures of students' academic performances (e.g., criterion-referenced measures, teacher-made tests, permanent-product information).
3. Uses appropriate informal and formal observation systems/techniques for collecting data on students' academic and social behavior.
4. Selects appropriate academic and social behaviors for intervention programs with students.
5. Uses assessment information to place students in appropriate instructional sequences.
6. Realistically appraises influence of situational variables that may affect an intervention program.

Behavioral Management Competencies

1. Arranges antecedent and consequent stimuli to change behavior in desirable directions.
2. Can establish and maintain a structured learning environment for students.
3. Uses various strategies for developing students' self-control.
4. Designs, implements, and evaluates effective behavior management programs for students.

5. Selects and successfully employs appropriate management strategies in various situations.
6. Arranges physical environment to facilitate management possibilities.
7. Selects appropriate reinforcers for use in motivating students.
8. Designs management programs to facilitate generalization and maintenance of acquired behaviors.

Communication/Consultation Competencies

1. Establishes and maintains open communication with students, other teachers, administrators, and parents.
2. Follows proper legal procedures regarding assessment, placement, programming, and consultation with parents and other professionals.

Personal Competencies

1. Remains calm in crisis, inflammatory, or provocative situations.
2. Provides an acceptable model of self-control for students.
3. Maintains flexibility in managing students' behavior and in administering their academic programs.
4. Objectively evaluates students' behavior.
5. Expresses joy and enthusiasm under appropriate circumstances.

continued

---

teachers in all of the competencies necessary to be effective teachers of behaviorally disordered students. Different students, circumstances, environments, support services, and teacher responsibilities will demand different personal and professional skills. In a very real sense, a teacher is never fully equipped to deal with every behavioral and instructional challenge posed by his or her students. There will always be new challenges for which teachers have not been fully prepared. The solution is ongoing acquisition and refinement of competence.

Categorical versus Noncategorical Preparation

An unresolved issue in the preparation of teachers for behaviorally disordered students is the degree to which training should focus exclusively on this population or be more generic

Box 11.2 continued

Instructional Competencies

1. Accurately analyzes students' strengths and weaknesses in given areas for planning an instructional sequence.
2. Adapts instructional materials for meeting long- and short-term objectives.
3. Provides effective individual and small group instruction.
4. Uses various strategies (e.g., modeling, imitation, rehearsal, inquiry, prompting, cueing, feedback, consequation, discussion, lecture) in isolation or in combination for providing appropriate instruction for students.
5. Selects and writes appropriate long- and short-term academic and social goals based on assessment information.
6. Selects appropriate placement for students in instructional sequences based on assessment information.
7. Uses continuous assessment to modify instructional activities for meeting students' instructional needs.
8. Teaches personal development skills such as: self-control, self-help, communication, taking responsibility, self-confidence, problem solving, aesthetics.

Administrative Competencies

1. Establishes and maintains a resource room, self-contained classroom, or residential school classroom and itinerant class for students.
2. Develops and implements appropriate IEPs for students.
3. Keeps appropriate records on students.
4. Functions as a member of a team for planning social and educational interventions with students.

Cognitive Competencies

1. Demonstrates knowledge of general child development.

Source: L. Polsgrove & H.J. Reith, "A new look at competencies required by teachers of emotionally disturbed and behaviorally disordered children and youth," in F. H. Wood (Ed.), *Teachers for secondary school students with serious emotional disturbances: Content of programs.* (Minneapolis, MN: Dept. of Psychoeducational Studies, University of Minnesota, 1978).

in orientation. That is, should teacher preparation be categorical or noncategorical?

In recent years there has been a movement toward more noncategorical special education teacher preparation. This movement has corresponded with a trend in the schools toward noncategorical educational programming for exceptional students, particularly those considered to have mild or moderate handicaps. This is usually meant to include children with emotional and behavioral disorders, learning disabilities, and mild to moderate mental retardation.

Greenough, Huntze, Nelson, and Simpson (1983, p. 5) reviewed literature on the issue and concluded that "arguments on both sides lean toward an emphasis on rhetoric, as opposed to empiricism." Arguments favoring noncategorical educational programming and teacher preparation include the following (Blackhurst, 1981; Brady, Conroy, & Langford, 1984; Heward, Cooper, Heron, Hill, McCormick, Porter, Stephens, & Sutherland, 1981):

- Categories of exceptionality are diagnostically indistinct and educationally irrelevant.
- Categories perpetuate detrimental labeling.
- Categories result in fragmented and inefficient delivery of educational services.
- Noncategorical training better prepares teachers to work with children representing a variety of educational characteristics.
- Noncategorical preparation is more compatible with competency-based preparation.

On the other side of this argument are the proponents of a more categorical approach. Huntze and Grosenick (1980), for example, have charged that the flexibility of noncategorically trained teachers sometimes comes at the expense of behaviorally disordered students. They believe that categorical preparation can provide greater attention to the specific issues and skills relevant to working with children with behavioral disorders. Proponents of a categorical orientation also cite the large body of category specific literature, research, and teacher trainer expertise.

This debate is not yet resolved. Categorical preparation proponents acknowledge the overlap in competencies needed by teachers of mildly to moderately handicapped students. Some noncategorical training advocates agree that noncategorical teacher preparation has tended to ignore preparation of teachers to deal with problem behavior (Greenough, et al., 1983). Actually, few teacher preparation programs are purely categorical or noncategorical in orientation. Many would be better characterized as multicategorical. They include generic introductory and supporting course work in the characteristics and education of exceptional children, together with preparation in characteristics and interventions specific to the more traditional categories of educational exceptionality.

For some teacher competencies, categorical treatment may be irrelevant, but for others it may not be. For example, there are some striking differences between the competencies that are important for teachers of learning disabled students and those for teachers of behaviorally disordered students. In a national survey, teachers of learning disabled students rated competence in teaching reading and other academic subjects as most important (Newcomer, 1982). They also rated their own proficiency highest in these skills. However, their ratings of the importance of behavior management skills fell only in the middle range for both importance and proficiency. As we discussed earlier, competence in behavior management is of utmost importance for teachers of students with personality and behavioral disorders.

Personal Characteristics of BD Teachers

As we have seen, personal traits such as warmth, maturity, flexibility, objectivity, self-control, and positive interpersonal skills have been included in most studies of teacher competencies. In the Cullinan, Epstein, and Schultz (1987, p. 68) study, for example, nearly all of the personal and professional traits were rated "highly important." Successful teachers of behaviorally disordered students are those who:

- model appropriate social-emotional, intellectual, and achievement skills;
- show fairness, sensitivity, empathy, persistence, and other crucial human values;
- express humor, joy, and enthusiasm under appropriate circumstances;
- remain calm and objective in crisis or stressful situations;
- establish and maintain rapport with other teachers, administrators, and other professionals;
- conduct professional activities in an ethical manner.

As critical as these characteristics are, they are difficult to measure and perhaps even more difficult to teach.

Maily (1975) has listed some positive and negative personal characteristics drawn from the Rutland Program (Developmental Therapy) at the University of Georgia. Maily lists energy, recognition of own strengths and weaknesses, a child centered orientation, and openness to new ideas, among others. She also lists undesirable characteristics, including combative, inconsistent, seductive, provocative, defensive, intolerant, compulsive, projecting, lethargic, threatened, and overreactive.

Although both positive and negative personal characteristics undoubtedly do affect a teacher's ability to work with behaviorally disordered students, little is known about what personality types are best suited for this profession. We have observed excellent teachers with widely divergent personalities. Some are excitable bundles of energy; others are calm and pensive. Some readily express warmth of feeling, both verbally and nonverbally; others are more taciturn and controlled in their emotional expression.

Nicholas Long and Ruth Newman (1971, p. 281) comment on this: "Some of the best teachers in the past, as in the present, are, in other realms of life, considered eccentric or painfully shy . . . But, in the classroom, 'odd ball' or not, many of these people seem to be able to marshal all their resources. Their pupils often love them and/or learn from them. It is not necessary to come off a mental health assembly line to be a good teacher. . . . Uniformity is not the goal for which to strive." Long and Newman suggest that teachers' self-awareness of their motivation to teach disturbed children is essential. "The more aware a teacher is of the hidden, as well as the obvious, reasons for teaching, the more fully will he be able to do his job and face its frustrations (p. 292).

Empathy

One teacher trait that has received some attention from researchers is empathy (Morgan, 1977; Scheuer, 1971). Morgan defines empathy as the "teacher's understanding of the meaning to the student of the classroom experiences in which they are mutually engaged. This understanding is reflected in the learning interaction by the way in which the teacher responds to the students" (p. 89). Empathy can mean *objective caring*. According to this view, teachers must genuinely care about their students and understand students' perceptions of their own worlds. Caring translates into interventions in the best interest of the child.

Being empathic also means that teachers attempt to be objective with students. Teachers must not allow emotional overinvolvement with students to impair their effectiveness. Teachers should also avoid both sentimentality and defeatist attitudes, and acknowledge the limitations of their intervention goals.

Effects of Students

Objective caring is not always easy to achieve. Robert Bloom (1983, p. 209) says, "We have specially designed buildings and classrooms, materials, techniques, curricula, and IEPs. But, as Fritz Redl often noted, what we often forget is that we also have ourselves." Difficulties in handling our own emotional reactions to students and their life conditions can sometimes interfere with teaching effectiveness. Bloom refers to these interfering emotional reactions with terms like *helplessness rage, anger at our teammates, envy of the young,* and *complexity shock.* He observes,

Time and again, positively and negatively, the emotional generators of our adult professional personalities are energized by the youngsters we teach and the circumstances in which we teach them. Refusal to recognize the emotional impact students have upon us and how that affects our professional work impairs our ability to establish rapport with youths, limits our instructional effectiveness, and establishes us as prime candidates for the despair and depression of teacher burnout. Accepting special education's interpersonal underworld allows us to disengage from unproductive conflicts, to forego battles with windmills in exchange for struggles with real dragons, and as a marvelous extra, to continue to grow as teachers and as human beings. (1983, p. 215)

Personal Preparation

There have been some deliberate attempts to teach affective competencies (e.g., Pattavina & Ramirez, 1980). Some teacher training programs, especially those with a more psychoeducational orientation, have included attention to teacher self-examination and personal growth (Balow, 1967b; Fagen, 1978; Spence, 1978). In the program at the Child Center in Oregon, a residential and day treatment program for seriously emotionally disturbed children, teacher competencies are determined by the general treatment goals for the children (Spence, 1978). These include the development of an adequate inner life (self-concept), interpersonal relations skills, and competencies for living. Thus, in addition to instructional competencies, trainees are expected to become nurturing parent models, to actively care for and about the child, and to be emotionally supportive to parents.

The Mark Twain School teacher internship program of the Montgomery County (Maryland) Schools includes a human relations group (Fagen, 1978). The purpose of the group is to enhance acceptance and awareness of self and others by sharing professional concerns in a mutually supportive setting. Interns have the opportunity to explore areas of human relations, including building trust and risk taking, seeking and providing feedback, listening and consulting, and confronting limits and expectations. Trainees also provide self-evaluations of their performance in these and other areas of competence, which are then compared and discussed with those of practicum supervisors and program staff.

It is essential that persons considering careers as teachers of children and adolescents with behavioral disorders examine their own fitness for this line of work. Professional aspirations, tolerance for emotional and behavioral deviance, energy level, self-awareness, and defensiveness are some attributes that prospective teachers should examine. Probably the best way to do this is to learn as much as possible about what the work actually entails. Prospective teachers can do this by seeking opportunities in the field for observation and participation as volunteers or paraprofessionals. Part-time and summer employment in special camps, recreational programs, summer schools, and institutions can also provide such firsthand experiences.

Working as a Member of a Team

The importance of being able to work as a member of a team and to serve as an advocate for behaviorally disordered students is included in many of the lists of important teacher competencies. Mackie et al. (1957) referred to the "ability to work with other professional groups," Feinberg and Wood (1978) to the ability to "work cooperatively with team members," and Polsgrove and Reith (1979) to the importance of establishing and maintaining "open communication with students, other teachers, administrators, and parents," and the ability to "function as a member of a team for planning social and educational interventions with students."

The role a teacher plays in collaborative intervention efforts depends partly on the individual needs of the students, the other service providers who are involved, and the service delivery model within which the teacher operates. Some roles, such as consulting and resource teacher, include major responsibilities for coordinating interventions with other school staff as well as personnel from community agencies, specialists, and families outside of schools. Even teachers who work in more restrictive environments such as institutions, special schools, or self-contained classrooms must work as members of a team with other special education staff members.

Many students with behavioral disorders have been treated inconsistently by adults. As a result, some have become masters of manipulation, playing one adult against the other. Communication among the adults involved with these children is necessary to establish consistent programming. In addition, teachers must identify and gain access to resources and services for their students. Utilizing the expertise of others not only benefits the student, but ultimately can relieve the teacher from the burden of total responsibility. Some ideas for facilitating communication and collaboration with other professionals, particularly within schools, were discussed in the last chapter. In the next chapter, we will suggest strategies for working with parents and other service providers and agencies.

Demographic Characteristics of BD Teachers

Teacher Shortages

There is a persistent shortage of teachers for behaviorally disordered children. Sharon Huntze and Judith Grosenick (1980) reported on human resources in the area of behavioral disorders. They found severe shortages of teachers for behaviorally disordered students. They attributed these to the combined effects of rapid growth in the number of identified students following the passage of PL 94–142, high attrition rates of teachers, and insufficient numbers of newly trained teachers.

More recent data, based upon surveys from states and territories, indicate that shortages of teachers for behaviorally disordered students remain acute. According to Smith-Davis, Burke, and Noel (1984), thirty-three states are experiencing shortages and in twelve of those the shortages are "extremely serious." They say, "When coupled with shortages in severe emotional disturbance . . . the findings suggest that mild to severe emotional disturbance is the single most vulnerable program area in special education where manpower is concerned" (p. 52).

According to a U.S. Department of Education (DOE) report on the status of implementation of PL 94–142 (1984), the number of identified "seriously emotionally disturbed" students increased by about 25 percent between the 1976–1977 and the 1982–1983 school year. Although this is still less than one-half of the estimated prevalence of 2 percent of the school-age population, it represents substantial growth over a relatively short time. The increase in size of this group has been due to greater efforts by state and local education agencies to serve previously underserved children.

With the increase in numbers of children served, there has also been an increase in the number of teachers to work with them. In the five years prior to the 1981–1982 school year, for example, the number increased from 21,700 to 29,100. However, during the last two years covered in the DOE report, the number of teachers actually declined slightly—a shift that is probably due to an increase in multicategorical or interrelated programs.

Age, Sex, Experience, and Delivery Models

Relatively little attention has been given to studying demographic characteristics of these teachers. What data do exist have usually been collected to describe subjects in studies with purposes other than determining demographics.

Existing data indicate that, as a group, teachers of behaviorally disordered students are relatively young and that a majority are female. Special education teachers as a group are relatively young because the field has experienced a rapid growth only since the mid-1970s. In a large representative sample of special education teachers from Kansas, including 125 teachers of behaviorally disordered children, nearly 45 percent were under thirty years of age (Zabel & Zabel, 1983). About 87 percent were female and 65 percent married.

Despite their youth, the group was highly educated and experienced. About 58 percent had master's degrees, many with additional graduate credits. They had a mean of 3.7 years of regular classroom experience and 5.3 years of special education teaching experience. Still, nearly one-half had no regular classroom experience. The most common amount of special education experience was only two years, with 55 percent having taught less than five years. In addition, only about 40 percent of the teachers were fully certified in special education when they began to teach.

Comparisons of BD teachers and other special education teachers indicate both similarities and differences. One noticeable difference is a higher percentage of male teachers (about 20 percent) than most other exceptionalities. Data from a national sample of secondary level teachers of behaviorally disordered students indicate that about 85 percent are under thirty-six years of age. More than 60 percent are female even at the secondary level, and nearly 60 percent are pursuing graduate level preparation. At the secondary level, about 60 percent work in resource and 25 percent in self-contained settings (Schmid, Algozzine, Maher, & Wells, 1984).

In a study of reintegration practices with behaviorally disordered students that included nearly 400 teachers in three midwestern states (Peterson, Zabel, Smith, & White, 1983), about equal numbers of teachers (about 40 percent) reported working in resource and self-contained settings. Another 6 percent taught in residential or institutional settings, and 14 percent worked in other service delivery roles. Nationally, according to the DOE report cited earlier, the largest number of teachers of seriously emotionally disturbed children are considered resource teachers (37.1 percent), followed closely by self-contained (33.6 percent), itinerant (21.4 percent), consultant (5.1 percent), home/hospital (2.1 percent), and work study (0.7 percent).

Temporary Certification

Because of shortages, many teachers of behaviorally disordered students enter the profession with temporary, or provisional, certifications. In most states, these teachers must possess regular teaching certification and complete specified, partial preparation in the area. In 1980, some states had as many as 80 percent of the teachers of behaviorally disordered children only temporarily certified; rural areas and mental health, and youth corrections facilities had the highest rates (Huntze & Grosenick, 1980). According to more recent data reported by Rutherford, Nelson, and Wolford (1985), only 28 percent of teachers in juvenile correctional facility schools have any special education certifi-

cation. Smith-Davis, Burke, and Noel (1984) charge that temporary certificates lower the quality of educational services to behaviorally disordered children and result in credibility problems with regular education personnel and parents.

Teacher Attrition and Burnout

Attrition rates for teachers of behaviorally disordered children and adolescents are higher than those of regular classroom teachers and other special education teachers (Huntze & Grosenick, 1980). Smith-Davis, et al. (1984) estimate that attrition due to burnout accounts for losses of teachers as high as 30 percent every three to four years, with a large proportion occurring within the first year of teaching.

Accurate data are hard to come by, since it is difficult to determine if some teachers who leave their jobs are taking similar positions elsewhere or are only temporarily leaving and plan to return later. The high demand for such teachers may actually contribute to greater mobility by providing employment opportunities. Because such a large proportion of these teachers are young, they also may be more likely to take temporary and extended leaves for personal reasons such as marriage and raising children.

In addition, the temporary certification situation probably contributes to high attrition rates. Teachers who have relatively little investment in the profession may be more likely to leave to pursue other kinds of employment. In addition, teachers who have not completed preparation programs may not be able to accomplish the requirements of their jobs, and be more susceptible to dissatisfaction and burnout.

Stress and Burnout

The teacher described in Box 11.3 is typical of one who experiences severe job-related stress. The term *burnout* has been used to refer to the psychological and physiological distress a per-

---

Box 11.3   Teacher Burnout

Four weeks into the school year, a first year teacher in a class for behaviorally disordered junior high students had quit, too physically exhausted to continue. By all accounts, she was well prepared for her job, having completed teacher preparation programs in both regular and special education. She had been a good student in her classes, had had successful experiences in student teaching, and had worked as a teacher aide in a state hospital school during two previous summers. She was enthusiastic, appeared to have realistic expectations of what she was getting into, and wanted to teach behaviorally disordered children, In short, she showed considerable promise. Even so, she could not cope with the situation in which she found herself.

Tears came easily when she attempted to deal with the behavior of her students and when she talked to others about the problems she was having. She dreaded each new day and was so exhausted that she went to bed at six P.M. Finally, with feelings of confusion and frustration, mixed with anger toward the students, administrators, and most of all herself, she asked for a leave of absence. "It was hell," she said. "I've lost all my self-confidence and don't think I ever want to go back." She is an example of a syndrome that many special and regular teachers experience—burnout.

Source: R. H. Zabel & M. K. Zabel, "Burnout: A critical issue for educators," in *Education Unlimited* (March 1980), p. 23.

---

son experiences as a result of job conditions (Freudenberger, 1974). Symptoms of distress include unhappiness and depression, lack of enthusiasm or interest in work, psychological distancing from clients and colleagues, and a variety of psychosomatic conditions such as tension headaches, backaches, and lack of energy. Sometimes, burnout is accompanied by excessive use of alcohol or drugs. Obviously, burnout can increase absenteeism and attrition and affect performance on the job.

Most attention given to burnout has concerned persons in human services professions. Researchers have examined the phenomenon among day-care staff (Maslach & Pines, 1977), mental health professionals (Pines & Maslach, 1978), police officers (Maslach & Jackson, 1979), and child care workers in residential treatment facilities (Freudenberger, 1974). Social service providers have received attention because they are "required to work intensely and intimately with people on a continuous basis. They learn about people's psychological, social and physical problems and are expected to provide aid or treatment of some kind. Some aspects of this job involve 'dirty work' . . . tasks particularly upsetting or embarrassing to perform" (Maslach & Pines, 1977, p. 100).

Many of the day-to-day responsibilities of teachers of students with behavioral disorders fall into this category. Such students confront teachers with verbal and physical abuse, engage in disruptive and uncooperative behavior, or are socially withdrawn, distant, and depressed. In his observations on his needs as a teacher of adolescent emotionally disturbed students, Jon Bell (1979) cites the importance of making the school environment safe for students and himself, avoiding power struggles, and dealing with depression. He says, "The hardest part of the work is dealing with depression—theirs and mine. They are depressed because they have been lonely and failing for so long and they don't believe it is going to get any better. I get depressed because they are at high risk, and if I am not successful with them, they probably will not have many more chances" (p. 172).

Some attention has been given to the burnout problem among teachers of behaviorally disordered students (Lawrenson & McKinnon, 1982; Zabel & Zabel, 1982) and among special educators generally (Bensky, Shaw, Grouse, Bates, Dixon, & Beane, 1980; Fimian, 1986; Weiskopf, 1980; Zabel & Zabel, 1982, 1983).

One study (Zabel & Zabel, 1982, 1983) used the responses of 600 special education teachers to the Maslach Burnout Inventory (MBI) to measure burnout, and then related these findings to several personal and professional factors. The MBI asks respondents to rate the frequency with which they experience feelings related to three factors: emotional exhaustion, depersonalization, and personal accomplishment. More frequent feelings of emotional exhaustion and depersonalization coupled with fewer feelings of personal accomplishment are viewed as correlates of burnout.

Thus, burnout should not be considered an absolute condition, but a matter of degree. One teacher may be relatively more or less burned out than another. According to the Zabels's research, teachers of behaviorally disordered students as a group are at higher risk for burnout than other teachers of exceptional children. This group had the highest average scores on the measure of depersonalization and were second only to teachers of hearing impaired students on the emotional exhaustion factor. They were, however, in about the middle range on the measure of personal accomplishment.

Approximately one-fourth of the teachers of behaviorally disordered students fell into a high burnout group (i.e., at least one standard deviation above the sample mean) on both the emotional exhaustion and depersonalization measures. Although this was considerably higher than any other group, certainly not all teachers of behaviorally disordered students are burned out. Some, in fact, are in the least burned-out group. Nevertheless, a relatively high proportion of BD teachers seem to experience a high frequency of feelings associated with burnout. This is a concern that merits some attention.

Age, Experience, and Training. Additional analyses in the Zabel and Zabel study (1984) clarified relationships between burnout and specific personal and job-related factors. For example, there appears to be a linear relationship between age and burnout. Generally, older, more experienced, and more highly trained teachers are less burned out than younger teachers, those with less experience, and those with less training. Of course, the age, training, and experience factors are difficult to separate. Together, they can contribute to the development of teaching skills and coping strategies. In addition, older, more experienced, more highly trained teachers might be considered the survivors, since those who do experience difficulty are likely to leave the profession early.

Interestingly, certain job-related conditions such as length of work week, number of students, and availability of a paraprofessional or team teacher do not appear to be directly related to burnout among special education teachers. It may be that the number of students a teacher has is not the critical factor, although teachers who reported they had too many students were significantly more emotionally exhausted than those who considered their caseload about right or too few. This finding corresponds with other research indicating the influence of heavy work loads on teacher burnout (Kyriacou & Sutcliffe, 1978).

Students' Ages and Service Delivery Models. Although differences were not dramatic among teachers with burnout judged according to the age level of their students, teachers at the junior high level did score somewhat higher on burnout measures than teachers at other age levels. Teachers in service delivery models at either end of the continuum (consulting teachers and those in institutions) were found to be at relatively high risk for burnout. It is not surprising that teachers in institutional settings score high, since by and large they work with more severely handicapped children. The role of consultant is also demanding. Consulting teachers often have not been specially trained for this role, they may have unreasonably large caseloads of students spread over large geographic areas, and may not identify with a particular school, staff, or group of students. Consequently, they may have less access to the intrinsic or psychic rewards of teaching that Lortie (1975) has identified as so important.

Perceptions of Support. One of the most striking results of the burnout research involves teachers' perceptions of support. There is an inverse relationship between perceptions of support from colleagues, parents, and especially administrators, and the measures of burnout. The higher the teachers' burnout scores, the lower their ratings of support from each of these potential sources. The relationship between support from administrators and job-related burnout is especially clear. In a study of BD teachers who had left their jobs, Lawrenson and McKinnon (1982) found that the most commonly cited reason for leaving the job was "hassles with administration." The most common job dissatisfactions were "lack of administration support," "inconsistent support staff," and "clerical and paperwork." Another frequently cited reason for leaving teaching was the inability "to have a long-term effect on students due to outside influences."

A Teacher Stress and Burnout Model

Zabel, Boomer, and King (1984) proposed the model of teacher stress and burnout depicted in Box 11.4. It is an adaptation of the Nicholas Long Pupil Stress Cycle discussed in Chapter 9 (Long & Duffner, 1980; Long & Fagen, 1981). The model consists of a series of components that have a dynamic relationship with one another. Beginning at the top of Box 11.4, moving down and then clockwise, these components are *Expectations, School Experiences, Feelings, Behavior,* and *Others' Reactions.* Within each component, the teacher's experience is presented along a positive (+) to negative (−) continuum. Positive experiences place the teacher at less risk for burnout; negative experiences at greater risk. As in the Maslach view of burnout discussed above, burnout is presented as a relative, rather than an absolute, condition.

Expectations. The Expectations component is placed outside the stress and burnout cycle, but it both affects and is affected by the other components. Teachers of students with behavioral disorders, like all teachers, approach their professions with expectations about the kinds of students, colleagues and supervisors, facilities, and resources they will encounter in their profession. They have expectations for their roles as teachers and their competence in fulfilling those roles.

Expectations may be formed early, beginning even prior to professional training, in what Nemser (1983) refers to as pretraining. Kyriacou and Sutcliffe (1978, p. 4) identify the following individual teacher characteristics: "biographical details (e.g., sex, teaching experience), personality traits (e.g., anxiety proneness, flexibility-rigidity), higher order needs (e.g., need for self-actualization), ability to meet or cope with demands, and the teacher's beliefs-attitudes-values system." Teacher expectations are derived from many factors, including the teacher's own socialization experiences in family, school, and community. They are also influenced by the nature of their preservice professional preparation. Long and Newman (1980) have suggested several reasons people choose teaching as a profession. Some of these reasons contribute to a generally positive, optimistic set of expectations; others to more negative expectations.

Experiences. Initial expectations are countered with reality as the teacher embarks on his or her career. Students with behavioral disorders present special challenges for many teachers. By definition, these children pre-

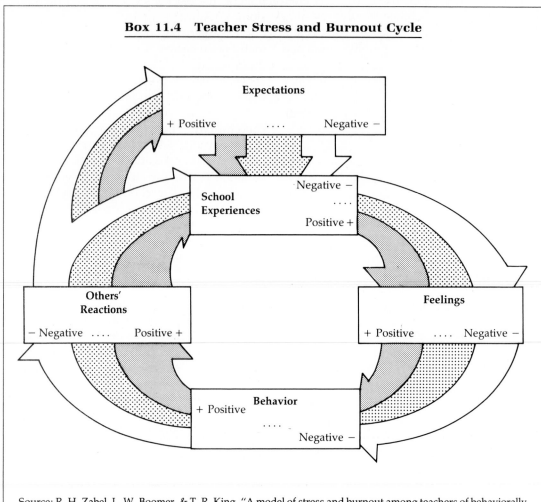

Box 11.4   Teacher Stress and Burnout Cycle

Source: R. H. Zabel, L. W. Boomer, & T. R. King, "A model of stress and burnout among teachers of behaviorally disordered students," *Behavioral Disorders*, 9 (1984), pp. 215–221.

sent too much inappropriate and too little appropriate behavior in school, making it more difficult for some teachers to reap rewards from their work.

Lortie (1975) identified three sources of potential reward for teachers—extrinsic (e.g., money, status), ancillary (e.g., location, schedule), and intrinsic (e.g., satisfaction from achieving positive results with students). For most teachers, intrinsic rewards are the central motivators.

Achievement of positive results with problem students (improved social and academic skills) can be difficult to come by and often unstable, and subject to many influences beyond the teacher's control. In the Lawrenson and McKinnon study (1982), one of the most frequently cited reasons for teachers leaving the profession was their perception of the absence of long-term effects on their students' behavior. However, one of the most frequently cited sources of satisfaction for teachers was "self-achievement on the job" as measured by student achievement academically and in management of behavior.

What sense of achievement can teachers experience working with behaviorally disordered students? William Morse (1983, p. 9) observed that "we must . . . forego the normal expectations if we are to work with the disturbed. It is normal to want to be liked, to want to be helpful, and even to actually be helpful . . . One has to get one's satisfaction from knowing we are doing the right thing to help, though change may be too delayed to give us the desired feedback."

Feelings. A variety of positive and negative feelings can be generated by the teacher's perception of the teaching experience. Of course, more positive experiences would be expected to result in more positive feelings; more negative experiences in more negative feelings. Negative feelings about work can include emotional exhaustion, expressed as apathy or anger, and depersonalization, expressed in alienation and resentment toward students, parents, and colleagues. Teachers' feelings result from both the emotionality and provocative behavior of pupils and their own personal needs (Bloom, 1983). Thus, one teacher may feel anger or fear from encounters with verbally abusive students, while another may be frustrated by a student's withdrawal. As mentioned earlier, Bloom has referred to some of the common emotional reactions such as rage, anger, shock, paranoia, and despair. Such feelings are elicited not only by students, but by fellow teachers, parents, administrators, and other personnel as well.

Rubenstein and Rezmierski (1983, p. 61) have emphasized the effects of adults' conflicted feelings about behaviorally disordered students on the reactions of school systems to such behavior:

For adults who work with this population of students, the dynamic seems to be that too often the human cognitive processes are overpowered by the affective processes; the ability to reason and think becomes secondary to the feelings which are aroused. Time and efforts which should be focused upon the students are refocused to meet the adults' own needs. . . . Adults often have negative feelings of anger, frustration, fear, despair, and helplessness at the same time they feel the need to nurture, support, help, and teach these students.

Teacher Behavior. Teachers' behavior, according to this model, results from their feelings, although there are individual differences in how feelings are displayed. For example, some teachers overtly communicate anger or enthusiasm, while others suppress such emotions and only covertly express them. Many may not even recognize the strong emotions underlying their behavior.

Negative teacher behavior includes physical exhaustion, psychosomatic ailments, absenteeism, frequent use of sarcasm and criticism of others, sleeping and eating problems, excessive use of drugs and alcohol, and increased conflict with others inside and outside school. Attrition may be a behavioral manifestation of negative feelings, although not necessarily the most serious. Continuing to work while being apathetic or hostile is more detrimental to the teacher and to everyone he or she encounters.

Reactions of Others. The last component in the model consists of others' reactions to teacher behavior. Those who behave in positive or negative ways toward students, colleagues, parents, and supervisors are generally expected to be treated in kind. There are clear relationships between burnout and perceptions of support from others (Zabel & Zabel, 1982).

Because of the nature of their work, teachers of behaviorally disordered students tend to be isolated from potential sources of support. Students and their parents often have limited capacities for providing support. Some are so needy of support themselves they can quickly deplete a teacher's resources. Also, teachers are sometimes physically segregated from other professional staff. They may have little relief from responsibility for supervision of students to allow for interaction with others who might empathize. In addition, other school staff sometimes regard them as "emotionally disturbed teachers." Building principals and other teachers are sometimes unhappy about having special programs in their school, and the educational philosophies of special and regular educators may differ. This does not mean that teachers of behaviorally disordered students will not encounter supportive colleagues, but that some colleagues may be disinterested and even hostile.

Sometimes BD teachers are caught in the middle of conflicts between students and the school. Rubenstein and Rezmierski (1983) say, "students who cause confusion between expectations and behavior, who threaten adults' needs for order, respect, and compliance, stimulate structuring activities on the part of the system." Sometimes those structuring activities conflict with special educators' perceptions of appropriate services to students. Despite being at odds with the system, the special educator must still be able to work within it.

According to the stress and burnout model, teachers who are caught in a cycle of unfulfilled expectations will experience negative feelings, will express those feelings in their behavior, and will receive reactions in kind. Thus, burnout results from the cumulative effect of unrealized expectations and negative experiences.

Of course, consideration of teacher stress and burnout cannot be limited to experiences within school. Stress encountered beyond the school walls affects and is in turn affected by job-related stress. The kinds of economic, psychological, reality, and developmental stresses, discussed by Long and Fagen (1981), that children bring with them to school also operate for their teachers. Thus, to cope with stress and prevent burnout, teachers must address factors in their lives both within and beyond their jobs.

Stress Reduction and Burnout Prevention

Although there has been considerable attention to methods for stress reduction, we know little about their effectiveness. Just as stress and burnout are manifested in different symptoms by different individuals, so do interventions vary from teacher to teacher. In the Zabel, Boomer, and King model, stress and burnout are viewed as products of the interaction between individual teachers and job conditions. The model has implications both for the types of strategies that may be helpful and the targets for those strategies. Stress reduction and burnout prevention efforts must be undertaken by teacher preparation programs, by schools, and by teachers themselves.

In the Expectations phase of the model, deliberate preservice preparation for teachers about the realities they will encounter might serve as one intervention. Such preparation might include attention directed specifically at stress and burnout through forthright presentation and discussion of factors that can contribute to stress. An understanding is necessary of the kinds of personality and behavioral problems that are likely to be encountered and their effects on teachers, the demands of the teacher's roles, and the influence of school environments. Development of the teacher competencies we discussed earlier, together with opportunities to practice those skills in the field, is crucial.

Prospective teachers must also assume personal responsibility for honestly assessing their own fitness, both in terms of skills and disposition, for this type of work. "While youthful enthusiasm is a desirable thing and is greatly needed in the schools today, understanding of one's limitations and what can practically be accomplished is critical. Without it, grand visions of rapid change are likely to be shattered, leaving in their wake a young professional who may no longer have the confidence to do things which are actually within reach" (Greer & Wethered, 1984, p. 527).

In the Feelings phase of the Stress and Burnout Model, teachers must objectively and critically examine the nature of their feelings toward students, parents, and colleagues. They should try to separate their own emotional needs from those of others, whether students, parents, or colleagues. As Redl said, teachers must "find out where [their] own heads are." They can also examine the relationships between their feelings and behavior to determine if their behavior is warranted, if it is constructive, if it contributes additional distress for themselves, and whether it interferes with their therapeutic efforts with students. In addition, teachers should question how their behavior affects others in their ecosystems.

It is important that administrators, supervisors, and teachers themselves attempt to provide support for each other—particularly for younger, inexperienced teachers. From all available evidence, it appears that early professional experiences are critical to survival (Cook & Leffingwell, 1982). Young, inexperienced teachers should not be placed in impossible situations and allowed to "sink or swim." Support and offers of support by others should be frequent and visible. There exist a variety of forms that such support might take. For example, it is possible to provide administrative arrangements such as assigning more than one special education teacher to a building, arranging team teaching situations, and organizing regular staff meetings expressly for the purpose of exchanging ideas and providing mutual support. However, such meetings must avoid degeneration into complaint sessions, which can make participants feel even worse and more helpless by generating even more negative expectations.

Shaw, Bensky, and Dixon (1981) have provided guidelines for assessing both individual and organizational stress and strategies for managing stress and preventing burnout among special educators. Although acknowledging possible

beneficial outcomes of stress such as heightened awareness, motivation, and creativity, they point out that an inability to cope with stress can lead to burnout.

Shaw et al. (1981) categorize coping strategies as either cognitive or affective/physical, and describe burnout prevention in terms of relational, structural, and organizational strategies. The key to successful management of stress and enhancement of health is not to master all possible techniques, but to recognize that everyone operates according to a different formula in both the experience of stress and in remedies for it.

Ultimately, it is an individual's responsibility to develop ways of dealing with stress in one's professional and personal life. Shaw, et al. (1981) suggest the following sequence of steps:

1. establishing self-responsibility and motivation for change
2. awareness of the factors and variables in the teacher's own formula
3. discovery of and experience with techniques that assist the teacher in conflict situations
4. refinement and modification to fit the teacher's individual style

Following recognition of self-responsibility and the need for change, teachers must assess their own strengths and weaknesses, in much the same way as for a student in development of an IEP. One way to do this is by answering the questions in Box 11.5.

When these questions have been answered, the individual can explore ways to increase professional and personal satisfactions and decrease the dissatisfactions. The teacher may even wish to continue with the IEP analogy by writing goals, setting necessary objectives for meeting those goals, and designing strategies for implementation.

Cognitive Strategies

Shaw, Bensky, and Dixon (1981) outline several potentially helpful cognitive strategies including

---

Box 11.5   Professional and Personal Satisfaction Questionnaire

"What are the sources of greatest satisfaction in my *job?*"

"What are the sources of greatest dissatisfaction in my *job?*"

"What are the sources of greatest satisfaction in my *personal life?*"

"What are the sources of greatest dissatisfaction in my *personal life?*"

---

cognitive reprogramming, changing states of consciousness, and visualization. These are ways of changing how a person perceives potentially stressful events. Shaw et al. believe that deliberate attempts to visualize stressful situations, experiences, and feelings can lead to ideas for more productive behavior in the future.

Earlier, we discussed the importance of teachers having realistic expectations for their jobs. Greer and Wethered (1984, p. 325) have analyzed burnout in terms of learned helplessness: "If people expect their responses to have little effect on the outcome, then the probability of initiating actions designed to solve problems or to overcome obstacles will decrease, and if the individual's expectations are that actions are doomed to failure they are likely to deny information that control is possible." One potential cognitive strategy is self-examination of what causes personal and job-related stress and consideration of alternative perceptions of those experiences.

Affective/Physical Strategies

Interventions included in the affective/physical strategies category do not deal with causes of stress, but with ways of handling physical symptoms such as tension headaches, backaches, exhaustion, and rapid heart rate. Strategies suggested by Shaw, et al. (1981) are

relaxation techniques, including meditation, biofeedback, breathing exercises, and guided imagery. Each of these can be learned and practiced to help an individual gain control over physiological symptoms of stress (Bernstein & Borkovek, 1973). In an experimental study involving teachers and paraprofessionals working with severely behaviorally disordered adolescents, Schloss, Sedlak, Wiggins, and Ramsey (1983) found that relaxation training and systematic desensitization significantly reduced teacher stress when dealing with aggressive student behavior.

For some people, regular exercise such as running, vigorous walking, biking, aerobics, and swimming provides outlets for stress. Persons who regularly exercise often feel more energetic than those who do not. Another physical strategy is the development of more healthy lifestyles, through better diets, regular patterns of eating and sleeping, and the elimination or reduction of smoking and alcohol consumption.

Relational Strategies

Relational strategies include the fostering of positive attitudes about oneself and one's job (Shaw, et al., 1981). One strategy is learning to accept and acknowledge positive feedback from others ("moment of glory"). Recognition of positive accomplishment from colleagues, students, supervisors, or others should not be routinely denied, but accepted with appropriate expressions of appreciation. C. Michael Nelson (1983) suggests that teachers recruit reinforcement for themselves by learning about their colleagues, making friends among them, reinforcing others' behavior, and offering and providing help and support to others. Such interaction can extend beyond teachers and administrators to janitors, secretaries, and others in the school support staff system. Taylor and Salend (1983) have proposed that teachers develop a network support system including school personnel, community resources and services, parent organizations, professional development resources, and personal development opportunities.

There are times when it is important to affirm, albeit covertly, "Damn, I'm good!" Certainly, it is not constructive to shrug off others' positive remarks as misperceptions, while taking negative perceptions to heart. It can also be helpful to "look for the silver lining" when things do go wrong, to recognize that situations might be even worse, and to look for evidence of progress. When things do go wrong, the teacher may even use that as an opportunity for growth, asking, "What have I learned from this?" and "How will this experience help me in the future?"

One way teachers can foster more positive perceptions of their jobs is to make their workplace as enjoyable and comfortable as possible. Teachers usually have considerable influence over the physical arrangements and decoration of their classrooms or offices. Consequently, they can create physical environments that are comfortable and inviting for themselves and for their students. Some ideas for creating therapeutic classroom environments are included in our earlier discussion of psychoeducational interventions (Chapter 9).

Teachers can also attempt to enhance collegial relationships with other teachers and staff. Because some jobs tend to isolate BD teachers from colleagues, extra effort may be necessary. Nelson (1983) urges special educators to be visi-

ble within their schools. He encourages greater participation in normal teacher duties such as club sponsorship and bus duty, working where colleagues can see and interact with them such as the teachers' lounge, and making the special program part of the school by bringing other staff and students into their room for student clubs and staff meetings. Although opportunities for interaction are limited for some teachers, reasonable efforts to participate in school social events, staff parties, local education associations, and extracurricular activities can contribute to acceptance by others.

Shaw, et al. (1981) also make several suggestions for meeting teachers' personal needs, including taking "mental health days" when needed. There are times when a teacher may need a break, an opportunity for a breather. Stressful, conflict-causing situations sometimes build to intolerable levels. The cycle may be interrupted by occasionally taking a day off.

Many teachers seek learning experiences through course work or adult education to acquire additional professional skills, develop leisure-time skills, provide distraction from stressful experiences, and cultivate support groups. Some find that budgeting "worry time" can be helpful. By scheduling a period of time each day devoted to worries, a person may be able to avoid a pervasive preoccupation with those concerns. Writing down those stressors also helps some people focus on them and develop ameliorative strategies while avoiding free-floating anxiety.

Structural Strategies

Shaw, et al. (1981) have described several structural strategies for preventing burnout. Several involve ways to organize time. As a first step, it is necessary that teachers know how they spend their time. It may be helpful to monitor actual use of time. This can be done by devising a self-observation chart, such as the one in Box 11.6. Frequently, teachers have misperceptions about how they use their time. Once data

Box 11.6   One Week Monitoring of Use of Time

Monday, April 15

8:00–8:30	Prepare for the day
8:30–9:20	Travel from administrative office to first school
9:20–9:30	Prepare for students
9:30–10:00	Meet with students
10:00–10:10	Prepare for next group
10:10–10:25	Consult with classroom teacher
10:25–10:30	Gather students
10:30–11:00	Meet with students
11:00–11:05	Transfer to other building
11:05–11:30	Meet with student
11:30–11:50	Travel to second school
11:50–12:00	Consult with teacher
12:00–12:30	Meet with student
12:30–1:00	Lunch downtown
1:00–1:20	Travel to third school
1:20–1:30	Consult with teacher and plan for student
1:30–2:00	Meet with student
2:00–2:15	Travel to fourth school
2:15–2:35	Meet with school counselor about today's staffing
2:35–3:20	Meet with student for the last time
3:20–3:30	Prepare for staffing with school psychologist
3:30–4:00	Staffing
4:00–4:20	Travel home

Monday's totals: teaching (3 hours and 10 minutes), consulting (50 minutes), preparation and planning (1 hour and 40 minutes), travel (2 hours and 10 minutes), and lunch (30 minutes).

Tuesday, April 16

8:00–9:00	Plan and prepare for the day and complete paperwork
9:00–9:15	Travel to first school
9:15–10:00	Meet with student
10:00–10:15	Travel back to administrative office

10:15–10:30	Consult with teacher and plan for next student
10:30–11:00	Meet with student
11:00–11:30	Meet with two students
11:30–12:05	Lunch
12:05–12:10	Travel to local school
12:10–12:15	Prepare for students
12:15–12:50	Meet with students
12:50–1:00	Visit administrative board office
1:00–2:30	Plan for group of students
2:30–3:30	Meet with group of students
3:30–4:10	Consult with social worker regarding student
4:10–4:20	Prepare for next day

Tuesday's totals: teaching (3 hours and 20 minutes), consulting (1 hour and 5 minutes), preparation and planning (2 hours and 45 minutes), travel (35 minutes), and lunch (35 minutes).

Wednesday, April 17

8:00–8:30	Pack and prepare for the day
8:30–9:20	Travel to first school
9:20–9:30	Prepare for students
9:30–10:00	Meet with students
10:00–10:30	Meet with other students
10:30–11:30	Test student
11:30–11:50	Travel to second school
11:50–12:00	Consult with teacher
12:00–12:30	Meet with student
12:30–1:15	Lunch downtown with student's mother
1:15–1:30	Travel to third school
1:30–2:00	Meet with student
2:00–2:35	Return to administrative office
2:35–3:25	Preassessment
3:25–3:30	Travel to another school in town
3:30–4:10	Prestaffing conference

Wednesday's totals: teaching (2 hours), consulting (10 minutes), preparation and planning (2 hours and 10 minutes), travel (2 hours and 5 minutes), evaluation (1 hour), and lunch (45 minutes).

continued

Box 11.6   continued

Thursday, April 18

7:45–8:00	Prepare for the morning
8:00–8:35	Travel to first school
8:35–8:45	Consult with teachers
8:45–9:45	Meet with student
9:45–9:50	Consult with teacher
9:50–10:25	Return to school in home district
10:25–10:30	Prepare for students
10:30–11:00	Meet with student
11:00–11:30	Meet with students
11:30–11:35	Return phone call from a parent
11:35–12:00	Home for lunch
12:00–12:05	Travel to another school in town
12:05–12:15	Consult with teacher
12:15–12:45	Meet with student
12:45–1:40	Teach ASSET group
1:40–2:00	Complete paperwork for staffing
2:00–2:55	Travel to neighboring community for staffing
2:55–3:30	Consult with school psychologist and complete paperwork
3:30–4:40	Introduce new student into my program
4:40–5:30	Travel home

Thursday's totals: teaching (3 hours and 25 minutes), consulting (1 hour and 5 minutes), preparation and planning (1 hour and 50 minutes), travel (3 hours), and lunch (25 minutes).

Friday, April 19

8:00–10:00	Catch-up time for paperwork and planning for next week
10:00–11:00	Observe student
11:00–11:30	Consult with teachers
11:30–12:15	Lunch
12:15–12:30	Prepare for afternoon
12:30–12:45	Travel to first school
12:45–1:00	Consult with teachers
1:00–2:00	Lead ASSET group
2:00–2:15	Travel back to office
2:15–2:30	Prepare to test a student
2:30–3:25	Test a student
3:25–4:00	Office time to prepare for Monday moring

Friday's totals: teaching (1 hour), consulting (45 minutes), preparation and planning (3 hours and 5 minutes), travel (30 minutes), evaluation (1 hour and 55 minutes), and lunch (45 minutes).

Week totals:

Teaching	12 hours, 55 minutes
Consultation	3 hours, 55 minutes
Preparation & Planning	11 hours, 30 minutes
Travel	8 hours, 20 minutes
Evaluation	2 hours, 55 minutes
Lunch	3 hours
Total time worked	42 hours, 35 minutes
Average daily time	8 hours, 31 minutes

are tabulated, decisions can be made about how time might be allocated more efficiently, and how more time might be spent in more rewarding activities. In Box 11.6, the itinerant/consulting teacher in a rural special education district was surprised to learn that she spent about one-fifth of her time in travel between the schools she served, since it was broken up into many small amounts of time. She subsequently shared the information with her supervisor and together they rearranged her schedule to make her travel more efficient. Some teachers may use a similar approach to monitor their time

away from their jobs to help determine ways of increasing efficiency and involvement in rewarding activities.

The time demands of administrative tasks such as record keeping are frequently cited as stressors for many teachers. As part of time management strategies, it may be helpful to examine the data management system. Setting up efficient filing systems for curricular materials, tests, diagnostic materials, student records, and supplies requires an initial investment of time, but can result in more time available for other uses. In the same fashion, systems for collecting and summarizing students' academic and behavioral performance contribute to more efficient use of time. Some data management systems, particularly those that provide regular documentation of student performance, have been discussed in earlier sections. They are essential for teachers in designing students' programs and assessing progress. Frequently, paraprofessionals and even the students themselves can be trained to collect and summarize data.

For some teachers, it is important to have a transition time between school and home. One experienced teacher has learned to stop thinking about home and begin thinking about school at the halfway point during the ride to school. On her way home, she reverses her attention at the same point. Some find it helpful to leave their work at school as much as possible to allow for more undistracted involvement with family, friends, and other activities, although it may mean arriving earlier or staying later at school.

However individual teachers find to schedule their time on the job to be satisfying and efficient, it is important to cultivate a satisfying personal life beyond the job. This may mean involvement with family, community, organizations, hobbies, and activities that can serve as a counterbalance to job-related stress. Still, teachers must also exercise some care to avoid overextension. As Shaw, Bensky, and Dixon (1981, p. 27) caution, "if outside activities become so dominant that you get to school so exhausted or do not have time to fulfill professional responsibilities, burnout will surely ensue."

An additional structural strategy is the clarification of roles and responsibilities with supervisors. Specification of student caseload, nature and amount of support services, and other responsibilities should be jointly determined at the outset of a job and the beginning of each academic year, and renegotiated as necessary. Supervisors may be unaware of particular burdens a teacher is experiencing, and may be able to provide assistance after they are informed.

There are also times when a teacher may have to say no to additional responsibilities when they impair his or her ability to deliver appropriate services to students. Sometimes, additional responsibilities and assistance can be negotiated. For example, a teacher may agree to assume additional duties if relieved of some existing responsibilities through additional staff support.

Professional Growth

Teachers also should be open to change, innovation, and new opportunities. For some, change from one job role to another, from one school setting to another, or from one age level of students to another may provide both respite and fresh challenges. One teacher who has been observed by one of the authors over seven to eight years has successively taught in an elementary, self-contained BD classroom, a secondary program for mentally retarded students, a regular third grade class, and is now teaching in a junior high BD resource room. Since all of these positions have been within the same school district and most in the same building, there has been some continuity among colleagues, support services, supervisors, and physical environment. In this case, the special education director and principal supported her mobility, and the changes are professionally stimulating. For others, this much change and adjustment might be overwhelming.

Teachers should also seek opportunities for professional growth. They may do this independently by seeking and developing new materials and trying new methods. It can be helpful to view teaching as a series of experiments. The answers to what may work, or work best, are not always known before materials and methods are tried. Students with personality and behavioral problems are always presenting new challenges and teachers are faced with dilemmas that are not easily or fully resolved. Thus, teachers who actively seek ways to be more effective, while avoiding discouragement when those attempts do not succeed, can experience professional invigoration. Learning from colleagues, taking additional professional courses, reading relevant professional journals, and visiting other programs can be important sources of professional development.

There are expanding opportunities for involvement in professional organizations for educators of students with behavioral disorders. The most prominent of these is the Council for Children with Behavior Disorders (CCBD), a division of the Council for Exceptional Children (CEC). These organizations promote the interests of exceptional children and special educators in the United States and Canada. They include international, state and provincial, and even local organizations that sponsor regular annual conferences, attempt to influence legislation affecting special education, and publish journals on special educational issues.

The Council for Children with Behavioral Disorders (CCBD) gives special attention to the education of children with emotional and behavioral disorders. CCBD participates in the annual international CEC convention and supports topical and regional conferences as well. For example, CCBD has cosponsored national conferences on behaviorally disordered adolescents and has supported several regional conferences. There are now more than twenty state CCBD federations (Guetzloe, 1984). These provide opportunities for professional and social interaction and communication of common interests and concerns within states and provinces through conferences, retreats, and newsletters. Members of CCBD receive the quarterly journal *Behavioral Disorders*, which includes research, presentation of interventions and program descriptions, a forum for introducing provocative ideas and issues, and a newsletter reporting activity of the CCBD executive committee and announcing events of interest to the membership. Recently, CCBD has also sponsored a monograph, *TEACHING: Behaviorally Disordered Youth*, directed at teachers of behaviorally disordered students (Zabel, 1985, 1986a, 1987).

Another organization of interest to some special educators is the American Orthopsychiatry Association, a national association of social workers, special educators, psychiatrists, psychologists, and others involved in mental health professions, especially with children and families. For additional ideas on professional journals that publish material of interest to persons involved in the education of students with personality and behavioral disorders, the reader is encouraged to study the bibliography of this text and then to examine selected journals in libraries.

Other opportunities for professional growth are also available. In some states, independent organizations sponsor newsletters and conferences. The New York Special Educators of Emotionally Disturbed (NYSEED) is one example. In the midwest, a consortium of professionals, including teacher educators, teachers, administrators, and state departments of education personnel sponsor the annual Midwest Symposium for Leadership in Behavior Disorders each February in Kansas City, Missouri.

Professional activities such as these provide opportunities for teachers to learn from one another, stay abreast of current thinking and innovative practice within the field, influence public policy, provide professional leadership, and develop professional and social ties with those who have similar interests.

A final strategy suggested by Shaw, Bensky, and Dixon (1981) for preventing burnout is to consider career options. These may include other roles within special or regular education such as changes in the service delivery model or alternative job role (e.g., work-study coordinator, consultant, supervisor, placement team coordinator, administrator).

For some, careers outside of special education, or even outside of education, should be considered. Teaching students with personality and behavior disorders is not for everyone. Special educators frequently have talents that can be used in a wide variety of occupations. For some individuals, alternative professional opportunities may contribute less stress and greater satisfaction.

No one can expect a life completely free of stress. Given the nature of working with behaviorally disordered students, some stress "goes with the territory." The goal should be to minimize debilitating distress. There are no unequivocal solutions, but the strategies outlined above offer some possibilities to enhance the quality of professional and personal lives. Readers who wish additional, more detailed discussions of techniques for dealing with stress and burnout are encouraged to read the Shaw, Bensky, and Dixon (1981) monograph published by CEC.

Summary

The competence of teachers of behaviorally disordered students is critical to educational interventions. In this chapter we examined a variety of topics concerned with these teachers. We have seen that important teaching competencies for regular and special educators overlap, but that certain additional understandings, skills, and personal characteristics are important for teachers of these students. Although there has been some evolution in what are considered necessary competencies, there has also been a good deal of consensus among teachers and teacher educators.

We also looked at preparation of teachers and at some of the controversies surrounding preparation such as categorical versus noncategorical training, and provisional certification. Certain demographic characteristics of teachers were discussed in this context. Finally, we gave considerable attention to factors related to the occupational hazards of stress and burnout. Although teachers of behaviorally disordered students are at risk, there are several strategies that may help ameliorate stress and prevent burnout, to make this profession highly rewarding.

CHAPTER 12

The School–Home Partnership

Overview

Introduction

Judy Larson, a teacher in a middle school program for severely behaviorally disordered students, is a recipient of the "Teacher of the Year" award from the Council for Exceptional Children (CEC). When an interviewer asked her about the role of parents in her program, she responded:

"Parents are a very important part of my classroom. They can make the difference between success or failure in the student's attempt to change behavior.

"The parents of my students are welcome to come into the class, telephone, or set up an appointment to discuss any problems regarding their children. Many times I find myself just listening to concerns that don't have anything to do with the classroom. The wealth of information parents can provide to help the school staff in working with students can be very helpful. Each time a parent tries to assist in this manner, it renews my faith in the fact that parents do the very best they know how with the skills they have acquired" (Larson, 1987).

Throughout this book we have emphasized an ecological perspective on children's behavioral disorders. This integrative approach has proposed that behavior problems can be neither understood nor treated in isolation. Personality and conduct problems are not simply malfunctions of a child's personality, but represent aberrant patterns of interaction within the child's ecosystems. There is a lack of a goodness of fit between the child and the ecosystem.

In earlier chapters we examined conceptual models of emotional disturbance. Several (e.g., psychodynamic, behavioral, social learning) emphasize the personal and social forces that can contribute to problem behavior. Central among these is the influence of the family, particularly parents, on the emotional and behavioral adjustment of children. Our discussion of personality problems and conduct disorders stressed research and theory concerning the effects of dysfunctional family patterns and children's disordered behavior.

The ecological perspective acknowledges not just the family but the multiple factors that make up the child's entire school-home environment. It also recognizes the countervailing influences the child has on the family. Even in our discussion of dysfunctional families, we cautioned about drawing one-dimensional, cause-effect conclusions about the effects of families on individual child adjustment. As Thomas, Chess, and Birch (1968) showed, emotional and behavioral deviance appears to result from a combination of child temperamental traits interacting with the social environment. One corollary of this finding is that family problems are sometimes the result of a child whose temperamental traits strain parental toleration. Sometimes, a difficult child may exacerbate already existing family tensions and conflicts.

Certainly, some parent-child interaction patterns that we discussed in earlier chapters (e.g., overprotection, rejection, and double-bind communication), as well as marital conflicts, marital schism, and divorce, place children at risk for behavioral disorders (Guidubaldi & Perry, 1984). Still, many children who experience these stressors seem able to cope with them and do not develop serious personality or conduct disorders.

Importance of Parent Involvement

The ecological perspective acknowledges that the family does not operate in an ecological vacuum. Social, economic, and cultural forces have an impact on the family and its individual members. The availability of resources and services can enhance or limit how a family is able to meet its needs.

The importance of meaningful parent involvement in educational programs for their children has been discussed in our chapters on assessment (Chapter 3), designing individual educational programs, and determining appropriate placements (Chapter 10). In our discussion of assessment, for example, we detailed legal requirements to inform and obtain consent from parents to engage in individual assessment that might lead to the identification and placement of their child. In addition, we stressed that parents can be excellent sources of information about their child. Their intimate knowledge can

aid educators' understanding of the child's personal and educational history, as well as provide information about current circumstances that affect performance and behavior.

A good deal has been written about the importance of special educators actively involving parents in the education of their exceptional children (Kroth, 1975; Kroth & Simpson, 1977; Losen & Losen, 1985; Paul, 1981; Schultz, 1987; Shea & Bauer, 1985). Our chapters describing behavioral (Chapter 8) and psychoeducational (Chapter 9) interventions have tended to emphasize school-based programs. However, we have also pointed out how some of these interventions can be adapted to involve parents and other family members. For example, contracting is a behavioral intervention that can involve both school and home. Home-school contingency plans can be designed for parents to provide back-up support at home for their child's school performance (Swassing, 1984). Social skills training programs, as presented in our chapter on psychoeducational interventions, sometimes rely on homework that has students practice newly learned skills at home and in other environments outside of school.

As we have stressed earlier, the right of parents to participate in identification, programming, and placement decisions is ensured by PL 94-142. This legal right is based on the assumption that parents have interests and knowledge that can contribute to their child's education. Professional literature generally supports this assumption (Shea & Bauer, 1985). Many special educators have advocated the need for the systematic training of parents in order that they may be kept abreast and involved. This chapter examines special considerations for communication and participation with parents of behaviorally disordered students. Our discussion will include the determination of parents' needs, interests, and skills for involvement, as well as strategies for enhancing their participation to contribute to their child's educational program.

Special Considerations with Parents of Behaviorally Disordered Children

Parents of behaviorally disordered children have some similar characteristics with parents of other types of handicapped children. Yet there are some real differences, too. A diagnosis of exceptionality is usually a traumatic experience for family members. Roger Kroth (1975) has discussed the emotional stages that parents of handicapped children experience in the process of recognizing their child's handicap: shock, denial, guilt, sorrow, withdrawal, fear, overprotectiveness or rejection, and, finally, acceptance. With some types of exceptionality an educational diagnosis may be no surprise. In fact, in the case of some physical and intellectual disabilities, family members often have long been aware of the handicaps, although perhaps not fully informed of their educational implications. Because most behaviorally disordered children look "normal" there is often no apparent reason for their disordered behavior.

Parents of behaviorally disordered students experience some of the same feelings as other parents, but not necessarily in the same sequence. Some, for example, continue to feel guilty about their possible causal role in the child's problems. Many parents are embarrassed about the social stigma that frequently accompanies personality and conduct problems. Some defensively deny that their child has problems. Some blame schools for the problems, or at least for not solving the problems. In some cases, parents' views may be legitimate.

Being a parent is difficult even under the best of circumstances. Parenting a disabled child is particularly challenging. Parents of children considered behaviorally disordered must also deal with the stigma associated with emotional and behavioral deviance and the common, though often unfair, assumption that they have caused the problems through inadequate parenting. Even when the existing evidence points strongly in this direction, it should be remembered that parents encounter life experiences over which they may have little control. In any case, an assignment of blame is fruitless. Although understanding family history, dynamics, current conditions, and resources may be integral in designing and implementing effective interventions, pointing the finger at the family or any other single source of a child's maladjustment serves no useful purpose. In the remainder of this chapter we will look closely at some ways parents can be involved in the education of behaviorally disordered children.

Assessing Parents

There are as many kinds of families as there are people who compose them. The variations in family constellations, ways of interacting, personalities, economics, and social factors are virtually limitless. Consider, for example, the many varieties of family structures a child may experience. They include:

- intact
- single parent
- divorced
- separated
- foster
- adoptive
- recombined

A large and increasing proportion of children are part of nontraditional families (i.e., live in a situation other than with both biological parents). It is not uncommon, for example, for children to be assigned to the joint custody of divorced parents. They may spend a period of time, such as one to two years, with one parent and then the next period of time with the other. Or, they may live with one parent on weekdays and the other on weekends.

Without making any qualitative judgments of the relative advantages and disadvantages to a child from such arrangements, it is clear that family dynamics can become more complex simply by virtue of the number of people and environments with which the child must interact. Such nontraditional family arrangements also present challenges to schools for communicating with and involving parents in their child's education. In addition, some behaviorally disordered children and adolescents live in group homes, residential treatment facilities, mental health, and correctional facilities.

Families are not static entities. They are constantly changing and evolving as a result of changing physical, intellectual, emotional, social, economic, and cultural factors. Families are influenced by factors both internal and external to them. For example, a family with an alcoholic father may at times focus its attention on the drinking problem and its related problems of lost income, the father's absence from the home, physical and verbal abuse, and the social stigma of alcoholism. A variety of circumstances may alter this situation. The father may obtain treatment for alcoholism or periodically stop drinking and resume a contributory or at least benign role in the family. The problems associated with the alcoholism may diminish, allowing the family to devote more attention to other issues. On the other hand, the marriage may dissolve. This might result in lowered tensions associated with the neglect, abuse, and stigma, but might also bring increased economic stresses for the family and require a reshuffling of the remaining familial relationships.

Recognizing that many permutations of every pattern exist, it may be helpful from an educational perspective to think in terms of four general types of families. These we categorize as involved, overwhelmed, unresponsive, and hostile.

Involved Parents

Most parents of behaviorally disordered students are actively concerned about and involved in their child's education and treatment at some level. These are parents who tend to the basic needs of their child. To the best of their abilities, they see that their child is adequately fed, clothed, and cared for.

In addition, they assume a supportive role in their child's education. They participate in parent-teacher and IEP conferences. They respond to school-home communications. Some may participate in parent support groups and actively seek support for their children and themselves from school and nonschool resources. A few even participate in collaborative interventions with schools and serve as advocates for their own and other exceptional children (Simpson & Poplin, 1981).

There are also parents who have the interest and desire to be involved directly in their child's educational program, but because of other demands (work or child-care responsibilities) must limit their involvement. Nevertheless, their support and encouragement can be important contributions.

Overwhelmed Parents

Unlike involved parents, overwhelmed parents seem to have neither the energy, resources, or, sometimes, the know-how to be actively involved in their child's education. There are a variety of reasons parents are overwhelmed. Some are exhausted by repeated failure to solve their child's problems, and have given up. Some have experienced chronic economic stress due to unemployment or underemployment. For example, in a single parent family supported by welfare, the family may face chronic, insufficient financial resources to meet even basic needs for food, shelter, and clothing (Edelman, 1987). The family may be forced to live in housing projects in disorganized neighborhoods where crime and drugs are ever-present realities.

In addition to problems at school, the child may also present problems at home and in the neighborhood. Parents may have tried to solve the child's problems but have met with repeated failure. They may have sought outside support but found it lacking. They and other family members may encounter behavioral, emotional, or legal problems that they are ill-equipped to handle. In short, overwhelmed parents not only have very little energy and skills left for school involvement, but have depleted their own resources. Many overwhelmed parents have given up solving their child's problems or are focused on more pressing survival issues.

Unresponsive Parents

Unresponsive parents are sometimes difficult to recognize. Some are obsessively involved in arenas such as careers or social activities that do not include their child. Although some of these parents have the financial and intellectual potential to contribute to their child's well-being, other interests and involvements take precedence. The result is a type of neglect in which there is inadequate supervision, extreme permissiveness, and absent role models. Some unresponsive parents express willingness to participate but fail to follow through on their commitments.

Other unresponsive parents are intimidated by school personnel, and so maintain a distance. Parents' own lack of education and cultural and language differences sometimes affect their willingness to become involved with schools. Others are insecure in the role of parent and feel uneasy about having a child who is considered to have problems. Whatever the reasons for their unresponsiveness, they cannot be counted on for reliable support and involvement in their child's educational program.

Hostile Parents

There is a minority of parents who are actually hostile toward educators. Hostility is sometimes overtly, but more often covertly, expressed. Some of these people have had unhappy experiences in their own schooling. They may have experienced academic failure and conflicts with school authorities.

Some parents disagree with the diagnosis of their child as behaviorally disordered. Kaufman, Swan, and Wood (1980) found significant discrepancies between teachers' and psychoeducational evaluators' and parents', particularly black

parents', ratings of children's behavior problems. Kaufman, et al. speculate that sociocultural and socioeconomic factors influence perceptions of behavior disorders.

Some parents do not approve of specific educational methods used with their child. They may not, for example, believe that time-out is an appropriate measure, or they may disapprove of the way it is used. Some parents do not believe that their children should be "bribed" with reinforcers to modify their behavior. Others may want the schools to stick with academic interventions and not attempt to be therapists for their children. In some cases, of course, hostile parents' distrust develops out of legitimate concerns about the mistreatment of their child.

Some hostile parents avoid direct interaction with school personnel, yet share their criticisms with their children. The result can be not only lack of support but a real undermining of the school's efforts. For others, involvement is punctuated by active and direct conflict. Losen and Losen (1985) have outlined several ways educators can defuse conflicts with belligerent and defensive parents. They include:

- avoid confrontations at team meetings
- if possible, defer decisions until major conflicts are resolved
- appeal to a sense of reason for the child's sake
- openly acknowledge that parents have an intelligent point of view
- directly acknowledge, discuss, and deal with sources of parent hostility
- obtain independent consultation when necessary

When parent-school conflicts arise, the immediate goal should be to avoid counterdefensive behavior. Parents should be reassured that school personnel are also concerned with the child's best interests. Teachers and other school personnel should attempt to clarify the conflicts and try to deal with them calmly and objectively. When possible in conflict situations, attempts should be made to defer discussion to a later time when tempers have cooled and when more objective parties can be included.

The most difficult situations involve dealing with emotionally unstable parents and those with alcohol or drug problems. Sometimes, these parents are unresponsive, passive, and despondent. Others are consistently confrontational and unpredictable. They may disrupt meetings with antagonistic outbursts, threaten legal action or even, though rarely, physical retaliation. In such cases, school-home interactions may be no more than routine and ritual. They are best handled with calm reassurance about the good intentions of school personnel and attempts to correct and clarify parent perceptions.

Fortunately, few parents can be characterized as either unresponsive or hostile. Most parents have their child's best interest at heart and want their child to succeed in school. Many parents who are initially hostile and unresponsive become trusting toward schools after they see their child making progress in a special program. Of course, even involved and supportive parents sometimes disagree about the educational services their child should be or is receiving. In addition, the patterns of parent involvement outlined above are not unique to parents of behaviorally disordered students. They are also found among parents of well-adjusted children.

Each of these patterns provides challenges for special educators, particularly teachers of behaviorally disordered students. The challenge for dealing with involved parents is how to channel their interests and energies to benefit the child. The challenge for dealing with overwhelmed parents is helping them meet their family's basic needs so they can retain some energy for dealing with their child. For unresponsive parents, channels of communication must be established so they can understand how their involvement can contribute to the growth and adjustment of their child. The challenge for dealing with hostile parents is defusing their distrust of schools and demonstrating that the school personnel also have their child's best interest at heart.

Obviously, these are not easy tasks. However,

given the opportunity, support, and encouragement, most parents can become involved at some level in their child's education. In some cases, the level of involvement may consist only of not undercutting the school's efforts. For other parents, involvement may be limited to receiving information from school. For others, it may mean active involvement in educational planning and actual participation in interventions. In the following sections, we will examine some of the ways teachers and other school personnel can facilitate various levels of parent involvement.

Limits of the Teacher as Family Therapist

Teachers and other educators are not typically trained to be family therapists. Their involvement with parents and other members of their students' families should be limited and they should not be expected to answer all of a family's needs. Certainly, in cases where families are experiencing severe social-emotional difficulties, where there is serious psychopathology, where there is child abuse and neglect, alcohol and drug abuse, and marital difficulties, teachers and other educators cannot cure all problems. The educator's primary responsibility is to the student. There are even occasions when teachers must take an adversarial role with parents in the interest of protecting a child. For example, when the teacher suspects or has actual evidence of child abuse, the teacher is obligated to report it to appropriate civil authorities.

In most cases, sources of formal and informal services and support beyond the school must also be involved in the treatment of behaviorally disordered children. These include, but are not limited to, extended families, churches, community and recreational resources, physicians, social welfare agencies, corrections, public and private counselors, mental health services, and child protection agencies. For many behaviorally disordered children, school is the one support system in which they are actively involved. This does not mean that schools must independently attempt to meet all of a child's needs. It does mean, however, that school personnel, particularly teachers, frequently must help parents find those additional sources of services for their children.

Communication Strategies and Skills

Parents of exceptional students differ in their needs and desires for involvement in their child's educational programs. Roger Kroth (1980) has proposed a model of parent involvement that divides involvement into two areas: (1) the need and desire to receive professional service, and (2) provide parental service. In each of these areas, Kroth says there are different levels of participation determined by how many (all, most, some, few) might be expected to participate. For example, nearly all parents could provide some information regarding their child's social and school history. Most parents can provide relevant information and participate in the IEP process. Some might participate in a parent support group or attend parent education workshops. Only a few might volunteer their services in the classrooms or form and conduct parenting workshops. Kroth believes that lower levels of participation are a prerequisite to higher levels.

Levels of Involvement

Alexander, Kroth, Simpson, and Poppelreiter (1982) have distinguished different levels of parent involvement according to the following hierarchy: awareness; knowledge and information; meaningful exchanges and interaction; and skill acquisition and training. Educators should determine the level of participation each parent wishes to attain and then strive to increase parental involvement in ways that benefit the child.

At the awareness level, it is a legal requirement that parents be informed about laws and regulations pertaining to educational programs for handicapped children. In addition, they need to know their child's and their own rights. (In Chapter 3 we outlined the points at which parents need to be involved in the assessment process.)

Contributions to the Assessment Process

Parents can be a valuable source of several types of information. In assessing both type and degree of behavioral problems, for instance, it can be important to determine similarities and differences in home and school perceptions. Educators' understanding of the nature of behavior problems, as well as the design and implementation of interventions, can be aided by an understanding of parents' views. Parents can provide information about their child in settings other than school, about interventions that have been attempted at home, about family involvement in other support systems within the community, about relationships within the family and other social groupings, and about the developmental status of the child and family.

These kinds of information may be gathered in structured interviews conducted by the BD teacher or consultant, school social worker, or school psychologist. Sodac, Nichols, and Gallagher (1985) suggest that parent interviews should include the following types of information:

1. Information about the problem—nature, frequency, severity, effect on family members, causes, contributing factors, and attempted solutions.
2. Developmental landmarks—significant physical, emotional, and social milestones, diseases, and injuries.
3. Family roles—patterns of authority and discipline, problem-solving approaches, and relationships within the family.
4. Family origins—information about extended family, health, and social relationships.
5. Family network—social involvements within the family and community for each family member.

6. Significant stress factors—past and current potential stress factors, including illnesses, deaths, separations, moves, changes in family constellations, occupations, and financial conditions.
7. Educational history—child's initial and subsequent adjustments to school and previous academic and behavioral functioning of the child and educational experiences of other family members.

Parents' perceptions of their child can be collected in a format that is appropriate to the child and the family. The interview may take the form of a written questionnaire, a structured interview, or some combination of both. Obviously, the parents' writing and verbal skills, willingness, and ability to provide this kind of information must be considered. Parents' right to privacy should be respected, and only information that is relevant to understanding the child and to designing interventions should be solicited. Roger Kroth and Richard Simpson (1977) have provided the following guidelines for conducting a parent interview: It should be conducted in a private, quiet setting. It should be held in a positive atmosphere, although the interviewer should be prepared for hidden motivations. The interviewer should attend to both verbal and nonverbal responses. Parents' right to privacy should be respected.

In addition to their contributions to educational assessment, parent interviews provide other potential benefits. They sometimes help parents understand their child, what is expected of the child in school, and relationships between home and school behavior (Sodac, et al., 1985). In addition, a parent interview can lay the foundation for ongoing family involvement with the school.

IEP Development

The IEP process discussed in Chapter 10 should provide a means of meaningful exchanges and interactions between parents and the other members of the IEP team. To ensure this is a worthwhile process, educators must attempt to arrange meeting times convenient to parents, provide parents with information about the purpose of the meeting and format, avoid professional jargon and insider professional language (so that parents are not unduly intimidated), and actively solicit parents' ideas, information, and support. It helps to assign a team member to meet parents at the door, offer coffee, and be responsible for introductions among team members. Since parents are often the only nonprofessionals at the meeting, each person might wear a name tag identifying his or her professional role.

IEP meetings should include an agreement on a plan for regular communication between the school and parents that relates progress on identified objectives. The importance of parent involvement in the IEP process cannot be overstressed. If IEP development increases parents' belief in the value of the special education plan and their trust in educators, they are more likely to provide ongoing support for it.

When students are placed in a behavior disorders program, it can be helpful to ask parents about the ways they would like to be involved in their child's program. Shea and Bauer (1985) have designed a Parents' Needs Form (included in Appendix E) to help determine the types of involvement the parents desire or will accept.

A companion Parent Activities Form is found in Appendix F. This form asks parents to indicate the ways they might contribute to their child's development. The possibilities range from *Help my child learn* to *Teach my child to express feelings in a socially acceptable manner*. With this information, the teacher may talk with parents, provide readings, arrange parent group meetings, or arrange social worker contacts to address these topics.

Communication with Parents

Preferences of Parents and Teachers

There are several ways that parents and teachers can communicate regarding the performance of behaviorally disordered students. However, parents and teachers of behaviorally disordered students do not always concur on preferred types of communication. In a study involving a large, geographically diverse sample of teachers and parents of behaviorally disordered students, McCarney (1986) asked respondents to rate their preferences of twenty potential types of parent-teacher communication. Although the ratings of the two groups did not differ significantly for half of the items, they did differ for the other ten.

According to parents, the five most preferred types of communication were:

- phone calls from teacher to parent (93.9%)
- report cards (90.4%)
- parent-teacher conference at school (88.5%)
- phone calls from parent to teacher (86.5%)
- student's work sent home by teacher (84.9%)

Teachers' top five types of communication, in order, were:

- parent-teacher conference at school (95%)
- phone calls from teacher to parent (94.5%)
- IEP meeting (92.9%)
- phone calls from parent to teacher (84.9%)
- parent-teacher conference including student (80%)

According to both parents and teachers, telephone communication and parent-teacher conferences at school are mutually valued forms of communication.

Teachers, however, did not view either report cards or students' work sent home by teacher as highly as did parents. The two groups also differed concerning the value of IEP meetings and parent-teacher conferences that included the student; parents preferred both of these less than teachers.

Although the most preferred modes of communication can help guide the selection of communication strategies, it is also instructive to know which received the least favorable ratings. In the McCarney study, parents' lowest preferences were for the following types of communication:

- parent-teacher conference at home (51%)
- parent group meeting (51%)
- parent-teacher conference including other adults (44.2%)
- PTA meetings (38.9%)
- parent-teacher meeting other than at home or school (38.8%)

Teachers' lowest preferences corresponded with several of these (parent-teacher meetings other than school or home, 47.8%; parent group meetings, 45.8%; PTA meetings, 23%). Also, few teachers expressed a preference for either parent classroom observation (45.9%) or parent drop-in meeting with the teacher (39%), both items that considerably more parents rated high.

McCarney (1986) concluded that parents and teachers do agree on some of the most and least useful types of communication, but they also disagree on some others that have great potential for improving school-home relations and enhancing students' school success. It is difficult to know if the rated preferences are based on actual experiences using the types of communication, or if they are simply speculations on potential types of communication. Some types may not have been preferred, because the respondents had no experience with them.

We cannot conclude from the McCarney study that some types of parent-school communication should be avoided simply because they are not preferred by most teachers and parents. Rather, some of these may need to be approached differently so they are more useful for parents and teachers alike. Also, even though only a minority prefer a particular type of communication, it may be effective for those persons. Educators should attempt to determine individual parent preferences and try to accommodate them. It may also be helpful for parents and teachers to discuss why some are preferred and others are not. Finally, it must be remembered that some parents of exceptional children prefer limited involvement with school when they believe it will benefit themselves, their child, or their family (MacMillan & Turnbull, 1983).

Communication Considerations

In any plan for parent-teacher communication, individual conditions as well as preferences must be considered. Some of these are the availability of a telephone, transportation, parent work schedules, needs for child care, and fluency in English. Also, parents sometimes can be overburdened with expectations from teachers for involvement at school and should be allowed not to be actively involved if they wish (Kroth, 1980; Winton & Turnbull, 1981).

Types of Communication and Involvement

In addition to legal requirements for parental involvement in the assessment (Chapter 3) and IEP (Chapter 10) processes, there are several ways parent involvement can be facilitated. Some of these require relatively minimal and passive involvement; others require substantial and active participation and contributions to the child's educational programs. We are not suggesting that every program should use all of the following strategies, but rather that methods be tailored to the needs of students, the needs and interests of parents, and the capabilities of the school, especially the teacher.

Parent Handbooks

When a student is placed in a special education program, and at the beginning of each school year, a handbook can be used as a means to communicate a variety of useful information to parents. It can be a reference book that adds to parents' understanding of the special program and that helps them prepare their child for it. Schools sometimes prepare parent handbooks; sometimes individual teachers prepare handbooks about their classrooms. Although the specific contents of parent handbooks will differ according to the nature of the program, they may include the following:

- lists of necessary school supplies
- daily schedules
- school year calendar that highlights important events such as holidays, parent-teacher conferences, and parent group meetings
- summary of books and programs used with the student
- sample progress report forms
- suggested procedures for visiting the school or classroom
- guidelines for communicating with the teacher
- classroom and school rules and consequences of infractions
- overview of behavior management techniques (e.g., token economy, time-out) and other interventions (e.g., affective education, social skills training)
- bus and cafeteria rules
- names, professional roles, and telephone numbers of relevant school personnel
- list of the available social services outside of school

Samples of suggestions for visiting school and guidelines for special conferences are included in Box 12.1.

Parent Information Meetings

Periodically, and particularly near the beginning of the school year, parent information meetings should be scheduled. These can provide opportunities to inform parents of the nature and purpose of the special program, introduce staff members, answer questions, and solicit parents' questions and concerns. In some school districts, a designated parent facilitator organizes and leads these meetings. In others, special education administrators, teachers, or other special services staff serve as facilitators. Meetings may be open to all parents or limited to those whose children are in a particular program.

The purpose of these meetings is primarily informational. Speakers may discuss topics like special education services available in the school district, parent participation in developing IEPs

---

Box12.1 Suggestions for Visiting School

We'd like you to visit our school whenever you can. Because we want you to see a typical school program, we ask you to observe these rules:

1. Check in at the office before entering the classroom.
2. During discussion and formal group activities, please remain seated and do not converse with the children.
3. During work periods you may move around the room and watch the children at work or look at our materials.
4. Jot down any questions and comments for discussion with the teacher later.

We hope you enjoy your visit.

Special Conferences

You may wish to schedule a special conference with me concerning your child. Any time you wish to speak to me, you may call the school and the secretary will take a message. I am at school at 7:40 A.M. and I usually leave at 4:00 P.M. If these times are not convenient, we can try to schedule a more suitable time to meet. Your comments and concerns are important to me, so feel free to contact me at these times.

---

and in parent-teacher conferences, or community mental health services.

Progress Reports

In addition to report cards on academic performance that usually correspond to those used in regular programs, daily and weekly reports of academic and behavioral performance provide another means of communicating with parents. In Chapter 8 we included an example of a weekly report card, associated with a token economy, that could be used with students who are integrated in departmentalized regular classes. That kind of weekly report card serves as motivation for the student, provides ongoing evaluative data for the teacher, and can be collected and used to make programming decisions. Weekly report cards can also be sent home to parents to inform them of their child's performance, or kept and shared with them at parent-teacher conferences.

Regular reports that parents sign, comment on, and return to school can ensure that teachers, parents, and the student have common information about what is happening in school (Hutton, 1983). Box 12.2 contains an example

of a report form that could be used on a daily basis with elementary level students. Parents can review, sign, and return it with their child the following day. This report form can also be easily adapted to a weekly schedule.

A variation of report forms is the special achievement certificate that can be sent home to inform parents of their child's special achievements. Box 12.3 contains two examples. Similar achievement awards are available from commercial publishers, although they can also be designed by teachers to fit a particular program. Some teachers post several kinds of award certificates and allow students to choose which they wish to take home. Certificates may be used both to reward student accomplishment and to inform parents, who frequently do not have a history of positive communications, about their child.

Newsletters

Class and school newsletters provide another vehicle for communicating with parents (Imber, Imber, & Rothstein, 1979). They can provide information about school activities, past and upcoming special events, and recognition of stu-

---

Box12.2   Example of a Report Form

Report Card For: _____   Date: _____

😊 GREAT   😐 FAIR   🙁 POOR

Spelling
Work Complete
Behavior

Reading
Work Complete
Behavior

Math
Work Complete
Behavior

Social Studies/Science
Work Complete
Behavior

Music/PE/Library
Work Complete
Behavior

Morning Exercises
Work Complete
Behavior

A.M. **Recess**
Behavior

P.M. **Recess**
Behavior

Parent Signature _____   Comments _____

---

dent accomplishments. Weekly or monthly newsletters may routinely include information such as a calendar of events and lunch menus, as well as feature articles on upcoming field trips, special presentations, and parent meetings. Often, much of the writing, printing, and distribution can be undertaken by students, particularly at the upper elementary and secondary levels. Articles may profile teachers, describe programs, and report on field trips; students' creative writing, poetry, and drawings might be included.

Telephone Communication

According to the McCarney (1986) study, one of the most preferred types of communication for both teachers and parents is via the telephone.

It is convenient and allows for direct, two-way communication. Some teachers like to talk with parents on a regular, perhaps weekly, basis to inform them of their child's performance. The telephone also permits more immediate communication about events that have occurred during the school day that parents need to know about and that teachers need information or feedback on. The telephone can also provide a more personal means of communication than written notices about upcoming parent-teacher conferences, parent group meetings, and IEP meetings. When home-based interventions have been implemented, the telephone allows for ongoing communication about them.

Home-school communication systems that use automatic telephone answering devices can provide a convenient method of parent-teacher

Box 12.3   Sample Recognition Awards

AWARD OF ACHIEVEMENT

This certifies that _____

has achieved highly in _____

OFFICIAL
———
SEAL

_____   /_____/_____

Signature   Date

GOOD-NEWS-GRAM:

_____

_____

_____

_____

_____   /_____/_____

Signed   Date

interaction (Minner, Beane, & Prater, 1986; Test, Cooke, Weiss, Heward, & Heron, 1986). The answering machine can record messages from teachers to parents, as well as allowing parents to leave messages for school personnel. With this system, teachers can inform parents of current and upcoming class activities and academic assignments. They can make suggestions for reinforcing school activities and behavior at home and can report on individual student behavior and performance at school. Confidentiality can be provided by using code numbers rather than students' names. Minner, et al. (1986) suggest that teachers use recorded telephone messages to improve student self-concept and parents' perceptions of their children by reviewing daily activities and making at least one positive comment about each student. In addition, parents can indicate that they have heard the teacher's recorded message, report any significant events to the teacher, and request further communication if desired.

Parents sometimes use telephone communication with the teacher to obtain ideas, support, and encouragement to deal with their child at home. Teachers can often help parents simply by serving as an objective listener, reflecting on parents' thoughts and feelings.

Parent-Teacher Conferences

Another of the communication techniques preferred by both parents and teachers of behaviorally disordered students is the parent-teacher conference. Conferences typically occur at school, usually in the classroom, but are sometimes arranged at the student's home or another location. Although a home visit may be convenient for parents and provide insights for the teacher about the student's home life, parents and teachers are frequently uncomfortable meeting in the home.

Parent-teacher conferences can be used to provide information on student performance, discuss plans for future interventions, and enlist parent support and ideas. A major advantage of parent-teacher conferences is that they involve face-to-face communication. Both verbally and nonverbally, these direct encounters can help build mutual trust that contributes to supportive relationships between parents and teachers.

An obvious disadvantage of conferences is that they can be difficult to schedule at a mutually agreeable time. On scheduled conference days, teachers should attempt to coordinate the timing of conferences with the student's other teachers and with teachers of siblings who may be in the same school.

Sometimes a parent-teacher conference is arranged to address a specific issue. For example, the teacher may wish to discuss with parents the prospects for reintegrating a student into a less restrictive educational placement, before the teacher meets with the multidisciplinary team. Or, the teacher may want to enlist parent participation in a behavior management plan, to discuss with parents the need for and potential sources of counseling or other resources for the student and the family.

In the Developmental Therapy program, Peggy Wood (1975) has suggested several topics special educators should keep in mind to direct their exchanges with parents. She suggests the following:

- clarify the objectives of conferences
- identify current objectives for the student
- explain how the program attempts to meet the objectives
- discuss how the objectives and the student's behavior may have changed since previous meetings
- determine if parents have noted changes at home

It is important both to report on progress, problems, and changes in students' programs, and to obtain parents' perceptions of problems, goals, and growth. Teachers can determine which activities parents are using at home, what objectives are a high priority for them, and what kinds of participation are reasonable to expect. Wood stresses the importance of conveying a sense of confidence that the child is progressing by providing evaluative data and samples of student performance.

In both telephone and face-to-face communication with parents, teachers should attempt to be positive. As noted earlier, parents often have had little positive communication from school personnel about their child. Thus, teachers should use every opportunity to contact parents about the accomplishments of their children. When problems or crises must be reported, they will then be balanced by these positive reports. Even when discussing problems, the teacher should maintain a positive problem-solving tone.

At the conclusion of telephone and face-to-face communications, the content should be summarized to affirm the consensus of parents and teacher, and plans for future communication made. To provide a written record, teachers should maintain a log of all conversations with parents.

School Programs

Some schools schedule annual or semiannual open houses and other programs (e.g., music programs, field days, art displays). Behaviorally disordered students can often participate in them. These programs provide informal opportunities for families to go to schools and classrooms to appreciate and recognize their children's performances.

Parent Volunteers

Some parents are interested and able to provide direct assistance to their child's special education program. They may, for example, prepare snacks for class parties. A few may be able to contribute more actively by participating in behavior management projects, providing mutual support for other parents, preparing supplies for classroom activities, and chaperon-

ing field trips. Some parents may even be interested in serving on parent advisory committees that serve as advocates for exceptional students and their families.

Teachers of behaviorally disordered students cannot expect that many parents will be able to assume these roles, although a few will. A parent volunteer questionnaire such as that devised by Shea and Bauer (1985) in Appendix G can help teachers determine how parents' interests and skills can best be used.

Parent Support Groups

One of the striking results of the McCarney study is the relatively low preference expressed by both parents and teachers for parent support groups. This may result from lack of experience in groups or the discomfort parents may feel identifying with such a group. Still, the efficacy of parent groups for some parents should not be categorically disregarded.

Groups can be formed to meet a variety of goals. They may be informational, instructional, or provide mutual support. Many include activities related to all three of these goals. Parent groups can also take a variety of forms. Some are limited to parents of behaviorally disordered students; others may include parents of any exceptional children and other interested parents. Some support groups are led by school social workers, psychologists, or trained parent facilitators. Others are led by a BD teacher, coordinator, or consulting teacher.

Although all parents of handicapped children face some degree of loneliness in raising their children, parents of behaviorally disordered children have the added burden of social stigma. As we have previously discussed, a child's emotional and behavioral disorders are commonly, although often incorrectly, viewed as a reflection of poor parenting. Consequently, parents experience feelings of guilt, self-blame, remorse, and apprehension in facing school authorities. They frequently prefer that others not know that their child is considered behaviorally disor-

---

Box 12.4   Sample Letter to Target Group of Parents

Saratoga Elementary School
Lincoln, Nebraska

1988–1989 School Year:

Dear Parents:

Parenting is an enjoyable and rewarding job. It is also a demanding one, and requires many skills.

Sometimes it is possible to acquire parenting skills from one another by sharing ideas and experiences. In addition, sometimes it is helpful for one parent who is experiencing a troublesome situation with a child to visit with another parent who has experienced the same situation. We all need support, understanding, and a chance to be "revitalized."

In an effort to offer support, Saratoga sponsors a Parent Support Group. This support group meets one evening per month at Saratoga Elementary School, and is offered to parents of children enrolled in special education programs. Activities include discussions, group problem solving, short informational talks, and time for socializing. Topics discussed include: talking to children; how to praise and criti-

cize; effective ways to resolve conflict; helping sources; working with schools; and how to communicate effectively and painlessly with your child. We hope you'll show your support by becoming a member of this group.

If you would be interested in participating in this Parent Support Group, please indicate by marking the "Yes" line below, and have your child return this to Kathie Phillips, Room 102, Saratoga Elementary School. More detailed information will be sent to those who indicate interest. Thank you.

Sincerely,

Kathie Phillips
Teacher, Room 102

Saratoga Elementary School
Lincoln, Nebraska

Please return to Room 102, Kathie Phillips

_____ Yes
_____ No
Child's Name _____
Parent's Name _____

Source: K. Phillips, "Parents as Partners: Developing Parent Support Groups." In M. K. Zabel (Ed.), *TEACH-* *ING: Behaviorally Disordered Students* (Reston, VA: Council for Exceptional Children, 1985), p. 31.

---

dered. Many parents feel their children's problems should be hidden. A reflection of this stigma is the absence of any national organization of parents, such as those that have been formed to advocate for mentally retarded, learning disabled, or physically handicapped children. The National Society for Autistic Children (NSAC) includes many parents and other family members of autistic children, but as we pointed out in Chapter 6, autism is generally believed to have an organic, rather than environmental, etiology.

Kathryn Phillips (1985), a teacher of behaviorally disordered children as well as a parent of a son with behavioral disorders, has shared her experiences in forming and facilitating a parent support group. Given the need, yet the reluctance, of parents to participate in mutual support groups, Phillips considers the initial development and recruitment of members the most difficult task facing the group leader. She suggests several strategies. First, a letter explaining the group's purpose and possible functions can be sent to parents. (See Box 12.4 for an example.) The idea for a parent group can be presented at staff meetings, parent-teacher conferences, IEP meetings, and in other telephone and face-to-face contacts with parents. School administrators, school social workers and psychologists, and BD consultants should be informed of the group's existence so they can inform interested parents.

Once a group has been contacted and a meeting time and place arranged, planning the initial meeting is critical. Phillips believes that the group leader must determine group members' goals and their preferences for the structure and format of meetings. A warm-up activity that facilitates getting to know one another is helpful. One possibility is providing a few minutes for one group member to tell another about himself or herself. Then each parent can introduce another to the rest of the group. Phillips also suggests beginning with a sentence completion task, including statements such as:

- The most enjoyable thing about being a parent is _____ .
- The most frustrating thing about being a parent is _____ .
- I love it when _____ .
- I don't like it when _____ .
- Something I do well as a parent is _____ .
- Something I need to focus on as a parent is _____ .

It is important to include positive statements in this type of activity. The completed sentences can be used as the basis for a discussion in which parents share their responses as they feel comfortable.

Although some groups may generate their own ideas for topics and activities, it can be helpful to have a schedule partially planned for future meetings. This can be determined by using a parent questionnaire. A sample agenda designed by Phillips is included in Box 12.5.

Each meeting may consist of a planned activity, such as a talk or discussion led by a professional on a topic of interest to the group. Professionals should be selected who can communicate with parents without intimidating them or talking down to them. Meetings should allow time for members to ask questions and raise concerns.

Phillips cautions that the group leader must be prepared to troubleshoot. Chief among potential problems is the placement of too much reliance on the group leader as the expert who can solve all problems and answer all questions. When this happens, the leader may redirect questions to the group. Another potentially serious problem is the situation when some parents need more professional counseling and support than the group can provide, but who still use it in place of other resources. In such a situation, the group can provide support and assistance to these individuals to find additional sources of support.

The individual needs of group members must be met if the group is to be successful. For example, questions can be directed at group members who seldom participate or deflected from persons who tend to dominate discussions.

Counseling Parents

In communication with parents, it is not always easy to determine how much counseling and support from the teacher is helpful to parents in dealing with their child and related family problems. Counseling parents may exact more time, emotional energy, and expertise than a teacher can realistically provide together with other responsibilities. Some teachers find it helpful to specify to parents when they can be reached by telephone and when they can schedule conferences. Just as some parents rely on parent groups to provide more support and expertise than they can offer, so, too, do some expect too much from teachers.

Teachers must be sensitive to the limits of their own expertise and refer and encourage parents to sources of support and assistance

---

Box 12.5   Sample Agenda for Parent Support Group Meetings

September—Introduction
        Warm-up activity
        Reasons for starting the group
        Group's goals identified
October—Talking to children
        Active listening
November—How to develop responsibility in
        children
December—Discipline techniques
January—Sibling rivalry
        Peer pressure

February—Sex education
        Juvenile justice system
March—Community resources that offer
        professional help to families
April—Working with the schools
May—Social gathering
        End-of-year party
        Summer group plans

Source: K. Phillips, "Parents as Partners: Developing Parent Support Groups." In M. K. Zabel (Ed.), *TEACH-* *ING: Behaviorally Disordered Students* (Reston, VA: Council for Exceptional Children, 1985), p. 32.

---

from other appropriate personnel in school as well as outside of school. To expect teachers to accept responsibility to solve all student problems is unfair to their students, their families, and to the teachers themselves. Although teachers and other educators can communicate with parents, and can encourage parent involvement in their child's education, growth, and development, they are only one of several potential team members. Other school personnel, including regular classroom teachers, administrators, parent facilitators, school social workers, and psychologists have special expertise and professional roles that should be drawn upon. Outside of school, there are a variety of human services professionals who can be called upon to provide counseling to behaviorally disordered students and their families.

Summary

In one way or another, parents of behaviorally disordered students have a tremendous influence on their child's success in school. Yet, the history of their child's problems in school, family stress associated with behavioral disorders, and the social stigma of being a parent of a child with behavioral disorders frequently erect barriers to involvement with school programs by parents of these students.

Still, most parents can be involved in their child's education at one of the levels we discussed. Many can provide information relevant to the identification and assessment of educational needs, can participate in the development of IEPs and determination of appropriate placements, and can provide ongoing support for those programs. A few may even play direct roles in interventions. For some parents, however, involvement with school may be limited to the passive reception of communication from school personnel. In this chapter, we have discussed a variety of ways teachers and other educators can assess and then attempt to facilitate parent involvement.

Behind legal requirements and professional testimonials like Judy Larson's at the outset of this chapter is a recognition that the purpose of parent involvement is not simply to make educational interventions more effective. The ultimate goal is for behaviorally disordered children to function more successfully throughout their ecosystems. School is but one environment the child inhabits. The home and community are others. Consequently, interventions involving behaviorally disordered students must effect changes not only in the child, but in school, home, and community environments as well. Teachers and other educators can effect changes in students' behavior that carry over into those other environments.

Equally important are the improvements in parent attitudes toward and treatment of their children that teachers can accomplish through the various types of parent communication and involvement presented in this chapter. Improving parents' views of their children, helping them gain better understanding, become more tolerant and skilled in dealing with their children, and assisting parents in locating and using appropriate services and support outside of school are implicit in ecological approaches.

Appendix A: Steps in Quality Decision Making

STEP I: **Initial Classroom or Home Adjustments**

Entry Decisions:

Is the student's behavior sufficiently disordered that intervention is necessary? (Decision maker: The person(s) disturbed by the behavior, teacher, parent, etc.)

If *yes:* An intervention is planned by the person(s) disturbed by the behavior.

If *no:* No intervention is undertaken.

Procedures:

No formal referral is made.

Suggestions may be sought informally from others.

Efforts to change the behavior(s) of concern are implemented primarily by the person(s) directly concerned.

Exit Decisions:

Have the initial classroom or home adjustments applied been effective in assisting the student to resume making educational progress? (Decision maker: The person(s) disturbed by the behavior, teacher, parent, etc.).

If *yes*: No further action is necessary.

If *no*: Move to Step II.

STEP II: **Prereferral Activities**

Entry Decisions:

Same as exit decisions for Step I.

Procedures:

Teacher or parent brings student's problem behavior to the attention of others in the school who may be able to provide assistance. Possible resource persons at this step include other teachers, the principal, counselors, and area education agency staff such as consultants, social workers, or psychologists.

No formal referral procedures are initiated at this point in the process.

No special education services other than informal consultation are provided at this time.

The person(s) directly concerned about the problem behavior direct intervention efforts. Either direct or indirect service may be supplied by home, community, or other school personnel.

Exit Decisions:

Have the Step II interventions applied been effective in assisting the student to resume making educational progress? (Decision maker: The person(s) disturbed by the problem behavior, teacher, parent, etc., in informal consultation with others who may have been contacted regarding the problem.)

If *yes*: Decide which of the following alternatives is most appropriate: (a) continue the Step II intervention or (b) return to a Step I intervention as a less restrictive level of intervention or (c) discontinue all special intervention as the least restrictive level of intervention.

*If *no*: Decide which of the following alternatives is most appropriate: (a) Seek other Step II intervention strategies as the least restrictive alternative or (b) move to Step III.

STEP III: **Referral for Special Education Services—Eligibility**

Entry Decisions:

Same as exit decisions for Step III until a formal referral is made.

Once a formal referral is made: Is the student's problem behavior sufficiently severe to justify development of a formal assessment plan? (Decision makers: Area education agency staff charged with screening referrals in consultation with person(s) directly disturbed by the student's behavior, those who have provided intervention advice or assistance at Steps I and II, and other area education agency staff whose advice may be helpful.)

*If *yes*: Proceed to implement Step III procedures.

*If *no*: Require additional Step II interventions. Extend offer of informal assistance from area education agency staff.

Exit Decisions:

Is the student's behavior sufficiently disordered that special education services are necessary if he/she is to benefit from education? (Decision makers: The multidisciplinary team with the concurrence of the parents.)

*If *yes*: Proceed to Step IV.

*If *uncertain*: Review the assessment plan and plan for the collection of missing or additional information. Schedule continuation of meeting of team for time after additional assessment has been completed.

*If *no*: Require additional Step II interventions. Extend offer of informal assistance from area education agency staff.

STEP IV: **Referral for Special Education Services—Placement**

Entry Decisions:

Assumes a *yes* on exit decisions for Step III.

Procedures:

Having documented its decision that the student is sufficiently behaviorally disordered to require special education services to benefit from education, the multidisciplinary team proceeds to determine an appropriate altenative to the present placement. A coordinator for the placement planning phase is designated.

Although ongoing Step II interventions are continued during this time, the multidisciplinary team and the parents must now approve any major changes in placement or intervention strategy.

The alternative placement should be one in which the student is expected to show improved educational progress. It need not require direct special instruction but may include, or consist primarily of, related or supportive services.

The team may find it necessary to take time as permitted by due process requirements to investigate a variety of potential alternative placements so as to determine the best match between placement and student needs.

The final report of the team on its placement recommendation should specify the data on which the selection of a suitable alternative placement was based. Those responsible for providing direct and indirect service and monitoring implementation of the plan should be named. Data to be collected for monitoring and evaluation purposes should be specified. A timeline should be presented showing the date at which the effectiveness of the alternative intervention(s) will be reviewed.

*Parents must concur with the alternative placement plan.

Exit Decisions:

Has the team developed a plan for an alternative placement for the student with behavioral disorders that promises educational benefits for the student, is in the least restrictive setting possible given the nature of the student's disability, and is feasible to implement given the resources of the school district? (Decision makers: The multidisciplinary team with the concurrence of the parent.)

*If *yes*: The coordinator named by the team directs implementation of the plan.

*If *no*: The team should review the possible reasons before deciding on a new course of action. Does the team lack information on which to base its decision? (Solution: Collect needed information.) Is there a difference of opinion between the members of the team and the parent(s)? (Solution: Continue discussion and negotiation, with informal outside assistance if desired, or move to next level of formal due process conflict resolution procedures.) Does the district lack resources needed to implement the selected alternative option? (Solution: Inform appropriate administrators of need for additional resources.) (These are suggestions for meeting some problems often encountered at this step.)

STEP V: Implementation of the Special Education Plan

Entry Decisions:

Assumes a *yes* on exit decisions for Step IV.

Procedures:

Full responsibility for oversight of the student's educational process now rests with the multidisciplinary team, although direct services may continue to be provided through regular education personnel. Implementation of the placement plan is managed by the coordinator named by the team. The coordinator is also charged with assuring that the data needed by the team to evaluate the effectiveness of the alternative placement will be analyzed and organized for use at the designated time.

Direct and indirect regular or special services as specified in the plan are provided to the student in the least restricted educational environment feasible.

Exit Decisions:

Has the alternative placement plan been implemented? (Decision makers: The multidisciplinary team with the concurrence of the parents.)

*If *yes*: Proceed to consideration of the second exit question for Step V.

*If *no*: The team should review possible reasons. Are essential resources missing? (Solution: Inform administrators of need to seek additional resources.) Are resources available but implementation of plan is faulty? (Solution: Correct implementation procedure.) Is plan not feasible? (Solution: Recycle to Step III or Step IV as appropriate.) (These are suggestions for meeting some of the problems commonly encountered at this step.)

Have the interventions applied been effective in assisting the student to resume making educational progress? (Decision makers: The multidisciplinary team with the concurrence of the parents.)

*If *yes*: Decide which of the following alternatives is most appropriate: (a) Continue the Step V intervention or (b) return to a Step II intervention as less restrictive if it is reasonable to expect that the student will continue at least the present rate of educational progress or (c) discontinue all special intervention if it is felt to be no longer necessary as the least restrictive level of intervention.

*If *no*: Decide which of the following alternatives is most appropriate: (a) Recycle to Step IV and develop an alternative placement plan that the team and parents feel offers a better chance of assisting the student to make educational progress or (b) recycle to Steps III and IV, planning to develop a new assessment plan to collect data on which to base a new placement plan.

Note: An asterisk (*) indicates a decision for which a written rationale should be prepared, including reference to the data on which the team based its decision.

Source: F. H. Wood, "Decision making: Eligibility and programming options." In F. H. Wood, C. R. Smith, & J. Grimes (Eds.), *The Iowa Assessment Model in Behavioral Disorders: A Training Manual* (Des Moines, IA: State Department of Public Instruction, 1985), pp. 51–56.

Appendix B: Sample Referral Form

1. Name: _____ Birthdate: _____

   School: _____ Grade: _____

   Parent/Guardian: _____ Phone: _____

   Address: _____

   _____

2. Referrer(s):   Position(s):

3. Specific reasons for referral:

4. Preassessment interventions attempted to deal with each of the above:

   Results:

   Other interventions recommended by the preassessment team but not attempted?

5. Attendance information
   Schools attended and dates:

   Average number of absences per year:

   Number of absences this year:

6. Is the student of limited English proficiency?
   Is the student from bilingual or non-English-speaking home?

   Primary language: _____

7. Medical information
   School vision screening   Date: _____   Results: _____

   School hearing screening   Date: _____   Results: _____

   Other significant physical/medical information (e.g., seizures, allergies, injuries, medications):

8. Academic performance information from student's cumulative file:
   Achievement test scores/dates   Report card grades

   _____   _____
   _____   _____
   _____   _____
   _____   _____
   _____

   Has student been retained? _____   If so, reasons: _____

9. Previous referrals?   Dates:

   Previous evaluations?   Dates:
   If yes, summarize results and indicate action taken:

10. Extent of parent/guardian awareness of reasons for referral and nature of parent/guardian
    involvement:

Appendix C: Environmental Analysis

Linda E. Miller

Student's Name _____ Age _____
School _____ Grade _____
Teacher _____ Observer _____
Date _____ Time _____ To _____

Directions: Check *all* items that apply. Keep in mind that the analysis is of the environment
of the designated student and not of the classroom in general.

I. Learning Setting
   A. General Information
      1. Type of classroom:
         _____ Self-contained   _____ Open-space   _____ Team-teaching

      2. Person in charge:
         _____ Regular teacher   _____ Student teacher   _____ Other
         _____ Substitute   _____ Teacher Aide   (Specify) _____
         _____

      3. Time of Day: _____ A.M.   _____ P.M.
         Half of Period: _____ First   _____ Second

      4. No. of Students _____   No. of Adults _____   Ratio _____ To _____

      5. Subject being taught at time of observation: (If more than one, number in order of
         sequence)
         _____ Reading   _____ Language   _____ Handwriting
         _____ Math   _____ Music   _____ Health/Safety
         _____ Spelling   _____ Art   _____ P.E.
         _____ Social Studies   _____ Science   _____ Other_____
                                        (Specify)

6. Activity in progress: (If more than one, number in order of sequence)

_____ Teacher lecture _____ Seat work _____ Film
_____ Small Group _____ Student _____ TV
_____ General Class Directed _____ Lab
        Discussion _____ Demonstration _____ Learning
_____ Question & _____ Test Center Activity
        Answer _____ Independent _____ Other_____
                Student Project (Specify)

B. Space
  1. Seating arrangement: Please diagram and mark the designated pupil's seat with an X. Indicate youngsters in adjacent seats by name and/or sex.

Check (✔) if seat is next to:

_____ Bulletin board _____ Teacher's desk _____ Windows
_____ Bookshelves _____ Learning centers _____ Chalkboard
_____ Door to _____ _____ Heating/A.C.
                                                          unit

Visible from teacher's desk _____ Yes _____ No

  2. Spatial Areas

_____ Learning centers _____ Isolation booths
_____ Study areas _____ Free reading areas
_____ Other (specify) _____

  3. Room in relation to:
Bathrooms: _____
Drinking fountains: _____
Prinicpal's office: _____
Nurse's office: _____
Access to outside: _____
Media center: _____
Clothes hooks, lockers, coathall (describe): _____
_____

Rooms next door are: _____
_____

C. Props
  1. Furnishings:
    a. Pupil's desk:

_____ Correct size _____ Too large _____ Too small

Individual
Type: Attached   _____ Indiv. table, or desk with chair
_____ Right handed
_____ Left handed

Cluster
_____ Table w/chairs   _____ Number in cluster
_____ Desks w/chairs

Pupil's desk and/or work area: _____ Orderly   _____ Messy

b. Pupil's chair:
_____ Correct size   _____ Movable
_____ Too large   _____ Immovable
_____ Too small

c. Flooring
_____ Wood   _____ Tile   _____ Carpet

d. Lighting of room:
_____ Incandescent   _____ Adequate
_____ Fluorescent   _____ Inadequate

2. Bulletin boards:
_____ Teacher made   _____ Pupil made   _____ Commercial
Content (describe): _____

_____

_____

Arrangement (describe): _____

_____

3. Windows:
a. Location
_____ In door to hall
_____ Along wall (east, west, north south)–underline one
_____ Near ceiling (outside wall, hall wall)–underline one

b. Number _____

c. Size: _____ Large   _____ Small   _____ Floor-ceiling

4. Wall color: _____

5. Ventilation:
_____ Comfortable   _____ Stuffy   _____ Hot   _____ Chilly

*6. Pupil's supplies:
a. Pencils:
_____ Correct size   _____ Sharpened   _____ Own supply
_____ Too short   _____ Dull   _____ Available
_____ Too long   from teacher

    b. Crayons:

_____ Complete set (8 basic colors)	_____ In good condition	_____ Own supply
_____ Incomplete set	_____ Broken	_____ Available from teacher

    c. Marking pens: _____ Own supply   _____ Available from teacher

    d. Drawing paper: _____ Manilla   _____ Own supply
                                 _____ Newsprint   _____ Available from teacher

    e. Writing paper: _____ Wide lined   _____ Own supply
                                 _____ Narrow lined _____ Available from teacher
                                 _____ No lines

    f. Scissors: _____ Right handed   _____ Left handed

7. Chalkboard:

_____ Metal	_____ White	_____ White chalk	_____ Board
_____ Slate	_____ Green	_____ Yellow chalk	not
	_____ Black	_____ Marking pens	well erased

8. Extraneous or obtrusive noise which might interfere w/pupil concentration (describe):
_____
_____

D. Time schedule

Subject	Activity	Duration
		to
		to
		to
		to
		to
		to

II. Classroom Social Environment
   A. Peer Society
      1. Number of boys _____   Number of girls _____

     *2. Socioeconomic Background
        a. Range:

           Lower   Lower Middle   Middle   Upper Middle   Upper

        b. Predominantly:

           Lower   Lower Middle   Middle   Upper Middle   Upper

     *3. Age range: _____ yr. _____ mo.   to   _____ yr. _____ mo.

*4. Overall social maturity: (Use students' chronological age range as norm)
_____ young   _____ age appropriate   _____ mature

5. Ethnic mix (specify number):
_____ black   _____ Caucasian   _____ Indian   _____ Mexican
_____ Oriental   _____ other   American

6. Group climate
   a. Leadership (by students):   weak |___|___|___|___| strong
                                          1   2   3   4   5

                                    central |___|___|___|___| distributed
                                             1   2   3   4   5

   b. Attraction/Cohesion: many cliques |___|___|___|___| few cliques
      (between students)   1   2   3   4   5

                               many rejected   no rejected
                                    students |___|___|___|___| students
                                              1   2   3   4   5

   c. Norms (of students):   incongruent   congruent
                            w/teacher rules |___|___|___|___| w/teacher rules
                                             1   2   3   4   5

                                       weak |___|___|___|___| strong
                                             1   2   3   4   5

   d. Communication: infrequent |___|___|___|___| frequent
      (between students)   1   2   3   4   5

                          ambiguous |___|___|___|___| clear
                                     1   2   3   4   5

7. Student's approximate position in the "pecking order":
                                low |___|___|___|___| high
                                     1   2   3   4   5

8. Group role (if any) adopted by student:
   (describe: i.e., clown, scapegoat, bully, etc.) _____
   _____
   _____
   _____

9. Small group work
   * _____ Work cooperatively   * _____ Work in isolation
     _____ Work face-to-face   _____ Work facing same direction

*10. Students assist one another _____

11. Address teacher by name _____   Address teacher as "Teacher" _____

B. Teacher Characteristics and Teaching Style
   1. Sex of teacher: _____ Male _____ Female

  *2. Feeling tone manifested:
      _____ Anxious   _____ Quiet   _____ Courteous   _____ Self-
      _____ Relaxed   _____ Shouting   _____ Short-tempered   assured
      _____ Pleasant   _____ Cheerful   _____ Fair   _____ Indifferent

   3. Work with pupils
      _____ Total group   _____ Small group   _____ Individual
      Time allotment ratio: _____ to _____
                              group   individual

   4. Expression of feelings
      Reveals: _____ anger   _____ love   _____ sense of
                  _____ fear   _____ acceptance   humor
                  _____ sadness   _____ pride

      Expressed: _____ verbally   _____ facial expression
                  _____ voice tone _____ general demeanor

   5. Error behavior: _____ acknowledges own errors
                          _____ covers up errors

   6. Discipline:
      _____ Makes expectations clear
      _____ Follows through with "promised" consequences
      _____ Talks over precipitating behavior with child
              _____ clearly   _____ matter-of-factly   _____ angrily
              _____ interprets child's feelings about situation to him
      _____ Elicits commitment for improved behavior from child
      _____ Holds child responsible for own behavior
      _____ Accepts word of peers in learning of and acting upon misbehavior

      Consequences:
      * Those used: _____
      _____
      _____

      * Relation to "crime":   _____ appropriate   _____ too harsh
                                _____ too lenient
      * Timing with misdeed: _____ immediate   _____ delayed
      How long? _____
      * Effective? (i.e., misbehavior subsided)   _____ Yes   _____ No

  *7. Intervention into peer squabbles
      _____ Immediate   _____ Disciplines all involved   _____ Other
      _____ Delayed   _____ Disciplines only one   (specify)
      _____ Not at all   _____ Has squabblers settle it   _____

*8. Communication with parents

_____ at conference time only   _____ by phone

_____ routinely   _____ in person

_____ as needed   _____ by note

III. Instructional Dimensions

   A. Instructional Methods

      1. Teacher communication behavior   Teacher comments directed to:

         _____ Complimentary, courteous   _____ total group

         _____ Rude, belittling   _____ individuals

         _____ Teacher mediates all in-class communications

         Teacher adaptation to individual differences

         _____ Too complex   _____ Oversimplified

      2. Instructional Methods

         a. Questioning techniques of the teacher

            _____ Open-ended   _____ Accepts   _____ Presses for
            _____ Single, correct   unusual   immediate
                    answer   questions   response
                                     _____ Ignores,   _____ Encourages
                                             belittles them   taking time

         b. Planning

            _____ Plans for one activity at a time

            _____ Plans for student involvement in variety of activities

            _____ Selection of goals and purposes done primarily by teacher

            _____ Selection of goals and purposes is mutual student/teacher responsibility

            _____ Goals and purposes coincide with school curriculum units

         c. Direction giving

            _____ Highly specific, exact   _____ Leaves out details/allows
            _____ Incomplete   leeway
            _____ Unclear   _____ Allows for creativity
            _____ One step at a time   _____ Match a model
            _____ Multistep   _____ Multisensory
                                                 _____ Demonstration

         d. Class discussion

            _____ Humor accepted   _____ Discussion cut off
            _____ Levity unappreciated   _____ Expression of ideas
                                                         encouraged
                                                 _____ Pupil comments redirected
                                                         to encourage further dis-
                                                         cussion

*e. Evaluation of work

_____ Pupil evaluated   _____ Errors are belittled, impatience with them

_____ Teacher evaluated

_____ Group evaluated   _____ Encouragement, concern about errors shown

_____ Not evaluated

_____ Correction of errors expected   _____ Improvement suggested constructively

Pupil behavior:

_____ Hostile to criticism, argues   _____ Willingly admits, reveals errors

_____ Accepts/analyzes criticism

_____ Accepts/pleased with praise   _____ Afraid of errors

_____ Responds negatively to praise

f. Correction/marking method

_____ Number wrong   _____ Verbal comments, positive   _____ Wrong answers marked

_____ Number correct

_____ %   _____ Verbal comments, negative   _____ Correct answers marked

     _____ Both

* Feedback:

_____ that day   _____ on the spot   _____ next day

_____ later in activity

How much? _____

*g. Teacher's out of class availability to students:

_____ Between classes, periods   _____ Recess

_____ After school   _____ Before school

_____ Lunchtime   _____ Other (specify) _____

_____

B. Lessons

1. Assignments

_____ Single topic assignment for all

_____ Variety for individual interests

_____ Same difficulty level   _____ too hard   _____ too easy

_____ Variety for individual differences

_____ Same resources recommend to all

_____ Variety recommended

_____ Same assignment length for all   _____ too long   _____ too short

_____ Length varied for individual differences

_____ Assignment length appropriate

*2. Homework

_____ Assigned to everyone   _____ Parent involvement discouraged

_____ Only to slow students

_____ Only to accelerated students   _____ Parent involvement encouraged
_____ As appropriate
_____ Daily   _____ Parent involvement made explicit
_____ Not at all
    _____ Supplemental work
    _____ Reinforcement
    _____ Error correction

* C.   "Traffic Regulation System" (Class rules/procedures)

Entry into room: _____

Dismissal during hour for special needs: _____
_____

Dismissal at end of class period: _____

Pupil to pupil communication: _____

Materials passed out, collected: _____
_____

Pencil sharpening: _____

Transitional times: _____

Use of interest centers: _____

Clean up: _____

Obtaining free materials: _____

Stretch breaks: _____

Enforcement system:

    _____ Student monitors   _____ Teacher   _____ both

Rules clear to students?:   _____ Yes   _____ No   _____ Posted

Other rules imposed?:   _____ Frequently   _____ In advance of infraction
    _____ Rarely
    _____ Sometimes   _____ Following it

Rules made by: _____ Teacher   _____ Students   _____ Mutual agreement
    _____ School

Rules/Procedures observed?:   _____ Consistently   _____ Inconsistently

D.   Media Resources

1.   Type available

_____ Basic texts   _____ Filmstrips
_____ Workbooks   _____ 2x2 slides
_____ Supplementary texts   _____ 16mm films
_____ Library books   _____ 8mm films
_____ Reference books   _____ Records
    _____ Encyclopedias   _____ Audiotapes
    _____ Dictionaries   _____ Cassettes
    _____ Thesauruses   _____ Open reel
    _____ Almanacs   _____ Videotapes
    _____ Atlases
Other: _____

_____ Games, puzzles

_____ Kits (i.e., reading, math, science)

_____ Charts, posters, study prints

_____ Models, Diorama, specimens, Realia

_____ Transparencies (overhead)

_____ Maps

_____ Globes

_____ Toys

_____ Cards, flash or audio

2. Equipment (Appropriate for materials)

_____ Television set

_____ Videotape recorder

_____ Filmstrip/slide projector

_____ Filmloop projector

_____ 16mm film projector

_____ 8mm film projector

_____ Overhead projector

_____ Tachistoscope

_____ Screen

_____ Room darkening facilities (Drapes/shades)

_____ Filmstrip previewer

_____ Record player

_____ Audiotape recorder

_____ Cassette

_____ Open reel

_____ Audiotape player

_____ Earphones/headsets (No. _____)

_____ Listening center/jackbox

_____ Audio patch cards

_____ Audiocard reader (Lang. Master, EFI)

_____ Flannel board

_____ Chalkboards

_____ Bulletin boards

Other: _____

_____

_____

* Data to be obtained in interview with the teacher.

Source: L. Miller, J. Epp, & E. McGinnis. "Setting Analysis." In F. H. Wood, C. R. Smith, & J. Grimes (Eds.), *The Iowa Assessment Model in Behavioral Disorders: A Training Manual* (Des Moines, IA: State Department of Public Instruction, 1985), pp. 111–123.

Appendix D: Publishers of Several Behavior Rating Scales

Behavior Evaluation Scale
Pro-Ed
5341 Industrial Oaks Blvd.
Austin, TX 78735

Behavior Problem Checklist (Revised)
Herbert C. Quay
Box 248074
University of Miami
Coral Gables, FL 33124

Burks' Behavior Rating Scale
The Arden Press
8331 Alvarado Drive
Huntington Beach, CA 92646

Behavior Rating Profile: An Ecological
   Approach to Behavioral Assessment
Pro-Ed
5341 Industrial Oaks Blvd.
Austin, TX 78735

Child Behavior Checklist
Thomas Achenbach
Laboratory of Developmental Psychology
Bldg. 15K
National Institute of Mental Health
9000 Rockville Pike
Bethesda, MD 20205

Devereux Child Behavior Rating Scale
Devereux Elementary School Behavior
   Rating Scale
Devereux Adolescent Behavior Rating Scale
Devereux Foundation Press
Devon, PA 19333

Hahneman Elementary Behavior Rating
   Scale
Hahneman High School Behavior Rating
   Scale
George Spivack and Marshall Swift
Hahneman Community Mental
   Health/Mental Retardation Center
Department of Mental Health Services
Philadelphia, PA 19102

Appendix E: Parents' Needs Form

<u>Confidential</u>   Date: _____
Parent's name _____
Child's name _____

Introduction:

Listed below are several statements describing concerns common to the parents of exceptional children. The items may or may not concern you at this time. Please complete only those items that currently concern you.

The information on this form is used *only* to help plan and implement a parent-teacher-involvement program. All information is held in strict confidence.

Directions:

1. Read each statement carefully.
2. Circle the number on the 1–5 scale that most closely approximates your current need in each area. Circle *1* to indicate a low priority need and *5* to indicate a high priority need.
3. Below the 1–5 scale are several statements suggesting ways you may prefer to meet your stated needs. Please check only *two* of the four statements listed below each item.
4. You may write additional comments in the space provided.

I. I need the opportunity to discuss my feelings about my exceptional child and myself with someone who understands the problem.

(Circle the appropriate number.)

1	2	3	4	5
Low Priority				High Priority

(Check *only* two statements.)

_____ I prefer to talk to a professional.
_____ I prefer to talk to the parent of an exceptional child.
_____ I prefer to be referred to another agency for counseling.
_____ I prefer to read articles and books discussing the reactions of parents of exceptional children.

_____ I prefer _____
_____

II. I would like to talk with other parents and families who have exceptional children.

(Circle the appropriate number.)

1	2	3	4	5
Low				High
Priority				Priority

(Check *only* two statements.)

_____ I prefer to be in a discussion group.
_____ I prefer to participate in social gatherings (picnics, parties, potluck dinners).
_____ I prefer to meet informally.
_____ I prefer to participate in general meetings, workshops, lectures, demonstrations, and other informational gatherings.
_____ I prefer _____
_____

III. I would like to learn more about my child's exceptionality.

(Circle the appropriate number.)

1	2	3	4	5
Low				High
Priority				Priority

(Check *only* two statements.)

_____ I prefer to obtain information through reading.
_____ I prefer to observe teachers and other professionals working with my child and then discuss my observations.
_____ I prefer individual parent-teacher conferences.
_____ I prefer _____
_____

IV. I would like to learn more about how children develop and learn, especially exceptional children.

(Circle the appropriate number.)

1	2	3	4	5
Low				High
Priority				Priority

(Check *only* two statements.)

_____ I prefer to obtain information through reading.
_____ I prefer to participate in a formal behavior management training course.
_____ I prefer a parent-teacher discussion group.
_____ I prefer individual training in my home by a teacher or other professional.

_____ I prefer to attend meetings at which specialists present information on behavior management.

_____ I prefer _____

_____

VI. I would like to work with a teacher or other professional so that I can use the same instructional methods at home that the school uses.

(Circle the appropriate number.)

1	2	3	4	5
Low Priority				High Priority

(Check *only* two statements.)

_____ I prefer to observe my child in school.

_____ I prefer to attend a training program in observation.

_____ I prefer to attend a course in instructional methods.

_____ I prefer to work with the teacher in my child's classroom.

_____ I prefer in-home training by a teacher or other professional.

_____ I prefer to learn through readings, newsletters, telephone communication, and similar resources.

_____ I prefer _____

_____

VII. I would like _____

_____

(Circle the appropriate number.)

1	2	3	4	5
Low Priority				High Priority

(Write the appropriate statements.)

_____ I prefer _____

_____

_____ I prefer _____

_____

Comments:

Thank you.

Source: T. M. Shea & A. M. Bauer, *Parents and Teachers of Exceptional Children: A Handbook for Involvement* (Boston: Allyn & Bacon, 1985), pp. 337–339.

Appendix F: Parents' Activities Form

<u>Confidential</u>   Date: _____
Parent's name _____
Child's name _____

Introduction:

   Listed below are thirty-five topics and activities generally believed of interest to the parents of exceptional children. Not all parents are interested in any single item, nor is any parent interested in all the items.

   Your response to this questionnaire is used *only* to assist in planning and implementing a parent-teacher involvement program for you. All information is held in strict confidence.

Directions:

1. Read the entire form carefully.
2. In Column A check 15 items of interest to you.
3. In Column B rank 5 of the 15 items you checked in Column A. Number the item of highest priority to you 5, the next highest 4, and so on.
4. You may write additional comments in the space provided.

A	B	
_____	_____	1. Help my child learn.
_____	_____	2. Build my child's self-confidence.
_____	_____	3. Select activities to help my child learn (books, games, toys, projects, experiences).
_____	_____	4. Teach my child to follow directions.
_____	_____	5. Help my child enjoy learning.
_____	_____	6. Assist my child in language development.
_____	_____	7. Teach my child problem-solving skills.
_____	_____	8. Fulfill my role as (father) (mother) to my child.
_____	_____	9. Avoid emotional involvement in my child's emotional outbursts.
_____	_____	10. Protect my child from getting hurt.

_____ _____ 11. Care for my child when he or she is sick or injured.
_____ _____ 12. Discipline my child.
_____ _____ 13. Deal with my child's misbehavior.
_____ _____ 14. Teach my child respect for people and property.
_____ _____ 15. Teach my child to express feelings in a socially acceptable manner.
_____ _____ 16. Teach my child to show love, affection, and consideration for other family members.
_____ _____ 17. Teach my child to live in harmony with the family (television, bedtime, meals, sharing, responsibilities).
_____ _____ 18. Develop a positive and productive relationship with my child.
_____ _____ 19. Develop my problem-solving skills.

How can I obtain information on the following topics affecting my child:

_____ _____ 20. Art activities
_____ _____ 21. Creative dramatics
_____ _____ 22. Educational games and activities
_____ _____ 23. Exercise
_____ _____ 24. Health and hygiene
_____ _____ 25. Music
_____ _____ 26. Nutrition and diet
_____ _____ 27. Puppetry
_____ _____ 28. Recreation
_____ _____ 29. Sleep
_____ _____ 30. Toys

Other topics and activities of interest to me are:

_____ _____ 31. _____
_____ _____ 32. _____
_____ _____ 33. _____
_____ _____ 34. _____
_____ _____ 35. _____

Thank you.

Source: T. M. Shea & A. M. Bauer, *Parents and Teachers of Exceptional Children: A Handbook for Involvement* (Boston: Allyn & Bacon, 1985), pp. 340–341.

Appendix G: Parent-Volunteer Questionnaire

Date _____
Parent's name _____
Child's name _____ Telephone number _____
Teacher's name _____

Parents! We need your help. Please consider helping with the activities and projects listed on this questionnaire. Check all those activities for which you can volunteer service. Your participation will help us provide an interesting, stimulating, individualized educational program for your children.

Mother	Father	
_____	_____	I would like to assist in the classroom on a regular basis. The times I have available are:

	Days	Hours
	_____	_____
	_____	_____

Mother	Father	
_____	_____	I would like to assist *occasionally* in the classroom. (check one)

    a.   Contact me _____

    b.   I will contact the school _____

Mother	Father	
_____	_____	I would like to assist from my home.

In-Classroom Activities

Mother	Father	
_____	_____	Read a story to the children.
_____	_____	Assist children in a learning center.
_____	_____	Assist individual children with learning and remedial tasks.
_____	_____	Assist with the music program.
_____	_____	Assist with the art program.
_____	_____	Assist with the movement activities program.
_____	_____	Work puzzles and play table games with the children.
_____	_____	Help with cooking projects.
_____	_____	Assist with writing activities.
_____	_____	Assist with carpentry projects.
_____	_____	Assist with homemaking projects.
_____	_____	Assist with the care of classroom pets.

_____	_____	Assist with gardening and horticultural projects.
_____	_____	Assist children during recess, snack time, lunch, and free time.
_____	_____	Take a child for a walk.
_____	_____	Assist with field trips.

Home-Based Activities

_____	_____	Make instructional materials: games, flash cards, puppets, costumes, charts.
_____	_____	Type.
_____	_____	Help with costumes for dress-up events.
_____	_____	Cut out and catalog pictures from magazines, catalogs, and newspapers for instructional use.
_____	_____	Help repair classroom furnishings and instructional materials and equipment.
_____	_____	Help construct new furnishings and equipment for the classroom.
_____	_____	Organize parties for birthdays and holidays.
_____	_____	Babysit for parents who are volunteering their service to the classroom.
_____	_____	Care for classroom pets during vacations.
_____	_____	Make props and sets for plays, parties, and special events.
_____	_____	Make room and bulletin board decorations.
_____	_____	Make posters.
_____	_____	Assemble and staple materials.
_____	_____	Research and organize field trips.
_____	_____	Help plan and conduct parent activities, such as meetings, educational training programs, and conferences.
_____	_____	Research and contact sources for free instructional supplies (computer cards and paper, wood scraps, boxes, carpet, print shop discards, spools, pencils, paper).
_____	_____	Make items to sell for fund raising.
_____	_____	Assist with fund-raising activities.
_____	_____	Plan and organize social events.

What other activities could you help with?
  A. In the classroom:
  B. At home:

What other family members or friends are interested in volunteering services to the children?

  A. _____
  B. _____

Your comments, concerns, and questions are welcome.

Source: T. M. Shea & A. M. Bauer, _Parents and Teachers of Exceptional Children: A Handbook for Involvement_ (Boston: Allyn & Bacon, 1985), pp. 344–345.

Bibliography

Abarbanel, A. (1979). Shared parenting after separation and divorce: a study of joint custody. *American Journal of Orthopsychiatry, 49,* 320–329.

Achenbach, T. M. (1966). The classification of children's psychiatric symptoms: A factor-analytic study. *Psychological Monographs, 80* (Whole No. 615, 1–37).

Achenbach, T. M. (1978a). The child behavior profile: 1. Boys aged 6–11. *Journal of Consulting and Clinical Psychology, 46,* 478–488.

Achenbach, T. M. (1978b). Psychopathology of childhood: Research problems and issues. *Journal of Consulting and Clinical Psychology, 46,* 759–776.

Achenbach, T. M. (1982). *Developmental psychopathology.* New York: John Wiley & Sons.

Achenbach, T. M., & Edelbrock, C. S. (1978). The classification of child psychopathology: A review and analysis of empirical efforts. *Psychological Bulletin, 85,* 1275–1301.

Achenbach, T. M., & Edelbrock, C. S. (1979). The Child Behavior Profile: II. Boys aged 12–16 and girls aged 6–12 and 12–16. *Journal of Consulting and Clinical Psychology, 47,* 223–233.

Ainsworth, M. D. S. (1973). The development of infant-mother attachment. In B. C. Caldwell & H. R. Ricciuti (Eds.), *Review of child development research* (Vol. 3, pp. 1–94). Chicago: University of Chicago Press.

Akers, R. L. (1985). *Deviant behavior: A social learning approach.* Belmont, CA: Wadsworth.

Alberts-Corush, J., Firestone, P., & Goodman, J. T. (1986). Attention and impulsivity characteristics of the biological and adoptive parents of hyperactive and normal control children. *American Journal of Orthopsychiatry, 56,* 413–423.

Alexander, R. N., & Apfel, C. H. (1976). Altering schedules of reinforcement for improved classroom behavior. *Exceptional Children, 43,* 97–99.

Alexander, R. N., Kroth, R. L., Simpson, R. L., & Poppelreiter, T. (1982). The parent role in special education. In R. L. McDowell, G. W. Adamson, & F. H. Wood (Eds.), *Teaching emotionally disturbed children.* Boston: Little, Brown and Co.

Algozzine, B. (1977). The emotionally disturbed child: Disturbed or disturbing? *Journal of Abnormal Child Psychology, 5,* 205–211.

Algozzine, B. (1979). Social-emotional problems. In C. Mercer (Ed.), *Children and adolescents with learning disabilities.* Columbus, OH: Charles E. Merrill.

Algozzine, B., Christenson, S., & Ysseldyke, J. E. (1982). Probabilities associated with the referral to placement process. *Teacher Education and Special Education, 5,* 19–23.

Alley, G., & Deshler, D. (1979). *Teaching the learning disabled adolescent: Strategies and methods.* Denver: Love Publishing.

Alvin, J. (1975). *Music therapy.* New York: Basic Books.

American Psychiatric Association. (1968). *Diagnostic and statistical manual of mental disorders* (2nd ed.). Washington, DC: APA.

American Psychiatric Association. (1980). *Diagnostic and statistical manual of mental disorders* (3rd ed.). Washington, DC: APA.

Anderson, E. (1985). The A.M. Club. In M. K. Zabel

(Ed.), *TEACHING: Behaviorally disordered youth.* Reston, VA: Council for Children with Behavioral Disorders.

Apley, J. (1975). *The child with abdominal pains.* London: Blackwell.

Apter, S. J. (1977). Applications of ecological theory: Toward a community special education model. *Exceptional Children, 43,* 366–373.

Apter, S. J., & Conoley, J. C. (1984). *Childhood behavior disorders and emotional disturbance.* Englewood Cliffs, NJ: Prentice-Hall.

Arbuthnot, J., & Gordon, D. A. (1986). Behavioral and cognitive effects of a moral reasoning development intervention for high-risk behavior-disordered adolescents. *Journal of Consulting and Clinical Psychology, 54,* 208–216.

Arter, J. A., & Jenkins, J. R. (1979). Differential diagnosis—prescriptive teaching: A critical reappraisal. *Review of Educational Research, 49,* 517–555.

Atkeson, B. M., & Forehand, R. (1981). Conduct disorders. In E. J. Mash & L. G. Terdal (Eds.), *Behavioral assessment of childhood disorders* (pp. 185–219). New York: Guilford Press.

Axelrod, S. (1977). *Behavior modification for the classroom teacher.* New York: McGraw-Hill.

Ayllon, T., Layman, D., & Kandel, H. (1975). A behavioral educational alternative to drug control of hyperactive children. *Journal of Applied Behavioral Analysis, 8,* 137–146.

Backman, J., & Firestone, P. (1979). A review of psychopharmacological and behavioral approaches to the treatment of hyperactive children. *American Journal of Orthopsychiatry, 49,* 500–504.

Bakalar, J. S., & Grinspoon, L. (1984). *Drug control in a free society.* New York: Cambridge University Press.

Baker, E. M., & Stullken, E. H. (1938). American research studies concerning the "behavior type" of the exceptional child. *Journal of Exceptional Children, 4,* 36–45.

Balow, B. (1966). A program of preparation for teachers of disturbed children. *Exceptional children, 48,* 455–460.

Bandura, A. (1969). *Principles of behavior modification.* New York: Holt, Rinehart & Winston.

Bandura, A. (1974). *Psychological modeling: Conflicting theories.* New York: Lieber-Atherton.

Bandura, A. (1977). *Social learning theory.* Englewood Cliffs, NJ: Prentice-Hall.

Bandura, A., Ross, D., & Ross, S. A. (1961). Transmission of aggression through imitation of aggressive models. *Journal of Abnormal and Social Psychology, 63,* 575–582.

Bandura, A., Ross, D., & Ross, S. A. (1963). Imitation of film-mediated aggressive models. *Journal of Abnormal and Social Psychology, 66,* 3–11.

Bandura, A., & Walters, R. H. (1963). *Social learning and personality development.* New York: Holt, Rinehart & Winston.

Barker, R. G. (1968). *Ecological psychology: Concepts and methods for studying the environment of human behavior.* Palo Alto, CA: Stanford University Press.

Barkley, R., & Cunningham, C. (1978). Do stimulant drugs improve the academic performance of hyperkinetic children? A review of outcome studies. *Clinical Pediatrics, 17,* 85–92.

Barlow, D. H., Blanchard, E. B., Vermilyea, J. A., Vermilyea, B. B., & DiNardo, P. A. (1986). Generalized anxiety and generalized anxiety disorder: Description and reconceptualization. *American Journal of Psychiatry, 143,* 40–44.

Barnes, E. J. (1972). The black community and the science of positive self-concept for black children: A theoretical perspective. In R. Jones (Ed.), *Black psychology.* New York: Harper & Row.

Barr, K. L., & McDowell, R. L. (1972). Comparison of learning disabled and emotionally disturbed children on three deviant classroom behaviors. *Exceptional Children, 39,* 60–62.

Barton, L. E., Brulle, A. R., & Repp, A. C. (1983). Aversive techniques and the doctrine of least restrictive alternative. *Exceptional Education Quarterly, 3,* 1–6.

Bash, M. A., & Camp, B. W. (1980). Teacher training in the Think Aloud classroom program. In G. W. Cartledge & J. F. Milburn (Eds.), *Teaching social skills to children: Innovative approaches.* Elmsford, NY: Pergamon Press.

Bates, J. E., Freeland, C. A. B., & Lounsbury, M. L. (1979). Measurement of infant difficultness. *Child Development, 50,* 794–803.

Bateson, G., Jackson, D. D., Haley, J., & Weakland, J. (1969). Toward a theory of schizophrenia, In A. H. Buss & E.H. Buss (Eds.), *Theories of schizophrenia.* New York: Atherton Press. (Originally published in *Behavioral Science,* 1956, *1,* 251–264.)

Bauer, D. H. (1976). An exploratory study of developmental changes in children's fears. *Journal of Child Psychology and Psychiatry, 17,* 69–74.

Baumrind, D. (1978). Parental disciplinary patterns and social competence in children. *Youth and Society, 9,* 239–276.

Beavers, W. R. (1982). Healthy, midrange, and severely dysfunctional families. In F. Walsh (Ed.), *Normal family processes* (pp. 45–66). New York: Guilford Press.

Beck, A. T., & Emery G. (1985). *Anxiety disorders and phobias.* New York: Basic Books.

Becker, W. C. (1964). Consequences of different kinds of parental discipline. In M. L. Hoffman & L. W. Hoffman (Eds.), *Review of child development research* (pp. 169–208). New York: Russell Sage.

Behling, H. E., Jr. (1986). What research says about effective schools and effective classrooms. *Counterpoint* (May), 12–13.

Bell, J. (1979). Our needs and other ecological concerns: A teacher's personal view of work with 'secondary school-aged seriously emotionally disturbed children.' *Behavioral Disorders, 4,* 168–172.

Bell, R. Q. (1968). A reinterpretation of the direction of effects in studies of socialization. *Psychological Review, 75,* 81–95.

Bemporad, J. R., & Schwab, M. E. (1986). The DSM-III and clinical child psychiatry. In T. Millon & G. L. Klerman (Eds.), *Contemporary directions in psychopathology: Toward the DSM-IV,* (pp. 135–150). New York: Guilford Press.

Bender, L. (1947). Childhood schizophrenia: Clinical study of one hundred schizophrenic children. *American Journal of Orthopsychiatry, 17,* 40–55.

Bender, L. (1956). Schizophrenia in childhood: Its recognition, description, and treatment. *American Journal of Orthopsychiatry, 26,* 499–506.

Bender, L. (1966). D-lysergic acid in the treatment of the biological features of childhood schizophrenia. *Diseases of the Nervous System, 7,* 43–46.

Bender, L. (1971). The nature of childhood psychosis. In J. G. Howells (Ed.), *Modern perspectives in international child psychiatry* (pp. 649–684). New York: Brunner/Mazel.

Bensky, J. M., Shaw, S. F., Grouse, A. S., Bates, H., Dixon, B., & Beane, W. F. (1980). Public Law 94–142 and stress: A problem for educators, *Exceptional Children, 47,* 24–29.

Bents, R., Lakin, K. C., & Reynolds, M. C. (1980). *Class management.* Washington, DC: American Association of Colleges for Teacher Education.

Berger, P. A., & Rexroth, K. (1980). Tardive dyskinesia: Clinical, biological, and pharmacological perspectives. *Schizophrenia Bulletin, 6,* 102–116.

Bergman, P., & Escalona, S. K. (1949). Unusual sensitivities in very young children. *Psychoanalytic Study of the Child, 3/4,* 333–353.

Berkowitz, P. H., & Rothman, E. P. (1960). *The disturbed child: Recognition and psychoeducational therapy in the classroom.* New York: New York University Press.

Bernstein, D. A., & Borkovek, T. D. (1973). *Progressive relaxation training: A manual for the helping profession.* Champaign, IL: Research Press.

Bessell, H., & Palomares, U. (1973). *Methods in human development: Magic arch theory manual.* La Mesa, CA: Human Development Training Institute.

Bettelheim, B. (1950). *Love is not enough: The treatment of emotionally disturbed children.* New York: Free Press.

Bettelheim, B. (1955b). *Truants from life: The rehabilitation of emotionally disturbed children.* New York: Free Press.

Bettelheim, B. (1967). *The empty fortress.* New York: Free Press.

Bettelheim, B. (1974). *A home for the heart.* New York: Alfred A. Knopf.

Blackhurst, A. E. (1981). Noncategorical teacher preparation: Problems and promises. *Exceptional Children, 48,* 197–205.

Blackhurst, A. E., McLoughlin, J. A., & Price, L. M. (1977). Issues in the development of programs to prepare teachers of children with learning and behavior disorders. *Behavioral Disorders, 2,* 157–168.

Blankenship, C., & Lilly, M. S. (1981). *Mainstreaming students with learning and behavior problems: Techniques for the classroom teacher.* New York: Holt, Rinehart & Winston.

Blatt, B. (1976). On competencies and incompetencies, instruction and destruction, individualization and depersonalization: Reflections on the now-movement. *Behavioral Disorders, 1,* 89–96.

Bloom, R. B. (1979). Why that one? Some thoughts about instructional competencies for teachers of emotionally disturbed adolescents. In F. H. Wood (Ed.), *Teachers for secondary school students with serious emotional disturbance: Content for programs.* Minneapolis, MN: University of Minnesota, Department of Psychoeducational Studies.

Bloom, R. B. (1983). The effects of disturbed adolescents on their teachers. *Behavioral Disorders, 8,* 209–216.

Board of Education v. *Rowley.* 458 U.S. 176, 102 S. Ct. 3034 (1982).

Bolstad, O. D., & Johnson, S. M. (1972). Self-regulation in the modification of disruptive classroom behavior. *Journal of Applied Behavior Analysis, 5,* 443–454.

Bond, G. L., Tinker, M. A., & Wasson, B. B. (1979). *Reading difficulties: Their diagnosis and correction* (4th ed.). Englewood Cliffs, NJ: Prentice-Hall.

Borg, W. R. (1976). Changing teacher and pupil performance with protocols. *Journal of Experimental Education, 15,* 9–18.

Bower, E. (1981). *The early identification of emotionally handicapped children in school* (3rd ed.). Springfield, IL: Charles C. Thomas.

Bowman, P. J., & Howard, C. (1985). Race-related socialization, motivation, and academic achievement: A study of Black youths in three-generation families. *Journal of the American Academy of Child Psychiatry, 24,* 134–141.

Braaten, S. (1979). The Madison school program: Programming for secondary severely emotionally disturbed youth. *Behavioral Disorders, 4,* 153–162.

Braaten, S. (1982a). *Behavioral objectives sequence.* Minneapolis, MN: Minneapolis Public Schools, Special Education Programs.

Braaten, S. (1982b). A model for the differential assessment and placement of emotionally disturbed students in special education programs. In M. M. Noel & N. Haring (Eds.), *Progress or change: Issues in educating the emotionally disturbed* (Vol. 1). Seattle, WA: University of Washington, Program Development Assistance System.

Brady, M. P., Conroy, M., & Langford, C. A. (1984). Current issues and practices affecting the development of noncategorical programs for students and teachers. *Teacher Education and Special Education, 7,* 20–26.

Brantner, J. P., & Doherty, M. A. (1983). A review of time-out: A conceptual and methodological analysis. In S. Axelrod & J. Apsche (Eds.), *The effects of punishment on human behavior.* New York: Academic Press.

Brickman, A. S., McManus, M., Grapentine, W. L., & Alessi, N. (1984). Neuropsychological assessment of seriously delinquent adolescents. *Journal of the American Academy of Child Psychiatry, 4,* 453–457.

Brill, L. (1981). *The clinical treatment of substance abusers.* New York: Free Press.

Broden, M., Hall, R. V., & Mitts, B. (1971). The effect of self-recording on the classroom behavior of two eighth-grade students. *Journal of Applied Behavior Analysis, 4,* 191–199.

Brophy, J., & Good, T. (1974). *Teacher-student relationships: Causes and consequences.* New York: Holt, Rinehart & Winston.

Brown, L., & Hammill, D. D. (1978). *Behavior rating profile.* Austin, TX: Pro Ed.

Brown, L., Nietupski, J., & Harme-Nietupski, S. (1986). Criterion of ultimate functioning. In M.A. Thomas (Ed.), *Hey, don't forget about me!* Reston, VA: Council for Exceptional Children.

Bryan, T. H., & Bryan, J. H. (1978). *Understanding learning disabilities* (2nd ed.). Sherman Oaks, CA: Alfred Publishing.

Buckley, N. K., & Walker, H. M. (1971). Free operant teacher attention to deviant child behavior after treatment in a special class. *Psychology in the Schools, 8,* 275–284.

Bullock, L., Donohue, C., Young, J., & Warner, M. (1985). Techniques for the management of physical aggression. *The Pointer, 29,* 38–44.

Bullock, L. M., & Whelan, R. J. (1971). Competencies needed by teachers of the emotionally disturbed and socially maladjusted: A comparison. *Exceptional Children, 37,* 485–489.

Burks, H. F. (1977). Burks' Behavior Rating Scales (BBRS). Los Angeles: Western Psychological Services.

Buros, O. K., (Ed.). (1985). *The ninth mental measurements yearbook.* Lincoln, NE: University of Nebraska Press.

Cameron, J. R. (1978). Parental treatment, children's temperament, and the risk of childhood behavioral problems: 2. Initial temperament, parental attitudes, and the incidence and form of behavioral problems. *American Journal of Orthopsychiatry, 48,* 140–147.

Camp, B. W., & Bash, M. A. (1981). *Think aloud: Increasing social and cognitive skill, a problem-solving program for children.* Champaign, IL: Research Press.

Camp, B. W., Blom, G. E., Hebert, F., & VanDoorninck, W. J. (1977). "Think Aloud": A program for developing self-control in young aggressive boys. *Journal of Abnormal Child Psychology, 5,* 57–169.

Campbell, M. (1975). Pharmacotherapy in early infantile autism. *Biological Psychiatry, 10*, 399–423.

Campbell, M., Anderson, L. T., Meier, M., Cohen, I., Small A., Samit, C., & Sachar, E. (1978). A comparison of haloperidol and behavior therapy and their interaction in autistic children. *Journal of the American Academy of Child Psychiatry, 17*, 640–655.

Campbell, M., Anderson, L. T., Small, A. M., Perry, R., Green, W. H., & Caplan, R. (1982). The effects of haloperidol on learning and behavior in autistic children. *Journal of Autism and Developmental Disorders, 12*, 167–175.

Campbell, M., Cohen, I. L., & Small, A. M. (1982). Drugs in aggressive behavior. *Journal of the American Academy of Child Psychiatry, 21*, 107–117.

Campbell, M., Fish, B., Shapiro, T., & Floyd, A. (1972). Acute responses of schizophrenic children to a sedative and a "stimulating" neuroleptic: A pharmacologic yardstick. *Current Therapeutic Research, 14*, 759–766.

Campbell, M., & Green, W. H. (1985). Pervasive developmental disorders of childhood. In H. I. Kaplan & B. J. Sadock (Eds.), *Comprehensive textbook of psychiatry* (pp. 1672–1683). Baltimore, MD: Williams & Wilkins.

Cantor, S., Evans, J., Pearce, J., & Pezzot-Pearce, T. (1982). Childhood schizophrenia : Present but not accounted for. *American Journal of Psychiatry, 139*, 758–762.

Cantwell, D. P. (1982). Childhood depression: A review of current research. In B. B. Lahey & A. E. Kazdin (Eds.), *Advances in clinical child psychology* (Vol. 5, pp. 39–93). New York: Plenum Press.

Cantwell, D. P. (1983). Depression in childhood: Clinical picture and diagnostic criteria. In D. P. Cantwell & G. A. Carlson (Eds.), *Affective disorders in childhood and adolescence* (pp. 3–19). New York: Spectrum Medical and Scientific Books.

Capaldi, F. J., & McRae, B. (1979). *Stepfamilies: A cooperative responsibility*. New York: New Viewpoints/Vision Books.

Carey, W. B., McDevitt, S. C., & Baker, D. (1979). Differentiating minimal brain dysfunction and temperament. *Developmental Medicine and Child Neurology, 21*, 765–772.

Carpenter, R. L., & Apter, S. J. (1987). Research integration of cognitive-emotional interventions for behaviorally disordered children and youth. In M. C. Wang, H. J. Walberg, & M. C. Reynolds (Eds.), *The handbook of special education: Research*

and practice. Oxford, England: Pergamon Press.

Cartledge, G., & Milburn, J. F. (1980). The case for teaching social skills in the classroom: A review. *Review of Educational Research, 48*, 133–156.

Cartledge, G., & Milburn, J. F. (1986). *Teaching social skills to children*. Elmsford, NY: Pergamon Press.

Cartwright, C. A., & Cartwright, G. P. (1984). *Developing observation skills* (2nd Ed.). New York: McGraw-Hill.

Cartwright, G. P., Cartwright, C. A., & Ward, M. E. (1984). *Educating special learners* (2nd ed.). Belmont, CA: Wadsworth.

Chapman, W. E. (1977). *Roots of character education*. Schenectady, NY: Character Research Press.

Chess, S., Thomas, A., & Birch, H. G. (1967). Behavior problems revisited: An anterospective study. *Journal of the American Academy of Child Psychiatry, 6*, 321–331.

Claghorn, J. (1972). A double-blind comparison of haloperidol (Haldol) and thioridazine (Mellaril) in outpatient children. *Current Therapeutic Research, 14*, 785–789.

Coates, B. (1972). White adult behavior toward black and white children. *Child Development, 43*, 145–154.

Cobb, D., & Evans, J. (1981). The use of biofeedback techniques with school-aged children exhibiting behavioral and/or learning problems. *Journal of Abnormal Child Psychology, 9*, 251–281.

Coleman, M. C. (1986). *Behavior disorders: Theory and practice*. Englewood Cliffs, NJ: Prentice-Hall.

Coleman, M. C., & Gilliam, J. E. (1983). Disturbing behaviors in the classroom: A survey of teacher attitudes. *The Journal of Special Education, 17*, 121–129.

Conger, R. D. (1981). The assessment of dysfunctional family systems. In B. B. Lahey & A. E. Kazdin (Eds.), *Advances in clinical child psychology* (Vol. 4, pp. 199–243). New York: Plenum Press.

Cook, J. M. E., & Leffingwell, R. J. (1982). Stressors and remediation techniques for special educators. *Exceptional Children, 49*, 54–59.

Coopersmith, S. A. (1981). *Coopersmith self-esteem inventories*. Monterey, CA: Publishers Test Service.

Cornett, C. E., & Cornett, C. F. (1980). *Bibliotherapy: The right book at the right time*. Bloomington, IN: Phi Delta Kappa Educational Foundation.

Costello, C. G. (1981). Childhood depression. In E. J. Mash & L. G. Terdal (Eds.), *Behavioral assess-*

ment of childhood disorders (pp. 305–346). New York: Guilford Press.

Cottingham, P. (1975). Black income and metropolitan residential dispersion. *Urban Affairs Quarterly, 10,* 273–296.

Cowen, E., Pederson, A., Barbigian, H., Izzo, L., & Trost, M. (1973). Long-term follow-up of early detected vulnerable children. *Journal of Consulting and Clinical Psychology, 41,* 436–438.

Cox, A., Rutter, M., Newman, S., & Bartak, L. (1975). A comparative study of infantile autism and specific developmental receptive language disorder: II. Parental characteristics. *British Journal of Psychiatry, 126,* 146–159.

Creak, M. (1961). Schizophrenic syndrome in childhood. Progress report of a working party. *Cerebral Palsy Bulletin, 3,* 501–504.

Crohn, H. Sager, C. J., Rodstein, E., Brown, H. S., Walker, L., & Beir, J. (1981). Understanding and treating the child in the remarried family. In I. R. Stewart & L. E. Abt (Eds.), *Children of separation and divorce: Management and treatment* (pp. 293–317). New York: Van Nostrand Reinhold.

Cruickshank, W., Bentzen, F., Ratzeburg, F., & Tannhauser, M. (1961). *A teaching method for brain-injured and hyperactive children.* Syracuse, NY: Syracuse University Press.

Cullinan, D., Epstein, M. H., & Dembinski, R. J. (1979). Behavior problems of educationally handicapped and normal pupils. *Journal of Abnormal Child Psychology, 7,* 475–502.

Cullinan, D., Epstein, M. H., & Kauffman, J. M. (1982). The behavioral model and children's behavior disorders: Foundation and evaluations. In R. L. McDowell, G. W. Adamson, & F. H. Wood (Eds.), *Teaching emotionally disturbed children.* Boston: Little, Brown and Co.

Cullinan, D., Epstein, M. H., & Schultz, R. M. (1987). Important SED teacher competencies to residential, local, and university authorities. *Teacher Education and Special Education, 9,* 63–70.

Cullinan, D., Epstein, M., & Lloyd, J. (1983). *Behavior disorders of children.* Englewood Cliffs, NJ: Prentice-Hall.

Cytryn L., & McKnew, D. H. (1972). Proposed classification of childhood depression. *American Journal of Psychiatry, 129,* 149–155.

Dahl, E. K., Cohen, D. J., & Provence, S. (1986). Clinical and multivariate approaches to the nosology of pervasive developmental disorders. *Journal of the American Academy of Child Psychiatry, 25,* 170–180.

Daniels, W. D. Jr. (1980). Tumbling my way to success. In N. J. Long, W. C. Morse, & R. J. Newman (Eds.), *Conflict in the classroom: The education of emotionally disturbed children* (4th ed.). Belmont, CA: Wadsworth.

Darby, J. K. (1976). Neuropathologic aspects of psychosis in children. *Journal of Autism and Childhood Schizophrenia, 6,* 339–352.

David, O. J., Clark, J., & Voeller, K. (1972). Lead and hyperactivity. *The Lancet, 2,* 900–903.

DeMagistris, R. J., & Imber, S. C. (1980). The effects of life space interviewing on academic and social performance of behaviorally disordered children. *Behavioral Disorders, 6,* 12–25.

Dembinski, R. J., Schultz, E. W., & Walton, W. T. (1982). Curriculum intervention with the emotionally disturbed student: A psychoeducational perspective. In R. L. McDowell, G. W. Adamson, & F. H. Wood (Eds.), *Teaching emotionally disturbed children.* Boston: Little, Brown and Co.

DeMyer, M. K., Barton, S., Alpern, G. D., Kimberlin, C., Allen, J., Yang, E., & Steele, R. (1974). The measured intelligence of autistic children. *Journal of Autism and Childhood Schizophrenia, 4,* 42–60.

DeMyer, M. K., Barton, S., DeMyer, W. E., Norton, J. A., Allen, J., & Steele, R. (1973). Prognosis in autism: A follow-up study. *Journal of Autism and Childhood Schizophrenia, 3,* 199–246.

DeMyer, M. K., & Ferster, C. B. (1962). Teaching new social behavior to schizophrenic children. *Journal of the American Academy of Child Psychiatry, 1,* 443–461.

DeMyer, M. K., Hingtgen, J. N., & Jackson, R. K. (1981). Infantile autism reviewed: A decade of research. *Schizophrenia Bulletin, 7,* 388–451.

DeMyer, M. K., Pontius, W., Norton, J. A., Barton, S., Allen, J., & Steele, R. (1972). Parental practices and innate activity in normal, autistic, and brain-damaged infants. *Journal of Autism and Childhood Schizophrenia, 2,* 49–66.

Deno, E. (1970). Special education as developmental capital. *Exceptional Children, 37,* 229–237.

Deno, S., & Mirkin, P. K. (1977). *Data-based program modification.* Reston, VA: Council for Exceptional Children.

De Sanctis, S. (1971). On some varieties of dementia praecox. In J. G. Howells (Ed.), *Modern perspectives in international child psychiatry* (pp. 590–609).

New York: Brunner/Mazel. (Reprinted from *Rivista Sperimentale di Freniatria*, 1906, *32*, 141–165.)

Deshler, D. D., & Schumaker, J. B. (1986). Learning strategies: An instructional alternative for low-achieving adolescents. *Exceptional Children, 52*, 583–590.

Deshler, D. D., Schumaker, J. B., & Lenz, B. K. (1984). Academic and cognitive interventions for LD adolescents: Part 1. *Journal of Learning Disabilities, 17*, 108–117.

DesLauriers, A. M. (1978). Play, symbols, and the development of language. In M. Rutter & E. Schopler (Eds.), *Autism: A reappraisal of concepts and treatment.* New York: Plenum Press.

DesLauriers, A. M., & Carlson, C. (1969). *Your child is asleep.* Homewood, IL: Dorsey Press.

Despert, J. L. (1938). Schizophrenia in children. *Psychiatric Quarterly, 12*, 366.

Despert, J. L. (1965). *The emotionally disturbed child—then and now.* New York: Robert Brunner.

Despert, J. L. (1968). *Schizophrenia in children.* New York: Robert Brunner.

Dewey, J. (1938). *Experience and education.* New York: Collier.

Deykin, E. Y., & McMahon, B. (1979). The incidence of seizures among children with autistic symptoms. *American Journal of Psychiatry, 136*, 1310–1312.

Dietz, D. E., & Repp, A. C. (1983). Reducing behavior through reinforcement. *Exceptional Education Quarterly, 3*, 34–36.

Dinkmeyer, D. (1982). *Developing understanding of self and others—revised* (DUSO-R). Circle Pines, MN: American Guidance Service.

Dollard, J., & Miller, N. E. (1950). *Personality and psychotherapy.* New York: McGraw-Hill.

Donnellan, A. M. (1984). The criterion of the least dangerous assumption. *Behavioral Disorders, 9*, 141–150.

Dorval, B., McKinney, J. D., & Feagans, L. (1982). Teacher interaction with learning disabled children and average achievers. *Journal of Pediatric Psychology, 17*, 317–330.

Drake, H. (1981). Helping children cope with divorce: The role of the school. In I. R. Stewart & L. E. Abt (Eds.), *Children of separation and divorce: Management and treatment* (pp. 147–172). New York: Van Nostrand Reinhold.

Dreger, R. M., & Miller, K. S. (1968). Comparative psychological studies of Negroes and whites in the United States: 1959–1965. *Psychological Bulletin, 70* (Supplement), 1–58.

Dreyer, S. S. (1985). *The bookfinder* (Vol. 3). Circle Pines, MN: American Guidance Service.

Dupont, H. (1977). Toward affective development: Teaching for personal development. In *Proceedings of a Conference on Preparing Teachers to Foster Personal Growth in Emotionally Disturbed Students.* Minneapolis, MN: University of Minnesota, Department of Psychoeducational Studies.

Dupont, H., & Dupont, C. (1979). *Transition.* Circle Pines, MN: American Guidance Service.

Dupont, H., Gardner, O. W., & Brody, D. S. (1974). *Toward affective development* (TAD). Circle Pines, MN: American Guidance Service.

DuPont, R. L. (1984). *Getting tough on gateway drugs: A guide for the family.* Washington, DC: American Psychiatric Press.

Edelbrock, C., Costello, A. J., & Kessler, M. D. (1984). Empirical corroboration of the attention deficit disorder. *Journal of the American Academy of Child Psychiatry, 23*, 285–290.

Edelbrock, C. S., & Achenbach, T. M. (1980). A typology of child behavior profile patterns: Distribution and correlates for disturbed children aged 6–16. *Journal of Abnormal Child Psychology, 8*, 441–470.

Edelman, M. W. (1987). *Families in peril: An agenda for social change.* Cambridge, MA: Harvard University Press.

Edgar, E. (1987). Secondary programs in special education: Are many of them justifiable? *Exceptional Children, 53*, 555–561.

Eggers, C. (1978). Course and prognosis of childhood schizophrenia, *Journal of Autism and Childhood Schizophrenia, 8*, 21–36.

Einstein, E. (1982). *The stepfamily: Living, loving, and learning.* New York: Macmillan.

Eisenberg, L. (1957). The fathers of autistic children. *American Journal of Orthopsychiatry, 27*, 715–724.

Eisenberg, L., & Kanner, L. (1956). Early infantile autism: 1943–1955. *American Journal of Orthopsychiatry, 36*, 556–566.

Elias, M. J. (1983). Improving coping skills of emotionally disturbed boys through television-based social problem solving. *American Journal of Orthopsychiatry, 53*, 61–72.

Elliott, S. N., Witt, J. C., Galvin, G. A., & Peterson, R. L. (1984). Acceptability of positive and reductive behavioral interventions: Factors that influence teachers' decisions. *The Journal of School Psychology, 22,* 353–360.

Emery, R. E. (1982). Interparental conflict and the children of discord and divorce. *Psychological Bulletin, 92,* 310–330.

Empey, L. T. (1967). Delinquent subcultures: Theory and recent research. *Journal of Research in Crime and Delinquency, 4,* 32–42.

Engelhardt, D., Polizos, P., & Waizer, J. (1975). CNS consequences of psychotropic drug withdrawal in children: A follow-up report. *Psychopharmacology Bulletin, 11,* 6–7.

Epstein, M. H., & Cullinan, D. (1983). Academic performance of behaviorally disordered and learning disabled pupils. *The Journal of Special Education, 17,* 303–307.

Epstein, M. H., & Olinger, E. (1987). Use of medication in school programs for behaviorally disordered pupils. *Behavioral Disorders, 13,* 138–145.

Erikson, E. (1959). *Identity and the life cycle: Selected papers by Erik H. Erikson.* New York: International Universities Press.

Erikson, E. (1963). *Childhood and society.* (2nd ed.) New York: W. W. Norton.

Erikson, E. (1964). *Insight and responsibility.* New York: W. W. Norton.

Erikson, E. (1968). *Identity: Youth and crisis.* New York: W. W. Norton.

Etaugh, C. (1980). Effects of nonmaternal care on children: Research evidence and popular views. *American Psychologist, 35,* 309–319.

Etscheidt, S., Stainback, S., & Stainback, W. (1984). The effectiveness of teacher proximity as an initial technique of helping pupils control their behavior. *The Pointer, 28,* 33–35.

Evans, S. S., Evans, W. H., & Mercer, C. D. (1986). *Assessment for instruction.* Boston: Allyn and Bacon.

Evans, W. H., Evans, S. S., Schmid, R. E., & Pennypacker, H. S. (1985). The effects of exercise on selected classroom behaviors of behaviorally disordered adolescents. *Behavioral Disorders, 11,* 42–51.

Evertson, C., Hawley, W., & Zlotnick, M. (1984). *The characteristics of effective teacher preparation programs: A review of research.* Nashville, TN: Vanderbilt University, Peabody Center for Effective Teaching.

Eysenck, H. J. (1976). The learning theory model of neurosis—a new approach. *Behavior Research and Therapy, 14,* 251–268.

Eysenck, H. J. (1977). *Crime and personality.* London: Routledge and Kegan Paul.

Eysenck, H. J., & Prell, D. B. (1951). The inheritance of neuroticism: An experimental study. *Journal of Mental Science, 97,* 441–467.

Fagen, S. A. (1978). Sustaining our teaching resources: A public school-based internship in special education. In C. M. Nelson (Ed.), *Field-based teacher training: Applications in special education.* Minneapolis, MN: University of Minnesota, Department of Psychoeducational Studies.

Fagen, S. A., Long, N., & Stevens, D. (1975). *Teaching children self-control: Preventing emotional and learning problems in the elementary school.* Columbus, OH: Charles E. Merrill.

Faretra, G., Dooher, L., & Dowling, J. (1970). Comparison of haloperidol and fluphenazine in disturbed children. *American Journal of Psychiatry, 126,* 1670–1673.

Farley, R. (1977). Trends in racial inequalities: Have the gains of the 1960's disappeared in the 1970's? *American Sociological Review, 42,* 189–208.

Feagans, L. (1974). Ecological theory as a model for constructing a theory of emotional disturbance. In W. C. Rhodes & M. L. Tracy (Eds.), *A study of child variance (Vol. 1): Conceptual models* (pp. 323–389). Ann Arbor: University of Michigan Press.

Feagans, L., & McKinney, J. D. (1981). The pattern of exceptionality across domains in learning disabled children. *Journal of Applied Developmental Psychology, 1,* 313–328.

Federal Register. (1977). *Regulations implementing Education for All Handicapped Children Act of 1975* (Public Law 94-142), (August 23), 42474–42518. Author.

Fein, D., Pennington, B., Markowitz, P., Braverman, M., & Waterhouse, L. (1986). Toward a neuropsychological model of infantile autism: Are the social deficits primary? *Journal of the American Academy of Child Psychiatry, 25,* 198–212.

Fein, D., Skoff, B., & Mirsky, A. F. (1981). Clinical correlates of brainstem dysfunction in autistic children. *Journal of Autism and Developmental Disorders, 3,* 303–314.

Feinberg, F. C., & Wood, F. H. (1978). Goals for teachers of seriously emotionally disturbed children. In F. H. Wood (Ed.), *Preparing teachers to develop and maintain therapeutic educational environments.* Minneapolis, MN: University of Minnesota, Department of Psychoeducational Studies.

Feingold, B. F. (1975). *Why your child is hyperactive.* New York: Random House.

Feingold, B. F. (1976). Hyperkinesis and learning disabilities linked to the ingestion of artificial food colors and flavors. *Journal of Learning Disabilities, 9,* 551–559.

Feldman, D. (1964). Psychoanalysis and crime. In B. Rosenberg, I. Gerver, & F. W. Howton (Eds.), *Mass society in crisis* (pp. 50–58). New York: Macmillan.

Fenichel, C. (1971). Psychoeducational approaches for seriously disturbed children in the classroom. In N. J. Long, W. C. Morse, & R. G. Newman (Eds.), *Conflict in the classroom* (2nd ed.). Belmont, CA: Wadsworth.

Fenichel, C. (1974a). Carl Fenichel. In J. M. Kauffman & C. D. Lewis (Eds.), *Teaching children with behavior disorders: Personal perspectives.* Columbus, OH: Charles E. Merrill.

Fenichel, C. (1974b). Special education as the basic therapeutic tool in treatment of severely disturbed children. *Journal of Autism and Childhood Schizophrenia, 4,* 177–186.

Fenichel, O. (1945). *The psychoanalytic theory of neurosis.* New York: W. W. Norton.

Ferster, C. B. (1961). Positive reinforcement and behavioral deficits of autistic children. *Child Development, 32,* 437–456.

Ferster, C. B., & DeMyer, M. K. (1961). The development of performances in autistic children in an automatically controlled environment. *Journal of Chronic Disease, 13,* 312–345.

Fiedler, N. L., & Ullman, D. G. (1983). The effects of stimulant drugs on curiosity behaviors of hyperactive boys. *Journal of Abnormal Child Psychology, 11,* 193–206.

Fimian, M. J. (1986). Social support, stress, and special education teachers: Improving the work situation. *The Pointer, 31,* 49–53.

Firestone, P., Crowe, D., Goodman, J. T., & McGrath, R. (1986). Vicissitudes of follow-up studies: Differential effects of parent training and stimulant medication with hyperactives. *American Journal of Orthopsychiatry, 56,* 184–194.

Fiscus, E. D., & Mandell, C. J. (1983). *Developing individualized education programs.* St. Paul, MN: West.

Fishburne, P. M., & Cisin, I. (1980). *National survey on drug abuse: Main findings: 1979.* Rockville, MD: National Institute on Drug Abuse (NIDA).

Fitts, W. (1965). *Tennessee self-concept inventory.* Nashville, TN: Counselor Recordings and Tests.

Fitzgerald, G. E. (1982). *Practical approaches for documenting behavioral progress of behaviorally disordered students.* Des Moines, IA: Drake University, Midwest Regional Resource Center.

Fleck, S. (1985). The family and psychiatry, In H. I. Kaplan & B. J. Sadock (Eds.), *Comprehensive textbook of psychiatry* (4th ed., pp. 273–294). Baltimore, MD: Williams & Wilkins.

Folstein, S., & Rutter, M. (1977). Genetic influences and infantile autism. *Nature, 265,* 726–728.

Forness, S. R. (1979). Normative behavioral data as a standard in classroom treatment of educationally handicapped children. In R. B. Rutherford, Jr. & A. G. Prieto (Eds.), *Monograph in behavioral disorders.* Reston, VA: Council for Exceptional Children.

Forness, S. R., Sinclair, E., & Russell, A. T. (1984). Serving children with emotional or behavior disorders: Implications for educational policy. *American Journal of Orthopsychiatry, 54,* 22–32.

Frances, A., & Schiff, M. (1976). Popular music as a catalyst in the induction of therapy groups for teenagers. *International Journal of Group Psychotherapy, 26,* 393–398.

Francescani, C. (1982). MARC: An affective curriculum for emotionally disturbed adolescents. *Teaching Exceptional Children, 14,* 217–222.

Frank, G. H. (1965). The role of the family in the development of psychopathology. *Psychological Bulletin, 64,* 191–205.

Frank, S. M., Allen, D. A., Stein, L., & Myers, B. (1976). Linguistic performance in vulnerable and autistic children and their mothers. *American Journal of Psychiatry, 133,* 909–915.

Frankel, F. (1976). Experimental studies of autistic children in the classroom. In E. Ritvo, B. J. Freeman, E. Ornitz, & P. Tanguay (Eds.), *Autism: Diagnosis, current research, and management* (pp. 185–194). New York: Spectrum Publications.

Franks, C. M., Wilson, G. T., Kendall, P. C., & Brownell, K. D. (1984). *Annual review of behavior therapy* (Vol. 10). New York: Guilford Press.

French, A. P. (1979). "Depression in children"–the development of an idea. In A. French & I. Berlin (Eds.), *Depression in children and adolescents* (pp. 17–28). New York: Human Sciences Press.

Freud, S. (1930). *Civilization and its discontents.* London: Hogarth Press.

Freud, S. (1936). *The problem of anxiety.* New York: Psychoanalytic Quarterly Press.

Freudenberger, H. J. (1974). Staff burnout. *Journal of Social Issues, 30,* 1959–1965.

Friedlander, S., Pothier, P., Morrison, D., & Herman, L. (1982). The role of neurological-developmental delay in childhood psychopathology. *American Journal of Orthopsychiatry, 51,* 102–107.

Frommer, E. A. (1967). Treatment of childhood depression with antidepressant drugs. *British Medical Journal, 1,* 729–32.

Gadow, K. D. (1979). *Children on medication: A primer for school personnel.* Reston, VA: The Council for Exceptional Children.

Gadpaille, W. J. (1980). Psychiatric treatment of the adolescent. In H. I. Kaplan & B. J. Sadock (Eds.), *Comprehensive textbook of psychiatry* (4th ed., pp. 1805–1812). Baltimore, MD: Williams & Wilkins.

Gajar, A. (1979). Educable mentally retarded, learning disabled, emotionally disturbed: Similarities and differences. *Exceptional Children, 45,* 470–472.

Gallagher, J. J. (1976). James J. Gallagher. In J. M. Kauffman & D. P. Hallahan (Eds.), *Teaching children with learning disabilities: Personal perspectives.* Columbus, OH: Charles E. Merrill.

Gast, D. L., & Nelson, C. M. (1977a). Legal and ethical considerations for the use of time-out in special education settings. *Journal of Special Education, 11,* 457–467.

Gast, D. L., & Nelson, C. M. (1977b). Time-out in the classroom: Implications for special education. *Exceptional Children, 43,* 461–464.

Gaylord-Ross, R. J., Haring, T. G., Breen, C., & Pitts-Conway, V. (1984). The training and generalization of social interaction skill with autistic youth. *Journal of Applied Behavior Analysis, 17,* 229–247.

Gaylord-Ross, R. J., & Pitts-Conway, V. (1983). Social behavior development in integrated secondary autistic programs. In N. Certo, T. G. Haring, & R. York (Eds.), *Public school integration of the severely handicapped: Rational issues and progressive alternatives* (pp. 197–219). Baltimore, MD: Paul H. Brooks.

Georgotas, A. (1980). Affective disorders: Pharmacotherapy. In H. I. Kaplan & B. J. Sadock (Eds.), *Comprehensive textbook of psychiatry* (4th ed., pp. 822–833). Baltimore, MD: Williams & Wilkins.

Gersten, R., Woodward, J., & Darch, C. (1986). Direct instruction: A research-based approach to curriculum design and teaching. *Exceptional Children, 53,* 17–31.

Gillberg, G., & Schaumann, H. (1982). Social class and infantile autism. *Journal of Autism and Developmental Disorders, 12,* 223–228.

Gillberg, G., Terenius, L., & Lonnerholm, G. (1985). Endorphin activity in childhood psychosis. *Archives of General Psychiatry, 42,* 780–783.

Gittelman, M., & Birch, H. G. (1967). Childhood schizophrenia: Intellect, neurological status, perinatal risk and family pathology. *Archives of General Psychiatry, 17,* 271–278.

Gittelman, R., Mannuzza, S., Shenker, R., & Bonagura, N. (1985). Hyperactive boys almost grown up: I. Psychiatric status. *Archives of General Psychiatry, 42,* 937–947.

Glasser, W. (1965). *Reality therapy.* New York: Harper & Row.

Glasser, W. (1969). *Schools without failure.* New York: Harper & Row.

Glen, D., Rueda, R., & Rutherford, R. (1984). Cognitive approaches to social competence with behaviorally disordered youth. In J. K. Grosenick, S. L. Huntze, E. McGinnis, & C. R. Smith (Eds.), *Social/affective interventions in behavioral disorders.* Columbia, MO: University of Missouri–Columbia, Department of Special Education, National Needs Analysis in Behavior Disorders Project.

Glidewell, J. C., & Swallow, C. S. (1969). *The prevalence of maladjustment in elementary schools.* Chicago: University of Chicago Press.

Glueck, S., & Glueck, E. (1950). *Unraveling juvenile delinquency.* New York: Commonwealth Fund.

Glueck, S., & Glueck, E. (1962). *Family environment and delinquency.* Boston: Houghton Mifflin.

Glueck, S., & Glueck, E. (1968). *Delinquents and nondelinquents in perspective.* Cambridge, MA: Harvard University Press.

Goddard, H. H. (1912). *The Kallikak family: A study in the heredity of feeble-mindedness.* New York: Macmillan.

Goldstein, A. P., Sprafkin, R. P., Gershaw, N. J., & Klein, P. (1980). *Skill-streaming the adolescent: A structured approach to teaching prosocial skills.* Champaign, IL: Research Press.

Goldstein, A. P., Sprafkin, R. P., Gershaw, N. J., & Klein, P. (1983). Structured learning: A psychoeducational approach for teaching social competencies. *Behavioral Disorders, 8,* 161–170.

Goldstein, H. S. (1984). Parental composition, supervision, and conduct problems in youths 12 to 17 years old. *Journal of the American Academy of Child Psychiatry, 23,* 679–684.

Good, T. L. (1981). Teacher expectations and student

perceptions: A decade of research. *Educational Leadership, 38,* 415–421.

Gottman, J., & McFall, R. (1972). Self-monitoring effects in a program for potential high school dropouts. *Journal of Consulting and Clinical Psychology, 39,* 273–281.

Gould, M. S., & Shaffer, D. (1986). The impact of suicide in television movies: Evidence of imitation. *New England Journal of Medicine, 315,* 690–694.

Graham, P., Rutter, M., & George, S. (1973). Temperamental characteristics as predictors of behavior disorders in children. *American Journal of Orthopsychiatry, 43,* 328–339.

Graubard, P. S. (1969). Utilizing the group in teaching disturbed delinquents to learn. *Exceptional Children, 35,* 267–272.

Graubard, P. S. (1973). Children with behavioral disabilities. In L. Dunn (Ed.), *Exceptional children in the schools.* New York: Holt, Rinehart & Winston.

Graziano, A., & De Giovanni, I. S. (1979). The clinical significance of childhood phobias: A note on the proportion of child-clinical referrals for the treatment of children's fears. *Behavior Research and Therapy, 17,* 161.

Graziano, A. M. (1978). Parents as behavior therapists. In M. Hersen, R. Eisler, & P. M. Miller (Eds.), *Progress in behavior modification.* New York: Academic Press.

Greenough, K. N., Huntze, S. L., Nelson, C. M., & Simpson, R. L. (1983). *Noncategorical versus categorical issues in programming for behaviorally disordered children and youth.* Columbia, MO: University of Missouri–Columbia, Department of Special Education, National Needs Analysis/Leadership Training Project.

Greer, J. G., & Wethered, C. E. (1984). Learned helplessness: A piece of the burnout puzzle. *Exceptional Children, 50,* 526–530.

Gresham, F. M. (1979). Comparison of response cost and time-out in a special education setting. *Journal of Special Education, 13,* 199–208.

Gresham, F. M. (1981). Social skills training with handicapped children: A review. *Review of Educational Research, 51,* 139–176.

Gresham, F. M. (1984). Social skills and self-efficacy for exceptional children. *Exceptional Children, 51,* 253–261.

Grief, J. (1979). Fathers, children and joint custody. *American Journal of Orthopsychiatry, 49,* 311–319.

Grosenick, J. K. (1971). Integration of exceptional children into regular classes: Research and procedures. *Focus on Exceptional Children, 3,* 1–8.

Grosenick, J. K. (1986). *Program effectiveness: Current practices and future prospects.* Paper presented at Midwest Symposium for Leadership in Behavioral Disorders, 28 February, at Kansas City, MO.

Grosenick, J. K., & Huntze, S. L. (1980). *National needs analysis in behavior disorders: Severe behavior disorders.* Columbia, MO: University of Missouri, Department of Special Education.

Grosenick, J. K., & Huntze, S. L. (1983). *More questions than answers: Review and analysis of programs for behaviorally disordered children and youth.* Columbia, MO: University of Missouri–Columbia, Department of Special Education, National Needs Analysis/Leadership Training Institute.

Grosenick, J. K., Huntze, S. L., Kochan, B., Peterson, R. L., Robertshaw, C. S., & Wood, F. H. (1982a). *Disciplinary exclusion of seriously emotionally disturbed children from public schools.* Des Moines, IA: Drake University, Midwest Regional Resource Center.

Grosenick, J. K., Huntze, S. L., Kochan, B., Peterson, R. L., Robertshaw, C. S., & Wood, F. H. (1982b). *National needs analysis in behavior disorders: Psychotherapy as a related service.* Columbia, MO: University of Missouri, Department of Special Education.

Gross, M. D., Tofanelli, R. A., Butziris, S. M., & Snodgrass, E. A. (1987). The effect of diets rich in and free from additives on the behavior of children with hyperkinetic and learning disorders. *Journal of the American Academy of Child and Adolescent Psychiatry, 26,* 53–55.

Grossman, H. (Ed.) (1973). *Manual on terminology and classification in mental retardation* (rev. ed.). Washington, DC: American Association on Mental Deficiency.

Group for the Advancement of Psychiatry (1966). *Psychopathological disorders in childhood: Theoretical considerations and a proposed classification* (GAP Report No. 62).

Group for the Advancement of Psychiatry (1973). *The joys and sorrows of parenthood.* New York: Charles Scribner's Sons.

Guetzloe, E. (1984). CCBD newsletter. *Behavioral Disorders, 10,* 75–78.

Guidubaldi, J., & Perry, J. D. (1985). Divorce, socioeconomic status, and children's cognitive-social competence at school entry. *American Journal of Orthopsychiatry, 54,* 459–468.

Hacker, A. (1983). *U/S: A statistical portrait of the American people.* New York: Viking Press.

Hall, R. V., Hawkins, R. P., & Axelrod, S. (1975). Measuring and recording student behavior: A behavior analysis approach. In R. A. Weinberg & F. H. Wood (Eds.), *Observation of pupils and teachers in mainstream and special education: Alternative strategies.* Minneapolis, MN: University of Minnesota, Leadership Training Institute/Special Education.

Hallahan, D. P., & Kauffman, J. M. (1977). Labels, categories, behaviors: ED, LD, and EMR reconsidered. *Journal of Special Education, 11,* 139–149.

Halperin, J. M., Gittelman, R., Katz, S., & Struve, F. A. (1986). Relationship between stimulant effect, electroencephalogram, and clinical neurological findings in hyperactive children. *Journal of the American Academy of Child Psychiatry, 25,* 820–825.

Hammill, D., & Larsen, S. (1978). The effectiveness of psycholinguistic training, *Exceptional Children, 41,* 5–14.

Hammill, D., Leigh, L. E., McNutt, G., & Larsen, S. C. (1981). A new definition of learning disabilities. *Learning Disabilities Quarterly, 4,* 336–342.

Hanna, G., Dyck, N., & Holen, M. (1979). Objective analysis of achievement-aptitude discrepancies in LD classification. *Learning Disabilities Quarterly, 2,* 32–38.

Hanson, D. R., & Gottesman, I. I. (1976). The genetics, if any, of infantile autism and childhood schizophrenia. *Schizophrenia Bulletin, 6,* 209–234.

Haring, N. G., & Fargo, G. A. (1969). Evaluating programs for preparing teachers of emotionally disturbed children. *Exceptional Children, 36,* 157–162.

Harms, J. M., Etscheidt, S. L., & Lettow, L. J. (1986). Extending emotional responses through poetry experiences. In M. K. Zabel (Ed.), *TEACHING: Behaviorally disordered youth* (Vol. 2), Reston, VA: Council for Exceptional Children.

Harper, L. V. (1975). The scope of offspring effects: From caregiver to culture. *Psychological Bulletin, 82,* 784–801.

Harrington, R. G. (1984). Assessment of learning disabled children. In J. Weaver (Ed.), *Testing children.* Kansas City, MO: Test Corporation of America.

Harris, K. R. (1982). Cognitive-behavior modification: Application with exceptional students. *Focus on Exceptional Children, 15,* 1–16.

Harris, K. R. (1985). Definitional, parametric, and procedural considerations in time-out interventions and research. *Exceptional Children, 51,* 279–288.

Harris, S. L. (1982). A family systems approach to behavioral training with parents of autistic children. *Child and Family Behavior Therapy, 4,* 21–35.

Harris, W. J. (1984). The Making Better Choices program. *The Pointer, 29,* 16–19.

Healy, W., & Alper, B. (1941). *Criminal youth and the Borstal System.* New York: The Commonwealth Fund.

Hechtman, L., & Weiss, G. (1983). Long-term outcome of hyperactive children. *American Journal of Orthopsychiatry, 53,* 532–541.

Hechtman, L., Weiss, G., & Perlman, T. (1984a). Hyperactives as young adults: Past and current substance abuse and antisocial behavior. *American Journal of Orthopsychiatry, 54,* 415–425.

Hechtman, L., Weiss, G., & Perlman, T. (1984b). Young adult outcome of hyperactive children who received long-term stimulant treatment. *Journal of the American Academy of Child Psychiatry, 23,* 261–269.

Heller, T. (1930). About dementia infantilis. Reprinted in J. G. Howells (Ed.). (1969). *Modern perspectives in international child psychiatry.* New York: Brunner/Mazel.

Heron, T. E. (1978). Punishment: A review of the literature with implications for the teacher of mainstreamed children. *Journal of Special Education, 12,* 243–252.

Heron, T. E., & Harris, K. C. (1982). *The educational consultant: Helping professionals, parents, and mainstreamed students.* Boston: Allyn and Bacon.

Hersh, R. H., & Walker, H. (1982). *Great expectations: Making schools effective for all students.* Eugene, OR: Department of Special Education.

Hetherington, E. M. (1979). Divorce: A child's perspective. *American Psychologist, 34,* 851–858.

Hetherington, E. M. (1984). Stress and coping in children and families. In A. B. Doyle, D. Gold, & D. S. Moskowitz (Eds.), *Children in families under stress: New directions for child development* (pp. 7–34). San Francisco: Jossey Bass.

Hetherington, E. M., Arnett, J., & Hollier, A. (1985). The effects of remarriage on children and families. In P. Karoly & S. Wolchik (Eds.), *Family transition.* New York: Garland Press.

Hetherington, E. M., Cox, M., & Cox, R. (1985). Long-term effects of divorce and remarriage on the adjustment of children. *Journal of the American Academy of Child Psychiatry, 24,* 518–530.

Hetherington, E. M., & Martin, B. (1972). Family interaction and psychopathology in children. In

H. C. Quay & J. S. Werry (Eds.), *Psychopathological disorders of childhood* (pp. 30–82). New York: John Wiley & Sons.

Heuchert, C. M., Morrisey, D., & Jackson, S. R. (1980). TREES: A five-day residential alternative school for emotionally disturbed adolescents. In N. J. Long, W. C. Morse, & R. G. Newman (Eds.), *Conflict in the classroom: The education of emotionally disturbed children*. Belmont, CA: Wadsworth.

Heward, W. L., Cooper, J. O., Heron, T. E., Hill, D. S., McCormick, S., Porter, J. T., Stephens, T. M., & Sutherland, H. A. (1981). Noncategorical teacher training in a state with categorical certification requirements. *Exceptional Children, 48,* 206–212.

Hewett, F. M. (1967). A hierarchy of competencies for teachers of emotionally handicapped children. *Exceptional Children, 33,* 459–467.

Hewett, F. M. (1968). *The emotionally disturbed child in the classroom: A developmental strategy for educating children with maladaptive behavior.* Boston: Allyn and Bacon.

Hewett, F. M. (1981). Behavioral ecology: A unifying strategy for the '80's. In R. Rutherford, A. Prieto, & J. McGlothlin (Eds.), *Severe behavior disorders of children and youth.* Reston, VA: Council for Exceptional Children.

Hewett, F. M., & Forness, S. R. (1977). *Education of exceptional learners.* Boston, Allyn and Bacon.

Hewett, F. M., & Taylor, F. D. (1980). *The emotionally disturbed child in the classroom: The orchestration of success* (2nd ed.). Boston: Allyn and Bacon.

Hewett, F. M., Taylor, F. D., & Artuso, A. A. (1969). The Santa Monica Project: Evaluation of an engineered classroom design with emotionally disturbed children. *Exceptional Children, 46,* 523–529.

Hewitt, L. E., & Jenkins, R. L. (1946). *Fundamental patterns of maladjustment: The dynamics of their origin.* Springfield, IL: State of Illinois.

Himmelweit, H. T. (1953). A factorial study of "children's behavior problems." In H. J. Eysenck (Ed.), *The structure of human personality.* London: Methuen.

Hingtgen, J. N., & Bryson, C. Q. (1972). Recent developments in the study of early childhood psychoses: Infantile autism, childhood schizophrenia, and related disorders. *Schizophrenia Bulletin, 5,* 8–54.

Hirschi, T., & Hindenlang, M. J. (1977). Intelligence and delinquency: A revisionist review. *American Sociological Review, 42,* 571–587.

Hlidek, R. (1979). Creating positive classroom environments. In M. C. Reynolds (Ed.), *What research and experience say to the teacher of exceptional children: Classroom social environments.* Reston, VA: The Council for Exceptional Children.

Hobbs, N. (1966). Helping disturbed children: Ecological and psychological strategies. *American Psychologist, 21,* 1105–1115.

Hobbs, N. (1974). Nicholas Hobbs. In J. M. Kauffman & C. D. Lewis (Eds.), *Teaching children with behavior disorders: Personal perspectives.* Columbus, OH: Charles E. Merrill.

Hobbs, N. (1978). Perspectives on re-education. *Behavioral Disorders, 3,* 65–66.

Hobbs, S. A., & Forehand, R. (1977). Important parameters in the use of time-out with children. A reexamination. *Journal of Behavior Therapy and Experimental Psychology, 9,* 365–370.

Hodgman, C. H. (1985). Recent findings in adolescent depression and suicide. *Journal of Developmental and Behavioral Pediatrics, 6,* 162–170.

Hoffman, L. W. (1979). Maternal employment: 1979. *American Psychologist, 34,* 859–865.

Hoffman, L. W. (1984). Effects of maternal employment on the child—a review of the research. *Developmental Psychology, 10,* 204–228.

Holinger, P. C., & Offer, D. (1982). Prediction of adolescent suicide: A population model. *American Journal of Psychiatry, 139,* 302–307.

Homme, L., Csanyi, A. P., Gonzales, M. A., & Rechs, J. R. (1969). *How to use contingency management in the classroom.* Champaign, IL: Research Press.

Hood-Smith, N. E., & Leffingwell, R. J. (1984). The impact of physical space alteration on disruptive classroom behavior: A case study. *Education, 104,* 224–230.

Hsu, L. K. G., Wisner, K., Richey, E. T., & Goldstein, C. (1985). Is juvenile delinquency related to an abnormal EEG? A study of EEG abnormalities in juvenile delinquents and adolescent psychiatric inpatients. *Journal of the American Academy of Child Psychiatry, 24,* 310–315.

Huber, F. (1976). A strategy for teaching cooperative games: Let's put back the fun in games for disturbed children. In N. J. Long, W. C. Morse, & R. G. Newman (Eds.), *Conflict in the classroom* (3rd. ed.). Belmont, CA: Wadsworth.

Huntze, S. L. (1985). A position paper of The Council for Children with Behavioral Disorders. *Behavioral Disorders, 10,* 167–174.

Huntze, S. L. (1987). Cooperative interface of schools

and other child care systems for the behaviorally disordered. In M. C. Wang, H. J. Walberg, & M. C. Reynolds (Eds.), *Handbook of special education: Research and practice.* Oxford, England: Pergamon Press.

Huntze, S. L., & Grosenick, J. K. (1980). *National needs analysis in behavior disorders: Human resource issues in behavior disorders.* Columbia, MO: University of Missouri–Columbia, Department of Special Education.

Hutt, S., & Hutt, C. (1970). *Behavior studies in psychiatry.* Oxford, England: Pergamon Press.

Hutton, J. B. (1983). How to decrease problem behavior at school by recording desirable behavior at home. *The Pointer, 28,* 25–28.

Imber, S. C., Imber, R. B., & Rothstein, C. (1979). Modifying independent work habits: An effective teacher-parent communication program. *Exceptional Children, 46,* 218–229.

Imig, D. G. (1982). *An examination of the teacher education scope: An overview of the structure and form of teacher education.* Washington, DC: American Association of Colleges of Teacher Education.

Ingraham v. Wright, 430 U.S. 651 (1977).

Jackson, P., & Lahaderne, H. (1967). Inequalities of teacher-pupil contacts. *Psychology in the Schools, 4,* 204–211.

Jacob, T. (1975). Family interaction in disturbed and normal families: A methodological and substantive review. *Psychological Bulletin, 82,* 33–65.

Jacobson, D. S. (1978). The impact of marital separation/divorce on children: II. Interparental hostility and child adjustment. *Journal of Divorce, 2,* 3–20.

James, A. L., & Barry, R. J. (1980). A review of psychophysiology in early onset psychosis. *Schizophrenia Bulletin, 6,* 506–525.

Johnson, D. R., Bruininks, R. H., & Thurlow, M. L. (1987). Meeting the challenge of transition service planning through improved interagency cooperation. *Exceptional Children, 53,* 522–530.

Johnson, D. W., & Johnson, R. T. (1975). *Learning together and alone: Cooperation, competition, and individualization.* Englewood, NJ: Prentice-Hall.

Johnson, J. E. (1981). The etiology of hyperactivity. *Exceptional Children, 47,* 348–354.

Johnson, R. T., & Johnson, D. W. (1983). Effects of cooperative, competitive, and individualistic learning experiences on social development. *Exceptional Children, 49,* 323–329.

Johnston, J., Campbell, L. E. G., & Mayes, S. S. (1985).

Latency children in post-separation and divorce disputes. *Journal of the American Academy of Child Psychiatry, 24,* 563–574.

Johnston, L. D., Bachman, J. G., & O'Malley, P. M. (1977). *Drug use among American high school students 1975–1977.* Rockville, MD: National Institute on Drug Abuse (NIDA).

Joint Commission on the Mental Health of Children. (1970). *Crisis in child mental health: Challenge for the 1970's.* New York: Harper & Row.

Jurkovic, G. J. (1980). The juvenile delinquent as a moral philosopher: A structural developmental perspective. *Psychological Bulletin, 88,* 709–727.

Kalter, N., Riemer, B., Brickman, A., & Chen, J. W. (1985). Implications of parental divorce for female development. *Journal of the American Academy of Child Psychiatry, 5,* 538–544.

Kandel, D. B. (1973). Adolescent marihuana use: Role of parents and peers. *Science, 181,* 1067–1070.

Kandel, D. B. (1974). Inter- and intra-generational influences on adolescent marihuana use. *Journal of Social Issues, 30,* 107–135.

Kandel, D. B., Kessler, R. C., & Margulies, R. Z. (1978). Antecedents of adolescent initiation into stages of drug use: A developmental analysis. In D. B. Kandel (Ed.), *Longitudinal research on drug use: Empirical findings and methodological issues* (pp. 73–79). Washington, DC: Hemisphere.

Kanfer, F. H., & Karoly, D. (1972). Self-control: A behavioristic excursion into the lion's den. *Behavior Therapy, 3,* 398–416.

Kanner, L. (1943). Autistic disturbances of affective contact. *Nervous Child, 2,* 250–271.

Kanner, L. (1949). Problems of nosology and psychodynamics of early infantile autism. *American Journal of Orthopsychiatry, 19,* 416–426.

Kanner, L. J. (1969). The children haven't read those books. *Acta Paedopsychiatrica, 36,* 2–11.

Kardiner, A., & Ovesey, L. (1968). *The mark of oppression: Explorations in the personality of the American Negro.* Cleveland, OH: Meridian Books.

Kaufman, A. S., Swan, W. W., & Wood, M. M. (1980). Do parents, teachers, and psychoeducational evaluators agree in their perceptions of the problems of black and white emotionally disturbed children? *Psychology in the Schools, 17,* 185–191.

Kaufman, K. F., & O'Leary, K. D. (1972). Reward, cost, and self-evaluation procedures for disruptive adolescents in a psychiatric hospital. *Journal of Applied Behavior Analysis, 5,* 293–309.

Kauffman, J. M. (1979). An historical perspective on disordered behavior and an alternative conceptualization of exceptionality. In F. H. Wood & K. C. Lakin (Eds.), *Disturbing, disordered or disturbed: Perspectives on the definition of problem behavior in educational settings* (pp. 49-70). Reston, VA: Council for Exceptional Children.

Kauffman, J. M. (1984). Saving children in the age of Big Brother: Moral and ethical issues in the identification of deviance. *Behavioral Disorders, 10,* 60-70.

Kauffman, J. M. (1986). *Characteristics of children's behavior disorders* (3rd ed.). Columbus, OH: Charles E. Merrill.

Kauffman, J. M., & Hallahan, D. P. (1979). Learning disability and hyperactivity (with comments on minimal brain dysfunction). In B. B. Lahey & A. E. Kazdin (Eds.), *Advances in clinical psychology* (Vol. 2, pp. 71-105). New York: Plenum Press.

Kauffman, J. M., McCullough, L. L., & Sabornie, E. J. (1984). Integrating exceptional students: Special problems involving the emotionally disturbed/behaviorally disordered. *B. C. Journal of Special Education, 8,* 201-210.

Kavale, K. (1981). Functions of the Illinois Test of Psycholinguistic Abilities (ITPA): Are they trainable? *Exceptional Children, 47,* 496-510.

Kavale, K. (1982). The efficacy of stimulant drug treatment for hyperactivity: A meta-analysis. *Journal of Learning Disabilities, 15,* 280-289.

Kavale, K., & Forness, S. R. (1983). Hyperactivity and diet treatment: A meta-analysis of the Feingold hypothesis. *Journal of Learning Disabilities, 16,* 324-330.

Kavale, K., & Forness, S. R. (1984). A meta-analysis of the validity of Wechsler Scale profiles and recategorization: Patterns or parodies? *Learning Disabilities Quarterly, 7,* 136-156.

Kavale, K., & Mattson, P. D. (1983). "One jumped off the balance beam": Meta-analysis of perceptual motor training. *Journal of Learning Disabilities, 16,* 165-173.

Kavale, K. A., & Nye, C. (1984). The effectiveness of drug treatment for severe behavior disorders: A meta-analysis. *Behavior Disorders, 9,* 117-130.

Kazdin, A. E. (1982). The token economy: A decade later. *Journal of Applied Behavior Analysis, 15,* 431-445.

Kazdin, A. E., & Bootzin, R. R. (1972). The token economy: An evaluative review. *Journal of Applied Behavior Analysis, 5,* 343-372.

Kelly, T. J., Bullock, L. M., & Dykes, M. K. (1977). Behavioral disorders: Teachers' perceptions. *Exceptional Children, 43,* 316-318.

Kendler, D. S., Heath, A., Martin, N. G., & Eaves, L. J. (1986). Symptoms of anxiety and depression in a volunteer twin population. *Archives of General Psychiatry, 43,* 213-221.

Kendler, K. S., & Eaves, L. J. (1986). Models for the joint effect of genotype and environment on liability to psychiatric illness. *American Journal of Psychiatry, 143,* 279-289.

Keogh, B. K. (1971). Hyperactivity and learning disorders: Review and speculation. *Exceptional Children, 38,* 101-109.

Keogh, B. K. (1986, July). Research issues in the study of learning disabilities. *Counterpoint,* 6-7.

Kerr, D. H. (1983). Teaching competence and teacher education in the United States. In L. S. Sykes & G. Sykes (Eds.), *Handbook of teaching and policy.* New York: Longman.

Kerr, M. M., & Nelson, C. M. (1983). *Strategies for managing behavior problems in the classroom.* Columbus, OH: Charles E. Merrill.

Kerr, M. M., Shores, R. E., & Stowitschek, J. J. (1978). Peabody's field-based special teacher education program: A model for evaluating competency-based training. In C. M. Nelson (Ed.), *Field-based teacher training: Applications in special education.* Minneapolis, MN: University of Minnesota, Department of Psychoeducational Studies.

Kessler, S. (1980). The genetics of schizophrenia: A review. *Schizophrenia Bulletin, 6,* 404-416.

King, C., & Young, R. D. (1982). Attentional deficits with and without hyperactivity: Teacher and peer perceptions. *Journal of Abnormal Child Psychology, 10,* 483-495.

Kirk, S. (1963). *Proceedings of the Annual Meeting of the Conference on Exploration into the Problems of the Perceptually Handicapped Child* (Vol. 1). Chicago.

Kirk, S. A., & Chalfant, J. C. (1984). *Academic and developmental learning disabilities.* Denver: Love Publishing.

Kirk, S. A., McCarthy, J. J., & Kirk, W. D. (1968). *The Illinois test of psycholinguistic abilities* (rev. ed.). Urbana, IL: University of Illinois Press.

Kitson, G. C., & Langlie, J. D. (1984). Couples who file for divorce but change their minds. *American Journal of Orthopsychiatry, 54,* 469-489.

Klein, M. (1932). *The psychoanalysis of children.* London: Hogarth Press.

Knight, C. J., Peterson, R. L., & McGuire, B. (1982). Cooperative learning: A new approach to an old idea. *Teaching Exceptional Children, 14,* 233–238.

Knoblock, P. (1983). *Teaching emotionally disturbed children.* Boston: Houghton Mifflin.

Kohlberg, L. (1969). Stage and sequence: The cognitive-developmental approach to socialization. In D. A. Goslin (Ed.), *Handbook of socialization theory and research.* Chicago: Rand McNally.

Kohlberg, L. (1976). Moral stages and moralization. In R. Lickona (Ed.), *Moral development and behavior: Theory, research, and social issues.* New York: Holt, Rinehart & Winston.

Korn, S. J., & Gannon, S. (1983). Temperament, cultural variation, and behavior disorder in preschool children. *Child Psychiatry and Human Development, 13,* 203–212.

Kotulak, R. (1986). Youngsters lose way in maze of family instability. *Chicago Tribune,* September 1, Section 6, p. 1.

Kounin, J. S. (1967). An analysis of teachers' managerial techniques. *Psychology in the Schools, 4,* 221–227.

Kounin, J. S. (1970). *Discipline and group management in classrooms.* New York: Holt, Rinehart & Winston.

Kounin, J. S., Friesen, W. V., & Norton, A. E. (1966). Managing emotionally disturbed children in regular classrooms. *Journal of Educational Psychology, 57,* 1–13.

Kounin, J. S., & Gump, P. V. (1974). Signal systems of lesson settings and the task-related behavior of preschool children. *Journal of Educational Psychology, 66,* 554–562.

Kovacs, M. (1986). A developmental perspective on methods and measures in the assessment of depressive disorders: The clinical interview. In M. Rutter, C. E. Izard, & P. B. Read (Eds.), *Depression in young people* (pp. 435–465). New York: Guilford Press.

Kozloff, M. A. (1973). *Reaching the autistic child.* Champaign, IL: Research Press.

Kroth, R. L. (1975). *Communicating with parents of exceptional children: Improving parent-teacher relationships.* Denver: Love Publishing.

Kroth, R. L. (1980). Mirror model of parental involvement. *The Pointer, 25,* 18–22.

Kroth, R. L., & Simpson, R. L. (1977). *Parent conferences as a teaching strategy.* Denver: Love Publishing.

Kurita, H. (1985). Infantile autism with speech loss before the age of thirty months. *Journal of the American Academy of Child Psychiatry, 24,* 191–196.

Kyriacou, C., & Sutcliffe, J. (1978). Teacher stress and satisfaction. *Educational Research, 21,* 89–96.

Lahey, B. B., Schaughency, E. A., Strauss, C. C., & Frame, C. L. (1984). Are attention deficit disorders with and without hyperactivity similar or dissimilar disorders? *Journal of the American Academy of Child Psychiatry, 23,* 302–309.

Lambert, L., Essen, J., & Head, J. (1977). Variations in behavior ratings of children who have been in care. *Journal of Child Psychology and Psychiatry, and Allied Disciplines, 18,* 335–346.

Lambert, N. M., Sandoval, J., & Sassone, D. (1978). Prevalence of hyperactivity in elementary school children as a function of social system definers. *American Journal of Orthopsychiatry, 48,* 446–463.

Lambert, N. M., Windmiller, M., Sandoval, J., & Moore, B. (1976). Hyperactive children and the efficacy of psychoactive drugs as a treatment intervention. *American Journal of Orthopsychiatry, 46,* 335–352.

Lancioni, G. E. (1982). Normal children as tutors to teach social responses to withdrawn mentally retarded schoolmates: Training, maintenance, and generalization. *Journal of Applied Behavior Analysis, 15,* 17–40.

LaNeve, R. (1979). The Mark Twain School: A therapeutic educational environment for emotionally disturbed students. *Behavioral Disorders, 4,* 183–192.

LaPouse, R., & Monk, M. A. (1958). An epidemiologic study of behavior characteristics in children. *American Journal of Public Health, 48,* 1134–44.

LaPouse, R., & Monk, M. A. (1964). Behavior deviations in a representative sample of children. Variation by sex, age, race, social class and family size. *American Journal of Orthopsychiatry, 34,* 436–46.

Larson, J. (1987). An inside look at the 1986 Clarissa H. Hug Teacher of the Year: An interview with Judy Larson. *Teaching Exceptional Children, 19,* 37–39.

Lawrenson, G. M., & McKinnon, A. J. (1982). A survey of classroom teachers of emotionally disturbed: Attrition and burnout factors. *Behavioral Disorders, 8,* 41–49.

Leckman, J. F., Weissman, M. M., Merikangas, K. R., Pauls, D. L., & Prusoff, B. A. (1983). Panic disorder and major depression: Increased risk of depression, alcoholism, panic and phobic disorders in families of depressed probands with panic disorder. *Archives of General Psychiatry, 40,* 1055–1060.

Leese, S. (1974). *Masked depression.* New York: Jason Aronson.

Lennox, C., Callias, M., & Rutter, M. (1977). Cognitive characteristics of parents of autistic children. *Journal of Autism and Childhood Schizophrenia, 7,* 243–261.

Lerner, J. (1981). *Learning disabilities* (3rd ed.). Boston: Houghton Mifflin.

Levine, M., & Rappaport, L. A. (1984). Recurrent abdominal pain in school children: The loneliness of the long distance physician. *Pediatric Clinics of North America, 31,* 969–991.

Levy, D. (1966). *Maternal overprotection.* New York: W. W. Norton.

Lewin, K. (1951). Psychological ecology. In D. Cartwright (Ed.), *Field theory in social science: Selected theoretical papers by Kurt Lewin* (pp. 170–187). New York: Harper & Row.

Lewis, D. O., Lewis, M., Unger, L., & Goldman, C. (1984). Conduct disorder and its synonyms: Diagnoses of dubious validity and usefulness. *The American Journal of Psychiatry, 141,* 514–519.

Lewis, H. (1954). *Deprived children.* London: Oxford University Press.

Lewis, J. M., Beavers, W. R., Gossett, J. T., & Phillips, V. A. (1976). *No single thread: Psychological health in family systems.* New York: Brunner/Mazel.

Lewis, W. W. (1970). Ecological planning for disturbed children. *Childhood Education, 46,* 306–310.

Lewis, W. W. (1975). From Project Re-ED to ecological planning. In H. DuPont (Ed.), *Educating emotionally disturbed children* (2nd ed.). New York: Holt, Rinehart & Winston.

Lewis, W. W. (1981). Ecological factors in successful residential treatment. *Behavioral Disorders, 6,* 149–156.

Lidz, T., Fleck, S., & Cornelison, A. R. (1965). *Schizophrenia and the family.* New York: International Universities Press.

Links, P. S. (1980). Minor physical anomalies in childhood autism. Part II. Their relationship to maternal age. *Journal of Autism and Developmental Disorders, 3,* 287–296.

Lloyd, J. W. (1987). Direct academic interventions in learning disabilities. In M. C. Wang, H. J. Walberg, M. C. Reynolds (Eds.), *The handbook of special education: Research and practice.* Oxford, England: Pergamon Press.

Loeber, R., & Dishion, T. (1983). Early predictors of male delinquency: A review. *Psychological Bulletin, 94,* 68–99.

Long, N. J. (1979). The conflict cycle. *The Pointer, 24,* 6–11.

Long, N. J., & Duffner, B. (1980). The stress cycle or the coping cycle? The impact of home and school stresses on pupils' classroom behavior. In N. J. Long, W. C. Morse, & R. G. Newman (Eds.), *Conflict in the classroom* (4th ed.). Belmont, CA: Wadsworth.

Long, N. J., & Fagen, S. A. (1981). Therapeutic management: A psychoeducational approach. In G. Brown, R. L. McDowell, & J. Smith (Eds.), *Educating adolescents with behavior disorders.* Columbus, OH: Charles E. Merrill.

Long, N. J., Morse, W. C., & Newman, R. G. (1980). *Conflict in the classroom: The education of children with problems* (4th ed.). Belmont, CA: Wadsworth.

Long, N. J., & Newman, R. G. (1971). The teacher and his mental health. In N. J. Long, W. C. Morse, & R. G. Newman (Eds.), *Conflict in the classroom* (2nd ed.). Belmont, CA: Wadsworth.

Long, N. J., & Newman, R. G. (1976). Managing surface behavior of children in school. In N. J. Long, W. C. Morse, & R. G. Newman (Eds.), *Conflict in the classroom: The education of children with problems* (3rd ed.). Belmont, CA: Wadsworth.

Lopez, R. E. (1965). Hyperactivity in twins. *Canadian Psychiatric Association Journal, 10,* 421–426.

Lortie, D. C. (1975). *Schoolteacher: A sociological study.* Chicago: University of Chicago Press.

Losen, S. M., & Losen, J. G. (1985). *The special education team.* Boston, Allyn and Bacon.

Lovaas, O. I., Berberich, J. P., Perloff, B. F., & Schaeffer, B. (1971). Acquisition of imitative speech by schizophrenic children. In A. Graziano (Ed.), *Behavior therapy with children.* Chicago, Aldine.

Lovaas, O. I., Freitas, L., Nelson, K., & Whalen, C. (1967). The establishment of imitation and its use for the development of complex behavior in schizophrenic children. *Behaviour Research and Therapy, 5,* 171–181.

Lovaas, O. I., Schaeffer, B., & Simmons, J. Q. (1965). Building social behavior in autistic children by use of electric shock. *Journal of Experimental Research in Personality, 1,* 99–109.

Lovitt, T. (1980). *Writing and implementing an IEP: A step-by-step plan.* Belmont, CA: Pitman Learning.

Luepnitz, D. (1982). *Child custody: A study of families after divorce.* Lexington, MA: Lexington Books.

Mackie, R. P., Kvaraceus, W. C., & Williams, H. M. (1957). *Teachers of children who are socially and emotionally maladjusted.* Washington, DC: U.S. Government Printing Office.

MacMillan, D., & Turnbull, A. (1983). Parent involvement with special education: Respecting individual preferences. *Education and Training of the Mentally Retarded, 18,* 4–9.

Madsen, C. H., Becker, W. C., & Thomas, D. R. (1968). Rules, praise, and ignoring: Elements of elementary classroom control. *Journal of Applied Behavior Analysis, 1,* 139–150.

Maertens, B. K., Peterson, R. L., Witt, J. C., & Cirone, S. (1986). Teacher perceptions of school-based interventions: Ratings of intervention effectiveness, ease of use, and frequency of use. *Exceptional Children, 52,* 213–223.

Maheady, L., Duncan, D., & Sainato, D. (1982). A survey of use of behavior modification techniques by special education teachers. *Teacher Education and Special Education, 5,* 9–15.

Maher, C. A., & Bennett, R. E. (1984). *Planning and evaluating special education services.* Englewood Cliffs, NJ: Prentice-Hall.

Mahler, M. S. (1952). On child psychosis and schizophrenia, autistic and symbiotic infantile psychoses. *Psychoanalytic Study of the Child, 7,* 286–305.

Maily, B. L. (1975). School liaison and field services. In M. M. Wood (Ed.), *Developmental therapy.* Baltimore, MD: University Park Press.

Martin, H. P., Burgess, D., & Crnic, L. S. (1984). Mothers who work outside of the home and their children: A survey of health professionals' attitudes. *Journal of the American Academy of Child Psychiatry, 23,* 472–478.

Maslach, C., & Jackson, S. (1979). Burned out cops and their families. *Psychology Today* (May), 59–62.

Maslach, C., & Pines, A. (1977). The burnout syndrome in the day care setting. *Child Care Quarterly, 6,* 100–113.

Mason-Brothers, A., Ritvo, E. R., Guze, B., Mo, A., Freeman, B. J., & Funderbunk, S. J. (1987). Pre-, peri-, and postnatal factors in 181 autistic patients from single and multiple incidence families. *Journal of the American Academy of Child and Adolescent Psychiatry, 26,* 39–42.

Mattison, R., Cantwell, D. P., Russell, A. T., & Will, L. (1979). A comparison of DSM-II and DSM-III in the diagnosis of childhood psychiatric disorders. *Archives of General Psychiatry, 36,* 1217–1222.

Maziade, M., Caperaa, P. Laplante, B., Boudreault, M., Thivierge, J., Cote, R., & Boutin, P. (1985). Value of difficult temperament among 7-year-olds in the general population for predicting psychiatric diagnosis at age 12. *American Journal of Psychiatry, 142,* 943–946.

Maziade, M., Cote, R., Boudreault, M., Thivierge, J., & Caperaa, P. (1984). The New York longitudinal studies model of temperament: Gender differences and demographic correlates in a French-speaking population. *Journal of the American Academy of Child Psychiatry, 23,* 582–587.

McAdoo, W. G., & DeMyer, M. K. (1978). Personality characteristics of parents. In M. Rutter & E. Schopler (Eds.), *Autism: A reappraisal of concepts and treatment* (pp. 251–267). New York: Plenum Press.

McAllister, L. W., Stachowiak, J. G., Baer, D. M., & Conderman, L. (1969). The application of operant conditioning techniques in a secondary classroom. *Journal of Applied Behavior Analysis, 2,* 277–285.

McCarney, S. B. (1986). Preferred types of communication indicated by parents and teachers of emotionally disturbed students. *Behavioral Disorders, 12,* 118–123.

McCarthy, J. M., & Paraskevopoulos, J. (1969). Behavior patterns of learning disabled, emotionally disturbed, and average children. *Exceptional Children, 36,* 69–74.

McCauley, R. (1977). Elements of educational programming. *Iowa Perspectives,* (May).

McCauley, R. W., Hlidek, R., & Feinberg, F. (1977). Impacting social interactions in classrooms: The classroom management and relationship program. In F. H. Wood (Ed.), *Preparing teachers to foster personal growth in emotionally disturbed students.* Minneapolis, MN: University of Minnesota, Department of Psychoeducational Studies.

McDaniel, E. A., Sullivan, P. D., & Goldbaum, J. L. (1982). Physical proximity of special education classrooms to regular classrooms. *Exceptional Children, 49,* 73–75.

McDermott, P. A. (1980). Prevalence and constituency of behavioral disturbance taxonomies in the regular school population. *Journal of Abnormal Child Psychology, 8,* 523–536.

McDermott, P. A. (1981). The manifestation of problem behavior in ten age groups of Canadian school children. *Canadian Journal of Behavioral Science, 13,* 310–319.

McGee, G. G., Krantz, P. J., Mason, D., & McClannahan, L. E. (1986). A modified incidental-teaching procedure for autistic youth: Acquisition and generalization of receptive object labels. *Journal of Applied Behavior Analysis, 16,* 329–338.

McGinnis, E. (1984). Teaching social skills to behaviorally disordered elementary students. *The Pointer, 28,* 5–12.

McGinnis, E., & Goldstein, A. P. (1984). *Skillstreaming the elementary school child.* Champaign, IL: Research Press.

McGinnis, E., Sauerbry, L., & Nichols, P. (1985). Skillstreaming: Teaching social skills to children with behavioral disorders. *Teaching Exceptional Children, 17,* 160–167.

McGinnis, E., Scott-Miller, D., Neel, R., & Smith, C. (1985). Aversives in special education programs for behaviorally disordered students: A debate. *Behavioral Disorders, 11,* 295–304.

McGlothlin, J. E. (1981). The school consultation committee: An approach to implementing a teacher consultation model. *Behavioral Disorders, 6,* 101–107.

McGrath, P. J., & Feldman, W. (1986). Clinical approach to recurrent abdominal pain in children. *Journal of Developmental and Behavioral Pediatrics, 7,* 56–61.

McMahon, R. C. (1980). Genetic etiology in the hyperactive child syndrome: A critical review. *American Journal of Orthopsychiatry, 50,* 145–150.

McManus, M., Brickman, A., Alessi, N. E., & Grapentine, W. L. (1985). Neurological dysfunction in serious delinquents. *Journal of the American Academy of Child Psychiatry, 24,* 481–486.

Meichenbaum, D. (1977). *Cognitive-behavior modification: An integrative approach.* New York: Plenum Press.

Meichenbaum, D., & Goodman, J. (1979). Training impulsive children to talk to themselves: A means of developing self-control. *Journal of Abnormal Psychology, 77,* 115–126.

Mercer, C. D., & Mercer, A. R. (1985). *Teaching students with learning problems* (2nd ed.). Columbus, OH: Charles E. Merrill.

Mesinger, J. F. (1985). Commentary on "a rationale for the merger of special and regular education" or, is it now time for the lamb to lie down with the lion? *Exceptional Children, 51,* 510–512.

Mezzich, A. C., Mezzich, J. E., & Coffman, G. A. (1985). Reliability of DSM-III vs. DSM-II in child psychopathology. *Journal of the American Academy of Child Psychiatry, 24,* 273–280.

Michael, A. (1987). A trip to Boys Town, *Behavior in Our Schools, 1,* 2–7.

Michelson, L., Foster, S. L., & Ritchey, W. L. (1981). Social-skills assessment of children. In B. B. Lahey & A. E. Kazdin (Eds.), *Advances in clinical child psychology* (Vol. 4, pp. 119–166). New York: Plenum Press.

Mikkelsen, E. J. (1982). Efficacy of neuroleptic medication in pervasive developmental disorders of childhood. *Schizophrenia Bulletin, 8,* 320–332.

Miller, L. C., Barrett, C. L., & Hampe, E. (1974). Phobias of childhood in a prescientific era. In A. Davids (Ed.), *Childhood personality and psychopathology: Current topics.* New York: John Wiley & Sons.

Miller, L. C., Barrett, C. L., Hampe, E., & Noble, H. (1972). Factor structure of childhood fears. *Journal of Consulting and Clinical Psychology, 39,* 264–268.

Miller, L. E. (1979). Setting analysis data in the identification of emotionally disabled pupils. In C. R. Smith & J. Grimes (Eds.), *The identification of emotionally disabled pupils: Data and decision making.* Des Moines, IA: Iowa Department of Public Instruction.

Miller, L. E., Epp, J., & McGinnis, E. (1985). Setting analysis. In F. H. Wood, C. R. Smith, & J. Grimes (Eds.), *The Iowa assessment model in behavioral disorders: A training manual.* Des Moines, IA: Iowa Department of Public Instruction.

Minner, S., Beane, A., & Prater, G. (1986). Try telephone answering machines. *Teaching Exceptional Children, 19,* 62–63.

Moffitt, T. E., Gabrielli, W. F., Mednick, S. A., & Schulsinger, F. (1981). Socioeconomic status, IQ, and delinquency. *Journal of Abnormal Psychology, 90,* 152–156.

Mogar, R. E., & Aldrich, R. W. (1969). The use of psychedelic agents with autistic schizophrenic children. *Behavioral Neuropsychiatry, 1,* 44–52.

Morgan, S. B. (1984). Helping parents understand the diagnosis of autism. *Journal of Developmental and Behavioral Pediatrics, 5,* 78–85.

Morgan, S. R. (1977). Personality variables as predictors of empathy. *Behavioral Disorders, 1,* 83–88.

Morrison, J. R., & Stewart, M. A. (1971). The psychiatric status of the legal families of adopted hyperactive children. *Archives of General Psychiatry, 28,* 888–891.

Morse, W. C. (1959). The life space interview. *American Journal of Orthopsychiatry, 29,* 27–44.

Morse, W. C. (1963). Working paper: Training teachers in life space interviewing. *American Journal of Orthopsychiatry, 33,* 727–730.

Morse, W. C. (1971). Education of maladjusted and disturbed children. In N. J. Long, W. C. Morse, & R. G. Newman (Eds.), *Conflict in the classroom: The education of children with problems* (2nd ed.). Belmont, CA: Wadsworth.

Morse, W. C. (1982). The place of affective education in special education. *Teaching Exceptional Children, 14,* 209–211.

Morse, W. C. (1985). *Pursuit of excellence for the behavior disordered.* Paper presented at the Midwest Symposium for Leadership in Behavior Disorders, Kansas City, MO.

Mosher, R. L., & Sprinthall, N. A. (1971). Psychological education: A means to promote personal development during adolescence. *The Counseling Psychologist, 2,* 3–80.

Munoz, F. U. (1983). Family life patterns of Pacific islanders: The insidious displacement of culture. In G. J. Powell (Ed.), *The psychosocial development of minority group children* (pp. 248–257). New York: Brunner/Mazel.

Muscott, H. S., & Bond, R. (1985). *Bridging the gap between residential treatment and public school programs: A model for expanding the continuum of special educational services through transitional education.* Paper presented at Fitting the Pieces Together: A Multidisciplinary Conference on Children and Adolescents in Conflict, New York: Teachers College, Columbia University.

Muscott, H. S., & Bond, R. (1986). A transitional education model for reintegrating behaviorally disordered students from residential treatment centers to public school programs. In M. K. Zabel (Ed.), *TEACHING: Behaviorally disordered youth.* Reston, VA: Council for Exceptional Children.

Myers, K. M., Burke, P., & McCauley, E. (1985). Suicidal behavior by hospitalized preadolescent children on a psychiatric unit. *Journal of the American Academy of Child Psychiatry, 24,* 474–480.

Nadelson, C. C. (1979). The women's movement and changing sex roles. In J. D. Noshpitz (Ed.), *Basic handbook of child psychiatry (Vol. 4): Prevention and current issues* (pp. 386–397). New York: Basic Books.

National Center for Health Statistics. (1981). *Monthly Vital Statistics Report,* (September 17). Hyattsville, MD: National Center for Health Statistics.

National Center for Health Statistics. (1984). *Monthly Vital Statistics Report, 32* (September 21). Hyattsville, MD: National Center for Health Statistics.

National Commission on Excellence in Education (1983). *A nation at risk: The imperative for educational reform.* Washington, DC: U.S. Department of Education.

National Commission on Excellence in Teacher Education. (1985). A call for change in teacher education. *The Chronicle of Higher Education, 30*(1), 13–20.

Neel, R. S. (1978). Research findings regarding the use of punishment procedures with severely behavior disordered children. In F. H. Wood & K. C. Lakin (Eds.), *Punishment and aversive stimulation in special education: Legal, theoretical and practical issues in their use with emotionally disturbed children and youth.* Minneapolis, MN: University of Minnesota, Department of Psychoeducational Studies.

Neel, R. S., McDowell, R. L., Whelan, R. J., & Wagonseller, B. R. (1982). The management of behavior and the measurement of behavior change. In R. L. McDowell, G. W. Adamson, & F. H. Wood (Eds.), *Teaching emotionally disturbed children.* Boston: Little, Brown and Co.

Nelson, C. M. (1983). Beyond the classroom: The teacher of behaviorally disordered pupils in a social system. In R. B. Rutherford, Jr. (Ed.), *Monograph in behavioral disorders.* Reston, VA: Council for Exceptional Children.

Nelson, C. M., & Rutherford, R. B. (1987). Behavioral interventions with behaviorally disordered students. In M. C. Wang, H. J. Walberg, & M. C. Reynolds (Eds.), *The handbook of special education: Research and practice.* Oxford, England: Pergamon Press.

Nelson, C. M., & Stevens, K. B. (1981). An accountable consultation model for mainstreaming behaviorally disordered children. *Behavioral Disorders, 6,* 82–91.

Nelson, C. M., & Stevens, K. B. (1983). Time-out revisited: Guidelines for its use in special education. *Exceptional Education Quarterly, 3,* 56–67.

Nemser, S. F. (1983). Learning to teach. In L. S. Shulman & G. Sykes (Eds.), *Handbook of teaching and policy.* New York: Longman.

Newcomer, P. L. (1982). Competencies for professionals in learning disabilities. *Learning Disabilities Quarterly, 5,* 241–252.

Nichols, P. (1986). Down the up staircase: The teacher as therapist. In M. K. Zabel (Ed.), *TEACHING: Behaviorally disordered youth.* Reston, VA: Council for Exceptional Children.

Niles, W. J. (1986). Effects of a moral development discussion group on delinquent and predelinquent boys. *Journal of Counseling Psychology, 33,* 45–51.

Oberklaid, F., Prior, M., & Sanson, A. (1986). Temperament of preterm versus full-term infants. *Jour-*

nal of Developmental and Behavioral Pediatrics, 7, 159–162.

Oden, S. (1980). A child's social isolation: Origins, prevention, intervention. In G. Cartledge & J. F. Miburn (Eds.), Teaching social skills to children: Innovative approaches. New York: Pergamon Press.

Oden, S., & Asher, S. R. (1977). Coaching children in social skills for friendship making. Child Development, 48, 495–506.

Ohio Social Acceptance Scale. (1979). Adaptive behavior development. Columbus, OH: The Ohio State University Research Foundation.

Ojemann, R. (1967). Incorporating psychological concepts in the school curriculum. Journal of School Psychology, 5, 195–204.

O'Leary, K. D. (1980). Pills or skills for hyperactive children? Journal of Applied Behavior Analysis, 13, 191–204.

O'Leary, K. D. (1984). Marital discord and children: Problems, strategies, methodologies and results. In A. V. Doyle, D. Gold, & D. S. Moskowitz (Eds.), Children and families under stress: New directions for child development (pp. 35–46). San Francisco: Jossey Bass.

O'Leary, K. D., & Johnson, S. B. (1979). Psychological assessment. In H. C. Quay & J. Werry (Eds.), Psychopathological disorders of childhood. New York: John Wiley & Sons.

O'Leary, K. D., Kaufman, K. F., Kass, R. E., & Drabman, R. S. (1970). The effects of loud and soft reprimands on the behavior of disruptive students. Exceptional Children, 37, 145–155.

Oppenheimer, E. (1985). Drug taking. In M. Rutter & L. Hersov (Eds.), Child and adolescent psychiatry: Modern approaches (pp. 491–500). London: Blackwell Scientific Publications.

Ornitz, E. M., Atwell, C. W., Kaplan, A. R., & Westlake, J. R. (1985). Brain-stem dysfunction in autism. Archives of General Psychiatry, 42, 1018–1025.

Ornitz, E. M., & Ritvo, E. R. (1976). The syndrome of autism: A critical review. American Journal of Psychiatry, 133, 609–621.

Osmond, H. (1973). The background to the niacin treatment. In D. Hawkins & L. Pauling (Eds.), Orthomolecular psychiatry. San Francisco: W. H. Freeman.

Pattavina, P., & Ramirez, R. R. (1980). Generic affective competencies: A common bond between regular and special educators. Paper presented at the CEC International Convention, Philadelphia, PA.

Patterson, G. R. (1974). Interventions for boys with conduct problems: Multiple settings, treatments, and criteria. Journal of Consulting and Clinical Psychology, 42, 471–481.

Patterson, G. R. (1982). Coercive family process. Eugene, OR: Castalia Publishing.

Patterson, G. R. (1986). Performance models for antisocial boys. American Psychologist, 41, 432–444.

Paul, J. (Ed.) (1981). Understanding and working with parents of children with special needs. New York: Holt, Rinehart & Winston.

Paul J. L., & Epanchin, B. C. (1982). Emotional disturbance in children: Theories and methods for teachers. Columbus, OH: Charles E. Merrill.

Pauling, L. (1973). Orthomolecular psychiatry. In D. Hawkins & L. Pauling (Eds.), Orthomolecular psychiatry. San Francisco: W. H. Freeman.

Paulson, G., Rizui, A., & Crane, G. (1973). Tardive dyskinesia as a possible sequel of long-term treatment with phenothiazines. Clinical Pediatrics, 14, 953–955.

Persson-Blennow, I., & McNeil, T. F. (1979). A questionnaire for measurement of temperament in six-month-old infants: Development and standardization. Journal of Child Psychology and Psychiatry, 20, 1–13.

Peterson, D. R. (1961). Behavior problems of middle childhood. Journal of Consulting Psychology, 25, 205–209.

Peterson, R. L., Zabel, R. H., & Smith, C. R. (1986). Reintegration of behaviorally disordered students: A replication. Paper presented at International Convention, Council for Exceptional Children, New Orleans.

Peterson, R. L., Zabel, R. H., Smith, C. R., & White, M. A. (1983). Cascade of services model and emotionally disabled students. Exceptional Children, 49, 404–408.

Pfeffer, C. R., Zuckerman, S., Plutchik, R., & Mizruchi, M. S. (1984). Suicidal behavior in normal school children: A comparison with child psychiatric inpatients. Journal of the American Academy of Child Psychiatry, 24, 416–423.

Phillips, D. P., & Carstensen, L. L. (1986). Clustering of teenage suicides after television news stories about suicide. New England Journal of Medicine, 315, 685–689.

Phillips, E. L. (1968). Achievement Place: Token reinforcement procedures in a home-style rehabilitation setting for "pre-delinquent" boys. Journal of Applied Behavior Analysis, 1, 214–223.

Phillips, E. L. (1981). Supportive therapies. In G. Brown, R. L. McDowell, & J. Smith (Eds.), *Educating adolescents with behavior disorders.* Columbus, OH: Charles E. Merrill.

Phillips, E. L., Fixsen, D. L., Phillips, E. A., & Wolf, M. M. (1979). The teaching family model: A comprehensive approach to residential treatment of youth. In D. Cullinan & M. H. Epstein (Eds.), *Special education for adolescents.* Columbus, OH: Charles E. Merrill.

Phillips, E. L., Phillips, E. A., Fixsen, D. L., & Wolf, M. (1971). Achievement place: Modification of the behavior of pre-delinquent boys with a token economy. *Journal of Applied Behavior Analysis, 4,* 45–59.

Phillips, E. L., & Weiner, D. N. (1966). *Short-term psychotherapy and structured behavior change.* New York: McGraw-Hill.

Phillips, K. (1985). Parents as partners: Developing parent support groups. In M. K. Zabel (Ed.), *TEACHING: Behaviorally disordered students* (pp. 29–36). Reston, VA: Council for Exceptional Children.

Piaget, J. (1932). *The moral judgment of the child.* London: Routledge & Kegan Paul.

Piaget, J., & Inhelder, B. (1969). *The psychology of the child.* New York: Basic Books.

Piers, E., & Harris, D. (1969). *Piers-Harris children's self-concept scale.* Nashville, TN: Counselor Recordings and Tests.

Piggott, L. R., & Gottlieb, J. S. (1973). Childhood schizophrenia: What is it? *Journal of Autism and Childhood Schizophrenia, 3,* 96–105.

Pines, A., & Maslach, C. (1978). Characteristics of staff burnout in mental health settings. *Hospital and Community Psychiatry, 29,* 233–237.

Polizos, P., Engelhardt, D., Hoffman, S., & Waizer, J. (1973). Neurological consequences of psychotropic drug withdrawal in schizophrenic children. *Journal of Autism and Childhood Schizophrenia, 3,* 247–253.

Pollack, M., Gittelman, M., Miller, R., Berman, P., & Bakwin, R. (1970). *A developmental, pediatric, neurological, psychological, and psychiatric comparison of psychotic children and their sibs.* Paper presented at the American Orthopsychiatric Association.

Pollack, M., & Woerner, M. G. (1966). Pre- and perinatal complications and "childhood schizophrenia": A comparison of five controlled studies. *Journal of Child Psychology and Psychiatry, 7,* 235–242.

Polsgrove, L. (1979). Self-control: Methods for child training. *Behavioral Disorders, 4,* 116–130.

Polsgrove, L. (1982). Return to baseline: Some comments on Smith's (1981) reinterpretation of time-out. *Behavioral Disorders, 8,* 50–52.

Polsgrove, L., & Nelson, C. M. (1982). Curriculum intervention according to the behavioral model. In R. L. McDowell, G. W. Adamson, & F. H. Wood (Eds.), *Teaching emotionally disturbed children.* Boston: Little, Brown and Co.

Polsgrove, L., & Reith, H. J. (1979). A new look at competencies required by teachers of emotionally disturbed and behaviorally disordered children and youth. In F. H. Wood (Ed.), *Teachers for secondary school students with serious emotional disturbance: Content of programs.* Minneapolis, MN: University of Minnesota, Department of Psychoeducational Studies.

Polsgrove, L., & Reith, H. J. (1983). Procedures for reducing children's inappropriate behavior in special education settings. *Exceptional Education Quarterly, 3,* 20–33.

Polsky, H. (1962). *Cottage six: The social system of delinquent boys in residential treatment.* New York: Russell Sage Foundation.

Porter, B., & O'Leary, K. D. (1980). Marital discord and childhood behavior problems. *Journal of Abnormal Child Psychology, 80,* 287–295.

Powell, G. J. (1983). Coping with adversity: The psychosocial development of Afro-American children. In G. J. Powell (Ed.), *The psychosocial development of minority group children* (pp. 49–76). New York: Brunner/Mazel.

Poznanski, E. O. (1979). Childhood depression: A psychodynamic approach to the etiology of depression in children. In A. French & I. Berlin (Eds.), *Depression in children and adolescents* (pp. 46–48). New York: Human Sciences Press.

Premack, D. (1965). Reinforcement theory. In D. Levine (Ed.), *Nebraska symposium on motivation.* Lincoln, NE: University of Nebraska Press.

Prieto, A. G., & Rutherford, R. B. (1977). An ecological assessment technique for behaviorally disordered and learning disabled children. *Behavioral Disorders, 2,* 169–175.

Prieto, A. G., & Zucker, S. H. (1981). Teacher perceptions of race as a factor in the placement of behaviorally disordered children. *Behavioral Disorders, 7,* 34–38.

Purcell, K. (1975). Childhood asthma: The role of family relationships, personality, and emotion. In A. Davids (Ed.), *Child personality and psychopathology: Current topics* (Vol. 2). New York: John Wiley & Sons.

Purvis, J., & Samet, S. (1976). *Music in developmental therapy: A curriculum guide.* Baltimore, MD: University Park Press.

Quay, H. C. (1986). A critical analysis of DSM-III as a taxonomy of psychopathology in childhood and adolescence. In T. Millon & G. L. Klerman (Eds.), *Contemporary directions in psychopathology: Toward the DSM-IV* (pp. 151–165). New York: Guilford Press.

Quay, H. C., & Cutler, R. L. (1966). Personality patterns of pupils in special education classes for the emotionally disturbed. *Exceptional Children, 32,* 197–301.

Quay, H. C., & Peterson, D. R. (1975). *Behavior Problem Checklist.* Manual available from D. R. Peterson, Graduate School of Applied Professional Psychology, Busch Campus, P. O. Box 88199, Piscataway, NJ 08854.

Rachman, S., & Seligman, M. E. P. (1976). Behavior of withdrawn autistic children: Effects of peer social initiations. *Behaviour Research and Therapy, 14,* 333–338.

Rank, O. (1929). *The trauma of birth.* New York: Harcourt Brace Jovanovich.

Raths, L., Harmin, M., & Simon, S. (1966). *Values and teaching.* Columbus, OH: Charles E. Merrill.

Red Horse, J. (1983). Indian family values and experiences. In G. J. Powell (Ed.), *The psychosocial development of minority group children* (pp. 258–274). New York: Brunner/Mazel.

Redl, F. (1976). The concept of the therapeutic milieu. In N. J. Long, W. C. Morse, & R. J. Newman (Eds.), *Conflict in the classroom: The education of emotionally disturbed children.* Belmont, CA: Wadsworth.

Redl, F. (1980). The concept of the life space interview. In N. J. Long, W. C. Morse, & R. J. Newman (Eds.), *Conflict in the classroom: The education of emotionally disturbed children.* Belmont, CA: Wadsworth.

Redl, F., & Wineman, D. (1951). *Children who hate.* New York: Free Press.

Redl, F., & Wineman, D. (1952). *Controls from within.* New York: Free Press.

Reeves, J. C., Werry, J. S., Elkind, G. S., & Zametkin, A. (1987). Attention deficit, conduct, oppositional, and anxiety disorders in children: II. Clinical characteristics. *Journal of the American Academy of Child and Adolescent Psychiatry, 26,* 144–155.

Reid, M. K., & Borkowski, J. G. (1984). Effects of methylphenidate (Ritalin) on information processing in hyperactive children. *Journal of Abnormal Child Psychology, 12,* 169–186.

Reynolds, M. C. (1962). A framework for considering some issues in special education. *Exceptional Children, 28,* 367–370.

Reynolds, M. C. (1976). *New alternatives through a new cascade.* Paper presented 23 November at the Sixth Annual Invitational Conference on Leadership in Special Education Programs.

Reynolds, M. C., & Birch, J. (1982). *Teaching exceptional children in all America's schools* (rev. ed.). Reston, VA: Council for Exceptional Children.

Rhode, G., Morgan, D. P., & Young, K. R. (1983). Generalization and maintenance of treatment gains of behaviorally handicapped students from resource to regular classrooms using self-evaluation procedures. *Journal of Applied Behavior Analysis, 16,* 171–188.

Rhodes, W. C. (1967). The disturbing child: A problem of ecological management. *Exceptional Children, 33,* 449–455.

Rhodes, W. C. (1970). A community participation analysis of emotional disturbance. *Exceptional Children, 36,* 309–314.

Rhodes, W. C. (1974). Introductory overview. In W. C. Rhodes & M. L. Tracy (Eds.), *A study of child variance (Vol. 1): Conceptual models* (pp. 11–36). Ann Arbor, MI: University of Michigan Press.

Rhodes, W. C., & Paul, J. L. (1978). *Emotionally disturbed and deviant children: New views and approaches.* Englewood Cliffs, NJ: Prentice-Hall.

Rhodes, W. C., & Tracy, M. L. (Eds.). (1974). *A study of child variance (Vol. 2): Interventions.* Ann Arbor, MI: University of Michigan Press.

Rice, R. E. (1984). *Toward reform in teacher education: Strategies for change.* Reflections on a conference at Wingspread sponsored by the Johnson Foundation and the Fund for the Improvement of Postsecondary Education.

Richards, E. A. (Ed.). (1951). *Proceedings of the Mid-century White House Conference on Children and Youth.* Raleigh, NC: Health Publications Institute.

Richter, N. C. (1984). The efficacy of relaxation training with children. *Journal of Abnormal Child Psychology, 12,* 319–344.

Rie, H. E. (1966). Depression in childhood: A survey of some pertinent contributors. *Journal of the American Academy of Child Psychiatry, 5,* 653–685.

Rie, H. E., Rie, E. D., Stewart, S., & Ambuel, J. P. (1976). Effects of Ritalin on underachieving children: A replication. *American Journal of Orthopsychiatry, 46,* 313–322.

Rimland, B. (1964). *Infantile autism.* New York: Appleton-Century-Crofts.

Rimland, B. (1973). High-dosage levels of certain vitamins in the treatment of children with severe mental disorders. In D. Hawkins & L. Pauling (Eds.), *Orthomolecular psychiatry.* San Francisco: W. H. Freeman.

Rist, R. (1970). Student social class and teacher expectations: The self-fulfilling prophecy in ghetto education. *Harvard Educational Review, 40,* 411–451.

Ritvo, E. R., Freeman, B. J., Mason-Brothers, A., Mo, A., & Ritvo, A. M. (1985). Concordance for the syndrome of autism in 40 pairs of afflicted twins. *American Journal of Psychiatry, 142,* 74–77.

Robbins, D. R., & Alessi, N. E. (1985). Depressive symptoms and suicidal behavior in adolescents. *American Journal of Psychiatry, 142,* 588–592.

Robin, A., Schneider, M., & Dolnick, M. (1976). The turtle technique: An extended case study of self-control in the classroom. *Psychology in the Schools, 13,* 449–453.

Robinson, L. H. (1984). Outpatient management of the suicidal child. *American Journal of Psychotherapy, 38,* 399–412.

Rock, N. (1974). Childhood psychosis and long-term chemo- and psychotherapy. *Diseases of the Nervous System, 35,* 303–308.

Rose, T. L. (1983). A survey of corporal punishment of mildly handicapped students. *Exceptional Education Quarterly, 3,* 10–19.

Rosenberg, H. E. (1973). On teaching the modification of employer and employee behavior. *Teaching Exceptional Children, 5,* 140–142.

Rosenberg, H. W., & Graubard, P. (1975). Peer use of behavior modification. *Focus on Exceptional Children, 7,* 1–10.

Rosenberg, M. (1979). *Conceiving the self.* New York: Basic Books.

Rosenshine, B. (1976). Classroom instruction. In N. L. Gage (Ed.), *The psychology of teaching methods: The seventy-fifth yearbook of the National Society for the Study of Education.* Chicago: The University of Chicago Press.

Rosenthal, D. (1971). *Genetics of psychopathology.* New York. McGraw-Hill.

Rosenthal, M. J., Finkelstein, M., Ni, E., & Robertson, R. E. (1959). A study of mother-child relationships in the emotional disorders of children. *Genetic Psychology Monographs, 60,* 65–116.

Rosenthal, M. J., Ni, E., Finkelstein, M., & Berkwits, G. K. (1962). Father-child relationships and children's problems. *Archives of General Psychiatry, 7*(5).

Rosenthal, P. A., & Rosenthal, S. (1984). Suicidal behavior by preschool children. *American Journal of Psychiatry, 141,* 520–525.

Ross, A. O. (1974). *Psychological disorders of children.* New York: McGraw-Hill.

Ross, M., & Salvia, J. (1975). Attractiveness as a biasing factor in teacher judgments. *American Journal of Mental Deficiency, 80,* 96–98.

Roy, L., & Sawyers, J. (1986). The double bind: An empirical study of responses to inconsistent communications. *Journal of Marital and Family Therapy, 12,* 395–402.

Rubenstein, M. F., & Rezmierski, V. (1983). Understanding nonproductive system responses to emotionally disturbed and behaviorally disordered students. *Behavioral Disorders, 9,* 60–67.

Rubin, R. A., & Balow, R. (1978). Prevalence of teacher-identified behavior problems: A longitudinal study. *Exceptional Children, 45,* 102–113.

Rumsey, J. M., Andreasen, N. C., & Rapoport, J. L. (1986). Thought, language, communication, and affective flattening in autistic adults. *Archives of General Psychiatry, 43,* 771–777.

Rumsey, J. M., Duara, R., Grady, C., Rapoport, J. L., Margolin, R. A., Rapoport, S. I., & Cutler, N. R. (1985). Brain metabolism in autism. *Archives of General Psychiatry, 42,* 448–455.

Rumsey, J. M., Rapoport, J. L., & Sceery, W. R. (1985). Autistic children as adults. *Journal of the American Academy of Child Psychiatry, 24,* 465–473.

Rutherford, R. B., Howell, K. W., & Rueda, R. (1982). Self-control instruction for behavior disordered students: Design and implementation. *Instructional Psychology, 9,* 91–99.

Rutherford, R. B., & Nelson, C. M. (1982). Analysis of the response contingent time-out literature with behaviorally disordered students in classroom settings. In R. B. Rutherford (Ed.), *Severe behavior dis-*

orders of children and youth (Vol. 5, pp. 79–105). Reston, VA: Council for Exceptional Children.

Rutherford, R. B., Nelson, C. M., & Wolford, B. I. (1985). Special education in the most restrictive environment: Correctional/special education. *Journal of Special Education, 19,* 59–71.

Rutherford, R. B., & Polsgrove, L. J. (1981). Behavioral contracting with behaviorally disordered and delinquent children and youth: An analysis of the clinical and experimental literature. In R. B. Rutherford, A. G. Prieto, & J. E. McGlothlin (Eds.), *Severe behavior disorders of children and youth* (Vol. 4). Reston, VA: Council for Exceptional Children.

Rutter, M. (1978). Diagnosis and definition of childhood autism. *Journal of Autism and Childhood Schizophrenia, 8,* 139–161.

Rutter, M. (1981). Psychological sequelae of brain damage in children. *American Journal of Psychiatry, 138,* 1533–1544.

Rutter, M. (1982). Syndromes attributed to "minimal brain dysfunction" in childhood. *American Journal of Psychiatry, 139,* 21–33.

Rutter, M. (1985). The treatment of autistic children. *Journal of Child Psychology and Psychiatry and Allied Disciplines, 26,* 193–214.

Rutter, M., & Lockyer, L. (1967). A five to fifteen year follow-up study of infantile psychosis. *British Journal of Psychiatry, 113,* 1169–1182.

Sabornie, E. J., & Kauffman, J. M. (1985). Regular classroom sociometric status of behaviorally disordered adolescents. *Behavioral Disorders, 10,* 191–197.

Safran, S. P., & Safran, J. S. (1985). Classroom context and teachers' perceptions of problem behaviors. *Journal of Educational Psychology, 77,* 20–28.

Salend, S. J., Esquivel, L., & Pine, P. B. (1984). Regular and special education teachers' estimates of the use of aversive contingencies. *Behavioral Disorders, 9,* 89–94.

Salvia, J., & Ysseldyke, J. E. (1981). *Assessment in special and remedial education.* Boston: Houghton Mifflin.

Salvia, J., & Ysseldyke, J. E. (1985). *Assessment in special and remedial education* (2nd ed.). Boston: Houghton Mifflin.

Sandoval, J., Lambert, N. M., & Sassone, D. M. (1981). The comprehensive treatment of hyperactive children: A continuing problem. *Journal of Learning Disabilities, 14,* 117–118.

Santrock, J. W., Warshak, R. A., & Elliott, G. L. (1982). Social development and parent-child interaction in father-custody and stepmother families. In M. E. Lamb (Ed.), *Nontraditional families: Parenting and child development* (pp. 289–331). Hillsdale, NJ: Lawrence Erlbaum.

Sapon-Shevin, M. (1980). Teaching cooperation in early childhood settings. In G. Cartledge & J. F. Milburn (Eds.), *Teaching social skills to children: Innovative approaches.* New York: Pergamon Press.

Satterfield, J. H., Hoppe, C. M., & Schell, A. M. (1982). A prospective study of delinquency in 110 adolescent boys with attention deficit disorder and 88 normal adolescent boys. *American Journal of Psychiatry, 139,* 795–798.

Schaffer, D., & Fisher, P. (1981). The epidemiology of suicide in children and young adolescents. *Journal of the American Academy of Child Psychiatry, 20,* 545–565.

Scheuer, A. L. (1971). The relationship between personal attributes and effectiveness in teachers of the emotionally disturbed. *Exceptional Children, 38,* 723–731.

Schloss, P. J., Miller, S. R., Sedlak, R. A., & White, M. (1983). Social-performance expectations of professionals for behaviorally disordered youth. *Exceptional Children, 50,* 70–72.

Schloss, P. J., Schloss, C. N., Wood, C. E., & Kiehl, W. S. (1986). A critical review of social skills research with behaviorally disordered students. *Behavioral Disorders, 12,* 1–14.

Schloss, P. J., Sedlak, R. A., Wiggins, E. D., & Ramsey, D. (1983). Stress reduction for professionals working with aggressive adolescents. *Exceptional Children, 49,* 349–354.

Schmid, R., Algozzine, B., Maher, M., & Wells, D. (1984). Teaching emotionally disturbed adolescents: A study of selected teacher and teaching characteristics. *Behavioral Disorders, 9,* 105–112.

Schneider, M., & Robin, A. (1974). *Turtle manual.* Washington, DC: U.S. Office of Education. (ERIC Document Reproduction Service No. ED 128 680.)

Schniedewind, N., & Salend, S. J. (1987). Cooperative learning works. *Teaching Exceptional Children, 19,* 22–25.

Schopler, E., Andrews, C. E., & Strupp, K. (1979). Do autistic children come from upper-middle-class parents? *Journal of Autism and Developmental Disorders, 9,* 139–152.

Schreibman, L., O'Neill, R. E., & Koegel, R. L. (1983). Behavioral training for siblings of autistic children. *Journal of Applied Behavior Analysis, 16,* 129–138.

Schroeder, S. R., Lewis, M. H., & Lipton, M. A. (1982). Interactions of pharmacotherapy and behavior therapy among children with learning and behavior disorders. In K. D. Gadow & I. Bialer (Eds.), *Advances in learning and behavioral disorders* (Vol. 2). Greenwich, CT: JAI Press.

Schultz, J. B. (1987). *Parents and professionals in special education.* Boston: Allyn and Bacon.

Schulz, J. B., & Turnbull, A. P. (1983). *Mainstreaming handicapped students: A guide for classroom teachers.* Boston, Allyn and Bacon.

Schumaker, J. B., Deshler, D. D., Alley, G. R., & Warner, M. M. (1983). Toward the development of an intervention model for learning disabled adolescents. *Exceptional Education Quarterly, 3,* 45–50.

Scruggs, T. E., & Mastropieri, M. A. (1986). Academic characteristics of behaviorally disordered and learning disabled students. *Behavioral Disorders, 11,* 184–190.

Sears, R. R., Maccoby, E. E., & Levin, H. (1957). *Patterns of child rearing.* New York: Harper & Row.

Segal, J., & Yahraes, H. (1979). *A child's journey.* New York: McGraw-Hill.

Sells, S. B. (1963). An interactionist looks at the environment. *American Psychologist, 18,* 696–702.

Sells, S. B. (1966). Ecology and the science of psychology. *Multivariate Behavioral Research,* 131–141.

Sevcik, B. M., & Ysseldyke, J. E. (1986). An analysis of teachers' prereferral interventions for students exhibiting behavioral problems. *Behavioral Disorders, 12,* 109–117.

Shafer, M. S., Egel, A. L., & Neff, N. A. (1984). Training mildly handicapped peers to facilitate changes in the social interaction skills of autistic children. *Journal of Applied Behavior Analysis, 17,* 461–476.

Shafii, M., Carrigan, S., Whittinghill, J. R., & Derrick, A. (1985). Psychological autopsy of completed suicide in children and adolescents. *American Journal of Psychiatry, 142,* 1061–1064.

Shapiro, S. K., & Garfinkel, B. D. (1986). The occurrence of behavior disorders in children: The interdependence of attention deficit disorder and conduct disorder. *Journal of the American Academy of Child Psychiatry, 25,* 809–819.

Shaw, S. F., Bensky, J. M., & Dixon, B. (1981). *Stress and burnout: A primer for special education and special services personnel.* Reston, VA: Council for Exceptional Children.

Shea, T. M., & Bauer, A. M. (1985). *Parents and teachers of exceptional children: A handbook for involvement.* Boston, Allyn and Bacon.

Shields, J. (1954). Personality differences and neurotic traits in normal twin schoolchildren. *Eugenics Review, 45,* 213–246.

Shores, R. E., & Haubrich, P. A. (1969). Effect of cubicles in educating emotionally disturbed children. *Exceptional Children, 36,* 21–24.

Siegel, A. (1984). Working mothers and their children. *Journal of the American Academy of Child Psychiatry, 23,* 486–488.

Simon, S. B., Howe, L. W., & Kirschenbaum, H. (1972). *Values clarification: A handbook of practical strategies for teachers and students.* New York: Hart.

Simon, S. B., & O'Rourke, R. D. (1977). *Developing values with exceptional children.* Englewood Cliffs, NJ: Prentice-Hall.

Simpson, R. L., & Poplin, M. S. (1981). Parents as agents of change. *School Psychology Review, 10,* 15–25.

Simpson, R. L., & Sasso, G. M. (1982). Use of behavioral strategies with behaviorally disordered children and youth: A perspective. In C. R. Smith & B. J. Wilcots (Eds.), *Iowa monograph: Current issues in behavior disorders—1982.* Des Moines, IA: Iowa Department of Public Instruction.

Sindelar, P. T., & Deno, S. L. (1980). The effectiveness of resource programming. In N. J. Long, W. C. Morse, & R. G. Newman (Eds.), *Conflict in the classroom: The education of emotionally disturbed children.* Belmont, CA: Wadsworth.

Sindelar, P. T., King, M. C., Cartland, D., Wilson, R. J., & Meisel, C. J. (1985). Deviant behavior in learning disabled and behaviorally disordered students as a function of level and placement. *Behavioral Disorders, 10,* 105–112.

Skiba, R., & Casey, A. (1985). Interventions for behavior disordered students: A quantitative review and methodological critique. *Behavioral Disorders, 10,* 239–252.

Skinner, B. F. (1974). *About behaviorism.* New York: Alfred A. Knopf.

Slavin, R. E. (1980). Cooperative learning. *Review of Educational Research, 50,* 315–342.

Slavin, R. E. (1983). *Cooperative learning.* New York: Longman.

Sleeter, C. E. (1986). Learning disabilities: The social construction of a special education category. *Exceptional Children, 53,* 46–54.

Small, J. G. (1975). EEG and neurophysiological studies of early infantile autism. *Biological Psychiatry, 10,* 385–397.

Smith, C. R. (1981). Policy issues in providing psychotherapy and counseling. In F. H. Wood (Ed.), *Perspectives for a new decade: Education's responsibility for seriously disturbed and behaviorally disordered children and youth* (pp. 97–108). Reston, VA: Council for Exceptional Children.

Smith, D. E. P. (1981). Is isolation room a punisher? *Behavioral Disorders, 6,* 247–256.

Smith, D. E. P. (1982). Time-out as reduced environmental stimulation (RES): A reply to Polsgrove. *Behavioral Disorders, 7,* 53–55.

Smith-Davis, J., Burke, P. J., & Noel, M. M. (1984). *Personnel to educate the handicapped in America: Supply and demand from a programmatic viewpoint.* College Park, MD: University of Maryland, Department of Special Education, Institute for the Study of Children and Youth.

Sodac, D., Nichols, P., & Gallagher, B. (1985). Pupil behavioral data. In F. H. Wood, C. R. Smith, & J. Grimes (Eds.), *The Iowa assessment model in behavioral disorders: A training manual.* Des Moines, IA: Iowa Department of Public Instruction.

Spence, J. (1978). Clinical educator: A direction in training for seriously emotionally disturbed children. In C. M. Nelson (Ed.), *Field-based teacher training: Applications in special education.* Minneapolis, MN: University of Minnesota, Department of Psychoeducational Studies.

Spitz, R. (1945). Hospitalism: An inquiry into the genesis of psychiatric conditions in early childhood. *Psychoanalytic Study of the Child, 1,* 53–74.

Spivack, G., & Swift, M. S. (1966). The Devereux Elementary School Behavior Rating Scales: A study of the nature and organization of achievement relative to disturbed classroom behavior. *Journal of Special Education, 1,* 71–90.

Spivack, G., & Swift, M. S. (1973). The classroom behavior of children: A critical review of teacher-administered rating scales. *Journal of Special Education, 7,* 269–292.

Spivack, G., & Swift, M. S. (1977). The Hahnemann High School Behavior Rating Scale. *Journal of Abnormal Child Psychology, 5,* 299–307.

Spivack, G., Swift, M. S. & Prewitt, J. (1971). Syndromes of disturbed classroom behavior: A behavioral diagnostic system for elementary schools. *Journal of Special Education, 5,* 269–292.

Sprague, R. L. (1983). Behavior modification and educational techniques. In M. Rutter (Ed.), *Developmental neuropsychology.* New York: Guilford Press.

Sprague, R. L., & Werry, J. (1974). Psychotropic drugs in handicapped children. In L. Mann & D. Sabatino (Eds.), *Second review of special education* (pp. 1–50). Philadelphia, PA: JSE Press.

Stayton, D. J., Hogan, R., & Ainsworth, M. D. S. (1971). Infant obedience and maternal behavior: The origins of socialization reconsidered. *Child Development, 42,* 1057–1069.

Stearns, R., & Rosenshine, B. (1981). Advances in research on teaching. *Exceptional Education Quarterly, 2,* 1–9.

Steinhausen, H., Gobel, D., Breinlinger, M., & Wohlleben, B. (1984). Maternal age and autistic children. *Journal of Developmental and Behavioral Pediatrics, 5,* 343–345.

Steinhausen, H., Gobel, D., Breinlinger, M., & Wohlleben, B. (1986). A community survey of infantile autism. *Journal of the American Academy of Child Psychiatry, 25,* 186–190.

Steinman, S. (1981). The experience of children in a joint custody arrangement: A report of a study. *American Journal of Orthopsychiatry, 51,* 403–414.

Steinman, S. B., Zemmelman, S. E., & Knoblauch, T. M. (1985). A study of parents who sought joint custody following divorce: Who reaches agreement and sustains joint custody and who returns to court. *Journal of the American Academy of Child Psychiatry, 24,* 554–562.

Stephens, T. M. (1977). *Teaching skills to children with learning and behavior disorders.* Columbus, OH: Charles E. Merrill.

Stephens, T. M. (1978). *Social skills in the classroom.* Columbus, OH: Cedars Press.

Sternberg, L., & Taylor, R. L. (1981). The insignificance of psycholinguistic training: A reply to Kavale. *Exceptional Children, 49,* 254–256.

Stewart, M. A., & Olds, S. W. (1973). *Raising a hyperactive child.* New York: Harper & Row.

Stierlin, H. (1972). *Separating parents and adolescents.* New York: Quadrangle Books.

Stierlin, H., Levi, L. D., & Savard, R. J. (1973). Centrifugal versus centripetal separation in adolescence: Two patterns and some of their implications. In S. Feinstein & P. Giovacchini (Eds.), *Annals of the American Society for Adolescent Psychiatry* (Vol. 2). New York: Basic Books.

Stokes, T. F., & Baer, D. M. (1977). An implicit technology of generalization. *Journal of Applied Behavior Analysis, 10,* 349–367.

Strain, P. S. (1985). Programmatic research on peers as intervention agents for socially isolated classmates. *The Pointer, 29,* 22–29.

Strang, J. J., & Connell, P. Clinical aspects of drug and alcohol abuse. (1985). In M. Rutter & L. Hersov (Eds.), *Child and adolescent psychiatry: Modern approaches* (pp. 501–515). London: Blackwell Scientific Publications.

Strauss, A. A., & Lehtinen, L. (1947). *Psychopathology and education of the brain-injured child*. New York: Grune & Stratton.

Sudak, H. S., Ford, A. B., & Rushforth, N. B. (1984). Adolescent suicide: An overview. *American Journal of Psychotherapy, 38,* 350–363.

Sugai, G. (1985). Recording classroom events: Maintaining a critical incidents log. *Teaching Exceptional Children, 18,* 98–102.

Sulzer-Azeroff, B., & Mayer, G. R. (1977). *Applied behavior analysis procedures with children*. New York: Holt, Reinhart & Winston.

Suran, B. G., & Rizzo, J. V. (1983). *Special children: An integrative approach*. Glenview, IL: Scott, Foresman.

Sutherland, E. H., & Cressey, D. R. (1966). *Principles of criminology*. Philadelphia: J. B. Lippincott.

Swan, W. W., Brown, C. L., & Jacob, R. T. (1987). Types of service delivery models used in the reintegration of severely emotionally disturbed/behaviorally disordered students. *Behavioral Disorders, 13,* 99–103.

Swap, S. M. (1974). Disturbing classroom behaviors: A developmental and ecological view. *Exceptional Children, 41,* 163–172.

Swap, S. M. (1978). The ecological model of emotional disturbance in children: A status report and proposed synthesis. *Behavioral Disorders, 3,* 186– 196.

Swap, S. M., Prieto, A. G., & Harth, R. (1982). Ecological perspectives of the emotionally disturbed child. In R. L. McDowell, G. W. Adamson, & F. H. Wood (Eds.), *Teaching emotionally disturbed children*. Boston: Little, Brown and Co.

Swassing, C. I. (1984). Helping your child adjust to junior high school: A home-school contingency plan. *The Pointer, 29,* 4–7.

Talbot, N. B. (1976). *Raising children in modern America: What parents and society should be doing for their children*. Boston: Little, Brown and Co.

Taylor, F. D., Artuso, A. A., Soloway, M. M., Hewett, F. M., Quay, H. C., & Stillwell, R. J. (1972). A learning center plan for special education. *Focus on Exceptional Children, 4,* 1–7.

Taylor, L., & Salend, S. J. (1983). Reducing stress-related burnout through a network support system. *The Pointer, 27,* 5–9.

Terestman, N. (1980). Mood quality and intensity in nursery school children as predictors of behavior disorder. *American Journal of Orthopsychiatry, 50,* 125–138.

Test, D. W., Cooke, N. L., Weiss, A. B., Heward, W. L., & Heron, T. E. (1986). A home-school communication system for special education. *The Pointer, 30,* 4–7.

Thomas, A., & Chess, S. (1976). Evolution of behavior disorders into adolescence. *American Journal of Psychiatry, 133,* 539–542.

Thomas, A., & Chess, S. (1977). *Temperament and development*. New York: Brunner/Mazel.

Thomas, A., & Chess, S. (1984). Genesis and evolution of behavioral disorders: From infancy to early adult life. *American Journal of Psychiatry, 141,* 1–9.

Thomas, A., Chess, S., & Birch, H. G. (1968). *Temperament and behavior disorders in children*. New York: New York University Press.

Treffert, D. A. (1970). Epidemiology of infantile autism. *Archives of General Psychiatry, 22,* 431–438.

Tucker, J. A. (1980). Ethnic proportions in classes for the learning disabled: Issues in nonbiased assessment. *Journal of Special Education, 14,* 93–105.

Turnbull, A. P., Strickland, B. B., & Brantley, J. C. (1982). *Developing and implementing individualized education programs*. Columbus, OH: Charles E. Merrill.

U.S. Bureau of the Census, (1981, March). *Current population reports: Marital status and living arrangement* (Series P-20, No. 372). Washington, DC: U.S. Government Printing Office.

U.S. Congress. Federal Public Law 94-142, *Congressional Record*, 94th Congress, November 29, 1975, 12, 173–196.

U.S. Department of Education, (1984). *Implementation of Public Law 94–142: The Education for Handicapped Children Act* (Sixth annual report to Congress). Washington, DC: Special Education Programs (ED/OSERS), Division of Educational Resources.

Vacc, N. A., & Kirst, N. (1977). Emotionally disturbed children and regular classroom teachers. *Elementary School Journal, 77,* 309–317.

Varley, C. K. (1984a). Attention deficit disorder (the hyperactivity syndrome): A review of selected issues. *Journal of Developmental and Behavioral Pediatrics, 5,* 254–258.

Varley, C. K. (1984b). Diet and the behavior of children with attention deficit disorder. *Journal of the American Academy of Child Psychiatry, 23,* 182–185.

Vega, W. A., Hough, R. L., & Romero, A. (1983). Family life patterns of Mexican-Americans. In G. J.

Powell (Ed.), *The psychosocial development of minority group children* (pp. 194–215). New York: Brunner/Mazel.

Veltkamp, L. J. (1975). School phobia. *Journal of Family Counseling, 3,* 47–51.

Virden, T. (1984). Supportive peer groups: A behavior management program for children. In J. K. Grosenick, S. L. Huntze, E. McGinnis, & C. R. Smith (Eds.), *Social/affective interventions in behavioral disorders.* Columbia, MO: University of Missouri–Columbia, Department of Special Education, National Needs Analysis in Behavior Disorders Project.

Visher, E. B., & Visher, J. S. (1979a). *Stepfamilies: A guide to working with stepparents and stepchildren.* New York: Brunner/Mazel.

Visher, J. S., & Visher, E. B. (1979b). Stepfamilies and stepchildren. In J. D. Noshpitz (Ed.), *Basic handbook of child psychiatry: Prevention and current issues* (Vol. 4, pp. 347–353). New York: Basic Books.

Volkmar, F. R., & Cohen, D. J. (1985). The experience of infantile autism: A first-person account by Tony W. *Journal of Autism and Developmental Disorders, 15,* 47–54.

Volkmar, F. R., Cohen, D. J., & Paul, R. (1986). An evaluation of DSM-III criteria for infantile autism. *Journal of the American Academy of Child Psychiatry, 25,* 190–197.

Volkmar, F. R., Stier, D. M., & Cohen, D. J. (1985). Age of recognition of pervasive developmental disorder. *American Journal of Psychiatry, 142,* 1450–1452.

Vorrath, H., & Brendtro, L. (1974). *Positive peer culture.* Chicago: Aldine.

Wachs, T. D., & Gruen, G. E. (1982). *Early experience and human development.* New York: Plenum Press.

Waelder, R. (1960). *Basic theory of psychoanalysis.* New York: International Universities Press.

Wahler, R. G. (1976). Deviant child behavior within the family: Developmental speculations and behavior change strategies. In H. Leitenberg (Ed.), *Handbook of behavior modification and behavior therapy.* Englewood Cliffs, NJ: Prentice-Hall.

Wahler, R. G. (1980). The insular mother: Her problems in parent-child treatment. *Journal of Applied Behavior Analysis, 13,* 207–219.

Walker, H. M. (1979). *The acting-out child: Coping with classroom disruption.* Boston: Allyn and Bacon.

Walker, H. M. (1983). Applications of response cost in school settings: Outcomes, issues, and recommendations. *Exceptional Education Quarterly, 3,* 47–55.

Walker, H. M., & Buckley, N. (1972). Programming generalization and maintenance of treatment effects across time and across settings. *Journal of Applied Behavior Analysis, 5,* 209–224.

Wallace, G., & Larsen, S. C. (1978). *Educational assessment of learning problems.* Boston: Allyn and Bacon.

Wallace, G., & McLoughlin, J. A. (1979). *Learning disabilities: Concepts and characteristics* (2nd ed.). Columbus, OH: Charles E. Merrill.

Wallerstein, J. S. (1984). Children of divorce: Preliminary report of a ten year follow-up of young children. *American Journal of Orthopsychiatry, 54,* 444–458.

Wallerstein, J. S. (1985a). Children of divorce: Preliminary report of a 10-year follow-up of older children and adolescents. *Journal of the American Academy of Child Psychiatry, 24,* 545–553.

Wallerstein, J. S. (1985b). Children of divorce: Recent research. *Journal of the American Academy of Child Psychiatry, 24,* 515–517.

Walls, R. T. (1977). Behavior checklists. *Behavioral assessment: New directions in clinical psychology.* New York: Brunner/Mazel.

Waterhouse, L., Fein, D., Nath, J., & Snyder, D. (1986). Critique of DSM-III diagnosis of pervasive developmental disorders. In G. Tischler (Ed.), *DSM-III: An interim appraisal.* Washington, DC: American Psychiatric Association.

Watson, J. B. (1913). Psychology as the behaviorist views it. *Psychological Review, 20,* 158–177.

Weakland, J. H. (1976). The double-bind hypothesis of schizophrenia and three-party interactions. In C. E. Sluzki & D. C. Ransom (Eds.), *Double-bind: The foundation of the communicational approach to the family.* New York: Grune & Stratton.

Weinberg, R. A., & Wood, F. H. (Eds.). (1975). *Observation of pupils and teachers in mainstream and special education settings: Alternative strategies.* Reston, VA: Council for Exceptional Children.

Weinberg, W., & Rehmet, A. (1983). Childhood affective disorder and school problems. In D. P. Cantwell & G. A. Carlson (Eds.), *Affective disorders in childhood and adolescence: An update* (pp. 109–128). New York: SP Medical and Scientific Books.

Weiskopf, P. E. (1980). Burn-out among teachers of exceptional children. *Exceptional Children, 47,* 18–23.

Weissman, M. M., Leckman, J. F., Merikangas, K. R., Gammon, G. D., & Prusoff, B. A. (1984). Depression and anxiety disorders in parents and children. *Archives of General Psychiatry, 41,* 845–852.

Wender, E. H. (1986). The food additive-free diet in the treatment of behavioral disorders: A review.

Journal of Developmental and Behavioral Pediatrics, 7, 35–48.

Werry, J. S., & Quay, H. C. (1971). The prevalence of behavior symptoms in younger elementary school children. *American Journal of Orthopsychiatry, 41*, 136–143.

Werry, J. S. (1972). Psychosomatic disorders (with a note on anesthesia, surgery, and hospitalization). In H. C. Quay & J. S. Werry (Eds.), *Psychopathological disorders of childhood*. New York: John Wiley & Sons.

Werry, J. S. (1982). Pharmacotherapy. In B. B. Lahey & A. E. Kazdin (Eds.), *Advances in clinical child psychology* (Vol. 5, pp. 283–321). New York: Plenum Press.

Werry, J. S., Reeves, J. C., & Elkind, G. S. (1987). Attention deficit, conduct, oppositional, and anxiety disorders in children. I. A review of research on differentiating characteristics. *Journal of the American Academy of Child and Adolescent Psychiatry, 26*, 133–143.

Westoff, L. A. (1977). *The second time around: Remarriage in America*. New York: Viking Press.

Whelan, R. J. (1977). Human understanding of human behavior. In A. J. Pappanikou & J. L. Paul (Eds.), *Mainstreaming emotionally disturbed children*. Syracuse, NY: Syracuse University Press.

White, L. (1974). Organic factors and psychophysiology in childhood schizophrenia. *Psychological Bulletin, 81*, 238–255.

White, M. A. (1980). *Iowa monograph: Strategies for planning and facilitating the reintegration of students with behavioral disorders*. Des Moines, IA: Iowa Department of Public Instruction.

White, W. J., & Wigle, S. E. (1986). Patterns of discrepancy over time as revealed by a standard-score comparison formula. *Learning Disabilities Research, 2*, 14–20.

Whiteside, M. F. (1981). A family systems approach with families of remarriage. In I. R. Stewart & L. E. Abt (Eds.), *Children of separation and divorce: Management and treatment* (pp. 319–336). New York: Van Nostrand Reinhold.

Whiting, J. W., & Child, I. L. (1969). *Child training and personality development*. New Haven: Yale University Press. (Originally published 1953.)

Wiederholt, J., Hammill, D. D., & Brown, V. L. (1983). *The resource teacher: A guide to effective practices* (2nd ed.). Austin, TX: Pro-Ed.

Williams, J. B. W. (1985). The multiaxial system of DSM-III: Where did it come from and where should it go? *Archives of General Psychiatry, 42*, 175–186.

Williams, J. E., & Morland, J. K. (1976). *Race, color, and the young child*. Chapel Hill, NC: University of North Carolina Press.

Williams, R. J., & Algozzine, B. (1980). Teachers' attitudes toward mainstreaming. *Elementary School Journal, 80*, 63–67.

Wilson, J. Q., & Herrnstein, R. J. (1985). *Crime and human nature*. New York: Simon & Schuster.

Wilson, W. J. (1978). *The declining significance of race: Blacks and changing American institutions*. Chicago: University of Chicago Press.

Wing, L., Yeates, S. R., Brierly, L. M., & Gould, J. (1976). The prevalence of early childhood autism: Comparison of administrative and epidemiological studies. *Psychological Medicine, 6*, 89–100.

Winsberg, B. G., & Yepes, L. E. (1978). Antipsychotics (major tranquilizers, neuroleptics). In J. S. Werry (Ed.), *Pediatric psychopharmacology: The use of behavior modifying drugs in children* (pp. 234–273). New York: Brunner/Mazel.

Winton, P. J., & Turnbull, A. P. (1981). Parent involvement as seen by parents of preschool handicapped children. *Topics in Early Childhood Special Education, 1*, 11–19.

Wise, F., & Miller, N. B. (1983). The mental health of the American Indian child. In G. J. Powell (Ed.), *The psychosocial development of minority group children* (pp. 344–361). New York: Brunner/Mazel.

Wolfensberger, W. (1972). *The principle of normalization in human services*. Toronto: National Institute on Mental Retardation.

Wood, F. H. (1968). Behavior modification techniques in context. *CCBD Newsletter, 5*, 12–15.

Wood, F. H. (1973). Negotiation and justification: An intervention model. *Exceptional Children, 39*, 185–189.

Wood, F. H. (1978). The influence of public opinion and social custom on the use of corporal punishment in schools. In F. H. Wood & K. C. Lakin (Eds.), *Punishment and aversive stimulation in special education: Legal, theoretical and practical issues in their use with emotionally disturbed children and youth*. Minneapolis, MN: University of Minnesota, Department of Psychoeducational Studies.

Wood, F. H. (1979). Defining disturbing, disordered, and disturbed behavior. In F. H. Wood & K. C. Lakin (Eds.), *Disturbing, disordered or disturbed? Perspectives on the definition of problem behavior in educa-*

tional settings. Reston, VA: Council for Exceptional Children.

Wood, F. H. (1979). *Pupil Observation schedule* (rev. ed.). Unpublished manuscript. Minneapolis, MN: University of Minnesota, Department of Educational Psychology.

Wood, F. H. (1981). The influence of personal, social, and political factors on the labeling of students. In F. H. Wood (Ed.), *Perspectives for a new decade: Education's responsibility for seriously emotionally disturbed and behaviorally disordered children and youth.* Reston, VA: Council for Exceptional Children.

Wood, F. H. (1982). Affective education and social skills training: A consumer's guide. *Teaching Exceptional Children, 14,* 212–216.

Wood, F. H. (1985). Issues in the identification and placement of behaviorally disordered students. *Behavioral Disorders, 10,* 219–228.

Wood, F. H., & Braaten, S. (1983). Developing guidelines for the use of punishing interventions in the schools. *Exceptional Education Quarterly, 3,* 68–75.

Wood, F. H., & Hill, B. K. (1983). Aversiveness and frequency of use of commonly used interventions for problem behavior. In R. B. Rutherford (Ed.), *Severe behavior disorders of children and youth* (Vol. 6). Reston, VA: Council for Exceptional Children.

Wood, F. H., & Lakin, K. C. (1978). *Punishment and aversive stimulation in special education: Legal, theoretical and practical issues in their use with emotionally disturbed children and youth.* Minneapolis, MN: University of Minnesota, Department of Psychoeducational Studies.

Wood, F. H., & Lininger, R. (1982). Services to the seriously behaviorally disordered/emotionally disturbed students in rural communities. In R. B. Rutherford (Ed.), *Monograph in behavioral disorders: Severe behavior disorders of children and youth.* Reston, VA: Council for Children with Behavioral Disorders.

Wood, F. H., Smith, C. R., & Grimes, J. (1985). *The Iowa assessment model in behavioral disorders: A training manual.* Des Moines, IA: Iowa Department of Public Instruction.

Wood, F. H., & Zabel, R. H. (1978). Making sense of reports on the incidence of behavior disorders/emotional disturbance in school-age populations. *Psychology in the Schools, 15,* 45–51.

Wood, M. M. (Ed.). (1975). *Developmental therapy: A textbook for teachers as therapists for emotionally disturbed young children.* Baltimore, MD: University Park Press.

Wood, M. M. (Ed.). (1981). *Developmental therapy sourcebook* (Vols. 1 & 2). Baltimore, MD: University Park Press.

Wood, M. M. (Ed.). (1986). *Developmental therapy in the classroom: Methods for teaching students with social, emotional, or behavioral handicaps.* Austin, TX: Pro-Ed.

Wood, M. M., & Swan, W. W. (1978). A developmental approach to educating the disturbed young child. *Behavioral Disorders, 3,* 197–209.

Wren, C. G. (1984). *The coping with series* (rev. ed.). Circle Pines, MN: American Guidance Service.

Yamamoto, J., & Kubota, M. (1983). The Japanese-American family. In G. J. Powell (Ed.), *The psychosocial development of minority group children* (pp. 237–247). New York: Brunner/Mazel.

Yates, A. J. (1970). *Behavior therapy.* New York: John Wiley & Sons.

Young, J. G., Cohen, D. J., Brown, S. L., & Caparulo, B. K. (1978). Decreased urinary free catecholamines in childhood autism. *Journal of the American Academy of Child Psychiatry, 17,* 671–678.

Ysseldyke, J. E., Algozzine, B., Shinn, M., & McGue, M. (1982). Similarities and differences between underachievers and students classified learning disabled. *Journal of Special Education, 16,* 73–85.

Ysseldyke, J. E., Thurlow, M., Graden, J., Wesson, C., Algozzine, B., & Deno, S. (1983). Generalizations from five years of research on assessment and decision making: The University of Minnesota Institute. *Exceptional Education Quarterly, 4,* 75–93.

Zabel, M. K. (Ed.). (1985). *TEACHING: Behaviorally disordered youth* (Vol. 1). Reston, VA: Council for Exceptional Children.

Zabel, M. K. (Ed.). (1986a). *TEACHING: Behaviorally disordered youth* (Vol. 2). Reston, VA: Council for Exceptional Children.

Zabel, M. K. (1986b). Timeout use with behaviorally disordered students. *Behavioral Disorders, 12,* 15–21.

Zabel, M. K. (1987). *TEACHING: Behaviorally disordered youth* (Vol. 3). Reston, VA: Council for Exceptional Children.

Zabel, M. K., & Zabel, R. H. (1983). Burnout among special education teachers: The role of age, experience, and training. *Teacher Education and Special Education, 6,* 255–259.

Zabel, R. H. (1978a). Providing education for emotionally disturbed children in the least restrictive environment. *Educational Considerations, 5,* 5–8.

Zabel, R. H. (1978b). Recognition of emotions in facial expressions by emotionally disturbed children. *Psychology in the Schools, 15,* 119–126.

Zabel, R. H. (1981). Behavioral approaches to behavioral management. In G. Brown, R. L. McDowell, & J. Smith (Eds.), *Education of adolescents with behavior disorders.* Columbus, OH: Charles E. Merrill.

Zabel, R. H. (1982). Etiology, characteristics, and interventions with autistic children: Implications for delivery of services. In R. Peterson & J. Rosell (Eds.), *Current topics in the education of behaviorally impaired children* (pp. 1–15). Lincoln, NE: University of Nebraska–Lincoln, Barkley Memorial Center.

Zabel, R. H. (1987). Preparation of teachers for behaviorally disordered students. In M. C. Wang, H. J. Walberg, & M. C. Reynolds (Eds.), *Handbook of special education: Research and practice.* Oxford, England: Pergamon Press.

Zabel, R. H., Boomer, L. W., & King, T. R. (1984). A model of stress and burnout among teachers of behaviorally disordered students. *Behavioral Disorders, 9,* 215–221.

Zabel, R. H., Peterson, R. L., & Smith, C. R. (In press). Availability and usefulness of assessment information for behaviorally disordered students: A replication. *Diagnostique.*

Zabel, R. H., Peterson, R. L., Smith, C. R., & White, M. A. (1981). Placement and reintegration information for emotionally disabled students. In F. H. Wood (Ed.), *Perspectives for a new decade: Education's responsibility for seriously disturbed and behaviorally disordered children and youth.* Reston, VA: Council for Exceptional Children.

Zabel, R. H., Peterson, R. L., Smith, C. R., & White, M. A. (1982). Availability and usefulness of assessment information for emotionally disabled students. *School Psychology Review, 11,* 433–437.

Zabel, R. H., Peterson, R. L., Smith, C. R., & White, M. A. (1983). Use of time as reported by teachers of emotionally disabled students. *The Pointer, 27,* 44–47.

Zabel, R. H., & Wood, F. H. (1977). *Efficacy of interventions with emotionally disturbed children: A review of literature.* Minneapolis, MN: University of Minnesota, Department of Psychoeducational Studies, Advanced Training Institute for Teacher Trainers for Seriously Emotionally Disturbed Children.

Zabel, R. H., & Zabel, M. K. (1980). Burnout: A critical issue for educators. *Education Unlimited* (March), 23–25.

Zabel, R. H., & Zabel, M. K. (1982). Factors involved in burnout among teachers of exceptional children. *Exceptional Children, 49,* 261–263.

Zentall, S. (1983). Learning environments: A review of physical and temporal factors. *Exceptional Education Quarterly, 4,* 90–115.

Zigler, E. F., & Child, I. L. (Eds.), (1973). *Socialization and personality development.* Reading, MA: Addison-Wesley.

Zimbardo, P. G. (1977). *Shyness.* Reading, MA: Addison-Wesley.

Zimbardo, P. G. (1977). *Shyness: What it is, what to do about it.* Reading, MA: Addison-Wesley.

Zionts, P. (1983). The rational-emotional approach. *The Pointer, 27,* 13–17.

Author Index

Subject Index